Professional
Team Foundation Server

Professional
Team Foundation Server

Jean-Luc David, Mickey Gousset, and Erik Gunvaldson

Wiley Publishing, Inc.

Professional Team Foundation Server

Published by
Wiley Publishing, Inc.
10475 Crosspoint Boulevard
Indianapolis, IN 46256
www.wiley.com

Published by Wiley Publishing, Inc., Indianapolis, Indiana

Published simultaneously in Canada

ISBN-13: 978-0-471-91930-8
ISBN-10: 0-471-91930-6

Manufactured in the United States of America

10 9 8 7 6 5 4 3 2 1

1B/QS/RR/QW/IN

Library of Congress Cataloging-in-Publication Data:

David, Jean-Luc, 1971-
Professional Team foundation server / Jean-Luc David and Mickey Gousset. . . [et al.].
p. cm.
Includes index.
ISBN-13: 978-0-471-91930-8 (paper/website)
ISBN-10: 0-471-91930-6 (paper/website)
1. Computer software--Development--Computer programs. 2. Teams in the workplace--Data processing. 3. Microsoft Visual studio. I. Gousset, Mickey. II. Title.
QA76.76.D47D365 2007
005.3--dc22

2006031030

Credits

Executive Editor
Robert Elliott

Development Editor
Sydney Jones

Technical Editors
Erik Gunvaldson
Marvel de Vries
Mario Rodriguez
Joe Sango

Production Editor
William A. Barton

Copy Editor
Maarten Reilingh

Editorial Manager
Mary Beth Wakefield

Production Manager
Tim Tate

Vice President and Executive Group Publisher
Richard Swadley

Vice President and Publisher
Joseph B. Wikert

Project Coordinator
Ryan Steffen

Graphics and Production Specialists
Carrie A. Foster
Lauren Goddard
Denny Hager
Barbara Moore
Lynsey Osborn
Alicia B. South

Quality Control Technician
Jessica Kramer

Media Development Specialists
Angela Denny
Kit Malone
Travis Silvers

Proofreading and Indexing
Techbooks

I'd like to dedicate this book to my lovely wife Miho, who has supported me through the writing of this book (and through all my projects).
— Jean-Luc David

This book is dedicated to my incredibly wonderful and beautiful wife, Amye. I can't begin to describe the support and love she has provided for me through this process, and I couldn't have done it without her. I love you, Mom, and Lea. — Mickey Gousset

About the Authors

Jean-Luc David works as a Developer Evangelist for Microsoft Canada. Prior to this role, he worked as a senior consultant, speaker, and author for Stormpixel Solutions based in Toronto, Canada. He has been writing code since the age of 12, and has been an ongoing active participant in user groups, online chats, and developer events. Most of his time is spent writing, creating courseware, speaking, and deploying Visual Studio 2005 Team System and .NET Framework 3.0 to companies in Canada and abroad.

Jean-Luc has been the lead author for several successful books including *Professional Visual Studio 2005 Team System, Professional WinFX Beta,* and *Professional Javascript*, 2nd edition, all published by Wrox Press. You can reach Jean-Luc at `support@stormpixel.com` or through his blog at `http://teamsystemrocks.com/blogs/jldavid/`.

Mickey Gousset is a current Microsoft Team System Most Valuable Professional (MVP) and works as a consultant for Notion Solutions, Inc., a company that focuses on helping clients adopt and use Microsoft Visual Studio Team System. He also runs the Team System Rocks! Web site (`www.teamsystemrocks.com`) and holds the position of Web master for the Memphis .NET User Group. Mickey holds B.S. degrees in both Physics and Computer Science from Mississippi State University, and also has the distinction of being in the first graduating class from the Mississippi School for Mathematics and Science, a specialized high school.

When not writing or working with computers, Mickey enjoys a range of activities such as playing Halo 2 (GamerTag: HereBDragons), cooking, blogging, and participating in local community theatre. But nothing takes the place of spending time with his two wonderful little girls, Emma and Meg, and his beautiful wife, Amye.

Erik Gunvaldson is a technology development manager within Microsoft's Enterprise Partner Group, focused on driving Software Factories with Microsoft's global partners. Prior to this role, Erik was a Microsoft Technical Evangelist, where he managed Microsoft's Technology Adoption Program (TAP) for Visual Studio 2005 Team System. Other roles that Erik's enjoyed at Microsoft include managing the development of Microsoft's Natural Language SDK and the Enterprise Knowledge Management program for application development. Before coming to Microsoft nine years ago, Erik was a software architect at large mutual funds company and a C++/Unix developer and team manager at a telecommunications company. Erik enjoys spending time with his wife Anna, daughter Katrina, son Lukas, his big lab Joe, and, when time affords, playing golf and tennis

Acknowledgments

I would like to first thank my good friend Mickey for cowriting and collaborating on the book. (May it be the first of many!) Your knowledge, honesty, and dedication are truly inspiring. A special thanks also goes out to Erik Gunvaldson for his technical knowledge and experience. This book would not be possible without the hard work of my editors—Bob Elliott (thanks for your ongoing support), Sydney Jones (my development editor who made the experience of writing the book an absolute joy), and the rest of the staff at Wiley Publishing. I would also like to acknowledge the technical support and encouragement from the great staff at Microsoft—Rob Caron, Tom Patton, Mario Rodriguez, Noah Coad, Ed Hickey, Sam Guckenheimer, and countless others. My fellow VSTS MVPs Joe Sango and Marcel de Vries provided excellent technical edits for the book. And lastly, thanks to my family, my good friend Chris Dufour, and last but not least my wife Miho—for your encouragement and support throughout the writing of the book. *—Jean-Luc David*

Thank you to Jean-Luc David, for giving me this chance to write this book with him, putting up with all of my endless late-night questions, and making this a great experience. You are an incredible author and a great friend. Next, to all those people who helped tech edit this book: Buck Hodges, Marcel deVries, Mario Rodriguez, Joe Sango, as well as anyone else I may have overlooked, thanks for all of your great feedback that has helped make this a better product. And thanks to Martin Woodward for his contributions and his help.

I'd like to give a very special thanks to the editors and publishers at Wiley Publishing, specifically Robert Elliot and Sydney Jones. Thank you both for your guidance and support. To Rob Caron and Korby Parnell, for hosting that Team System session on communities at Tech Ed 2004, which helped me end up where I am today. You've always been there for me when I needed it, and I will never forget it. Finally, to my departed father, Philip Gousset. Thanks Dad, for doing what you did to make me who I am today. *—Mickey Gousset*

Contents

Introduction

At the time of writing this, Visual Studio Team System has been out for several months. In my previous book, *Professional Visual Studio 2005 Team System* (also published by WROX—ISBN: 0-7645-8436-7), the focus was specifically on the features of the product. This book takes a slightly different approach—rather than look at features, we will look at common tasks and scenarios around the entire software development lifecycle (SDLC).

> **Team Foundation Server has an interesting history of codenames. The original codename for Visual Studio 2005 Team System is Burton (named after a ski equipment company). The majority of the features in Team Foundation Server include codenames derived from landmarks in North Carolina. (Microsoft has a development office based in Raleigh, NC.) For example, the Team Foundation Server SDK is codenamed Bodie (after the Bodie Island Lighthouse near Nags Head). Currituck is the codename for the Team Foundation Work Item Tracking feature (named after the Currituck Beach Lighthouse). The Cape Hatteras Lighthouse provided the namesake for Team Foundation Version Control. Finally, the Ocracoke Island Light provided the codename for Web and load testing. Rob Caron has provided a series of blog posts describing these landmarks in detail. You can read them at the following address:** `http://blogs.msdn.com/robcaron`**. The "Foundation" part of Team Foundation Server describes the foundation of support for team software development. The elements include source control, workflow, build services, and reporting.**

In case you've never heard of Team System, it is a new product developed by Microsoft to support not only developers but also other members of development teams such as architects, database professionals, testers, and product managers. Team System is much more than Visual Studio—it includes a world-class version control system, build server, a workflow and bug management system, reporting, and much more.

As companies start to work with Team System, they will inevitably encounter challenges such as implementing IT governance (Sarbanes-Oxley comes to mind), working within mixed environments (Java and .NET, for example), and setting up the product for large distributed environments. This book addresses these real-world challenges and much more. The contents are based on the practical experience of two Microsoft Team System Most Valuable Professionals (MVPs) and a host of sources within the product team.

Unlike other Team System books that may focus solely on developers, this book targets the project manager, administrators, and IT professionals. If you happen to be in one of these roles (or you are a consultant or systems integrator), you'll find a lot of great pragmatic information and step-by-step guidance within the pages of this book. We tell you how to handle a variety of tasks including setting up and administering Team System. This includes planning, project creation, and even properly completing a software project at the end of a development cycle.

The book provides a lot of depth on a variety of features in Team System; however it does not cover the whole of the product. For example, there is very little information provided about the Visual Studio 2005 Team Edition for Software Architects or Domain Specific Language (DSL) tools. If you would like a full overview of Team System, we would highly recommend you pick up *Professional Visual Studio 2005 Team System* published by WROX Press. All efforts have been made to diminish the overlap between books and in fact, you'll find them to be quite complimentary.

When deploying Team System, it's a natural tendency to be thinking about the development process. Thus you will probably be thinking about how your own teams are organized, continuous development, builds, refactoring, and so forth. However, it's important to look at a deployment on many levels (as shown in Figure IN-1):

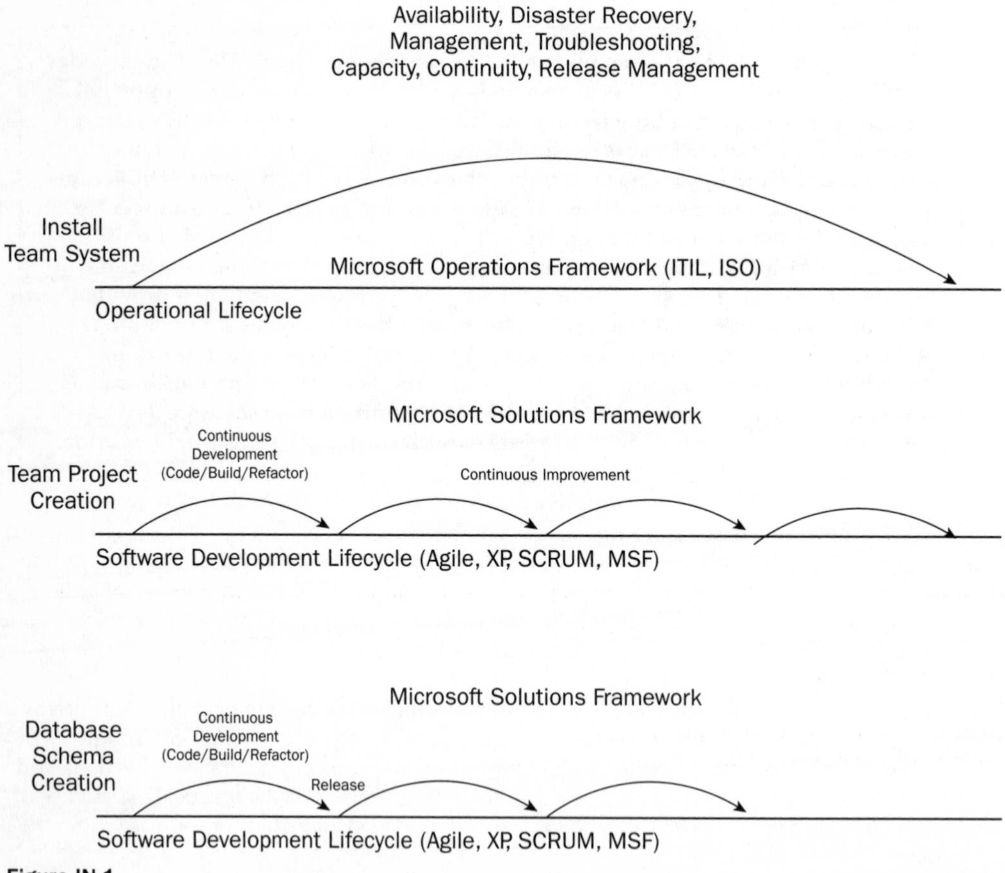

Figure IN-1

When you deploy and use Team System, there are multiple lifecycles you have to take into consideration:

- **Operational lifecycle**—Before even starting a single team project, you have to install and support Team Foundation Server, and the other components of Team System. Most users start team projects as soon as they install the product (as shown in Figure IN-1). However, the tasks related to the ongoing maintenance of the product overlap with many team projects. The Microsoft Operations Framework (MOF) based on the IT Infrastructure Library (ITIL) provides great guidance on how to manage your environment, including Team System.

- **Software development lifecycle**— The software development lifecycle (SDLC) is what drives Team System. You can use a variety of methodologies to drive your development efforts including the Microsoft Solutions Framework. Each Team Project has its own lifecycle, and within a Team Project, you may have a series of smaller iterations or milestones.
- **Data development lifecycle**— In May 2006, Microsoft announced the Team Edition for Database Professionals, which allows database developers and administrators alike to manage database schemas in very much the same way a software developer manages code. You'll notice in the graphic above that the data development lifecycle (DDLC) mirrors the lifecycle of a team project. You would be hard pressed to find an application that doesn't use a data driven infrastructure. Therefore, it's logical that the continuous creation, development, and release of database schemas occurs at the same time as your application development process.
- **Business continuity and resource management**—What is not represented in the previous figure is the business infrastructure required to run a successful software development company. Microsoft has many enterprise planning and management solutions such as Microsoft Dynamics, Microsoft Project Server, Microsoft CRM, and many others to handle the business side of operations.

When you start working with Team System, what you may not instantly realize is that it was fundamentally designed to implement and promote software engineering practices and process improvement. It also promotes transparency and friction free software development in the spirit of Agile development. A Team System deployment isn't just about installing a set of tools—it's an opportunity to revisit your practices; implement proper patterns and coding conventions; and set up the right scalable branching structures, adaptable builds, and predictable workflow.

Introducing Team Foundation Server

Team Foundation Server provides the underlying glue to Team System—it is the central integration point that provides a collaborative environment for all members of your team, regardless of role. Here are the main features of Team Foundation Server:

- **Team Foundation Version Control**— The version control system allows you to store both source code and other files in a controlled manner. It supports the kinds of features you would expect including branching and merging, shelving, and policies.
- **Team Foundation Build**— Team Foundation Build leverages MSBuild and takes it further, providing scalability for over five hundred developers. Team Foundation Build includes great features such as build customization, scripting, and test integration.
- **Work item tracking**— Using the work item tracking tools, you can assign and track bugs, tasks, and requirements within a software development project. Team System allows you to not only manipulate work items but also customize and extend them to fit your needs.

- **Team portal**—The Team Portal provides a centralized location to view all project activities and documentation. You can access the process guidance, download support documents, or retrieve the latest reports.
- **Team reporting**—The reporting features of Team System are built on top of SQL Server Reporting Services. They provide rich views of your project including indicators that will allow you to evaluate whether a project is healthy or not.
- **Team Foundation Core Services (TFCS)**—The Team Foundation Core Services is a set of Team Foundation APIs and services. It provides resources that allow you to create custom applications that interact with Team Foundation Server in very rich ways.
- **Project management**—Team System comes with a lot of support for project managers. You can organize the milestones and iterations of a project using the server, track the progress of a team using simple tools like Microsoft Excel, and even look at bug rates and code churn in the report component.

In the book, we provide not only information on Team Foundation Server but also on the rest of Team System. The question you might be asking yourself is—then why call the book *Professional Team Foundation Server?* The features of Team Foundation Server and Team System are so tightly (and nicely) integrated that it would be difficult, if not next to impossible to separate them and provide worthy coverage of the topic. Second, the book is organized to logically represent the various lifecycles from cradle to grave. It's no coincidence that the book opens up with a chapter called "Planning a Team System Deployment" and closes off with "Completing Software Projects."

Who Is This Book For?

Unlike other Wrox books, the target audience for this book is not primarily developers. Sure, Team System is a product oriented toward the process of software development. However, apart from the official documentation, a few blogs, and the Microsoft Forums, there isn't much substantial coverage anywhere on how to use the product end-to-end, how to perform essential tasks, and how to cope with special development environments.

The main target audience for this book is project managers and IT administrators—those who will administer the product on a daily basis, run a software project, set up users, security, and so forth. As a result, you can filter the chapters of the book based on each role.

Project Managers and Business Analysts

This book provides project managers with a great overview of how the software development life cycle is managed in Team System using Project Management Institute (PMI) principles outlined in the Project Management Body of Knowledge (PMBOK). We show you how to plan, set up, and track your software development projects and create custom project templates to fit your best practices and processes. We even show you how to complete the project at the end—including how to save your work and implement process improvement. The whole book is informative of course; however the following chapters will be especially interesting to project managers:

- **Chapter 1**—Planning a Team System Deployment
- **Chapter 9**—Creating Custom Development Tools
- **Chapter 10**—Extending the Windows SharePoint Team Portal
- **Chapter 11**—Administering and Customizing Work Items
- **Chapter 13**—Managing Your Team Projects
- **Chapter 14**—Effective Team Communication
- **Chapter 15**—Working with Geographically Distributed Teams
- **Chapter 16**—Monitoring Your Team Project Metrics Using SQL Server Reporting Services
- **Chapter 17**—Completing Software Projects

For business analysts (and business process analysts), this book provides a guide to converting business requirements into assets that fit perfectly into Team System. In addition, this book serves as a nice guide to pragmatically determine the return on investment (ROI) of a tool like Visual Studio 2005 Team System within your environment.

IT Administrators

In delving into this book, you might be quite surprised. It is very strongly oriented toward IT professionals. We cover such topics as security, backup/recovery, and setting up your network on Active Directory (AD)—all the common tasks you would come to expect from an operational perspective. Team System is a huge product including several versions of Visual Studio, Team Foundation Server, SQL Server 2005, and Windows Server 2003. It can be difficult to get a handle on all the specific and pragmatic operational information available for Team System. We attempt in this book to sum it all up for you in a convenient format. If you are an IT professional, the chapters that will likely interest you include the following:

- **Chapter 1**—Planning a Team System Deployment
- **Chapter 2**—Advanced Installation and Tools Migration
- **Chapter 3**—Configuring Team Foundation Build
- **Chapter 4**—Setting Up Security
- **Chapter 5**—Team Foundation Server Backup and Recovery
- **Chapter 12**—Setting Up Team Foundation Version Control
- **Chapter 15**—Working with Geographically Distributed Teams
- **Chapter 17**—Completing Software Projects

> **One of the things that might jump out about these topics is that they reflect some of the requirements outlined in the IT Infrastructure Library (ITIL). This is not a coincidence—the book does not comprehensively cover all of ITIL but certainly provides a baseline, and a great starting point.**

Developers

If you are a developer and you also play the role of the project manager (or you are setting up Team System for a small team of developers), then this book will be quite useful for you. If you are just a pure programmer, Part III (Extensibility and Customization) includes some great info on creating custom tools that integrate with Team Foundation Server, developing custom SharePoint components (for the project portal), customizing work items, creating reports, working with Team Version Control, and scripting Team Foundation Build (Team System's enterprise-class build engine). The book also serves as a great map to provide you with a big picture look at the product. You will definitely want to take a closer look at the following chapters:

- **Chapter 8**— Managing Schemas Using Team Edition for Database Professionals
- **Chapter 9**—Creating Custom Development Tools
- **Chapter 10**—Extending the Windows SharePoint Team Portal
- **Chapter 11**—Administering and Customizing Work Items
- **Chapter 12**—Setting Up Team Foundation Version Control

Database Professionals

What exactly is a database professional? If you look at the functionality of Team Edition for Database Professionals, the tool provides support for both the database administrator and the database developer. The database administrator can back up, administer, and deploy database schemas very easily without impacting the production database. The database developer provides you with the ability to do unit testing on schemas and stored procedures to refactor and build database projects as first-class citizens within your development environment. Databases can now be stored in version control, integrated in the server, and much more.

> **IT administrators are greatly encouraged to look at the administration chapters mentioned earlier in the introduction. The same applies to database developers and the developer chapters.**

Enthusiasts

Team System is primarily designed for large software development teams. So what if you are an enthusiast or a micro ISV (Independent Software Vendor)? Can you still use the product? Some of the core advantages of Team System are the management of work item tasks and larger scale user and project management. In most cases, these features will be of little use to you. What may be useful to you is the build engine, version control system, and, to some limited degree, the project portal. One of the great benefits of this book is that you will learn how software development works on a higher order of scale, which may help you from a career perspective if you wish to work for a large development team or you just want a greater understanding of the product.

If you are a consultant, this book is practically a how-to guide. A lot of the information in the book is based on practical experience implementing and deploying Team Foundation Server. Therefore, if you have to wear the project manager/IT professional/developer hats all at once, this book is written for you.

What Does This Book Cover?

This book covers the tasks required to configure and run Team Foundation Server. You'll get this information within the context of the software development life cycle. Team System is a huge product with countless moving parts. In fact, each section of this book can be made into a book itself! We go into a good level of depth—enough to allow you to be productive. You'll also find links to external resources.

Think of this book as a manual for Team System. A lot of books on the market provide good information on individual features of the product. This book is designed to walk through the tasks to put the product into action and provide real-world information on Team System beyond the scope of the official product documentation.

How This Book Is Structured

We have divided this book into four logical sections. These sections cover both tasks within the entire software development life cycle and the operational implementation of Team System in real world scenarios. The sections in the book include:

- **Deployment and Administration**—The first step in deploying any product is the planning stage. The first five chapters walk through the process of deploying and configuring Team System within your development environment and help you make that transition as seamless as possible.
- **Project Creation**—Once Team System is in place, you'll need to create the team project that will support the process of developing software. In the three chapters in this section, you learn how to customize a process to your needs and put it into play.
- **Extensibility and Customization**—Default projects in Team System will not always fit your needs. You will sometimes need to change or modify components to better fit the way you are used to working. The extensibility and customization portion of the book shows you how to make Team System work for you.
- **Management**: How is a project supposed to be handled in Team System? The product documentation may provide you with the right direction; however this book is designed to take it further. We look at nontechnological concepts, such as team communication, which are of the highest order of importance in a working development team. We'll show you things that the manual simply can't show you, and frame it within real-world scenarios.

Figure IN-2 shows a conceptual view of how each section fits into the big picture of both the operational and the software development lifecycles. The graph isn't completely accurate, because in many cases you will be implementing tasks throughout each lifecycle. For example, you will be continuously implementing and maintaining your servers using backup and recovery strategies. You will be using extensibility and customization to continuously improve your process. For example, you will be constantly implementing custom policies, custom reports and other extensibility hooks to help your team avoid repeating past mistakes, and to automate tasks that are taking your team a long time to accomplish. Realistically, you would want to constantly roll out your improvements into new process templates whenever a new project is envisioned.

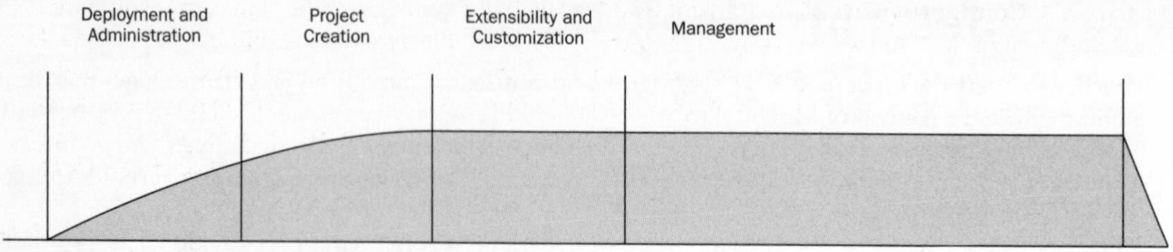

Operational and Software Development Lifecycles

Figure IN-2

Deployment and Administration

If you are a server administrator or an IT professional, this section will greatly interest you. We cover topics such as planning, migrating tools and processes, configuring the build engine, and setting up security and a disaster recovery plan.

Chapter 1: Planning a Team System Deployment—In this chapter, you get an overview of Team Foundation Server—including a look at the architecture, components, and a brief overview of Team System as a complete product. The next task that is covered is the process of compiling the data for your project. For example, what are the requirements of the projects? Next is deployment planning, including capacity planning, paying close attention to the network architecture and topologies, deployment models, and even virtualization. We also look at security and test planning. Once a deployment plan has been conceived, it's important to determine whether your current hardware infrastructure supports Team System. You will find out everything you need to know, including what hardware is unsupported. Next we look at software requirements including required service packs and software components. What if you are already using tools to perform tasks such as source control or testing? (This is probably the case for a lot of software development teams.) You will learn how to migrate your current source control, work item tracking, reporting, build engine, and testing tools. In the migration portion of the book, we provide you with decision flowcharts to help you in the process of figuring out the best migration approach to take according to best practices. The final part of the chapter looks at licensing models and provides you with avenues to obtain copies of Team System. These topics are of particular interest to IT professionals.

Chapter 2: Advanced Installation and Tools Migration—When installing Team System, how do you handle the difficult situations and how do you migrate existing tools to the new platform? The standard documentation doesn't necessarily provide that information, which is the reason it's found in this book. The first part of the chapter defines the different IT roles within your organization and the elements found in your network infrastructure. We then look at the different installation options including the multiserver installations and the single-server installation. When looking at these installation options in detail, you'll find out the best practices to set up the application tier (AT), the data tier (DT), and the client tier (CT). Next is virtualization—you'll get an overview of the virtualization technologies available that work with Team System and the appropriate use and settings including how to work virtual servers within your existing network. The next topic is Team Explorer, the plugin that allows Visual Studio 2005 to connect to, and administer Team Foundation Server. You will get in-depth information about Team Explorer and details on how to effectively connect it to Team Foundation Server. You also learn other options for controlling the server. Finally, we review the migration path of your existing tools to Team System, including source control and work item tracking.

Chapter 3: Configuring Team Foundation Build—The build engine is at the core of any software development project. In many processes (especially Agile methodologies), the build will provide the key indicator of whether the project is on track. You'll get an overview of the Team Foundation Build architecture and the components of the build process (including types, reports, and execution). Next, we look at common build scenarios including common builds, nightly builds, weekly builds, and continuous integration (CI)—probably one of the most requested build configurations for the product. The chapter also includes a section on setting up the build server including information that will help you understand how builds are managed, how to set up build servers, setting up a common build site, and configuring security roles and permissions. This leads up nicely to the next chapter, which deals with the ever-important matter of security.

Chapter 4: Setting Up Security—One of the challenges in implementing security is that it is never simple. In Team System, you have to worry about role security, project security, server security—in fact, every component in Team System has a security feature built-in. If you are planning to deploy Team System in a real-world environment, these are important considerations! The chapter opens up with an overview of the Team Foundation Server security model. This includes a look at how Team Foundation Server manages groups, how global roles are defined, and permissions that are set for all groups. Next, you learn about security within certain components of Team System including Windows SharePoint Services, SQL Server Reporting Services, and other important parts of the server. Roles play an important part in the administration of security and get a lot of coverage. Some of the topics you will discover include creating and adding users to the system using Team System's graphical user interface and command-line tools. You then learn how to manage all the security roles on the server. Once the groups and roles have been defined, you will find out how to secure Team Foundation Server and common access security issues (and more importantly, the ways you can work around them). The chapter rounds up with security best practices, properly patching and updating your server (and other components), and logging and auditing to help you keep on top of your system security.

Chapter 5: Team Foundation Server Backup and Recovery—Security is all-important, but equally important is setting up a disaster recovery strategy. A hardware issue or user error may inadvertently cause data loss. Data (especially assets such as source code) is the lifeblood of a software development company. Losing data not only means losing time but also money. In this chapter, you learn how to troubleshoot problem situations by reviewing log files and learning about the various sources of support for help. Next, we review common installation errors—this overview will help you get around common problems experienced by users. The chapter also examines common administration problems and how they can affect your system. We then learn about disaster recovery in detail (including how it relates to Team System). Topics include server interdependencies, built-in backup tools, third-party tools, and the steps in writing an effective disaster recovery plan. Finally, we dig deeper in each of the components of Team System (SQL Server 2005, Team Foundation Server, and the client tools) and we learn how to not only recover from a disaster but also take proactive steps to avoid the disaster in the first place!

Project Creation

Once the proper planning and the Team System infrastructure have been put into place, the next step is to create a software development project. The project creation part of the book covers topics such as process template customization, the details in creating a Team System project, and finally configuration of that project. This portion of the book will be of special interest to project managers. Developers may also be interested in the process of customizing templates for project creation.

Chapter 6: Incorporating Your Process Using Microsoft Solutions Framework—This chapter looks at the Microsoft Solutions Framework and other processes available within Team System. First, you get an overview of the two process templates available in the product (MSF for Agile Software Development and MSF for CMMI Process Improvement). Next, you learn how to customize these preexisting templates to fit your particular process development needs by editing XML files or using third-party tools. A good portion of the chapter looks at the anatomy of a custom process template—specifically, we look at the Conchango implementation of Scrum within Team System. The last part of the chapter tells how to compile and create documentation (which can be viewed by all members of your team using the project site) and how to integrate your new methodologies into Team Foundation Server.

Chapter 7: Project Creation and Team Building—In the past, Visual Studio was a tool used by teams of developers but there was no integrated tool to allow you to work with developers, testers, and architects as a team. This chapter starts out by defining the differences between a team project and a Visual Studio 2005 project. Next, we walk through the process of creating a new team project including specifying settings, and a process template for your project. In the creation of a project, you may encounter common mistakes including permission errors and other problems. We teach you how to deal with them. Finally we look at the roles in your software development team, how they compare to MSF, and how to implement a project based on the roles.

Chapter 8: Managing Schemas Using Team Edition for Database Professionals—Once you have set up your team project, the next step is setting up your application infrastructure including your data tier. Team Edition for Database Professionals provides the tools to administer and develop data driven software applications. In this chapter, you learn about this Team Edition, including how to back up your database and work on it offline, how to develop a database using unit tests and the refactoring tools, how to use the build functionality within Team Edition for Database Professionals, and how to compare and release your database against a production system. Finally, we show you how to create a custom data generator.

Extensibility and Customization

Team System is an interesting product unlike any that has been developed by Microsoft. It is actually not designed to run right out of the box—software development teams should customize the tool to fit their needs before it is deployed. You'll see a lot of evidence for this in the wide breadth of customization and extensibility support within Team Foundation Server. This section will be of particular interest to project managers (who will want the customizations implemented) and developers who will actually perform the customizations in many cases.

Chapter 9: Creating Custom Development Tools—You will find in some cases that Team System requires add-ins to fit your particular development environment. This chapter shows you how to extend and customize Team System (and Visual Studio 2005). The first part of the chapter defines the difference between extensibility and customization and shows examples supporting these two concepts. Next, we look at the Team Foundation Object Model and see how it allows you to create custom applications that interact with many components within Team Foundation Server. Next, we look at the services on Team Foundation Server that are accessible—the collection of these services is called the Team Foundation Core Services (TFCS). You learn about registration, notifications, linking, and user groups, and common structure capabilities on the server. Next, we look at eventing with a concrete case study of how you can autogenerate a work item when a scenario is submitted. Finally, we look at Visual Studio 2005 programmability, including macros, and present the resources available through the Visual Studio Industry Partner (VSIP) program.

Chapter 10: Extending the Windows SharePoint Team Portal—The project portal provides you with a centralized area to manage and view the project details; however, the Team System documentation provides very little information on how to extend the portal. In this chapter, you get an overview of the portal components (including WSS files, site definitions, and elements) and a detailed technical review. Next, we get our hands dirty to create and customize Web Parts that integrate with Team System. (Specifically, we'll add a work item browser to the Team Portal.) You'll learn the entire process from creation to deployment. The chapter also provides information on how to customize your portal using a browser and Microsoft FrontPage, and then how to deploy your portal within a process template.

Chapter 11: Administering and Customizing Work Items—In terms of workflow, work items are an important feature of Team System. This chapter starts out by giving you a good look at common work item concepts including the object model (OM) and the application program interface (API). After reading the chapter, you'll be intimately aware of the components of work items and how these components fit in the grand scheme of things. Next we examine the default work item types available in Team System's default process templates. You also learn about the tools that are available to manipulate work items, including Visual Studio 2005 and `WITImport/WITExport`. What is the proper way of working with and deploying work items? The chapter covers topics such as properly naming work items in play, and adding support for features such as alerts, source control integration, and work item history. The second part of the chapter shows you how to customize your work items. You learn a little more about work item internals and the tools and resources available in the Extensibility toolkit. You will find out how to import and export work items, customize existing work items, test your work items, create queries, and much more. The chapter wraps up with a look at the future direction of work items in the next version of Team System.

Chapter 12: Setting Up Team Foundation Version Control—Microsoft designed Team Foundation Version Control is a brand new source control system. In this chapter, you learn how to configure the source control features using the Team System user interface. You also learn how to integrate and navigate version control using the Source Control Explorer. We look at important features such as changesets, check-in policies, branching and merging, and shelving. Finally, the chapter examines how to migrate projects residing in Microsoft Visual SourceSafe and other third-party tools to Team System's version control solution.

Management

Once you have deployed Team System, created a project, and customized it to your needs you then need project managers to put the software development project into play. The chapters in this section deal with the all important day-to-day management details such as communication (including setting up an infrastructure for large distributed teams), monitoring project metrics (and identifying problems), and then the all-important process of wrapping up a project, which includes performing a postmortem that will bring up information which will benefit your future projects.

Chapter 13:Managing Your Team Projects—In this chapter, you learn how to work with your team members. You may be wondering how this fits in with Team System, especially with Team Foundation System. Some of the topics we tackle include setting up status meetings and managing time and milestones. Team System offers many possibilities for setting up and administering these important tasks. In particular, we look at the core project management tasks including communication, metrics, and the steps to take to wrap up software development projects. The next chapters build on this and cover in detail all the responsibilities and tools available to the project manager. Finally, we look at test case management, specifically, how to incorporate tests from Team Edition for Software Developers and Team Edition for Software Testers into your check-in and build processes.

Chapter 14: Effective Team Communication—This chapter covers the challenges of communicating as a team and examines the current communication methods in use (including e-mail, telephone, and file shares). We provide you with best practices on improving communication using Team Foundation Server and cross-platform communication. The chapter provides a case study on implementing alerts via Instant Messenger (IM). Finally, we look at other communication tools such as TeamLook and Groove 2007.

Chapter 15: Working with Geographically Distributed Teams—Working with a team distributed across many countries and continents can be a challenge on a logistical and operational level. This chapter helps you set up Team System to simplify the administration tasks and set up an infrastructure that will scale on that level. The first part of the chapter shows you how you can identify the challenges within your particular company and how to set up communication channels across great distances. The next part of the chapter examines the tools available in Team System to simplify working with geographically distributed teams. In particular, a lot of attention is placed on the Team Foundation Server proxy, including installation steps and configuration, and the distributed load testing tools. Finally, we examine some of the ways you can enable foreign language support and internationalization within Team Foundation Server.

Chapter 16: Monitoring Your Team Project Metrics Using SQL Server Reporting Services—One of the key ways you can judge the health of a project is by using the metrics available through the Team Reporting feature in Team System. First, you get an overview of SQL Server 2005 internals, specifically the architecture of SQL Server Reporting Services. Once you understand the architecture, you get an overview of how to administer the database server. Some of the topics covered include the structure of the data warehouse cube, fact and history tables, schemas, and data regions. One of the key architectural components of the reporting service is the online analytical processing (OLAP) component. You get a view of the architectures, data warehouse cubes, and parameters. The Microsoft Solutions Framework (MSF) provides a good guide to let you know what reports should be looked at and how to interpret them. Next, you learn how to access the reports on Team Foundation Server. Next, you learn the all-important topic of how to customize your project reports using Report Designer, Report Builder, and Microsoft Excel to get the project data you need. Finally, you learn how to manage the data warehouse and set security permissions on reports including Team Foundation report site permissions and role-based security.

Chapter 17: Completing Software Projects—What do you do when your project has been completed? This chapter shows you how to export and save your project and settings. After your project has been completed, you may opt to do a project and server postmortem. This process may yield new optimizations for your development process. As a result, you may develop a new set of best practices. These optimizations can then be integrated into your project template, including changes in your work items and documentation. How do you delete a project (or port over a project to another server)? This chapter shows you how to delete a project using `DeleteTeamProject` and uninstalling Team System as a whole. Finally, we examine new future directions for Team Foundation Server and Team System.

What You Will Need to Use the Book

To use the book, you will at a minimum require a copy of a Team Edition (for example, Architect, Developer, Tester, or Database Professional—preferably Team Suite), Team Foundation Server, and all applicable components installed on your system. Even if you are implementing this product within your work environment, we highly recommend that you install a test copy on a virtual drive (or download a

VirtualPC image from MSDN) to try out the examples contained within. You also need other Microsoft products such as Windows Server 2003, Office, and VirtualPC; please refer to the Team System `readme` for more details. Chapter 2 provides a step-by-step guide to installing the product on a virtual drive.

If you are simply evaluating Team System, you can download a trial copy of it from the Microsoft Web site at `www.microsoft.com/vstudio/`.

Source Code

As you work through the examples in this book, you may choose either to type in all the code manually or to use the source code files that accompany the book. All of the source code used in this book is available for download at `www.wrox.com`. Once at the site, simply locate the book's title (either by using the Search box or by using one of the title lists) and click the Download Code link on the book's detail page to obtain all the source code for the book.

Because many books have similar titles, you may find it easiest to search by ISBN; this book's ISBN is 0-471-91930-6 (changing to 978-0-471-91930-8 as the new industry-wide 13-digit ISBN numbering system is phased in by January 2007).

Once you download the code, just decompress it with your favorite compression tool. Alternately, you can go to the main Wrox code download page at `www.wrox.com` to see the code available for this book and all other Wrox books.

Errata

We make every effort to ensure that there are no errors in the text or in the code. However, no one is perfect, and mistakes do occur. If you find an error in one of our books, such as a spelling mistake or a faulty piece of code, we would be very grateful for your feedback. By sending in errata, you may save another reader hours of frustration, and you will be helping us provide even higher quality information.

To find the errata page for this book, go to `www.wrox.com` and locate the title using the Search box or one of the title lists. Then, on the book details page, click the Book Errata link. On this page, you can view all errata that has been submitted for this book and posted by Wrox editors. A complete book list, including links to each book's errata, is also available at `www.wrox.com/misc-pages/booklist.shtml`.

If you don't spot "your" error on the Book Errata page, go to `www.wrox.com/contact/techsupport.shtml` and complete the form there to alert us about the error you have found. We'll check the information and, if appropriate, post a message to the book's errata page and fix the problem in subsequent editions of the book.

p2p.wrox.com

For author and peer discussion, join the P2P forums at `http://p2p.wrox.com`. The forums are a Web-based system for you to post messages relating to Wrox books and related technologies and to interact with other readers and technology users. The forums offer a subscription feature to e-mail you topics of interest of your choosing when new posts are made to the forums. Wrox authors, editors, other industry experts, and your fellow readers are present on these forums.

At `http://p2p.wrox.com` you will find several different forums that will help you not only as you read this book, but also as you develop your own applications. To join the forums, just follow these steps:

1. Go to `http://p2p.wrox.com` and click the Register link.
2. Read the terms of use and click Agree.
3. Complete the required information to join, as well as any optional information you wish to provide and click Submit.
4. You will receive an e-mail message with information describing how to verify your account and complete the joining process.

You can read messages in the forums without joining P2P, but, in order to post your own messages, you must join.

Once you join, you can post new messages and respond to messages other users post. You can read messages at any time on the Web. If you would like to have new messages from a particular forum e-mailed to you, click the Subscribe to this Forum icon by the forum name in the forum listing.

For more information about how to use the Wrox P2P, be sure to read the P2P FAQs for answers to questions about how the forum software works as well as many common questions specific to P2P and Wrox books. To read the FAQs, click the FAQ link on any P2P page.

Part I
Deployment and Administration

1

Planning a Team System Deployment

It can't be stated enough that planning is an essential part of any process. Without planning, you may unnecessarily complicate the deployment process or, worse yet, miscalculate what your needs are and have to reinstall the product. (As a consultant who has deployed Team System hundreds of times, I speak from experience.)

Deployment does not necessarily mean just the installation of the product. Once Team System has been installed, you must configure it correctly. (For example, you must set up the proper permissions, change the process template to match the target environment, and handle other details including source code migration and extension or customization of tools to make them interact with Team Foundation Server). If you are a consultant, you'll often get client requests to install Team System in, say, two days. Team Foundation Server takes at the very least a day to correctly install and configure in an enterprise environment. Working on a two-day engagement to deploy Team System is the equivalent of asking a home builder to build a house from scratch in two weeks! It's best to set the proper expectations with your clients, work out a deployment plan, and work out realistic timeframes.

In this chapter, you learn the major components of Team System and how to plan your deployment based on your capacity and needs. The final part of the chapter discusses strategies to help you migrate your existing tools and data to Team System.

Team Foundation Server Overview

One of the big challenges of working on a software development team is getting all the members of the team to collaborate seamlessly. There are always so-called silos that are created for each role on a team. For example, developers like to live in Visual Studio and can easily relate to development talk and issues, whereas most project managers have no Visual Studio experience whatsoever; they are used to working with Excel spreadsheets working up use cases, scenarios, and project milestones.

Architects map out application designs in Visio, testers use testing tools. The groups and roles are quite different. Trying to integrate it all is difficult and requires a lot of coordination — and frequently intercession — on the part of the project manager, who must set up status meetings and track deliveries from a number of sources.

To successfully deploy Team System, you'll need cooperation from the entire development team, and especially the operations team. Installing Team System involves setting up accounts in Active Directory, changing firewall port settings, prepping hardware, making sure the licensed software is available on DVD or on a network share, and so forth. Get the operations team involved early in the process and get them to read the Team Foundation Server installation guide (and quiz them on it). Both of these steps will make the deployment process a lot easier.

Team System (and specifically Team Foundation Server) provides tooling and a framework to simplify collaboration between team members. The server allows you to communicate with anyone on your team using a number of tools including the Visual Studio editions, Microsoft Excel, Microsoft Project, and Team Explorer. All team members get access to a common set of services including a Team Portal, version control, build engine, and reporting. Everything is integrated in one location. All of this means that you need fewer status meetings, and you get more transparency and clarity with regards to the work being done within a project.

Team System can be viewed as three logical tiers: the client tier, which includes the Team Editions of Visual Studio 2005; the application tier, in other words, Team Foundation Server; and the data tier (SQL Server 2005), which provides the data management and storage support behind the scenes. This very basic architecture can be seen in Figure 1-1.

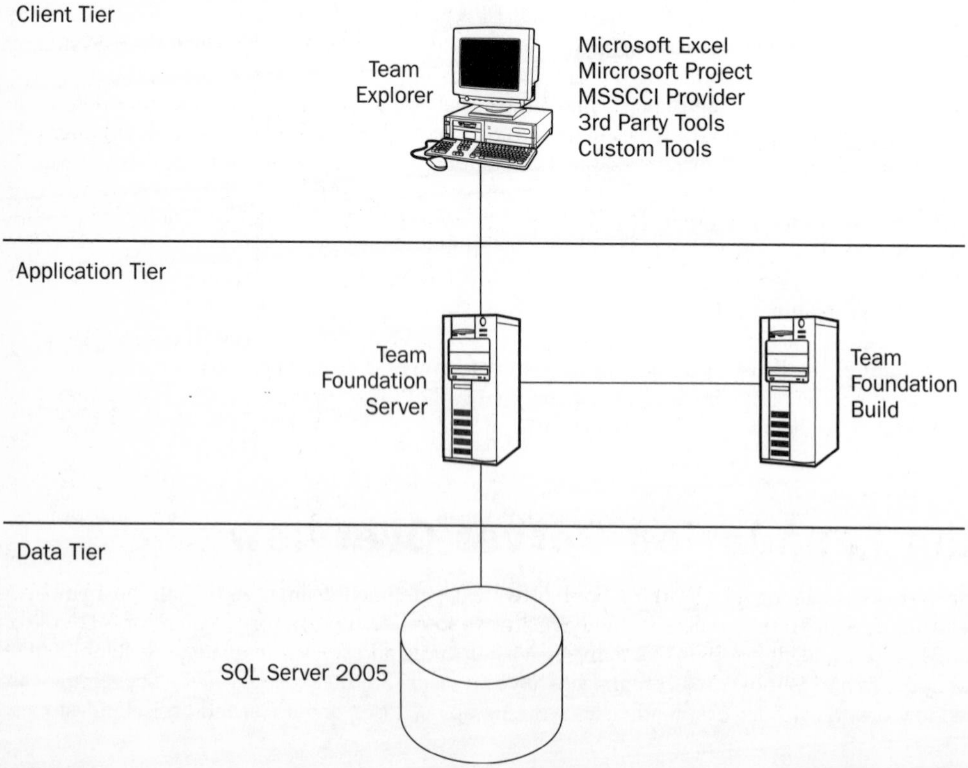

Figure 1-1

When you are planning a deployment, it is important to consider what deployment scenario will work best for your needs and what client/server configuration will give you the best bang for your buck in terms of management and configurability. Let's start by looking at the essential parts that make up the client and server components of Team System.

Team System Overview

Team Foundation Server plays a very important part in Team System. It is the collaborative suite that supports the entire software development life cycle (SDLC). Prior versions of Visual Studio supported developers only and everyone else had to rely on third-party products to achieve any kind of integration. The different tiers of Team System can be further broken down into its client and server components.

> **Brian Harry has posted on his blog a Visio diagram outlining how Team System was deployed within Microsoft. Specifically, it maps out the overall topology of both server and components. You can download the Visio file at the following link:** `http://blogs.msdn.com/bharry/archive/2006/08/22/712746.aspx`.

Client Components

Here is a listing of Team System's core client components. You can't really talk about a server without discussing how the clients interact with the server (of course). Along with these clients, the Team Foundation Server API (also known as the Team Foundation Core Services) contains methods that allow you to programmatically connect to Team Foundation Server (and create your own custom clients).

- **Visual Studio 2005 Team Editions** — Even though this is a book on Team Foundation Server, we would be remiss not to cover client features and how they integrate with Team Foundation Server. Refer to the individual editions below for details on the coverage level.
    - **For software architects** — Unfortunately, this book has little to no coverage of the architecture tools. If you are interested in Team Edition for Software Architects, we would like to refer you to *Professional Visual Studio 2005 Team System* (Wrox Press, ISBN: 0764584367).
    - **For software developers** — For developers, the book covers version control management (Chapter 12) and extensibility (Chapters 9 through 11).
    - **For software testers** — For testers, refer to Chapter 15 for information about the Team Test Load Agent. We also cover test case management to a limited degree in Chapter 13.
    - **For database professionals** — Chapter 8 is devoted to Team Edition for Database Professionals and how the data development lifecycle ties into the software development lifecycle.
    - **Visual Studio 2005 Team Suite** — Visual Studio 2005 Team Suite integrates the features of Team Edition for Software Architects, Team Edition for Software Developers, and Team Edition for Software Testers. Starting late 2006, Team Suite will also include Team Edition for Database Professionals.

- **Team Explorer** — Team Explorer ships on the Team Foundation Server media and provides connectivity between Visual Studio 2005 and Team Foundation Server. You can learn more details about Team Explorer in Chapter 2.
- **Third Party Tools** — There are a number of third-party companies developing tools for Team Foundation Server. When appropriate, we have provided you with links to these complementary tools.
- **MSSCCI Provider (for Visual Studio 6.0 and 2003)** — Many companies have made investments in .NET 1.0 and .NET 1.1, and need to support Visual Basic 6.0. The Microsoft Source Code Control Interface provider allows these IDEs to connect to Team Foundation Server.
- **Microsoft Office Excel 2003** — Microsoft Excel is used as a project management tool within Team System. (A developer or any other team member can also use it to manage their work items.) You can learn how to make the most out of Excel in Chapter 13.
- **Microsoft Project 2003** — Microsoft Project has special capabilities and limitations that are documented in Chapter 13.

Server Components

These server components provide the infrastructure backbone for Team System. In this book, we examine each one of these in detail:

- **Team Foundation Server** — Team Foundation Server is comprised of a number of components and services. The installation of the product is covered in Chapter 2, you learn about backup and recovery strategies in Chapter 5, right up to retirement in Chapter 17.
- **Team Foundation Build** — Team Foundation Build provides an automated, integrated build experience. You can learn a great deal more about Team Foundation Build in Chapter 3.
- **Team Test Load Agent** — The Team Test Load Agent is composed of an Agent and Controller, which allows you to test Web applications against a profile of a thousand users or more. There is coverage of these tools in Chapter 15.
- **Team Foundation Server Proxy** — Team Foundation Server Proxy is a tool that helps improve the performance of Team Foundation Version Control over HTTP. We cover the proxy in Chapter 15.
- **Team Foundation Core Services** (TFCS) — Team Foundation Core Services is a set of services and APIs that allow you to extend Team Foundation Server. You can learn more about extensibility in Chapter 9.
- **Active Directory domain controller** — If you are working within a big enterprise, Active Directory (AD) is essential for the management of your user's roles and credentials. You'll find deep coverage of AD in Chapters 2 and 4.
- **Mail server** — Team Foundation Server has the ability to leverage a mail server to send out alerts to your team members. The alert and eventing infrastructure is covered in several chapters, most notably in Chapter 14.

Compiling Your Project Data

There is key data you should compile to plan a deployment. Otherwise, you may be unprepared for the installation and it may be unnecessarily complicated. Here are some of the data points you should collect:

- **Hardware infrastructure** — This includes a full audit of all the target systems that will be used alongside Team System. This audit should be undertaken in consultation with your operations team. Equipment usually takes time to order, therefore you may want to consider dates — a nontrivial requirement because they will affect the dates in which you can start the deployment. Part of the hardware infrastructure review includes writing a maintenance plan, which includes backup/recovery, a maintenance task list for administrators to perform regularly, and so forth. Your operations team should be deeply involved in this process.
- **Software infrastructure** — List all the software required for the deployment, and the software currently in place in your environment. The software check may reveal systems with incompatible software, in which case the operations team must upgrade the target systems before starting the deployment process. A close consultation with your operations team is key to obtaining a solid understanding of the target environment. Another element that can't be understated is licensing. Do you have all the necessary licenses for Team System? A good place to start is look at the 1:1 correspondence between the software you need and licenses you need. After that, you will need to look at client access licenses (CALs) for those who will be accessing Team Foundation Server without a Team Edition.
- **Network infrastructure** — Your network infrastructure may appear deceptively simple, but there are many things to consider including security settings, user account settings, topology challenges, and so forth. For example, if you have governance rules in place, your user accounts may have special restrictions such as password policies that will complicate a deployment. Another scenario is that ports may need to be opened on your network to allow Team Foundation Server communication to flow through. In order for the ports to be opened, a security audit might be required. It's important to note not only the components that are required, but also the process behind those components.
- **Project documentation** — Find all documents relating to your software development process and the documents supporting that process, including templates, lists, and so on. If some of these seem ad hoc, not to worry. Team System provides a solid mechanism for aggregating and publishing software project assets.
- **Build requirements** — The complexity of your build may depend on many factors, including what type of software you are developing, if you are building a multiplatform or distributed solution, and so forth. The key information you will want to record includes what needs to be built, what you are expecting as a release at the end of the build process, and if any special tasks are required along the way (for example, automatically copying files via FTP to another server).
- **Source code** — How much source code do you have? Where is it stored? What policies and procedures have you put in place to track versions and integrate source code? You must document all of this to decide how you will migrate the code and what approach to take to configure Team Foundation Version Control.

Another thing you can do that can't be understated is creating a checklist before deployment. Figure 1-2 shows the installation checklist available in the Visual Studio Team Foundation Installation Guide. It breaks down the installation steps for both single-server and dual-server deployments.

You can create a personal checklist in Excel that reflects the software, hardware, and tasks you need to accomplish to successfully deploy Team System. Figure 1-3 shows an inventory of software, which you can check off as you obtain it. Once all the software has been checked off the list, for example, you know that you are ready for the deployment.

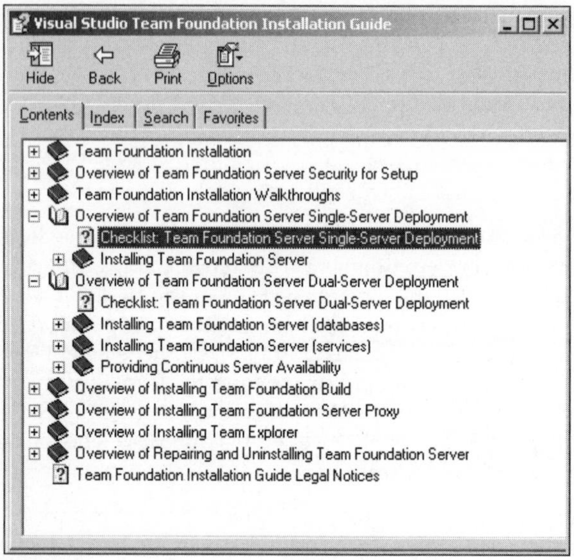

Figure 1-2

	A	
1	Team Foundation Server Deployment Checklist	
2		Description
3		**Software Requirements** (*on DVD or accessible network share*)
4		- Windows Server 2003
5		- Windows Server 2003 R2
6		- Team Foundation Server RTM
7		- Visual Studio 2005 Team Editions (for each team member)
8		- Team Edition for Software Developers
9		- Team Edition for Software Testers
10		- Team Edition for Software Architects
11		- Team Edition for Database Professionals
12		- Team Suite (for Team Foundation Build server)
13		- Windows SharePoint Services Service Pack 2
14		- Microsoft SQL Server 2005
15		- Developer Edition
16		- Standard Edition
17		- Professional Edition
18		- Enterprise Edition
19		- Microsoft Office 2003 Professional
20		- Microsoft Office 2007 Professional

Figure 1-3

Planning a Deployment

Installing and deploying a product such as Visual Studio 2005 Team System involves a lot of preplanning and forethought. You must consider variables such as capacity, scale, disaster recovery planning, backups, and the underlying infrastructure. There are several important sources you can refer to that will help in your deployment efforts:

- **Existing infrastructure documentation** — If your company had to write up a disaster recovery plan (which may have stemmed from the Year 2000 fiasco), then you are in a great position as all your software and assets have been catalogued.
- **Visual Studio Team Foundation Planning Guide** — Along with the Installation Guide (`TFSInstall.chm`) and Administration Guide (`TFSAdmin.chm`), the Planning Guide will provide you with hints on what to look at in the planning process. Unlike the other guides (which are also great tools to help you plan your deployment), the Planning Guide (`TFSPlanning.chm`) is not available on the Team Foundation Server CD or DVD.
- **Microsoft Operations Framework (MOF)** — The Microsoft Operations Framework provides guidance on the proper implementation of technology based on Microsoft's own internal experience and practices derived from the IT Infrastructure Library (ITIL). You can learn more about MOF at `microsoft.com/technet/itsolutions/cits/mo/mof/`
- **Governance documents** — Your company may need to follow strict or specific rules for legal reasons. You need to consider these governance rules and practices when planning your deployment.

Some of the key questions you have to ask include whether you'll need one or two Team Foundation Servers (depending on the scale of your team). Will you need a proxy server? (In other words, will you support geographically distributed teams?) Do you need more than one build server? If so, where will they be installed? Do you need to create load tests with more than a thousand simulated users? If so, a test rig may be required. Here is a more in-depth look at these variables and how they may affect your implementation of Team System.

Capacity Planning

The best way to look at capacity planning is by thinking about and looking at scenarios. First, we look at the performance and scope of a deployment. Next, we look at deployment on a small and then a larger scale.

Performance and Scope

Team System was designed to work with a single Team Foundation Server instance at the core. Microsoft is currently investigating scenarios where multiple Team Foundation Servers instances are used to scale up to larger sized teams. However, note that Team Foundation Server does not currently support clustering and mirroring. (However, this is supported on the SQL Server 2005 data tier, which is really the key area because all project assets are stored in the database.) Team Foundation Server supports a warm standby scenario, if an issue should occur. For more information about availability within Team System, refer to "Ensuring Team Foundation Server Availability" on MSDN at `http://msdn2.microsoft.com/en-us/library/ms253159.aspx`. The Microsoft Operations Framework also has information about service management functions, including availability management, at `http://www.microsoft.com/technet/itsolutions/cits/mo/smf/smfavamg.mspx`.

The responsiveness of Team System depends greatly on the amount of memory you have in your Team Foundation Server and, most important, your SQL Server 2005 instance. The more memory and processor power you can add in, the better your user experience will be.

In planning your deployment, you must consider whether you will use Team Foundation Server for one or two configurations. Some of the questions you might be asking yourself include the following:

- How many users will you support?
- Are Proxy Servers required (for distributed version control support)?
- Will you support clusters of remote users?
- Where on your network is your build server?
- Do you need test rig and how many test users will you simulate?
- Will you integrate with Active Directory?

Small-to-Medium Deployments

There are two fundamental scenarios to consider for small-to-medium deployments: Let's first define a small-to-medium deployment as one to 2,000 users.

A one-user scenario may include a customer evaluating a demo version of the product, a consultant giving a presentation on Team System (perhaps through a single machine VirtualPC install), or even a small learning environment to help a group of users experiment with the product. The one-user version of Team System is usually installed on a single machine and may contain demo or evaluation versions of the product (rather than the full retail version of the product). The single machine install contains all the components of Team System including the client tier (CT), build engine, data tier (DT), and application tier (AT).

The second scenario in small-to-medium deployments is for two to 2,000 users. In this scenario, Team System is installed on a single server and deployed to a small team. Because there are multiple users, the client tier (in other words, Visual Studio) is installed on machines separate from those with the application tier and data tiers. This allows multiple users to access a single instance of the server. You can also optionally install Team Foundation Build on a separate machine or even on the client's desktop. This deployment model is configured to support workgroups or Active Directory.

Enterprise Deployment

The final scenario to consider is the very large team of more than 2,000+ developers, testers, and architects (assuming a dual-server install). To go beyond 2,000 users, you need to bump up the processor scale and performance along with memory on both the application and database tiers. A large infrastructure requires larger capacity, security, manageability, and support for geographically distributed software teams. Team System supports a large team by dividing the tiers on different machines. (Note that a single machine will not support anywhere near 2,000 users.) To support such a large number of users, you must use Active Directory 2000 or 2003. (Otherwise, from an operational perspective the management of the users and shifting needs will require more overhead than can be afforded.) Team Foundation Proxy allows distributed teams to access the source control portion of the product. You can optionally set up multiple build servers, multiple proxies, and, in some cases, multiple Team Foundation Server!

At the time of writing, Microsoft is internally evaluating Team System as a tool to manage ambitious development projects such as Windows or Office. In fact, the Team Foundation Proxy was designed to effectively tackle latency challenges with remote teams. The Prescriptive Architectural Guidance Group, as well as a number of other small organizations, is currently deploying Team Foundation Server.

For updates about how Team System can scale for larger teams, we highly recommend you look at Brian Harry's blog at `http://blogs.msdn.com/bharry/`.

Network Topologies

Depending on your target environment, the network topology may present a special set of challenges. Here are common deployment models that you may encounter:

Single-Server Deployment (Workgroup Configuration)

A single-server deployment is the simplest configuration option you can pick. It is advised if you want to deploy Team System for testing purposes or for very small teams. Typically, the single-server deployment is set up using a workgroup configuration (although it is possible to set it up on a domain).

We define a single server as a 2.2 GHz Pentium IV or Athlon, with 1 gigabyte (GB) of memory that will support a team of 50 or less. If you double the memory, support goes to 250. If you use dual-processor support on both machines with 4GB memory, support for 500 users is obtained. You may also wish to consider your build requirements, which may further determine the machine sizing.

The MSDN Subscriber Download site provides virtual machine images of a single-server deployment, which makes it very handy for you to test and evaluate Team System in a lab-like environment. You can deploy these virtual machines using either Microsoft VirtualPC (VPC) or Microsoft Virtual Server. VPC requires at least 1.5 gigabytes of memory for even modest usability. Two gigabytes is highly suggested.

The workgroup version of the Team System installation process has a couple of notable limitations. One of the limitations is that the domain users can't login to the server. (See multiserver deployment for details.) Second, your passwords and user accounts must be synchronized with Team Foundation Server. Otherwise, users will not be able to log in to the server.

Dual-Server Deployment

If you are planning to divide the tiers on separate machines, note that you should set up your servers on a domain. In order for your components to access the domain, it is *extremely* important for you to set up your `TFSSETUP`, `TFSREPORTS`, and `TFSERVICE` accounts using domain accounts. Otherwise, `TFSSERVICE` will be unable to effectively interoperate and authenticate with the domain controller.

Architecting Your Active Directory (AD) Structure

To set up and configure Team Foundation Server in dual-server deployment, you must use computers that are joined to an Active Directory domain. With the Workgroup edition, you have the choice whether you want to join it (or not). If you are working within a large infrastructure, Active Directory will be a given for managing your users on Team Foundation Server.

There are several reasons you would want to use Active Directory over the workgroup configuration. First, from a convenience perspective, you can implement single sign-on. Active Directory has security features that help prevent scenarios such as unwanted clients or servers running on your network. Second, and most important of all, is manageability. In Workgroup mode, you have to manually add all users and groups to the server; if you have hundreds of users, this can be a pain from an administrative standpoint because all changes made to the external network will have to be replicated locally on Team Foundation Server. For example, if a developer decides to leave a company running Team System, the administrator will have to remove privileges from not only the network, but also the server.

Team Foundation Server supports Active Directory 2000 and Active Directory 2003. (Windows NT is not supported.) Team Foundation Server will interact with Active Directory 2000 in native mode; mixed mode is not supported. Specifically, Team Foundation doesn't support NT4 and so does not support AD2000 mixed mode. It does support AD2003 mixed mode. Team Foundation Server also supports one-way trusts, full trusts, explicit trusts, and cross-forest trusts.

Team Foundation Server does not support a configuration of the application and data tiers on separate domains (or subdomains). You can't mix domains and workgroups either; they have to be on the same domain. Finally, make sure that your network isn't using Windows NT 4.0 Domain Controllers.

Test Deployment Using Virtualization

You can test your deployment using a variety of tools including Microsoft Virtual PC (VPC) and Microsoft Virtual Server. Virtual PCs are not just for testing. There is a trend to deploy VSTS on the workstation as a VPC. This makes it far easier for developers to get around IT-mandated machine configurations and is simpler to install. They can also be used for evaluation and training. Also, some organizations have adopted VPC on the Team Foundation Server side. Often this is used for evaluation, but also more and more for pilot efforts. There are many advantages to doing so, especially in a test environment:

- Virtual images created from one product are compatible with the other
- There is no need to reinstall Team Foundation Server. The virtual image can be redeployed to a production server quite easily.
- You can create a base installation of Team Foundation Server that allows you to restore the server to a pristine state rather than try to clean up the projects.

Almost all the features of Team System work within a virtual environment with the exception of profiling. The profiler will not work with 100-percent precision in a virtualized environment, because of virtual driver limitations. Think of it; the profiler uses the core system as a baseline to execute the tests. If the core environment is virtualized, it is difficult if not impossible to get accurate performance readings.

> **After Visual Studio 2005 Beta 2, the profiler does work with VPC; however, the profiler under VPC does not go down to the bare metal as originally planned. The dev/test team removed the exception that detects whether you are on a virtual machine. It is now left up to the user to know what the profiler meaning is. For most users, this is quite fine, as they want only a relative view of their hot spots, not an absolute view.**
>
> **Andy Leonard documented a way to configure a virtual domain controller with Team Foundation Server. You can read the details on his Web site:** `vsteamsystemcentral.com/dnn/`.

Client Planning

Before attempting to install any software within a large-scale environment, it is quite important to plan your deployment. Microsoft itself is still learning how to effectively deploy Team Foundation Server. Because there are so many variables, it is impossible for us (or Microsoft) to provide absolute guidance in all deployment scenarios. However, we can provide best practices based on our personal experience and expertise.

Team Editions

Microsoft has designed three versions of Visual Studio 2005 to support three roles in your typical software development team: Team Edition for Software Developers, Team Edition for Software Testers, and Team Edition for Software Architects. Before you deploy these products, you have to determine which edition best fits your team members. If there is an overlap between responsibilities or tools, then you can install Team Suite.

Team Suite

Team Suite encompasses the functionality of all the other Team Editions. It is useful to install on Team Foundation Build to get the full range of testing capabilities. Project managers should definitely get a copy of the suite product to be able to view architecture, development, and test solutions across the entire project.

Team Explorer

In most development roles, you are required to connect to Team Foundation Server, be it to generate a work item, upload source code, or run a build. Each instance of Visual Studio that will be performing these tasks needs Team Explorer and an accompanying client access license (CAL).

A project manager who has never used Visual Studio can use Microsoft Excel or Project integration to connect to Team Foundation Server. Keep in mind that Team Explorer will have to be installed regardless on their systems — the Office plug-in gets installed as part of the Team Explorer install process — and the project manager's system will also require a CAL.

The only roles that don't require Team Explorer are the client and upper management. They can examine the project portals and reporting features; the only requirement is a browser. No client CALs are required to view content on the Reporting site or the Project Portal.

There are other Team Explorer–like client tools developed by third-party vendors for the Team Foundation Server; these include Teamplain (a Web interface to interact with the work item database) and Teamprise (a Team Explorer–like plug-in for Eclipse developers).

Security Planning

To correctly configure your security within Team Foundation Server, you have to put some thought into what users and roles you will define within your development environment. You must consider several layers of security:

- Network security (enforced by Active Directory)
- Operating System security on the machine hosting Team Foundation Server
- Security within Team Foundation Server
- Security on a project level

Roles (as defined by the Microsoft Solutions Framework) play a main part in determining security settings. Would you want any developer on your team to create or delete projects on the fly? Probably not. Applying proper least-privileged user account (LUA) principles to your access controls is the best approach. In a nutshell, LUA advocates providing users with just enough privileges to do their job — no more, no less.

Where should you start? The first thing you can do is look at your current Active Directory user and group configuration. If possible, map and define groups within Active Directory that correspond to the roles defined by Team System. For example, architect, developer, tester, and project manager.

To save administrative headaches, you can map these groups to the groups within Team Foundation Server by adding the domain groups as part of the server groups. This will simplify the task of adding users in Active Directory and will provide a single point of contact for all user administration.

Here is a practical example: let's say a tester is promoted to be a test lead (which entails project management tasks). You can simply change the user in Active Directory from the tester group to the project management group. As a result, the permissions will trickle down to Team Foundation Server and the new test lead will gain more control over server functionality.

In a workgroup install, you must manually make changes on both the target operating system and within Team Foundation Server. As this is more administrative overhead, consider using the workgroup installation only if you manage a small number of users.

Refer to Chapter 4 for detailed information about configuring and administering security within Team Foundation Server.

Creating a Test Plan

Before you install Team System, you must consider who will be implementing tests, and how tests will be implemented. If you are running a large project, you may require additional build and test rigs to support the extra load. Testing can be done manually or as part of a build. You should think about what best practices you want to put into place to create an environment that fosters test driven development (TDD).

All tests will run seamlessly as part of a build with the exception of manual tests. As a best practice, you should create dedicated test runs of manual tests. The two reasons are that it will make the tests easier to administer and will not impede the run of automated tests.

You should also look at all the tests available in Team System to see which ones you can leverage. Frequent testing improves the quality of your code and, as a result, improves productivity. Chapter 13 has some coverage on how to implement test case management.

Test Rig Considerations

If you try to run a load test with more than a few users within Visual Studio 2005, Visual Studio may become unresponsive or you may experience performance problems at the outset. If you want to run capacity and performance tests, it is best to use a remote test rig (consisting of a test load agent and controller) to run the tests without affecting the overall operating environment.

Using the test runs that you can configure using Team Edition for Software Testers, you can use a test controller to manage several load agents situated on several machines. By distributing the load, you can most effectively test your applications without loss of productivity. It goes without saying that the larger the project, the more test rigs will be required. Let's now look at the individual components. The Team Test Load Agent is discussed in detail in Chapter 15.

Hardware Requirements

The best source of information for system requirements is the installation documentation. One reason we are discussing the hardware requirements in this chapter is because a lot of practical information is not covered in the documentation.

> **One of the hardware components you can never have enough of is memory. The more memory you have installed on your target machines, the more satisfactory your experience with Team System will be in terms of responsiveness and capacity. If you are to choose which machine to add the memory, choose the database server, as it will deliver the optimal results.**

Team Foundation Server

According to the documentation, Team Foundation Server requires a minimum of 1 gigabyte of RAM. (This includes the application tier and the data tier.) Based on private testing, you are better off assigning at least 2 gigabytes of RAM for the server (one gigabyte for the server component, one gigabyte for SQL Server 2005).

Team Foundation Server has preset capacity limits. Read the capacity document at `http://blogs.msdn.com/bharry/archive/2005/11/28/497666.aspx` to learn more about the number of work items the software can handle in heavier load situations.

Team Foundation Build

The hardware requirements for Team Foundation Build requirements are the same as the Visual Studio 2005 system requirements for the most part, except that support is limited to Windows XP Professional with SP2 and Windows Server 2003 with SP1 Standard or Enterprise Edition. If you have a small project with 5 to 20 users, Team Foundation Build requires at minimum a single processor running 766 GHz, an 8-gig hard drive and 256MB of memory. At the most, in a large project (spanning 250 users or more), Team Foundation Build requires a CPU with dual processors running at 2.8 GHz, 80GB of hard drive space, and at least 2GB of RAM.

Build requirements also are based on the duration of the project build. If less than 30 minutes, 1.5 GHz with 512MB RAM is fine. For medium size team with projects taking less than two hours to build, 2.6 GHz with 1GB RAM. For a large team, you will want dual 2.8 GHz with 2GB RAM.

SQL Server 2005

In a dual-server scenario, the data tier of Team Foundation Server requires a CPU with a single (or dual) processor(s) running at 2.2 GHz, 80GB of hard drive space, and 2GB of RAM. This should be ample to support from 100 to 250 users.

If your team is much larger, you should spec out your target server-class machine to have at least a CPU with quadruple processors running at 2.2 GHz, 150GB of free hard drive space, and at the minimum 4GB of RAM.

Visual Studio 2005

At the bare minimum, Visual Studio 2005 requires a CPU with a 2.0 GHz processor, 512MB of RAM, and 8GB of free hard drive space. Even though Microsoft states that 512MB is enough, my practical experience has shown that 1GB is the minimum required for any acceptable level of performance. Microsoft's recommended hardware requirements include a 2.6 GHz processor, 1GB of RAM, and 20GB of free hard drive space.

Other Tools

The minimum specification for a test agent (also known as a test rig) is a single processor running at 600 GHz, 1GB of hard drive space, and at the very least 256MB of RAM. The maximum requirement (assuming you have over 250 users) is a CPU with dual processors running at 2.8 GHz, 8GB of free hard drive space, and at least 2GB of memory.

The test controller has slightly different specifications. The minimum specification (roughly 5 to 20 users) is a CPU with a single processor running at 600 MHz, 1GB of hard drive space, and 256MB of RAM. For larger projects (and a greater number of users) you should spec out a machine with a single processor running at 2.6 GHz, 48GB of hard drive space, and, at the very minimum, 1GB of RAM.

64-Bit Support

Team Foundation Server (the application tier) will not run on 64-bit systems; you must install it on a 32-bit machine. As a result, you obviously can't set up a single-server install (application tier and data tier) on a single 64-bit system. The data tier (SQL Server 2005) will run on a 64-bit machine, you just need to install SQL Server 2005 64-Bit Edition. Team Foundation Build and Visual Studio 2005 will run on 64-bit machines but only in WOW64 compatibility mode.

Software Requirements

To successfully deploy Team Foundation Server, you must take into account the software requirements of each of the components. Here is a drill down of all the required software and additional practical considerations.

Required Service Packs and Software Components

At the time of writing, Team Foundation Server itself does not require any service packs. However, we have outlined the service packs for the components that Team Foundation Server depends on (for example, the operating system).

Team Foundation Server

Team Foundation Server requires Microsoft Windows Server 2003 with Service Pack 1 (SP1). It will not correctly function on any other current operating systems. To function correctly, the following software components must be installed: Windows SharePoint Services Service Pack 2 (SP2), Internet Information Server 6.0 (IIS, which is packaged with Windows Server 2003), and SQL Server 2005 Standard Edition and above. The key for a successful deployment is installing the components in the right order and correctly configured. The most accurate and complete source of information is the Visual Studio Team Foundation Installation Guide (`TFSInstall.chm`). The guide can be found on the CD or DVD installation media for Team Foundation Server.

SQL Server 2005

SQL Server 2005 has more flexibility than Team Foundation Server with regards to the operating system (again, assuming that you install the data tier [DT] on a separate machine than the application tier [AT]). SQL Server 2005 requires at least Windows 2000 Advanced or Datacenter Edition with Service Pack 4 or higher. It is fully supported on Windows 2003 Enterprise or Datacenter Edition, or Windows Small Business Server 2003 Service Pack 1 Standard or Premium Edition.

SQL Server 2005 has 64-bit support. If you try to run SQL Server 2005 32-bit edition on a server that has an x64 bit processor, it will run in Windows On Windows (WOW64) compatibility mode. Otherwise, SQL Server 2005 will effectively run Windows 2003 Service Pack 64-bit X64 Standard, Enterprise, or Datacenter Edition.

Team Foundation Server requires at the very least SQL Server 2005 Standard Edition to run.

Team Foundation Build

Team Foundation Build can only be installed on Windows XP Professional with Service Pack 2 (SP2) and Windows Server 2003 with Service Pack 1 (SP1) Standard or Enterprise Edition.

Visual Studio 2005 and Team Explorer

Visual Studio 2005 will install on Windows 2000, Windows XP Home and Professional, and Windows Server 2003. Note that Visual Studio 2005 is not supported on the Windows 2000 Datacenter Server.

> **If you need to install Visual Studio 2005 on a pre-Service Pack 2 system, Aaron Stebner outlines the steps on his Web log at `http://blogs.msdn.com/astebner/`. This may be useful if your operations department hasn't yet deployed Service Pack 2 to all desktops or in test installations.**

All the editions of Visual Studio 2005 also require Internet Explorer 6.0 with Service Pack 1, Microsoft Office 2003 (or greater) with Service Pack 1, Microsoft Data Access Components (MDAC) Version 9.0, and the .NET Framework 2.0 (which is installed as part off the Visual Studio 2005 installation process).

Team Explorer has the same requirements as Visual Studio 2005. It can be used as a standalone tool (a stripped down version of Visual Studio 2005 without any code building functionality). If you have any of the Team Editions installed on your target machine, Team Explorer will install as a plug-in, providing access to Team Foundation Server. Team Explorer is available on the Team Foundation Server CD or DVD media. Figure 1-4 shows a screenshot of the standalone version of Team Explorer.

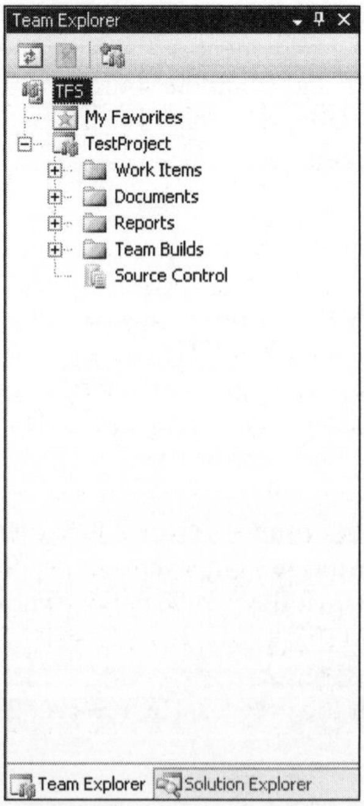

Figure 1-4

Other Tools

The test controller and test rigs are used to run load tests with a large number of simulated users on remote computers. The test controller requires Microsoft Windows Server 2003 with Service Pack 1 (any version of Windows Server 2003 will do), Microsoft SQL Express Edition, and the .NET Framework 2.0. The test rig must be installed on Microsoft Windows Server 2003 with Service Pack 1, Windows XP Professional with Service Pack 2, or Windows 2000 with Service Pack 4. The test rig also requires Microsoft SQL Express Edition and the .NET Framework 2.0.

Unsupported Software

If you want to integrate Microsoft Excel or Microsoft Project with Team Foundation Server, you must install Office 2003 before installing Team Explorer. Earlier versions of Office aren't supported.

If you are running any systems with Windows NT or Windows 98, you will have to upgrade them to Windows XP to connect them to Team Foundation Server.

Migrating and Integrating Your Existing Tools and Assets

When you look at how you can work within Team System, you have to consider whether it makes more sense to migrate or integrate your existing tools into Team System. Migration makes a lot of sense if you want to rid yourself of expensive third-party licensing agreements. For example, Team System provides the ability to do large-scale load tests and obviates the necessity of paying thousands of dollars to support and license a third-party tool.

Integration is a smart option if you have invested a lot of money on existing tools and you wish to leverage that investment. Integration is a little trickier because it often entails extra configuration and programming steps to make both systems "talk" to and integrate with each other. Let's take NUnit as an example of a tool that is very popular and does not have a great integration story with Team Foundation Server. Sure, you can migrate your NUnit code over to the Unit Test Framework within Team System using the migration tool. But if you want true integration with NUnit, you would have to create tools using Team Foundation Server's extensibility hook, which would perform the translation back and forth and allow Team Foundation Server to "understand" the code in build verification tests, during checkins, and so forth.

In this section, we will look at the core features of Team Foundation Server and discuss the challenges and resources available to help you migrate and integrate your existing solutions to Team System.

When making a decision about integration or migration, it is important to discuss the implications with a knowledgeable systems integrator or consultant. While a decision may seem straightforward, it may have cost, technical, and architectural implications. It is important that whoever you decide to work with has a solid background on Team System and your existing tools.

Version Control

Most of the core components of Team Foundation Server are designed to work with the .NET Framework 2.0. This makes Team System a very appealing candidate if you are planning to develop an application from scratch using Visual Studio 2005.

But what should you do if your application was built in VB6 or the .NET Framework 1.1? Here is a matrix covering the common scenarios you may encounter:

Scenario	Action
You have VB 6.0 or VC++ 6.0 and would like to import into Team Foundation Version Control.	You can choose to run Visual Studio 6.0 side-by-side with Visual Studio 2005. You can then import Visual Studio 6.0 projects into Team Foundation Version Control using the command-line tool or the MSSCCI client. Another option is to convert your code from VB or VC++ 6.0 to the .NET Framework 2.0. For example, if you attempt to open a VB 6.0 project in Visual Studio 2005, an upgrade wizard appears. There is also a lot of migration documentation on the MSDN Web site at `http://msdn2.microsoft.com/en-us/library/`.
You would like to import and build .NET 1.0 or 1.1 code in Team System.	In most cases, attempting to open and save a .NET 1.0 or 1.1 solution in Visual Studio 2005 will result in solution that will no longer open in Visual Studio 2002 or 2003. The reason for this is that Visual Studio 2005 supports the .NET Framework 2.0 only. So, what are your options? You can install Visual Studio 2002/2003 and Visual Studio 2005 side-by-side. By opening your older solutions in the older versions of Visual Studio, you will avoid any migration issues. However, until a Team Foundation Source Control plug-in is developed for Visual Studio 2003, the only way you will be able to import your code in Team Foundation Version Control is by using the version-control command-line tool. Another option is upgrading your application to the .NET Framework 2.0. This is facilitated by the built-in upgrade wizard. The downside is that you will have to deal with migration issues; however, the upside is that you will be able to import and export your source code using Team Explorer.

Scenario	Action
	There are two tools available to build .NET 1.1 within Team Foundation Build. The first tool is called MSBuild Toolkit and is available at `http://downloads.interscapeusa.com/MSBuildToolkit_v2_RC.msi`. The second tool is called MSBee — MSBuild Everett Environment. It is being developed by Microsoft. More information is available at `http://blogs.msdn.com/clichten/`.

For ASP.NET 1.0 or 1.1 code, there is a migration wizard to help you migrate your application to ASP.NET 2.0. The easiest way to migrate 1.0 Web services is to recreate them in 2.0 and copy and paste your source code.

> **Keep in mind that launching ASP.NET 2.0 Web sites will automatically launch the local Cassini Web Developer server by default. You should configure the virtual directory in your IIS server to host your application and set Visual Studio to launch without Cassini to get a similar experience as earlier ASP.NET applications. ASP 3.0 applications are compatible but will not compile.**

What if you have code designed for a different platform, for example, Java code? Team Foundation Version Control is versatile and can store different file types including Java projects. Obviously, code from other platforms will not integrate as nicely with the testing tools and the build engine. However, you could launch builds on other platforms using custom build tasks, and integrate external testing tools using either build tasks or generic tests.

Teamprise (`teamprise.com`), one of Microsoft's VSIP customers, has developed a plug-in to allow Eclipse to integrate with Team Foundation Version Control and Team Foundation's work item tracking. Before you decide to integrate code from other platform, however, you must first configure the file types by clicking on Team⇨Team Foundation Server Settings⇨Source Control File Types. The window shown in Figure 1-5 displays.

Simply add the required file type and you are ready to go. Be sure to select Disabled file merging if your files are binaries or nonsource code files.

> **You will have different levels of support for languages in Team System depending on the language. For example, there is great support for Java in the IDE, whereas other languages are "less" supported. Of course, you can integrate anything with Team System. All that is required is ingenuity and effort.**

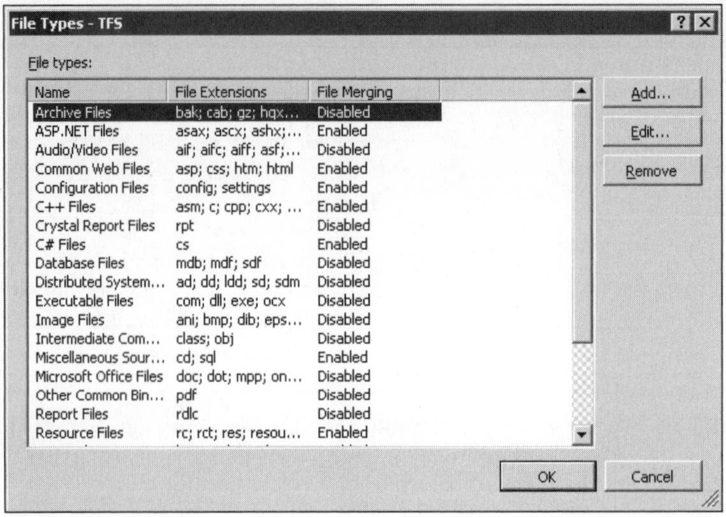

Figure 1-5

When looking at source control, the main question you have to ask yourself is if it makes more sense to maintain the current version or source-control system, or migrate your source projects to Team Foundation Version Control. If your company has invested tens and hundreds of thousands on a source-control system, it may not be in your best interest from a business perspective to migrate all your code. However, if you are planning new development using Visual Studio 2005 and the .NET Framework 2.0 (or .NET Framework 3.0), starting a project within Team System will be a good decision, as you will be able to leverage the deep integration between Visual Studio and Team Foundation Version Control.

> **One of the most important considerations in deciding whether to move your source code to Team System is your history. If the history isn't crucial, then you can check out all of your code and check it into Team Foundation Version Control. If it is important, then you may choose to migrate your code (using the Visual SourceSafe migration tool, a third-party tool like ComponentWare's Converter, or your own custom migration tool using the Team Foundation Version Control API), maintain the code in the existing repository, or even just keep an archive of your "old" code and begin new development on the new platform.**

Figure 1-6 contains a flowchart that will help you decide what approach to take in the migration (or archiving) of your existing code.

One of the most popular migration paths is moving code from Visual SourceSafe to Team System. Visual SourceSafe is a good tool for a small development projects with a small number of developers. However, it does not scale well if your team grows beyond a dozen developers and testers. Team Foundation Version Control is designed to manage large teams of developers and provides first time concurrent check-ins and rollback capabilities.

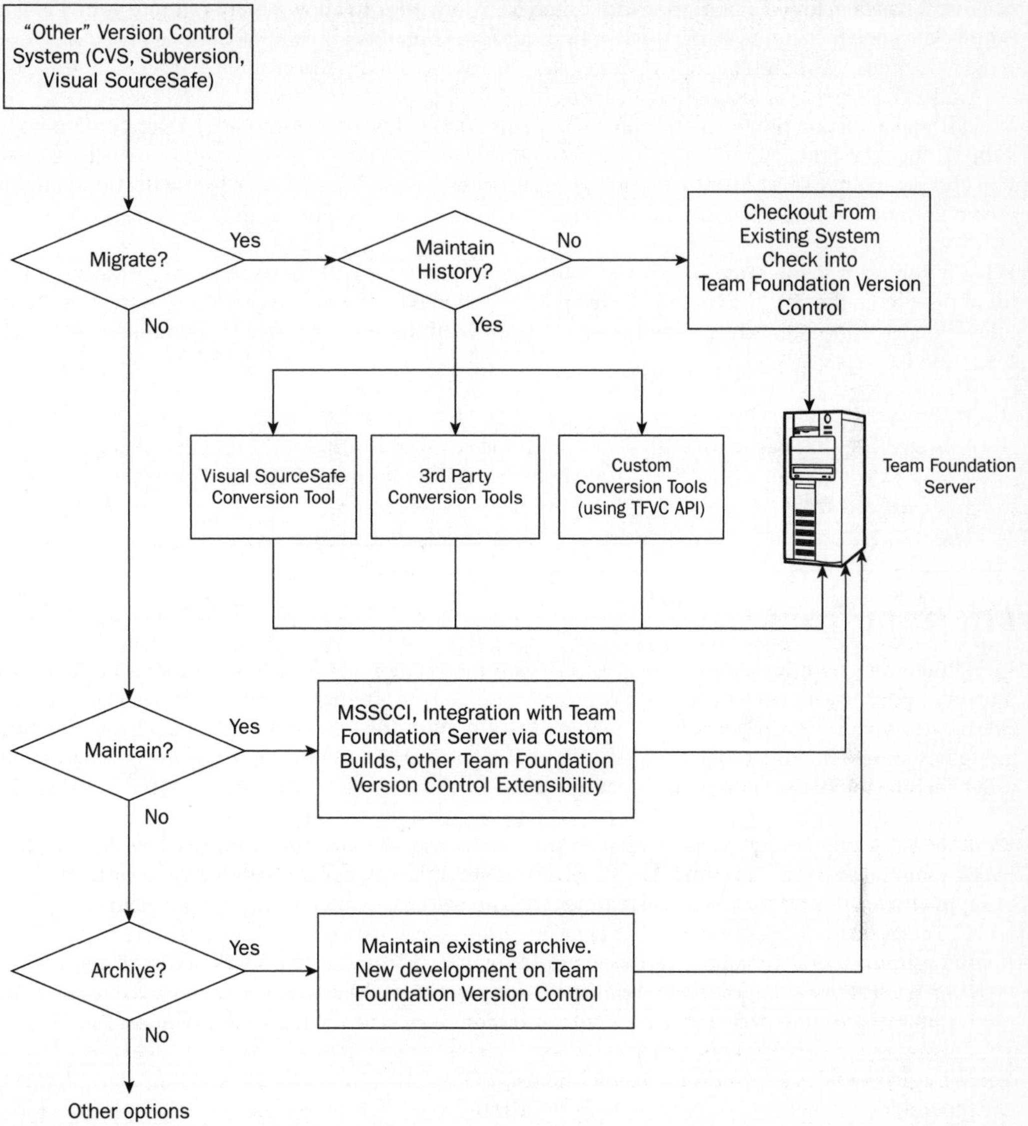

Figure 1-6

> **One of the biggest misconceptions about Team System's version control is that it is the new version of Visual SourceSafe. This is incorrect; Team System Version Control was written from scratch for Team System and uses SQL Server 2005 as a means of scaling to larger environments and infrastructures.**

Microsoft has developed a migration tool called VSSConverter to allow you to migrate your Visual SourceSafe code to Team System. You can find out more details in this MSDN article at `http://msdn2.microsoft.com/en-us/library/ms253060.aspx` and in Chapter 12 in this book.

What if you are using other version control systems such as CVS or SourceGear? Team System does not support these systems out of the box, but nothing prevents you from leveraging these systems directly. If you choose another source control system, keep in mind you will not be able to use the build engine. (Team Foundation Build pulls the sources out of source control before building them.)

What if you want to integrate an existing source-control system with Team System? Luckily, there are a lot of projects in the works to help you. Team Foundation Server provides a wide variety of APIs to allow you to connect and transmit information from Team Foundation Server to your source-control system and vice-versa.

> **Anything that has to do with extensibility is covered in Chapter 9, and can also be found within the Visual Studio 2005 Software Development Kit, which you can download from** `http://affiliate.vsipmembers.com/`.

Work Item Tracking

Work item tracking is an important feature of Team Foundation Server for two reasons: First, it provides a way for your team members to track workflow and collaborate right from within Visual Studio. Second, it provides the important link to implementing your process. For example, if the process you are using has a predefined iterative flow, you can create a series of tasks or requirements that will support and enact the iterations and establish your process.

Work item tracking is a baked-in and highly integrated way of managing your work within Team System. But what if you have invested work or budget on other tools? As with any other feature of Team System, you are not forced to use the feature. You can selectively pick what you prefer to use.

If you wish to move over your ClearQuest workflow to the Team System work item database, Microsoft provides a ClearQuest migration tool called WIConverter to help you out. You can learn more about the migration tool at `http://msdn2.microsoft.com/en-us/library/ms253046(en-US,VS.80).aspx`.

You may also be tracking workflow using Microsoft Office Project Server 2003. Fortunately, there are efforts under way to integrate both Team System and Project Server using a special connector. You can learn more about the connector at `gotdotnet.com/workspaces/workspace.aspx?id=b9f69ea5-ace1-4a21-846f-6222a507cc9c`.

The chart in Figure 1-7 shows the different decisions you can make in regards to migrating or integrating your existing work items within Team Foundation Server.

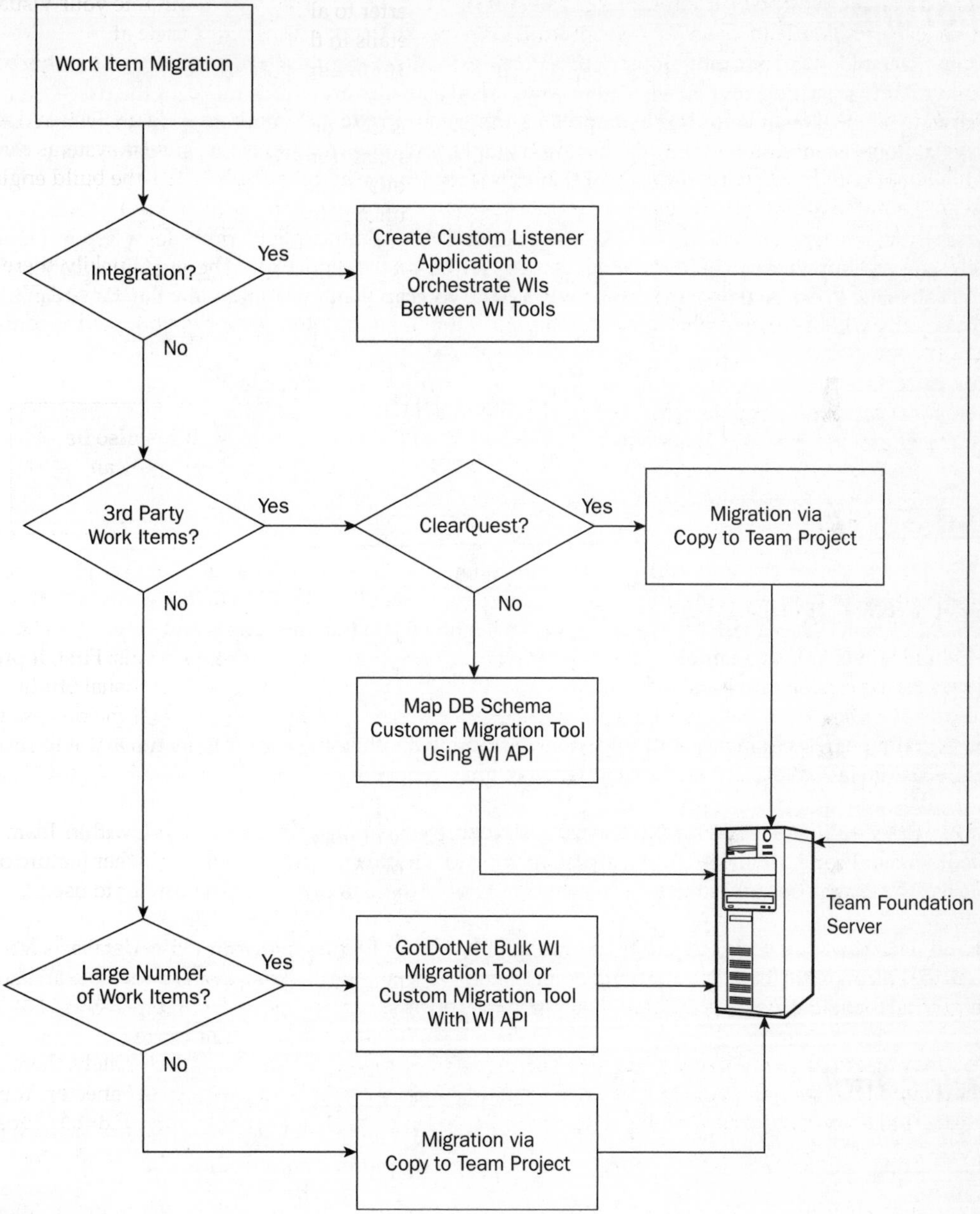

Work Item Migration
Integration?
Yes
No
Create Custom Listener Application to Orchestrate WIs Between WI Tools
3rd Party Work Items?
Yes
No
ClearQuest?
Yes
No
Migration via Copy to Team Project
Map DB Schema Customer Migration Tool Using WI API
Team Foundation Server
Large Number of Work Items?
Yes
No
GotDotNet Bulk WI Migration Tool or Custom Migration Tool With WI API
Migration via Copy to Team Project

Figure 1-7

Reporting

Team System does an amazing thing with reporting: It automatically aggregates project data such as build quality stats, bug counts, work item completion statistics and much more. In the past, you had to manually aggregate all your data by hand and import it into Excel to generate a report. Other tools like Crystal Reports provide the ability to generate graphs and other reports from raw data. One of the disadvantages with third-party tools is that they can be expensive.

Team System leverages SQL Server Reporting Services. Visual Studio 2005 provides a Report Designer to help you create new kinds of reports that can be viewed on the report site. The main idea here is that if you can bring in external data into SQL Server 2005, you can then mine and view the data in an integrated way within Team System.

You can create custom reports using the Report Designer or Excel. You can also create custom work items that contain reportable fields that can be integrated within a custom report. To learn how to create your own reports, refer to Chapter 16.

Build Server

One of the scenarios you may encounter is that you may want to transfer your NAnt scripts (or other build scripts) to Team System. Unfortunately, there is no established tool to help you do this. However, MSDN Channel 9 has a task equivalency chart that shows you the differences and similarities between MSBuild and NAnt. You can view the chart at `http://channel9.msdn.com/wiki/default.aspx/MSBuild.EquivalentTasks`.

In migrating or converting a script from one platform to another, the trick is sometimes just to find the right custom task to do the job. GotDotNet has a great repository of prebuilt custom build tasks at `http://www.gotdotnet.com/Community/UserSamples/Details.aspx?SampleGuid=2cb20e79-d706-4706-9ea0-26188257ee7d`. The GotDotNet project is called ".NET SDC Solution Build & Deployment Process & Tools." You can also download a number of useful open-source build tasks from Tigris. The download link is `http://msbuildtasks.tigris.org/`.

Figure 1-8 shows the decision path to determine if you want to integrate your existing tools (such as CruiseControl) with Team Foundation Server. If you want to migrate your tasks, then there are equivalency charts and custom tasks that will facilitate the process.

Testing Tools

Team System incorporates many testing tools including dynamic analysis, code analysis, manual testing, load testing, unit testing, ordered testing, Web testing, and performance testing.

NUnit Converter is a migration tool created by James Newkirk to port NUnit tests to Team System. Note that unit testing is fully integrated into the toolset as the Unit Test Framework. Note that this framework is available only in the Team Edition for Software Developers, Team Edition for Software Testers, and Team Suite versions of Visual Studio 2005. The migration tool is available on the NUnit Add-ons workspace on GotDotNet at `http://www.gotdotnet.com`.

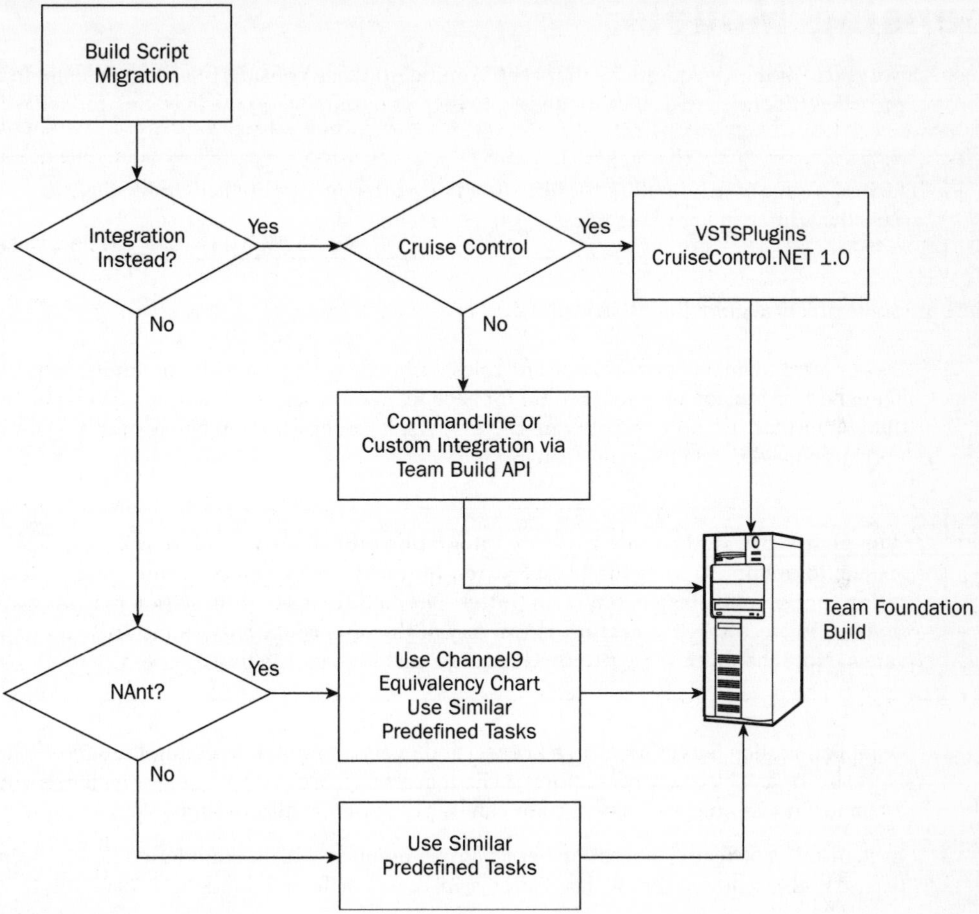

Figure 1-8

The converter tool is integrated in Visual Studio 2005 and requires the installation of the Guidance Automation Extensions to function.

In terms of load testing, Team System comes with an integrated tool. From a practical standpoint, one of the core advantages of the load-testing tool is that it is available to the entire software development team and is a great deal less expensive (from a licensing perspective) than other third-party tools. Another advantage is that the Team System load tester can support a great number of concurrent users.

Unfortunately, at the time of writing there aren't any migration tools to help you migrate Mercury Loadrunner tests to Team System. However, it is possible to integrate the Loadrunner tool using a generic test. The generic test allows you to run external executables (with parameters) and import results into Team System's testing framework.

Licensing Models

Cost is always one of the key questions that keep coming up when considering Team System. In this section, we provide guidance and a simplified view to help you understand the licensing model.

> **The best source of information for licensing is a whitepaper published on MSDN. To access the whitepaper, refer to** `http://go.microsoft.com/fwlink/?LinkId=55933`.

Here are some practical guidelines to consider:

- If your team members perform specific roles without overlap, consider obtaining a specific Team Edition version of Visual Studio for each team member. For example, developers would obtain the Team Edition for Software Developers. If there is overlap between roles, you should perhaps consider obtaining the Team Suite.

> **If you plan to use all the testing feature integration with Team Foundation Build, you should obtain a license for Team Edition for Software Developers and Team Edition for Software Testers (or Team Suite). The combination of these two products provides the necessary framework to run any of the tests commonly found in Team System. Note that both these products must be installed on the build server.**

- Team Foundation Server requires a license, and every computer accessing the server using Team Explorer (or any other client) requires a client access license (CAL). In some instances involving a remote "non-employee," a connector can be purchased to allow them access to the server.
- Each instance of Team Foundation Server Proxy requires a Team Foundation Server license. A license is also required for "warm" failover instances of Team Foundation Server.

Where to Get Team System

There are four primary ways of obtaining Team System:

- **Retail** — The components of Team System are available from retail outlets (such as Amazon.com). If you are buying the product retail, keep in mind that (a) you are paying full price, and (b) you are not going to benefit from Software Assurance (SA). Software Assurance guarantees that if Microsoft releases any Team System products off band (such as Team Edition for Database Professionals), you will get a license for it at no extra cost. It also applies if something like a "Team Foundation Server R2" gets released; you will be entitled to a copy.
- **Reseller** — Resellers such as SoftChoice provide good value because they have licensing experts that can find and tailor a licensing package to your situation and environment.
- **MSDN Subscriber Downloads** — If you get a combination of Partner, Academic or GSI Programs and own a MSDN subscription, you may also be able to benefit from substantial savings by upgrading to Team System. You can view more information about each option at the following link: `http://msdn.microsoft.com/vstudio/howtobuy/`.

Summary

This chapter introduced Team Foundation Server including its underlying architecture and the components of the product. Next, you learned how to compile your project data, including assessing security, client, and server requirements.

Later in the chapter, you learned how to plan a deployment and looked at the practical hardware considerations for the smooth operation of the product. You then looked at migration and integration scenarios for each one of the Team Foundation Server components. Finally, you learned about the Team System licensing model and a little about the costs involved.

In the next chapter, you will learn in detail about advanced installation topics and drill down on scenarios to put all of your planning into action.

2

Advanced Installation and Tools Migration

Now that we have discussed how to plan your Team System deployment, it's time to begin the actual installation of the product and its tools. This chapter is all about teaching you how to install the different pieces of Team Foundation Server (TFS), and how to migrate existing tools to Team Foundation Server. Installing Team Foundation Server has become much easier since the beta days of the project, as you might expect. You are going to learn how to install TFS over multiple servers, and how to consolidate the install onto a single server. As well, you will learn how to install Team Foundation Server Proxy, which can speed up access to the version control system for distributed teams, and the Team Foundation Build Server, which can be used to automate your build processes.

Virtualization technology is really starting to take hold like wildfire in enterprise organizations. It can be a very effective tool for testing new software, or for getting the most out of your servers. In this chapter, you learn about Microsoft's virtualization technology, how to create a virtual machine, and some tips for installing TFS on a virtual machine.

We then look at some of the administrative functions you may need to perform on your Team Foundation Server, and the different ways you can implement them. And finally, we have a brief discussion on how to migrate some of your existing tools, such as source control or work-item tracking, into Team Foundation Server.

Before we get started with the actual installation, however, we should discuss the different types of administrators for TFS, and what they expect from TFS. We also look at the user accounts that should be created before installation begins, and at the required Active Directory setup, if applicable.

Administrator Types

There are many different individuals perform various types of administrative function using Team Foundation Server. Each of them looks at Team Foundation Server in a different way to solve their problems, or make their daily work lives a little easier.

Enterprise IT Administrator

Everyone knows the enterprise IT administrator. He is the guy (or gal) who keeps the corporate infrastructure up and running. He watches and fixes problems with the network, makes sure e-mail is always working, and fixes problems with user accounts. He is concerned about the servers on his network, especially to ensure they are functioning properly. His daily concerns are for the reliability, availability, and performance of both his network and the servers on it.

He doesn't expect too much from Team Foundation Server. He just wants an application that works easily within the current security and software requirements of his organization. He also wants it to easily integrate into his existing disaster recovery procedures, so as not to create extra headaches for himself. That's not too much to ask, is it?

Team Foundation Server meets these expectations. It supports multiple deployment types, from a single server installation to multiple servers that will scale easily to meet demand. The servers can be members of an Active Directory domain, or a simple workgroup. Because most information concerning Team Foundation Server is stored in a database, integrating TFS into disaster recovery plans can be as simple as adding another database backup to the procedures.

Group IT Administrator

The Group IT administrator is usually a member of the development team. This person provides support to other members of the team. You know, the one everybody turns to for help, whether it is a programming question or a network issue. He is also the one who makes sure all the hardware and software systems used by the development team are in working order. He tries to keep everything running smoothly for the team members, so they can focus on their work.

He wants, from Team Foundation Server, an application with minimal administrative overhead. It also needs to provide good performance for the team. Additionally, he would love to have some sort of security control independent of the enterprise IT administrator. This would allow him to make the security changes necessary for people to do their jobs quickly and easily.

Team Foundation Server meets these expectations. Team Foundation provides excellent performance with a minimum of administrative maintenance. You can install multiple Team Foundation application servers, as needed. You can use the Team Foundation proxy server to speed up access to the version control system. Team Foundation Server also has its own built-in security model, giving the group IT administrator all the security powers needed for Team Foundation Server. For more on this security model, see Chapter 4.

Team Member/Developer

Everyone knows what the developer is responsible for, right? *Everything!* Just kidding (kind of). A member of the development team could be responsible for any aspect of the application. This includes designing an application, actually writing code, managing the nightly builds, or maintaining existing systems. Team members usually wear multiple hats and provide assistance on some or all the previous responsibilities mentioned.

What team members expect from Team Foundation Server is an application that deploys easily and quickly, has low administrative overhead, ties into their tool of choice, and enables them to complete their work in a more efficient manner.

Team Foundation Server meets these expectations. Team Foundation Server ties into Visual Studio 2005, Microsoft Word, Microsoft Excel, and Microsoft Project, allowing team members to use their tool of choice to complete their work. The functions of Team Foundation Server, including Work Item Tracking and Version Control, provide new and easy-to-use functionality, which will increase the efficiency and productivity of team members.

User Accounts

Before the installation of Team Foundation Server can begin, three user accounts must be created and configured as shown in the following table:

User Name	Description
TFSSETUP	This account is used to log on to the different computers and run the installation setup applications for Team Foundation Server.
TFSSERVICE	This account is used to run the different services that make up the Team Foundation Server. It is also used for different application pools related to Team Foundation Server.
TFSREPORTS	This account is used to access the data sources using SQL Server Reporting Services.

The user names listed in this table are sample names. You can use any name you would like. In this book, we have adopted these names for discussing the installation and configuration of Team Foundation Server.

The TFSSETUP account must be in the local Administrators group on each Team Foundation Server machine. The TFSSERVICE and TFSREPORTS accounts should *not* be in the local Administrators group.

In a multiserver installation, each machine must be a member of an Active Directory domain. The user accounts defined above *must* be members of that Active Directory domain.

In a single-server installation, the user accounts can either be members of an Active Directory domain or local user accounts on the machine. If the machine is a member of an Active Directory domain, the user accounts must be domain user accounts. If the machine is a member of a workgroup, then local user accounts may be used. Also, for a single-server installation, you can use the same account for the Team Foundation Server Setup and the Team Foundation Server Service account. The Reporting Services Account must still be a separate account.

Active Directory

If you are deploying a multiserver installation, all machines must be members of an Active Directory domain. When using machines that are members of an Active Directory domain, the Team Foundation Server requires that the domain *not* contain Windows NT 4.0 domain controllers.

For a Windows 2000 Active Directory domain, only native mode controllers are permitted. Mixed mode controllers are prohibited. If you attempt to use mixed mode controllers, the base Web services used by Team Foundation Server can't connect to the data tier. Everything may seem to install correctly, but you'll begin to receive really strange errors when using Team Explorer.

For a Windows 2003 Active Directory domain, only the standard mode controllers are permitted. Interim mode controllers are prohibited.

Installing Team Foundation Server

Now that we have discussed the user accounts necessary to install Team Foundation Server and the Active Directory requirements, let's get our hands dirty with the actual installation details. Make sure you follow the setup directions carefully to ensure your installation is a success. If you stray from the directions or try to take shortcuts, you will more than likely run into problems. Take the woodworker's advice: Measure twice; cut once.

> **The official Team Foundation Server installation guide from Microsoft can be downloaded at** `microsoft.com/downloads/details.aspx?familyid=e54bf6ff-026b-43a4-ade4-a690388f310e&displaylang=en.`

First, here is a brief overview of the Team Foundation Architecture. There is a data tier, consisting of SQL Server 2005. There is an application tier, consisting of Team Foundation Server and Windows SharePoint Services. Finally, there is a client tier, consisting of Team Explorer, which can be used as a standalone application or integrated into Visual Studio 2005.

Together, these constitute a base installation of Team Foundation Server. In addition, you can install the Team Foundation Server Proxy, to provide cached access to the version control system, and the Team Foundation Build Server, which provides help with build automation. These applications can be installed on the application tier or on separate machines.

Types of Installation

There are two main types of installations: multiserver installations and single-server installations.

- **Multiserver installation** — A multiserver installation places the data tier and application tier on separate machines. The Team System data tier components *must* be installed first. After the data tier installation is complete, you can install the application tier. If you wish to install the client tier on the same machine as the application tier, you need to first finish the installation of the application tier.
- **Single-Server installation** — A single server installation places the data tier and application tier on the same machine. If you wish to install the client tier on the same machine as well, you need to finish the installation of the other components first. The data tier must be installed before the application tier.

Multiserver Installation

In a multiserver installation, the data tier is installed on a separate machine from the application tier. This section covers the details of a multiserver installation.

The following list covers the prerequisites that must be completed before installing Team Foundation Server in a multiserver environment:

- All hardware and software requirements must be met. Refer to Chapter 1 for more information.
- All machines must be members of a permitted Active Directory domain. Refer to the "Active Directory" section earlier in this chapter for more information.
- All three users described previously (TFSSETUP, TFSSERVICE, TFSREPORTS) in this chapter must be created as domain accounts. Remember to add the TFSSETUP user to the local Administrators group on all machines involved in the setup process.

Once these prerequisites have been met, you can begin the installation of the data tier. Make sure you follow these steps in order. Don't be tempted to skip around or skip ahead. If you do, you may encounter problems with your installation. Refer to Chapter 5 for some of the more common installation errors and solutions.

Unless otherwise noted, you should log into every machine as the TFSSETUP user before doing any of the following installation steps.

Installing the Data Tier

The data tier is installed first in a multiserver installation. During this process, you will perform the following actions:

1. Set the base user permissions.
2. Install SQL Server 2005.
3. Install SQL Server 2005 Hotfix.

4. Make firewall modifications, as necessary.
5. Install Team Foundation Server databases.

> **The SQL Server 2005 instance for the data tier is specifically licensed for Team System and can't be used for other purposes.**

Setting the Base User Permissions

If you have completed the prerequisites, the TFSSETUP account is already a member of the local Administrators group on the machine. Verify this before proceeding to the next step of the installation. To do this, right-click My Computer, and select Manage. This opens the Computer Management window. Under System Tools, select Local Users and Groups, and then the Groups folder underneath that. Double-click the Administrators group to open it, and view its members. If you do not see the TFSSETUP account listed, click the Add button and add that account.

Installing SQL Server 2005

Team Foundation Server requires either Microsoft SQL Server 2005 Standard or Enterprise edition. Team Foundation Server itself includes a fully licensed copy of SQL Server 2005 Standard Edition, for use with Team Foundation Server only.

1. To start the SQL Server 2005 installation, log on to the data tier machine using the TFSSETUP user. Insert the SQL Server 2005 CD into your CD-ROM drive. If your CD-ROM drive is set to autorun, the SQL Server 2005 Start page will open. Otherwise, navigate to the CD using Windows Explorer, and double-click the splash.hta file to open the Start page. Under the Install heading on the Start page, click Server components⇨Tools⇨Books Online⇨Samples, to begin the SQL Server 2005 Setup Wizard.
2. The first window of the Setup Wizard is End User License Agreement. Select (check box) I accept the licensing terms and conditions, and click Next.
3. This opens the Installing Prerequisites page of the installation wizard. This installs the .NET Framework 2.0, Microsoft SQL Native Client, and Microsoft SQL Server 2005 Setup Support Files. Click Install to begin the installation of the prerequisites. Once this installation is done, click Next.
4. This starts the Microsoft SQL Server Configuration Wizard. Click Next. This opens the System Configuration Check Page, shown in Figure 2-1. If any problems are indicated on this page, they should be addressed before continuing with the installation. Note, that you will not be installing Reporting Services on the data tier. Thus, you can ignore any warning related to IIS feature requirements. Once everything is ready, click Next to continue with the installation.

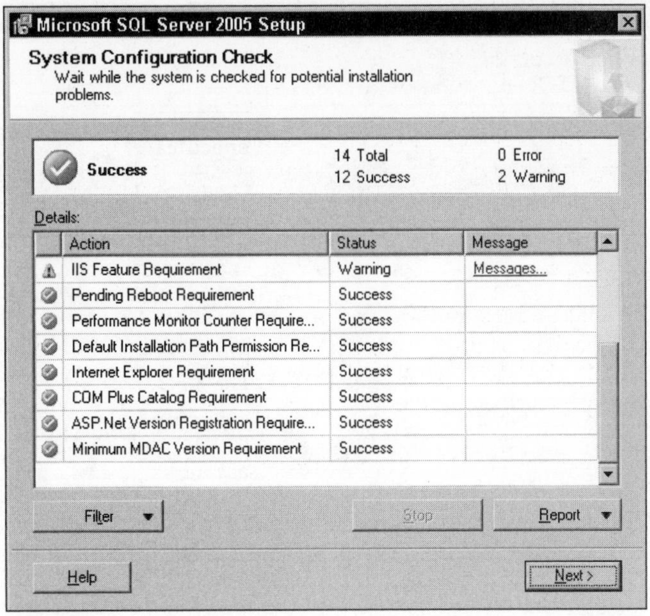

Figure 2-1

5. Next appears the Registration Information page. Fill out your name, company name, enter your registration key, and click Next.

   This opens the Components To Install page of the wizard. Select the following components:

   - SQL Server Database Services
   - Analysis Services
   - Integration Services
   - Workstation components, Books Online, and development tools

6. Notification services is not required by Team Foundation Server, so leave it unchecked. Click the Advanced button to open the advanced options. Under Database Services⇨Replication, select Entire Features Will Be Unavailable; then click Next.

7. This opens the Instance Name page. SQL Server 2005 for Team Foundation Server must be the default instance of SQL Server. Select Default Instance on this page and click Next.

8. The Service Account page opens, as shown in Figure 2-2. Select the Use the built-in System account radio button. Select Local System from the drop-down list. At the bottom of the page, check all the services check boxes; then click Next.

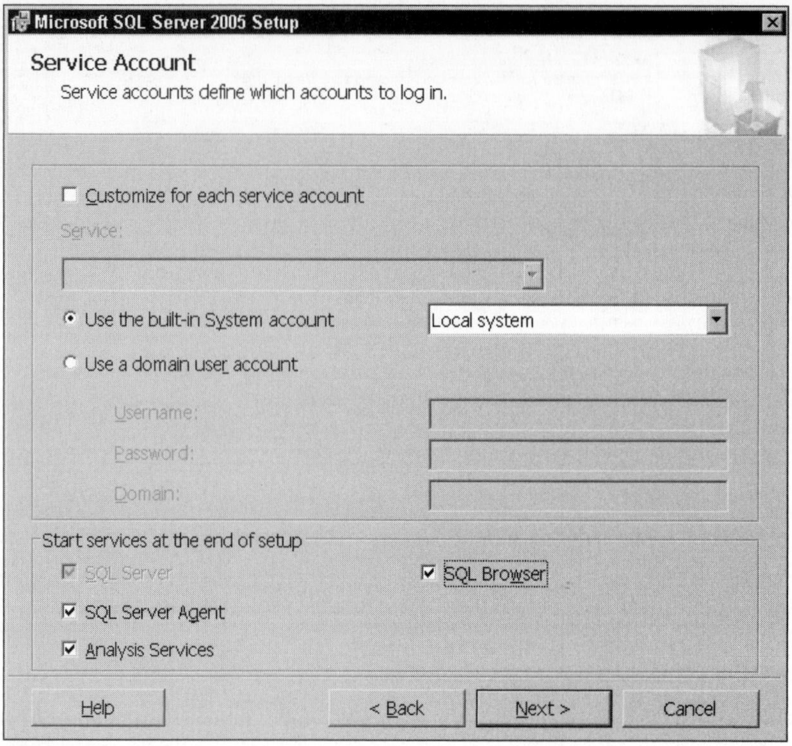

Figure 2-2

9. The Authentication Mode page appears. Leave the default as Windows Authentication; then click Next.
10. The Collation Settings page appears. Make sure to select the correct settings, as installing with the incorrect ones can mess things up. Select the correct collation for your language and click Next.
11. The Error and Usage Report Settings page appears. Both check boxes on this page are optional. If you wish to provide information on any errors that occur or on how you use SQL Server, check the appropriate box. Then click Next.
12. This takes you to the Ready To Install page. You can review all the options that have been selected through the wizard. If everything appears satisfactory, click Install to begin the installation. The Setup Progress page allows you to monitor each component as it is installed. Once the installation is finished, click Next. You can now choose to view a summary log of the installation. To complete the installation, click Finish to close the wizard.

Installing SQL Server 2005 HotFix

After the installation of SQL Server 2005 is complete, a hotfix needs to be applied to the database. This hotfix helps SQL Server Analysis Services with more efficient reporting. The easy way to apply this hotfix is to install Service Pack 1 for SQL Server 2005. By installing SP1 for SQL Server 2005, you get some general performance improvements with your database, besides the required hotfix.

If you don't want to install SP1, you can install just the hotfix. Before installing the hotfix, you need to turn off the SQL Server Browsing Service.

1. Go to Start⇨All Programs⇨Microsoft SQL Server 2005⇨Configuration Tools⇨SQL Server Configuration Manager, to open the SQL Server Configuration Manager. Once the window opens, click SQL Server 2005 Services in the left pane of the window. The right pane of the window now shows all the SQL Server services that are running. Right-click the SQL Browser Service and select Stop. This will stop that service. You are now ready to install the hotfix.
2. On the Team Foundation Server CD, find the SQLServerKB folder in the root of the CD. In this folder are three executables. Select the appropriate executable, based on your computer processor, and double-click it. This extracts the hotfix files and begins the installation of the hotfix. The Hotfix Installer window opens. Click Next.
3. This opens the End User Licensing window. Select the check box to agree to the license, and click Next. The window that opens shows you all the SQL Server instances running on the machine, and allows you to select which ones have the hotfix installed.
4. Click Next, and then Install, to begin the installation of the hotfix. Once the installation is done, click Next, and then click Finish.
5. Go back to the SQL Server Configuration Manager, right-click the SQL Browser Service, and select start to restart the service and you are done with this part of the installation.

Making Firewall Modifications

The following table contains the ports used by Microsoft SQL Server 2005. These ports should be opened in any intervening firewalls, to allow the data tier to communicate with the application tier and the client tier. If you are unsure how to modify your firewall settings, see your network administrator. If there is a firewall installed on the server itself, the setup application will open the appropriate ports.

Port	Protocol	Reason
1433	TCP	SQL Server
1434	TCP	SQL Browser Service
1444	TCP	SQL Monitoring
2382, 2383	TCP	Analysis Services

Installing Team Foundation Server Databases

Once SQL Server 2005 is installed, you need to install the databases needed for Team Foundation Server.

1. To start the installation, log onto the data tier machine using the TFSSETUP user. Insert the Team Foundation Server CD into your CD-ROM drive. If your CD-ROM drive is set to autorun, the Team Foundation Server Setup window shown in Figure 2-3 opens automatically. Otherwise, navigate to the CD using Windows Explorer, and double-click autorun.exe.

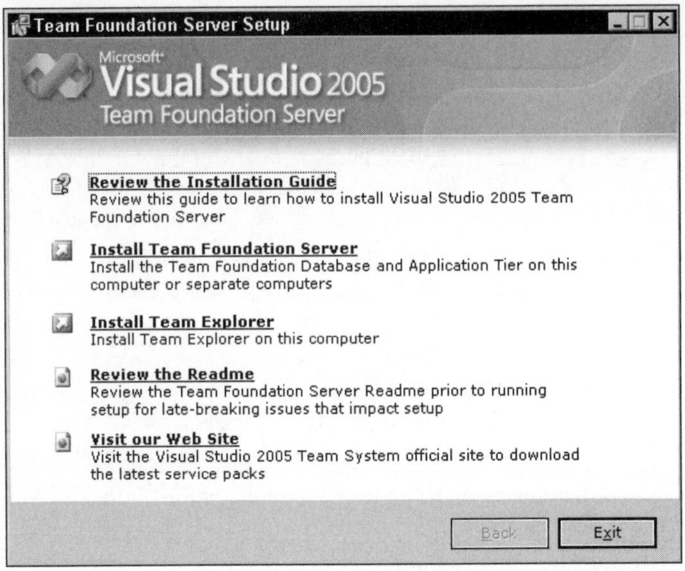

Figure 2-3

2. To install the Team Foundation databases, click Install Team Foundation Server, then Dual Server Installation, and finally Install The Team Foundation Databases Tier ONLY. This starts the Setup Wizard for installing the Team Foundation Server databases.
3. On the first page of the Setup Wizard, click Next to continue.
4. The next page is the End-User License Agreement. Check the I accept the terms of the License Agreement check box, and click Next.
5. This starts the System Health Check. If any problems are indicated, they should be addressed before continuing with the installation. Once everything is ready, click Next to continue with the installation. This opens the Destination Folder page. You can change the destination of the databases or accept the default. Click Next to continue with the wizard.
6. This opens the Ready To Install page. Click Install to complete the installation. Once the installation is completed, the Setup Completed Successfully page opens. Click Finish to exit from the wizard.

At this point, you have finished the installation of the data tier. Now let's move on to the application tier.

Installing the Application Tier

The application tier is installed next in a multiserver installation. During this process, you will perform the following actions:

- Set the base user permissions.
- Install Internet Information Server.
- Install Reporting Services.

- Install .NET Framework 2.0 HotFix.
- Install Windows SharePoint Services.
- Install Team Foundation Server.
- Make firewall modifications, as necessary.

Setting User Permissions

If you have completed the prerequisites, the TFSSETUP account is already a member of the local Administrators group on the machine. Verify this is the case before proceeding to the next step of the installation.

1. Right-click My Computer, and select Manage. This opens the Computer Management window.
2. Under System Tools, select Local Users and Groups, and then the Groups folder underneath that. Double-click the Administrators group to open it and view its members. If you do not see the TFSSETUP account listed, click the Add button and add that account. Also confirm the TFSSERVICE and TFSREPORTS users have been created.

Installing Internet Information Server (IIS)

Internet Information Server 6.0 (IIS) is used to provide Web services access to the Team Foundation Server databases.

1. To begin the IIS installation, log on to the data tier machine using the TFSSETUP user. Open the Control Panel and double-click Add or Remove Programs to open that application.
2. Click the Add/Remove Windows Components button on the left side of the Add or Remove Programs window.
3. Click the check box next to Application Server to select it, and then click Details. In the Application Server Details window, click the ASP.NET check box to select it, as Figure 2-4 shows.

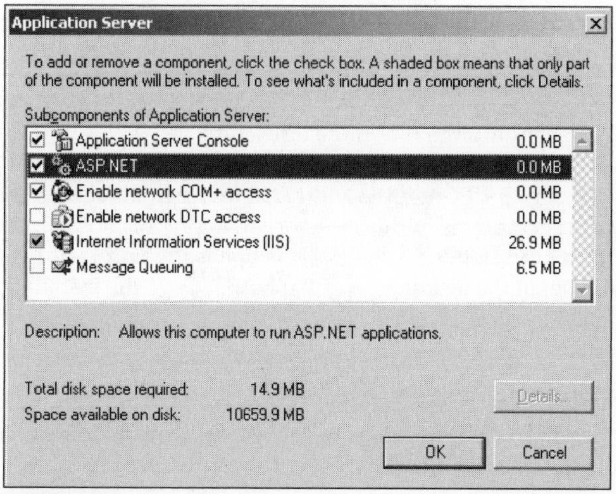

Figure 2-4

4. Click OK to close the Application Server Details Window. Click Next on the Windows Components Wizard window. This opens the Configuring Components window, which shows the status of the IIS installation.
5. Once IIS is installed, the Completing the Windows Components Wizard window opens. Click Finish to close this window and complete the IIS installation.

Next, visit the Windows Update site (`http://windowsupdate.microsoft.com`) to ensure you have the latest updates and security patches for IIS.

Installing Reporting Services

Installing Reporting Services is very similar to installing SQL Server 2005.

1. Follow the steps as listed in the previous section "Installing SQL Server 2005," until you reach the Components To Install section of the wizard. On the Components To Install page, select only Reporting Services, and click Next.
2. This opens the Instance Name page. SQL Server 2005 for Team Foundation Server must be the default instance of SQL Server. Select Default Instance on this page and click Next.
3. The Service Account page opens. Select the Use the built-in System account radio button. Select Network Service from the drop-down list. At the bottom of the page, check the Reporting Services check box; then click Next.
4. The next step of the wizard is the Report Server Installation Options page. Simply click Next to move on to the Error and Usage Report Settings Page. Both check boxes on this page are optional. If you wish to provide information on any errors that occur or how you use SQL Server, check the appropriate box. Then click Next.
5. This takes you to the Ready To Install page. You can review all the options that have been selected through the wizard. If everything appears satisfactory, click Install to begin the installation. The Setup Progress page allows you to monitor each component as it is installed. Once the installation is finished, click Next. You can now choose to view a summary log of the installation.
6. To complete the installation, click Finish to close the wizard.

Installing .NET Framework 2.0 HotFix

Once you have installed Reporting Services, you now have to install a hotfix for the .NET Framework, which allows ASP.NET to handle large files more efficiently.

On the Team Foundation Server CD, find the KB913393 folder in the root of the CD. In this folder are three executables. Run the executable in this directory to apply this hotfix to the server. You will be asked if you want to install this hotfix. Click OK. This opens the End User Licensing window. Click the I Accept button. This will begin the installation of the hotfix. Once the installation is done, click OK to finish the installation.

Installing Windows SharePoint Services 2.0 SP2

Windows SharePoint Services (WSS) provides the ability to create team-project portal sites for your Team Foundation projects. Team Foundation Server uses WSS 2.0 SP2.

1. To begin the WSS installation, log on to the application tier machine using the TFSSETUP user. Download Microsoft Windows SharePoint Services 2.0 with Service Pack 2 (`http://go.microsoft.com/fwlink/?linkid=55087`) and save the file to your local hard drive. Once the download is complete, double-click the stsv2.exe file to start the WSS Installation Wizard.
2. The first page of the wizard is the End User Agreement page. Check the I accept the terms in the License Agreement check box, and click Next to continue.
3. This opens the Type Of Installation page, shown in Figure 2-5. Select the Server Farm radio button, and click Next.

> **If you do not select Server Farm, Team Foundation Server will not be able to generate a new portal for each Team Project, and the Team Project creation process will fail.**

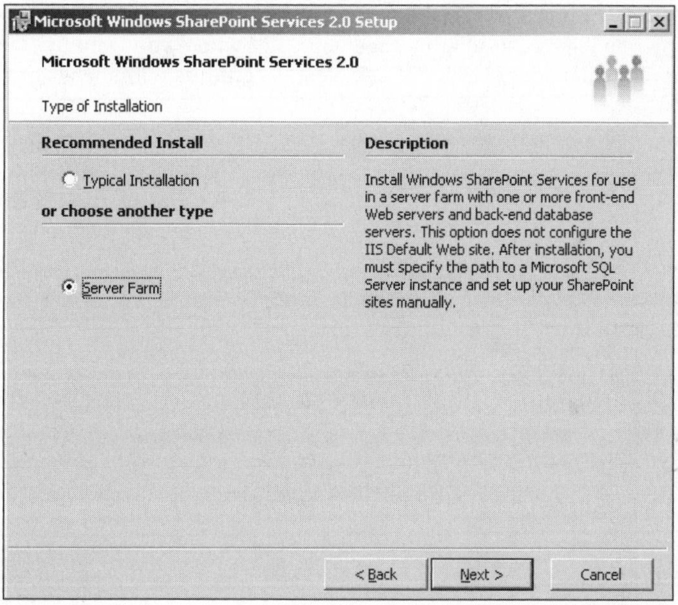

Figure 2-5

4. This takes you to the Summary page. Click Install to begin the installation.

When the installation is finished, a Web page opens to a configuration page for WSS. Do not make any changes to this page. Later, during the Team Foundation Server install, the installation program will make the configuration changes for you automatically. Do make a note of the port number for the site. This number is located in the URL in the Web browser `http://localhost:####`. You will need this port number to make firewall modifications later.

Finally, you should visit the Windows Update site (`http://windowsupdate.microsoft.com`) to ensure you have the latest updates and security patches of WSS. Once you have done this, reboot your server and continue the installation.

Installing Team Foundation Server Services

At this point, we are ready to install the Team Foundation Server Services on the application tier. These Web services provide access to Team Foundation Server functionality.

1. To start the installation, log on to the data tier machine using the TFSSETUP user. Insert the Team Foundation Server CD into your CD-ROM drive. If your CD-ROM drive is set to autorun, the Team Foundation Server Setup window opens automatically, as shown previously in Figure 2-3. Otherwise, navigate to the CD using Windows Explorer, and double-click autorun.exe.
2. Click Install Team Foundation Server. On the next page, click Dual Server Installation.
3. On the next page, click Install The Team Foundation Application Tier Only. This starts the Setup Wizard for installing the Team Foundation Server Application Tier.
4. The first page of the wizard is the Welcome to Setup page. Click Next to continue.
5. The next page is the End-User License Agreement. Check the I accept the terms of the License Agreement check box, and click Next. This opens the Destination Folder and Database Server page, shown in Figure 2-6. On this page you enter where you want the TFS files installed, and the name of the data tier machine. Click Next to continue with the wizard.

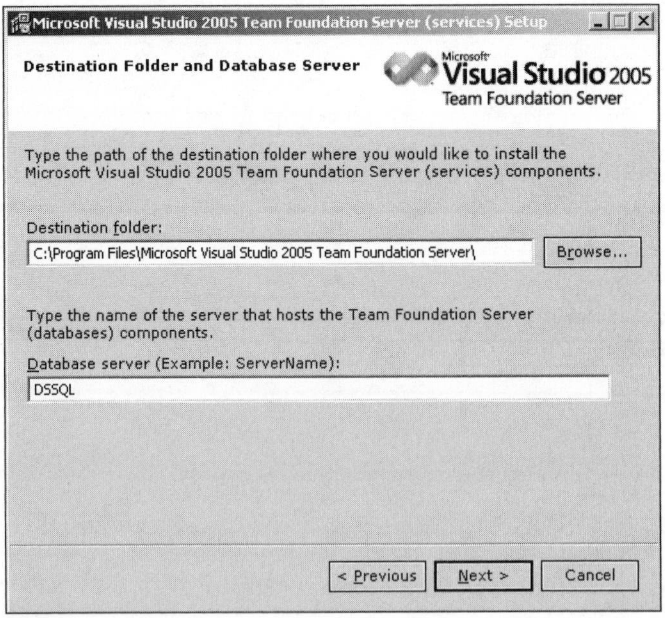

Figure 2-6

6. This kicks off the System Health Check. If this check shows any errors, review the detailed warning information and make the appropriate changes. Once you have resolved these errors, click Next. This opens the Service Account Page, shown in Figure 2-7. This is where you enter the user account used in the application pools for Team Foundation. Enter the name of the service account, for example TFSSERVICE, and the password. Click Next to continue.

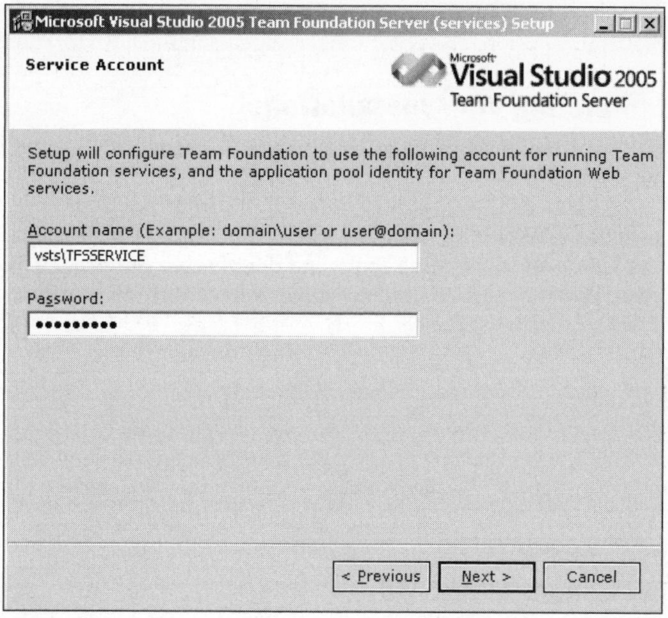

Figure 2-7

7. This opens the Reporting Data Source Account page. Enter the user account that will be used for accessing data in SQL Server for reporting purposes. Enter the name of the reports account (for example, TFSREPORTS) and the password. Click Next to open the Team Foundation Alerts page.
8. You can specify the SMTP server you wish to use, as well as who the e-mails should appear to be from. Click Next to continue.
9. This takes you to the Ready To Install page. Click Install to begin the installation. Once the installation is finished, the Setup Completed Successfully page opens. Click the Finish button to exit the Setup Wizard.

Making Firewall Modifications

The following table contains the ports used by Windows SharePoint Services and Team Foundation Server. These ports should be opened in any intervening firewalls, to allow the application tier to communicate with the data tier and the client tier.

Port	Protocol	Reason
80	TCP	WSS, Reporting Services
Variable	TCP	SharePoint Administration
8081	TCP	Team Foundation Server
8080	TCP	Team Foundation Proxy Server
9191	TCP	Team Foundation Build Remoting

To find the SharePoint Administration port, go to Administrative Tools in the Control Panel, and open SharePoint Central Administration. The port number appears in the URL for the Web site.

Verifying and Completing Your Installations

Now that you have completed the installation of all the components, you should verify that everything was installed correctly.

To verify IIS was installed correctly, log on to the machine using the TFSSETUP account. Open the Control Panel, double-click Administrative Tools, and double-click Services. This opens the Services window. Look for the following Service Display Names and confirm they are started:

- IISADMIN
- WWWSERVICE

To verify SQL Server 2005 was installed correctly, open the Services window on the data tier machine, and look for the following Service Display Names to confirm they are started:

- SQL Server (MSSSQLSERVER)
- SQL Server Agent (MSSQLSERVER)
- Analysis Services (MSSQLSERVER)
- Reporting Services

For more information on verifying a SQL Server 2005 installation, see `http://msdn2.microsoft.com/en-us/library/ms217409`.

To verify SQL Server Reporting Services was installed correctly, log on to the application tier using the TFSSETUP account. Open Internet Explorer, and navigate to `http://<servername>/ReportServer`. This should take you to the Reporting Services Web site. For more information, consult the Online Help at `http://msdn.microsoft.com/library/default.asp?url=/library/en-us/RSinstall/htm/gs_installingrs_v1_4q61.asp`.

To verify Windows SharePoint Services was installed correctly, log on to the application tier using the TFSSETUP account. Open the Control Panel, and double-click Administrative Tools. Then double-click SharePoint Central Administration. This should open the SharePoint Portal Site in your Web browser.

To verify Team Foundation Server was installed correctly on the application tier and is communicating with the data tier, you can use the command-line tools. These tools are addressed in more detail in Chapter 4. For now, you can log on to the application tier machine using the TFSSETUP account and open a command prompt. Run the following command:

```
C:\Program Files\Microsoft Visual Studio 2005 Team Foundation Server\Tools\
TFSSecurity.exe /g /server:<TFS Server Name>
```

This should return a list of the global groups defined in Team Foundation Server.

At this point, you have completed your multiserver installation of Team Foundation Server. Remember to add any users of Team System to the appropriate Team Foundation Server groups and give them the correct Team Foundation Server rights, so they are able to access the appropriate resources. See the section "Giving Users Team Project Create Ability" later in this chapter for more information.

All installation logs for the Team Foundation Server installation are located at `C:\Documents and Settings\TFSSETUP\Local Settings\Temp` **and begin with "**`dd_`**". If you have any problems with your installation, these log files can provide key information to help you or someone at the MSDN forums solve your problem.**

Single-Server Installation

This section covers a single-server installation of Team Foundation Server. We will install the data tier and application tier on the same physical machine.

The following list contains the prerequisites that must be completed before installing Team Foundation Server in a single server environment:

- All hardware and software requirements must be met. Refer to Chapter 1 for more information.
- If the machine is a member of an Active Directory domain, it must be a permitted Active Directory Domain.
- All three users described earlier (TFSSETUP, TFSSERVICE, TFSREPORTS) must be created. Remember to give the TFSSETUP account administrative access to the machine. If the machine is a member of an Active Directory domain, the user accounts should be domain accounts. If the machine is a member of a workgroup, the user accounts should be local accounts on the machine.

Once these prerequisites have been met, you can begin the installation. During this process, you will perform the following actions:

- Set the base user permissions.
- Install Internet Information Server.
- Install SQL Server 2005.
- Install SQL Server 2005 Hotfix.
- Install .NET Framework 2.0 HotFix.
- Install Windows SharePoint Services SP2.
- Install Team Foundation Server.

Again, make sure you follow these steps in order. Don't be tempted to skip around or skip ahead. If you do, you may encounter problems with your installation. Refer to Chapter 5 for some of the more common installation errors and solutions.

Setting User Permissions

If you have completed the prerequisites, the TFSSETUP account is already a member of the local Administrators group on the machine. Verify this before proceeding to the next step of the installation:

1. Right-click My Computer, and select Manage. This opens the Computer Management window.
2. Under System Tools, select Local Users and Groups, and then the Groups folder underneath that.
3. Double-click the Administrators group to open it, and view its members. If you do not see the TFSSETUP account listed, click the Add button and add that account. Also, confirm the TFSSERVICE and TFSREPORTS users have been created.

Installing Internet Information Server (IIS)

The instructions for installing IIS in a single-server installation are the same as a multiserver installation. Refer to the previous section on "Installing Internet Information Server" for detailed instructions.

Installing SQL Server 2005

The instructions for installing SQL Server 2005 in a single server installation are very similar to the multiserver installation. Basically, they are a combination of what you did on the data-tier installation and installing Reporting Services on the application tier. Refer to the previous section called "Installing SQL Server 2005" for detailed instructions and firewall modifications. When you get to the Components to Install section of the installation, make sure to select Reporting Services along with the other services you are selecting. Note: Do *not* install the Team Foundation Server Databases at this time. We cover that installation later in this chapter.

Installing the SQL Server 2005 HotFix

The instructions for installing this hotfix in a single-server installation are the same as a multiserver installation. Refer to the previous section called "Installing the SQL Server 2005 Hotfix" for detailed instructions.

Installing the .NET Framework 2.0 HotFix

The instructions for installing this hotfix in a single-server installation are the same as a multiserver installation. Refer to the previous section called "Installing the .NET Framework 2.0 Hotfix" for detailed instructions.

Installing Windows SharePoint Services 2.0 SP2

The instructions for installing WSS in a single-server installation are the same as a multiserver installation. Refer to the previous section called "Installing Windows SharePoint Services 2.0 SP2" for detailed instructions and firewall modifications.

Installing Team Foundation Server Services

To start the installation of Team Foundation Server Services using a single-server installation, log onto the machine using the TFSSETUP user. Insert the Team Foundation Server CD into your CD-ROM drive. If your CD-ROM drive is set to autorun, the Team Foundation Server Setup window opens automatically, as shown in Figure 2-3. Otherwise, navigate to the CD using Windows Explorer and double-click autorun.exe. Then follow these steps:

1. Click Install Team Foundation Server.
2. On the next page, click Single Server Installation. This starts the Setup Wizard.

At this point, the installation is the same as the multiserver installation. Refer to the section of that installation entitled "Installing Team Foundation Server Services" for detailed instructions.

During the single-server installation, on the Destination Folder page, you do not enter the name of the database server. The single-server installation knows the machine it is running on is also the database server. This installation also installs the appropriate databases required for Team Foundation Server.

Verifying and Completing Your Installations

The instructions for verifying and completing an installation in a single-server installation are the same as those for a multiserver installation. Refer to the previous section called "Verifying and Completing Your Installations" for detailed instructions.

Installing Team Foundation Server Proxy

Team Foundation Server Proxy gives you the ability to cache source-control files, allowing quicker access to those files. This section covers how to install the Team Foundation Server Proxy. The proxy server itself is covered in depth in Chapter 15.

Here are the prerequisites that must be completed before installing Team Foundation Server Proxy:

- ❑ All hardware and software requirements must be met. Refer to Chapter 1 for more information.
- ❑ If the machine is a member of an Active Directory domain, it must be a permitted Active Directory Domain.
- ❑ All three users described previously (TFSSETUP, TFSSERVICE, TFSREPORTS) must be created. Remember to give the TFSSETUP account administrative access to the machine. If the machine is a member of an Active Directory domain, the user accounts should be domain accounts. If the machine is a member of a workgroup, the user accounts should be local accounts on the machine.
- ❑ Team Foundation Server must already be installed, either on the same machine or on a separate machine.

Important Considerations

Team Foundation Server itself already uses the proxy's caching ability. It is built in. So installing Team Foundation Server Proxy on the same physical machine as Team Foundation Server will not provide any real benefit.

In a typical LAN setting, having a separate Team Foundation Server Proxy does allow you to offload the processing from the application server. However, the limiting factor is more the data tier than the application tier, so you still will not gain much of a performance improvement.

Where Team Foundation Server Proxy really shines is in a fully distributed WAN environment. A separate machine in this environment, running Team Foundation Server Proxy, will provide a tremendous performance increase in accessing source control files.

Before installing Team Foundation Server Proxy, you must install Internet Information Server (IIS). You can use the same instructions presented earlier in this chapter. If you are installing the proxy server to a separate server from the Team Foundation Server, make sure you have installed the .NET 2.0 Framework on your build server.

To do this, open Control Panel, run Add/Remove Programs, and look at the installed applications, to see if the framework is installed. If it is not, you can easily download it from `microsoft.com`. Also, if you are installing to a separate machine, you need to install the .NET Framework 2.0 Hotfix. (See the previous section in this chapter titled "Installing the .NET Framework 2.0 HotFix.")

Once IIS is installed, you can install the Team Foundation Server Proxy application:

1. Insert the Team Foundation Server installation CD and navigate to the \proxy folder. Double-click the setup.exe file to start the Team Foundation Server Proxy Setup Wizard.
2. Clicking the Next button takes you to the End-User License Agreement and Product Key page. On this page, you can accept the terms of the license agreement and enter your product key. Clicking Next takes you to the System Health Check page. Once the System Health Check is complete, click Next to open the Destination Folder for installation.
3. Keep the default destination and click Next. The next step of the wizard is the Cache Folder page, which specifies where the data will be cached on the server.
4. Accept the defaults on this page and click Next. This opens the Service Account page of the wizard.
5. On this page, you enter the user id and password of the Service Account you created earlier, such as TFSSERVICE. Clicking Next opens the Ready To Install window, where you can verify everything you entered. Click Install to begin installation.
6. Clicking Install opens the Installing Components window. This window allows you to monitor the progress of the installation. Once the installation has completed, the Setup Completed Successfully window opens.
7. Click Finish to exit the window. Internet Explorer opens with some final instructions on how to configure the proxy server. Follow these instructions and your proxy server will be ready to go.

Installing Team Foundation Build Server

Team Foundation Build is a server used to automate building and sharing your Visual Studio 2005 solutions. This section covers how to install the Team Foundation Build Server.

> **Team Foundation Build can be installed on the application tier machine. However, this could lead to performance issues with both the build process and with access to Team Foundation Server. It makes more sense to install Team Foundation Build on a separate server, just for use with build automation.**

Here are the prerequisites that must be completed before installing Team Foundation Server Proxy:

- ❑ All hardware and software requirements must be met. Refer to Chapter 1 for more information.
- ❑ Team Foundation Server must already be installed, either on the same machine or on a separate machine.

When you are ready to begin installation, follow these steps:

1. Insert the Team Foundation Server installation CD and navigate to the \build folder. Double-click the `setup.exe` file to start the Team Foundation Build Setup Wizard.
2. Clicking the Next button takes you to the End-User License Agreement and Product Key page. On this page, you can accept the terms of the license agreement and enter your product key. Clicking Next takes you to the System Health Check page. Once the System Health Check is complete, click Next to open the Destination Folder for installation page.
3. The default destination cannot be changed, so simply click Next to continue.
4. The next step of the wizard is the Service Account page. On this page, you enter the user id and password of the Service Account you created earlier, such as TFSSERVICE. Clicking Next opens the Ready To Install window, where you can verify everything you entered. Click Install to begin installation.
5. Clicking Install opens the Installing Components window. This window allows you to monitor the progress of the installation. Once the installation has completed, the Setup Completed Successfully window opens.
6. Click Finish to exit the window.

Using Virtualization

Virtualization software is software that emulates computer hardware. Virtualization software allows you to run multiple operating systems on the same computer, at the same time. Each of these operating systems acts as a separate physical computer, complete with its own hard drive, memory, network connections, and so on.

There are two main uses for virtualization software in a Team Foundation Server context:

- Server consolidation
- Software testing

By installing multiple virtual machines (VM) on one powerful computer, you can take advantage of unused resources. Most servers use 20 percent or less of their resources, such as processor and RAM. Installing multiple VMs on a server allows you to take full advantage of the hardware, allowing you to push the utilization of server resources as far as possible. This also leads to less physical servers to have to maintain. Expensive computer hardware is used to its fullest potential, and less money is being spent on new hardware.

VMs also assist in software testing. Many times, you want to test an upgrade to a mission-critical application in a test environment as close to that of production as possible. However, acquiring the hardware to create this environment can be very expensive. Using VMs, you can create a test network very similar to your production network, but at less cost than purchasing duplicate hardware. VMs are also useful for testing patches before pushing them out to your corporate machines. As well, VMs make evaluating new software, particularly beta software, a relatively painless experience.

In this section, we talk about Microsoft's virtualization solutions, and give you the basics of how to install Team Foundation on a VM, for either evaluation or production purposes.

Overview of Microsoft Virtual Server and Virtual PC

Microsoft currently has two virtualization systems on the market: Virtual PC and Virtual Server. The two products have many of the same features in common, including file architecture, networking, and disk options.

Using a similar file architecture allows for the transfer of VMs between instances of Virtual PC and Virtual Server. Virtual PC and Virtual Server both use configuration files (.vmc) to store the basic information concerning the virtual machine. The virtual hard disk files are stored with a `.vhd` extension.

Virtual PC and Virtual Server both allow network communication between virtual machines and physical machines. There are various network options available.

Hard disk options include the use of undo and differencing disks. Undo discs allow you, for a given session with your VM, to save everything that has changed on the VM, or discard it, leaving your VM in its initial state before it was started. A differencing disk is a virtual hard disk associated with another virtual hard disk. Think of this as a parent-child relationship. You can create a virtual hard disk that contains Windows XP. Then you can create a new VM, with a differencing disk, that points to the Windows XP hard disk. Your new VM will now boot using the operating system on the original hard disk, but all changes that you make (such as installing new applications), will be applied to the differencing disk. You can have multiple VMs that all use the same base virtual hard disk, with this one caveat: You cannot apply any changes to the base virtual hard disk. If you do, all related differencing disks become invalid and all data on those disks is effectively lost.

Finally, you will find you achieve a performance increase if you run your VM on an external hard drive, separate from your main operating system.

We will be using differencing disks in an example later in this section. For this section, we will be using Virtual PC. However, these same instructions can be applied to Virtual Server with relatively few changes. Also, when I refer to "host operating system," I'm referring to the operating system running on the physical hardware. When I refer to "guest operating system," I'm referring to the operating system running inside the VM.

If you have installed Virtual PC, you can find the help file at `C:\Program Files\Microsoft Virtual PC\Documentation\English\vpc.chm`. This file is an excellent resource for understanding Virtual PC and all of its options.

Microsoft Virtual Server and Virtual PC are now 100-percent free, and can be downloaded from `microsoft.com`.

Hardware/Software Requirements

The following are the minimum hardware/software requirements for Virtual PC:

- 400 MHz Pentium-compatible process (1 GHz recommended)
- 20MB disk space

- ❑ Host operating system: Windows XP Professional, Windows 2000 Professional, or Windows XP Tablet PC Edition

Virtual PC supports the following guest operating systems: MS-DOS 6.22, Windows 95, Windows 98, Windows ME, Windows 2000, Windows NT 4.0, Windows XP, and OS/2. With Virtual PC Service Pack 1 installed, Windows Server 2003 is also supported. Refer to the Virtual PC help file for the latest information concerning required memory and hard disk space.

There are two versions of Virtual Server: Standard Edition and Enterprise Edition. Each supports multiple processors, processor types, and operating systems. Refer to the Virtual PC help file for the latest information.

The guest operating systems for Virtual Server include all listed above for Virtual PC. In addition, it also supports Windows NT Server 4.0 Enterprise Edition SP6a.

Determining How Many Virtual Machines to Run

While there is no hard and fast rule for how many virtual machines you should run on a particular piece of hardware, there are some common sense guidelines to follow.

Each virtual machine is going to need memory, probably more than the minimum amount listed in the help file. At the same time, the host operating system is also going to need memory to continue to function. You need to make sure you have allocated enough memory to the host operating system, so it can function effectively.

Each virtual machine is also going to use processor power. Virtual PC supports single processors only, so all VMs running with Virtual PC will use the same processor. There are some options for determining how much processor time a particular machine gets. Using Virtual Server, if you are running on a multiprocessor machine, you can assign a separate processor to each VM, if you have them.

Based on how much memory you have to spare for your VMs and how much processing power you have, you will probably have to run some tests to determine the ideal number of VMs to run on your hardware.

Creating a Base Virtual Machine

This section guides you through the process of using Virtual PC to create a Windows Server 2003 virtual machine with the latest patches installed. You can then use this VM as a base hard disk for installing your Team Foundation Server components. You will use differencing disks, which allows you to install the operating system only once.

1. Open the Microsoft Virtual PC Console. This is accessed using Start➪All Programs➪Microsoft Virtual PC.
2. Click New to start the New Virtual Machine Wizard. Once the wizard starts, click Next. Figure 2-8 shows the Options page of the wizard.

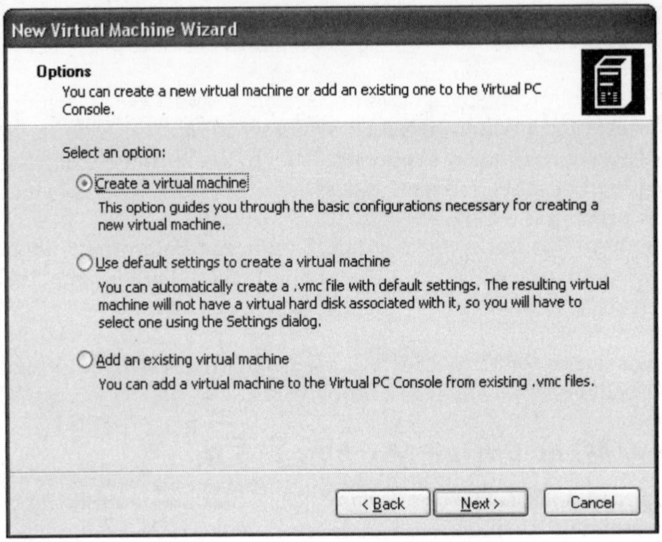

Figure 2-8

3. You have three options: create a virtual machine, use default settings to create a virtual machine, or add an existing virtual machine. Here, you are going to use the default, which is to create a virtual machine. Click Next.

4. This step of the wizard asks you for the name and directory for your .vmc file, which is the configuration file for your virtual machine. Enter the name and select a directory; then click Next.

5. This takes you to the next step of the wizard where you can select the guest operating system you want to install on the VM. For this example, select Windows Server 2003. Clicking Next allows you to configure the amount of RAM for the machine, as shown in Figure 2-9.

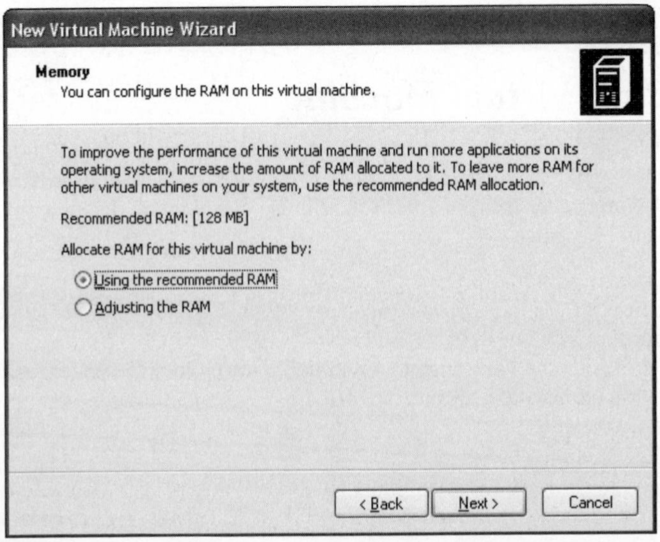

Figure 2-9

6. For now, accept the defaults. This can always be changed later in the settings of the virtual machine. Click Next. This step of the wizard allows you to create or select a virtual hard disk to use with this virtual machine.

7. Select a new virtual disk and click Next. Enter the name and directory of the virtual hard disk.

   It defaults to the same directory as your .VMC file, and with the same name as your .vmc file, but with a .vhd extension. For now, just accept the defaults. You have the option of changing some of the hard drive configuration options later.

8. Clicking Next takes you to the last step of the wizard. Click Finish to create the virtual machine. Once the machine is created, it appears in the Virtual PC Console, as shown in Figure 2-10.

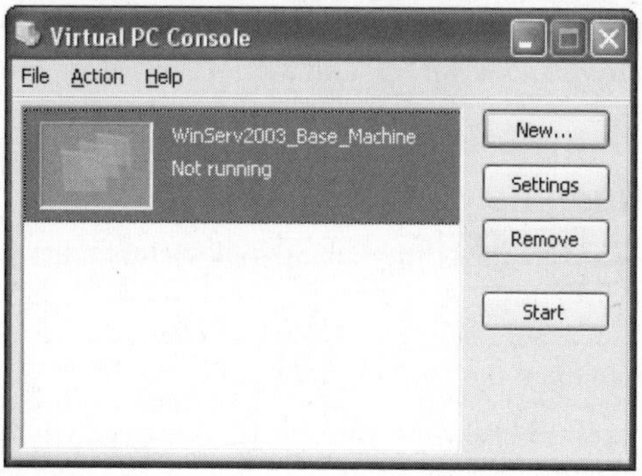

Figure 2-10

The wizard has created the virtual hard disk for you. It defaults to a dynamically expanding virtual hard disk, with a maximum size of 16GB.

Now you need to install the operating system. Insert a Windows Server 2003 Standard Edition disk into the CD drive of the physical computer. Before you start the VM, we recommend increasing the amount of memory used by it. Clicking Settings opens the settings for the VM, allowing you to change things such as memory and network configurations. Open the Settings window and change the memory to be 1024 MB. Next, click Start on the Virtual PC Console, to start the virtual machine you just created.

When the machine starts, it should recognize the CD drive and try to boot from the disk. If it does not recognize the drive, then select CD⇨Use Physical Drive D: to make the VM use the drive. Install Windows Server 2003 as normal, following the installation directions.

After installing Windows Server 2003, click Action⇨Install or Update Virtual Machine Additions. This installs the Virtual Machine Additions, which add some extra functionality to your VMs. Reboot the VM after installing the additions. Once the machine has rebooted, you can select Edit⇨Settings, to open the Settings Window for this VM. In the Networking section, select Shared Networking (NAT), to allow this VM to use the network card and Internet access of the host machine. Then, using Internet Explorer and Windows Update, download all the latest patches and apply them to the guest operating system to ensure the system is secured.

Once the guest operating system has been patched, shut down the virtual machine. You do this just like a regular machine, by selecting the Start button, and then Shutdown. Once the machine is shut down, navigate to the folder where you stored the .VHD and .VMC files. Right-click both the files and set them to be read-only. This ensures you cannot make changes to these files. Remember, you are going to use these files as the base image for your differencing disks, so this step ensures you don't corrupt your base image.

At this point, you have a base image of Windows Server 2003, which you can use for future servers.

Installing Team Foundation Server Components on a Virtual Machine

You now have a base image to use to create our other server virtual machines. In this section, you create a VM based off a differencing disk virtual hard drive. We look at how to install the components of Team Foundation Server on that drive and wrap up with a brief discussion on how to configure your new VM for network connectivity.

Creating the Virtual Machine

The first thing you need to do is create a differencing disk virtual hard drive.

1. From the Virtual PC Console, select File⇨Virtual Disk Wizard. This opens the Virtual Disk Wizard. Click Next to open the Disk Options page.
2. Select Create A New Hard Disk, and click Next. This opens the Virtual Disk Type page. You can create a new Virtual Hard Disk or a new Virtual Floppy Disk. Select the Hard Disk options and click Next.
3. This opens the Virtual Hard Disk Location page. You can select the name and location of the virtual hard disk you are creating. Enter this information and click Next. This opens the Virtual Hard Disk Options page, shown in Figure 2-11.

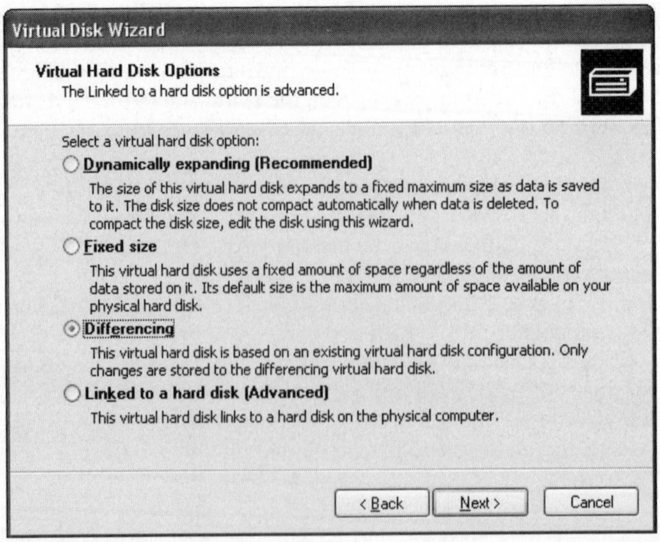

Figure 2-11

You have four options: Dynamically expanding, fixed, differencing, and linked to a hard disk. Click the Differencing option, and click Next. This opens the Difference Virtual Hard Disk page. This is where you select the parent virtual hard disk. Go ahead and select the Windows Server 2003 hard disk you created in the previous section. Click Next to go to the final page of the wizard. Click Finish to create the differencing hard disk. Once the disk is created, a window opens to let you know it was created successfully.

Now that you have created the virtual hard disk, you need to create the new virtual machine. You are going to follow almost the same steps as in the previous section, "Creating a Base Virtual Machine," with a few of changes:

1. Use a different name on the Name and Location page.
2. Instead of creating a new virtual hard disk, select to use An Existing Virtual Hard Disk.
3. When you select to use an existing virtual hard disk, there will be an extra step where you select which hard disk to use. Select the differencing disk we just finished creating in this section.
4. Continue the remaining steps.

You will now see the new virtual machine listed in the Virtual PC Console. Select the virtual machine and click Start to start the machine. The machine starts up just like it is supposed to, as shown in Figure 2-12.

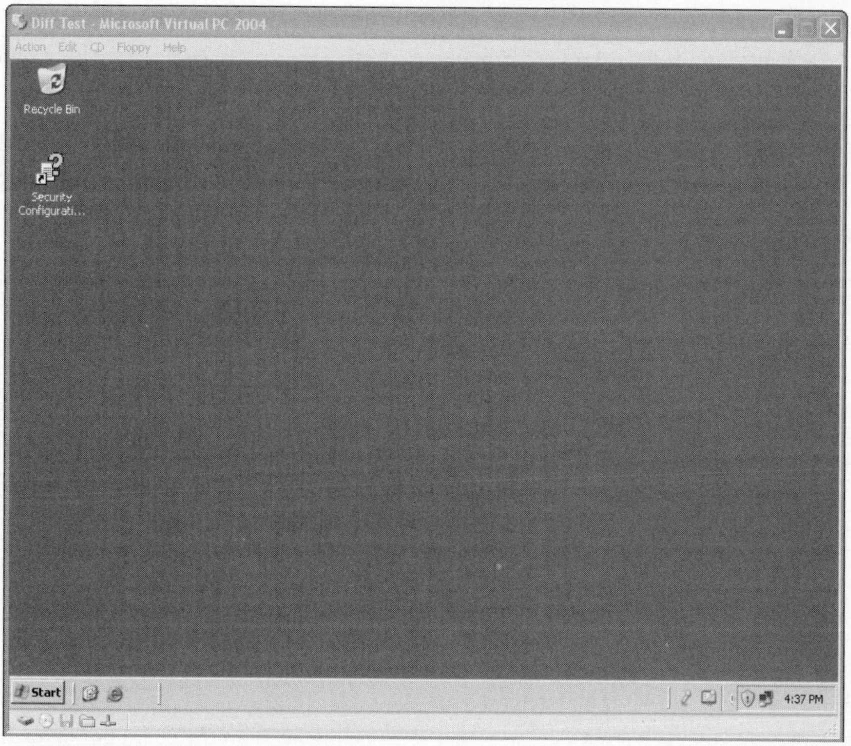

Figure 2-12

> **At this point, you have your virtual machine up and running. It is just a computer like any other. You can insert your installation media into your physical CD-ROM drive on your computer, and your virtual machine will recognize and use it. Follow the steps listed previously in this chapter to install Team Foundation Server.**

Configure Network for Virtual Machines

Network options with Virtual PC include:

- **Not Connected** — Used if the machine is not going to be connected to a network. This can speed up the virtual machine, because it is not checking for a network controller.
- **Local** — Allows virtual machines to talk to each other only. This is great for a test environment. The VMs will not access any of the network resources from the host machine. This is a private network between virtual machines.
- **Shared Networking** — The VM is connected to a private network created by VPC. This includes a virtual DHCP server and NAT server. The VMs can then access most TCP/IP resources that the host operating system can access.
- **Network Adapter On Physical Computer** — VM connects directly to the network connection on the host operating system. The VM acts as a separate physical machine on the same network.
- **Microsoft Loopback Adapter** — Can be used to create a more complex network environment on a single physical computer, without installing multiple physical network cards.

You can specify up to four emulated network adapters for a VM. If you are running several VMs on one machine for testing purposes, more than likely you will use Local networking. Otherwise, you will have to choose the networking option that makes the most sense for your environment and what you are trying to accomplish.

Understanding Team Explorer

Team Explorer is the client interface to Team Foundation Server. You can run Team Explorer by itself, or, if you install Visual Studio 2005 on the same machine as Team Explorer, it will integrate itself into the Visual Studio 2005 development environment.

Team Explorer is a free product, and can be downloaded as an .iso from Microsoft. You are required to have a client access license (CAL) to connect Team Explorer to an instance of Team Foundation Server. As a final note, it is very important that you install Team Explorer on your Team Foundation Server instance. Otherwise, you can't set up permissions and your server will be dead in the water.

Installing the Prerequisites

The following list explains the prerequisites that must be installed on the client tier before installing Team Explorer:

- All hardware and software requirements must be met. Refer to Chapter 1 for more information.
- Microsoft Excel 2003 and Microsoft Project Professional 2003 must be installed. If you have not done a Complete Installation of these products, make sure to install the .NET Programmability Support. Otherwise, you will not be able to use Excel and Project to access the Team System integration features.

Internet Explorer Enhanced Security Configurations

This section applies only if you are installing Team Explorer onto a Windows Server 2003 machine. In this case, you need to apply the Windows 2000 default Internet Explorer security settings. This enables Team Foundation functionality for Team Explorer.

Open the Control panel, and double-click Add or Remove Programs. This opens the Add or Remove Programs window. Click the Add/Remove Windows Components button on the left side of the window. This opens the Windows Component Wizard.

Uncheck the Internet Explorer Enhanced Security Configuration check box and click Next. The wizard disables the enhanced security configuration. Once it is done, click Finish to exit the wizard.

> **You will need to close any open instances of Internet Explorer to ensure this change is applied.**

Installing Team Explorer

To start the Team Explorer installation, insert the Team Foundation Server CD into your CD-ROM drive. If your CD-ROM drive is set to autorun, the Team Foundation Server Setup window opens automatically, as shown in Figure 2-3. Otherwise, navigate to the CD using Windows Explorer, and double-click autorun.exe and follow these steps.

1. From the Server Setup page, click Install Team Foundation Client. This starts the Team Explorer Setup Wizard. The first page of the wizard is the Welcome To Setup page. Click Next to move on.
2. The next page is the End-User License Agreement. Check the I accept the terms of the license agreement check box, enter your product key, and click Next.
3. This starts the System Health Check. If any problems are indicated, they should be addressed before continuing with the installation. Once everything is ready, click Next to continue with the installation. This opens the Destination Folder Page. You can change the destination folder, or accept the default. Click Next to continue with the wizard.
4. This takes you to the Ready To Install page. Click Install to complete the installation. Once the installation is completed, the Setup Completed Successfully page opens. Click Finish to exit from the wizard.

Connecting Team Explorer to Team Foundation Server

If you install Team Explorer on the same machine as Visual Studio 2005, it integrates into the Visual Studio 2005 IDE. If you install Team Explorer on a machine by itself, its looks remarkably similar to VS2005. However, even though it looks like Visual Studio, it contains only the functionality for interacting with Team Foundation Server.

1. To open Team Explorer and/or Visual Studio 2005, from the Start Menu, navigate to Programs⇨Microsoft Visual Studio 2005⇨Microsoft Visual Studio 2005. Note: On a machine with just Team Explorer installed, it is still referred to as Visual Studio 2005, and you would use the previous method to open the application.
2. First, you need to add a Team Foundation server to connect to. Open Team Explorer or Visual Studio 2005. The Team Explorer Window should open by default. If it does not, select View⇨Team Explorer to open this window.
3. From the Tools menu, select Connect to Team Foundation Server. This opens the Connect to Team Foundation Server window, shown in Figure 2-13.

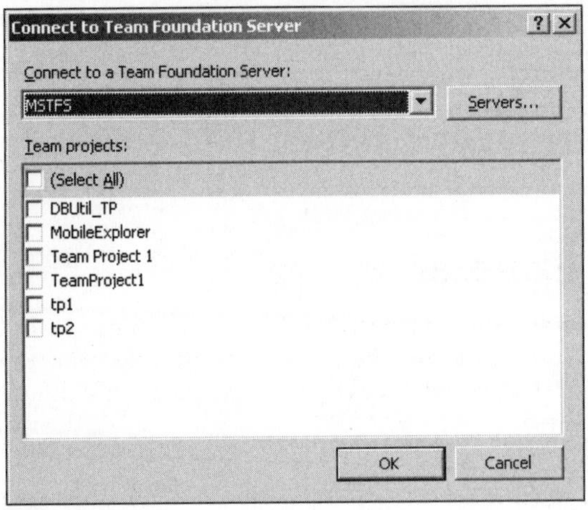

Figure 2-13

You may see your server listed in the drop-down list. If so, select it. You can also select any team projects you would like to add to the Team Explorer as well, as long as you have permissions to access those projects.

If you do not see your server in the drop-down list box, click the Servers button. This opens the Add/Remove Team Foundation Server window.

4. To add a server, click the Add button. Enter the Team Foundation Server name and click OK. Click Close to close the Add/Remove Team Foundation Server window. Your Team Foundation Server now appears in the drop-down list of the Connect To Team Foundation Server window. You can now select your server and projects, and click OK.

The Team Foundation Server, along with any projects selected, now appear in the Team Explorer window.

Configuring Team Explorer to Use Team Foundation Server Proxy

If you are using the Team Foundation Server Proxy, you must configure Team Explorer to use the Proxy server.

1. To do so, open Visual Studio 2005 or Team Explorer. From the menu at the top of the IDE, select Tools⇨Options. This opens the Options window, shown in Figure 2-14.

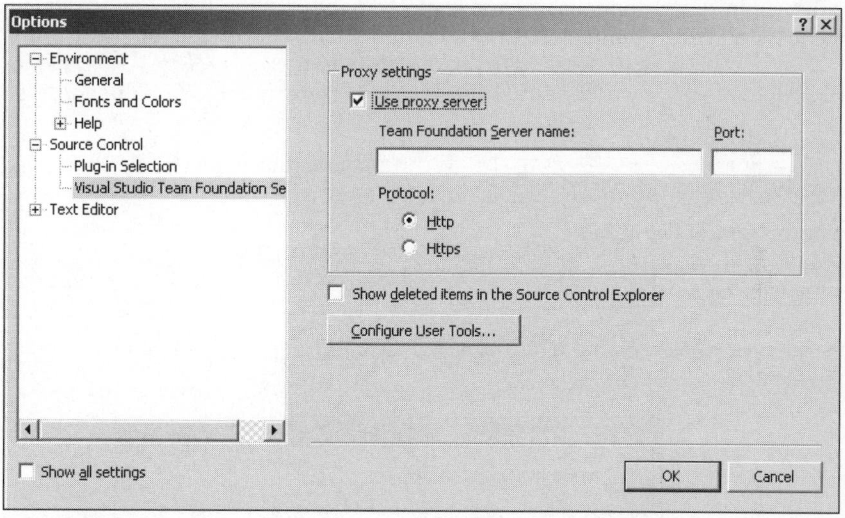

Figure 2-14

2. Click the plus sign (+) beside Source Control on the right side of the window to expand it, and then click Visual Studio Team Foundation to view the properties.
3. Check the Use Proxy Server check box. In the Team Foundation Server Name box, enter the name of the Team Foundation Server Proxy you wish to use. In the Port box, enter the port for the Proxy server. This will probably be either 8080 or 8081. In the Protocol drop-down list, select http. Finally, click OK to save and apply the changes.

Accessing Administrative Functions

The administrative functions for Team Foundation Server can be accessed using either Team Explorer or the command-line tools. You must be a member of the global Team Foundation Administrators group to perform administrative functions.

Here are some typical administrative functions:

- Creating new groups
- Setting group permissions and members

The command-line tools provide extra functionality not found in Team Explorer, such as the ability to delete team projects and modify the service account used. The following sections cover some of the basic administrative tasks using both Team Explorer and the command-line tools.

Using Team Explorer

Probably the two most common tasks will be creating groups and adding/removing users from groups. Let's look at how you perform each of those tasks.

To access the administrative options in Team Explorer, right-click the Team Foundation Server. From the context menu, select Team Foundation Server Settings. This gives you the following four options:

- Security
- Group Membership
- Process Template Manager
- Source Control File Types

To create a new group:

1. Select Group Membership. This opens the Global Group Membership window, shown in Figure 2-15.

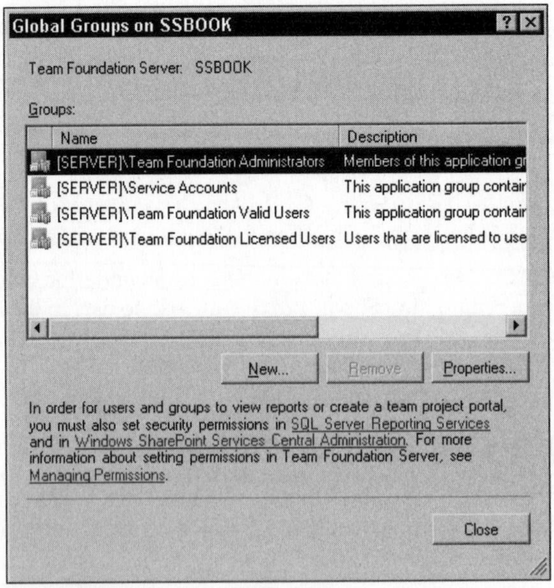

Figure 2-15

2. Click New to open the Create Team Foundation Server Group.
3. Enter the Group Name and description, and click OK to create a new group.

To add and remove users from a group, open the Global Group Membership Window. Select the group, and click Properties. This opens the Team Foundation Server Group Properties window.

From here, you can add or remove users from your group. You can also add other Team Foundation Server groups to your group.

To set the permissions for your new group from the Team Explorer window, right-click the server and click Security from the context menu. This opens the Global Security window, as shown in Figure 2-16.

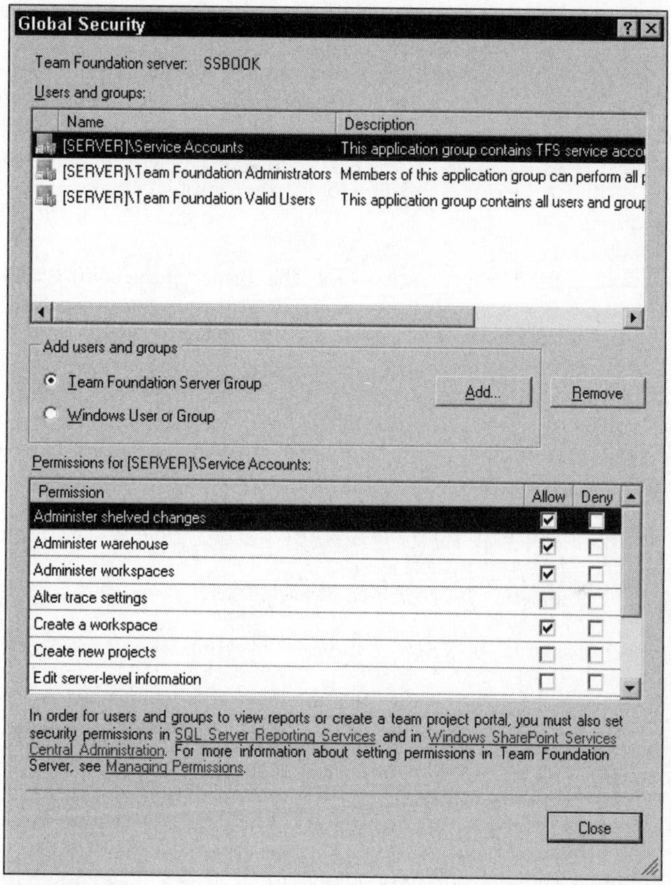

Figure 2-16

Using the Command Line

Pretty much anything that can be done using Team Explorer can also be done using the command-line tools. In fact, the command-line tools allow you to do some things you can't do in Team Explorer, such as delete a team project or optimize the database.

The command-line tools are made up of several executables, located at either `C:\Program Files\Microsoft Visual Studio 2005 Team Foundation Server\Tools` or `C:\Program Files\Microsoft Visual Studio 8\Common7\IDE`. Some of the most common tools used for administrative tasks include the following:

- **TFSSecurity.exe** — This tool is handles group security.
- **TFSAdminUtil.exe** — This tool handles changes to the service account and allows you to optimize the database.
- **TFSDeleteProject** — This tool is used to delete Team Projects.

In addition to the tools listed above, there are several others, such as TFSFieldMapping, witimport, and witexport, which also can be useful. Consult the documentation (`http://msdn2.microsoft.com/en-us/library/ms253088(en-US,VS.80).aspx`) for more information on these tools.

Let's look at how we can use the command-line tools to accomplish what was done in the previous section, using Team Explorer.

To create a new group, use the TFSSecurity.exe tool. The format of the command is:

```
TFSSecurity.exe /server:<ServerName> /gcg <GroupName> <Optional Group Description>
```

So, to add a group called GlobalTestGroup, you would do the following:

```
TFSSecurity.exe /server:SSBOOK /gcg GlobalTestGroup "this is a description of the
GlobalTestGroup"
```

You can also use TFSSecurity.exe to add users to a group. The format of the command is:

```
TFSSecurity.exe /server:<ServerName> /g+ n:<GroupName> <domain\user>
```

To add the Developer1 user from the VSTS domain to the group we just created, you would use the following command:

```
TFSSecurity.exe /server:SSBOOK /g+ n:GlobalTestGroup ssbook\Developer1
```

So, did this really create the group and add this user to them? If you open the Global Group Membership window in Team Explorer, you see the GlobalTestGroup group you just created.

If you go to the properties of that group, you see the user you added, as shown in Figure 2-17.

To remove users from a group, you would use TFSSecurity.exe and the following format:

```
TFSSecurity.exe /server:<ServerName> /g- n:<GroupName> <domain\user>
```

To remove Developer1 from the GlobalTestGroup, you would use the following command:

```
TFSSecurity.exe /server:SSBOOK /g- n:GlobalTestGroup ssbook\Developer1
```

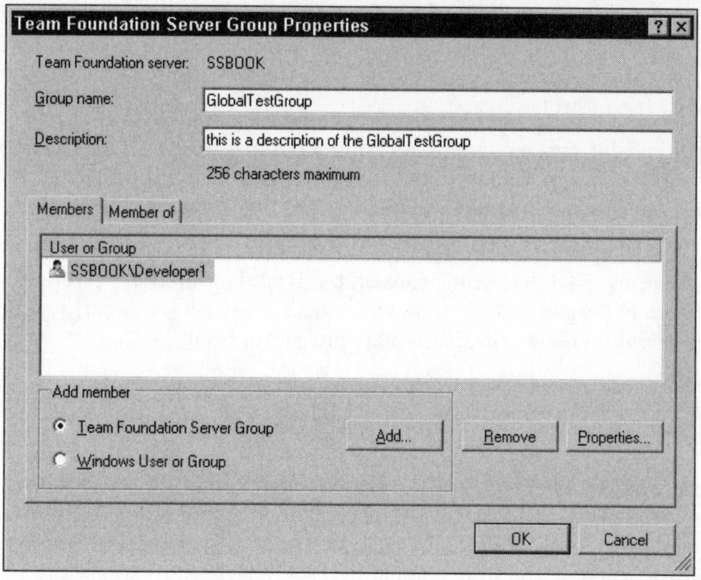

Figure 2-17

There are a multitude of switches and options for use with the command line tools. Consult the help files, or at the command line, type a `/?` (forward slash, question mark) after the tool name to receive help.

Giving Users Team Project Create Ability

One of the first things you will want to do is to give users the ability to create Team Projects. However, this is not quite as straightforward as it sounds. Besides being given the appropriate security permissions on the Team Foundation Server, a user must also be given rights to both Windows SharePoint Services and SQL Reporting Services. Remember, when a team project is created, it also creates a team portal for the project using WSS and allows reporting using Reporting Services. The user must have the appropriate access at all three levels to create a team project. Before you let this stress you out, you may not be creating team projects as often as you think. It all depends on how you decide to organize yourself. The best advice I can give you is to have a trusted IT person who has administrative privileges on the Team Foundation Server create any projects for your groups; and have the appropriate member information from the project managers.

> **There is a Team Foundation Server Administration Tool, currently under development at CodePlex, that provides a graphical interface for administering Team Foundation Server. For more information, visit** `codeplex.com/Wiki/View.aspx?ProjectName=TFSAdmin`**.**

You can create an Active Directory group to easily manage who has team project creation rights. Add this group to Team Foundation Server, as well as WSS and Reporting Services. This section shows you how to do this.

1. Create an Active Directory group to contain the users who need project creation rights. You may have to work with your local network administrator to achieve this. For this example, call that group TFS Project Creators. Once the Active Directory group is created, add the users who need this ability to this group.
2. Next, you need to create a new Team Foundation Server group for creating team projects. This will be a global group. Call it Team Project Creators. Using the instructions in the previous section, you can create this group and add your Active Directory group (TFS Project Creators) to the group.
3. Now, you need to set the permissions on the Team Foundation Server group. Again, using the instructions in the previous section, you can go to the Global Security window and give your Team Foundation Group the Create new projects option.

   The Team Foundation Server group, Team Project Creators, now has the ability to create new projects on the Team Foundation Server. However, you still need to add the Active Directory group to Windows SharePoint Services and Reporting Services.
4. The Active Directory group needs to be given Administrator access to Windows SharePoint Services. To do this, on the Team Foundation Server, open Control Panel, go to Administrative Tools, and select SharePoint Central Administration. This opens the browser to the WSS Central Administration Web site, shown in Figure 2-18.

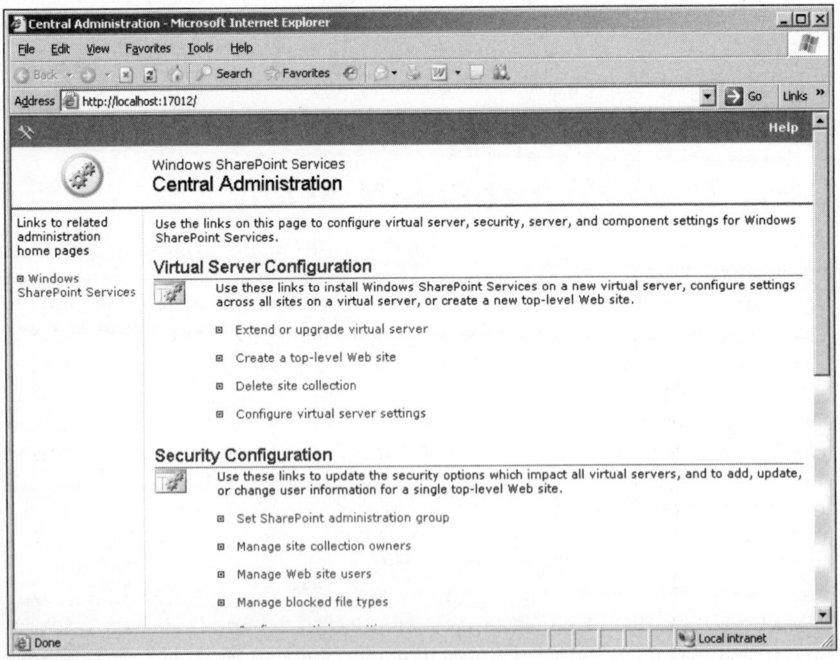

Figure 2-18

5. On this page, under the Security Configuration, click the Set SharePoint administration group link. This takes you to a page where you can specify a group to which you wish to provide Administrative Access to WSS. Enter the Active Directory group and click OK. The AD group now has the appropriate access to WSS.

6. The last step is to give the AD group access to Reporting Services. The AD group must be set up as a Content Manager in Reporting Services. To do this, go to the data tier machine and open a Web browser. Navigate to `http://localhost/reports`. Click the Properties tab. Click the New Role Assignment button. This takes you to the New Role Assignment page, shown in Figure 2-19.

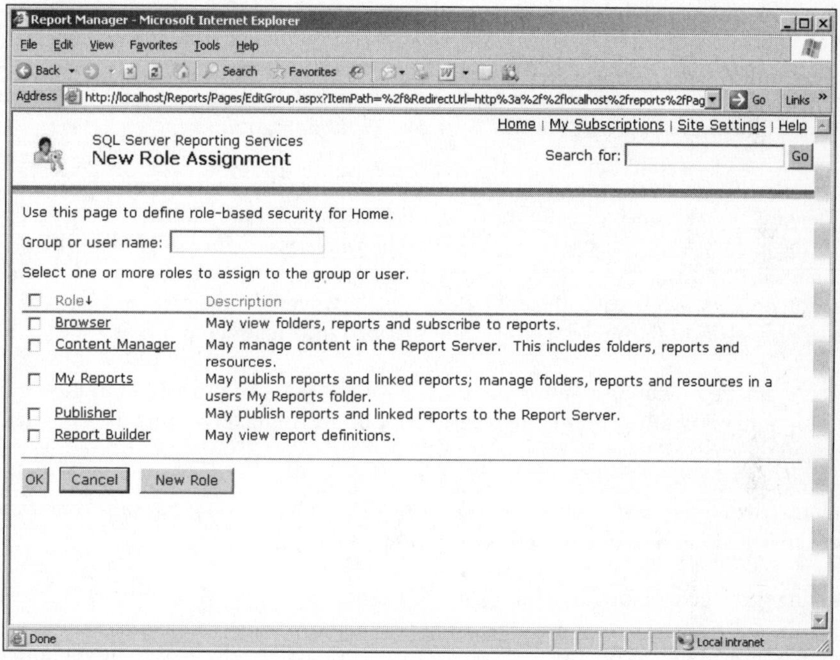

Figure 2-19

7. Enter the name of the AD group and check the Content Manager check box, then click OK.

At this point, anyone who is a member of the AD group TFS Project Creators has the ability to create a new project. As new people need the project creation ability, all you have to do is add them to the AD group.

> **With the workgroup edition of Team Foundation Server, there is a group called Team Foundation Licensed Users. Since the workgroup edition is limited to five users, anyone who wants to access TFS must be in that group as well.**

Migrating your Tools to Team Foundation Server

If you are a development shop, then you probably have certain tools you prefer to help with your development, such as a source-control system. Microsoft is taking steps to try to make it easy to convert from some of the major tools to using Team System and Team Foundation Server.

Version Control

Microsoft has provided a tool that allows you to migrate from Visual Source Safe (VSS) 6.0 to Team Foundation Source control. The migration can be broken into two phases. In the first phase, you analyze the VSS database; in second phase, you do the actual migration from the VSS database to Team Foundation Source Control. One of the best sources of information on this tool comes from Akash Maheshwari's blog (`http://blogs.msdn.com/akashmaheshwari`).

The first phase in the analysis is to determine whether you need to migrate, or whether you can simply pull the "leaves" of the branch directly into Team Foundation Server. This may depend on whether you care about the history. This phase is going to generate some reports for you, indicating the potential data loss that may occur during the migration. Using these reports, you should be able to configure some of the migration options to minimize this loss. Be aware, however, that some data loss is unavoidable. This is due to some aspects of the VSS data not being mapped into Team Foundation.

Once you are satisfied with the results from the first phase, you can proceed with the actual migration. Once the migration is complete, you will receive a report detailing any errors or warnings encountered during the migration.

While a detailed walkthrough of the conversion process is outside the scope of this book, we will present a high-level overview and refer you to more information.

The following is the general process for migrating from VSS to Team Foundation.

First, you need to install VSS on the machine on which you will be doing the conversion. Remember, the VSS database that you will be migrating must be version 6.0. If it is an older version, use the DDUPD utility (`http://msdn.microsoft.com/library/default.asp?url=/library/en-us/guides/html/vstskupgradingvisualsourcesafe.asp`) to upgrade the database. Make sure you install VSS 2005 on the conversion machine as well. To decrease the migration time, it is recommended that you copy the VSS database to a local directory on the conversion machine. Also, running the Analyze.exe (`http://msdn.microsoft.com/library/default.asp?url=/library/en-us/guides/html/vsgrfss_analyze.asp`) application can help to find and fix any integrity and corruption issues before you begin the analysis and migration of the database.

The VSS Converter application uses SQL Express in the migration process. SQL Express needs to be installed on the conversion machine, before the analysis and migration are started. Make sure you have administrator rights on SQL Express before you continue. Also, make sure you install Team Explorer on the conversion machine. The VSS converter application is part of the client portion of Team Explorer. Before you start the migration, make sure you are a member of the Team Foundation Administrator group in Team Foundation.

At this point, you are ready to run your analysis. Remember, the migration process is going to be time consuming, depending on the amount of data involved. It could be a day or longer, for a nontrivial sized repository. The process may also generate a fair amount of warnings, many of which can be discarded as being benign. One recommendation is to migrate sources one team at a time, which will typically be one folder. Once you know which folders to migrate, you will create the settings file. This is an XML file containing all the options for the migration. Once this file is ready, you run the VSS Converter application to begin your analysis. For more detailed information on the analysis phase, refer to the MSDN Library: Preparing To Migrate from Visual SourceSafe to Team Foundation (`http://msdn2.microsoft.com/en-us/library/ms181246`).

After the analysis is finished, a report file is generated. This file indicates the data loss that may occur during the migration. As mentioned previously, some of this data loss can be prevented, but there will be some loss. At this point, you should make sure the potential data loss will not have a significant impact on your organization before you continue. The analysis phase will also generate a user map file. This file shows all the users who have performed any sort of operation on the folders that were analyzed. This file is used to map VS users to Team Foundation users. This is an optional step.

Finally, we are ready to perform the actual migration. Before you begin, make sure you have identified the destination folders in Team Foundation for each folder in VSS. If the destination folder already exists, it must be empty. If the destination folder does not exist, the VSS Converter application will create it automatically. Next, you need to make modifications to the settings file to prepare it for migration. At this point, you are ready to run the VSS Converter application and migrate the database. For more detailed information on the migration phase refer to the MSDN Library: Migrating from Visual SourceSafe to Team Foundation (`http://msdn2.microsoft.com/en-us/library/ms181247`).

Once the VSS Converter application is finished, you need to review the report file, to see what errors and warnings occurred during the migration.

Once the migration is complete, you will need to change the source-control bindings of the solution files from VSS to Team Foundation. (See `http://blogs.msdn.com/nagendra/archive/2005/09/30/475633.aspx` for more information.)

Microsoft has also mentioned a conversion tool for use with Rational ClearCase. However, at this point, there is no information on the tool, when it will be available, or how it will work.

Work Item Tracking

Microsoft is also working on a tool that will allow you to migrate existing Rational ClearQuest work items into the Team Foundation work item tracking system. This conversion utility, CQConverter.exe, is included with Team Foundation Server. For detailed information on using this conversion utility, refer to the MSDN Library: Walkthrough: Migrating ClearQuest Work Items to Team Foundation (`http://msdn2.microsoft.com/en-us/library/ms181248(en-US,VS.80).aspx`).

Summary

In this chapter, we examined the various expectations of different types of Team Foundation Server users. We covered in detail how to install Team Foundation Server in both a multiserver and a single-server installation. We also showed how to install the proxy and build servers.

Next, we presented an overview of virtualization software and showed how to set up a virtual machine for evaluating Team Foundation. We discussed how, using both Team Explorer and the command-line tools, to install Team Explorer and how to administer Team Foundation.

Finally, we covered how to migrate some of your existing tools to Team Foundation Server.

3

Configuring Team Foundation Build

Build automation is an important process in the software development lifecycle. The ability to have your application automatically compiled for you on a regular schedule can be extremely empowering. Whether you are running your builds infrequently, nightly, or every time there is a code change, the status of a build can give a good indication of the overall health of the project.

Team Foundation Build was primarily designed by the Microsoft India Development Center. The original codename for Team Foundation Build is BigBuild.

In a perfect world, you would have a set of machines completely devoted to doing your builds. Your build software would allow you to perform the following tasks quickly and easily:

- Clean the build machine to prepare it for the next build
- Move the latest source code from the repository to the build machine
- Compile the code
- Run tests against the compiled application
- Store the build results in an easily consumable format

However, you never do seem to live in the perfect world, do you? Finding one product that easily integrates into your environment and does all these things is usually impossible. Most of the time, you are kludging together different scripts to try to automate the process as best you can. Even then, you still can't get the integration you really want. Team Foundation Build server is here to change all of that.

Your build is at the center of your development process. Think about it, if your build breaks, then you don't have a product to show for it! One of the most important policies you can implement is a build break policy — if someone breaks the build, they have to stay behind until it is fixed. It's a mindset that is very prevalent in the agile development community and within Team System — build in quality early in the process, and continuously. If you are serious about your builds, you should consider designating a member of your team as a release manager. You can learn more about the release management role in Chapter 17.

Team Foundation Build server has been referred to as a "build lab in a box." It provides the functionality of a public build lab, integrates smoothly with Visual Studio Team System, and is relatively easy to get up and running. And all of those tasks we mentioned earlier? Team Foundation Build server provides the ability to automate *all* of them. That said, remember, at the time of this writing, that this is the first version of Team Foundation Build, and some features are still developing. Some of those will be touched on in this chapter. This is not meant to be a discouraging statement, far from it. Team Foundation Build is a good first version; it will only get better.

If you are interested in the build process, along with the software configuration management and release management practices within Microsoft, a book we highly recommend is Vincent Maraia's *The Build Master: Microsoft's Software Configuration Management Best Practices.*

This chapter focuses on Team Foundation Build server, specifically on how to configure it. We start by giving you an overview of the Team Foundation Build server architecture, explain how it works, and look at some of the build reporting options. Then we talk about some common build scenarios, including nightly builds and Continuous Integration. Finally, we give even more details on how to configure your Team Foundation Build server.

Team Foundation Build Overview

In conjunction with Team Foundation Server and Team Explorer, Team Foundation Build server allows you to create an end-to-end build process. You can retrieve code from Team Foundation Source Control, compile it, run tests against the compiled code, release the builds onto a file server, update work items accordingly, and publish build reports of the information. Moreover, you can do all of this using a five-step wizard.

Team Foundation Build (or Team Build as it is sometimes referred to) uses a build engine called MSBuild. MSBuild is the new XML-based build engine of the .NET Framework 2.0, and is distributed as part of the framework. You can make use of MSBuild using Visual Studio or the command line, it's your choice. MSBuild uses XML files to help configure the build process. Team Foundation Build is a build automation tool. It follows a series of tasks to complete a build, utilizing MSBuild where appropriate to help with the process.

Let's look at the architecture that makes up Team Foundation Build, and then drill down into how we configure and run these builds, and how we can view the results.

Architecture

Team Foundation Build is designed to be used in conjunction with Team Foundation Server and its associated components. It's easiest to think of the Team Foundation Build architecture as broken into four distinct parts, as shown in Figure 3-1:

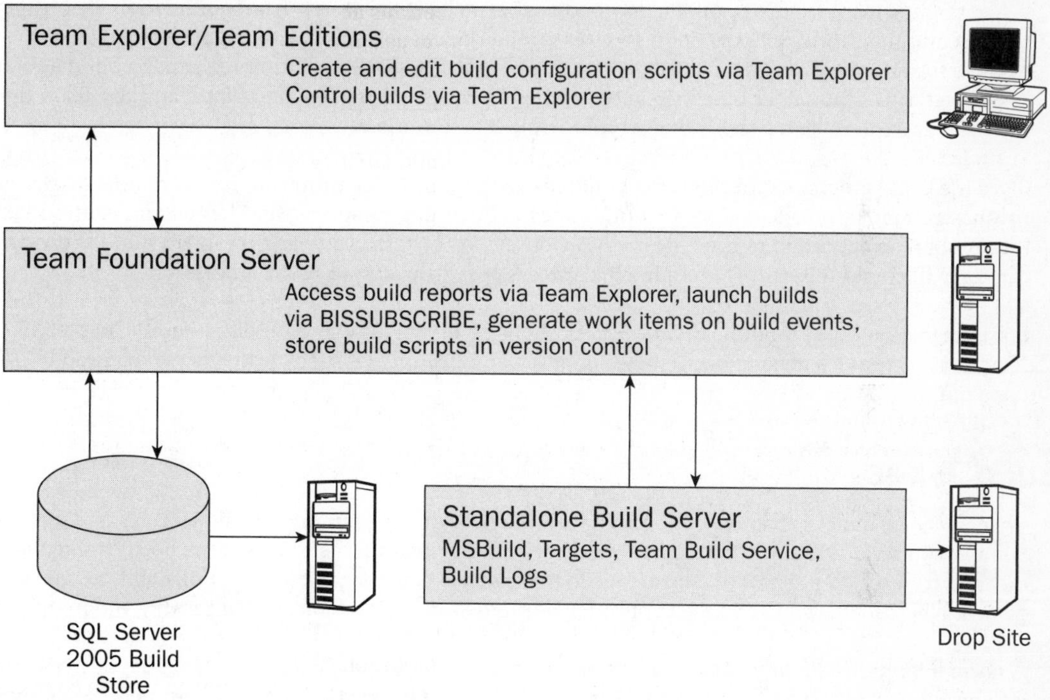

Figure 3-1

- **Team Explorer/Team Editions** — You use Team Explorer, running on your client machine, to create, run, and view the results of your builds. Using Team Explorer, you can create and run builds. Then, using the Team Build Browser, you can view the results of a build, either while it is running or once it has finished. Team Explorer, in conjunction with the Team Build Browser, gives you full control of your build process from your client machine.
- **Team Foundation Server** — Team Foundation Server provides access to the Team Foundation Build Web services, which help coordinate each step of the build process. It also provides access to the version control system, for both retrieving build scripts and code to compile, and to the work item tracking system, enabling the generation of work items from the build events. The Team Foundation Server also provides the data store for Team Foundation Build, which stores all the information related to the build, such as build configurations and build results.
- **Standalone build server** — The build server is the physical machine where the build takes place. In most instances, you have a separate build machine on which you run the actual build. This tier has a build service running on it, which executes each step in the build based on instructions and information sent to it from the Team Foundation Server. If you will be running tests against the build, you will need to have either Team System for Testers or Team System Team Suite installed.

- **Drop site** — This server is where the build files are placed once the build has finished running. This could be the same server as the build server, or just another server on your network. The build server needs access to this server to drop files onto this server.

Using Team Explorer on your client machine, you create a build type, which defines the steps that will be taken in the build process. You can version control this build type using Team Foundation Server. When you are ready, you kick off the build process from Team Explorer. Team Foundation Server then begins communicating with the build services on the standalone build server, working together to retrieve files from the version control system, copy those files to the build server, run the build and any associated tests, and gather information on the build process. Using Team Explorer and the Team Build Browser, you can track the status of the build while it is running.

Once the build process is complete, the built files are placed on the drop site. Team Foundation Server finishes gathering information on the build process, including its success and failure, and stores that information for reporting purposes. Finally, again using Team Explorer and the Team Build Browser, you can view the build reports to determine the success or failure of your build process.

For information about multiple build configurations of Team Foundation Build, refer to Chapter 15. Now that you have a general understanding of the architecture, let's look into what is required to configure a build.

Build Types

Projects can be built in a variety of different ways, depending on your organizational rules and methods. Some organizations like to have nightly builds, where they take all the code that has been checked in that day and try to build it. Some organizations do this weekly. Some organizations implement *continuous integration,* where they try to build the application as many times as possible during the day and night.

A normal build usually involves several steps, such as retrieving the latest code from the source-control system, compiling the code, running tests and analysis, and generating reports. Most people use some sort of *build scripts* to automate this process. Team Foundation Build is no different. In Team Foundation Build, these scripts are called a *build type.*

A Team Foundation build type allows the user to define all the steps necessary for a particular build to execute, as well as any specific parameters needed for the build. Using Team Explorer and the New Team Build Type Creation Wizard, you can easily create a build type. The build type is just an XML file. Once it has been created, it is stored in your project in the Team Foundation Source Control system. From there, you can easily check it out and modify the file to work with your specific build environment, should you so choose. You can also configure multiple build types, which allows you to specify different configurations for your nightly builds as opposed to your continuous integration builds. After all, each build type is nothing more than a different build script that contains different steps and different configurations, depending on what you are trying to achieve with the build.

In the rest of this section, we walk through creating a build type using the wizard, and examine the files created. Later in this chapter, we briefly discuss how to modify an existing build type.

Before you can create a build type, you need the Team Foundation "Administer a build" privilege. Please see "Setting Up Team Foundation Build Server" later in this chapter for more information. Also, before you can create a build type, you need to have created a team project and connected that team project to the Team Foundation Version Control system. You must also have an actual code project associated with the team project and checked into the version control system.

Assuming all those pieces are in place, let's move on to creating an actual build type with the wizard:

1. In Team Explorer, navigate to the Team Builds folder located under your Team Project. Right-click the Team Builds folder, and select New Team Build Type. This starts the New Team Build Type Creation Wizard.
2. In the first step of the wizard, you enter in a name for your build type, and an optional description. Clicking Next takes you to the next step of the wizard, where you select the solutions you wish to build, as shown in Figure 3-2.

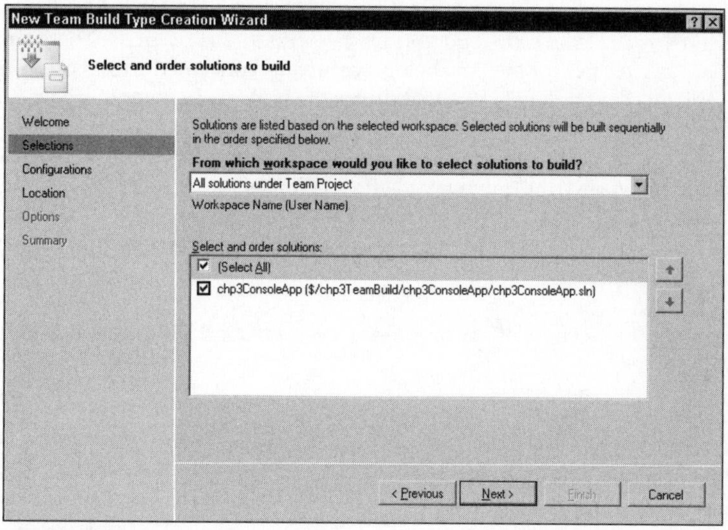

Figure 3-2

3. First you need to select which workspace you want to pull files from to create the build. You can choose to view solutions that are located in the current team project only. Or, you can select a particular workspace, which might have solutions from multiple team projects. Being able to create a build from a previously created workspace can help with getting to correct disk mappings, such as to external assembly references. Once you have selected a workspace, you need to select the solution or solutions you want to include in the build. Using the up- and down-arrows to the right of the window, you can reorder the solutions, to ensure they build in the correct order. Once you are done, click Next.

   This opens the build configuration page. You can use one build type to create multiple builds of your solution. For example, you could create a Debug build and a Release build for the x86 platform, at the same time. Using the Configuration drop-down list, you can select either Debug or Release. Using the Platform drop-down list, you can select from any of the following platforms: x86, x64, Win32, Itanium, or Any CPU. Selecting a new row in the table allows you to add another configuration to the build type. You can add as many configurations as you would like.
4. Click Next to move to the Select Build Location step of the wizard. On this page, you enter the name of the build machine and the directory on the build machine (example: `c:\build`) where the build is to take place. You also enter the drop location for the build type. This is the location where the final compiled files are placed, so you can review and use them as appropriate. It is important that this location be a file share that everyone has write access to, and that the build

service account, for example TFSSERVICE, has the appropriate rights to modify data located there. Please see the section "Setting Up a Common Build Drop Site" later in this chapter for detailed information.

5. The next step of the wizard allows you to configure which tests, if any, you would like to run against the compiled code. You can run static code analysis, or unit tests that you have configured. Select the options you want to run, and click Next. Click Finish on the summary page to create the build type.

Once the build type is created, you can see it under the Team Builds folder in Team Explorer. When the build type is created, it is automatically checked in to the version control system at `$/{Team Project Name}/TeamBuildTypes/{Name Of The Build Type}/TFSBuild.proj`. There are some other files created and put there as well, but for the time being, we are just concerned with the TFSBuild.proj file. This build type file contains the MSBuild script that drives the build process for this particular configuration.

Unfortunately, there is no graphical interface for making changes to a build type. Once you have created a build type using the wizard, the only way to effect changes is to modify the `TFSBuild.proj` file by hand. At this point, a quick look at the sections of the `TFSBuild.proj` file would be helpful. `TFSBuild.proj` is just an MSBuild XML file. It is broken up into sections that correspond back to the wizard you used to create it.

First up is the description section, offset by `<Description>` tags. This is the description associated with the build type:

```
<Description>Your Description Here</Description>
```

Next, the build machine is specified, using the `<BuildMachine>` tag:

```
<BuildMachine>machine1</BuildMachine>
```

If you build server changes, you would need to change the server name here, to ensure the appropriate build server is used.

You specify the Team Project you want to build using the `<TeamProject>` tag:

```
<TeamProject>MyTeamProjectName</TeamProject>
```

The build directory and drop location are listed using `<BuildDirectoryPath>` and `<DropLocation>`, respectively:

```
<BuildDirectoryPath>c:\buildir</BuildDirectoryPath>
```

and

```
<DropLocation>\\dropmachine\\droploc</DropLocation>
```

The `<RunTest>` tag enables or disables testing:

```
<RunTest>false</RunTest>
```

The <RunCodeAnalysis> tag enables or disables static code analysis:

```
<RunCodeAnalysis>Default</RunCodeAnalysis>
```

If you need to add more solutions to this build type after its initial creation, you need to add another <SolutionToBuild> tag to the appropriate item group in the file:

```
<SolutionToBuild Include="$(SolutionRoot)\SolutionPath\Solution.sln />
```

To add different configuration types, you add a new <ConfigurationToBuild> section:

```
<ConfigurationToBuild Include="Debug|Any CPU">
<FlavorToBuild>Debug</FlavorToBuild>
<PlatformToBuild>Any CPU</PlatformToBuild>
</ConfigurationToBuild>
```

This configuration section creates a Debug release of the application that runs on any CPU.

There is more information contained in the TFSBuild.proj file, but this gives you enough to have a general understanding of its contents. Consult the online help (http://msdn2.microsoft.com) for more information. The TFSBuild.proj file itself is also commented very well, making it easy to understand what is going on.

Build Execution

Once a build type has been created, you can execute a build. This can be done using Team Explorer or from the command-line tools. When a build is executed, it moves through each step of the build type and performs the necessary actions, including retrieving code from the repository, running tests, and creating build metrics for reporting purposes.

> **You must have the Team Foundation Server start or resume a build security rights to run a build.**

To execute a build using Team Explorer, open Team Explorer, and navigate to the Team Project you want to build. From the Build menu, select Build <Team Project>. In Team Explorer, you can also right-click the Team Builds folder and select Build <Team Project>. This opens the Build dialog box, shown in Figure 3-3. From the Build type drop-down list, select the build type you want to use for this build. Under Build location, you can change the build machine to be used by selecting a new machine from the drop-down list, or you can leave the default, which is the build machine configured with the build type. You can also change the default directory that the build will use, or leave the one configured with the build type.

> **Make sure your build directory has enough space to hold the build. Running out of space will lead to failed builds.**

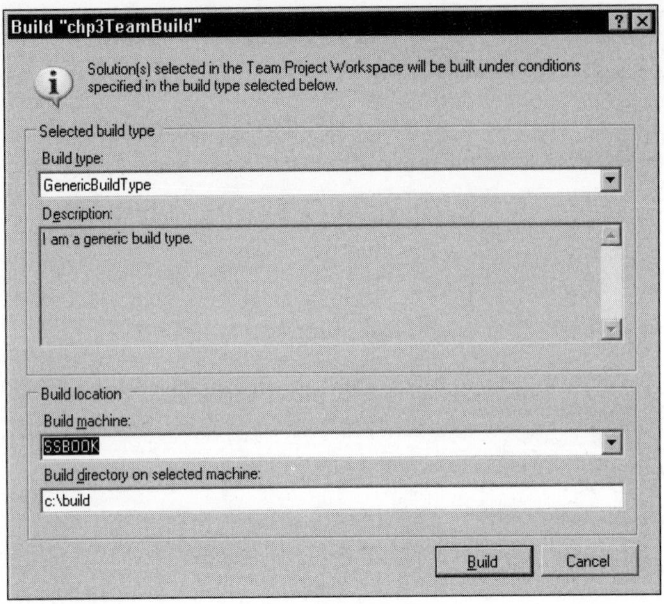

Figure 3-3

Now all you have to do is click the Build button in the dialog box to start the build process.

To start the build process using the command-line tools, you will use TFSBuild.exe application to schedule a build using the Windows scheduler. The Team Foundation Server Scheduler does not provide the ability to schedule builds, so you have to set this up yourself, as you will see later in this chapter. This application is located at `C:\Program Files\Microsoft Visual Studio 8\Common7\IDE`. There are four commands used in conjunction with this tool: delete, help, start, and stop. Here is the general syntax for starting a build using the command line tools:

```
TFSBuild.exe start <teamfoundationserver> <teamproject> <buildtype>
[/machine:buildmachine] [/d:builddirectory].
```

So, to build the same project we built previously with the wizard, you would do the following:

```
TFSBuild.exe start SSBOOK chp3TeamBuild GenericBuildType
```

Where `SSBOOK` is the name of my Team Foundation Server, `chp3TeamBuild` is the name of my team project, and `GenericBuildType` is the build type I have created.

Please consult the online help (`http://msdn2.microsoft.com`) for more information on the other commands associated with `TFSBuild.exe`.

While the build is running, you can use the Team Build Browser or the Team Build report to monitor the build status. To open the Team Build Browser, first open Team Explorer. In the Team Builds node of the specific Team Project, click All Build Types to open the Team Build Browser. This shows a summary of all completed builds and builds that are currently in progress. The information in the Team Build Browser is automatically refreshed during the build process.

To view more detailed information concerning the build process, open the Team Build report for the particular build type that is running. From the Team Build Browser, double-click the build you are interested in to open the report. This shows you, among other things, the detailed status of each step in the build process. The build information in the report is automatically refreshed during the build process.

Let's look at some Team Foundation Build internals. Figure 3-4 shows the build process in sequence. The tasks in the hexagons are built into the `Microsoft.TeamFoundation.Build.targets` file. The target elements within the file help coordinate the project building process. The task elements define what should trigger within the build. You learn how to modify targets and tasks later in the chapter.

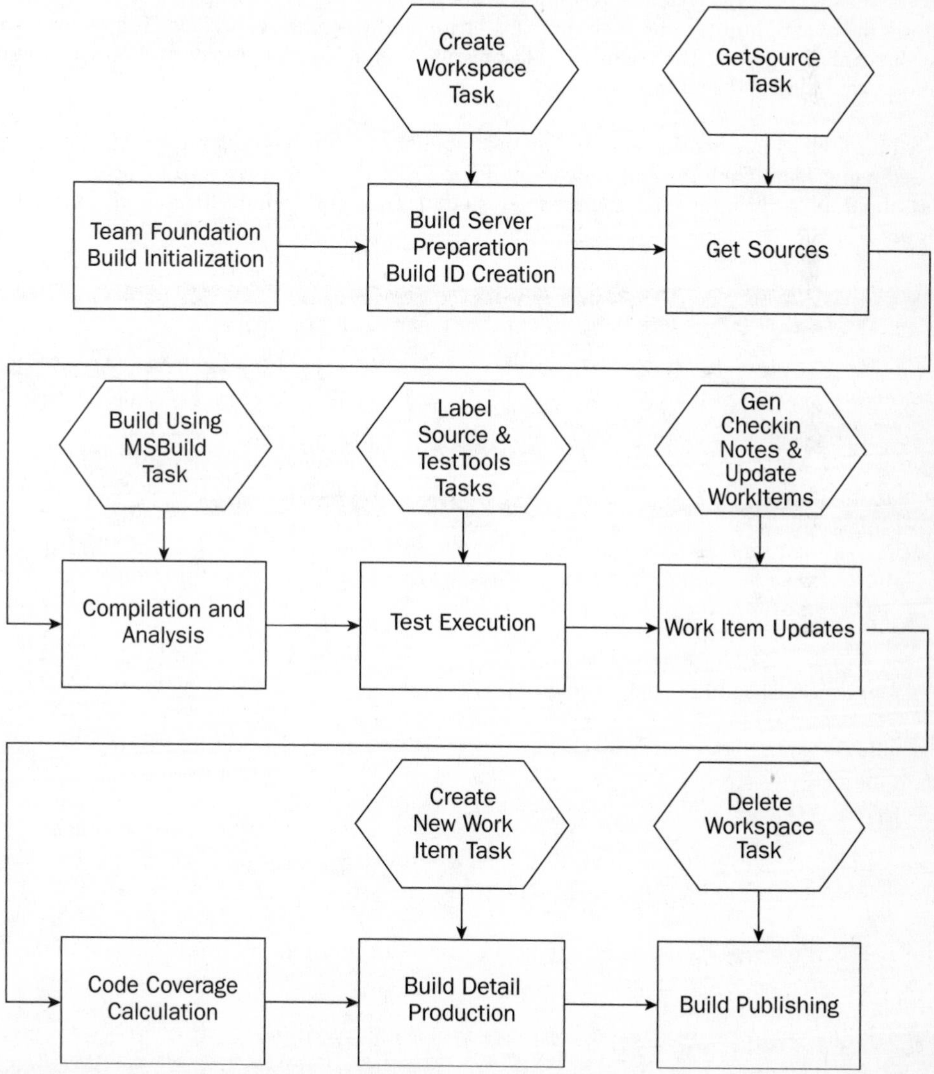

Figure 3-4

> **You must have Team Foundation Server view project level information permissions to view build reports and statuses.**

Build Report

Once the build process is complete, a report is generated containing detailed information about the build and its results. This report contains detailed information, including a list of all the build steps, information on which work items were resolved, new work items which were created, test execution information, and the overall build status, including any errors and warnings generated. The report also contains active links to changesets, work items, and test results to enable you to really drill down and understand what occurred during the build.

All the build report information is stored on the data tier of Team Foundation Server, and can be accessed using Team Explorer. Navigate to the Team Project you are interested in, open the Team Builds folder, and double-click the build you are interested in. This will open the Team Build Browser, as shown in Figure 3-5.

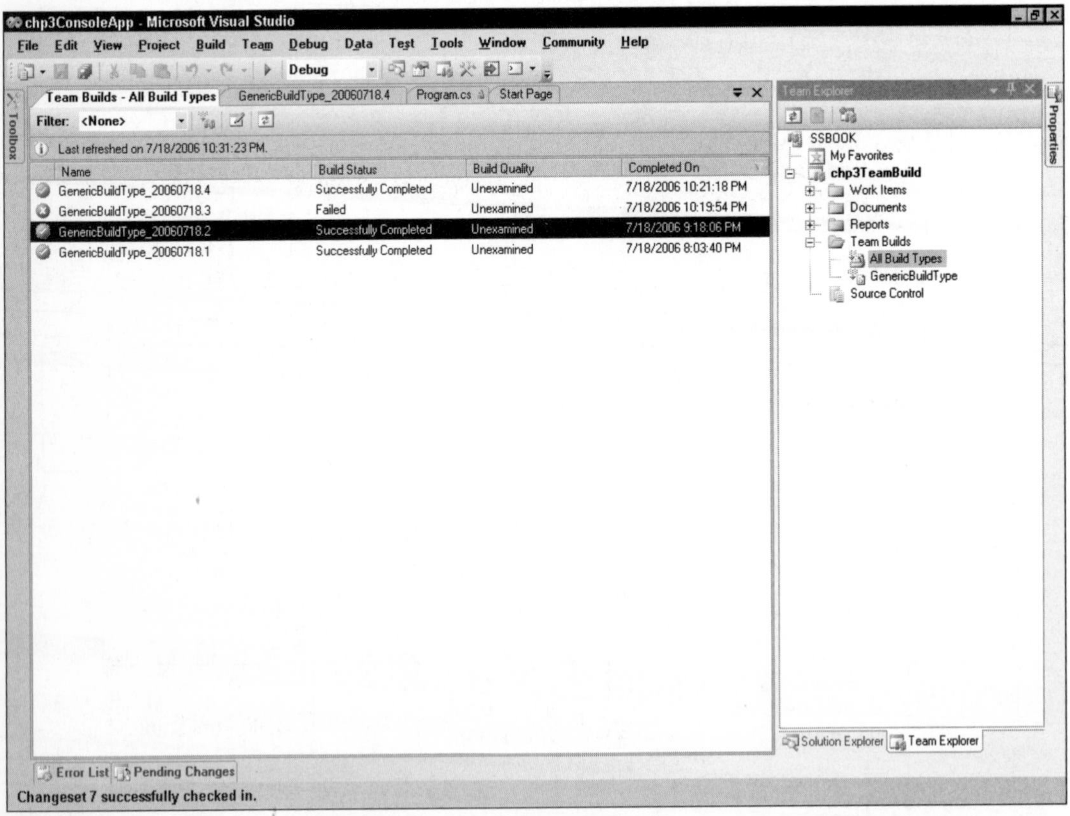

Figure 3-5

Double-click a specific build to view a detailed build report, as shown in Figure 3-6 and Figure 3-7.

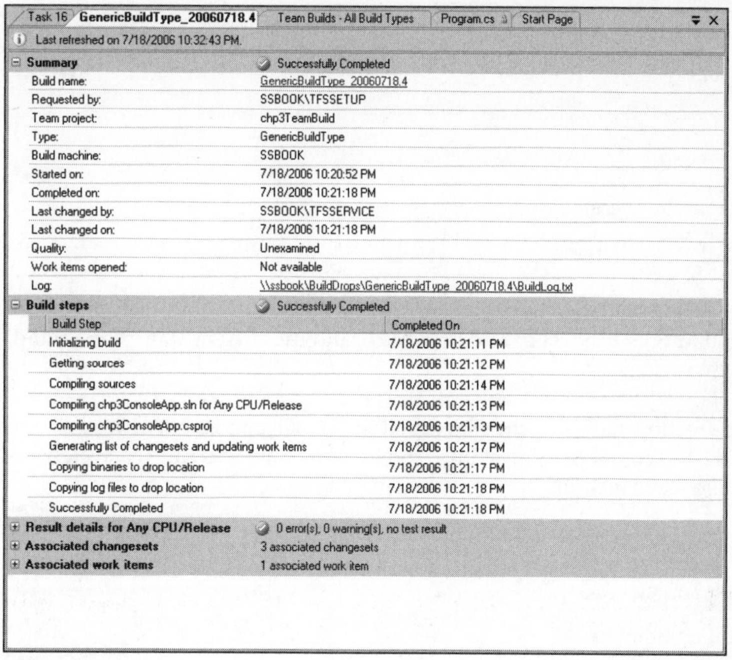

Figure 3-6

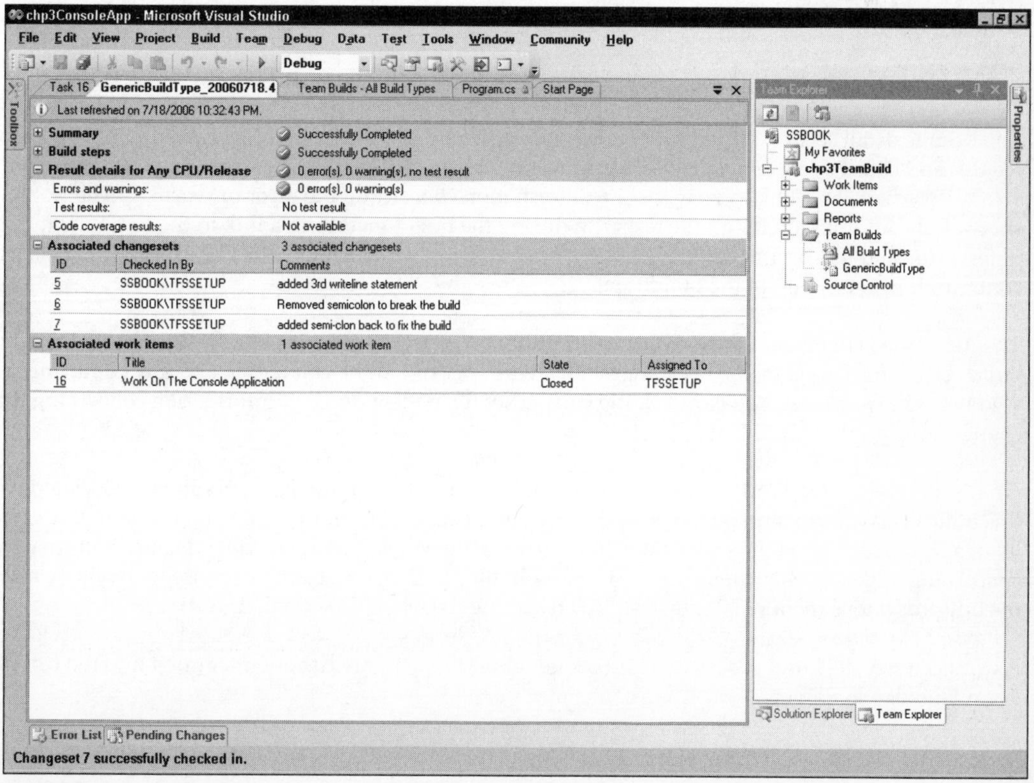

Figure 3-7

A Build Report can contain up to five different sections:

- Summary
- Build steps
- Result details
- Associate changesets
- Associated work items

The Summary section contains the basic information about the build, including the build name, who ran the build, the build type used, start and end dates, and the current state of the build, as well as a few other pieces of information.

The Build Steps section shows all the steps used by a particular build, as well as whether the build was successful. Each step contains a timestamp, showing the date and time each step was initiated. Some of the possible build steps include:

- Initializing Build
- Getting Sources
- Compiling Sources
- Running Tests
- Getting changesets and updating work items
- Copying binaries and log files to drop location
- Completion status (Successfully completed, Failed, Stopped)

The Results detail section contains information concerning any errors and/or warnings generated, test results, and code coverage results. With errors and warnings, it displays compilation and static analysis errors. You can click a link to view specific information concerning the error or warning. The test results show all the information for all the tests run during the build, including a link to the test, total number of tests run, and test results, such as passed or failed. There will be a Results Detail section for each build configuration you set up in the build type.

The Associated changeset section contains information concerning which changesets are contained in the build. This information includes Changeset ID, who checked in the changeset, and any comments associated with the changeset. You can click the Changeset ID to view detailed information concerning the changeset.

Finally, the Associated Work Items section contains information about any work items associated with this build. This information includes the Work Item ID, name, check-in action associated with the work item, and who modified this work item. You can click the Work Item ID to view detailed information concerning a specific work item. This is important information, especially for those who will be testing the build, as it tells them what they need to be looking for when they do their testing.

As you can see, the build process and subsequent build reports are deeply integrated into the rest of Team Foundation Server.

Common Build Scenarios

We spoke earlier in this chapter on the different ways projects can be built. Some organizations use nightly builds, some weekly, and some even implement a process called continuous integration, where the application is built multiple times during the day and night.

In this section, we are going to look at these scenarios, and examine some ways we can use Team Foundation Server, as well as other tools, to implement them.

Typical Builds

When we refer to a *typical build*, we are talking about kicking off a build type from within Team Explorer. We discussed how to do this earlier in the chapter. Just right-click the Team Builds folder in Team Explorer, and select Build <Team Project>. You always have the option of starting a build whenever the mood strikes you, by using either Team Explorer or the command-line tools.

For a more structured approach to building your apps, you will need to use the command-line tools, as well as the Windows Scheduler, as the next section shows.

It's worth pointing out here why you might be interested in different builds. You may want to run a build every hour that does compilations only, but no testing. This would help ensure that only code that compiles is being entered into the repository. You may then want a nightly build that, besides running the compile, does some basic testing. Finally, you may want to have a weekly build that does all of the above, but with more extensive testing.

Nightly Builds

A nightly build can be a good indicator of the health of your application and of the daily progress the developers have made with the application. By viewing the results of the nightly build, you can gain a better understanding of where problems are occurring in the development process and take the appropriate action.

This first version of Team Foundation Server does not automate the process of a nightly build for you. To implement nightly builds, you will need to make use of the Team Foundation Build command-line tools and the Windows Scheduler.

Before you begin, make sure your drop directory folder (the folder where the build will be placed once it has been created) and all server permissions have been configured. Also, make sure you have created the build type to be used.

Once that has been done, you need to create a batch (.bat) file on your build server. This batch file will contain all the build commands you wish to run. For example, you could create a batch file called nightly.bat, and put this following line of code in it:

```
TFSBuild start MSTFS TeamProject1 BuildType1 /machine:TFSBuild /d:C:\Drop1
```

When this batch file is executed, it tells the command-line tools to start executing a build, using the Team Foundation Server named MSTFS, the team project named TeamProject1, and the build type BuildType1. In addition, it specifies using the build machine TFSBuild, and using `C:\Drop1` as the location for performing the build. This would override these same values located in the build type.

At this point, any time we wanted to run a build using these parameters, we can just run this batch file. So how do we get this to run on a nightly basis? That's where Windows Scheduler comes in.

1. Open Windows Scheduler by going to Control Panel and double-clicking Scheduled Tasks. Click the Add Scheduled Task option to start the Scheduled Task Wizard. Click Next to move off the first page of the wizard.
2. Click Browse, and select the batch file you just created. Go ahead and name the task. Set the frequency to run daily, and specify the time you would like it to run at.
3. Finally, select an account with the appropriate rights to run a build on the build server. The account should have the Team Foundation Server Start a build rights. Otherwise, you will be unable to run any build commands from the command line. Click Next to finish and close the wizard.

At this point, your nightly build is ready to go. If you wanted to change the build so that it runs over a different period, such as weekly, all you have to do is modify the scheduled task appropriately.

Weekly Builds

A weekly build is pretty much the same thing as a nightly build, executed once a week instead of every night. Some organizations find it more effective to view their code over this extended period.

To implement a weekly build, you follow the same steps as outlined in the previous section on nightly builds. However, when configuring Windows Scheduler, set the schedule to run weekly instead of daily.

Continuous Integration (CI)

Kent Beck, in his book *XP Explained*, defines continuous integration (CI) as the process of integrating and building the system every time a task is completed. CI is used extensively by *Agile* methodologies (`www.agilealliance.com`), which use the status of the build as a key indication of project performance and progress. You can learn more about Agile methodologies in Chapter 6.

Let's discuss a little of the theory behind CI, and some things to think about if you are considering implementing it. For CI to be effective, two things must be true. First, any code that is checked into the version control system must compile. If a developer checks in a piece of code that he knows is broken, then he knows the build is going to fail. Second, all your unit tests should be in the version control system, and should run successfully against the code in the system. This allows you to keep a history of your tests, and to ensure your app is meeting the functional requirements.

For the above conditions to work effectively, your developers need to be checking their code in frequently. If a developer keeps code out for an extended period, his portion may work when he checks his code back in; it may, however, break the code of others, because their updated code does not play nice with his. Besides checking in his code frequently, a developer should also grab the latest code of the other developers from the system and run it against his code changes before checking his code back in. This helps to ensure that his code runs effectively with the latest changes in the version control system; it also helps to ensure an effective build of the entire application.

One recommendation when implementing CI is to kick off a build any time new code changes are checked into the repository. While this may be an ideal case, in practice it can lead to problems, especially if you have a long build cycle, which could lead to overlapping builds. If you are interested in using Team Foundation in this way, you will have to do some custom coding. Chapter 9 provides an overview of the Team Foundation Object Model and Team Foundation Core Services, and is a great place to learn more about that.

> **For a good example of how to implement continuous integration in this manner, check out the Vertigo Software Team System blog at** `http://blogs.vertigosoftware.com/teamsystem/archive/2006/07/14/3075.aspx`**.**

It might be more effective to use standard build times when implementing CI — for example, every hour or every four hours. You can easily modify the process outlined earlier in the nightly builds section to run on any CI schedule you would like.

You can read about Microsoft continuous integration and download a sample at `http://msdn.microsoft.com/library/default.asp?url=/library/en-us/dnvs05/html/ConIntTmFndBld.asp`.

Customizing and Extending Team Foundation Build

Team Foundation Build provides out-of-the-box capabilities for creating basic build types. But, what if you have special needs during the build — for example, you have to trigger a third-party testing tool during the build process? These scenarios are not uncommon — therefore it is important to understand how Team Foundation Build can be extended and customized. There are also some limitations that you should understand.

Team Foundation Build is built upon MSBuild, therefore most (if not all) of the limitations that apply to MSBuild also apply to Team Foundation Build. For example, Team Foundation Build is primarily designed for building .NET Framework 2.0 applications. If you want to build anything else, you have to customize the build process.

Team Foundation Build does not support deployment projects. (However, it does support the Web deployment project.) Out-of-the-box, you have no user interface to modify the build scripts

> **Although there are no prebuilt tools to modify Team Foundation Build scripts, there are a few really interesting projects on the Web. The first is a Windows Presentation Foundation sample in the Windows SDK called GUI for MSBuild. You can download the sample at** `http://windowssdk.msdn.microsoft.com/en-us/library/ms756489.aspx`**. There is also another free tool called the MSBuild Sidekick that you download at** `http://www.attrice.info/msbuild/`**.**

In the current version of Team Foundation Build, you have to manually check out the TfsBuild.proj file, edit the XML, and then check back in the file. Team Foundation Build does not contain built-in extensions such as continuous integration, rolling build, and gauntlet (a build configuration in use at Microsoft). There are also no built-in management capabilities — you can't just dynamically select a build machine and automatically prepare it. Team Foundation Build also doesn't support build queuing or requests.

> **If you want to track the progress of your builds on your desktop, you can download a Team Foundation Build Notification tool. The notifications are very similar to the e-mail notifications that appear at the bottom right of your screen when you receive mail in Outlook 2003. You can download the tool and source code at** `http://blogs.msdn.com/abhinaba/archive/2006/08/09/293234.aspx`**.**

What exactly does this mean? There are tons of opportunities for developers to build on (forgive the pun) the Team Foundation Build platform. The Team Foundation Build API is well documented within the Visual Studio 2005 SDK and provides opportunities to trigger and configure your builds in really interesting ways. You can download the Visual Studio 2005 SDK at: `http://msdn.microsoft.com/vstudio/extend/`.

Existing Build Tasks

There may be circumstances where you will need to FTP files to another directory, create your own custom clean build, run third-party tools, and so forth. Fortunately, there is a vibrant development community around MSBuild tasks. Here are the two primary resources:

- **MSBuild Tasks on Tigris.org**: This is an open-source effort to compile different MSBuild tasks. You can access the forums for help in implementing the tasks (`http://msbuildtasks.com`), or you can download the binaries at `http://msbuildtasks.tigris.org`.
- **Microsoft Services (UK) Enterprise Solutions Build Framework (SBF):** This is a list of over a hundred useful MSBuild tasks compiled by Microsoft Services UK. You can download them from `GotDotNet` at `gotdotnet.com/codegallery/codegallery.aspx?id=b4d6499f-0020-4771-a305-c156498db75e`.

The MSBuild EXEC task allows you to run external applications with specific arguments. You can use the following parameters along with this task: Command, ExitCode, IgnoreExitCode, WorkingDirectory, and so forth.

Custom Build Tasks

Within your basic build type, you can incorporate custom build tasks that trigger any functionality that you want. The `UsingTask` element points to an assembly (which is usually located somewhere on your build server). The following build task adds information into the build log. You can use the same template to make the build server do pretty much anything. Here are the required steps to create a custom build task:

1. Launch Visual Studio 2005 Team Suite and select File⇨New⇨Project.
2. Select the C# Class Project type and name the project `CustomBuildTask`.
3. Once the project loads in Solution Explorer, rename `Class1.cs` to `BuildTask.cs`.
4. Right-click your solution in the Solutions Explorer and select Properties.
5. Change the assembly name and default namespace to `BuildTask`.
6. Close the solution properties.
7. Right-click the References folder.
8. Add the following references to your project:

```
Microsoft.Build.Framework
Microsoft.Build.Utilities
```

9. Edit `BuildTask.cs`.
10. Change the source code as follows. Notice the references to `Microsoft.Build.Framework` and `Microsoft.Build.Utilities`, The `Execute` method launches your build task during the build process:

```
using System;
using System.Collections.Generic;
using System.Text;

using Microsoft.Build.Framework;
using Microsoft.Build.Utilities;
using System.Diagnostics;
using System.IO;

namespace BuildTask
{
public class LogMessage : Task
{

public override bool Execute()
{
LogMessage();
return true;
private void LogMessage()
{
Log.LogMessage("Hello World");
}
}
}
```

11. Build your solution.
12. Save your solution.
13. Copy the DLL you created (`CustomBuildType.dll`) to the root of the C:\ drive (or any preferred directory on your build server).

Registering Your Custom Task

Here is how you can register your new task within a preexisting build type:

1. Open the Source Code Explorer (View⇨Other Windows⇨Source Code Explorer).
2. Checkout your target build type.
3. Edit `TfsBuild.proj`.
4. Replace `</Project>` with the following code (substituting `<solution path>` with the path to the project .dll you built earlier):

```
<UsingTask TaskName="BuildTask.LogMessage"

AssemblyFile="C:\<solution path>\CustomBuildTask.dll" />
<Target Name="BeforeDropBuild">
<LogMessage SourceDir="$(SolutionRoot)" />
</Target>
</Project>
```

Advanced Build Scenarios

When working with Team Foundation Build, there may be common scenarios that will fall outside the purview of simply creating a basic build task. Here are the three top scenarios and some strategies to implement them.

Building .NET v 1.1 and VB 6.0 Code

Team Foundation Build does not support building .NET Framework 1.1 code out of the box. Fortunately, Microsoft has worked on an open-source initiative called MSBee — an unsupported power toy built by the Developer Solutions Team that will allow you to build .NET 1.1 solutions using Visual Studio 2005 (a common scenario and much-requested feature). You can learn more about MSBee at `http://blogs.msdn.com/clichten/`.

`MSBee` allows developers to build managed applications in Team Foundation Build and Visual Studio 2005 that target the .NET Framework version 1.1. You can download a copy on GotDotNet: `gotdotnet.com/codegallery/codegallery.aspx?id=9ac94da5-8e5a-4a33-beda-9b8d00970371`.

If you choose not to use the toolkit, you have the following options:

1. Use `devenv`.
2. Override the `AfterCompile` target.
3. Use the `EXEC` task to invoke `devenv` and build appropriately.

You can learn more about this process by reading the following blog post: `http://blogs.msdn.com/nagarajp/archive/2005/10/26/485368.aspx`.

To build Visual Basic 6.0 code, Visual Basic 6.0 (the IDE) must be installed on the build server. Use the same `EXEC` task steps to call the VB compiler that will build the code.

Building ASP.NET Applications

Building ASP.NET applications is nontrivial due to version control and deployment specific challenges. The best thing you can do is to review the following TechNote as a starting point: `http://msdn.microsoft.com/vstudio/teamsystem/reference/technotes/team_build/build_asp_proj.aspx`.

- You may need to debug build errors as a result of building ASP.NET solutions. You can learn debugging tips at `http://blogs.msdn.com/nagarajp/archive/2005/10/18/482491.aspx`.
- Be sure to choose the right platform configuration. If possible use the Visual Studio 2005 Web Deployment Projects at `http://msdn.microsoft.com/asp.net/reference/infrastructure/wdp/default.aspx`.

Setting Up Team Foundation Build Server

Thus far in this chapter, you have learned what Team Foundation Build Server is and how it works. We've overviewed the architecture, explained some of the different parts, and discussed how to implement several different build scenarios.

In this last section of the chapter, you are going into a more detail concerning how to set up and manage the Team Foundation Build Server. We talk about managing builds, utilizing multiple build servers, and security permissions, among some other topics. As always, the online help (`http://msdn2.microsoft.com`) is also a great place to obtain information related to Team Foundation Build Server.

Managing Builds

In reality, you can manage your builds and your build process any way you want. Team Foundation Build does provide a couple of ways to help you with that management.

We've discussed previously the Team Foundation Build Reports and the detailed information they contain. Obviously, those provide a great management overview of specific builds. Let's shift our focus to the Team Build Browser. The Team Build Browser provides a different yet effective view of the build information.

Figure 3-4 shows a view of the Team Build Browser. To open the Team Build Browser, you can double-click All Build Types in the Team Builds folder of your Team Project, or you can double-click a specific build type. If you choose a specific build type, it will only display information for builds of those types. If you choose All Build Types, then all the build reports for all the build types will be displayed.

The Team Build Browser displays Build Name, Build Status, Build Quality, and Completed On date. Notice that each Build Name is the name of a build type, followed by an underscore, a date, a period and then a number, representing the number of times the build type has been run that day. For example, if you have a build type named BuildType1, and you ran the build type on July 18, 2006, and it was the third time that day you had run the build, the Build Name would appear as BuildType1_20060718.3.

If you go look in the drop directory for the build, you will see a directory with the same name as the build. This directory contains all the different compiled configurations from the build.

There is a drop-down list at the top of the Team Build Browser, which you can use to determine which builds are shown. The filter options include None, Today, Yesterday, This Week, Last Week, and Last 4 Weeks. You can use this filter to narrow the range of builds you want to look at.

To examine the details of a particular build, you can double-click the build name to open the build report. Once you have examined the build, you should return to the Team Build Browser and change the Build Quality to the appropriate value. That way, other people who examine the build information will know the current state of that build. To do this, simply select the Build Quality column for the appropriate build in the Team Build Browser. The column becomes a drop-down list box, from which you can change the build quality. The default options for Build Quality are Initial Test Passed, Lab Test Passed, Ready For Deployment, Ready for Initial Test, Rejected, Released, UAT Passed, Under Investigation, and Unexamined. In addition, you can easily add your own build quality states, by selecting the Edit option from the Build Quality drop-down list.

You must have the Team Foundation Server Edit build status permission to change the Build Quality.

Setting Up Build E-Mail Notifications

You can configure Team Foundation Server to notify you via e-mail when different events occur. With regards to Team Foundation Build, you can receive e-mails whenever a build status changes or a build is completed. To do this, you need to modify your project alerts.

To open the Project Alerts window, open Team Explorer and navigate to the team project you are interested in. Right-click the team project, and select Project Alerts. This opens the Project Alerts window, shown in Figure 3-8:

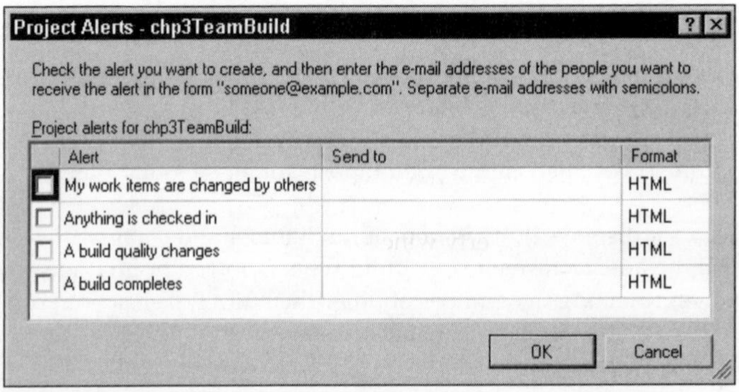

Figure 3-8

Using this window, you can specify which events you are interested in receiving notifications for. You enter your e-mail address, and also specify the format: HTML or Text.

When you receive a build notification e-mail, it contains a link to a build detail Web page. You can click this link to view the detailed build information. The e-mail also contains some basic build information, such as the name of the build, when it was started, when it completed, and its quality, as well as links to the build log.

Setting Up Multiple Build Servers

You can have as many build servers in your environment as you would like. Remember, if a build server is going to run tests against the build, then Visual Studio Team Test Edition or Team Suite Edition must be installed on the machine. This means you must have a license for Visual Studio Team Test for each build server you want to run tests on.

When you configure a build type, you specify a build server and a directory on that build server to be used during the build process. You might think, for the same project, you have to create another build type in order to run the build on a different build machine, but that is not the case. Remember, when you start a build from Team Explorer, it opens the Build window, as shown in Figure 3-3. Using this window, you can override the defaults in the build type, and specify a different build machine or build directory. You cannot, however, change the drop location. For that, you do have to create a new build type.

You can do the same thing from the command line, using `/machine` and `/d` commands.

Setting Up a Common Build Drop Site

The build drop site is where the final build files are deposited, after the build has been completed. In this drop directory is a directory named for each build. Inside each build directory are directories containing the files for each configuration listed in the build type for that particular build.

The drop directory is not automatically shared. Therefore, you need to share the directory out, so that it can be accessed via the UNC (`\\server\share`) location. To create a share, open Windows Explorer on the machine where the build will be dropped. This can be the build machine, or a separate machine just for evaluating built programs. Navigate to the folder where you want to drop the built applications, and right-click the folder name. From the context menu, select Sharing and Security. This opens the property window for the folder to the Sharing tab, shown in Figure 3-9.

Click the Share this folder radio button. Enter the name for the share. Now click the Permissions button to open the Permissions window for the share. Add the service account used to run the Team Build Service, for example, TFSSERVICE, and give them Read and Change permissions on the share. Click OK to save your changes and return back to the properties window for the folder.

Next, click the Security tab in the property window of the folder. Add the service account used to run the Team Build Service, and give it write access. Click the Apply button to apply the changes, and then click OK to close the window. At this point, your drop directory is configured correctly.

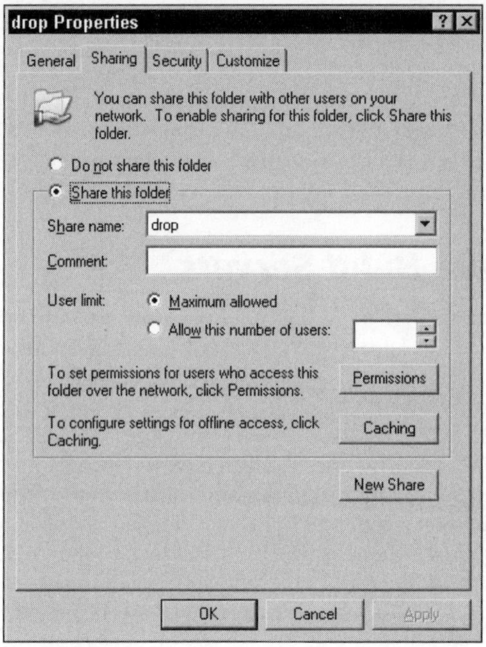

Figure 3-9

Team Foundation Build Security Permissions Overview

As Chapter 4 of this book covers in some detail, and as we have already previously mentioned, Team Foundation Server manages its own list of security rights and permissions. Each section of Team Foundation Server has its own set of permissions, and team build is no exception. In some of the previous sections of this chapter, we mention the appropriate security permissions needed to perform particular tasks. In this section, we are going to briefly mention the Team Foundation build security permissions and what they allow you to do.

The following is a list of all the Team Foundation Server security permissions that apply to Team Foundation Build:

- **Administer a build** — This permission is required to create a new build type, edit an existing build type, or delete an existing build type.
- **Edit build quality** — This permission is required to change the build quality status in the Team Build Browser.
- **View project-level information** — The permission is required to view build reports and to subscribe to e-mail notifications.
- **Start a build** — This permission is required to start, stop, and restart builds.
- **Write to build operational store** — This permission is required to be able to write the results of builds to the data tier.

Best Practices

Here are some core best practices related to Team Foundation Build:

- Avoid modifying the `Microsoft.TeamFoundation.Build.Targets` file. The reason is that Microsoft reserves the right to make changes to the file at any time. Instead, put your customizations into your `tfsbuild.proj` file.
- Avoid having dependencies across team projects and try to have all the related or dependent solutions or projects under the same team project. It will make your project files a lot easier to manage. Use project-to-project references in your `.csproj` file as much as possible and avoid file references. If you are working on Web projects, use the Web Deployment Project (`http://msdn.microsoft.com/asp.net/reference/infrastructure/wdp/`).
- To troubleshoot Team Foundation Build issues and to gather best practices, refer to "Troubleshooting Guide for Team Build," a white paper available at `http://forums.microsoft.com/MSDN/ShowPost.aspx?PostID=154526&SiteID=1&PageID=1`.
- The build server should be installed on a client, not the application or data tier, in order to avoid possible security problems related to the build service running with higher security permissions.
- Avoid synching redundant files and folders in your build. Do the work upfront by choosing the right workspace template while creating the build type itself.
- Once you have successfully set up the build and have run one successful build, set the `SkipInitializeWorkspace` flag with `ForceGet` set to false to avoid deleting and recreating the same workspace again and again.

Summary

You started out this chapter learning about exactly what build automation was. We then moved on to Team Foundation Build Server and its architecture. We discussed build types, how to create them, and some of the details of the `TFSBuild.proj` file. We talked about how to execute a build using a build type, from both Team Explorer and using the command-line tool, TFSBuild.exe. We also talked about the Team Build Browser and build reports, which show the status and results of builds.

We discussed some of the common build scenarios, such as nightly builds and continuous integration, giving examples of how to implement these scenarios using Team Foundation Build.

Finally, we covered how to manage your builds, how to set up multiple build servers and e-mail notifications, and how to configure your build drop site. We wrapped everything up with a brief overview of the Team Foundation Build security permissions.

One thing you may have noticed from the past two chapters is the variety of security permissions needed to accomplish different things using Team Foundation Server. The next chapter goes into some detail on the Team Foundation Server security model, including all the different permissions, groups, and roles required for Team Foundation Server.

Best Practices

4

Setting Up Security

Security. It seems like no matter which way you turn in the IT world today, you run into that word. And for good reason. As our world becomes more and more connected, security becomes even more important. Team Foundation Server was built with security in mind, with the idea that the server be easy to secure yet also easy to manage.

To really understand how to secure Team Foundation Server, you need to look at three different categories. First, you need to examine the environment in which the Team Foundation Servers are deployed. Next, you need to look at how users to Team Foundation Server are authenticated. Finally, you need to understand how users are authorized to perform specific actions using Team Foundation Server. Most of this chapter covers authorization, but let's touch on the other two points briefly.

In your environment, you want to make sure that your clients can talk to the Team Foundation Server application tier, that the Team Foundation Server application tier can talk to the database tier, and that any unauthorized connections are not allowed. As mentioned in Chapter 2, several different ports need to be maintained to allow the different pieces of Team Foundation Server to communicate effectively. As well, be advised the database tier server(s) and the application tier server(s) must be on the same network segment, and cannot be separated by firewalls. You can also use HTTPS and Secure Socket Layer (SSL) to use the Team Foundation Server Web services, as opposed to using the default HTTP connections. This provides one more layer of protection for your system.

You should be aware though, that HTTPS and SSL provide point-to-point security between the client tier and the application tier only. Any data located on the client tier, application tier, or data tier is still readable by anyone with access to the machine, such as administrators. Team Foundation Server does not use any sort of data encryption. So, if you are working with any kind of security sensitive data, you might require some sort of additional measure, such as an application to sit between Team Foundation Server and the client tier, which could encrypt the information.

Windows integrated authentication is used in several different places to ensure valid accounts are being used:

- Between Team System clients and the Team Foundation Server application tier
- Between the Team Foundation Server application and data tiers

User and groups that are being authenticated can be members of an Active Directory domain, or members or a workgroup tied to the servers. Integrated authentication provides the best secure method of authenticating your users, as opposed to basic clear text authentication, which sends the password unencrypted in the communication.

> **Integrated authentication is also referred to as strong authentication.**

The rest of this chapter covers how users are authorized to perform specific actions in Team Foundation Server. You will learn about the security model used by Team Foundation Server, and how to modify each aspect of that model, using both a graphical user interface (GUI) and the command-line tools. We cover some of the security access problems that are commonly encountered, and finish the chapter with a look at some best security practices concerning Team Foundation Server.

Team Foundation Server Security Model Overview

Team Foundation Server uses the concept of permissions to allow certain people to do certain things, while restricting others from doing the same thing. For example, to create a new workspace, your user account, or a group that contains your user account, must have the Create a workspace permission. Team Foundation Server has permissions for most things, from being able to access a project, to being able to start a build. This enables you to fine-tune user's access to team projects and to Team Foundation Server. There are two explicit settings for each permission in Team Foundation Server: Allow and Deny. The Allow setting enables a particular permission. Unless permission is set to Allow, the user or group cannot use that particular permission.

The Deny setting disables a particular permission. The Deny setting always overrides the Allow setting. For example, if you are a member of two different groups, and one group has Allow set for a particular permission, and the other group has Deny set for the same permission, you will *not* be able to use that permission. Even though one of the groups you are a member of has that permission allowed, because of your membership in the other group, you are blocked.

By default, most permissions are set to neither Allow or Deny. Basically, they are left unset, which is technically a setting of its own. If permission is not explicitly set to Allow or Deny, then by default, the user is denied access to that permission. Team Foundation Server would rather be too stingy with its permissions than too generous.

The Team Foundation Server Security Model also allows for inheritance of security permissions. This ties back into the ability to unset a permission. If you are a member of two different groups, and one group has a permission set explicitly, and it is not set at all in the other group, then inheritance allows you to use the permission as it is set in the first group.

Finally, you can also set security permissions in other parts of Team Foundation Server, specifically in Version Control and in the Work Item Tracking Areas section. The Version Control permissions can be set at the server level all the way down to the individual file level, while the Work Item Tracking Areas section is set at the project level only.

How Team Foundation Server Manages Groups

Team Foundation Server was designed to be easy to administrate. As such, it has its own built-in security model. This permits the Team Foundation Server administrator to deal with security issues, such as creating new groups, adding users to groups, and assigning group permissions, without having to have full access to the Active Directory or other network resources. By providing both UI and command-line tools, the Team Foundation Server administrator can use the tools he feels comfortable with to modify any security permissions.

Team Foundation Server has two levels of groups. Global groups are groups that exist at the server level. These groups provide access to the different server-level permissions. Project groups are groups that exist on the individual project level. These groups provide access to the different project-level permissions.

In addition to these two group levels, which are built into Team Foundation Server, you must also administer groups within Windows SharePoint Services and SQL Server Reporting Services to grant users the ability to create new team projects. Team Foundation Server's security groups are specific just to Team Foundation Server. But the project creation process also requires the ability to set up a Windows SharePoint Services Web site, and the ability to create reports in SQL Server Reporting Services. Therefore, the user needs administrative rights to these other groups. Currently there is no way to give these rights through Team Explorer.

There is, however, an unsupported downloadable tool that provides one common interface to administer users on all three platforms. It's called the Team Foundation Server Administration Tool, and can be found at `codeplex.com/Wiki/View.aspx?ProjectName=TFSAdmin`. It is worth looking into, as it should save you some time doing administrative work.

Now that we have briefly touched on the different groups, let's dive into each one in more detail.

Built-In Global Groups

Team Foundation Server comes installed with three global groups:

- Team Foundation Administrators — This group can perform any operation on Team Foundation Server and have total administrative control. It should be restricted to a small number of users.
- Team Foundation Valid Users — This group allows users access to the Team Foundation Server. It automatically contains any users or groups added to Team Foundation Server
- Service Accounts — This groups contains the service accounts used by Team Foundation Server.

If you are running Team Foundation Server Workgroup edition, there is a fourth group, called Team Foundation Licensed Users. This group explicitly lists the users who have access to the Team Foundation Server. It can contain a maximum of five users, as the Workgroup Edition is restricted to a five-user maximum.

You can also create new global groups and assign them global-level permissions, as needed. All groups are added to the Team Foundation Valid Users group automatically when created.

Just as there are global groups, there are global permissions related to those groups. The following table shows the different global-level permissions in Team Foundation Server. The Permission column is the name of the permission. The Action ID column specifies the parameter to use when setting this permission via the command-line tools. Notice that some of the rows do not have an Action ID. That is because you will use a different command-line tool, which does not require an Action ID, for setting those permissions. You learn more about that later in this chapter.

The following table shows global level permissions:

Permission	Which Means	Action ID
Administer shelved changes	You can delete someone else's shelved changes.	No Action ID for this
Administer warehouse	You can change warehouse settings.	ADMINISTER_WAREHOUSE
Administer workspaces	You can create and delete workspaces for other users.	No Action ID for this
Alter trace settings	You can change trace settings on the Team Foundation Server.	DIAGNOSTIC_TRACE
Create a workspace	You can create a workspace.	No Action ID for this
Create new projects	You can create new team projects.	CREATE_PROJECTS
Edit server-level information	You can edit global groups and their permissions. You can also edit project groups and their associated permissions.	GENERIC_WRITE
Manage process template	You can export, create, edit, and import process templates into Team Foundation Server.	MANAGE_TEMPLATE
Trigger events	You can fire a project alert event in Team Foundation Server. This permission is usually restricted to the service accounts.	FIRE_EVENT
View server-level information	You can view global group membership and permissions but cannot make any changes.	GENERIC_READ
View system synchronization information	You can monitor synchronization of event changes, such as access control list (ACL) changes.	SYNCHRONIZE_READ

This table shows the default Allow permissions assigned to each global group:

Group	Default Allow Permissions
Team Foundation Administrators	Team Foundation Administrators have Allow access on all permissions. This cannot be changed.
Team Foundation Valid Users	Create a workspace
	View server-level information
Service Accounts	Administer shelved changes
	Administer warehouse
	Administer workspaces
	Create a workspace
	Trigger events
	View system synchronization information

Built-In Project Groups

When you create a new team project, project level groups are created for you automatically. What groups are created and what project level permissions those groups have depend on the process model you selected when you created the team project. If you use the MSF for Agile Software Development process, you get the following groups:

- Build Services
- Contributors
- Project Administrators
- Readers

In addition, the three default global groups, mentioned previously, are also added to the project. You can also create new project-level groups, and give them the appropriate permissions. As with global permissions, there are also project-level permissions. These are permissions that are applied to a specific Team Project. The following table shows the project level permissions for Team Foundation Server:

Permission	Which Means	Action ID
Administer a build	You can create, edit, and delete build types, as well as stop builds that are in progress.	ADMINISTER_BUILD
Delete this project	You can delete projects from Team Foundation Server.	DELETE
Edit build quality	You can edit build quality of a build.	EDIT_BUILD_STATUS
Edit project-level information	You can edit the project-level information of a team project.	GENERIC_WRITE

Table continued on following page

Permission	Which Means	Action ID
Publish test results	You can add and remove test results from team project portal.	PUBLISH_TEST_RESULTS
Start a build	You can start a build using a build type.	START_BUILD
View project-level information	You can view all build information for builds within a team project.	GENERIC_READ
Write to build operational store	You can update the build database store.	UPDATE_BUILD

This table shows the default Allow permissions assigned to each project group and global group for the MSF for Agile Software Development process model:

Group	Default Allow Permissions
Build Services	Edit build quality
	Publish test results
	Start a build
	View project-level information
	Write to build operational store
Contributors	Publish test results
	Start a build
	View project-level information
Project Administrators	Project administrators have Allow access on all permissions. This cannot be changed.
Readers	View project-level information
Team Foundation Valid Users	View project-level information
Team Foundation Administrators	Team Foundation Administrators have Allow access on all permissions. This cannot be changed.

Managing Security in Other Groups

While most of the security settings are handled by Team Foundation Server, you may still need to manage security settings in a couple of other areas. These are in Windows SharePoint Services and SQL Server Reporting Services. To be able to create new Team Projects, you must have the appropriate security settings in WSS and SQL Server Reporting Services. Besides having the TFS Create New Projects permission, a user must have administrative privileges on both WSS and Reporting Services. These privileges are required *only* if you are wanting to give a user or group the ability to create new team projects. "Giving Users Team Project Create Ability" in Chapter 2 describes in detail how to configure these privileges.

Security in Other Parts of Team Foundation Server

You can set security permissions in two other sections: Version Control and Work Item Tracking Areas and Iterations.

The following table shows the Version Control Permissions:

Permission	Which Means
Read	You can read the contents of a folder or file.
Check out	You can check files out of the repository.
Check in	You can check files into the repository.
Label	You can apply a label to items in the repository.
Lock	You can lock an item so no one else can update it.
Revise other users' changes	You can change another user's check-in notes or changeset comments.
Unlock other users' changes	You can remove a lock someone else has on a file.
Undo other users' changes	You can undo a pending change from someone else.
Administer labels	You can make changes to the labels of another user.
Manipulate security settings	You can set the security permissions on folders and files.
Check in other users' changes	You can check in changes made by another user.

This table shows the default Allow permissions assigned to each project group and global group in Version Control for the MSF for Agile Software Development process model. Again, these default permissions are dependent on the process model chosen when the Team Project is created:

Group	Default Allow Permissions
Build Services	Read
	Check out
	Check in
	Label
	Lock
Contributors	Read
	Check out
	Check in
	Label
	Lock

Table continued on following page

Group	Default Allow Permissions
Project administrators	Project administrators have Allow access on all permissions.
Readers	Read
Service accounts	Service accounts have Allow access on all permissions. This cannot be changed.
Team Foundation administrators	Team Foundation administrators have Allow access on all permissions. This cannot be changed.

Using Version Control Explorer, you can get very granular with your security permissions, applying them at the server level, folder level, or even to individual files.

The other section is the Work Item Tracking Areas and Iterations. The following table shows lists the permissions for this section:

Permission	Which Means	Action ID
Create and order child nodes	You can create new child nodes and reorder existing child nodes.	CREATE_CHILDREN
Delete this node	You can delete area nodes.	DELETE
Edit this node	You can rename area nodes.	GENERIC_WRITE
Edit work items in this node	You can edit work items in an area node.	WORK_ITEM_WRITE
View this node	You can view security settings for an area node.	GENERIC_READ
View work items in this node	You can view work items in an area node.	WORK_ITEM_READ

This table shows the default Allow permissions assigned to each project group and global group for the MSF for Agile Software Development process model:

Group	Default Allow Permissions
Build services	Edit work items in this node
	View this node
	View work items in this node
Contributors	Edit work items in this node
	View this node
	View work items in this node
Project administrators	Project administrators have Allow access on all permissions. This cannot be changed.

Group	Default Allow Permissions
Readers	View this node
	View work items in this node
Team Foundation valid users	View this node
Team Foundation administrators	Team Foundation administrators have Allow access on all permissions. This cannot be changed.
The user who created the project	Edit this node

Managing Security Groups in Team Foundation Server

As mentioned previously, Team Foundation Server manages most of its own security groups. (The exceptions being security for Windows SharePoint Services and SQL Server Reporting Services.) And just as with Team Build in the previous chapter, you have the option of managing security from the user interface or by using the command-line tools.

Managing groups can be broken down into three different tasks: creating new TFS groups, adding users to the new groups, and associating security permissions with the new groups. In this section, you learn how to accomplish all three of these tasks using both Team Explorer and the command-line tools. You also learn about setting security permissions for Version Control and Work Item Tracking Area level permissions.

The ability to add new groups and set security permissions from the command line allows you to create administrative scripts to help you quickly and easily manage security on your Team Foundation Server. You can also make use of customized process templates to set up the groups and permissions on your team project at the time it is created. This allows you to create multiple projects with the same permissions in a very efficient manner.

Creating New Groups Using the GUI

As mentioned earlier in this chapter, there are two levels of groups: global and project. You use nearly identical steps in creating a new group for either.

To create a new global group, open Team Explorer and right-click Team Foundation Server. From the context menu that opens, select Team Foundation Server Settings, and then Group Membership. This opens the Global Group Membership window, shown in Figure 4-1.

To create a new project group, open Team Explorer and right-click the Team Foundation Server project you are interested in. From the context menu that opens, select Team Project Settings, and then Group Membership. This opens the Project Group Membership window, shown in Figure 4-2.

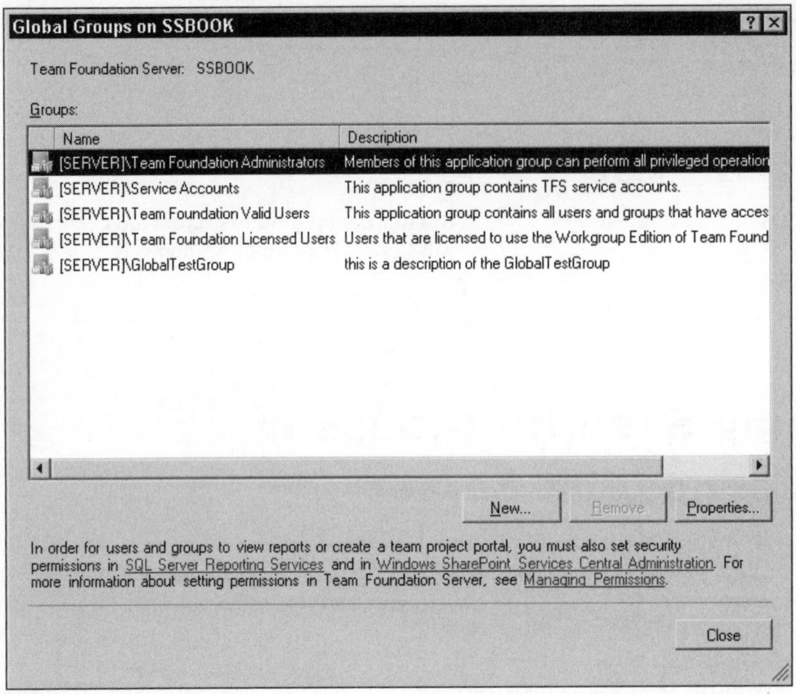

Figure 4-1

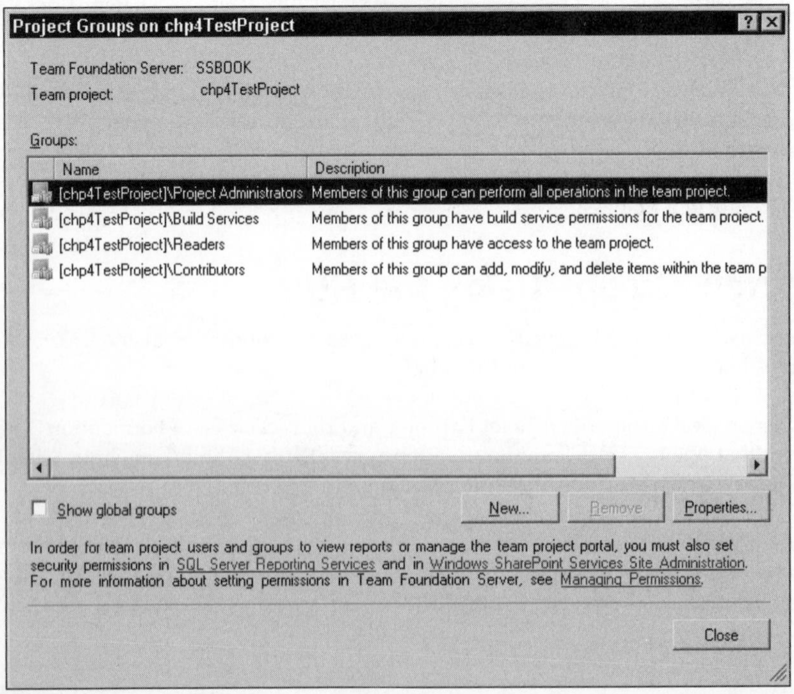

Figure 4-2

As you can see, both windows appear very similar. In the Project Group Membership window, there is a check box called Show Global Groups. You can choose to view or hide the Global groups in this window, depending on whether the box is checked.

Both windows work the same way. To create a new group, click New. This opens the Create Team Foundation Server Group window, as shown in Figure 4-3.

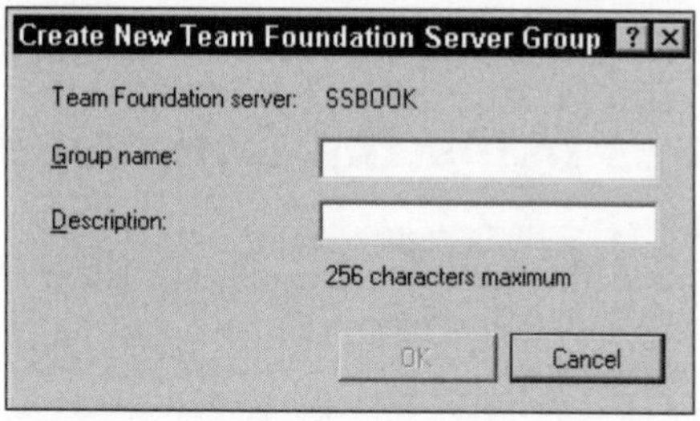

Figure 4-3

Once this window opens, you can enter your new group name and description. As an example, let's create a Global group called MyGlobalGroup. Enter **MyGlobalGroup** as the group name, and **I am a test group on the global level** as the description; then click OK. This returns you to the Project Group Membership window, where your new group now appears, as shown in Figure 4-4.

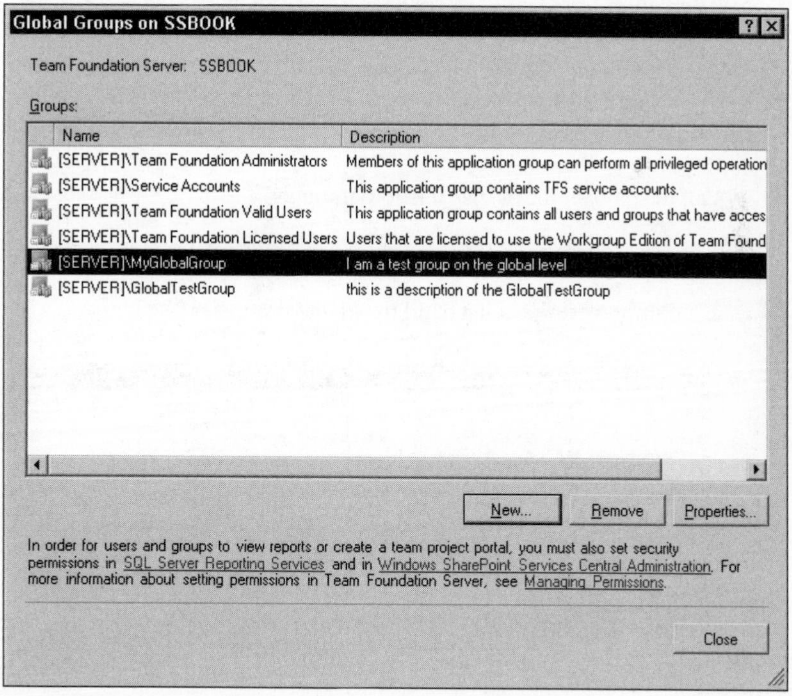

Figure 4-4

You can follow the same steps listed above to create a project-level group. Just start with the Project Group Membership window instead of the Global Group Membership window.

> **You can tell the difference between a global group and a project group by what is appended in front of the group name. Global groups are appended by [SERVER], where as project groups are appended by the Team Project name in brackets.**

Creating New Groups Using the Command Line

The TFSSecurity utility is used to create new groups via the command line. This utility is located by default in the `Program Files\Microsoft Visual Studio 2005 Team Foundation Server\tools` directory on the Team Foundation Server.

> **In older versions of documentation you will see this utility referred to as gssutil.**

To create a new global group, you use the /gcg parameter:

```
TFSSecurity /server:[TeamFoundationServerName] /gcg GroupName [GroupDescription]
```

The / server switch identifies the Team Foundation Server you are working with, and is a required switch. So to create a new global group called GlobalTestGroup on the Team Foundation Server SSBOOK, you would use the following command:

```
TFSSecurity /server:SSBOOK /gcg GlobalTestGroup "this is a description of the
GlobalTestGroup"
```

To display a list of all the global groups, use the `/g` parameter

```
TFSSecurity /server:SSBOOK /g
```

Figure 4-5 shows the output, which is a list of all the global groups:

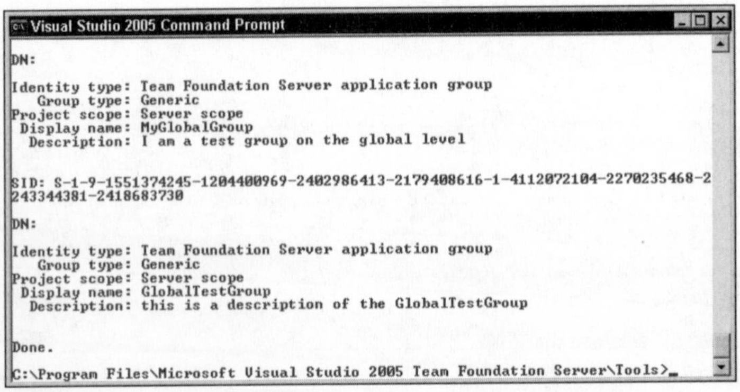

Figure 4-5

You can see the new group you just created is displayed.

To create a new project level group you use the `/gc` parameter. Here is the syntax:

```
TFSSecurity /server:[TeamFoundationServerName] /gc scope GroupName
[GroupDescription]
```

Scope is the URI (Uniform Resource Indicator) of the team project you want to create the group in. GroupName is the new group name, and GroupDescription is the optional group description. To find the URI, open Team Explorer, right-click the Team Project, and select Properties. This opens the Properties window. Under the Misc section is a property names URL. This is the URI of the team project, and will be in a format similar to this: `vstfs:///Classification/TeamProject/b1ed6e97-b84e-48e8-a74c-5ecd166ca2d1`. So to add a new project group, called TestCmdGroup, to the chp4TestProject Team Project, you would run the following code:

```
TFSSecurity /server:SSBOOK /gc vstfs:///Classification/TeamProject/b1ed6e97-b84e-
48e8-a74c-5ecd166ca2d1 TestCmdGroup
```

After running the above statement, if you view the project groups for chp4TestProject, the new group, TestCmdGroup, is added. Figure 4-6 shows the Project Groups window for chp4TestProject, after the statement has been run:

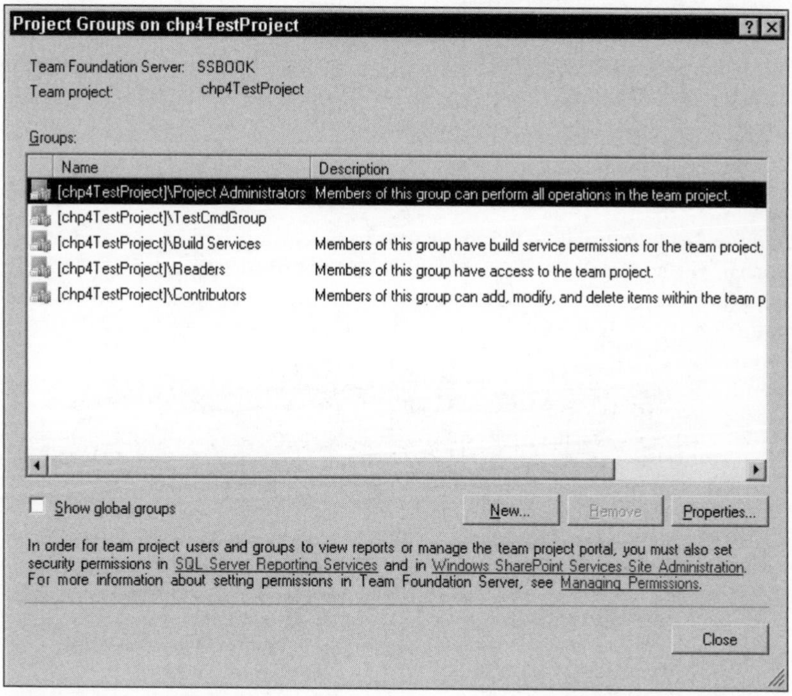

Figure 4-6

Adding Users to Groups Using The GUI

You now have a new group, called TestCmdGroup, added to your project. Next, you need to add some users to this group. Open the Project Group Membership window as discussed in the previous section. Select TestCmdGroup, and click the Properties button. This opens the Team Foundation Server Group Properties window, as shown in Figure 4-7.

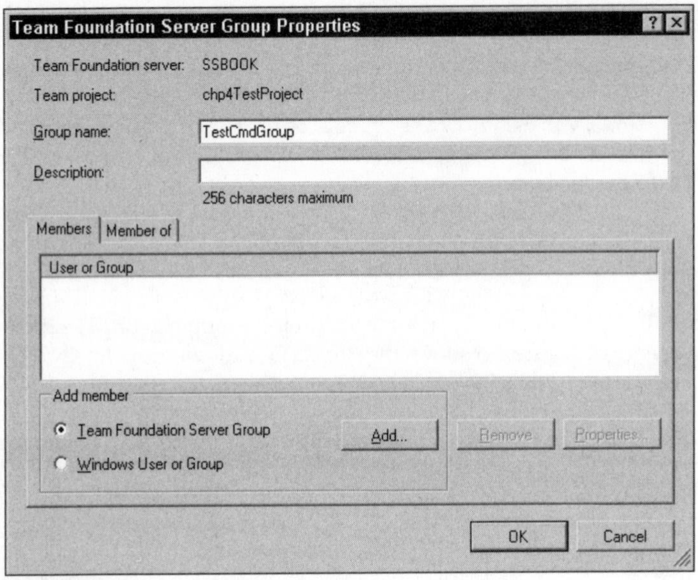

Figure 4-7

You can add other Team Foundation Server groups to this group, or you can add other Windows users or groups, such as from your Active Directory. Select the appropriate radio button option. To add a Team Foundation Server group, select that option and click Add. This opens the Add Groups window, as shown in Figure 4-8.

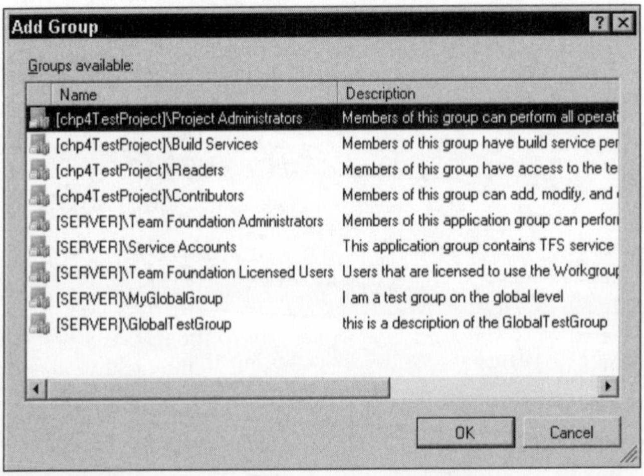

Figure 4-8

The only groups listed are the groups that are members of this project.

From this window, you just select the group you want to add, and click OK.

To add a Windows user or group, select the appropriate options and click Add. This opens the Select Users or Groups window, as shown in Figure 4-9.

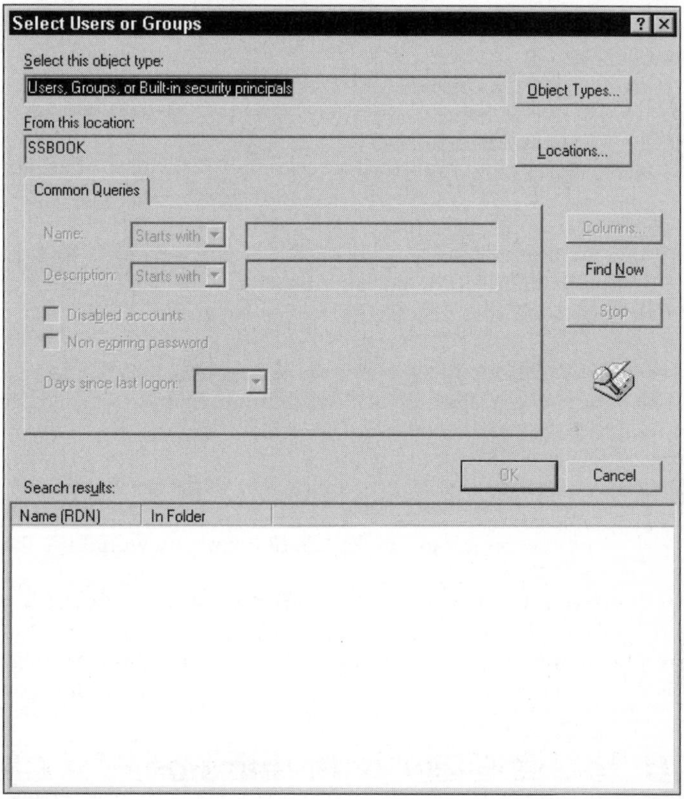

Figure 4-9

Using this window, you can find the users or groups you want to add from your Windows domain or workgroup.

To add users to a global group, you follow the same steps as listed previously, except you open the Global Group Membership window to begin with.

To remove a user, open the Team Foundation Server Group Properties window, as described previously. Select the user or group you want to remove, and click the Remove button.

> **You can click the Member Of tab of the Team Foundation Server Group Properties window, to see which Team Foundation Server groups this group is a member of. Currently, it is a member of the Team Foundation Valid Users group, whom they were added to automatically when the group was created.**

Adding Users to Groups Using the Command Line

Again, you use the TFSSecurity application to add users to groups using the command line. The general syntax for adding a user is:

```
TFSSecurity /server:[TeamFoundationServerName] /g+ GroupIdentity MemberIdentity
```

GroupIdentity is the global or project group; MemberIdentity is the user or group you want to add to the GroupIdentity.

To specify identity, you use the `n:` identity specifier. The syntax is `n:[domain\]name`. For project groups, the domain is the Team Project name, and the name is the display name of the group. If the domain is omitted, it is assumed you are referring to a global group.

Adding a new user to a global group is easy. Let's say you want to add the user Developer1, located in the VSTS domain, to your new global group MyGlobalGroup, that you created previously. You would use the following syntax:

```
TFSSecurity /server:SSBOOK /g+ n:MyGlobalGroup VSTS\Developer1
```

To add Developer1 to your new project group, TestCmdGroup, you would use the following code:

```
TFSSecurity /g+ n:[chp4TestProject]\TestCmdGroup VSTS\Developer1
```

You can use many other options with TFSSecurity, such as deleting and renaming groups, and removing users from groups. See the online help (`http://msdn2.microsoft.com`) for more information.

Using the GUI to Set Security Permissions for Groups

So far, we have talked about how to create new global and project level groups, and how to add users to those groups. The groups don't do you any good though, if they don't have any security permissions assigned to them. Remember from the earlier discussion that if a group is not set to explicitly allow a security permission, then the system defaults to denying access to that permission.

To set security permissions for global groups, open Team Explorer and right-click Team Foundation Server. From the context menu, select Team Foundation Server Settings, then Security. This opens the Global Security window, shown in Figure 4-10.

Once here, you can add other groups to the Global Security window using the Add button. You can enable permissions by checking the Allow check box, or disable them by checking the Deny check box. Simply select the appropriate group and then the appropriate permissions. Clicking the Close button will save all your changes.

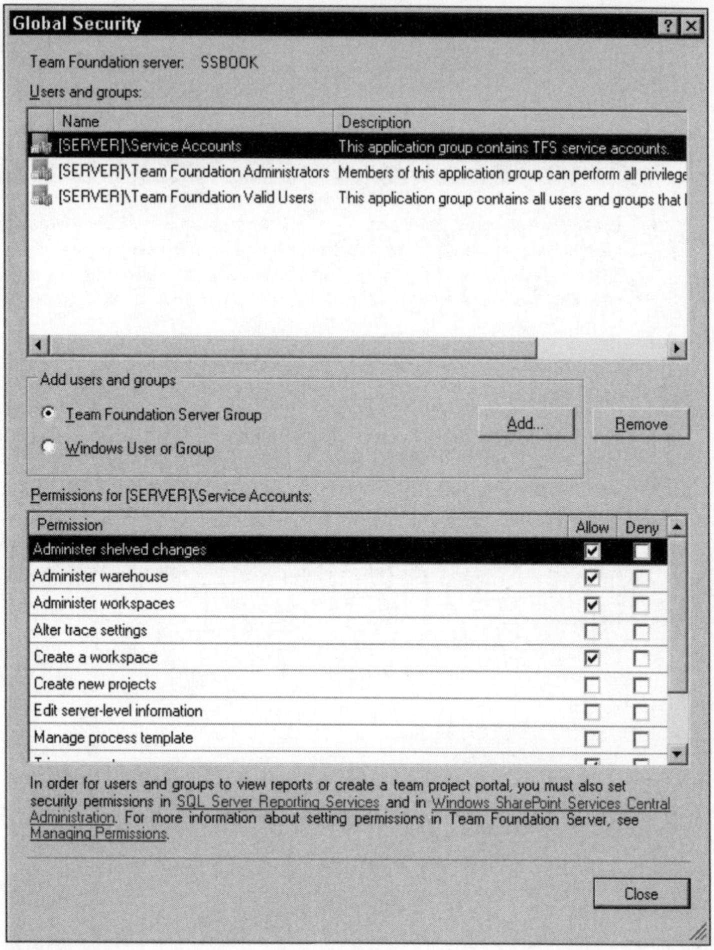

Figure 4-10

Do not change the default permissions given to the original global groups. This could cause Team Foundation Server to act erratically.

To set security permissions for project level groups, open Team Explorer and right-click Team Project. From the context menu, select Team Project Settings, then Security. This opens the Project Security window, shown in Figure 4-11.

Notice the new project groups you created earlier are not listed here. You will need to add them, using the Add button. Once you have added them, you can enable the group permissions as needed. Clicking the Close button will save all your changes.

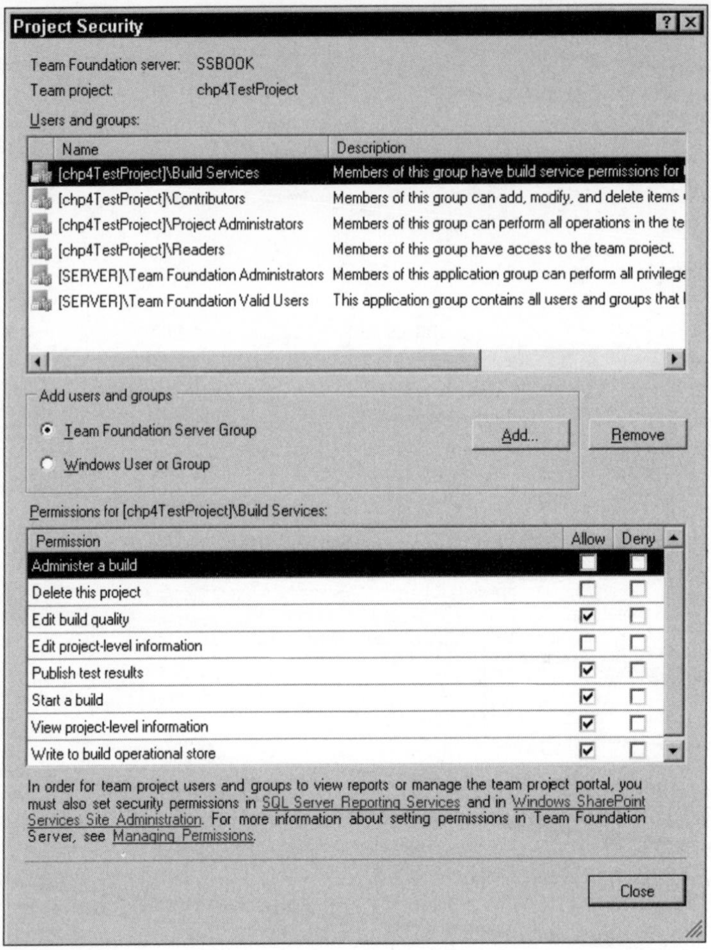

Figure 4-11

> **Do not change the default permissions given to the original project groups. This could cause Team Foundation Server to act erratically.**

Using the Command Line to Set Security Permissions

To set security permissions from the command line, you have to choose the appropriate tool. Which tool to use depends on the security permission you are trying to set.

For any of the permissions that deal with the version control system, use the version control command-line utility, tf.exe. This utility is located in the `Program Files\Microsoft Visual Studio 8\Common7\IDE` directory on any machine on which Visual Studio Team System is installed. All the permissions listed in the Version Control table earlier in this chapter can be set with this utility. In addition, the following global permissions can be set with it as well:

- Administer shelved changes
- Administer workspaces
- Create a workspace

The general syntax for using the tf.exe utility is:

```
tf command item[/options]
```

There are a variety of commands that can be used, all of which are documented in the online help (http://msdn2.microsoft.com).The command you are interested in for this section is the Permission command. For example, to give your global group, MyGlobalGroup, the ability to read from the root of the version control system, use the following code:

```
tf permission /server:SSBOOK /allow:Read /group:MyGlobalGroup $/
```

You can also use wildcards if you like. Let's say you wanted to give your project level group, TestCmdGroup, Allow rights for all the version control permissions for the chp4TestProject. You could run the following code:

```
tf permission /server:SSBOOK /allow:* /group:[chp4TestProject]\TestCmdGroup
$/chp4TestProject
```

There are a variety of options that can be used with the Permissions command, including `/allow`, `/deny`, `/group`, and `/user`, just to name a few. The online helps lists in detail all these options and how to use them.

The following is a list of possible options to use with the Permissions command. The online help lists details on all these options and how to use them.

- **/allow** — Lists the source control permissions to allow
- **/deny** — Lists the source control permissions to deny
- **/group** — Name of the group to modify permissions for
- **/inherit** — All parent permissions are inherited
- **/recursive** — Applies this command to all subdirectories
- **/remove** — Lists source control permissions to remove
- **/server** — The Team Foundation Server you want to access
- **/user** — Name of the user to modify permissions for

For all other permissions, you need to use the TFSSecurity.exe utility, which was touched on earlier in the chapter.

Managing Security for Other Areas

We have discussed how to set permissions on global groups and project groups, but you have not been shown how to set version control permissions or work item tracking area level permissions yet. The next two sections touch on those topics.

Version Control

All version control permissions can be controlled using the command-line utility, tf.exe. Please see the previous section for information on using this utility to set version control permissions.

You can also modify version control permissions using the Source Control Explorer. To open the Source Control Explorer, select the View menu option in Visual Studio 2005, and then select Other Windows, then Source Control Explorer. This opens the Source Control Explorer window, as shown in Figure 4-12.

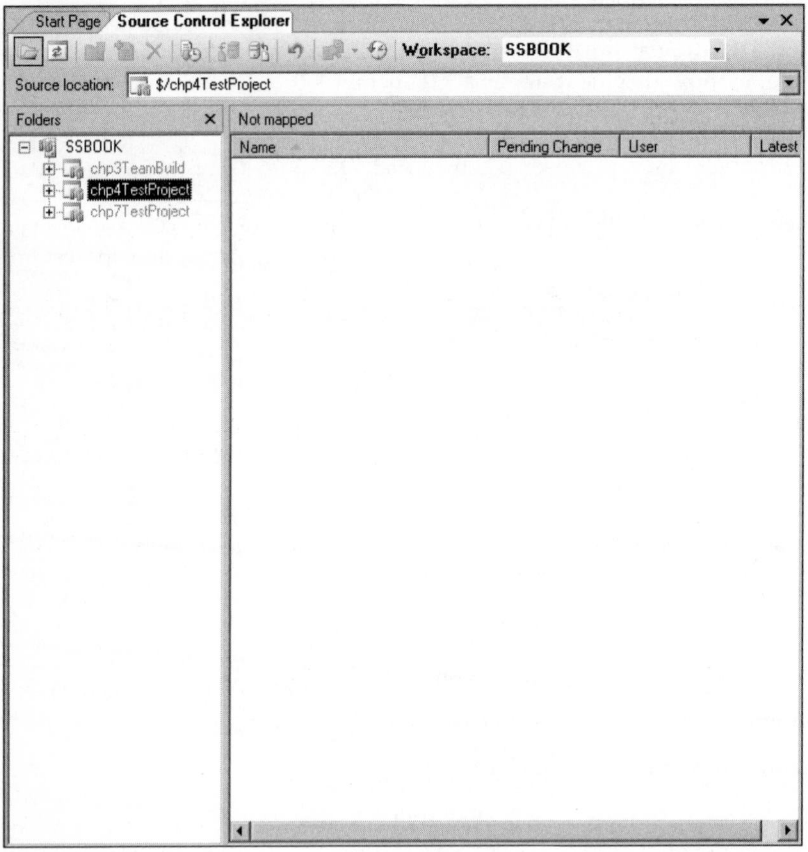

Figure 4-12

Once you have the Source Control Explorer open, you can set security permissions from the server level all the way down to individual files in particular projects. You can control how granular you need to get, depending on your situation. You need to develop some sort of guidelines of how your team is going to work the version control permissions, and what level of granularity you are going to enforce them at. If everyone on the team has the ability to change these settings to any level they want, this could lead to an administrative nightmare.

To modify the security permissions, right-click the file or folder you want to modify, and select Properties. This opens the Properties window. Click the Security Tab on that window, as shown in Figure 4-13.

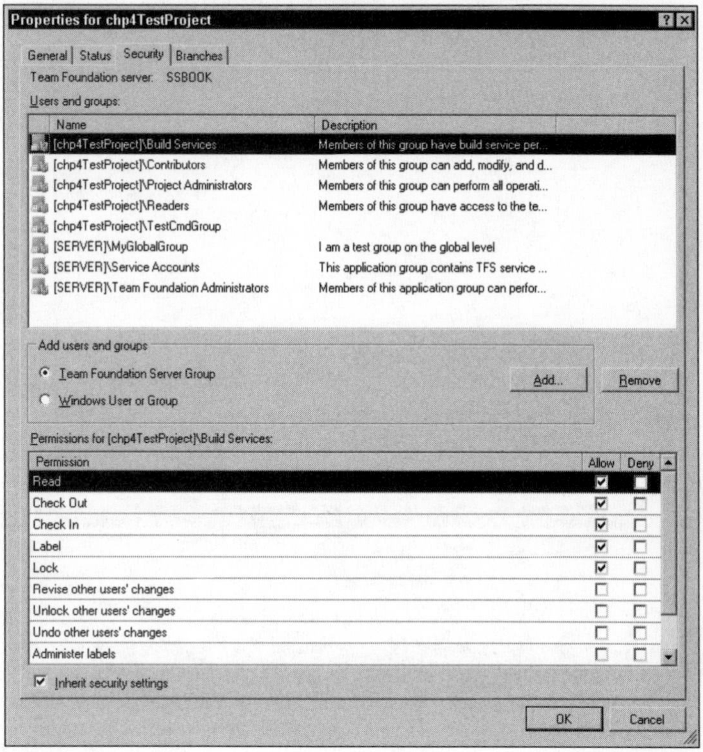

Figure 4-13

From this window, you can easily add more users and groups, remove users and groups, and give them the appropriate permissions needed to do their job.

Setting Work Item Tracking Areas Permissions

All Work Item Tracking Areas permissions can be set at the command line, using the TFSSecurity.exe tool. As you would expect, just as there was for Version Control, there is a graphical interface for this as well.

Right-click your Team Project, select Team Project Settings, then Areas and Iterations. This opens the Areas and Iterations window, as shown in Figure 4-14.

Select the area on which to modify security, and click the Security button. This opens the Area Node Security window, shown in Figure 4-15.

Have you noticed how all these security windows look the same? As you can guess, you use this window just like you do all the others.

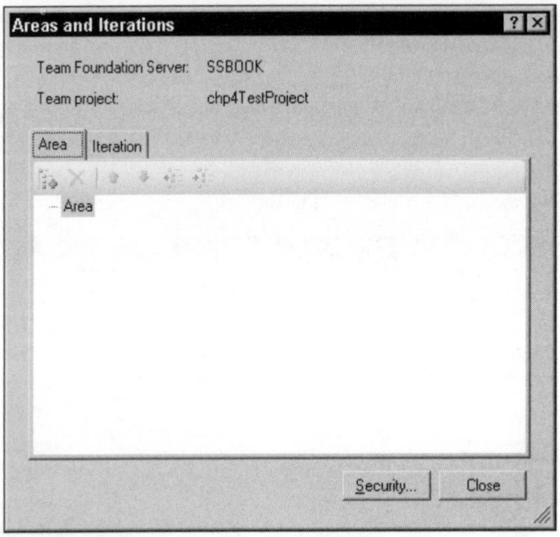

Figure 4-14

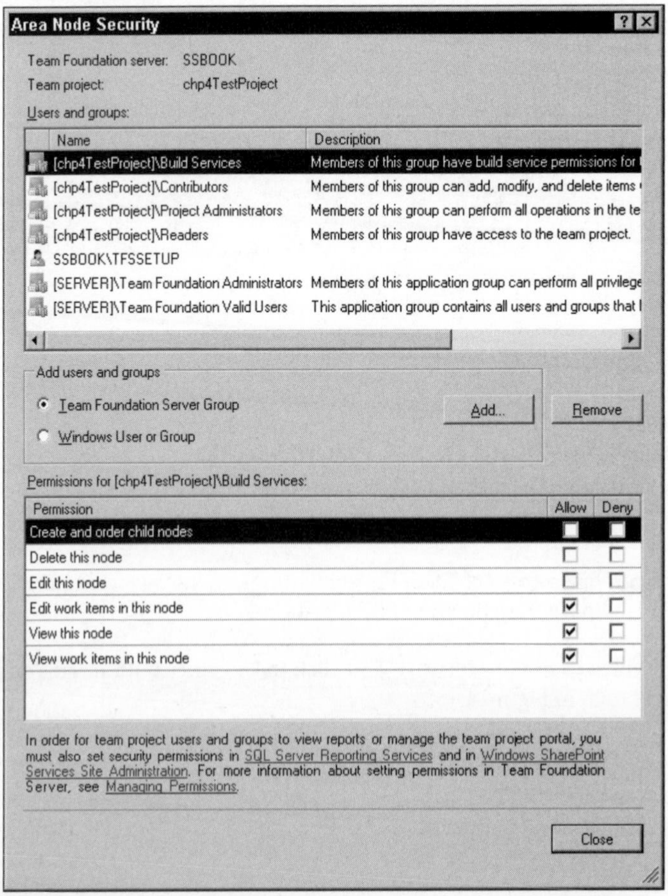

Figure 4-15

Common Security Access Problems

This section discusses the two common security access problems that you encounter. If you have been following the guidelines outlined in this book, more than likely you will not run into either of these issues. However, they occur often enough to make it worth discussing them here.

If you are having security issues, the MSDN Forums are a great resource (`http://msdn.microsoft.com/forums`). Many Microsoft employees and knowledgeable users monitor these forums, and will more than likely be able to answer any questions you might have, or at least point you in the right direction.

User Cannot Connect to Team Foundation Server

A user must be a member of the Team Foundation Valid Users group to connect to a Team Foundation Server using Team Explorer. If a user is not a member of this group, then when they try to add a Team Foundation Server to their Team Explorer, they will receive a TF31003 error message, stating that the user account does not have permission to connect to the Team Foundation Server.

The solution for this problem is to have your Team Foundation administrator add the user to either the Team Foundation Valid Users group, or to a group which is also a member of the Team Foundation Valid Users group. The latter option is the preferred method.

User Cannot Create a Team Project

If a user tries to create a new team project, and does not have sufficient rights, they may encounter the TF30172 error message, stating you do not have permission to create a new team project. This error message means the user does not have the global security permission Create A Project.

To correct this issue, you need to have your Team Foundation Administrator add the user to a group which has this permission set to Allow. Also, ensure the user is not a member of any group that has this permission set to Deny. Remember, Deny always overrides Allow.

You may receive other error messages, such as being unable to communicate with SQL Reporting Services, or with Windows SharePoint Services. Chapter 2 discusses how a user also has to have certain rights within both these services, which are not set in Team Foundation Server. Refer to Chapter 2 for more information.

Security Best Practices

Security is an ongoing process, and best practices will obviously change over time. However, you should always keep some basic security principles and ideas in mind when dealing with Team Foundation Server and other servers in general. It is important to note that Team Foundation Server ships out of the box with secure defaults, and you should not modify how Team Foundation Server communicates between its different tiers without good reason.

First, you should never use SQL Server Authentication to connect between Team Foundation Server and the data tier. Nor should you use it to connect between Windows SharePoint Services and the data tier. When using SQL Server Authentication, the username and password are not encrypted as they are sent from one server to another. This could allow someone snooping on your network to access this information. When using Windows integrated authentication, the identity of the IIS application pool is used in the authentication process. As well, when using Windows integrated authentication, a password is *never* sent over the wire.

Second, you should always make sure your servers are up to date with the latest patches, for both the operating system and any applications that are running on the server. If you have a patch management system in place at your organization, you can easily use that to make sure your servers have the latest updates. Otherwise, you should visit the Windows Update site regularly, to make sure you obtain the latest security updates. In addition, you should visit the Visual Studio Team System Web site at `http://msdn.microsoft.com/vstudio/teamsystem` to see whether there are any new patches or security updates for Team Foundation Server. You should make use of Microsoft Virtual PC and Virtual Server, to create an image that is identical to your Team Foundation Server setup. This allows you to test any changes or patches before applying those changes to a production environment.

Finally, you should have some system in place for auditing and testing the security settings on your Team Foundation Server. You should monitor the Windows event logs to look for any errors or suspicious activity.

> **When you create a new Team Foundation Server group, you should thoroughly test the group to make sure it cannot access any areas of the Team Foundation Server for which you have not planned.**

Team Foundation Server has a database called TFSActivityLogging, where Team Foundation Server can track the activity against the server. To enable activity logging, you have to turn it on. On the Team Foundation Server, go to Program Files\Microsoft Visual Studio 2005 Team Foundation Server\Web Services and open the `web.config` file. The `<appSettings>` tag contains the following key: `<add key="commandLogging" value="None"/>`. To enable activity logging, you need to change the value to one listed in the following table:

Value	Which Means
None	No logging
OnError	Log Web methods that encounter errors
ReadWrite	Log Web methods that change the databases
Normal	All of the above, as well as any Web methods that do not change the databases
Lightweight	All of the above, as well as any Web methods that have minimal database access
All	All of the above, as well as any Web method request details if available

After you make the change, commands against the Team Foundation Server will be logged. To query the information in the database, simply open SQL Server Management studio and run queries against the TFSActivityLogging database. In its simplest form, a query could just be:

```
select * from tbl_Command
```

You can also get more detailed with your queries, as needed. This could be a great source of information concerning how your Team Foundation Server is being used. Be aware, however, that turning on logging will require some resources from your server, so you might see a slight performance decrease.

Summary

Security is a big area, and there is no way we can touch on every aspect of it in this chapter. You have, however, learned some key ideas regarding security and Team Foundation Server, which should help you in securing your servers.

At the beginning of this chapter, we discussed the Team Foundation Server environment and how users are authenticated into the system. We then began an in-depth look at the Team Foundation Server Security Model and the different groups and permissions associated with the model. Next, we showed you how to take advantage of the security model, using both the graphical user interfaces and the command-line tools.

We discussed some of the common security access issues you will encounter with Team Foundation Server; and wrapped everything up by discussing some security best practices and showing how to enable activity logging on Team Foundation Server.

With a good understanding of Team Foundation Server security under your belt, we can now move on to discussing disaster recovery options. Chapter 5 discusses some troubleshooting tips for Team Foundation Server, and then provides instructions on how to ensure a successful backup of your Team Foundation Server data.

5

Team Foundation Server Backup and Recovery

Disasters strike when you least expect them. You need to be prepared for *any* emergency from a hurricane blowing away your datacenter to all the hard drives in your database server failing at the same time. Being prepared can mean the difference between having your organization up and running in 48 hours, versus priming your resume to look for a new job.

However, you can't just run off willy-nilly, set up a quick database backup job, and think that you are ready for any disaster. There is more to it than that. You need a plan, a written guideline for people to follow in case of an emergency. Moreover, you need to test that plan, constantly. Because if you don't test it and it fails, well, you may find yourself with a new interest in the job market.

This chapter covers the basics of disaster recovery. Whole books can be written on the subject, so we cover the basics here and we direct you to resources where you can learn more. Learning about disaster recovery in general before delving into Team Foundation Server specifics will help you to think about and create your own specific disaster recovery plan for your installation of Team Foundation Server. We briefly cover different backup tools, and then disaster recovery as it applies to Team Foundation Server. You also get an overview of SQL Server 2005 recovery modes, which play an integral part in determining your backup strategy for Team Foundation Server, and SQL Server in general.

Finally, in the remainder of the chapter, you learn step-by-step how to back up and restore Team Foundation Server to the same server or to a new machine.

Disaster Recovery Overview

Disasters come in all shapes and sizes. From natural disasters, such as tornadoes and floods, to hardware failure to accidentally dropping a table from a database. A disaster can strike at any time and how prepared you are can make all the difference. Given that, here are some things to ponder when thinking about disaster recovery.

To fully be prepared, you need to have a *disaster recovery plan*. This written checklist of everything that needs to happen in the event of an emergency will be a key to getting your organization up and running as quickly and efficiently as possible. Once something bad happens, people shouldn't have to think, they should be able follow a plan that has proven results.

Proven results means the plan has been thoroughly tested. You need to constantly test your disaster recovery plan. This provides several benefits. You have confidence in knowing your plan works. You are able to find any deficiencies in your plan, such as out-of-date material, and make the appropriate corrections. Finally, you gain experience in putting your plan into action, which, in the event of a real emergency, allows you to know what to expect.

When planning for an emergency, you should also see how much of the plan can be automated. As you learn later in this chapter, a good bit of SQL Server's backup and recovery can be automated using maintenance plans. Automation can save you time and prevent errors that occur from having to do something manually.

Given all this, let's briefly touch on what to think about when creating your disaster recovery plan. These considerations include an overview of the options that exist for backing up your data in Windows as well as when using third-party tools.

The Disaster Recovery Plan

A disaster recovery plan is a comprehensive, written plan of actions that need to be taken before, during, and after a disaster has occurred. It should be constantly tested, to ensure that all elements of the plan are still valid.

For a comprehensive recovery plan from a disaster affecting your business, you need to consider all the different areas of your organization and plan accordingly. Depending on the size of your business, this could be a massive undertaking. A good source to start with for this, and any disaster recovery needs in general, is *Disaster Recovery Journal* (`drj.com`). This publication offers a lot of free material related to disaster recovery, including sample plans, checklists, and other useful information.

Typically, a disaster recovery plan contains the following information:

- Information on location of backup hardware and software
- A communication list of people to contact in the event of an emergency, including people who will perform the recovery and those who will confirm the recovery works
- Some sort of organizational chart, so everyone involved knows who is responsible for what
- A list of the different recovery scenarios, along with a detailed checklist of each step required to perform each scenario
- A priority list of the recovery scenarios, listing which ones are most important, so that those involved in the recovery know which systems and scenarios have priority

This is by no means a comprehensive list, but it should give you an idea of some of the things to include in your plan.

Built-In Windows Backup Tools

Team Foundation Server runs on Windows Server 2003 and you can make use of the Windows Server 2003 Backup and Restore Wizard to configure your server backup options. To start the Backup and Restore Wizard, open a command prompt and type **NTBackup**. For in-depth information on how to use the Windows Server 2003 backup tool, refer to the following Microsoft TechNet Article: `microsoft.com/technet/prodtechnol/exchange/guides/DROpsGuide/321d275e-1a79-4cc0-972a-de757b7a2e1c.mspx`.

SQL Server 2005 has built-in tools for backing up databases and related items. We explore those tools later in this chapter.

Third-Party Backup Tools

A variety of third-party tools, including Symantec's Backup Exec, Legato's NetWorker, and Computer Associates' ARCserve, are available for backing up information. One of the major advantages of these tools is that they provide the ability to back up your database data as well as any other files related to your deployment. Of course, you can do the same thing with a combination of NTBackup and SQL Server 2005 tools. However, many of the third-party tools provide extra bells and whistles to make disaster recovery a much simpler process.

Disaster Recovery Applied to Team Foundation Server

Team Foundation Server disaster recovery can be relatively easy. All the data related to Team Foundation Server, including version control files, work items, and reports, is stored on the data tier of Team Foundation Server. Therefore, backing up Team Foundation Server is *almost* as simple as performing a database backup of the data tier. You also need to make a backup of the Report Server encryption key, which is not handled by a simple database backup. There may also be log files from other sources such as Internet Information Server that you want to save. These would also need to be backed up, if you wished to have them for historical reasons.

Given that all the data related to Team Foundation Server is stored in SQL Server 2005, it makes sense to spend a little time giving a basic overview of backup and restore strategies as related to SQL Server. This is by no means a comprehensive overview, but it is intended to give you a foundation for understanding the rest of this chapter. The online MSDN Library (`http://msdn2.microsoft.com`) is full of detailed resources concerning SQL Server 2005 backup and recovery, and would be a great place to learn more about the topic.

SQL Server 2005 Backup and Restore Overview

Let's start this section off by talking about recovery models in SQL Server 2005. A *recovery model* is just a database property. It controls how transactions are logged in the database, whether the transaction log file needs to be backed up, and which restore operations are available for that database. You can specify a different recovery model for each database in SQL Server 2005, and can change the recovery model at any point. There are three types of recovery models: simple, full, and bulk logged.

> **A new database inherits its recovery model from the model system database.**

In *simple* recovery mode, the transaction log is not backed up. After a database backup has executed, any transactions that have been committed from the transaction log are truncated, freeing up space in the log. Also, only minimum database information is retained to ensure database consistency after a database is restored. Simple recovery mode is the easiest to use, but it comes with some risk as well. You can recover data only up until the last backup. If you have a database failure twelve hours after your last backup, then you lose the past twelve hours of information. Given this, you should keep your backup intervals short enough to limit your losses, but long enough to keep the backup from affecting production. You can use a combination of full and differential backups to achieve this. A full database backup backs up all the information in the database. A differential database backup backs up only changes made to the database since the last full or differential backup. Best practices dictate this recovery model is not suitable for production systems where it is unacceptable to lose recent changes. As such, it is not recommended to use this model on your Team Foundation Server data tier.

Full recovery mode provides much better protection against data loss. In this mode, the transaction log must be backed up. By logging all transactions against the database to the transaction log and making backups of those logs, a database can be recovered almost to its point of failure. For example, you could schedule a full backup every night at midnight, and then a transaction log backup every hour. This would allow you to restore the database to within an hour of its failure, or better yet, if the transaction log can be saved from the failed server, you can restore the data back to the point of failure. Given the critical nature of the files stored within Team Foundation Server, this is the recommended model to use on your Team Foundation Server data tier. It is also the default for most databases in SQL Server 2005.

Bulk-logged recovery mode is a subset of full recovery mode. It is mostly used when doing huge imports or index creation to help with performance. You should never need to use this mode with Team Foundation Server.

To view the current recovery model of a database, open SQL Server Management Studio by going to Start⇨All Programs⇨Microsoft SQL Server 2005, and selecting SQL Server Management Studio. After establishing the database connection, expand the Databases folder on the left, and drill down to the database in question. Right-click the database and select Properties from the context menu to open the Database Properties window. In the Select a Page pane, click the Options button. You can see the current recovery model of the database displayed in the Recovery model drop-down list box. To change the model, simply choose a different option from the Recovery model drop-down list box.

After you know which recovery model you are using, you can set up a maintenance plan to perform backups of your databases. A *maintenance plan* is a series of scheduled tasks that run at specific times against the database server. Here is a list of some of the possible tasks that can be handled by a maintenance plan:

- Checking the integrity of the database
- Shrinking the database
- Rebuilding and reorganizing database indexes
- Cleaning up the database history
- Backing up the database, using either a full, differential, or transaction log backup

Later in this chapter you learn step by step how to set up a maintenance plan for backing up Team Foundation Server.

Backing Up Team Foundation Server

Backing up Team Foundation Server mostly requires backing up the data tier. In addition, you need to back up the symmetric encryption key from the report server.

Backing Up the Team Foundation Server Databases

Eleven databases, shown in the following table, make up the Team Foundation Server data tier:

Database Name	Database Function
ReportServer	This is the SQL Server Reporting Services database. It contains all the reports, settings, and other information related to Reporting Services.
ReportServerTempDB	This is used by SQL Server Reporting Services to temporarily hold information needed for running reports.
STS_Config	This is used by Windows SharePoint Services to hold configuration information for the different Team Project WSS sites.
STS_Content_TFS	This is used by Windows SharePoint Services to hold the content of the different Team Project WSS sites.
TfsActivityLogging	This is used by Team Foundation Server to maintain a history of all Web server requests made to Team Foundation Server.
TfsBuild	This is used by Team Foundation Server to hold all build information and related data, such as test results.
TfsIntegration	This is used by Team Foundation Server to hold registration data on projects, areas, and iterations, among other items.
TfsVersionControl	This is used by Team Foundation Server to hold all information related to the Team Foundation version control system.
TFSWarehouse	This is the SQL Server Analysis Server database used by Team Foundation Server.
TfsWorkItemTracking	This is used by Team Foundation Server to hold all information related to work item tracking.
TfsWorkItemTrackingAttachments	This is used by Team Foundation Server to hold all attachments added to the work item tracking system.

Before you can back up these databases, or any database for that matter, you need to determine your priorities and strategy for backing up the information. This is a huge and detailed topic, and Microsoft has some very in-depth information for you on this. Please reference "Backing Up and Restoring Databases" in the SQL Server 2005 help (`http://msdn2.microsoft.com/en-us/library/ms186289.aspx`) for more information. Also, you need to make sure you have installed SQL Server Integration Services on the database. If you have not, you can simply reinsert your SQL Server 2005 media, restart the installation, and choose that option to install.

To back up these eleven databases, you can use the built-in tools provided by SQL Server 2005. Using SQL Server Management Studio, you can set up a maintenance plan to back up the databases as you feel appropriate. You can set up an individual maintenance plan for each database, or can back up all the databases using one maintenance plan. In the following steps, you learn how to set up a single maintenance plan to run a full backup on all the user databases. You can easily extrapolate these steps to set up differential backups as well, or to back up individual databases.

You will be performing all the following on the data-tier server.

1. Open the SQL Server Management Studio, by going to Start⇨All Programs⇨Microsoft SQL Server 2005, and then selecting SQL Server Management Studio. This opens the SQL Server Management Studio window, and prompts you for your connection information, as shown in Figure 5-1.

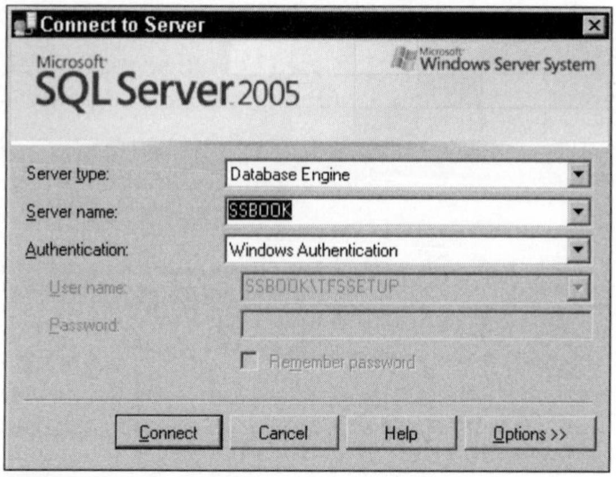

Figure 5-1

More than likely you are already logged in as the appropriate user if you are doing administrative tasks, so you should just be able to click Connect and move on. However, you can modify the information in the login box to change which server you are connecting to, the type of authentication you wish to use, and enter a valid user name and password, if required.

2. When you are in Management Studio, you need to kick off the Maintenance Plan Wizard to set up a new maintenance plan. On the left side of the Management Studio is a tree-view structure of the database server. Click the plus sign next to the Management folder to expand that folder. Right-click the Maintenance Plans option, and select Maintenance Plan Wizard from the context menu. As you would expect, this starts the Maintenance Plan Wizard.

   The first page of the wizard is just a welcome page. Click Next to move to the Select a Target Server page, shown in Figure 5-2.

   On this page you can name the maintenance plan, as well as give it a description. Best practices recommend you give the plan a descriptive name, so you can easily see the purpose of the plan. For this example, name the plan **TeamFoundationServerFullBackup**. You can also select which SQL Server to back up, how the backup user authenticates to the server, and even which user to use for running the maintenance plan. Leave these as their defaults, and click Next.

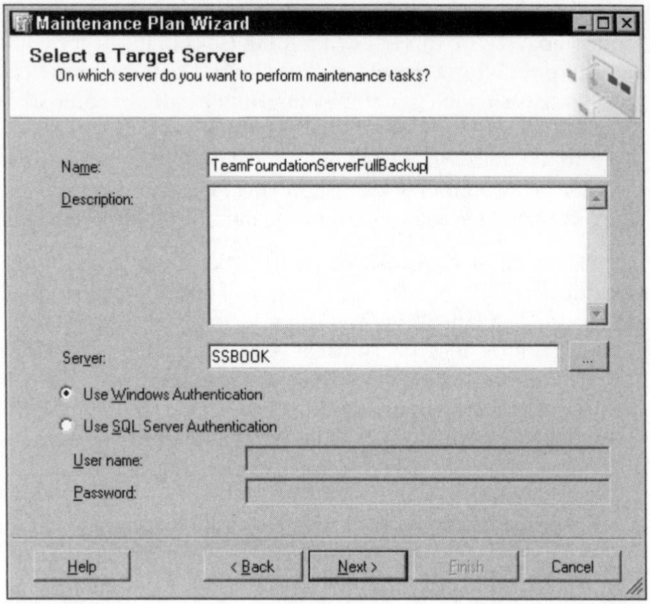

Figure 5-2

3. Figure 5-3 shows the next step of the wizard, the Select Maintenance Tasks page. You can choose to have a maintenance plan perform multiple functions, including shrinking the database or rebuilding indexes. To do so, simply check the check box of the task you wish to run. As mentioned earlier, you are doing a full backup in this example, so select Back Up Database (Full) and click Next.

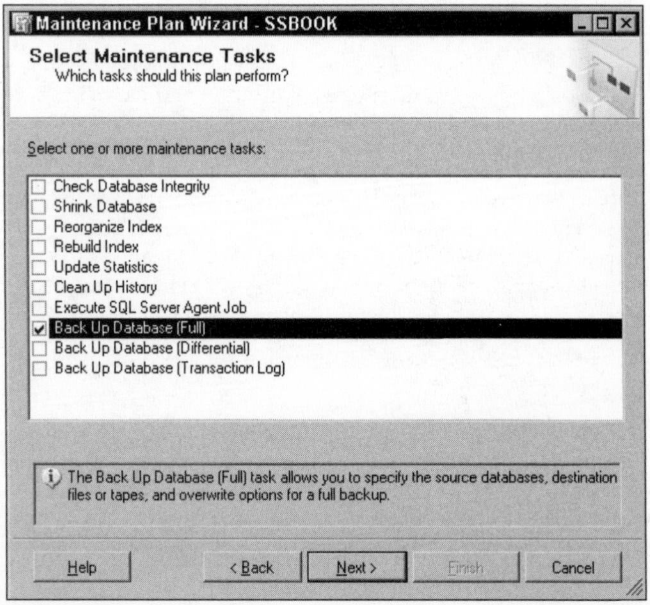

Figure 5-3

4. This opens the Select Maintenance Tasks Order page. If you selected multiple tasks to perform in the previous step, you use this page to put the tasks in the order you wish them to be performed. For example, if you selected both the Check Database Integrity task and the Back Up Database (Full) task, you might want the integrity task to run before the full database backup is performed. You would simply select the Check Database Integrity task in this window, and use the Move Up button to move it to the top of the list. You can also use the Move Down button to move tasks closer to the bottom of the list, in effect making them run after other tasks. In this example, you only have one task, so accept the defaults on this page and click Next.

5. This opens the Define Back Up Database (Full) Task page, shown in Figure 5-4. On this page, you can select the databases to back up, the type of backup to perform, and the backup destination, such as to a file or a tape drive. You can also specify whether the databases should be backed up across multiple files, or if a backup file should be created for each database being backed up. You can choose the folder to store the backup files in, the extension to give the files, and even create a subdirectory in the backup folder for each database, allowing for easier organization of your backups. Finally, you can verify the integrity of the backup once it has been performed, to ensure there has been no corruption of the backup files.

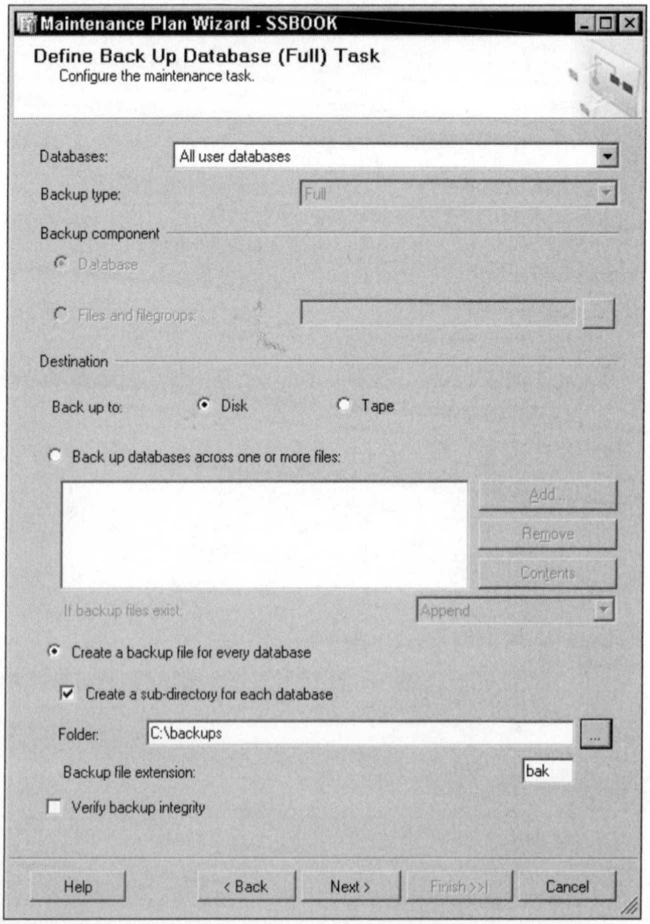

Figure 5-4

When you select a database from the drop-down list box, you are presented with four radio button options:

- All databases
- All system databases (master, msdb, model)
- All user databases (excluding master, msdb, model, tempdb)
- These databases, which is a check box list of all the databases on the server

Simply select the appropriate radio button for the task you are working on. For this example, from the Database drop-down list box, select All User Databases radio button, and click OK. This will back up all nonsystem databases.

> **You should create a separate maintenance plan to back up the system databases used by SQL Server 2005.**

6. Next you need to specify where the backup will be placed. Ideally, you would like the backups to be placed on a separate machine, which then archives the backup to tape or some other archival media. It is not recommended to backup directly to tape, as this will increase your backup time.

   For this example, select the Create a backup file for every database radio button, and check the Create a sub-directory for each database check box. In the Folder text box, enter **c:\backups**. Make sure this directory exists before you execute the maintenance plan. Optionally, you can check the Verify backup integrity check box. Once you have configured the backup task, click Next. This opens the Select Plan Properties window, shown in Figure 5-5.

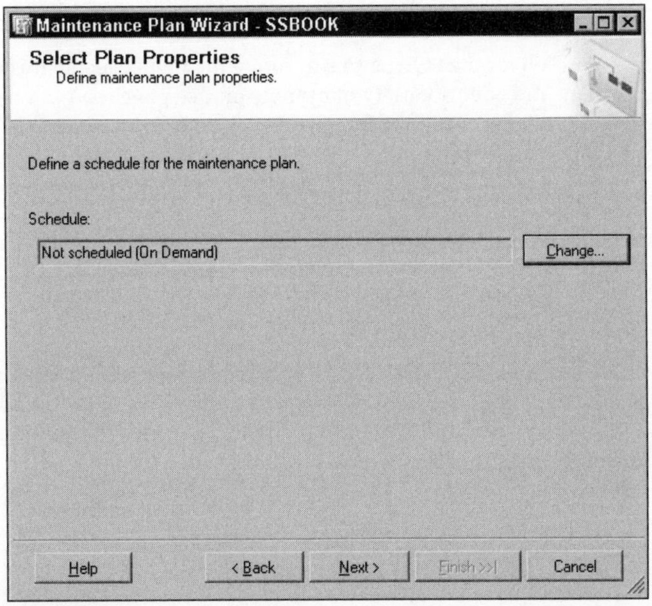

Figure 5-5

7. A maintenance plan defaults to Not Scheduled, meaning it will run only if you execute it. Ideally, you want your full backup to run weekly, or possibly even daily. For this example, you want to set the maintenance plan to run nightly at midnight. To do this, you click the Change button to open the New Job Schedule screen, shown in Figure 5-6.

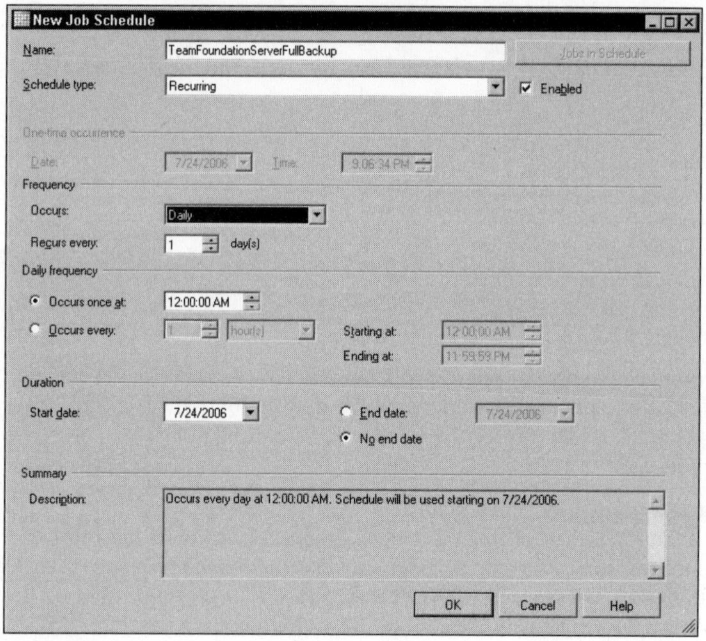

Figure 5-6

This creates a new job for the SQL Server to run, which will execute this full database backup maintenance plan. You have a variety of options on this page. You can name the job, and enable or disable it from running using the Enabled check box. You can select the appropriate schedule type from the following options:

- Start Automatically when SQL Server Agent Starts
- Start whenever the CPU(s) become idle
- Recurring
- One Time

For a One Time schedule, fill out the One Time Occurrence section, giving the job a date and time to run. For Recurring schedules, which will probably be the most used option, fill out the Frequency, Daily frequency, and Duration sections, as needed. Notice the Summary Description at the bottom of the page; it shows, in plain words, when the job is set to run.

For this example, enter in the name of your job. In this case, you can use the same name as the maintenance plan, **TeamFoundationServerFullBackup**. Set the Schedule Type to Recurring, the Frequency Occurs to Daily, and the Daily Frequency to 12:00:00 AM. Click OK to return to the Select Plan Properties window, and then click Next.

8. This opens the Select Report Options window. You can have the maintenance plan write a report out to specific directory. You can also have the report e-mailed. Clicking Next takes you to the final step of the wizard, the Complete the Wizard page.
9. Here you can review all the options you have chosen for your maintenance plan, and verify everything is correct before you have the plan built. If everything looks good, click Finish to build the plan.

A progress window opens and updates you on the creation of the maintenance plan. When the wizard is finished, you are alerted to the success or failure of the maintenance plan creation.

At this point in SQL Server Management Studio, in the Management Folder, and then in the Maintenance Plan folder, you can see the maintenance plan you just created. If you drill down under the SQL Server Agent node, and then the Jobs folder, you will see the job that was created to execute the maintenance plan nightly.

If you want to go ahead and run your maintenance plan, to ensure everything works, simply right-click the maintenance plan and select Execute from the context menu. Your maintenance plan will run, and you can verify the databases were backed up as expected.

Backing Up the Report Server Encryption Key

Besides backing up the databases, you also need to back up the SQL Server Reporting Services encryption key. SQL Server Reporting Services uses encryption keys to secure connections and other vital information. These keys are created during the installation of the server, and are required for the server to run. There are three types of keys used by Reporting Services: public, private, and symmetric. For purposes of this discussion, what each key is used for is not relevant. What is important, however, is that you back up the symmetric key. Without the symmetric key, Reporting Services will not work. If you have to restore the databases to a new server, and do not have a backup of the symmetric key, all the Reporting Services information will be useless.

Backing up the symmetric encryption key writes out a file containing the key. The key itself is scrambled using a password you have chosen when the file was created. You can then place this file in a directory where your backup software will find and archive it. Don't forget the password you used to create the file with. Without the password, you cannot recover the symmetric key from the file.

1. Go to Start⇨All Programs⇨Microsoft SQL Server 2005⇨Configuration Tools, and select Reporting Services Configuration. This starts the SQL Reporting Services Configuration tool. Enter the machine name and the instance name of the Report Server you wish to configure, as shown in Figure 5-7.
2. Enter in the appropriate information, and click Connect to open the configuration tool itself. This tool allows you to configure all the various aspects of the Report Server. This includes modifying virtual directories, service identities, and e-mail settings, just to name a few. Once in the configuration tool, click the Encryption Keys link on the left side of the tool. This opens the Encryption Key section of the tool, shown in Figure 5-8.

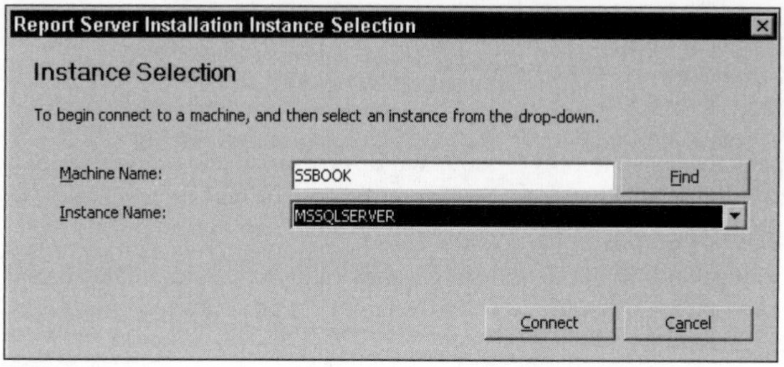

Figure 5-7

Figure 5-8

3. You have several different options here, including backing up, restoring, changing, or deleting the encryption key. You want to back up the key, so click the Backup button. Figure 5-9 shows the Encryption Key Information window that opens.

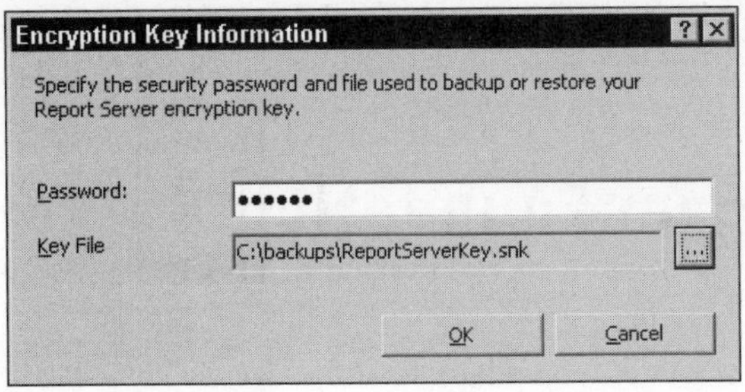

Figure 5-9

4. In the Password field, you enter a value to help scramble the key file. Do not forget what you enter here! Otherwise, the key file will be useless. You can click the ellipse button to select a directory and a name for your key file. Click OK to create the file. Once the file has been created, you should verify the file exists, and then archive it accordingly. Again, not to belabor a point, *do not* forget the password for your key file!

Instead of using the Reporting Services Configuration tool to back up the key file, you can use the RSKEYMGMT command-line tool. If you have deployed Team Foundation Server in a dual server or a cluster environment, you will have to use this tool in those instances, as the application tier does not support the Reporting Services Configuration tool described above.

The RSKEYMGMT command-line tool is located by default in the `C:\Program Files\Microsoft SQL Server\90\Tools\Binn` folder. The syntax for using this tool to backup the encryption key is:

```
RSKEYMGMT-e-f <FileName> -p <password>
```

So, to do the same example as above, but with the command-line tool, you would run the following:

```
RSKEYMGMT-e-f c:\backups\ReportServerKey.snk-p MyPassword
```

Restoring the Report Server Encryption Key (Optional)

If the encryption key for the report server has changed between the current state of the report server and the restore date of the backup files, then you will need to restore the report server encryption key. If the key has not changed, then you do not need to do anything, and can skip this section.

1. To restore the encryption key, open the Reporting Services Configuration Tool, as explained earlier. Enter the appropriate connection information and click Connect. Select Encryption Keys from the left side of the screen, then click Restore.
2. This opens the Encryption Key Information window, as you saw in Figure 5-9. Enter the password you selected for your key file, then click the ellipse button and select your key file.
3. Click OK to accept this file and password, and restore the key file to the reports server.

You have now backed up all the information necessary to restore Team Foundation Server. Up next, you learn how to restore that information.

Restoring Team Foundation Server to the Same Server

In some disaster recovery scenarios, you have to restore the data onto brand new hardware. However, sometimes you don't have a disaster situation where you need to use a new server. It could just be that the data has become corrupt in the database, and you want to roll back to an archived copy. In this section, you learn the steps required to restore a Team Foundation Server backup onto the original server. In a later section, you learn how to restore onto a new server.

> **To follow these instructions, you must have the data-tier Team Foundation Server from which the backups were taken in good working order.**

There are five steps involved in restoring a Team Foundation Server from its backup. These steps should be performed in the following order:

1. Stop Application Tier Services:
    a. On the application tier, open the Reporting Services Configuration Tool, as described previously, click the Server Status link; then click the Stop button. This will stop the report server.
    b. Next, open the Services window by clicking Start⇨Control Panel⇨Administrative Tools⇨Services.
    c. Right-click the following services and click Stop:
        - SharePoint Timer
        - TFSServerScheduler
    d. Finally, you need to stop Internet Information Server. To shutdown IIS, simply open a command prompt and type **iisreset /stop**.
2. Restore Team Foundation Server databases.
3. Recreate the Data Warehouse.
4. Start Application Tier Services:
    a. To restart IIS, simply open a command prompt and type **iisreset /start**.
    b. Open the Services window, right-click the following services, and click Start:
        - TFSServerScheduler
        - SharePoint Timer

c. Open the Reporting Services Configuration Tool, click the Server Status Link, and click the Start button.

5. Flush the Client Work Item cache.

Restoring Team Foundation Server Databases

To restore the Team Foundation Server databases, you once again make use of SQL Server Management Studio. Open SQL Server Management Studio as described previously. In the Object Explorer on the left side of the screen, select the plus sign beside the Databases folder to expand it. This folder lists all the databases installed on this SQL server. You have to restore each database individually. The following is a list of the databases you need to restore:

- ReportServer
- ReportServerTempDB
- STS_Config_TFS
- STS_Content_TFS
- TfsBuild
- TfsIntegration
- TfsVersionControl
- TfsWarehouse
- TfsWorkItemTracking
- TfsWorkItemTrackingAttachments

> **The TfsActivityLogging database is not restored, as it is not critical to the operation of Team Foundation Server; it can be restored if desired.**

1. To start the restore process on a database, right-click the database in SQL Server Management Studio. Select Tasks, then Restore, and then Database. This opens the Restore Database window, as shown in Figure 5-10.
2. In the Source to Restore section, click the From device radio button to select it. Click the ellipse button to open the Specify Backup window. Figure 5-11 shows the Specify Backup window.
3. Click the Add button, and select the appropriate backup file. Click OK to close this window and return to the Restore Database window. In the left pane of this window, select Options to view the different restore options. Check Overwrite the existing database. Make sure the paths in the Restore the database files section, for each file, are valid paths.

If everything looks good to you, click OK to close this window and restore the database. Remember, you have to perform this procedure on each individual database in Team Foundation Server.

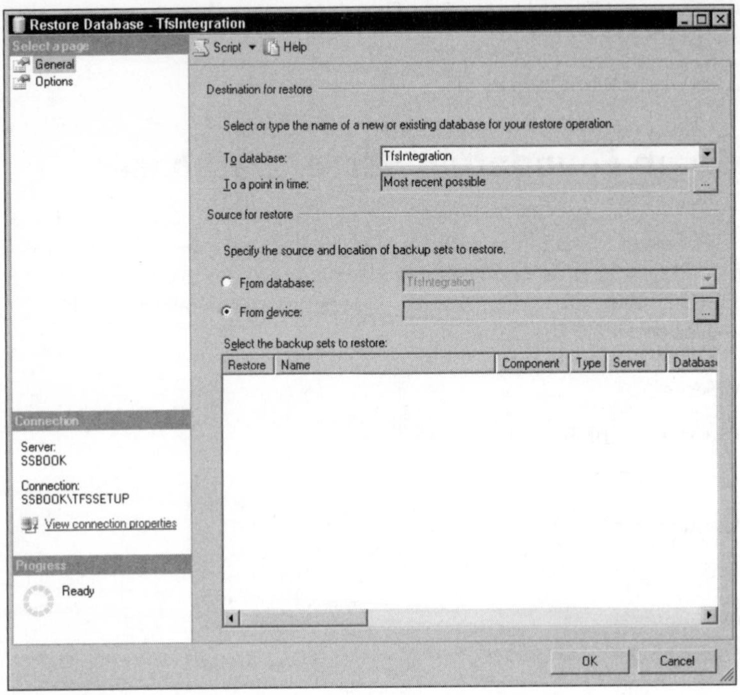

Figure 5-10

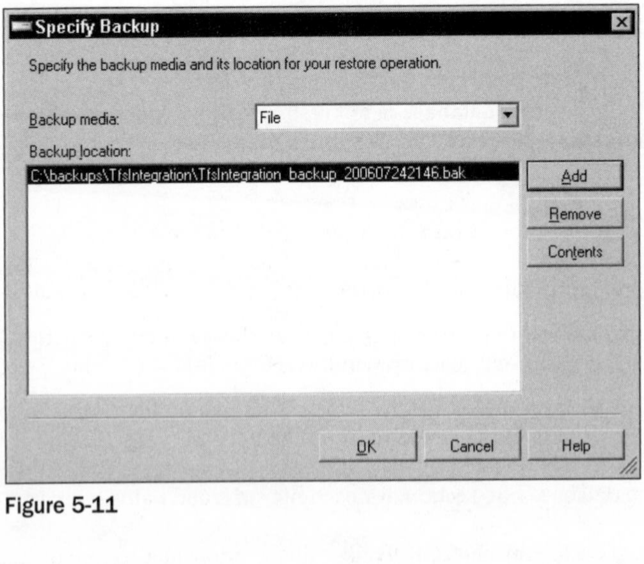

Figure 5-11

Recreating the Data Warehouse

Next, you recreate the data warehouse for Team Foundation Server. You do this from the application-tier machine using the setupwarehouse command-line tool. This command uses the TfsWarehouse database to recreate the Analysis Services data cube. On the application-tier machine, open a command prompt, and switch to the c:\Program Files\Microsoft Visual Studio 2005 Team Foundation Server\Tools directory. The format for running this command is:

```
Setupwarehouse-o-s <DataTierServer> -d TfsWarehouse-c warehouseschema.xml-ra
<ReportAccount> -a <ServiceAccount>
```

Where <DataTierServer> is the name of the data-tier server, <ReportAccount> is the report account you created when you installed Team Foundation Server, such as TFSREPORTS, and <ServiceAccount> is the account that runs the Team Foundation Services, such as TFSSERVICE. Figure 5-12 shows an example of running this command:

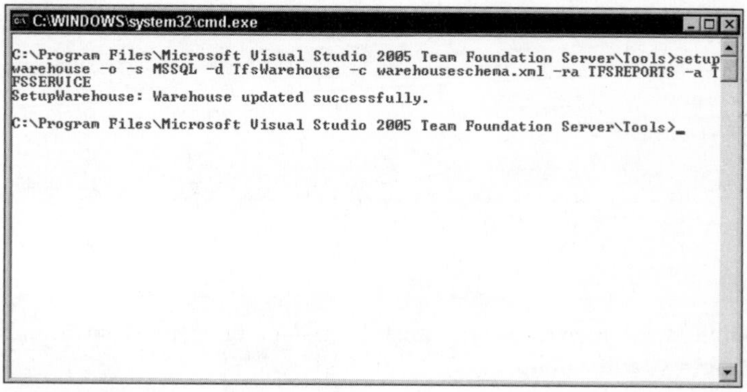

Figure 5-12

For more details on the setupwarehouse tool, type the following at a command prompt:

```
setupwarehouse /?
```

Refreshing the Work Item Cache on Client Machines

Finally, you need to force the client machines to refresh their work item cache.

1. To do this, open Internet Explorer on the application-tier server, and navigate to http://<appservername>:8080/WorkItemTracking/v1.0/ClientService.asmx. This opens the Client Service Web Service page, shown in Figure 5-13.

   The ClientService Web Service contains many different Web methods used by Team Foundation Server.

2. Click the StampWorkItemCache link to view the Web method. On the StampWorkItemCache Web method page, click the Invoke button to execute the method. A second blank Internet Explorer window may open while the method is running. Once the method is finished, close both Internet Explorer windows.

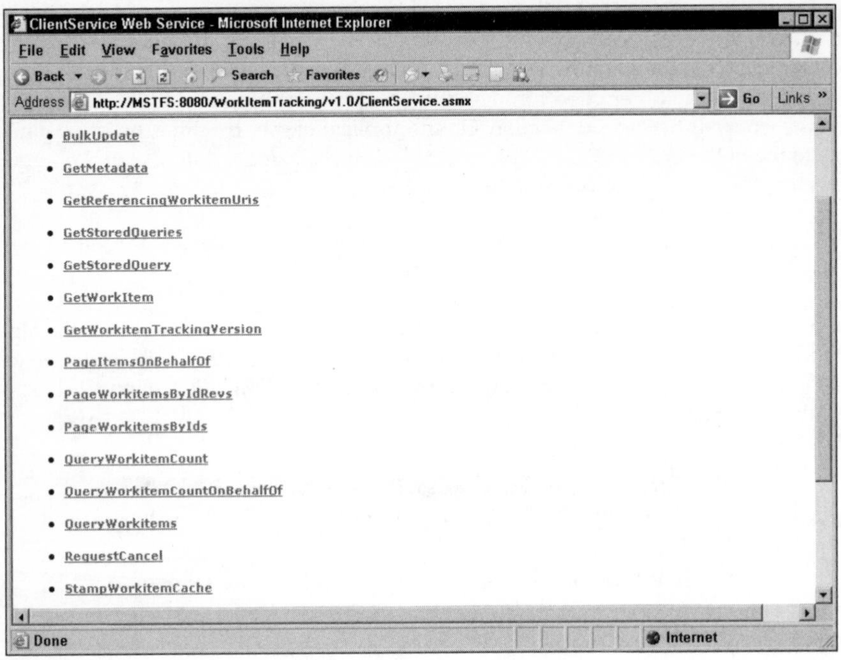

Figure 5-13

To refresh the work item cache, you must be a member of the Team Foundation Server Administrators group.

At this point, your Team Foundation Server has been restored. You should test to make sure you can connect to the application tier and the data tier from your client, and that all the data has been restored properly.

Restoring Team Foundation Server to a Different Server

At times, you are going to need to restore your backups to a different server. One example would be a disaster situation where the original server is lost. Another would be if you were moving from an old server to a new server, as in the case of upgrading your hardware. In any event, the following instructions walk you through how to restore your Team Foundation Server data to a new server.

To successfully migrate your server, you need to correctly identify all your live components. Brian Harry has created a utility called TFSVersionDetection to help you identify the version of Team Foundation Server you are using. You can download a copy of the tool at `www.bdharry.members.winisp.net/tools/TFSVersionDetection.zip`**.**

As a prerequisite before starting this operation, you must have a server that has a fresh install of the Team Foundation Server data tier. See Chapter 2 for more information and detailed instructions about how to set up a data tier server.

There are ten steps involved in restoring Team Foundation Server to a new server. These steps should be performed in the following order:

1. Configure and stop report server
2. Configure and stop IIS
3. Stop application-tier services
4. Restore Team Foundation Server databases
5. Recreate the data warehouse
6. Configure application tier to use data tier
7. Recreating report server connection strings
8. Configure Windows SharePoint portal sites
9. Start application-tier services
10. Flush client work item cache

Several of these steps have already been touched on in the previous section, so we refer you to those as appropriate.

The following steps are performed exactly as described in the previous section. Please reference those sections for detailed instructions on the following:

1. Restore Team Foundation Server databases
2. Start application-tier services
3. Flush client work item cache

Please refer to those sections as appropriate. The rest of this section will cover the remaining steps in the restore process.

Configure and Stop Report Server

You need to configure reporting services on the application tier to point to the new database server.

Open the Report Server Configuration Tool (Start⇨All Programs⇨Microsoft SQL Server 2005⇨ Configuration Tools⇨Reporting Services Configuration), then select the Database Setup link, as shown in Figure 5-14.

Type in the new database server name; then click the New button. This opens the SQL Connection dialog box. Enter **ReportServer** as the database name; then click OK. Your changes are automatically applied. Once that is finished, click the Windows Service Identity link. You need to reset the built-in account. To reset the built-in account value from the drop-down list box, select Network Service, then Local System, then Network Service again, then click Apply.

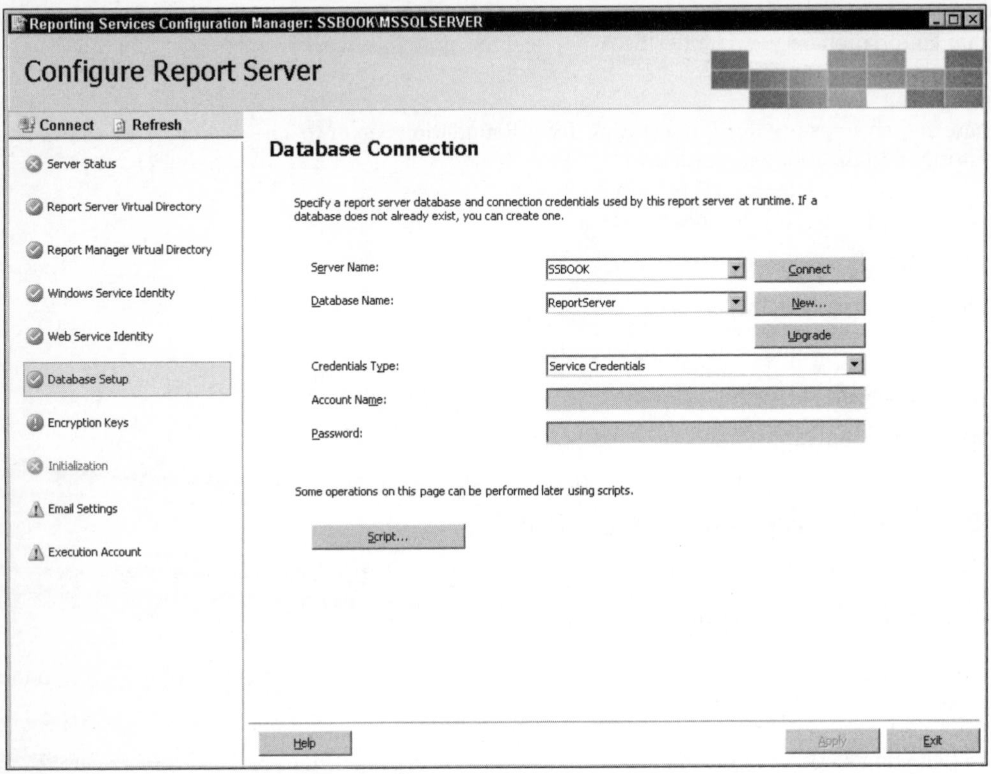

Figure 5-14

At this point, you have configured the report server to use the new data tier. Now you need to stop the server to continue the recovery process. To do this, click the Server Status link, then click the Stop button.

Configure and Stop IIS

Next, you need to stop the default Web site, so that you can remove Windows SharePoint Services from it. You will add WSS back later in the process.

Open the IIS Manager window (Start➪Control Panel➪Administrative Tools➪Internet Information Services (IIS) Manager). Expand the Web Sites node, right-click the Default Web site, and click Stop to stop the site.

Once the default Web site is stopped, open the Windows SharePoint Central Administration page (Start➪Control Panel➪Administrative Tools➪SharePoint Central Administration). This opens the administrative Web page for SharePoint. Click the Configure virtual server settings link, then click the Default Web site link. Click the Manage Content Databases link, followed by the STS_Content_TFS link. Finally, check the Remove content database check box, and click OK.

Go back to the Central Administration Page. Select the following links: Configure Virtual Server Settings➪Default Website➪Remove Windows SharePoint Services from Virtual Server. Select Remove without deleting content databases, and click OK.

Stop Services on the Application Tier

You need to stop the remaining services used by Team Foundation Server before continuing the restore process.

1. Open the Services window by clicking Start⇨Control Panel⇨Administrative Tools⇨ Services. Right-click the following services and click Stop:
   - ❑ SharePoint Timer
   - ❑ TFSServerScheduler
2. Open the IIS Manager Window (as described previously). Expand the Application Pools node, right-click the following pools, and click Stop:
   - ❑ ReportServer
   - ❑ TFS AppPool

Recreate the Data Warehouse

After all the databases have been restored, you have to recreate the data warehouse. First, you need to run the `setupwarehouse` command on the application tier as described in the previous section on restoring to the same server.

Once that is done, you need to run processing on the data warehouse. Open SQL Server Management Studio on the data tier. In the Connect To Server window, select Analysis Services as the Server type, then click Connect. Expand the Databases node, right-click the TFSWarehouse database, and click Process. This opens the Process Database window. Simply click OK to begin processing.

Connecting the Application Tier to the Data Tier

The data-tier name and IP address are stored in several locations throughout Team Foundation Server. If the name of the data tier changes, you need to update the Team Foundation Server application tier to point to the new data tier.

To connect the application tier to the new data tier, you need to use the TfsAdminUtil command-line utility. This utility is located at `C:\Program Files\Microsoft Visual Studio 2005 Team Foundation Server\Tools` on the application-tier server.

1. Open a command prompt and navigate to the above directory. The syntax for using TfsAdminUtil to connect to a new data tier is:

```
TFSAdminUtil.exe RenameDT <NewDataTierName>
```

   Where `<NewDataTierName>` is the name or the IP address of the new data-tier server. Figure 5-15 shows an example of running this command.

For more details on the TfsAdminUtil, run the following at a command prompt:

```
TfsAdminUtil /?
```

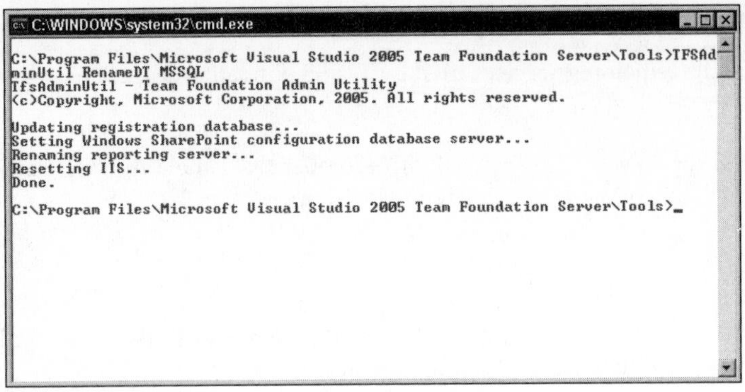

Figure 5-15

Re-creating Report Server Connection Strings

If you have a new data-tier name, you must update reporting services to use that name. On the application tier, start Internet Explorer and navigate to `http://<apptierservername>/reports`. This opens the home page of SQL Server Reporting Services. Click the TfsOlapReportDS link listed on this page. This opens the properties page for this data source, shown in Figure 5-16.

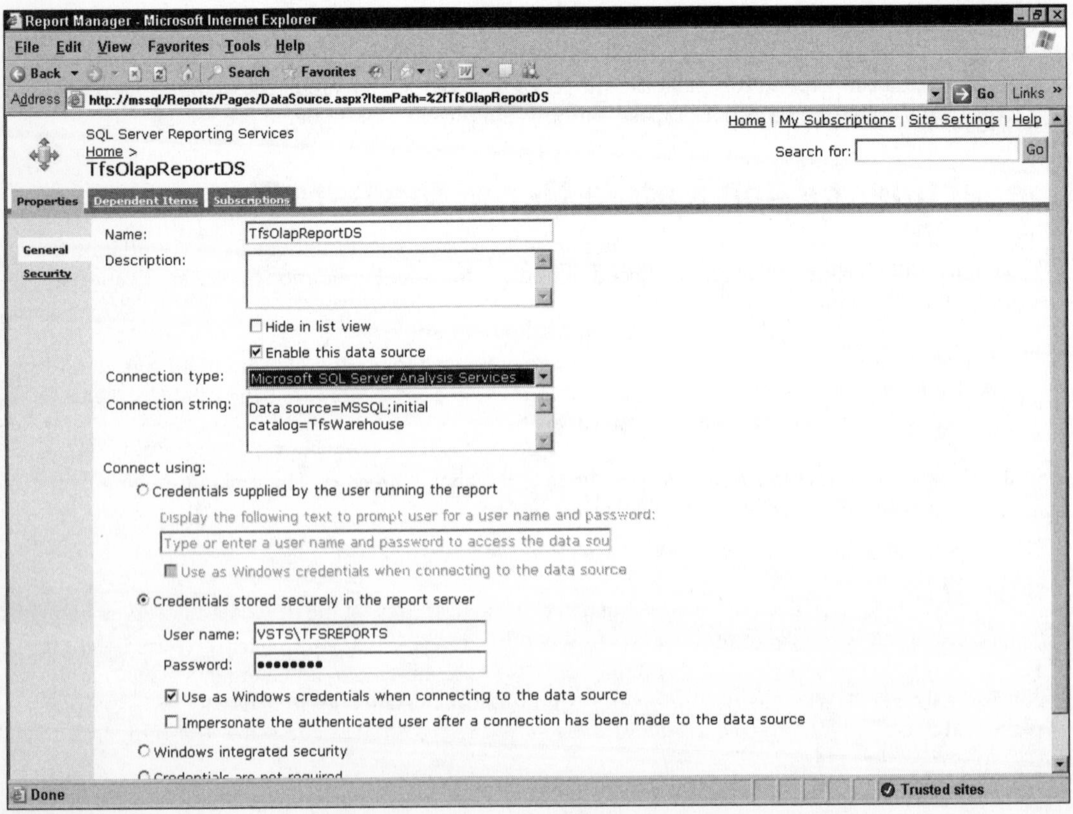

Figure 5-16

1. In the Connection Type drop-down list box, select Microsoft SQL Server Analysis Services. "Then modify the Connection String box to contain the new database value: `Data source=<newdatatier>;initial catalog=TfsWarehouse`, where `<newdatatier>` is the server name for the new data-tier server.
2. Select the Credentials Stored securely in the report server radio button. Enter in the Reports user (TFSREPORTS) and password, if not already filled. Make sure the Use as Windows credentials when connecting to the data-source check box is checked. Then click the Apply button.
3. Click the Home link at the top of the page, and then click the TFSReportDS link. This opens the properties window for this data source. In the Connection Type drop-down list box, select Microsoft SQL Server. Then modify the Connection String box to contain the new database value: `Data source=<newdatatier>;initial catalog=TfsWarehouse`, where `<newdatatier>` is the server name for the new data-tier server.
4. Select the Credentials Stored securely in the report server radio button. Enter in the Reports user (TFSREPORTS) and password, if not already filled. Make sure the Use as Windows credentials when connecting to the data source check box is checked. Then click the Apply button. You may now close out of this tool.

Configure Windows SharePoint Portal Sites

After the reporting services connection strings have been updated, you need to restore all the portal sites.

On the application tier, open the SharePoint Central Administration tool. Click the Set configuration database server link, enter the name of the new database server, select Connect to existing configuration database, and click OK.

Next, select the Set default content database server link, enter the name of the new database server, and click OK.

Click the Extend or upgrade virtual server link; then click the Team Foundation Server link. Click the Extend and map to another virtual server link. In the Server Mapping field, select Default Website. Click the use an existing application pool radio button, and select the pool to use from the drop-down list box. Finally, click OK.

Once you restart all your services, and flush the cache, your Team Foundation Server has been restored. You should test to make sure you can connect to the application tier and the data tier from your client, and that all the data has been restored properly.

Summary

You always need to be prepared in the event of an emergency; having a disaster recovery plan in place and knowing that plan works will make it much easier to handle such an emergency. This chapter has covered a lot of material, but two of the most important points are to have a disaster recovery plan in place and to consistently test your plan to make sure it works. That can't be stressed enough.

You learned about disaster recovery as it applies to Team Foundation Server, and delved into the different recovery modes of SQL Server 2005. It is very important that you select the appropriate recovery mode for SQL Server 2005 to ensure your data is backed up the way you want it and in the timeframe you need it.

Finally, you were presented with detailed instructions on how to back up and restore Team Foundation Server, including how to restore to the same data-tier machine or to a new server.

This chapter concludes Part I of this book, "Deployment and Administration." Now that you know how to set up your Team Foundation Server, it's time to move into how to use it. Part 2, "Project Creation," goes into the details of how to create your team projects and the different methods used by Team Foundation Server.

Part II
Project Creation

6

Incorporating Your Process Using Microsoft Solutions Framework

The Microsoft Solutions Framework (MSF) is a scalable, flexible framework incorporating Microsoft's software development principles, practices, and experience. The guidance that is included in MSF was gathered from a number of sources including Microsoft Consulting Service (MCS), partners and product groups. There are two process templates available in Team Foundation Server: MSF for Agile Software Development and MSF for CMMI Process Improvement. There has been some confusion as to the purpose of these templates and how they can be leveraged fully.

In this chapter, we provide an overview of these two process templates (and other processes that can be customized and integrated into Team System). We also look at the structure of a process template and learn how to customize it within an Agile scenario. Finally, you find out how to create process guidance that integrates nicely with Team System and techniques for deploying your customized design.

Understanding the Need for MSF

MSF was created as a response to customer demand. MCS used to receive calls from customers and partners asking such questions as How does Microsoft handle roles within a team? How does Microsoft structure projects? And so forth. Rather than continue fielding these questions, the MSF project was developed and the first version came out in 1991 to "codify" their process.

The Microsoft Solutions Framework is not a process methodology per se. It is a framework to help you create and instantiate processes.

MSF is constantly evolving. For example, each of the product teams at Microsoft has their own way of managing and developing software. Some of the approaches are successful, some less so. The lessons learned are rolled in (and show up) in each subsequent release of MSF.

The goals around MSF have also changed and evolved. One of the challenges in the IT industry is to get a handle on the risk and complexities of software development. Cost and time overruns are all too common—the sad truth is that too many of us use guesswork as an estimating tool. One common scenario in the companies I've seen is when the marketing, sales, or business analyst team hands off projects to the development team. A pressure is generated to deliver on time, to "time box" the project. Unfortunately, often there is no appreciation of the complexity of what is promised in the sale. The complexity of business requirements is escalating, therefore so is complexity of the software. To be fair to the sales staff, they have no measure to go by in determining what's workable and what isn't within a time frame.

In this pressured environment, the developer is usually the scapegoat responsible for the burden of the project. (Although we all know that the entire team should be responsible.) Stress builds as the developer must spend many overtime hours and suffer through sleep deprivation to reach the deadline. The quality of the software dips, bugs creep in, schedules slip, and the developer is ultimately to blame. Does this sound familiar?

There is a huge effort under way to find ways of regulating software development projects. Everyone is looking for a magical formula. So, what is being done about it? One of the successful approaches is by developing and using so-called mature processes. You can use statistical methods, engineering principles, manufacturing and scientific approaches, and adapt them to software development. Hence, the focus and terminology makes a big change—you are no longer *developing* software. You are now *engineering* software!

One of the ways the industry can measure the maturity of a process is through the Capability Maturity Model® Integration (CMMI) certification developed by the Carnegie Mellon Software Engineering Institute (SEI). Maturity isn't attained overnight; therefore, the focus is on a gradual evolution toward process improvement and maturity. What's interesting about CMMI is that it doesn't really endorse any specific process—it simply looks at and evaluates the results.

Heavy versus Light Processes

At this point, you might be thinking that all of this sounds rather heavyweight. So here we have a balancing act: On one side, we have a comprehensive systematic process but little in terms of agility. On the other hand, you can have lots of agility but very little in terms of predictability. The middle ground is to consider process as a tool to help us reach our goals. People are more important than process. (We are definitely not at a point where we can push a button and produce software—although code automation is something Microsoft is striving for in their vision for Software Factories.)

If you look at a process such as the Rational Unified Process (RUP), you'll come to realize that it is pretty darned complicated. The intent with RUP is to provide everything you could possibly need. Then it is up to you to whittle the process down, remove what isn't needed until you have something workable and manageable. The problem is that in reality, very few people have enough expertise to make the informed decisions of what to take out; therefore, many companies adopt the RUP process in its entirety with varying levels of success. MSF takes an opposite approach. It includes comparatively lean guidance and documentation. The intent is to provide a simple framework that you can then scale up as needed.

Some consider a process guidance document as a thick binder that sits on someone's desk. There is a disconnect between the process and the people using the process. Team System bridges the gap by incorporating process automation features and easy-to-get-to guidance anywhere from within the product. Mind you, not everything is automated, but it's relatively easy to adopt a process within your development project.

The previous version of the Microsoft Solutions Framework focused primarily on being a framework for developing processes. Version 4.0 introduces Agile concepts and patterns, security guidance, and, most importantly, a direct correlation between a process and results. Team System has many reports that provide a rich feedback mechanism to gauge if you are on the right track, or if you are veering badly.

As you are exploring different ways of managing software projects, you'll come to realize that there isn't a single process that will do the job. One of the common misconceptions about Team System is that you can and should develop a single template per company. A more realistic approach is to evaluate each software project as a different entity with different requirements. A company will end up with several processes (and templates) to fit each circumstance. MSF also does not necessarily need to be used in a development project. You can apply its principles to infrastructure and other nonsoftware related projects.

MSF for Agile Software Development

On February 13, 2001, a group of high-profile developers met in Snowbird, Utah to share new lightweight approaches in developing software. There was consensus that traditional, waterfall-based approaches actually hindered how developers write code. They discussed how Extreme Programming (XP) related to other light-development processes and they tried to come up with a unification of concepts. It is at that meeting that the term *Agile* was adopted and the Manifesto for Agile Software Development was written.

> **You can view the full text of the Manifesto for Agile Software Development at the following link:** `agilemanifesto.or/`.

Here follows a general overview of the Agile approach to software development. To begin, the process and tools should not take precedence over the developers. In contrast, large projects (such as government or military projects) require extensive documentation. It is an environment where Big Requirements Up Front (BRUF) are needed to an extent. It is quite clear, however, that the process of gathering reams of documentation will slow down the developer. The Agile methodology espouses the importance of working code over documentation. In contrast to Agile methodologies, many larger projects focus on the project specification as the be-all-and-end-all. In a waterfall approach, once you have laid out your plans, a large vehicle is set in motion; good or bad, your project will lumber forward. If there are flaws in your approach, all elements of your project will be affected by the flaws—kind of like a bunch of lemmings falling off a cliff. In Agile, what's important is the end customer and their wants and needs. During the course of developing software, you may find that a particular architecture doesn't work, or a problem comes up that wasn't accounted for in the initial design. An Agile developer can adapt to change for the benefit of the project and the benefit of the customer.

There are many misconceptions surrounding the Agile approach to software development. Some companies construe themselves as agile simply because they are small and don't have a process in place. (They develop software completely ad-hoc.) However, a true Agile approach is quite regimented. It involves more than just doing a bit of unit testing. Agile is a very specific test-first development approach with frequent refactoring, high iterations, frequent (if not continuous) builds, and a close connection with the customer.

> **There are others that believe that they are working with absolutely no processes in place. This is also untrue — when you write and check in code, even if the process isn't codified, it is still considered a process!**

MSF for Agile Software Development was developed by Randy Miller, a strong proponent of the Agile development community. This new process framework was developed with the goal of changing MSF to incorporate modern Agile principles. On his blog (`http://blogs.msdn.com/randymiller/`), Randy describes how the Agile movement has evolved; rather than focus on a specific approach (such as Scrum or XP), Randy says that proponents are now cherry picking and combining the elements that work. Randy calls this "Agile 2.0" (`http://blogs.msdn.com/randymiller/archive/2006/03/23/559229.aspx`).

Let's look at how Team System and MSF for Agile Software Development measure up to the Manifesto for Agile Software Development:

- One of the key principles of Agile is that people are more important than process or tools. In MSF for Agile Software Development, the team-of-peers concept comes into play. Each role has the equal responsibility of representing their constituencies. In other words, each person on the team has an equal say and an equal stake for the success or failure of a project. In this worldview, the thought leaders will emerge from the group no matter what their role is, and they will drive the development of the project (unlike a more formalized project manager/developer relationship). In Team System, the process is enacted in the tools, which allows the developer to be more Agile.
- In the manifesto, there is a greater emphasis placed on working code rather than documentation. Team System automanages a lot of the documentation, leaving the developer to be more productive. For example, a rich history of changes in work items is automatically maintained for *auditability*. The developer doesn't have to do anything apart from day-to-day work. Work items provide a lightweight way of creating and maintaining documentation. The individual work items may not look like much, but once you aggregate them and present them in a report format, what was done for the project and the progress so far emerge with great clarity.
- The Agile methodology maintains that the customer is more important than a set of specifications or contract provisions. MSF enacts this by incorporating the customer in the Team Model. The product manager advocates for the customer and has equal visibility and participation in the development process. Personas, as described later in this section, also play a role in representing the needs and wants of a target audience.
- Finally, the manifesto advocates being responsive rather than following a plan. MSF is built around overlapping iterations with incremental improvements in all stages of development. Because you are working within a team of peers, all members have a say at any stage of the development process, which in turn allows you to improve quality on all levels.

The incorporation of architecture as a component of MSF for Agile Software Development is controversial. The reason the architecture role is in there is because it accurately reflects of the environment of many Microsoft customers. There is also recognition that some planning before implementation isn't necessarily a bad thing, even in an Agile project. In his book *Extreme Programming Explained*, Kent Beck substitutes the concept of architecture with the concept of the "metaphor" to provide a clear vision of what you are trying to build. Some Agile proponents are slowly starting to advocate techniques such as Enough Design Up Front (ENUF) and continuous architectural refactoring as part of their development cycles.

Team System makes architecture Agile through tooling. It allows you to easily and quickly validate whether your designs work against an existing infrastructure, which allows you to refactor as needed. The Microsoft product teams have also devised a technique using *Shadow Modeling,* which allows you to apply lightweight architectural design on larger applications. You can read more about shadow modeling in this whitepaper written by Randy Miller: `stsc.hill.af.mil/crosstalk/2005/12/0512Miller.html`.

One of the traditional project management biases is that developers must be closely managed to make sure they deliver. However, the developers aren't the problem — the root of the problem for not shipping on time and cost overruns can be attributed directly to inaccurate estimation. In the real world, most developers have a tendency to *overdeliver* features, often trying to incorporate features they think will add value to the product or be needed in future versions. Agile methodologies such as XP and Scrum compensate for bad estimation techniques by taking the brunt of responsibility off the developers and sharing it with the entire development team. XP developers are "allowed" to be off by their estimates. In Scrum, the customer's expectation are managed to allow the developer to focus on a predefined set of features during a sprint, which allows a developer to work within a normal nine-to-five schedule, to focus on the code, and deliver on time.

Therefore, the key question is, How can we improve estimation? If the features keep changing and the complexity is hard to pin down, how can we assign timeframes to the tasks needed to do the job? When you deal with people instead of machines, it increases the complexity of variables you have to consider.

> **Barry Gervin, one of my colleagues, shared one of the ways that Agile development teams can get a handle on time and cost factors using arbitrary estimation units, specifically called NUTs (Nebulous Units of Time — a term and concept coined by Joshua Kerievsky). Essentially, you estimate the complexity of each feature using a scale of one to four, one being the simplest and four being the most complex. (This is very similar to the concept of Rough Order of Magnitude used as an estimation technique within MSF for Agile Software Development.) By measuring the time required to complete each task, you can profile your team and measure the amount of time required to complete one NUT of work, for example.**

To improve estimation on a software development project, you have to "unprogram" yourself from trying to guess time-to-task and substitute empirical principles that are more scientific. Each team will have its own dynamic and velocity — it is up to you to measure and profile your team in controlled circumstances to measure the true velocity of your team. Once you have gathered the necessary data and reverse engineered how your team works, it will then be possible for you to provide concrete realistic estimates. One of the issues with statistical analysis is that you need someone who is well versed in statistical analysis to correctly interpret the data. For example, if you look at lines of code, you may find that less code is being developed from one month to the next. On the surface, the natural tendency is to react negatively and interpret the results as a work slow down. The reality of the situation may be that the level of work is still within normal bounds and the code is being refactored and written more efficiently. Fortunately, Team System simplifies the statistical information by providing default templates that deliver easy-to-interpret results.

One of the characteristics of Agile software development is close customer interaction. When you deal with a large complex distributed development project, you can't always benefit from having the customer onsite. If you think of a large-scale project like building the Windows operating system, you could easily fill a huge metropolitan city with all the target customers! So, how to do deliver on a customer's needs, yet deal with scale? Microsoft has worked out an effective technique using *personas* — in fact, they played a key role in the development of Visual Studio. Personas are used as an interaction tool — to design one, you must create fictional character representations of your customers with different skill levels and goals. If you are familiar with *actors* and *roles* à la Unified Modeling Language (UML), you can think of personas as an instantiation of an actor in a role. A persona provides more fine-grained control as you define the wants, needs, and abilities of a user. If a persona is well designed, it will provide the essence of a customer, which can easily be imparted to developers. The concept of personas was popularized by Alan Cooper's book *The Inmates Are Running the Asylum.* You can learn more about the fascinating history of personas in Alan Cooper's newsletter hosted on his Web site at `cooper.com/content/insights/newsletters/2003_08/Origin_of_Personas.asp`.

In designing Visual Studio, Microsoft created three personas to target different developer types: Mort (a VB developer), Elvis (a C# developer), and Einstein (a C++ developer). These personas have been controversial in the Windows developer community, as they highlight language, work, and feature differences between C# and VB.

Working with MSF for Agile Software Development

So where is the starting point for MSF for Agile Software Development? First, as explained previously, MSF for Agile Software Development is a framework. If you have a process you are now using, your best bet is to customize MSF to make it fit nicely in your environment. But what if you don't have a satisfactory process? What if you simply would like to take MSF for Agile Software Development for a spin? Well, you can create an instantiation of MSF for Agile Software Development using the default template and the New Project Creation Wizard. The two process templates that ship with Team System have been road tested by many companies, including a council comprising of global systems integrators (GSI).

What you won't find here is a treatise on how to manage your project using Agile processes — there are literally thousands of books on the market on that particular topic! What you will learn here is how the basic template works and what the process is like. You can find the first hint of a development process in the work item *instance* (in other words, the list of work items that appear by default when you create a new team project using MSF for Agile Software Development). The requirements include:

- Create vision statement
- Create personas
- Brainstorm and prioritize quality of service requirements list
- Create iteration plan

The team project comes with *work products* (in other words, templates, documents, and spreadsheets) to help you manage your project. If you look at the Requirements folders in the documents related to your team project, you will notice a template for the vision statement called Vision.doc. What's more, if you open up the Vision Statement work item, you will find in the description a link to vision statement documentation within the MSF process guidance.

A huge part of the information you need to use the MSF for Agile Software Development process framework is included in the process guidance and associated templates. The Project Checklist.xls file contains a list of all the preliminary tasks that are required for implementation and is a recommended starting point.

You can start working on an MSF for Agile Software Development based project by defining your vision statement and creating personas. It should be a straightforward process because the templates are available as a starting point. Once you have completed that process, the next step is to define what quality standards are needed for the project to be signed off. Quality-of-service (QOS) requirements define constraints on functionality such as performance and security. A well-written QOS requirement includes empirical, reproducible details. For example, "Make the application secure" is an example of a bad QOS requirement since it is vague. A better QOS requirement is "Code must pass managed code analysis (FxCop) security rules." You can document the backlog of QOS requirements on the provided QOSRequirements.xls spreadsheet. What is great is that you can then easily synchronize the requirements on Team Foundation Server as work items. However, there is more work to be done before we do this. (In case you are interested, work item management is documented in Chapter 13.)

Microsoft has created a Threat Analysis & Modeling tool to figure out attack vectors within your service-oriented application. Once the tool analyzes the architectural design of your application (designed using the Team Edition for Software Architect designers), it provides a threat list that can be uploaded as a set of QOS requirements in Team Foundation Server. You can learn more about this tool at `http://blogs.msdn.com/threatmodeling/`.

Once you have completed these preliminary steps, it is time to organize and structure your project. MSF for Agile Software Development comes with an iteration plan already baked in. It's basically *Iteration0*, *Iteration1*, and *Iteration2*. A traditional approach in setting up iterations is breaking it down into predictable steps. For example: planning, development, testing and quality assurance, and production. An agilist will handle iterations quite differently — iterations are scopes of work including a list of high priority scenarios, tasks, and requirements. In a test driven development (TDD) approach, testing occurs before development; therefore, we can see right away that the traditional iteration structure doesn't quite work. Using an Agile methodology, rather than deal with large units of work passed from team to team, the work is distributed and broken down in smaller, easier to handle component parts. Admittedly, *Iteration0* is quite vague as an iteration name — you may want to personalize it to fit your needs and circumstance. One example of an Agile iteration plan is Scrum's Sprint Backlog.

Working with Areas, Scenarios, and Tasks

Areas provide another way of organizing your project. Think of an *area* as a category, or a logical grouping. If you are working on a commercial product, you can use the areas to represent different customers. You can also use areas to represent features or even groups that are working on the project. You can configure the areas and iterations for any given team project by right-clicking on it and selecting, Team Project Settings⇨Areas and Iterations.

In most software development projects, there is testing involved. Agile processes use continuous testing; more traditional, formalized processes designate a specific test phase. No matter what process you use, you will have to manage bugs at the end of an iteration (or project). A test plan is often necessary for working out a budget and pricing out bug fixes. You can work out how you will test a project using the test approach (which describes the tests in detail) and test development plan (which allows you to organize and prioritize your different tests). If bugs appear during any part of the process, you can add them to the bug triage list (Triage List.xls). This list allows you to sort out and prioritize your unchecked bugs and defects before assigning them within each iteration.

Next comes the *scenario*. A scenario differs from a use case, as a persona differs from an actor and a role. A use case indicates a generic list of occurrences with a generic actor/role. For example: "Customer A types in credit card number in form, clicks on the submit button, system responds with approval or rejection." A scenario uses a persona and personalizes the description: "Bob (*the persona*) accesses the Web form and types in '1234 5678 9012' then clicks on the submit button. Since the credit card number is invalid, Bob receives an error message and a link back to the entry form." The scenario provides a smart way of creating rich descriptions of expected behavior and features in your software. A well-written scenario not only shows a specific use, but also an important pattern of use.

As you might have guessed, there is a Scenario template (Scenario Description.doc) to assist you in writing the scenarios, and a scenario list (Scenarios.xls) to organize (and upload) scenarios once written.

Now that you've gathered your vision statement, personas, scenarios, QOS requirements, and tests, it is now time to open up Microsoft Project and develop your project plan (Development Project Plan.mpp). It is important to get the entire software development team involved in breaking down the scenarios and requirements into smaller component tasks. You first need to evaluate the architectural impact of each scenario. You can then break down each scenario and requirement into smaller, more granular tasks. According to MSF for Agile Software Development, each task must be design-oriented and should be easy to complete in one to three days by a single team member. In Microsoft Project, the layout will look something like Figure 6-1.

	Work Item ID	Title	Work Item Type	Duration	Start	Finish
1		⊟ **Scenario 1**	**Scenario**	**4 days**	**Mon 4/24/06**	**Thu 4/27/06**
2		Task 1	Task	1 day	Mon 4/24/06	Mon 4/24/06
3		Task 2	Task	1 day	Tue 4/25/06	Tue 4/25/06
4		Task 3	Task	2 days	Wed 4/26/06	Thu 4/27/06

Figure 6-1

The scenarios and tasks should be ordered by priority — the really important ones should be assigned to the first iteration. If you take a Scrum-like approach, you may want to solidly scope out the amount of work you are responsible for in each iteration.

Test Cases

Tests must also be organized. You should figure out which ones are ongoing test cases and which ones can be automated (as a managed code analysis rule or as part of a test list associated to the build process). You are now ready to assign the work items (scenarios and associated tasks) to your team members by synchronizing your list with Team Foundation Server.

During the course of the project, you may encounter blocking issues that will prevent certain tasks from being completed. In fact, it's inevitable. For example, you may find that you can't test a mobile application because of delays obtaining the actual mobile device. The tester who is responsible for testing the application on the device should create an issue work item, and then associate the work item to the blocked task work item. You incorporate this process in your day-to-day work. It will make it easier for a project manager to track, isolate, and manage the issues. Another mechanism for handling potential blocking issues in a project is the risk work item. At the beginning of your project, you can identify all risk within your project and then assign tasks to mitigate them.

Once the developer has completed all tasks related to a scenario, the scenario work item can then be assigned to the tester. This allows you to apply tests that can't be automated. Once testing is complete, the scenario can be wrapped up.

MSF for Capability Maturity Model Integration (CMMI) Process Improvement

Unlike other industries, software development has been around for a relatively short time. On an automobile assembly line, we can easily predict how many vehicles will be produced on any given day. In turn, this predictability provides an automobile company with the ability to be able to forecast what the profits will be for any given year and how much they are progressing. Now let's apply these principles to software development. How can you determine how much time it will take to build a feature or release a product? The short answer is that most of us don't even try — the conventional approach is to create artificial time limits and to impose these time limits on your development team.

Unfortunately, this approach doesn't work. A specification on a piece of paper may look deceptively simple, but in implementation may require a great deal of overhead. For example, let's look at a simple three-word instruction such as "build a car." What exactly does this mean? You have to create a functioning model of a vehicle, engineer or procure thousands of parts (or build them from scratch if they don't exist), walk through the process of assembling the automobile piece by piece, test it extensively (for security, emissions, etc.) and hopefully at the end, you'll have a functioning vehicle. The process involves a ridiculous amount of complexity, yet it appears deceptively simple on paper.

If you look at current statistics around the success and failure rates of software development projects around the world, you'll come to the realization that a huge number of projects are doomed to fail. Will your next project be part of this statistic?

> **For more information about these statistics, please refer to this revealing 1994 Standish Group report entitled the "CHAOS Report":** `standishgroup.com/sample_research/chaos_1994_1.php`.

So who is to blame for all these failures? The scapegoats are usually the developers who were unable to deliver the software or features within a set timeframe. The chief technology officer (CTO) who has to justify the expenses might be also blamed (and fired). It's difficult to provide visibility on how IT spends money. If you are a developer, you may want to blame the decision makers who have no concept of the scope and complexity of the requested software. The problem can't be attributed to a specific group — the problem exists in the way we currently manage our software development projects. This culture of blame and distrust fosters heavy documentation and process — this is something, as an industry, that we need to change. For example, in Japan there is more trust placed on the worker; also, there is a strong emphasis on shared ownership of responsibility.

Understanding the Need for CMMI Levels

Software companies (like companies in other industries) can't afford to have this level of uncertainty in the process. That is why the software industry has made inroads in developing techniques to improve predictability and reliability. The Capability Maturity Model Integration (CMMI) is one of the ways an organization can implement process improvement and show the level of maturity of a process. One of the primary goals of CMMI is the objective measurement of IT resources and assessing the maturity of an organization by using statistical and scientific approaches for the estimate, control, and objective measurement of software projects. By improving the maturity, we also improve productivity and profitability.

Philip Crosby, the former head of a major management consulting firm wrote *Quality is Free* and *Quality Without Tears*, two easy-to-read books on process quality improvement including. His writings were influenced by the works of Dr. W. Edward Deming and Dr. Joseph M. Juran — both pioneers in the field of quality management. Crosby's approach focuses on attaining zero defects. CMMI levels are strongly based on Crosby's Manufacturing Maturity Model. Levels 2 through 4 work for the elimination of special cause variation. Level 5 is the complete attainment of continuous improvement. Most of the training you can get today focuses on a Crosby-esque approach for doing things; as such it tends to be rigid and not very agile. Briefly, CMMI is used to track the maturity of any software design organization, from requirements to validation. The CMMI has six maturity capability levels outlined in the following table:

Capability Level	Description
0	**Incomplete Process**
1	**Performed Process.** You have little to no controls in your project. The outcome is unpredictable and reactive. Frequent instances of special cause variations. All the process areas for performed process have been implemented and work gets done. However, the planning and implementation of process has not yet been completed.
2	**Managed Process.** You have satisfied all the requirements for the implementation of a managed process. Work is implemented by skilled employees according to policies. Processes are driven according to specific goals such as quality and cost. Planning and review are baked into the process. You are managing your process.
3	**Defined Process.** You have a set of standard processes (or processes that satisfy a process area) within your organization that can be adapted according to specific needs.
4	**Quantitatively Managed Process.** All aspects of a project are quantitatively measured and controlled. Both your operational and project process are within normal control limits.
5	**Optimizing Process.** Continuous project improvement. CMMI Level 5 focuses on constant process improvement and the reduction of common cause variation. The project process is under constant improvement.

There are two models for implementing CMMI: the continuous model and the staged model. In the *continuous* model, elements such as engineering, support, project management, and process management are each composed of a set number of process areas. A *process area* is a description of activities for building a planned approach for improvement. Using the *staged* model, the process areas are set up according to the five maturity levels. MSF for CMMI Process Improvement was designed to support the staged model.

Capability Maturity Level 3

In Team System, one of the primary goals of MSF for CMMI Process Improvement is to gather Standard CMMI Appraisal Method for Process Improvement (SCAMPI) evidence to help a company to be appraised at a CMMI Level 3 process maturity according to the SEI. Another important goal of MSF for CMMI Process Improvement guidance is to provide a framework for creating a formal process within a software development team. In other words, storing information for the purpose of audits, process improvement, and quality assurance (QA). The CMMI specifications are quite detailed (over 700 pages long). Here are the characteristics of CMMI Level 3 (boiled down to three main points):

- CMMI Level 3 is customized to the organization's set of standard processes according to the organization's guidelines.
- CMMI Level 3 has a process description that is constantly maintained. This is implemented in Team System using work items and iterations.
- CMMI Level 3 must contribute work products, metrics, and other process improvement information to the organization's process assets. Process templates and the project site enable project managers to share metrics and documents with the rest of the team.

One of the differences between MSF for Agile Software Development and the MSF for CMMI Process Improvement frameworks is the nature of the process guidance. The process guidance in MSF for Agile Software Development implies a development process. MSF for CMMI Process Improvement has very specific process steps in the guidance. This makes a lot of sense if you look at the complexity and sheer number of CMMI requirements that need to be managed. The process guidance for MSF for CMMI Process Improvement is approximately 150 percent larger than MSF for Agile Software Development.

Statistics often fly in the face of what is generally perceived as common sense. For example, it's easy to perceive that controlling each line item of a task list will provide more predictive control over the process. This is completely wrong — change and variation are innate parts of the process. As long as the variation or fluctuation is within normal bounds (common-cause variation), the project is healthy. CMMI and other process improvement methods seek to deal with issues and situations that fall outside of normal boundaries (special or chance cause) variations.

Here is the main challenge with MSF for CMMI Process Improvement: CMMI was originally designed for the aerospace and defense industries. How do you take something that has heavy auditing and lack of trust in the process and make it accessible to hundreds of thousands of Visual Studio users (Microsoft's target audience) and get high adoption levels? How is it possible to take something like CMMI, make it smaller, manageable, and Agile?

MSF for CMMI Process Improvement takes a radical new approach for helping you pass your CMMI appraisals. David J. Anderson (the creator of MSF for CMMI Process Improvement) found a strong correlation between the work of W. Edwards Deming and Agile methodologies. Deming is considered the father of quality management, and his theories are the basis of Philip Crosby's work. MSF for CMMI Process Improvement offers a range of work products and reports to help eliminate special cause variation and is based on Deming's quality control and statistical process.

To learn more about MSF for CMMI Process Improvement, we would highly recommend you read David J. Anderson's book *Agile Management for Software Engineering—Applying the Theory of Constraints for Business Results* and visit his blog at `agilemanagement.net/Articles/Weblog/blog.html`.

Deming popularized statistical process control in the field of business and manufacturing in his theory of profound knowledge. To properly implement process controls, you must be able to identify the difference between common cause variations (CCVs) and special cause variations (SCVs). *Common cause variations* are natural fluctuations found in any process. *Special cause variations* are caused by special occurrences, environmental factors, and problems that affect a process. The challenge as a project manager is to correctly identify an instance of a special cause variation and reduce it. Complicating this goal is the fact is that these variations usually occur randomly. The reporting component of Team System provides visual metrics to measure factors such as project health. These charts can help you determine whether the upper control limits (UCLs) and lower control limits (LCLs) are within operational boundaries. Figure 6-2 illustrates the two varieties of variation and the attainment of process improvement.

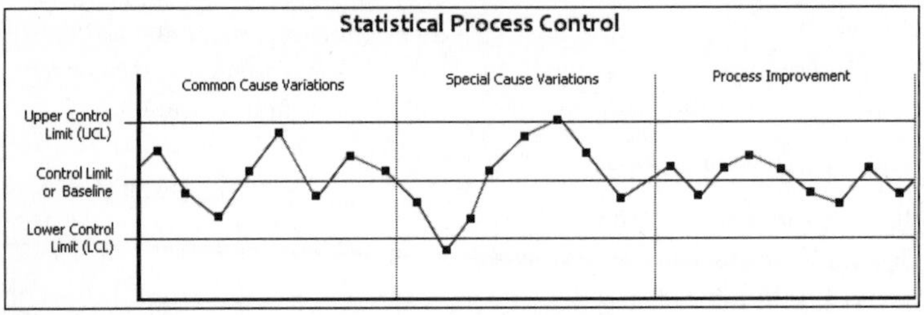

Figure 6-2

Another principle that influenced the development of MSF for CMMI Process Improvement is the theory of constraints (TOC) documented by Dr. Eliyahu M. Goldratt in his novel *The Goal*. The focus behind the theory is the goal of constant improvement. Constraints (as defined by Goldratt) are bottlenecks preventing you from reaching a specific goal. By identifying physical and nonphysical constraints, you can focus your energies on eliminating (or reducing) the constraints, making your process more effective.

A spreadsheet (MSF CMMI Reference.xls) was devised by David Anderson as a roadmap to create the process guidance. It contains all the SCAMPI requirements for CMMI Level 3 and mappings to what is contained in the process template.

Let's see how W. Edward Deming's fourteen principles from his book *Out of the Crisis* maps out to common Agile practices:

1. **Create constancy of purpose toward improvement of product and service, with the aim to become competitive, to stay in business, and to provide jobs.** The constant improvement of product (which is in our case, software) can be assured through continuous integration and refactoring, which are centerpieces of the Agile approach.
2. **Adopt the new philosophy.** Western management must take on leadership for change. This can be construed as advocating an adaptable approach in developing software (as opposed to having development run with heavy, monolithic processes). In the Agile approach and MSF for CMMI Process Improvement, developers are first-class citizens and advocates for code quality. The team-of-peers principle in MSF makes everyone on the team an equal and a thought leader, which benefits the project.
3. **Cease dependence on inspection to achieve quality.** Eliminate the need by building quality into the product in the first place. This principle is very akin to test driven development, where quality is assured early in the process.
4. **End the practice of awarding business based on a price tag.** Instead, minimize total cost. Move toward a single supplier for any one item, on a long-term relationship of loyalty and trust. This is akin to the Agile principle of keeping a close connection with the customer to be responsive to change and deliver right on target.
5. **Improve constantly and forever the system of production and service to improve quality and productivity, and thus constantly decrease costs.** Constant improvement of code can be achieved using test driven development, continuous integration, and constant refactoring. This closely resembles Deming's continuous improvement cycle that advocates Plan, Do, Check, and Act.
6. **Institute training on the job.** Agilists use pair programming and code reviews to improve knowledge sharing and quality of code. Unit testing code provides a solid, documented roadmap of customer requirements, which can then be picked up by any other developer.
7. **Institute leadership.** The aim of supervision should be to help people and machines — and gadgets — do a better job. In the Agile approach, the goal is to remove the supervision of people, create a vision to follow, and create an environment for great work.
8. **Drive out fear.** Fear can be driven out of a project by providing consistency, visibility, and transparency in the process. By deeply involving the customer, the Agile development shop provides an environment of trust. Team System provides visibility in your project on a continuous basis through metrics in project reports and by providing query views across all work items.
9. **Break down barriers between departments.** People in research, design, sales, and production must work as a team to foresee problems in production and use. The team-of-peers concept found in MSF encompasses this principle. A similar analogy in XP is the concept of collective ownership.
10. **Eliminate slogans, exhortations, and targets for the work force asking for zero defects and new levels of productivity.** Between the lines, you can read such slogans and the like as calls for the elimination of time to task and the need to individually calculate the velocity of your development team. Also implied by this principle is the need for mutual respect, which is reflected in many Agile processes such as Scrum and XP — also found in MSF for CMMI Process Improvement.
11. **Eliminate quotas, management by objective, and numerical goals.** The Agile approach uses nonnumerical ways of estimating, such as using NUTs and ROMs.

12. **Remove barriers that rob workers of their right to pride of workmanship.** Abolish merit ratings (and performance appraisals). Agile methodologies espouse joint ownership of work by everyone on the team. If you measure your work velocity using variation analysis rather than time to task or lines of code, you will realistically assess the performance of your team within an accepted baseline rather than worry about variables that are out of your control. In America, in some ways there is too much emphasis on the measurement of self. It is important to note that in other countries (such as Germany), it is illegal to measure the performance of an individual.

13. **Institute a vigorous program of education and self-improvement.** Using Agile modeling, pair programming, peer reviews, and promiscuous pairing (swapping partners), you can improve the abilities of your programmers.

14. **Put everyone in the company to work to accomplish the transformation.** In MSF for CMMI Process Improvement, the concept of the team of peers advocates that everyone on the team is a stakeholder in the project and is allowed to suggest and make changes to the process or product to improve it.

Deming also demonstrates agility through his PDCA Cycle (which stands for Plan, Do, Check and Act—the concept was originally developed by Walter A. Shewhart) as shown in Figure 6-3.

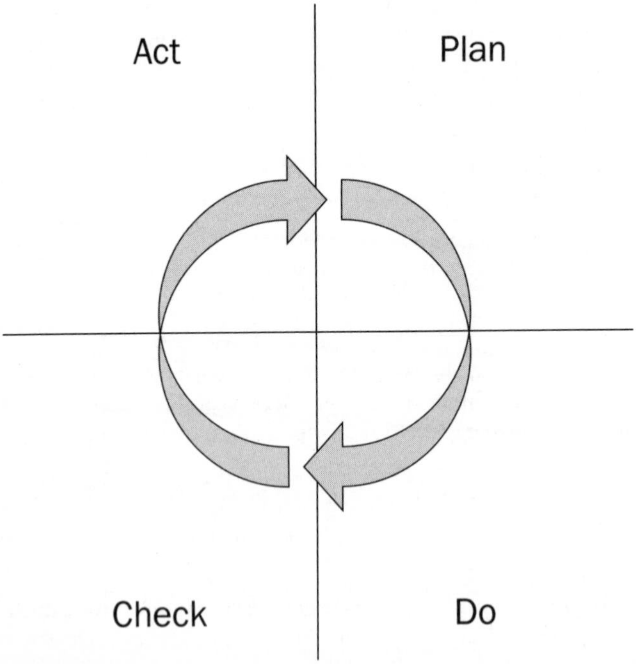

Figure 6-3

This cycle closely resembles the process behind the Agile approach of test driven development; however, one is applied to quality improvement, and the other applies to code improvement. Let's now compare these two processes:

- **Plan** — In the context of quality management, the Plan phase denotes the design or revision for process improvement. In testing, unit tests are written to assert business requirements before the implementation code is written. As you continue the process, unit tests are rewritten to improve code quality and fidelity with the requirements.
- **Do** — The Do phase is the implementation of process. The logical analogy in a test context is the implementation of code.
- **Check** — In a process context, Check tests the results of implementation. In a very similar way, unit testing can be automated during the build process to check the implementation of code to see if it breaks any of your coded assertions.
- **Act** — The Act phase is the decision-making process before the next implementation. This is where the process improvement occurs. In a testing context, if during testing your unit tests are not correctly capturing the requirements, they need to be refactored.

The framework for MSF for CMMI Process Improvement has been reviewed and accepted by prominent members of the SEI, including the originators of CMMI. MSF for CMMI Process Improvement covers 20 out of the 25 process areas. The missing process areas include:

- Supplier agreement management (SAM) — Level 2
- Organizational training (OT) — Level 3
- Organizational process focus(OPF) — Level 3
- Organizational environment for integration(OEI) — Level 3
- Integrated supplier management(ISM) — Level 3

> **David J. Anderson explains the reasoning for the missing process areas on his blog:** `agilemanagement.net/Articles/MSF/WhyTheMissingFive.html.`

Relative to other framework implementations of CMMI, MSF for CMMI Process Improvement is quite lean, characterized by a small number of work products, activities in the hundreds (not the thousands), and roughly 50 queries and reports. Microsoft's goal is to bring CMMI to the market for Visual Studio developers, add agility in a formalized process by incorporating Agile principles in the framework, and provide integrated tools to streamline and automate the adoption and management of processes that promote continuous improvement.

Project Planning Using Governance and Capacity

Fundamentally, a project is a collection of iterations. Within MSF, there is a loose approximate project plan, which encompasses end-to-end scenarios broken out into iterations. In a MSF for CMMI Process Improvement–based project, you have to consider the project on many levels. What activities are you undertaking to gather the SCAMPI evidence? What activities are you doing to incorporate governance in your project? What activities are actually driving the development itself? Here is a detailed breakdown of these activities (and how they overlap in places):

- The process of gathering SCAMPI evidence is documented in a work product spreadsheet called MSF CMMI Reference.xls. This spreadsheet is found in your general documents folder at the team project level. In the MSF for CMMI Process Improvement process guidance, there is also a CMMI tab, which is an appraiser's view to allow you to assess the way your process is coming along against the CMMI requirements. You'll notice that there isn't a one-to-one predefined list of work items generated against the CMMI reference list to provide you with a paint-by-numbers approach to get appraised. There is a reason behind this flexibility; you can define your own development process and measure it up against the list to see if you are on track.
- The governance process is documented very well in the MSF for CMMI Process Improvement process guidance. To get general information about governance, click the link on the left side of the screen on the main page of the process guidance screen. You can also see how governance works within your development cycle by looking at the Tracks view (Views⇨Tracks).
- Your development process is outlined in the process documentation but also as part of the work item *instance* (predefined collection of work items) that ships with MSF for CMMI Process Improvement.

With MSF, you can do postponed iteration planning. In other words, the function of the project is locked at iteration start, it's scenario based, and the scenarios are prioritized according to the value to the customer. Like many things in MSF, estimates are flexible. We would recommend that you refer to the Project Management Body of Knowledge (PMBOK) for a detailed rundown of estimation techniques. You can obtain the PMBOK from the Project Management Institute (`pmi.org`).

MSF for CMMI Process Improvement was designed with seven quality-of-service (QOS) requirements in mind: one customer-related and six software-related. Examples include customer requirements, security requirements, functionality requirements, and interaction requirements. Setting up your QOS requirements in advance allows you to filter activities by quality-of-service requirements and scenario later in the process.

All tasks in MSF for CMMI Process Improvement are structured according to entry criteria, tasks, and exit criteria (ETX). This structure provides level consistency and predictability in your process, which will help you track the natural flow of your project.

Tracking Your Project Progress

MSF for CMMI Process Improvement deals with the management of process rather than conformance to plan or specification. The MSF for CMMI Process Improvement framework not only provides you with documentation and workflow to obtain the SCAMPI evidence, but it also includes metrics to allow you to understand the variation within your projects. Because if it can't be accounted for, there's no way that you can control it!

One of the ways you can determine the capability of your process is by measuring it against Donald J. Wheeler's four-process state diagram (seen in Figure 6-4). Wheeler advocates that a process will never be at a standstill. It constantly shifts and moves from one state to another based on variation.

You'll notice that the top-right quadrant is the *ideal state*. This is a state where your processes are in control and you can analyze your reports to track down any problems that might come up. In the ideal state, there is a lot of predictability in your process; everything is coming up to specification. This is where you want to be in terms of capability and maturity.

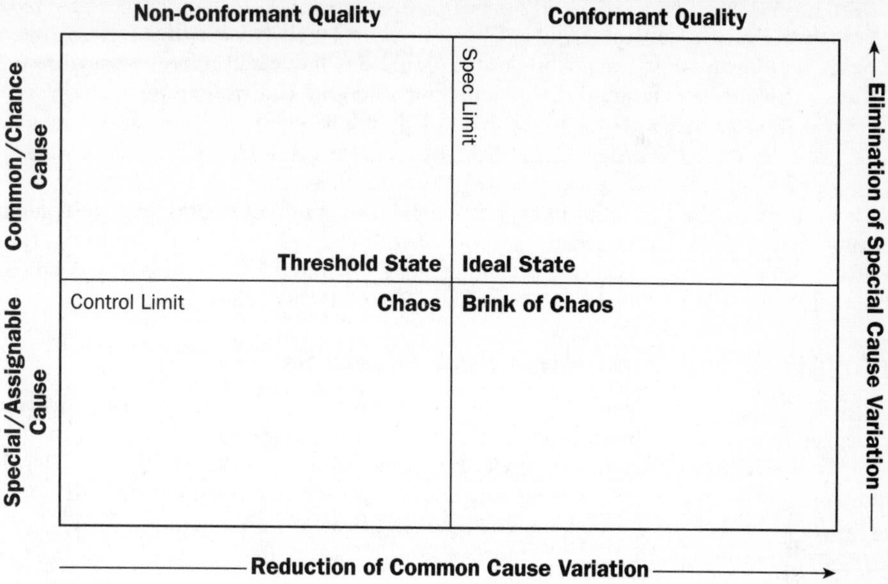

Figure 6-4

Let's look at the bottom-right quadrant. If you have an unstable process, but, for some reason or another, you are still hitting your targets, you are on the *brink of chaos*. This can occur if you manage a project using traditional time-to-task approach. What will happen is that *assignable cause variation* will creep into the project. Then you will start seeing the project fall off course, and worse yet, you won't know when it will occur. An example of this is a software project with complex features and a very tight timeframe. Everything looks fine initially — the project looks like it's on track. Then the inevitable happens — the estimation that was made does not correspond to your team's velocity and you are understaffed to deliver on time, developers decide to quit, and so forth — and the project slips out of control. The only way to correct a process that is on the brink of chaos is to identify and remove assignable cause variation. In other words, do a risk analysis at the beginning of the project. Recognize that you may be understaffed. Come up with a plan to mitigate the risk. Understand your velocity using loose or hard statistical methods and you will be back on the right track.

The top-left quadrant of the figure represents the *threshold state*. In this state, you are generating results but there is also unpredictability in your process. For example, you are running a project, but code is being produced inconsistently. You may have significant gaps of time where little to no code is being generated then, suddenly, the developers produce code in spurts of productivity. You manage to get through and deliver, but it's on the edge. You can move from a threshold state to an ideal state by improving your process, specifically, to reduce the amount of common cause variation.

In the lower-left quadrant is *chaos*. Chaos implies a process out of control, where you are constantly putting out fires. Sometimes specialized managers or consultants are brought in to establish order in a process. Unfortunately, unless you have a process improvement strategy in place, the pattern will continue to reoccur.

> **Statistical Process Control (SPC) is a huge topic and well outside the scope of this book. If you want a pragmatic book to explain how to apply it in real-world situations, we would recommend that you pick up and read *Understanding Statistical Process Control* by Donald J. Wheeler and David S. Chambers.**

In Wheeler's diagram, the Y-axis (north to south) represents on-time-on-budget development and is the specification limit. It is the management maturity of your process. The X-axis (left to right) represents how mature your development process is coming along. By moving from the bottom of the chart to the top, you are theoretically moving from CMMI Level 2 to CMMI Level 4.

Remaining Work and Cumulative Flow Diagrams

Cumulative flow diagrams are central in evaluating the effectiveness of your process. Such a diagram deemphasizes time-to-task estimation and makes you focus on tracking down your variation. Using an iterative cumulative flow diagram, you can look at your work in process (WIP). The WIP helps you predict lead time — you can use the IterationPlan.xls spreadsheet in the planning stage to work out the details. When the lead-time gets too long, you'll notice a dramatic dip in quality. That is because lead-time correlates to defects (or bugs).

If you consider a statistical analysis of your process, you'll notice a normalization process that occurs for your team. In the Agile approach, everyone works collaboratively; this normalization makes your process work closer as a common-cause system. Of course, this largely depends on the team — it has to execute on their process and methods very well.

Using a statistical approach, you can change fear into trust. MSF for CMMI Process Improvement has the resources to help you deal with fear. It provides the statistical visibility into your project. By working and buffering with variation, you can work in the true spirit of continuous improvement. Plan your scenarios according to priority. To prioritize, ask some of the following questions:

- Should we evaluate the amount of resources, time, and effort to allocate based on each task?
- What if a scenario appears to be more challenging than another?
- Should we allocate more time and/or effort if there is more complexity?

The rule of thumb is to use standard CMMI transaction cost; the underlying value will determine the iterations.

The *remaining work report* (Figure 6-5) is a classic example of a cumulative flow diagram. It indicates bottlenecks, queue of work and resources, how much work is left to be done, and when it will be done. The middle part represents work queuing for testing. The part on the left represents the difference between requirements of an iteration and the work that has been started, for example, work queuing for development.

You can measure a work remaining trend against a velocity report to indicate how quickly you are planning the process. It's very much like tack time on an assembly line. You can then track variation and averages over time to provide estimates and ask questions such as, What's the degree of variation? Can we normalize using training?

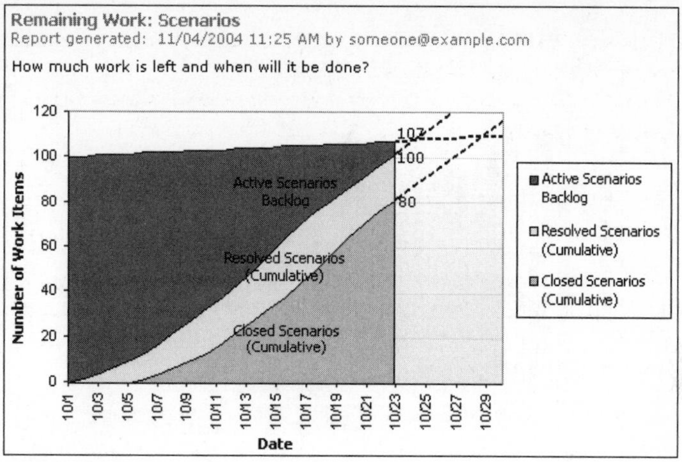

Figure 6-5

Velocity

A *velocity chart* has nothing to do with conformance to plan or specification. This report (Figure 6-6) will provide metrics on how long code stabilization will take within an iteration.

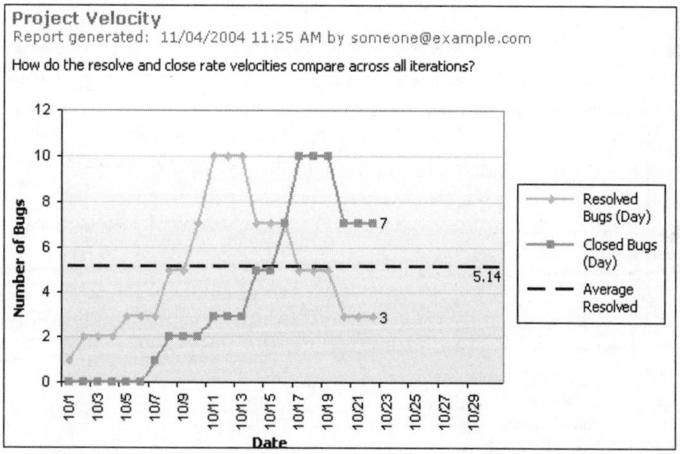

Figure 6-6

Triage

The *triage report* (Figure 6-7) represents proposed work queuing for approval. It includes tasks, risks for mitigations, requirements for scope, and more. The triage deals with project management artifacts including issues that are blocking work items. If you see the triage lines growing, it means that your velocity isn't good enough, and your process is slowing down.

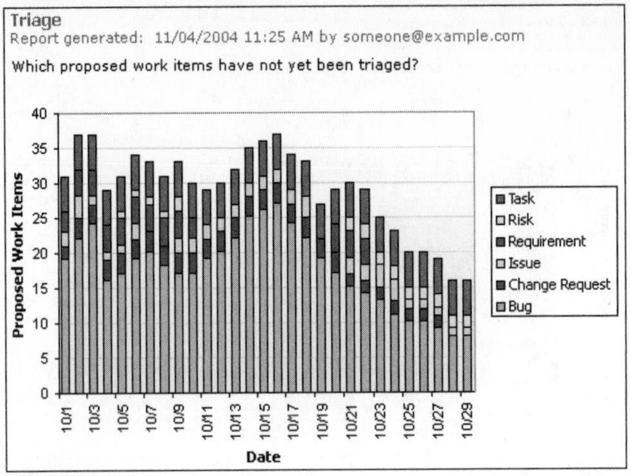

Figure 6-7

Bug Rates

The *bug rates report* (Figure 6-8) has similar information as cumulative flow diagram. It is a favorite report within Microsoft's internal teams. Cumulative flow diagrams are important; you shouldn't have to worry about variation.

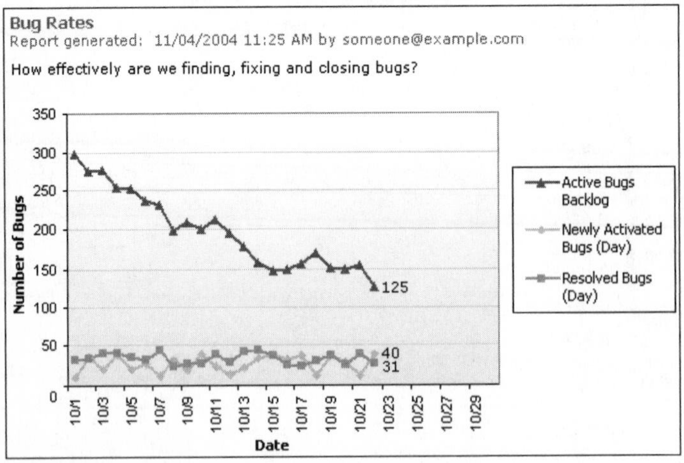

Figure 6-8

Quality Indicators

The *quality indicators report* (Figure 6-9) provides a powerful view into your project. It indicates the bugs, percentage of code coverage, and code churn against test results.

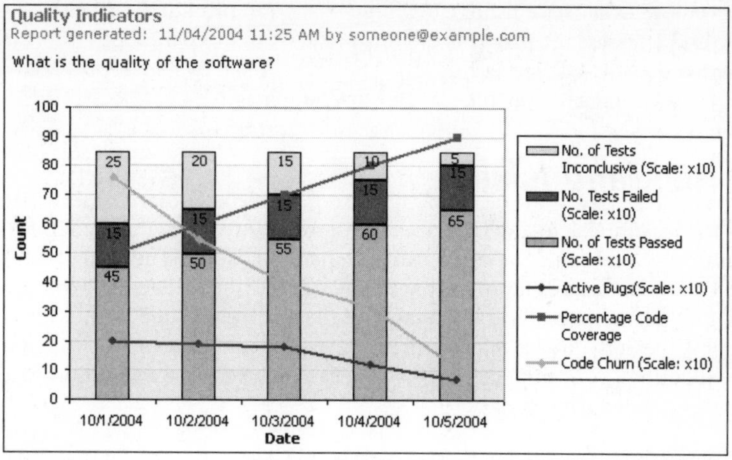

Figure 6-9

Unplanned Work

Here is how you can interpret the results of the *unplanned work report*. This report is generated for each iteration. The lighter color indicates work items that were generated at the beginning of the iteration. As you go along, new work items are added to the list — these additions are represented using the darker color (in the middle). There are three types of unplanned work: regressive work (in other words, work that was completed but must be done again due to bugs or defects found in the code), change requests, and scope change from a customer (otherwise known as *scope creep)*. You can use the unplanned work report (Figure 6-10) to give you the delta between planned and unplanned work, so you can add a buffer during your iteration planning cycle. This type of report is not commonly found in Agile methodologies.

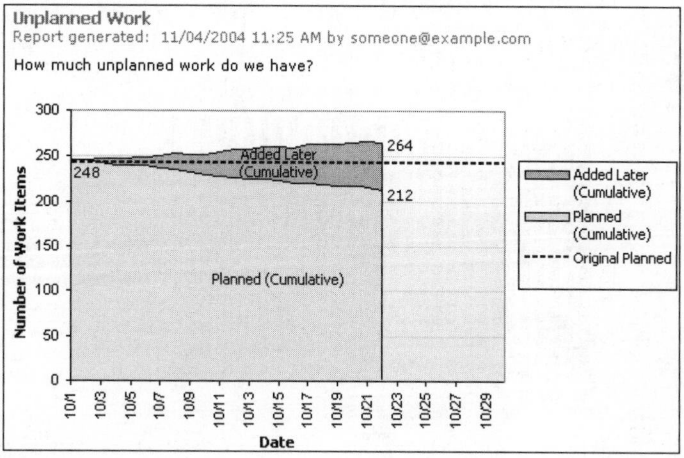

Figure 6-10

This is by no means an exhaustive list of CMMI reports, but it provides you with an overview of the techniques used to assess the progress of your project. For more in-depth information about extensibility and other features of SQL Server Reporting Services, Team System report analysis, and Business Intelligence (BI) related information, please refer to Chapter 16.

Managing Risk and Issues

It is important to measure risk in any CMMI-driven project. Anything that generates a 100-percent potential of causing special cause variation can be construed as risk. The goal of risk analysis is to identify a list of potential risks and analyze for likelihood of occurrence. You have to measure the impact on your schedule, budget, resources, and the quality of the work generated within the scope of the project. As with MSF for Agile Software Development, you can track and manage risks using a risk work item. Once you have identified your important risks, you can then propose mitigation schemes as a series of task work items associated to each risk.

You can also correlate issues work items with risk work items by looking at the issue logs with tracking links to the risk logs. Walter A. Shewhart introduced the concepts of assignable cause variation (predictable special cause variation) and chance cause variation (unpredictable variation in your project), which was embraced by Deming.

The diagram in Figure 6-11 shows the Issues and Blocked Work Items report, which is essentially a cumulative flow diagram used to track work items. It indicates any issues causing blockage in your process. When blocking issues do come up, you should create a work item. When you link the issue work item to the blocked work item, you can then track the issues more effectively. You can then use this report and the issue log to manage the issues and bring them back under control. Typically, you start with zero issues at the beginning and they build up as time goes on. Note that this report is not available in MSF for Agile Software Development, only in MSF for CMMI Process Improvement.

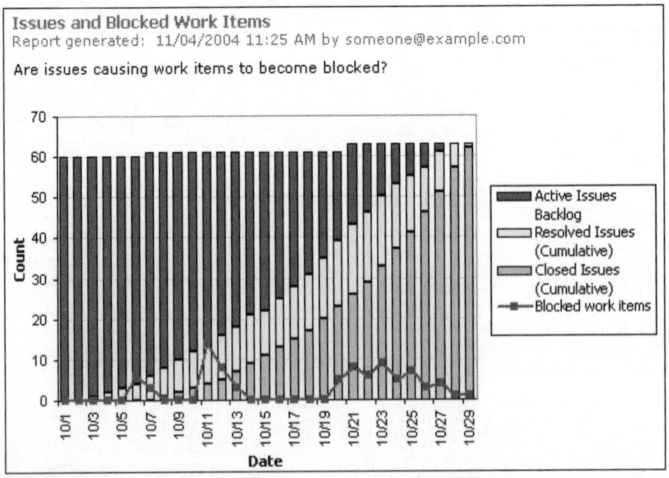

Figure 6-11

In MSF for CMMI Process Improvement, you can quantify all assignable cause variation using risk work items. Chance cause variation is harder to pin down, of course. You can use the issue work item to document issues that come up during the course of a project. If you are consistent with the way you document all your risks and issues, you will be able to learn and mitigate them in future projects. Using the Issues and Blocked Work Items report, you can use the evidence of impact to escalate issues for prompt resolution. The rate of resolved issues can serve as an indication of process maturity.

If you can't find risk in your project, you are either functioning at an extremely high level of process maturity, or you are having difficulty measuring the variation in your projects. As unpleasant as risk can be, it's important to recognize that you can't avoid it; you must adjust to working with risk. In MSF for CMMI Process Improvement, it's an important way we can empirically document and eliminate special cause variation from the environment.

MSF for CMMI Process Improvement has a defined methodology for dealing with risk. You should propose and devise mitigation schemes at the beginning of the project. An analysis has to be done to estimate risk and identify triggers for mitigation. Not all risk will cause show-stopping results. Using techniques such as Pareto's Principle (the 80/20 rule), you must prioritize what risks are the most important and what are their thresholds are for triggering a mitigation. (Working on tasks to mitigate risk will take your team away from the task of developing code—mitigation tasks should be worked on only if there is a real chance that it will adversely affect your project.) The prioritization of risk can be done using four factors: impact, cost, likelihood, and mitigation. As all projects will be affected by risk at one point or another, you should create a contingency plan and buffer to recover from risk. Once you have worked out the predictable risk factors, you can then enter them as work items (along with the mitigation tasks). For more detail on handling risk, refer to the documentation available in the MSF for CMMI Process Improvement process guidance.

MSF for CMMI Process Improvement is a radical new approach for helping companies get appraised at CMMI Level 3. It uses Agile techniques and principles based on Deming's variation model to mitigate risk and issues associated to your project. It also moves away from traditional definitions of a project to provide scientific and empirical insight in your process.

Team System is quite versatile because it is adaptable to any process and environment. What if you don't want to use the MSF model as the basis of your software development project? Luckily, there are third-party vendors and organizations working on process templates for established Agile and formal processes. Let's look at some of them.

Third-Party Processes

Many third-party vendors have designed process templates for Team System. Here is a breakdown of the resources currently at your disposal:

- **SCRUM**—Conchango has developed a fully featured Scrum template for Team System. You can download the template for free at `http://scrumforteamsystem.com`.
- **Essential Unified Process**—Ivar Jacobson, inventor of the Rational Unified Process has devised a lightweight, Agile process for Team System called the Essential Unified Process. You can learn more about this process and the process template at `ivarjacobson.com`.
- **Feature Driven Development**—Cognizant is working on a feature-driven development process template for Team System. You can learn more about it by downloading the following white paper: `http://download.microsoft.com/download/1/b/7/1b7cbbdc-50c9-4f53-8a82-5e583e5032dd/Cognizant%20FDD%20Implementation%20with%20VSTS.pdf`.

It is also important to note that Microsoft is continuously updating and improving the CMMI and Agile versions of MSF. They are also working on a Sarbanes-Oxley (SOX) compliant version of MSF. If you use systems such as Six-Sigma or feature-driven development, you can customize a template to meet your needs. Some companies may require special customized process templates for ITIL or the Canadian CICA 5900 requirements.

Rarely will a company adopt a process in its entirety. You have to modify and tailor any process to fit your needs. For example, you may have roles that don't quite fit those available by default in the MSF for Agile Software Development and MSF for CMMI Process Improvement process templates. Another possibility is that you have to modify the work items to be able to capture and store information that may be important to a company from a business perspective.

Understanding Process Templates

A process template is a series of XML files that define your team project. You have the choice of starting from scratch (which we wouldn't recommend unless you are extremely familiar with the schemas) or you can update a preexisting process template. To obtain an existing process template from Team Foundation Server, in Team Explorer right-click your server name, then select Team Foundation Server Settings⇨Process Template Manager. (You can alternatively access this option by clicking on Team⇨Team Foundation Server Settings⇨Process Template Manager.)

The Process Template Manager (Figure 6-12) allows you to upload, download, and delete templates. Select the MSF for Agile Software Development template and click download.

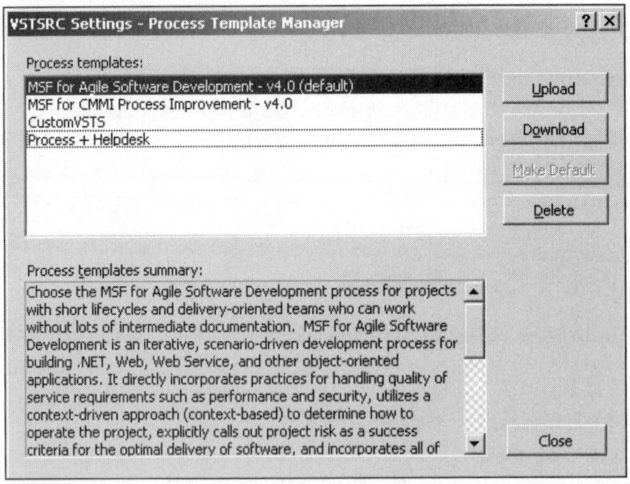

Figure 6-12

As a rule of thumb, you should use the MSF for Agile Software Development template as a starting point for creating customized templates. The reasoning behind this is that the MSF for CMMI Process Improvement template contains a lot of extra content to support the appraisal requirements for CMMI.

You should always try to start from a simple template and build up from there. (Otherwise, you will have to go backward and strip out the work products, work items, and other project artifacts you don't necessarily need.) The only exception to this rule is if you are designing a template for a project that requires a high level of governance, process improvement, and quality assurance (for example, audits).

For the sake of illustration, you should begin by downloading the MSF for Agile Software Development process template. On your system, you should see a folder for the template. Within the folder, you'll notice an XML file called ProcessTemplate.xml and several subfolders including the following:

- **Classification** — The files in this folder allow you to modify the iterations and areas to organize and structure your work items. A FileMapping.xml file allows you to create mappings from work item fields to Microsoft Project columns. This is extremely important when you start creating custom work items.
- **Groups and Permissions** — The groups and permissions portion of the template allows you to predefine the roles within your software development team, and the permissions associated to the roles. For example, if your software projects require the involvement of a helpdesk staff, you can define a special role that is defined every time you create a new project using your custom project templates.
- **Reports** — The reports portion of the template allows you to define which reports will appear in the project. You can remove some of the default reports and incorporate custom reports. The full process of creating customized reports is documented in Chapter 16.
- **Version Control** — The version control part of the template allows you to define the permissions your team members will have on Team Foundation's version control system. It also defines what kinds of checkin notes you want included in the project (in other words, what kind code reviews should be performed before checkin and who will perform them). Finally, you can set whether the version control allows multiple checkouts or exclusive checkouts.
- **Windows SharePoint Services** — The Windows SharePoint Services portion of the template does quite a lot. It can create document library folders on your SharePoint site and then add all of your custom work products (the templates you use in the course of working on a project, for example documentation you need to include in each project). You can also create a custom SharePoint site template and associate it to your process template. This means that whenever you create a new project, it will include your logo and your customized look-and-feel. Finally, the SharePoint site contains process guidance that you can build using the MSFWinBuild tool. (See the section titled "Compiling and Creating Documentation" later in the chapter.)
- **WorkItem Tracking** — The WorkItem Tracking folder contains definitions for your default work items (such as bugs, tasks, and issues). You can create and include your own work item types in this folder. You can also create custom work item queries. workitems.xml also defines a list of work items that will appear by default once a project is created. This list is called an *instance* — it allows you to set up a list of predetermined steps for each team project. For example, if you have to perform administrative tasks before starting a project you can explicitly set up work items for this purpose.

Global lists represent another customization you can make that is not explicitly indicated in the template. Let's say you create a work item that requires a drop-down list, you can include a custom list within that control.

In this chapter, we will not attempt to walk you through the minutiae of creating each part of the process template, because the process is well documented in the Visual Studio 2005 SDK and our companion book *Professional Visual Studio 2005 Team System*, published by WROX Press. If you are interested in advanced work item customization, we strongly recommend you look at Chapter 11 of this book.

What we do in this chapter is help you understand how to map business requirements to Team System and help you create process templates that work in the real world.

Using Process Template Editing Tools

Several tools are available to help you edit process templates; some are free and others are more commercially driven. Here is a rundown of the tools on the market:

- **Text/XML Editor** — In their native form, process templates are nothing more than XML documents. Therefore, if you have knowledge of XML, you can manually edit the XML file by adding, removing, and editing nodes on the XML tree using built-in text editing tools such as Notepad and Wordpad. There are also third-party XML editing tools such as XMLSpy by Altnova (`altova.com/features_xmlediting.html`).
- **Process Template Editor** — Joel Semeniuk has developed a free process template editor available for download on GotDotNet: `gotdotnet.com/Workspaces/Workspace.aspx?id=812a68af-5e74-48c6-9623-1a4469142a84`.
- **Work item type designer** — Darren Jefford has created a work item editor using the Domain Specific Language tools: `gotdotnet.com/workspaces/workspace.aspx?id=d03b00f5-7c5d-4e29-86b5-b966a04e1ed7`.
- **Third-party tools** — Osellus has designed a commercial ASP solution for designing process templates. You can learn more at `osellus.com`.

Creating Custom Process Templates

Some processes are extremely elaborate — you could write an entire book on how to customize a single process. The goal here is to get a big picture view of a process and look at how you can roll out the process into Team System.

Conchango Scrum Process Template

Scrum is an Agile process; developed by Ken Schwaber and Jeff Sutherland, it is focused on project management. It is a systematic approach to built-in predictability in your development process. If you want to learn the intricacies of Scrum, the best site to visit is `www.controlchaos.com`.

Conchango (`conchango.com`) has developed a Team System process template that allows any organization to implement Scrum on the Team System platform. In this section, we look at the different parts of the process template and explain the customizations that have been made to incorporate Scrum functionality and principles into Team System. You can download the template in question at the following link: `scrumforteamsystem.com`.

The easiest way to now modify a process template is the Process Template Editor. It was used to create portions of the Scrum process template. How do we know this? The work item definition for the Sprint work item contains the following line of code: `<WITD application="Work item type editor" version="1.0">`.

Classification

The Scrum programming process uses typical one-month iteration cycles called Sprints. Here is the structure of the Classification.xml file. The `ProjectLifecycle` structure type specifically defines iterations. (For example, you could easily change Iteration 0 to Sprint 0.)

```
<?xml version="1.0" encoding="utf-8" ?>
<tasks>
<task
id="UploadStructure"
name="Creating project structure"
plugin="Microsoft.ProjectCreationWizard.Classification"
completionMessage="Portfolio project structure created.">
<taskXml>
<Nodes>
<Node StructureType="ProjectLifecycle" Name="Iteration" xmlns="">
<Children>

<Node StructureType="ProjectLifecycle" Name="Iteration 0"></Node>
<Node StructureType="ProjectLifecycle" Name="Iteration 1"></Node>
<Node StructureType="ProjectLifecycle" Name="Iteration 2"></Node>
</Children>
</Node>
```

The Scrum template does not define any areas; however, you can define a list of predefined subcategories within each iteration. The `ProjectModelHierarchy` structure type applies to areas. The `MSPROJ` property points to a file called FileMapping.xml, which maps the fields from Microsoft Project and Team Foundation Server work items.

```
<Node StructureType="ProjectModelHierarchy" Name="Area" xmlns=""></Node>
</Nodes>

<properties>
<property name="MSPROJ" value="Classification\FileMapping.xml" isFile="true" />
</properties>
</taskXml>
</task>
</tasks>
```

Groups and Permissions

MSF for Agile Software Development includes three predefined security roles within the template. One of the modifications you can do to align it with Scrum is add additional roles. Scrum defines three primary roles: The Product Owner (such as a project manager or business analyst), the Team, and the Scrum Master. Here is the standard predefinition of the Reader, Contributor, and Build Services.

```
<?xml version="1.0" encoding="utf-8" ?>
<tasks>
<task id="GroupCreation1"
name="Create Groups and Permissions"
plugin="Microsoft.ProjectCreationWizard.Groups"
completionMessage="Groups and Permissions created.">
<taskXml>
<groups>
<group name="Readers" description="A group for those with read
 access across the project">
<permissions>
<permission name="GENERIC_READ" class="PROJECT" allow="true" />
<permission name="SUBSCRIBE_BUILD" class="PROJECT" allow="true" />
<permission name="GENERIC_READ" class="CSS_NODE" allow="true" />
<permission name="WORK_ITEM_READ" class="CSS_NODE" allow="true" />
</permissions>
</group>
<group name="Contributors" description="A group for those with
 general read/write permissions across the project">
<permissions>
<permission name="GENERIC_READ" class="PROJECT" allow="true" />
<permission name="PUBLISH_TEST_RESULTS" class="PROJECT" allow="true" />
<permission name="SUBSCRIBE_BUILD" class="PROJECT" allow="true" />
<permission name="GENERIC_READ" class="CSS_NODE" allow="true" />
<permission name="WORK_ITEM_READ" class="CSS_NODE" allow="true" />
<permission name="WORK_ITEM_WRITE" class="CSS_NODE" allow="true" />
<permission name="START_BUILD" class="PROJECT" allow="true" />
</permissions>
</group>
<group name="Build Services" description="Users in this group get
 permissions to run MSBuild for the sources in the Team project">
<permissions>
<permission name="GENERIC_READ" class="PROJECT" allow="true" />
<permission name="PUBLISH_TEST_RESULTS" class="PROJECT" allow="true" />
<permission name="GENERIC_READ" class="CSS_NODE" allow="true" />
<permission name="WORK_ITEM_READ" class="CSS_NODE" allow="true" />
<permission name="WORK_ITEM_WRITE" class="CSS_NODE" allow="true" />
<permission name="START_BUILD" class="PROJECT" allow="true" />
<permission name="UPDATE_BUILD" class="PROJECT" allow="true" />
<permission name="EDIT_BUILD_STATUS" class="PROJECT" allow="true" />
</permissions>
</group>
```

You can then add one of the Scrum roles, such as the Product Owner, within the template. Note that this role is not included in the Conchango template. We include it here for illustration:

```
<group name="Product Owner" description="The Product Owner role within
 the Scrum methodology.">
<permissions>
<permission name="GENERIC_READ" class="PROJECT" allow="true" />
<permission name="PUBLISH_TEST_RESULTS" class="PROJECT" allow="true" />
<permission name="SUBSCRIBE_BUILD" class="PROJECT" allow="true" />
<permission name="GENERIC_READ" class="CSS_NODE" allow="true" />
<permission name="WORK_ITEM_READ" class="CSS_NODE" allow="true" />
```

```
<permission name="WORK_ITEM_WRITE" class="CSS_NODE" allow="true" />
<permission name="START_BUILD" class="PROJECT" allow="true" />
</permissions>
</group>
</groups>
</taskXml>
</task>
</tasks>
```

SQL Server Reporting Services

The Scrum process has unique metrics to track. These include the Product Backlog, Sprint Backlog, Bug Count, Bug History, Priority, Delta Report, Retrospective Report, and the Sprint Burndown Chart (among others). Adding the Scrum report (and other reports) into the template requires that you created a custom .rdl file that has been designed using the Report Designer, Report Builder, and the Business Intelligence Development Studio (BIDS). The following highlighted code shows how to add a Scrum report into the process template.

```
<?xml version="1.0" encoding="utf-8" ?>
<tasks>
<task
id="Site"
plugin="Microsoft.ProjectCreationWizard.Reporting"
completionMessage="Project Reporting site created.">
<dependencies/>
<taskXml>
<ReportingServices>
<site />
</ReportingServices>
</taskXml>
</task>
<task id="Populate Reports"
plugin="Microsoft.ProjectCreationWizard.Reporting"
completionMessage="Project site created.">
<dependencies>
<dependency taskId="Site"/>
</dependencies>
<taskXml>

<ReportingServices>
<reports>
<report name="Product Burndown Chart"
filename="Reports\Product Burndown Chart.rdl"
folder=""
cacheExpiration="30">
<datasources>
<reference name="/TfsReportDS" dsname="TfsReportDS"/>
</datasources>
</report>
</ReportingServices>
</taskXml>
</task>
</tasks>
```

Team Foundation Version Control

Many elements of functionality can be controlled in VersionControl.xml, including security permissions with regards to access to the version control system. In Scrum, all members of the team are regarded as equals and there is inherent trust and transparency in the process. Here is an example of the Product Owner role added to Team Foundation Version Control (again, not included by default in the Conchango process template but shown here for illustration).

```
<?xml version="1.0" encoding="utf-8" ?>
<tasks>
<task
id="VersionControlTask"
name="Create Version Control area"
plugin="Microsoft.ProjectCreationWizard.VersionControl"
completionMessage="Version control Task completed.">
<dependencies/>
<taskXml>
<permission allow="Read, PendChange, Checkin, Label, Lock, ReviseOther,
 UnlockOther, UndoOther, LabelOther, AdminProjectRights, CheckinOther"
 identity="[$$PROJECTNAME$$]\Project Administrators"/>
<permission allow="Read, PendChange, Checkin, Label, Lock"
 identity="[$$PROJECTNAME$$]\Contributors"/>
<permission allow="Read" identity="[$$PROJECTNAME$$]\Readers"/>
<permission allow="Read, PendChange, Checkin, Label, Lock"
identity="[$$PROJECTNAME$$]\Build Services"/>

<permission allow="Read, PendChange, Checkin, Label, Lock, ReviseOther,
UnlockOther, UndoOther, LabelOther, AdminProjectRights, CheckinOther"
identity="[$$PROJECTNAME$$]\Product Owner"/>
```

Windows SharePoint Services

Here are the steps to modify our team portal. The first thing we can do is add a custom SharePoint template to change the look and feel and add the Scrum logo to the site.

```
<tasks>
<task
id="SharePointPortal"
name="Create Sharepoint Portal"
plugin="Microsoft.ProjectCreationWizard.Portal"
completionMessage="Project site created.">
<dependencies />
<taskXml>
<Portal>
<site template="Agile Software Development with Scrum" language="1033" />
```

You can then add libraries that incorporate documents that support the Scrum process. Instead of adding documentation to the team portal, Conchango opted to add two files (ProcessGuidance.html and AboutWorkItems.htm) that serve as redirectors to the `VSTSforTeamSystem.com` Web site.

```
<documentLibraries>
<documentLibrary name="Process Guidance"
description="Process Guidance for the team documents" />
</documentLibraries>
<folders>
```

```
<folder documentLibrary="Process Guidance" name="Supporting Files" />
</folders>

<files>

<file source="Wss\Process Guidance\ProcessGuidance.html"
documentLibrary="Process Guidance"
target="ProcessGuidance.html" />
<file source="Wss\Process Guidance\Supporting Files\AboutWorkItems.htm"
documentLibrary="Process Guidance"
target="Supporting Files/AboutWorkItems.htm" />
</files>
</Portal>
</taskXml>
</task>
</tasks>
```

Work Item Tracking

Here is the structure of workitems.xml. You'll find in this example a listing of the code defining the Sprint work item (Sprint.xml). You can find all the work items within your template in the folder called `WorkItemTracking/TypeDefinitions`. First, we need to give the work item a name and description:

```
<?xml version="1.0" encoding="utf-8" ?>
<WITD application="Work item type editor" version="1.0">

<WORKITEMTYPE name="Sprint">
<DESCRIPTION>Includes information about a particular Sprint</DESCRIPTION>
```

Next, we have to define a series of fields. Conchango has added customized fields such as Sprint Number to help track sprints. Notice that the field has been marked as reportable.

```
<FIELD name="Sprint Number"
refname="Conchango.VSTS.Scrum.SprintNumber" type="Integer" reportable="detail">
<HELPTEXT>The Sprint (iteration) number</HELPTEXT>
<REQUIRED/>
<CANNOTLOSEVALUE/>
</FIELD>
```

Conchango has also defined custom transitions for their work items. In the following example, they have defined a transition from "In Progress" to "Deleted." (The Deleted state is one of the ways you can eliminate work items without physically deleting them; see Chapter 17 for more details.) `Conchango.VSTS.Scrum.Audit` is a custom field that helps you track all changes happening to the work item.

```
<TRANSITION from="In Progress" to="Deleted">
<REASONS>
<DEFAULTREASON value="Item has been marked for deletion"/>
</REASONS>
<FIELDS>

<FIELD refname="Conchango.VSTS.Scrum.Audit">
<DEFAULT from="value" value="0" />
</FIELD>
</FIELDS>
</TRANSITION>
```

Once the fields and state transitions have been defined, you have to lay out the fields within a work item form. In the example below, the Sprint Number, Capacity, and Is Release Sprint are positioned under the title. Figure 16-13 shows the completed work item based on this code.

```
<FORM>
<Layout>
<Group>
<Column PercentWidth="100">
<Control Type="FieldControl"
FieldName="System.Title"
Label="Title"
LabelPosition="Left"/>
</Column>
</Group>

<Group>
<Column PercentWidth="50">
<Group Label="Planning">
<Column PercentWidth="100">

<Control Type="FieldControl"
FieldName="Conchango.VSTS.Scrum.SprintNumber"
Label="Sprint Number"
LabelPosition="Left"/>
<Control Type="FieldControl"
FieldName="Conchango.VSTS.Scrum.Capacity"
Label="Capacity"
LabelPosition="Left"/>
<Control Type="FieldControl"
FieldName="Conchango.VSTS.Scrum.IsReleaseSprint"
Label="Is Release Sprint?"
LabelPosition="Left"/>
</Column>
</Group>
```

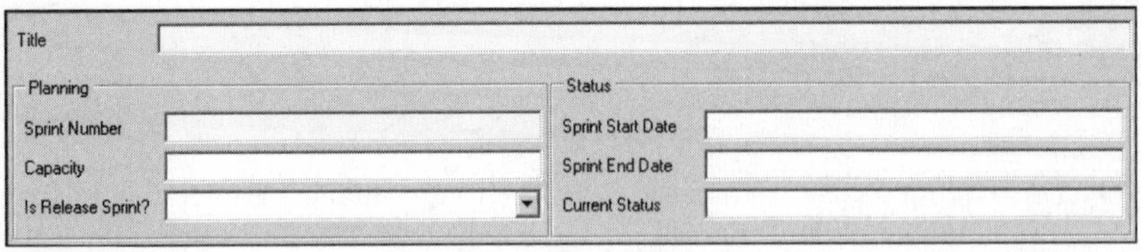

Figure 6-13

Once you have created your new type to represent a Sprint, you will need a new query to be able to retrieve them all from the work item database. Here is the structure of the `AllSprints.wiq` query; notice the inclusion of the Conchango custom fields (`Conchango.VSTS.Scrum.SprintNumber`, for example).

```
<?xml version="1.0" encoding="utf-8"?>
<WorkItemQuery Version="1">
<Wiql>
```

```
SELECT
[Conchango.VSTS.Scrum.SprintNumber],
[System.Title],
[Conchango.VSTS.Scrum.Capacity],
[System.State],
[Conchango.VSTS.Scrum.SprintStart],
[Conchango.VSTS.Scrum.SprintEnd]
FROM
WorkItems
WHERE
[System.TeamProject] = @project
AND
[System.WorkItemType] = 'Sprint'
AND
[System.State] &lt;&gt; 'Deleted'
ORDER BY
[Conchango.VSTS.Scrum.SprintNumber],
[Conchango.VSTS.Scrum.SprintStart]
</Wiql>
</WorkItemQuery>
```

Compiling and Creating Documentation

There are many ways to customize the documentation on the project portal. In the XML file defining the files included on the team portal (WssTasks.xml), you can include your own custom HTML files documenting your entire process. All you need to do is include the physical HTML file in the Supporting Files folder, and reference it in WssTasks.xml.

> **Note that there are a few filename dependencies to consider. For example, the main page of your document should be called ProcessGuidance.htm, in the folder path of** `Process Guidance/Supporting Files`**. (If you click Help➪Team Project Process Guidance, you will automatically jump to the ProcessGuidance.htm file in the current project.) Another one you should watch out for is AboutWorkItems.htm, which is accessible by clicking Work Items➪Team Project Process Guidance in any team project within Team Explorer.**

Another approach is to use the built-in MSF process guidance and make modifications to the guidance using Microsoft FrontPage 2003. All you need to do is connect to your team project using FrontPage 2003 (by clicking File➪Open Site) for your target team project. Expand the Supporting Documents node (within the Process Guidance folder). Double-click any of the .htm files (AboutRoles.htm for example) and make changes in the right pane. Once you are satisfied with the results, you can save the customized page on the server (or download a copy to your desktop to incorporate into a custom process template).

The MSF HTML Build Utility (`MSFWinBuild`) is an internal tool specifically designed by Microsoft to create the MSF process guidance. One of the challenges of MSF was representing the various links and dependencies between project artifacts. Just to give you an idea of the scale, MSF CMMI has approximately 13,000 pages of HTML and over 130,000 hyperlinks! The tool was designed to mitigate the load caused by the dynamic rendering of guidance pages, and reduce the complexity of building interconnected menus and hyperlinks. You can download the utility on the MSF Web site (`http://msdn.microsoft.com/vstudio/teamsystem/msf/`) or on the GotDotNet workspace (`gotdotnet.com/workspaces/workspace.aspx?id=c0ce8992-2955-4371-904b-1f93a9efffe6`).

All the process guidance content is stored in XML files. The MSFWinBuild utility uses a parameter file to denote the mapping and output directories of the process guidance. The utility will then incorporate the content and navigation. To run the utility, simply type the following:

```
> MSFWinBuild.exe Parameters.xml
```

Here is the structure of Parameters.xml, including the XML for navigation, mapping, and the Windows SharePoint Services tasks:

```
<?xml version="1.0" encoding="utf-8" ?>
<MSFWinBuild>
<NavXml>Custom\Process Guidance\Supporting Files\XML\Nav.xml</NavXml>
<MapXml>Custom\Process Guidance\Supporting
Files\XML\ProcessGuidanceMap.xml</MapXml>
<OutputXmlFile>Custom\Process Guidance\Supporting
Files\XML\ProcessGuidance.xml</OutputXmlFile>
<HtmlFile>C:\Custom\Process Guidance\Supporting
 Files\ProcessGuidance.htm</HtmlFile>
<OutputPath>Output\</OutputPath>
<WssXslFile>WssTasks.xsl</WssXslFile>
<WssOutputFile>WssTasks.XML</WssOutputFile>
</MSFWinBuild>
```

The MSFWinBuild utility allows the precise merging of XML files. The Map XML file uses the XInclude (`w3.org/TR/2003/WD-xinclude-20031110/`) standard.

```
<?xml version="1.0" encoding="utf-8"?>
<?mso-infoPathSolution PIVersion="1.0.0.0" language="en-us" name="urn:schemas-
microsoft-com:office:infopath:template:http---tempuri-org-XMLSchema-xsd"
solutionVersion="1.0.0.138" productVersion="11.0.6353"
href="file:///C:\Documents%20and%20Settings\v-
brtrau\Desktop\msf\working\Build%2064\Build%2064\Build%2064\Supporting%20Files\XML\
template.xsn" ?>
<?mso-application progid="InfoPath.Document"?><mstns:ProcessGuidance
xmlns:mstns="http://tempuri.org/XMLSchema.xsd"
xmlns:xsi="http://www.w3.org/2001/XMLSchema-instance"
xmlns:xhtml="http://www.w3.org/1999/xhtml"
xmlns:my="http://schemas.microsoft.com/office/infopath/2003/myXSD/2004-10-13T22:49:
49" xmlns:xd="http://schemas.microsoft.com/office/infopath/2003"
xmlns:xi="http://www.w3.org/2003/XInclude">
<mstns:Content>
<xi:include href="Roles.xml"
xpointer="xpointer(/mstns:Content/mstns:ContentItem)"/>
<xi:include href="WorkProduct.xml"
```

```
xpointer="xpointer(/mstns:Content/mstns:ContentItem)"/>
<xi:include href="WorkStream.xml"
xpointer="xpointer(/mstns:Content/mstns:ContentItem)"/>
<xi:include href="Activity.xml"
xpointer="xpointer(/mstns:Content/mstns:ContentItem)"/>
<xi:include href="Report.xml"
xpointer="xpointer(/mstns:Content/mstns:ContentItem)"/>
<xi:include href="Other.xml"
xpointer="xpointer(/mstns:Content/mstns:ContentItem)"/>
</mstns:Content>
```

For more information about the `MSFWinBuild` utility, please refer to the following MSDN documentation (`http://msdn2.microsoft.com/en-us/library/ms243790.aspx`) and the Process Template portion of the Visual Studio 2005 SDK.

> **Microsoft has released a series of articles on customizing the MSF process guidance using MSFWinBuild. You can view these articles at the following link:** `http://msdn.microsoft.com/library/en-us/dnvs05/html/MSF_customprocess.asp`.

Integrating Processes into Team System

Once you have customized the process template to your liking, you must reimport it into Team Foundation Server to share it with the rest of the project team members. A project manager can share your custom process by creating a new project using your process. You must, of course, also verify that the process has been imported successfully. Here are the steps to import a custom process template into Team Foundation Server:

1. Select Process Template Manager by clicking Team Foundation Server Settings within the Team menu. The Process Template Manager displays all current available processes.
2. Click the Upload button and select your process template description file (ProcessTemplate.xml) using the Upload Process Template dialog box.
3. As soon as you click Open, the process template imports into Team Foundation Server and appears on the list of available processes.
4. Close the Process Template Manager.

Deleting Process Templates

Sometimes, process templates are no longer needed because they have been replaced by newer versions or they have become obsolete. We strongly recommend that you export a copy of the process template you want to delete as a backup before you take the steps to delete it. To delete a process template, simply follow these steps:

1. Choose the Process Template Manager by selecting Team Foundation Server Settings from the Team menu. You then see a list of all the available process templates.
2. Pick a process template to delete and select Delete.

According to the Visual Studio 2005 SDK documentation, deleting a process template will not affect team projects that were created using the template. This is because a copy of all the artifacts from the process template (documents, source code repository, permissions) have been created on the server and the project is no longer tied to the template file. You can then change the default template by selecting a process and clicking the Make Default button. You can then close the Process Template Manager.

Testing Your Custom Process Template

There are two primary types of tests you would want to undertake with your custom process templates. The first kind is feature (or requirements) testing to determine whether all the customized features are available within your new template. The second type of testing you would want to undertake is usability testing: Will the feature break in certain circumstances? Does everything work as it should?

The most important guideline we can provide when editing process templates is to make small incremental changes and test your templates continuously. From this perspective, the process consists of making a minor change to the template, uploading the template to a nonproduction Team Foundation Server, creating a new team project using the template, testing your change, and starting all over again. Creating a process template this way is admittedly long and tedious, but will guarantee fantastic results in the end.

If you want to simply test and implement custom work items, you can use the `WITIMPORT` and `WITEXPORT` tools to modify work items in an existing project. The important advantage is that you don't have to create a brand new team project every time you want to test and deploy a custom work item. You can learn more about these tools on MSDN: `http://msdn2.microsoft.com/en-us/library/ms253088.aspx`.

Another important recommendation we can make is to create and test your process templates in a test environment before porting them over to a production environment.

Summary

In this chapter, we examined MSF in detail including the working details around MSF for Agile Software Development and MSF for CMMI Process Improvement. You found out about some of the third-party process template offerings and stepped through the process of customizing a new template to implement Scrum. You found out how to incorporate process guidance and documentation on the Team Portal using MSFWinBuild and most importantly, how to integrate your custom updates into Team System. In the next chapter, you will learn the next logical step in the development process, which includes establishing a Team Project and setting up your team and infrastructure.

7

Project Creation and Team Building

You have Team Foundation Server up and running, so now you have to figure out how to use it. In the previous chapter, you learned about process models, and the two models that are shipping with Visual Studio Team System: MSF Agile and MSF CMMI. Process models are only part of the picture. To fully utilize Team Foundation Server, you need to use a Team Project. In fact, you really can't do much with Team Foundation Server until you have a Team Project.

In this chapter, you learn what a Team Project is, from both a conceptual and physical perspective. You'll then move on to learn how to create a Team Project, and some of the errors that can occur during project creation. You'll read about project areas and iterations, which are ways of organizing the information in your Project. Finally, you'll learn about your project team, and revisit the roles associated with the MSF Agile process model.

Team Project Defined

So, what exactly is a Team Project? You can think about it in several ways. A *Team Project* is a collection of all the stuff that makes up your project in Team Foundation Server. That stuff can include work items, documents, code, test cases, and pretty much anything related to your project that can be stored in Team Foundation Server. The beauty of the Team Project is that everything related to the project is located in one logical space. You simply reference that Team Project to reference anything related to the project.

Maintaining all this information in one collection makes it easy to report on the project. All the information related to a Team Project is stored in SQL Server 2005 on the data tier, allowing easy access via SQL Server Reporting Services to project information. Also, each Team Project is its own silo of information, which allows all the information in the project to be unique to that project.

Team Explorer allows you to view this collection as a Team Project. When you create a Team Project, which you learn how to do later in this chapter, the process model you select defines the details of the Team Project, including work items and reports. Using Team Explorer, you can connect to the Team Project and access all the different work types associated with the project. You can also specify project areas and iterations, which allow you to add structure to your project.

Creating a New Team Project

Creating a Team Project is a very important step in utilizing Team Foundation Server. Almost everything the team does will be done within the constraint of the Team Project.

To make the products as easy to use as possible, Microsoft, with Team System and Team Foundation Server, has provided a variety of wizards to help speed up common tasks. With the New Team Project Wizard and an available process template, you can quickly and easily create a Team Project. Once the Team Project has been created, you can use Team Explorer to access the Team Project and make changes to the Team Project as it evolves.

To create a new Team Project, you must have the Team Foundation Server Create New Projects permission. Without this permission, you can't even run the New Team Project Wizard. See Chapter 4 for more information on how to set this and other Team Foundation Server permissions.

Finally, this is one of the few areas of Team Foundation Server where you cannot implement the same process via command-line tools. The process of creating a Team Project behind the scenes is rather involved. Thus, the only way to create a Team Project is via the New Team Project Wizard. You cannot use the command-line tools to create a new Team Project.

To start the New Team Project Wizard, first open Visual Studio 2005. From the File menu, select New➪ Team Project. Optionally, using Team Explorer, you can right-click the Team Foundation Server listed in Team Explorer, and select New Team Project from the context menu.

The New Team Project Wizard walks you through several pages of steps to create a new Team Project. The exact number of steps depends on the process template you select during project creation. In the following sections, you will be creating a Team Project based off the MSF Agile process, which ships with Visual Studio Team System.

Specifying your Team Project Settings

Figure 7-1 shows the first page of the wizard, the Specify the Team Project Settings page.

On this page, you enter the name of the Team Project. The name you pick for your Team Project should be one that other members of your team will easily recognize and understand. This name will be how others on your team find and access the Team Project.

Once you have entered the project name, click Next to move to the next step of the wizard.

Specifying a Process Template

The next page of the wizard is the Specify a Process Template page, as shown in Figure 7-2.

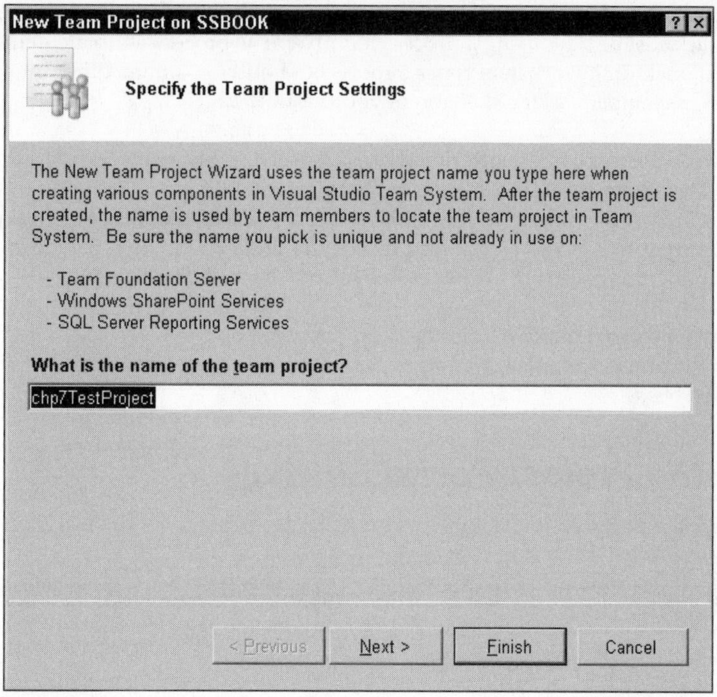

Figure 7-1

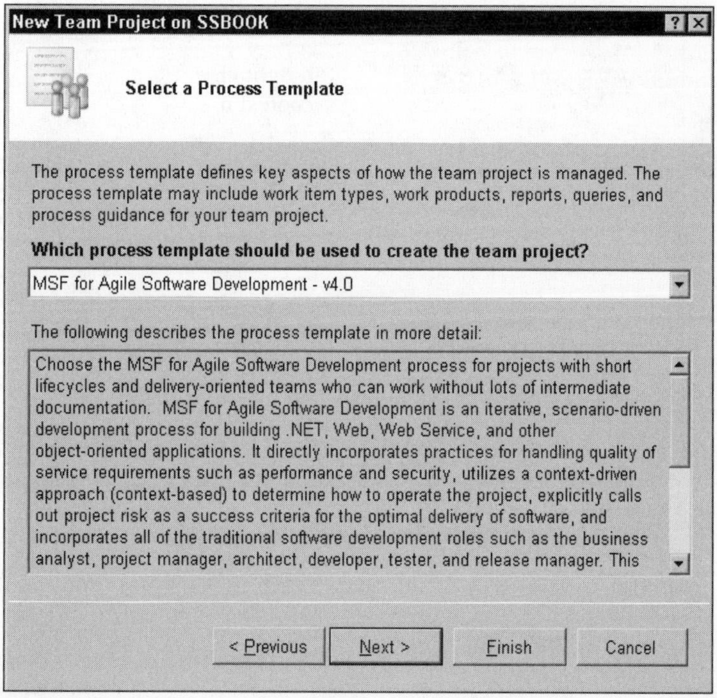

Figure 7-2

On this page, you select the process template you want to associate with this Team Project. Every Team Project you create must be built using a process template. The process template defines the key pieces of the Team Project, including work item types, reports, and queries, among other information. You can think of the process template as the skeleton of your Team Project.

Visual Studio Team System comes with two process templates: Microsoft Solution Framework (MSF) for Agile Software Development, also known as MSF Agile, and Microsoft Solution Framework for CMMI Process Improvement, also known as MSF CMMI. You can use either of these templates or you can develop your own process template and load it onto the Team Foundation Server for use during project creation. Third-party templates are also available for purchase or download.

When you select a process template from the drop-down list box, you can see a detailed description of the template in the process template summary area. Once you have selected the process template you want to use, click Next.

Specifying the Project Portal Settings

Figure 7-3 shows the next step in the wizard, specifying the settings for the project portal.

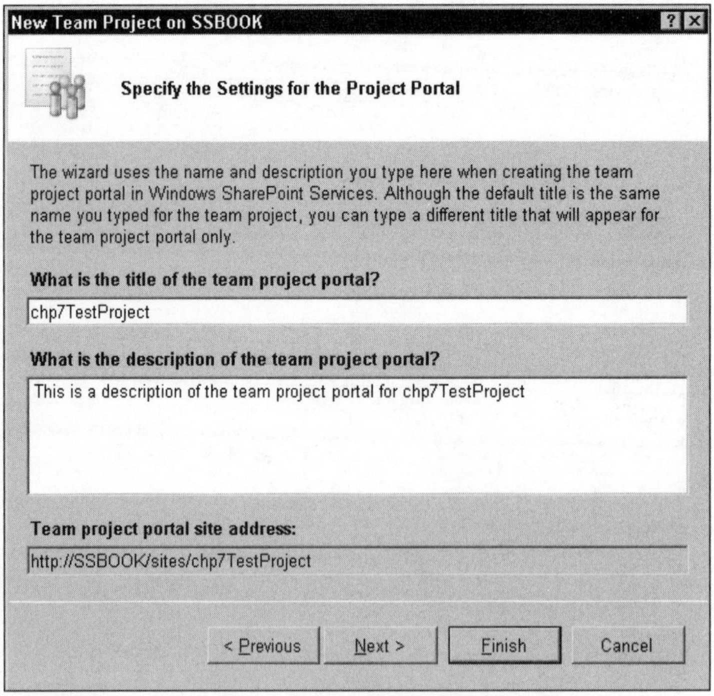

Figure 7-3

Every Team Project created on Team Foundation Server has its own Web site, called the project portal. This site, based on Windows SharePoint Services, provides access via a Web browser to project-related documents and information. It is a great way for all stakeholders in the project to stay on top of project information and progress.

The Team Project portal title defaults to the name of the Team Project. However, you can change the title to be anything you would like. Just make sure the title, if different from the Team Project, is descriptive enough to be identified by other Team Project members.

The Team Project portal description contains, as you would think, a description of the Team Project. This description is displayed on the project portal Web site. While this description is optional, you should go ahead and add one to provide more information to your project members.

The Team Project portal address field is not editable. This is the Web address of your project portal for this Team Project. The makeup of the address is as follows:

```
http://<Team Foundation Server Name>/sites/<Team Project Portal Title>
```

Once you have entered the portal title and optional description, click Next to move to the next step of the wizard.

Specifying the Version Control Settings

The next step of the wizard, Specify Version Control Settings, is shown in Figure 7-4.

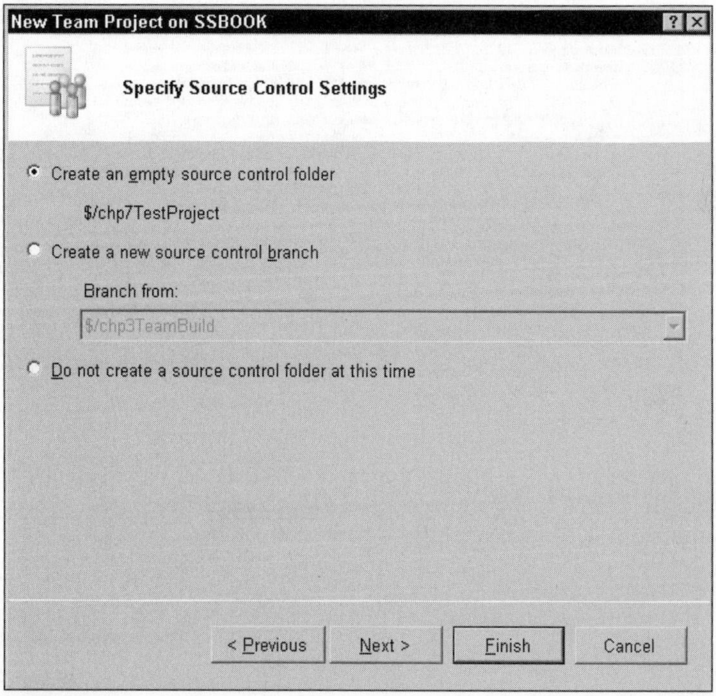

Figure 7-4

You have three different options for specifying the version control settings. The first is Create an empty version control folder. Selecting this radio button creates a folder off the root of the version control system with the same name as your Team Project name. Alternatively you can choose Create a new version control branch and then use the drop-down list box to specify which folder in the version control system to branch from. Chapter 12 has more details on branching. Finally, you can choose Do not create a version control folder at this time. Choosing this option does not connect your team project to the version control system. You will manually have to do this at a later point, using Team Explorer.

Once you have selected your option for version control, click the Next button.

Confirming the Team Project Settings

Figure 7-5 contains the next step of the wizard, the Confirm Team Project Settings page.

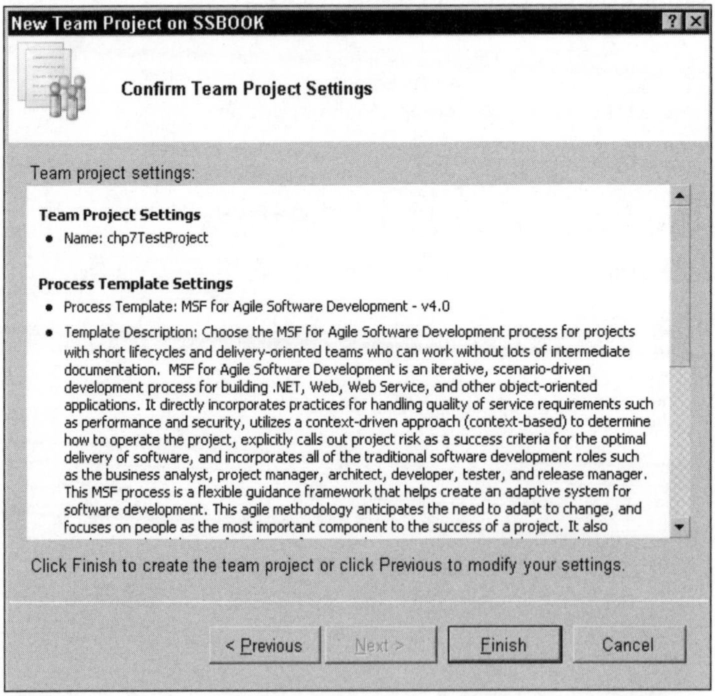

Figure 7-5

On this page, you can review all the options you have selected over the previous pages of the wizard. If you find something incorrect, or change your mind about a particular option, you can click Previous to return to the appropriate step of the wizard and make corrections.

If the information is correct, and you are ready to proceed with the creation of the project, click Finish. This begins the creation of the Team Project. The Team Project Creation Status Window opens, containing a status bar. This window shows you how long you have remaining in the project creation process. It also informs you of where you are in the creation process.

It may take several minutes for the project creation process to complete. Be patient!

During the project creation process, the wizard is using the information you entered, as well as the details from the process template, to create and configure the Team Project. If the wizard encounters an error while creating the Team Project, the error message will be displayed on the screen, and you will be prompted to take the appropriate steps to fix the error.

If the wizard completed successfully, then the Team Project Created page of the wizard opens.

Completing the Team Project

Figure 7-6 shows the final step of the New Team Project Wizard, the Team Project Created page.

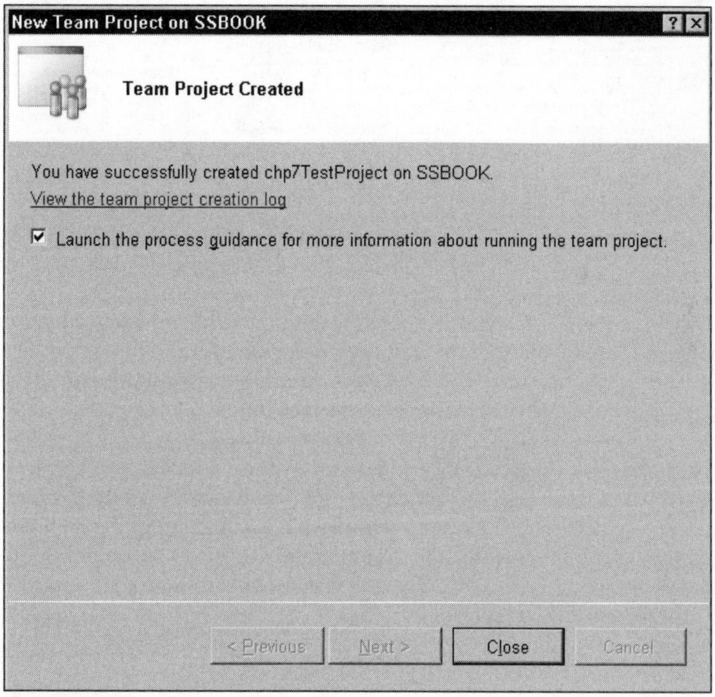

Figure 7-6

This page informs you that your Team Project was created successfully. As well, it presents you with a link and a checkbox option.

The link allows you to view the project creation log file. As you would expect, every step of the creation process is logged. This should make troubleshooting any problems easier. This log is located at `C:\Documents and Settings\<username>\Local Settings\Temp\VSTS_TeamProjectCreation_YYYY-MM-DD_HH.MM.SS.log`. Figure 7-7 shows part of the log from a successfully created Team Project.

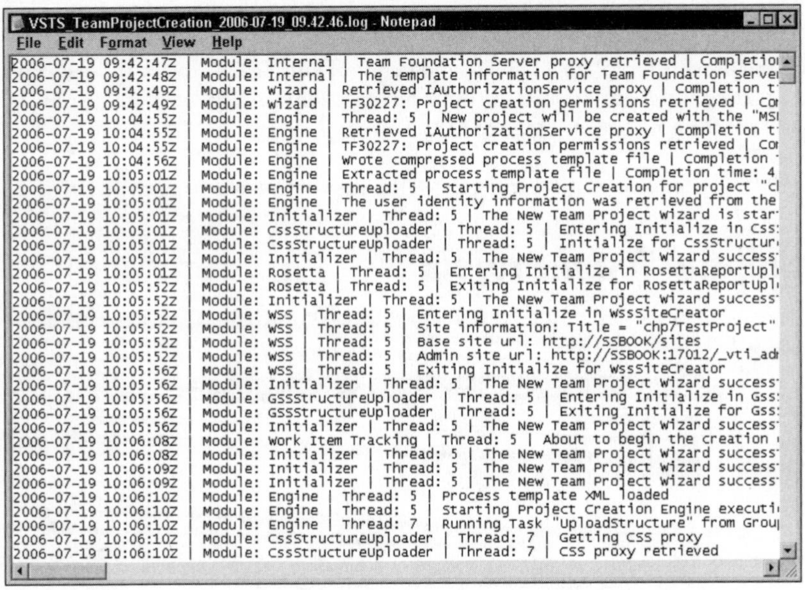

Figure 7-7

As you can see, this log file is not the most readable item. Should you encounter an issue with your project creation that you cannot troubleshoot, hang on to the log file, and head over to the MSDN Forums at `http://msdn.microsoft.com/forums`. Posting a question there, along with the part of your log file containing the errors, may result in some quick help for you.

The second option is to view the Process Guidance page of the process template you selected when you created your team project. The Process Guidance page is an overview of the process template and how to use it. It describes the different work items associated with the template, the roles of the different team members, and how team members interact, among other things. If you do not know anything about the process model you selected, this is a great place to start learning. Figure 7-8 shows the main page of the MSF Agile Process Guidance information.

To exit the New Team Project wizard at this point, simply click Close.

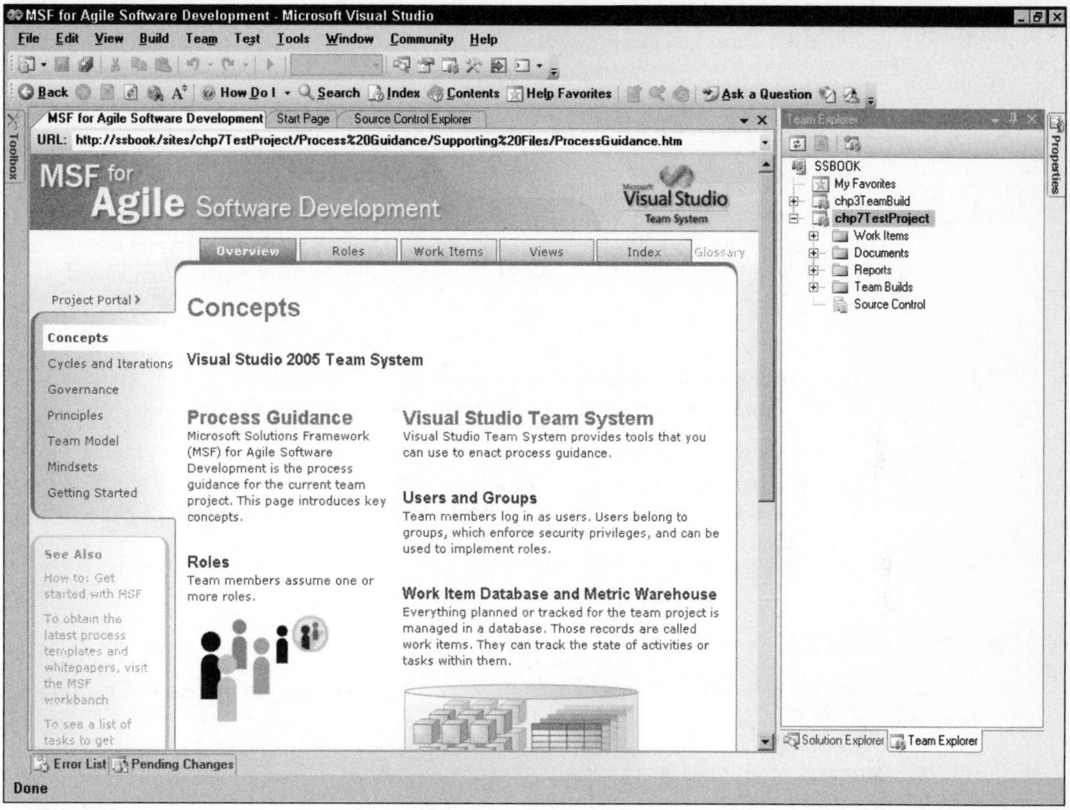

Figure 7-8

Common Project Creation Errors

Sooner or later you are probably going to run into a problem while trying to create a Team Project. Some of the errors may be easy to fix, such as a simple permission change. Others might be slightly more complicated. In this section, you will touch on some of the basic permission and network errors you may encounter while trying to create a Team Project.

For more information, you should consult the MSDN Online Help section entitled New Team Project Wizard Warnings and Errors (`http://msdn2.microsoft.com/en-us/library/ms244126.aspx`). Also, you should look to the MSDN Forums (`http://msdn.microsoft.com/forums`) for information and help.

Permission Errors

Permission errors are probably some of the first errors you will encounter. The following table contains some error messages you may encounter and possible solutions for each:

Error Code	Description	Possible Solution
TF30016	You do not have permission to create a new SQL Server Reporting Services site on the server.	Your user account needs to be added to the SQL Server Reporting Services Site Administrator group and Content Manager group. See Chapters 2 and 4 for more information.
TF30034	You do not have permission to create a new Team Project.	You have the Create new projects permission, but are encountering a permission error elsewhere, such as with an IIS virtual directory. Check the project creation log for the specific error information and set the permissions appropriately.
TF30172	You do not have permission to create a new Team Project.	Your user account needs the Team Foundation Server Create new projects permission.
TF30277	You do not have sufficient permissions on the Windows SharePoint Services to create a new site.	Your user account needs to be added to the Windows SharePoint Services Site Administrator group. See Chapters 2 and 4 for more information.

Network Errors

Network issues can also be a common source of problems when creating a Team Project. The following table contains some error messages you may see:

Error Code	Description
TF24023	Team Foundation Server Configuration Failure. The New Team Project Wizard work item component could not connect to the Team Foundation Server.
TF30005	The New Team Project Wizard group security component could not connect to the Team Foundation Server.
TF30015	The New Team Project Wizard could not connect to the specified SQL Server Reporting Services server.
TF30022	The New Team Project Wizard could not connect to the Windows SharePoint Services server.
TF30032	The New Team Project Wizard common structure component could not connect to the Team Foundation Server.
TF30320	The New Team Project Wizard could not retrieve the list of team projects on the Team Foundation Server.

These issues can be caused by various things, including the client computer not being connected to the network, a problem with the network, or the server you are trying to connect to being offline.

To fix this, you should first check that the client computer is connected to the network and can at least see the servers on the network. Next, confirm that the server in question, be it the data tier server or the application tier server, is up and running and connected to the network as well. Finally, review the project creation log for information related to the error. (Remember, it is located at `C:\Documents and Settings\<username>\Local Settings\Temp\ VSTS_TeamProjectCreation_YYYY-MM-DD_HH.MM.SS.log`.)

Don't forget to draw on the resources of your Team Foundation Server Administrator, the MSDN Help, and the MSDN newsgroups to solve your problem!

Configuring Project Areas and Iterations

One of the nice things about Team Projects is the concept of project areas and iterations. You can use these two hierarchies to help organize your work items and other information in the Team Project. A process template will usually define a base hierarchy for you, which you can then customize to fit the project. Once you have created your Team Project, you should configure the areas and iterations for the project, so team members can assign work items appropriately.

You can think of a project area as a logical division of your project, a breakdown of the components and features to include in the project. For example, you could look at your project from an architecture standpoint, and have a GUI area, a business object area, and a data access area. You can also have subsections as well, so in each area you can break things down into as much detail as you like. You can then use this structure to group your work items logically. This structure can be modified as the project progresses and changes.

The project iterations are the different lifecycle events into which the project can be divided. For example, if you were utilizing the classic waterfall model, you would have an iteration each for requirements gathering, design, development, testing, and deployment. Depending on the lifecycle model you will be following, you may have more or less iterations, or subcategories of iterations. As with the project areas, you can modify the iterations information as needed as the project progresses. The process template you chose when you created your Team Project defines the default areas and iterations for your Team Project. MSF Agile, for example, defines three default iterations, called Iteration0, Iteration1, and Iteration2. You can use iterations, in conjunction with project areas, to group your work items and other information into logical groupings, making the status of the project easy to understand.

Modifying Project Areas

As mentioned previously, you can modify the areas a project has, as well as add subcategories, at any point during the lifetime of the project. As a project progresses, it may make sense to reorder, change, or even delete project areas. Team Foundation Server gives you that flexibility, allowing you to make the most efficient use of the product.

> **You must have Team Foundation Server Edit Project-Level Information security permission to make changes to the project area information.**

To get started modifying the project areas, open Visual Studio 2005. From the Team menu, select Team Project Settings, and finally Areas and Iterations. Alternatively, from Team Explorer, you can right-click the Team Project, select Team Project Settings, and then Areas and Iterations. Figure 7-9 shows the Areas and Iterations window that opens.

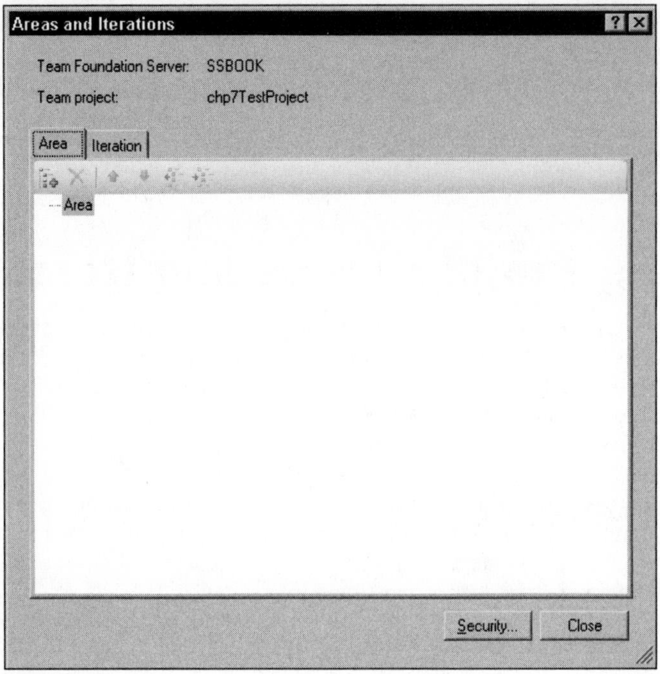

Figure 7-9

Select the Areas tab on this window. This window contains a toolbar with six options:

- **Add a child node** — Add a new area under the selected area
- **Delete node** — Delete selected area
- **Move a node up among its siblings** — Move selected area up in the hierarchy
- **Move a node down among its siblings** — Move selected area down in the hierarchy
- **Make selected node a sibling to its parent** — Make selected area a child of the area above it
- **Make selected node a child of its preceding sibling** — Make selected area a peer of the area above it

You can also right-click an area to open a context menu with the same options. Using the toolbar, you can configure the project areas as appropriate to your needs. Figure 7-10 shows an example of the project area configured as mentioned earlier, with a GUI area, a business object area, and a data access area.

When you are finished, click Close to save the changes.

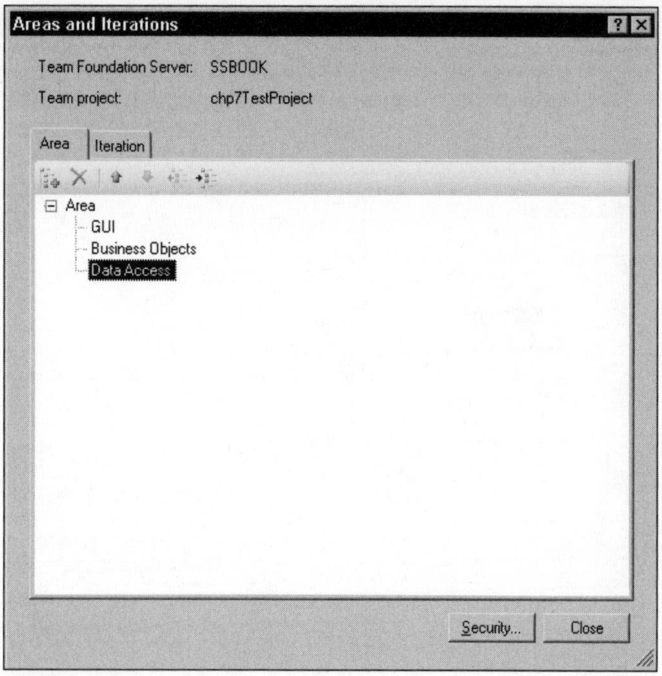

Figure 7-10

Modifying Project Iterations

You can modify the iterations that a project has, as well as add subcategories, at any point during the lifetime of the project. As with the project areas, as a project progresses, it may make sense to reorder, change, or even delete project iterations.

> **You must have Team Foundation Server Edit Project-Level Information security permission to make changes to the project area information.**

To get started modifying the project iterations, open Visual Studio 2005. From the Team menu, select Team Project Settings, and finally Areas and Iterations. Alternatively, from Team Explorer, you can right-click the Team Project, select Team Project Settings, and then Areas and Iterations.

Once on the Areas and Iterations window, select the Iterations tab. You will see the same toolbar as in the Areas tab. You configure the iterations in the same way you configure the Areas. Figure 7-11 shows an example of the project iterations configured using the standard waterfall method, as mentioned previously.

When you are finished, click Close to save the changes.

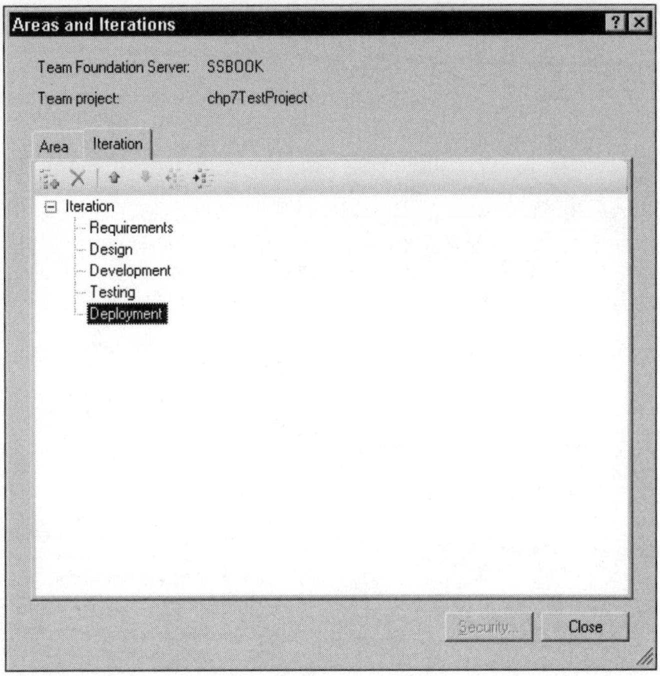

Figure 7-11

Using Microsoft Excel to Modify Project Areas and Iterations

You've already heard about how Team System and Team Foundation Server integrate with Microsoft Excel and Microsoft Project. Well, modifying the areas and iterations is yet another part of that integration. From within Microsoft Excel, you can select the Team menu, and then Edit Areas and Iterations. This opens the Areas and Iterations window, as shown in Figure 7-9, which is the same window used in Visual Studio. This allows you, the user, to make changes to areas and iterations, without leaving the comfort of the tool you like, in this case Microsoft Excel. This is just one more way that Visual Studio Team System and Team Foundation Server empower users to get their work done more efficiently.

Organizing Your Project Team

Creating your team project gives you an electronic repository for all your team information. But that is only one piece of the project puzzle. For a project to succeed, you need a project team of dedicated individuals from all aspects of the organization. All team members need to understand their role or roles. They need to be accountable for their actions, but not fearful of that accountability. One way to ensure this is to make sure lines of communication are always open between all team members.

Your project team should not consist of just technical people, such as the developers and testers. To really ensure the success of the project, as well as make the most of Team Foundation Server, you should also include the business users who requested and will be using the finished product, the managers who will oversee the project, and those who will help design and architect the project, to name just a few.

Team Foundation Server provides multiple ways to communicate the project status to everyone on the team. Using the project portal site, team members can stay up-to-date on the latest documentation and project status. Using Team Explorer, they can query Team Foundation Server to return the latest information on bugs, work items, and changes. Using Microsoft Excel they can view different lists of information from Team Foundation Server, as well as update that information. All these options serve to allow the team members to easily communicate with each other, as well as stay up-to-date on the status of the project.

Given this, let's take a brief look at the different roles that are defined in the MSF Agile process.

Understanding MSF Agile Team Roles

The MSF Agile Process Model defines six different roles for individuals who are involved with the Team Project. Each role has specific responsibilities, and one person can handle multiple roles, if required.

The following are the six roles, each with a short description of the role and its responsibilities. The following information was taken in part from the MSF Agile Process Guidance information that ships with Visual Studio Team System.

- **Business Analyst** — The Business Analyst role is responsible for defining the business needs of the application. Team members in this role also work with customers to understand their needs and turn those needs into requirements that the developers will use to build the application. They are advocates for the customer, and look out for the customer's needs and interest as related to the project.
- **Project Manager** — The Project Manager is responsible for delivering the project on time and within the defined budget. Project Managers handle the planning and scheduling duties that revolve around the project and monitoring the project status. They interact with Business Analysts, Architects, Developers, and Testers throughout the planning and managing of the project, and help ensure communication between the different roles.
- **Architect** — The Architects are responsible for designing the application, both its organizational and physical structure. They must take into account usability, maintainability, and security, among other things, during the design. The architecture of an application is extremely important, as it can effect how easy an application is to build and maintain.
- **Developer** — The Developers are responsible for building the application within the timeframe established by the Project Managers. In addition, they can contribute their ideas to the design of the application, help with the planning and deployment, and provide technical details as related to the project.
- **Tester** — The Testers are responsible for finding problems with the application and ensuring those problems can be fixed. This does not just mean finding problems with the code. Testers can also find problems in the design or deployment of the project. Once they have found a bug, they need to document its re-creation process, and then ensure the bug has been fixed in later versions of the project.

- **Release Manager** — The Release Managers are responsible for determining when a project is ready for deployment, and for deploying the product. They do this by creating a release plan, and working with the appropriate groups or departments to ensure a successful rollout.

Interchanging the Roles

You could have multiple roles involved in a large project. For example, a large project could have several Business Analysts and many Developers and Testers. But, for smaller projects or development shops, you may not need a team large enough to assign each role to a different person. In that instance, you will probably have a person who engages in multiple roles, as defined above.

A Developer might also wear the hat of an Architect or a Release Manager. A Business Analyst might also work as a Tester. There is no right and wrong way ultimately, though MSF Agile does give you some guidelines about which roles should not be combined with others. In the end, you should go with what works best for you and your environment.

For more detailed information on the MSF Agile process, you should visit the MSF for Agile Software Development Web site at `http://msdn.microsoft.com/vstudio/teamsystem/msf/msfagile`.

Summary

You've learned about how to set up Team Foundation Server, and the process models available with it. But this chapter took you to the next step, which was how to use the Team Project concept of Team System. At the beginning of this chapter, you learned what a Team Project actually is, a collection of all your stuff in the Team Foundation Server. You then learned how to create a Team Project using the New Team Project Wizard, and looked at some of the errors that can occur during project creation.

After that, you moved on to project areas and iterations. You learned how areas are just a logical breakdown of your project, while iterations are the different stages of your lifecycle model. Finally, you read about some things to take into account when developing your project team, and looked at the roles that are defined in the MSF for Agile Software Development process model. Remember, there are many different roles defined in that process model, and it is okay for someone to wear multiple hats, that is, take on multiple roles. For smaller projects, that is probably going to happen.

Now that you have learned how to create your Team Project, and a bit more about how to manage it, we are going to take a little detour and learn about a new edition to the Team System family. This new product is called Team Edition for Database Professionals, and is targeted at database administrators (DBAs) and database developers. As you'll see in the next chapter, it provides a lot of functionality for those roles that has been missing, and ties back into Team Foundation Server very nicely.

8

Managing Schemas Using Team Edition for Database Professionals

On May 31 2006, Microsoft announced a new Team Edition specifically targeted at database professionals called Team Edition for Database Professionals. A *database professional* can be defined as an architect, developer, administrator, or other professional that works within the SQL Server database (for example, a business intelligence specialist). The product is currently targeted at database developers and administrators, but future versions will provide support for architects (data modeling) and more features for IT operations.

This product fills a missing gap in the Team System family. You finally have a nice way to utilize all that Team Foundation Server has to offer, including version control and work item tracking, with your database schema. No more wondering what changes you made between your test database and your production database. No more question of whether you made a copy of that stored procedure before you added the new code. With Team Edition for Database Professionals, these and many other worries are taken care of.

This chapter is all about Team Edition for Database Professionals. We start this chapter with an overview of why this product is important, and how it fits into Team System. Then you delve into the details of how to use the product, including how to create a database project, and how to import and manage your database schema. You look at how to implement unit testing against your database, how to deploy your database changes, and even how to generate test data for the database.

This chapter was written using Community Technology Preview (CTP) 3 of Team Edition for Database Professionals. Many things may change between a CTP and the final release of the product. As such, some of this information may be inaccurate in relation to the released version.

Why This New Edition Is Needed

Today, you would be very hard pressed to find any application that doesn't have some sort of data component. Just as a developer would be responsible for code within the software development lifecycle (SDLC), the database professional is responsible for the development of data assets within the data development lifecycle (DDLC), which is illustrated in Figure 8-1.

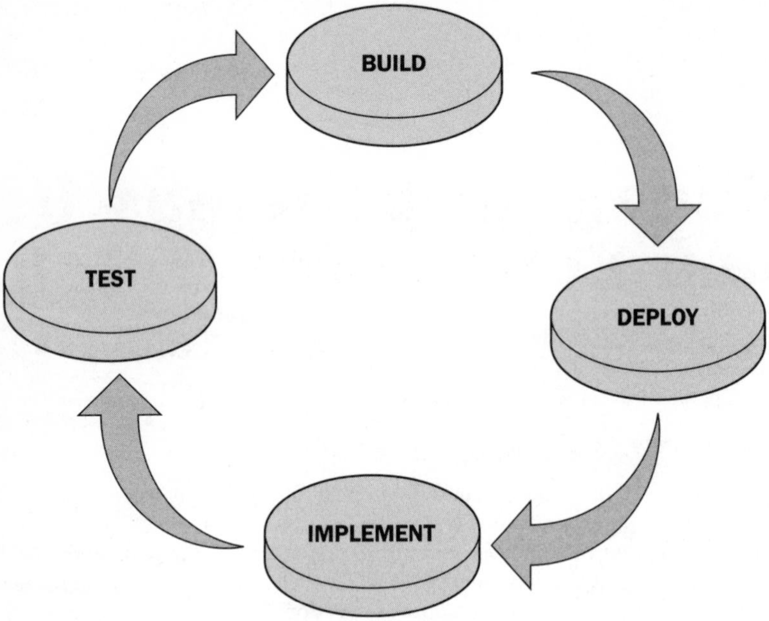

Figure 8-1

The important focus for most development companies is process improvement and predictability. The challenge is to find how a database professional can effectively apply engineering principles. First, the database schema is very hard to manage. How does one version a database? You can create snapshots but often, governance rules such as Sarbanes-Oxley prevent the extraction of data for such purposes. In addition, even with the best of intentions, you may lose data during backups. How do you test and deploy a database? A surprising number of database developers simply roll their changes into a production database without the benefit of testing. One of the big reasons for this is that the tools are simply not available or too expensive to use. A lot of the administrative tasks that you would associate with database management involve automation scripting to make a database easy to administer.

> **Team Edition for Database Professionals currently supports SQL Server 2005, SQL Server 2005 Express, and SQL Server 2000. It does not natively support Oracle, DB2, and other database vendors. (Although Microsoft expects that these platforms will be supported by third-party vendors using the extensibility model.)**

Team Edition for Database Professionals provides integration with Team Foundation Server to help manage several tasks within the DDLC. The challenge here is to provide database professionals with the tools to be able to work alongside agile development teams. Let's look at each task within the lifecycle:

- **Implement** — The implementation phase involves architectural and functional elements. The architectural part is the creation of a data model that fits the requirement of the target software application. This lightweight model is then translated into a database schema (the underlying structure of your tables, fields, and other database components), which can be updated offline and change-managed within Team Foundation Version Control. You also implement the application by creating the tables, views, stored procedures, functions, and types for use within the database. You have the choice of creating or generating new database schemas, or importing existing schemas and scripts from existing databases.
- **Test** — Just like a developer, database professionals can unit test entire databases, which ties in nicely with the Team Foundation test framework. All test results are pushed into the data warehouse, which allows you to aggregate metrics as a first class citizen alongside other test types (such as Web, load and manual tests, for example). Another really interesting feature is database refactoring. With the combination of unit testing, refactoring, continuous build and close connection with the rest of the team, the database professional can now develop using popular test driven development (TDD) approaches. One of the radical new features of the product is that you don't need a production database to perform these tests. You can work with the offline schema and simulate data using a powerful data generation utility.
- **Build** — Team Edition for Database Professionals comes with special MSBuild tasks that allow you to integrate your work into SQL Server 2000 or SQL Server 2005 using Team Foundation Build. You can also choose scripts that will run before and after the build.
- **Deploy** — Database assets can be stored alongside code in Team Foundation Version Control and can be deployed easily using the IDE. You can also compare and update a production schema against a schema in development, and deploy the changes.

Beyond these phases, Team Edition for Database Professionals has the same team integration functionality as the other Team Editions. In other words, you can communicate and collaborate with the rest of the development team using the Team System work item tracking database and control and manage your database-related assets using Team Explorer. Obviously, Team Foundation Server plays a key part in this integration.

One of the big challenges of working in an agile development environment is that you have to set up data infrastructure quickly, and it is often difficult to validate the work on many fronts. Many integration strategies have been tried in the past, such as scripting and modeling, which have been less than a great experience. The key problem is that up till now such work has been done on a production database. If you are working under time or financial constraints, it is difficult to implement a staging area for testing the application against the database before it is shipped out the door.

If you have used SQL Server 2005 at any length, you'll notice that development environment is considerably richer than SQL Server 2000, providing you with the ability to write stored procedures and other functional elements using .NET code against the SQL CLR. SQL Server 2000 is still fully supported; in fact, there is a strong argument for change-managing your queries and other assets, even from an operational perspective (for example, for backup and recovery scenarios).

The product team for Team Edition for Database Professionals designed the product around a persona called Data Dude. The name was coined by Eric Rudder (Microsoft's senior vice president for technical strategy) during an initial meeting about the product. Team Edition for Database Professionals is also sometimes referred to as Team System Data, Team Data, and TSData.

Like other parts of Team System, Team Edition for Database Professionals was conceived to improve the quality and predictability of the database development process. You can learn more about Team Edition for Database Professionals on the official MSDN site: `http://msdn.microsoft.com/vstudio/teamsystem/products/dbpro`.

The Data Development Lifecycle

Like your conventional software developer, the database developer can now enjoy support for each stage of the data development lifecycle. Let's look at the tools and functionality in detail. To do that, you are going to walk through each stage of the lifecycle using the Northwind database (one of the default databases in SQL Server) as an example. Along the way, you will learn the basics of how to use Team Edition for Database Professionals, and will see some of how it integrates into Team Foundation Server.

Implementation

The implementation phase consists of defining your database and building all the objects in it, such as tables, views, and stored procedures. Team Edition for Database Professionals helps you do this by storing your schema in a new Visual Studio Project, called a *database project*. It stores all the information about your database as SQL files, making them easy for database professionals to understand and modify.

Team Edition for Database Professionals does not support the use of graphical designers at this time. You must edit the raw SQL code to make all database changes. Support for graphical designers will be added in a future release.

For this example, you are going to see how to create a new database project, and then import the schema of an existing database into that project. We then cover how you can use the database project to manage your schema information, including how to use version control and work item tracking. Finally, you'll see how you can modify your database schema by adding a new table to your database.

Creating a Database Project

First thing you need to do is create a new database project.

1. Open Visual Studio, and select File⇨New⇨Project. This opens the New Project window, as shown in Figure 8-2.

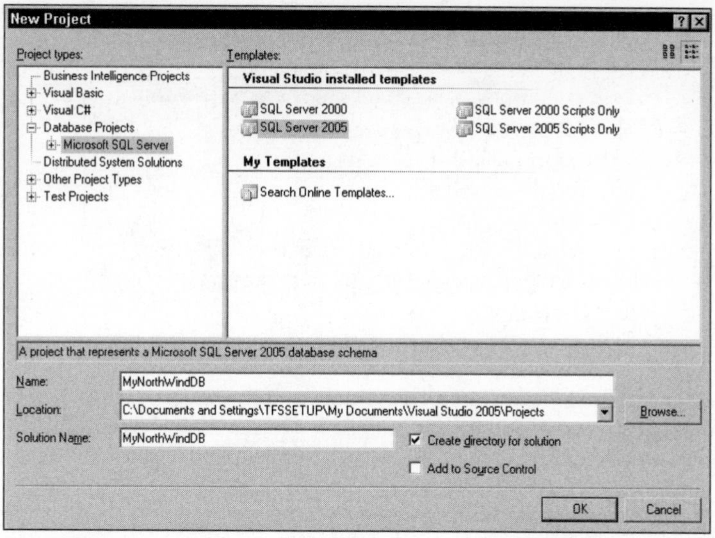

Figure 8-2

As you can see, there is a new section under Project types called Database Projects, and a section under that entitled Microsoft SQL Server. Team Edition for Database Professionals installs four templates for you to use, depending on whether you want to access SQL Server 2000 or SQL Server 2005.

2. In this case, you want to access the Northwind database on SQL Server 2005, so you select the SQL Server 2005 project template. Name your project **MyNorthWindDB**, leave everything else as the default, and click OK. This creates your database project., which you can see in the Solution Explorer.

Once you have created your database project, you can begin creating new database objects, or you can import the schema of an existing database. You are going to do the latter.

Importing Your Database Schema

Next, you want to import the schema of the Northwind database.

1. To do this, right-click the MyNorthWindDB project in the Solution Explorer, and select Import Database Schema. Figure 8-3 shows the Import Database Schema into Database Project window that opens.

2. In this window, you define the database from which you want to import the schema, and the database project where you wish to put that schema. You can click the New Connection button to set up a connection to your source database. In this instance, you are connecting to the Northwind database, and are going to store the database schema in the MyNorthWindDB database project. Click OK, and the process will proceed. This could take anywhere from a few seconds to a few minutes, depending on how complex your database is, so be patient.

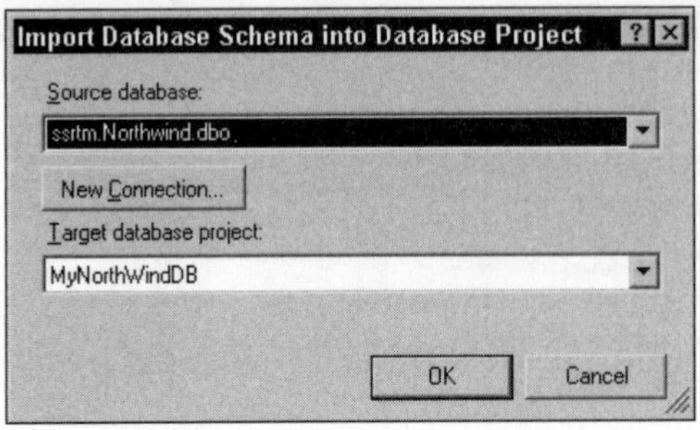

Figure 8-3

As you can see from Figure 8-4, all the database information, including tables, views, and stored procedures, has been added to your database project. Also in this figure you can see the SQL statement representation of the Categories table from the Northwind database.

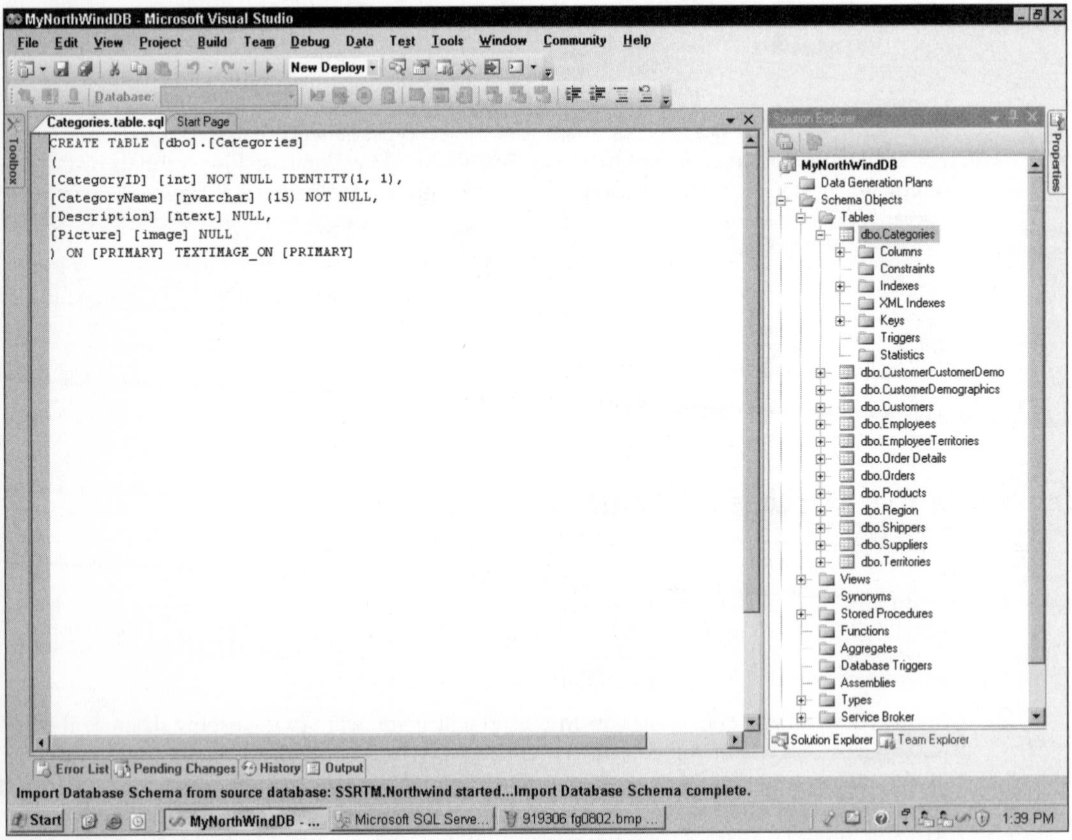

Figure 8-4

The cool thing is, all this database schema information is stored simply as multiple SQL statements in files. This makes it easy for a database professional to understand and modify information as needed.

Managing Your Database Schema

At this point, you have a database project that represents your Northwind database and contains the latest database schema of that database. Now you can begin making the database changes that are necessary for your project. However, before you do that, let's look at some of the ways you can manage your schema using the database project.

1. The first thing you will probably want to do is add your database project into the version control system. This allows you to track all changes made to any of your database objects. All you have to do is right-click the MyNorthWindDB project in Solution Explorer and select Add Project to Source Control. After all, the database project is just like any other project in Visual Studio, a collection of files. This opens the Add Solution to Source Control window, where you can select the Team Project you want to add your database project to, its location in the version control system, and the associated workspace.
2. Once you have added the files to the version control system, you need to check-in for the first time. Open the Pending Changes window and click the Check In button, to finish adding the files to the version control system. Your database schema is now under version control, and any changes you make to the schema will be tracked.

As you would suspect, you have access to all the version control features for this project, including branching, shelving, and associating database schema changes with work items. The database project is just another project in Visual Studio, so you access all these features the same way you always would.

There are three important folders in your database project. The Data Generation Plans folder contains any information related to data generation, which is covered later in this chapter. The Schema Objects folder holds all the objects that make up your database, such as tables and stored procedures. To add a new object, simply right-click the appropriate folder and select Add. To edit an existing object, double-click the object and it will open in the editor, where you can modify the SQL code. The Scripts folder contains SQL scripts that can run before or after you build your database project.

Modifying Your Database Schema

Now that you have imported your Northwind database, you need to add a new table to the database project.

1. In the solution explorer, under the MyNorthWindDB project, right-click the Tables folder located in the Schema Objects folder, and select Add⇨Table. This opens the Add New Item window, where you can select the Table template, and give your table a name.
2. Go ahead and name your table **CreditCard**. The table is added in the Tables folder, and an editor window opens in Visual Studio with a default table setup.
3. Modify the table to reflect Figure 8-5.

   As you can see, you are creating a table with a single column in it, called cc_number. This column will contain credit card numbers. Later in this chapter, you are going to learn how to create a custom data generator,to generate credit card numbers for testing. And yes, while this is a rather simple and incomplete example, it gives you a great jumping off point to delve into this more.

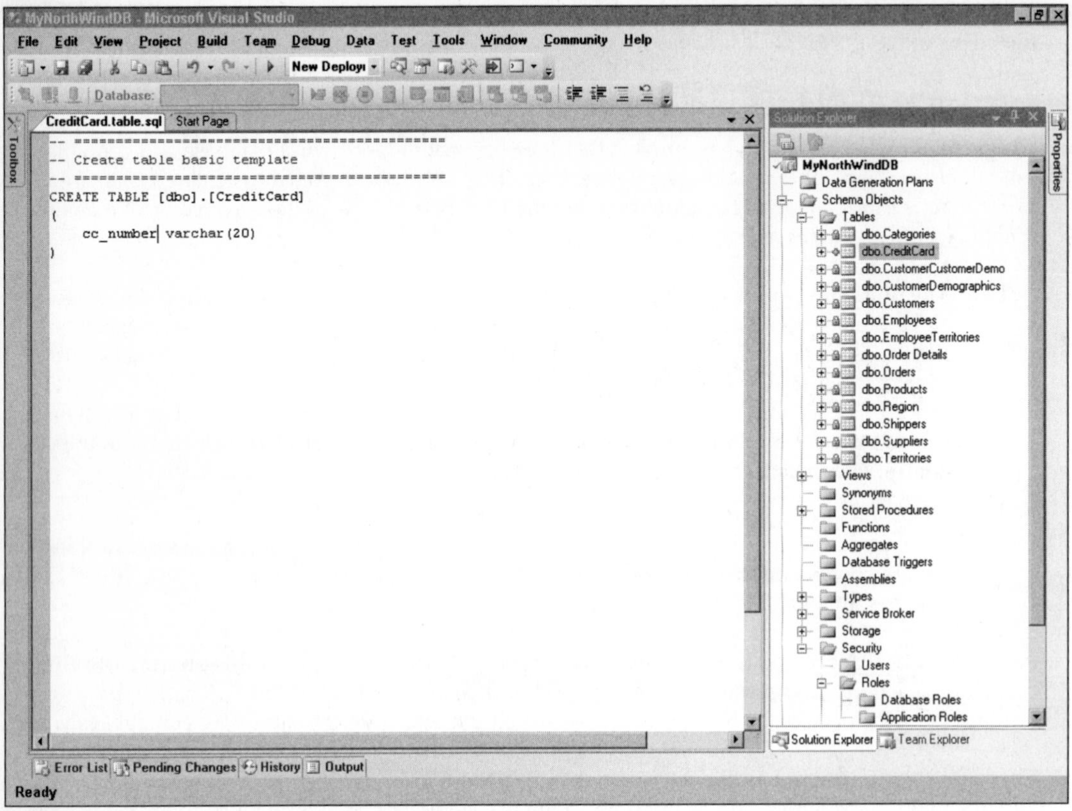

Figure 8-5

4. Once you have modified your table, click the save button. This new table has now been saved into your database project. If you have added your database project to your version control system, don't forget to check in your new table. Remember, you can also associate this check-in with any work items that are relevant. This table currently exists only on your local machine in your database project. Later in this chapter, you learn how to deploy your new database changes to either a test or a production server.

5. Let's also make a new stored procedure that will retrieve all the credit card numbers from our CreditCard table. Right-click the Stored Procedures folder in Solution Explorer, and select Add⇨Stored Procedure. Name the stored procedure **CCSelectAll**. Figure 8-6 shows the code for the stored procedure.

This stored procedure will retrieve all the rows from the cc_number column of the CreditCard table. Don't forget to save this stored procedure, and check it back into the version control system.

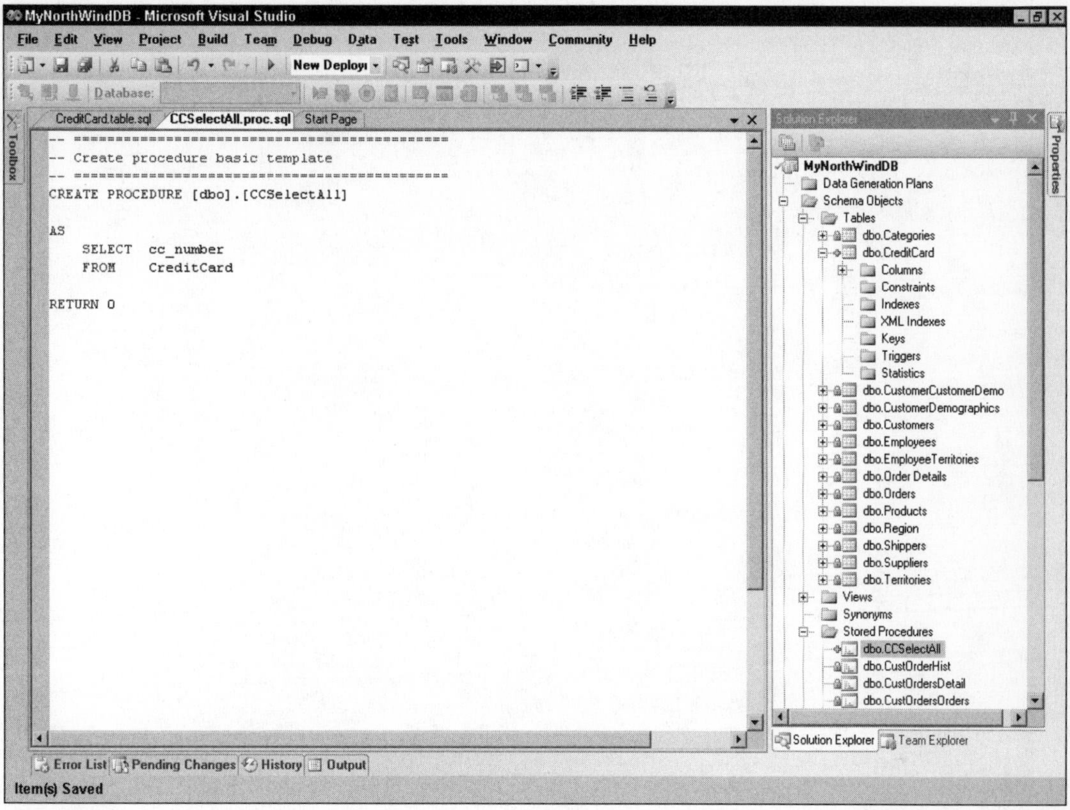

Figure 8-6

Building and Deploying

Before you can deploy your new database schema or update your existing database with your changes, you need to build the database project. This creates all the SQL scripts necessary to create your database schema, and verifies all the objects are valid. Once the database project has been successfully built, you can then deploy it to your test server or production server, as the case may be.

Building/Deploying Your Database Project

Before you build your database project, you need to define some project settings.

1. Right-click your database project in Solution Explorer, and select Properties to open the project properties window, shown in Figure 8-7.
2. On the Build tab, you specify the target database you want to deploy to. In this case, you are specifying a new database called NorthWindTestDB. When this database project is compiled, the SQL scripts will reflect that the database is to be deployed to the test server into a new database named NorthWindTestDB.

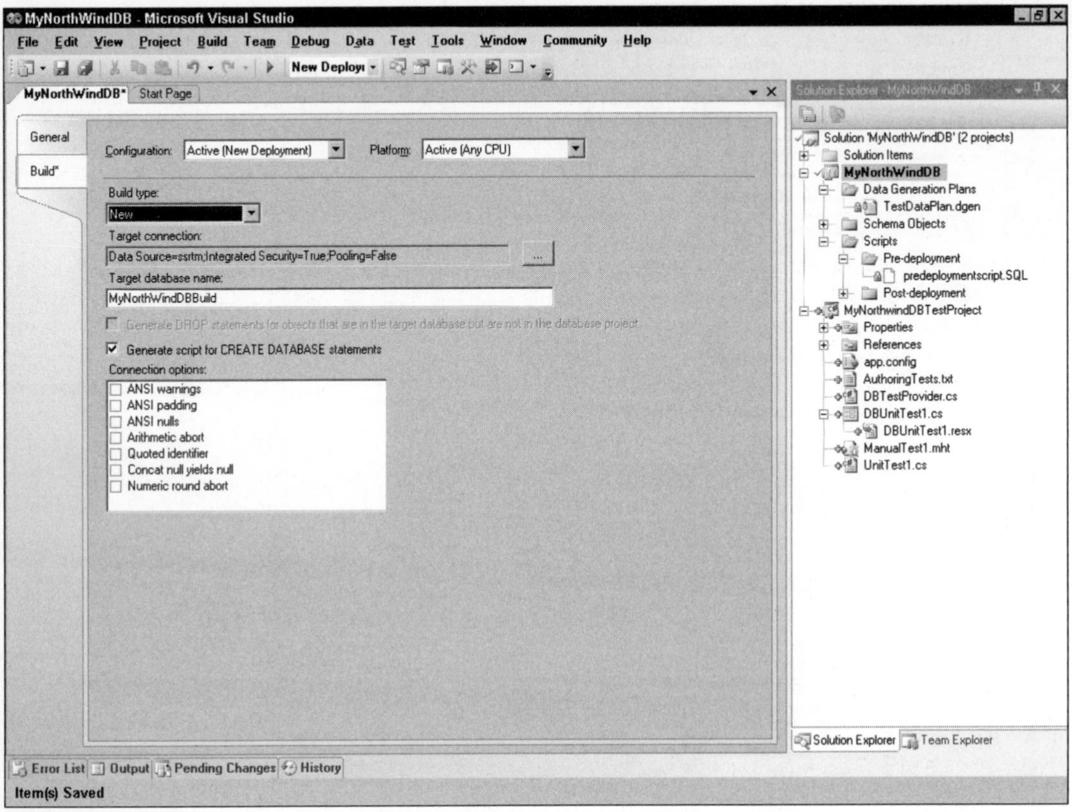

Figure 8-7

3. Save your changes and close this window.

4. To actually build your database project, right-click the database project and select Build MyNorthWindDB. The output window shows the success or failure of the build. For your test project, it should succeed. Once the project has been built, you can deploy it by right-clicking on the database project and selecting Deploy Selection. Go ahead and do this for the MyNorthWindDB project.

   If the deployment is successful, you will now see a new database on your SQL Server, named NorthWindTestDB, which contains your CreditCardNumber table. You have now created a test database for you to use with your unit testing.

One thing to consider is how you are going to deploy to an existing database. Some changes you make may require tables to be dropped and recreated, which can lead to a loss of data from that table. Team Edition for Database Developers is smart enough to realize when that might happen, and will warn you appropriately, but you should take care when deploying your updated schema, to ensure there is no data loss.

Team Edition for Database Developers allows for scripts that can run before your build script deploys, and after your build script has deployed. These scripts are not part of your database schema, but can be used to execute certain functionality during the deployment process, as necessary.

> **James Manning has blogged about how to script and monitor Team Foundation Server database jobs using PowerShell and SQL Server Management Objects (SMO). You can learn more by reading his blog post: http://blogs.msdn.com/jmanning/archive/2006/08/29/730482.aspx**

Comparing Schemas

Almost everyone has run into the situation where they have made changes to their local copy of the database while doing development, but can't remember what all their changes were. Team Edition for Database Developers also includes a nice feature called Schema Compare that helps solve this problem.

1. To get started, select Date⇨Schema Compare⇨New Schema Comparison. This opens the New Schema Comparison window, shown in Figure 8-8.

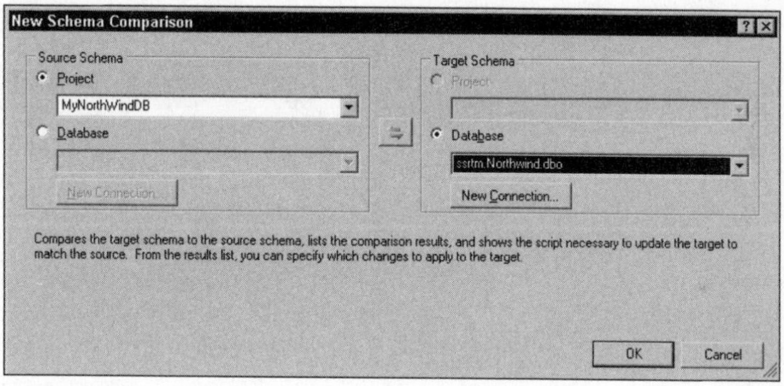

Figure 8-8

2. In this dialog, you can select your source schema and your target schema. Your source schema is usually your database project, though you could select another database if you wanted to compare the two. In the above example, you have selected your database project as the source schema, and the original production database as the target. Clicking OK begins the comparison. This may take anywhere from a few seconds to a few minutes, depending on the number of changes you have made, and the size of your database.

   Once the comparison is complete, the results will be displayed as shown in Figure 8-9.

   As you can see, there is a new table, CreditCardNumber, that does not exist in the target database, so the system is going to create this item for us. As well, it will create the stored procedure you created earlier as well. By selecting particular objects, you can view the differences between the source and target schemas. As well, at the bottom of the window you can view the SQL script that is being created dynamically for you, to make these changes in the target schema.

3. When you are satisfied, click Write Updates to make these changes to your target data source. You can also click Export to Editor to export this script to an editor, allowing you to modify it manually.

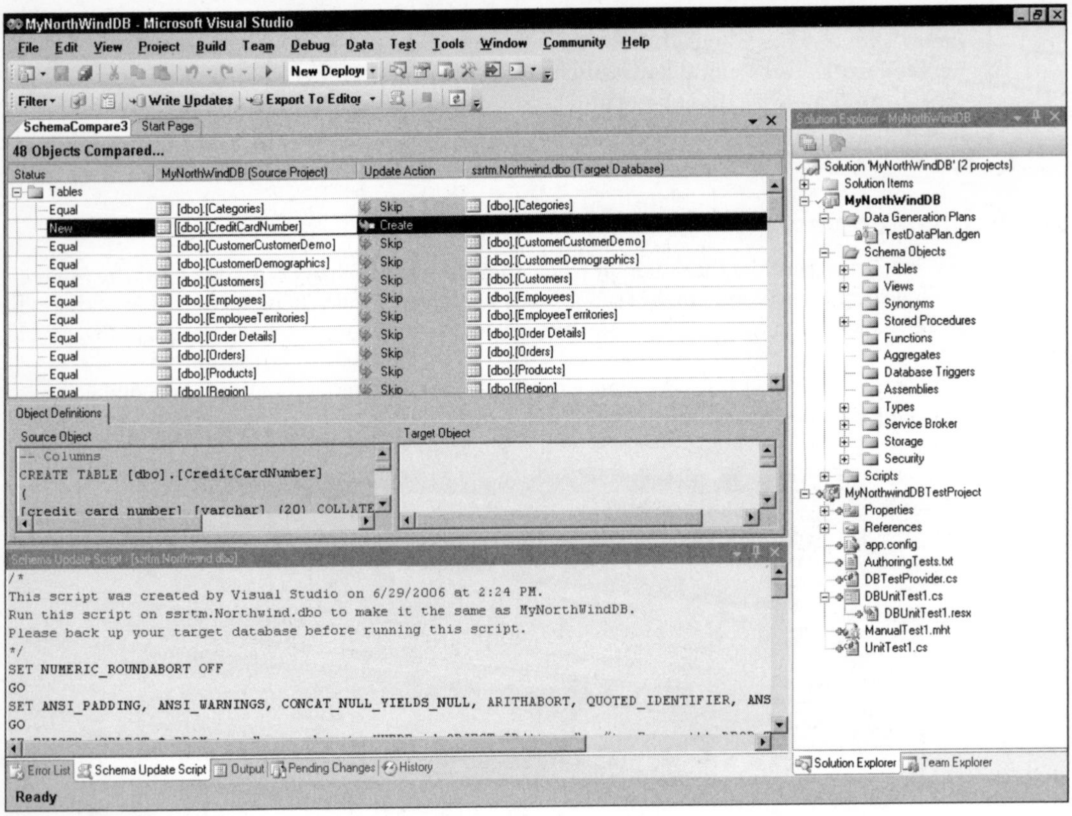

Figure 8-9

Testing

Team Edition for Database Professionals has support for unit testing built into it, allowing you to build detailed tests to verify the correctness of your database. It also supports refactoring, allowing you to change the name of a database column or table, and propagate that change throughout all the stored procedures and unit tests. Finally, a feature that will probably get a good bit of use is the data generation capabilities. Team Edition for Database Professionals will automatically generate test data for your database, freeing you to focus on more important testing matters.

Refactoring

Refactoring allows you to change a table name, and have that change automatically propagated throughout the entire database project, including your unit tests. This helps prevent errors from cropping up later in your application, due to a database change. For this example, let's change the name of the table you just created, CreditCard, to be CreditCardNumbers.

1. Right-click the CreditCard table and select Rename. This opens the Rename dialog box, as shown in Figure 8-10.

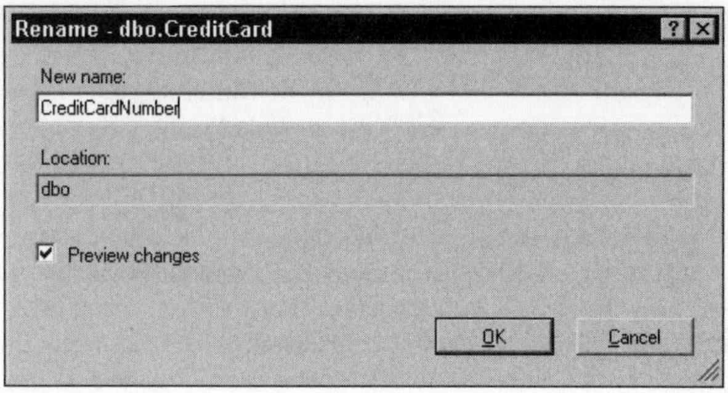

Figure 8-10

2. In this window, you enter the new name of the table, in this case **CreditCardNumber**. If you uncheck the Preview Changes check box, then the changes will be automatically propagated throughout your project. If you leave the box checked, then you will see all the changes that will be made and where they will be made. It is recommended that you leave this box checked, so you can preview the changes. Click OK to continue. Figure 8-11 shows the Preview Changes window that opens.

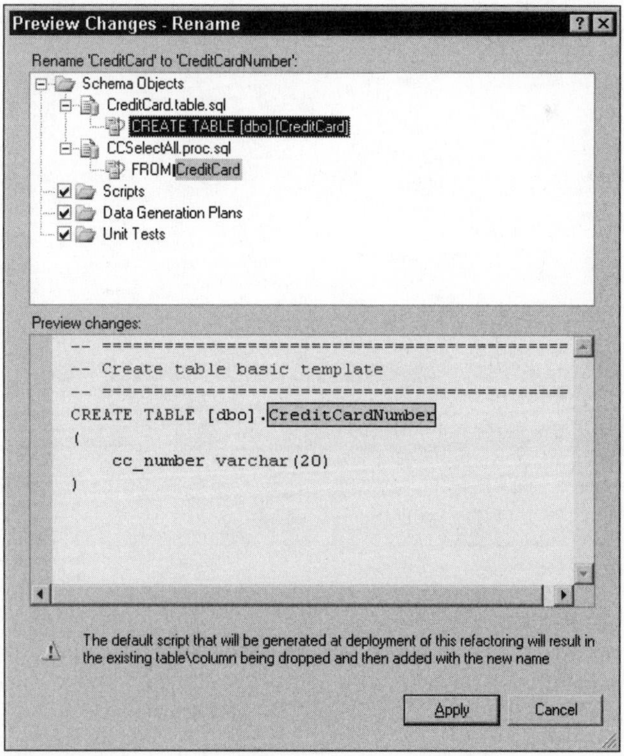

Figure 8-11

3. This window shows you all the different database objects that will be affected by the rename. In this case, the Create Table statement for the table and the CCSelectAll stored procedure will be changed. If you decide you do not want to make this change, you can click Cancel. If everything looks good, and you want to proceed, simply click Apply. This propagates the change throughout all the objects shown in the preview window.

While not exactly refactoring, so to speak, Team Edition from Database Professionals will warn you if you change a column in a table, and if that change will affect other objects in the schema. Double-click the CreditCardNumber table to open it in the editor. Change the column cc_number to be credit_card_number. When you save this change, the error list window opens, showing that the `CCSelectAll` stored procedure now contains an invalid column name, as shown in Figure 8-12.

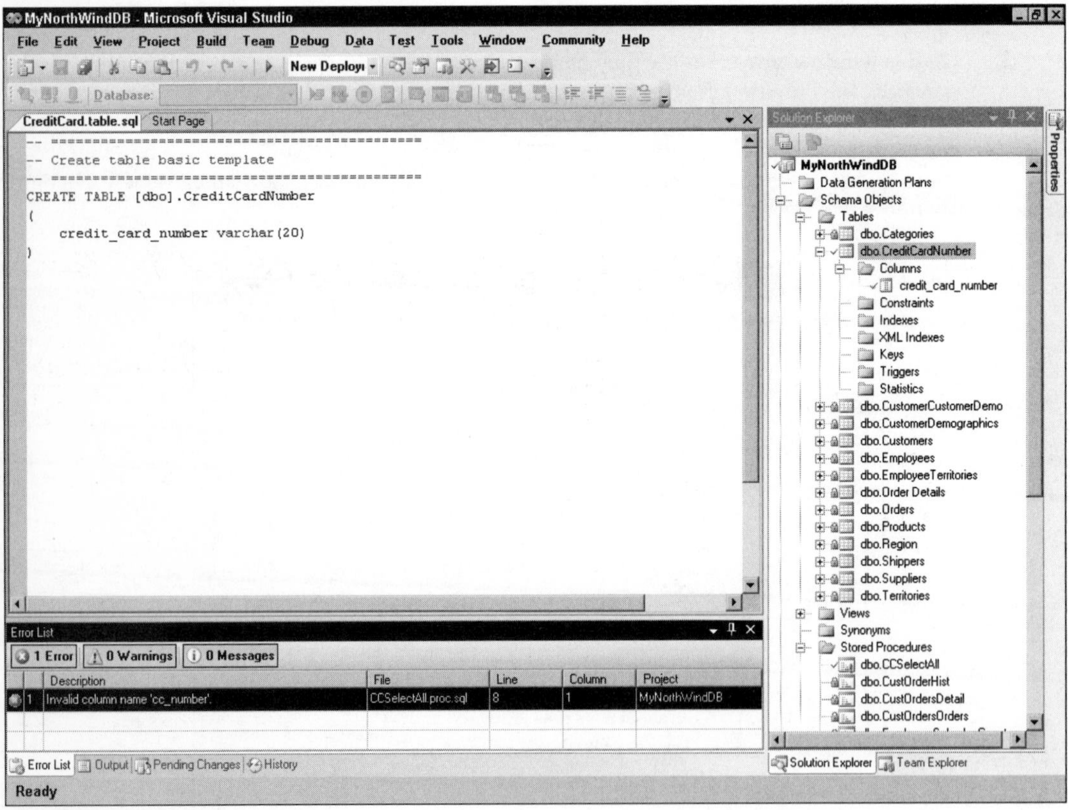

Figure 8-12

To fix this, open the `CCSelectAll` stored procedure, and change the column name to be **credit_card_number**. When you save your changes to the stored procedure, the error will disappear from the error list.

Data Generation

Data generation is probably the coolest and definitely one of the most useful features of Team Edition for Database Professionals. Data generation allows you to fill your database with test data. This data is based off the different column types in each of your tables, but it is gibberish, meaning that you can get meaningful results from the data, to verify your application is working, without having to worry about using sensitive data. No more siphoning data from your production database, or spending hours entering test data into your test database. By using data generation, with a few simple clicks, you can be up and running with test data.

Using the Data Generator, you can create either random or nonrandom data. You can run the data generator by itself, to populate your database, or you can tie it together with your unit tests, setting up the data in the database appropriately before the tests are run. The Data Generator supports the use of regular expressions, allowing you to format the data as you would like it. And finally, the Data Generator is fully extensible, allowing you to build your own data generator to create test data as you see fit.

Data generation starts with a data generation plan.

1. Right-click the Data Generation Plans folder in your database project, and select Add➪Data Generation Plan.
2. In the Add New Item window, enter a name for your plan, or accept the default. For this example, change the name to be **TestDataPlan**, and click Add. The data generation plan is created and opens in Visual Studio, as shown in Figure 8-13.

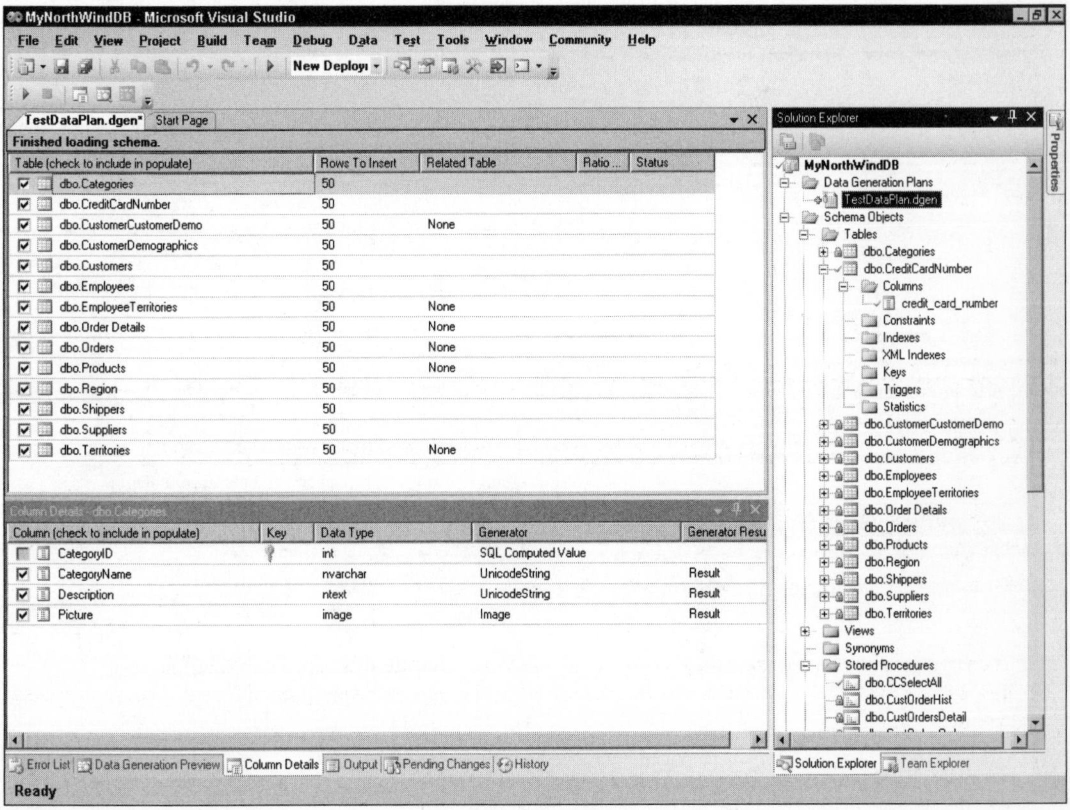

Figure 8-13

This window contains a lot of information. The top portion of the window shows all the tables in your database schema. It also shows how many rows will be added to this table. If you have a column in a table that is a foreign key in another table, the Related Table column allows you to tie those two tables together, making sure the foreign key matches correctly. Moreover, the Ratio to Related Table column allows you to specify the number of rows in the primary and any related tables, such as a one-to-one correspondence. You can select which tables to generate data for by selecting or deselecting them in the check box to the left. If the table you uncheck has a foreign key relationship to another table, you will not be able to completely uncheck the table until the related table is also unchecked. That is a safeguard to make sure there is data in all the required tables.

As you can see in Figure 8-13, the Categories table is selected in the top of the window. At the bottom of the window, you can see all the columns in the Categories table. You can select which columns you want to generate data for. You can see the data type of the column, and can specify the generator used to generate the data for that column. Team Edition for Database Professionals includes several data generators out of the box. Some of the included generators are ones for creating integers, floating point numbers, and strings, just to name a few. If you select a column, you can view the property information for the data generator selected for that column.

3. Select the CategoryName column of the Categories database, and view the Property window, as shown in Figure 8-14.

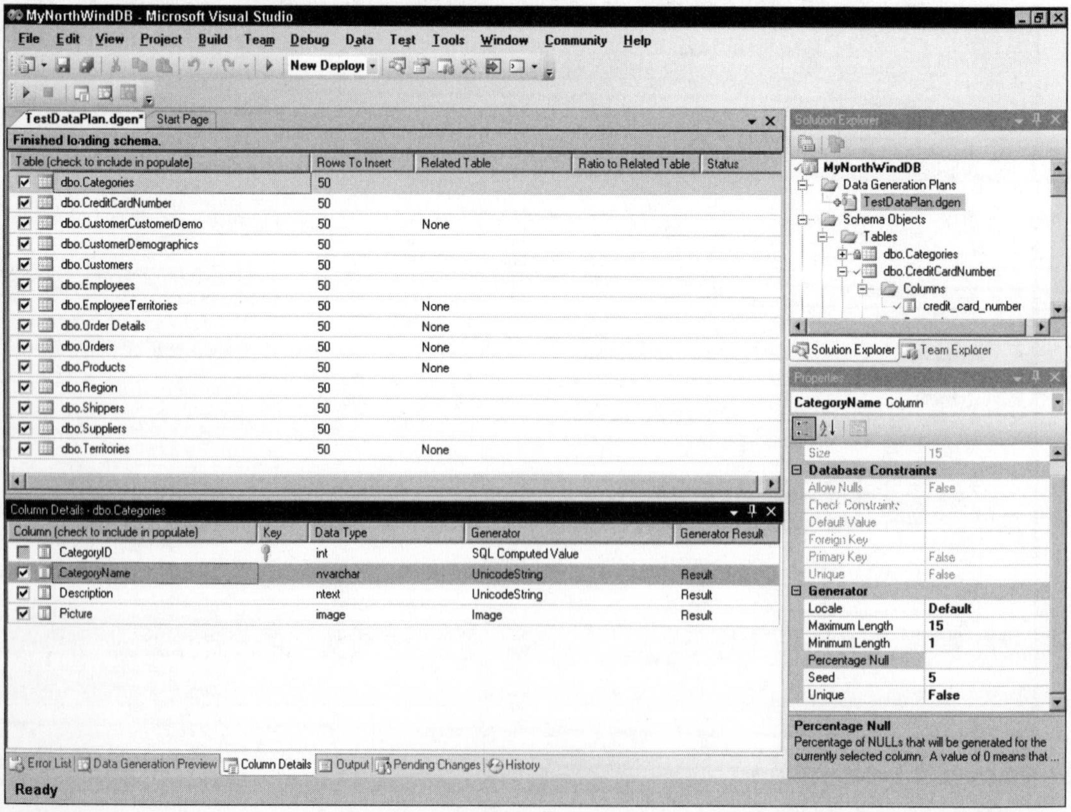

Figure 8-14

The property window allows you to configure the different aspects of the data generator for that column. For the above column, you can set the minimum and maximum length, and whether the column is unique or not. As well, you can specify how many of the column entries should be null, and can set the seed value that helps to generate the random values.

4. Uncheck all the tables in this data generation plan, and then check the CreditCardNumber table, so it is the only one selected. Select the CreditCardNumber table you created earlier. Select the credit_card_number column, and change the Generator value to be RegularExpression.

5. You can use regular expressions to create your random data in the database, allowing you more control over the data. For this example, you want numbers that are 16 digits, so you are going to use a regular expression to accomplish this. Go to the Properties window for this column, and set the Expression value to [0–9]{16}. This will generate a 16-digit number, which is what you want.

But how can you be sure the data will look like you want it to? If you look at Figure 8-13, you'll notice a tab at the bottom called Data Generation Preview. This tab shows you what the generated data will look like, before it is actually created, enabling you to verify it is how you wanted it. Figure 8-15 shows an example of this tab for the regular expression you just created.

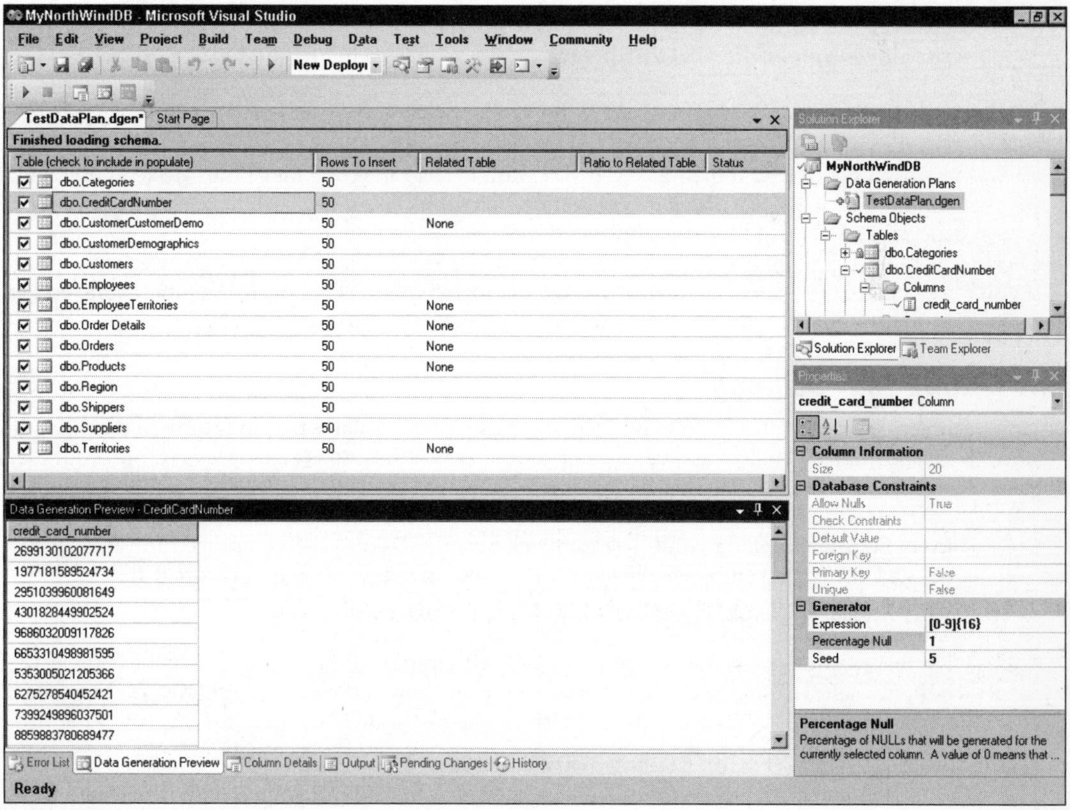

Figure 8-15

6. Notice the data are 16-digit numbers, similar to credit card numbers. However, some of the numbers are invalid, as credit cards do not normally start with a one or a two. You will address this later in the chapter when you develop a custom data generator for credit card numbers. For the time being, accept this limitation.

You can create a data generation plan that contains all the tables in the database, a plan for each individual table, or any combination in between. Use data generation in a way that makes the most sense to you. Remember, if you have added your database project to the version control system, your data generation plans are automatically version controlled as well, so make sure you check them in regularly.

At this point, you have the data generation plan, but you have not actually created or stored any data in a database.

1. To actually create the test data, open the data generation plan, then select Data⇨Data Generator⇨ Generate Data from the menu. You will be prompted to select the database you wish to generate data for.

> **Whatever you do, do not select your production database. If you do, you could overwrite all your production data with your generated data. That would be a bad thing.**

2. Select the NorthWindTestDB database that you created earlier as the target for your data generation, and click OK. You are asked if you want to clear the contents of the selected tables before continuing. Select Yes. The data generation plan thinks for a few seconds, and then displays the success or failure of the generation.

If you now open a SQL Query window and select the rows from the CreditCardNumber table, you will see the randomly generated data that was added to the table when you ran the plan.

Unit Testing Your Schema

Unit testing in Team Edition for Database Professionals works similarly to unit testing in the other versions of Visual Studio Team System. Let's create a unit test for the `CCSelectAll` stored procedure you created earlier.

1. In the Solution Explorer window, right-click the `CCSelectAll` stored procedure, and select Create Unit Tests. This opens the Create Unit Tests window, shown in Figure 8-16.

   You can select multiple stored procedures if you want.

2. For this example, name the test project **MyNorthwindTestProject**, make sure the CCSelectAll button is selected, and click OK. This starts the creation of the test project. You are prompted to select a database to execute your unit tests against, as shown in Figure 8-17.

3. Select the NorthwindTest database you created earlier. You can also choose to have your database schema deployed for you before the tests are run, and you can choose to have your data generation plan run before the tests are run. For your example, leave these unselected. Click OK to generate your test project.

   The unit test you have created will open for you automatically, as shown in Figure 8-18.

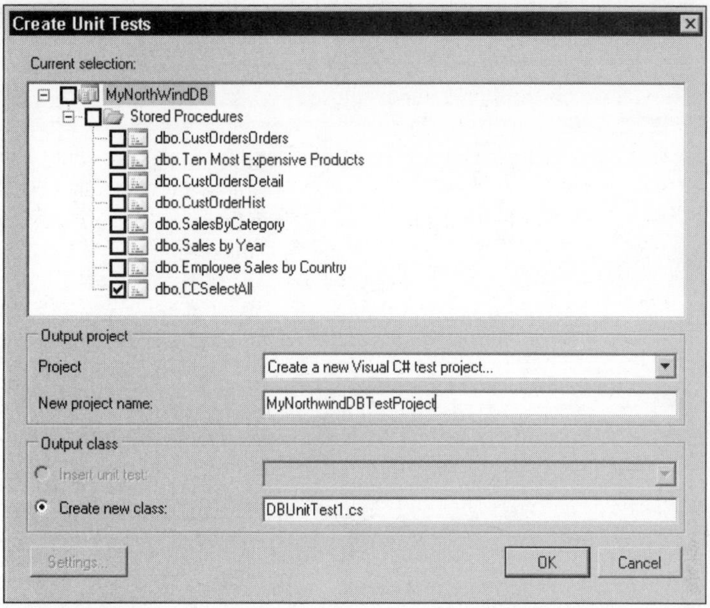

Figure 8-16

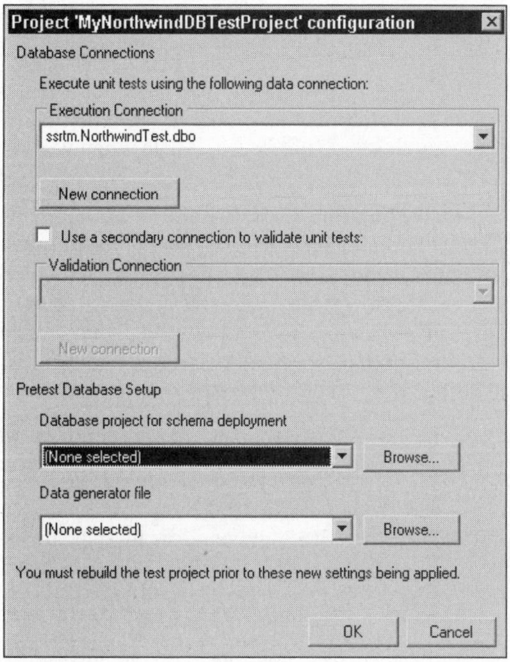

Figure 8-17

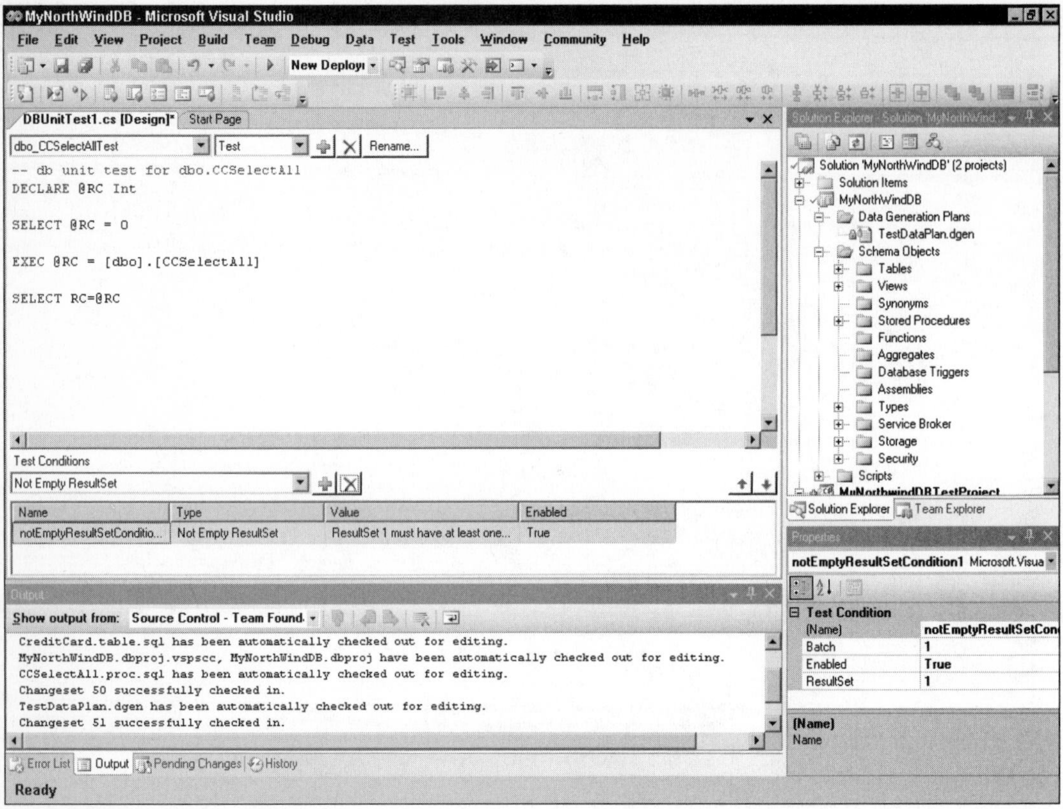

Figure 8-18

As you can see, the unit testing for stored procedures is slightly different than unit testing regular code. Initially it provides a nicer, high-level way to look at the testing, but don't worry, you can delve down into the C# code to create some detailed tests. For this example, you are going to stick with the high-level view. This unit test is going to call the `CCSelectAll` stored procedure. Pretty simple really. Notice that you can declare some test conditions for which you want to test. Team Edition for Database Professionals ships with several default test conditions, and you can add more if you want.

For this example, you are expecting a nonempty result set to be returned from the call to this stored procedure. You can easily add multiple test conditions by selecting them from the drop-down list box and clicking the plus sign.

4. To run this test, simply open the Test View window by selecting Test⇨Windows⇨Test View. Right-click the dbo_CCSelectAllTest and click Run Selection, just as you would any other unit test. As Figure 8-19 shows, the test has run successfully.

At this point, you can do anything else you would normally do, including publishing the test results to Team Foundation Server.

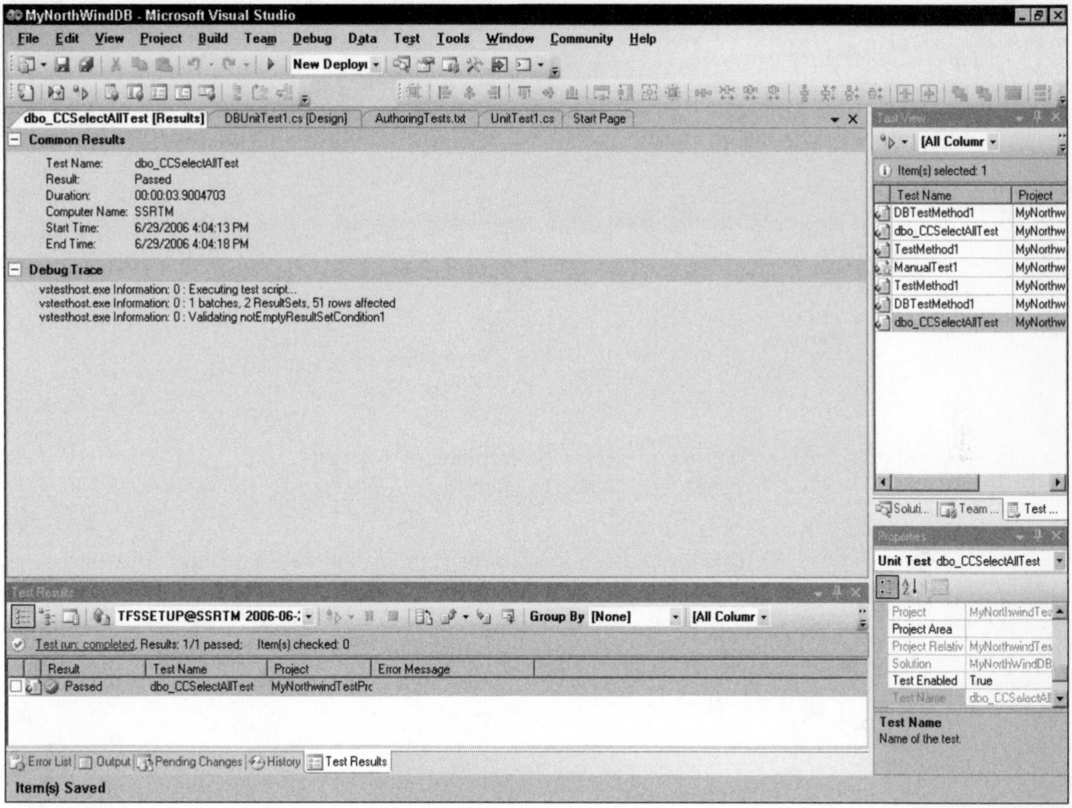

Figure 8-19

Building a Custom Data Generator

While the default data generators are very useful, especially the regular expression one, there may be times when those data generators just don't do quite what you want them to. At that point, you will need to create a custom data generator. In this section, you walk step-by-step through creating a custom data generator for credit card numbers. This data generator will create Visa (number begins with a four) or MasterCard (number begins with a five) numbers, and will even add dashes between the numbers as an optional setting.

1. To get started, create a new C# class library project in Visual Studio and name it **CreditCardNumberdg**.
2. Rename the Class1 file to be **CCNum**.
3. Next, add a reference to the Microsoft.VisualStudio.TeamSystem.Data.dll. This DLL is located at `c:\Program Files\Microsoft Visual studio 8\DBPro`. Once you have added that reference, add the following using statement to the top of your CCNum.cs file:

```
using Microsoft.VisualStudio.TeamSystem.Data.DataGenerator;
```

4. Add the `Generator()` attribute to the top of the `CCNum` class declaration:

```
[Generator()]
Public class CCNum
{
...
}
```

5. Your class also needs to inherit from the `Generator` abstract class, so make the following change:

```
[Generator()]
Public class CCNum : Generator
{
...
}
```

6. Right-click the Generator word, and select Implement Abstract Class, to stub out all the methods you must implement for this class. The only required method it creates is the `GenerateNextValues()` method.

7. Next, you want to create the input properties for your custom data generator. These properties can be set from the Properties window of Visual Studio. To create an input property, you create a public property and add the `Input()` attribute. Take the following code:

```
            public enum CreditCardTypes
{
V,
M,
A
}
private string _ccNumber;
private CreditCardTypes _creditCardType = CreditCardTypes.A;
private bool _includeDashes;


[Input()]
public CreditCardTypes CreditCardType
{
set { _creditCardType = (CreditCardTypes)value; }
}

[Input()]
public bool IncludeDashes
{
set { _includeDashes = value; }
}
```

First, you declared an enumerated type called `CreditCardTypes`. This type contains three values: `V` for Visa, `M` for MasterCard, or `A` for all numbers. Next you declared three variables. `_ccNumber` is our final credit card number. `_creditCardType` is the type of credit card to create. `_includeDashes` is a Boolean value that determines whether to include dashes in the credit card number.

Now you get to the two input properties. The first one, `CreditCardTypes`, creates a drop-down list of values for the user to choose from for the type of credit card to create. The second, `IncludeDashes`, allows the user to set this to true or false.

8. You have your input properties, and now need an output property. You declare a private variable to hold the credit card number, but you need a public property, decorated with the `Output()` attribute, to access this value.

```
        [Output()]
public string ccNumber
{
get { return _ccNumber; }
}
```

This creates a public property, `ccNumber`, which contains the credit card number.

9. The final coding step is to implement the GenerateNextValues method. This method is required, and is responsible for creating the actual test data. Here is the method for the example:

```
public override void GenerateNextValues()
{
Random randomNumber = new Random();



int tempNumber;
int i;
_ccNumber = "";

if (_creditCardType == CreditCardTypes.M)
_ccNumber = "5";
else if (_creditCardType == CreditCardTypes.V)
_ccNumber = "4";
else if (_creditCardType == CreditCardTypes.A)
{
tempNumber = randomNumber.Next(10);

_ccNumber = tempNumber.ToString();
}

for (i = 2; i <= 16; i++)
{
///Thread.Sleep(1);
tempNumber = randomNumber.Next(10);
_ccNumber += tempNumber.ToString();
if ((_includeDashes) && ((i % 4) == 0) && (i != 16))
_ccNumber += "-";
}

}
```

This method uses a random number generator to create the credit card numbers. First, it initializes the random number generator. Next, it checks to see which type of credit card was selected, and sets the first digit in the credit card number to the appropriate value. It then proceeds to loop fifteen times, creating the credit card number. It also checks to see if dashes are to be included in the number, and adds them as appropriate.

You have now created a custom data generator. However, you are not done yet. Next, you must sign your custom data generator with a strong name, before you register it.

1. To do this, right-click the project in Solution Explorer, and click Properties. On the properties window, check the Sign the assembly check box.

2. Select New File from the drop down-list box, and enter **ccnum.txt** as the key file name. Uncheck the Protect my key file with a password check box. Now save your changes to your project properties.

   Before you go any farther, save all your files and make sure your class library will build. If it does not, fix any errors, and then continue.

   Once you have created your generator, and signed it, you have to register it with Visual Studio to be able to use it:

3. Open the class library project you were just working on in Visual Studio. Select View⇨Other Windows⇨Command Window to open the command window in Visual Studio. Enter the following into the command window:

```
? System.Reflection.Assembly.LoadFrom([FilePath]).FullName
```

   In this line, `[FilePath]` is the path to the compiled DLL file. For your example, this should look similar to this:

```
? System.Reflection.Assembly.LoadFrom("C:\\Documents and Settings\\TFSSETUP\\My
Documents\\Visual Studio 2005\\Projects\\CreditCardNumberdg\\CreditCardNumberdg\\
bin\\Debug\\CreditCardNumberdg.dll").FullName
```

   Running this statement results in something similar to this:

```
"CreditCardNumberdg, Version=1.0.0.0, Culture=neutral,
PublicKeyToken=4826364792c75d48"
```

4. Save this information to a text file, as you will need it shortly. You need to add this information to the `Microsoft.VisualStudio.TeamSystem.Data.Extensions.xml` file. This file contains a `<type>` entry for each data generator used by Visual Studio. The format of the tag is:

```
<type>FullyQualifiedClassName,AssemblyName,Version,Culture,PublicKeyToken</type>
```

For your example, the type tag would look like this:

```
<type>CreditCardNumberdg.CCNum, CreditCardNumberdg, Version=1.0.0.0,
Culture=neutral, PublicKeyToken=4826364792c75d48</type>
```

5. Finally, copy the DLL to the `C:\Program Files\Microsoft Visual Studio 8\Common7\IDE\PrivateAssemblies` directory. Restart Visual Studio, and you are ready to use your custom data generator.

To test this, open the MyNorthWindDB database project, and open the data generation plan you created earlier in this chapter. Select the CreditCardNumber table. Notice how, for the credit_card_number column, you now have the option, under the Generator heading, for the CCNum generator you created earlier, as shown in Figure 8-20.

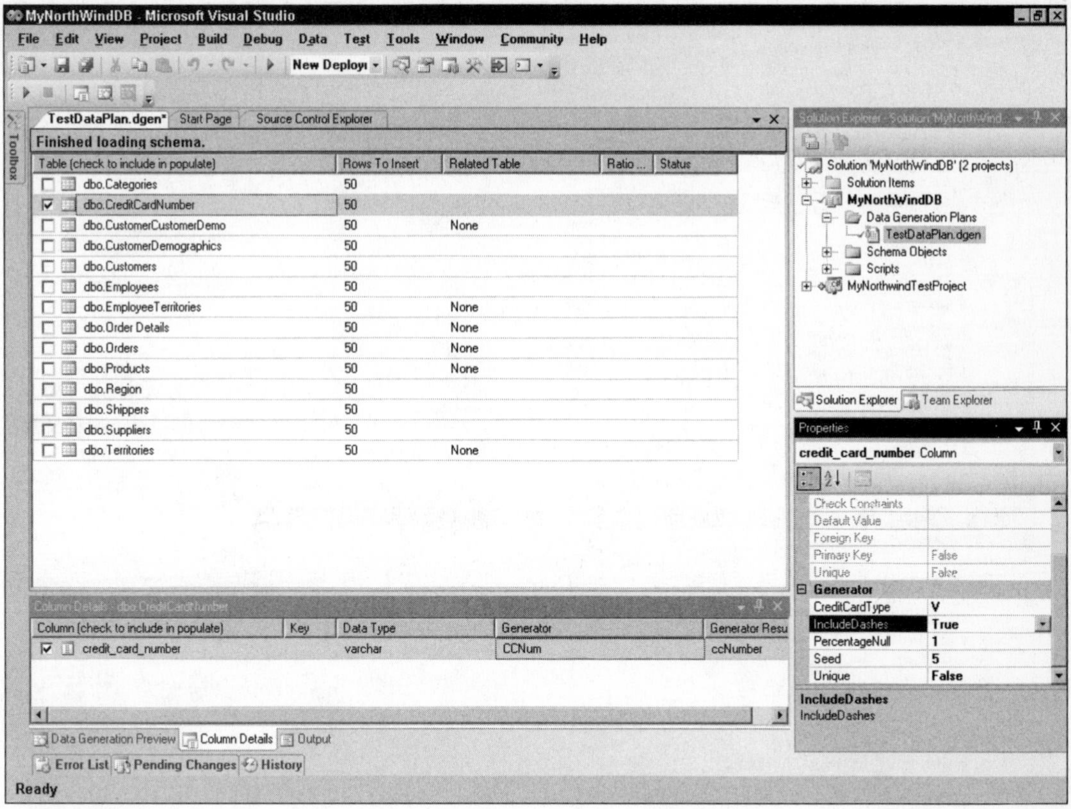

Figure 8-20

The two input options appear in the properties window. Set the CreditCardType to be V for Visa, and set the `IncludeDashes` property to `true`. If you preview the data, you will see that all the numbers begin with a `4`, indicating it is a Visa, and that the numbers are separated with dashes, as shown in Figure 8-21.

> **Notice how some of the numbers repeat. This is due to the random number generator, and how quickly the numbers are being created. You could add a pause in between each number to make each credit card number unique.**

There you have it; you have created your first custom data generator. Another possible data generator you might consider creating is a name generator, which reads names from a database or a file, and adds them to the tables. The possibilities are endless.

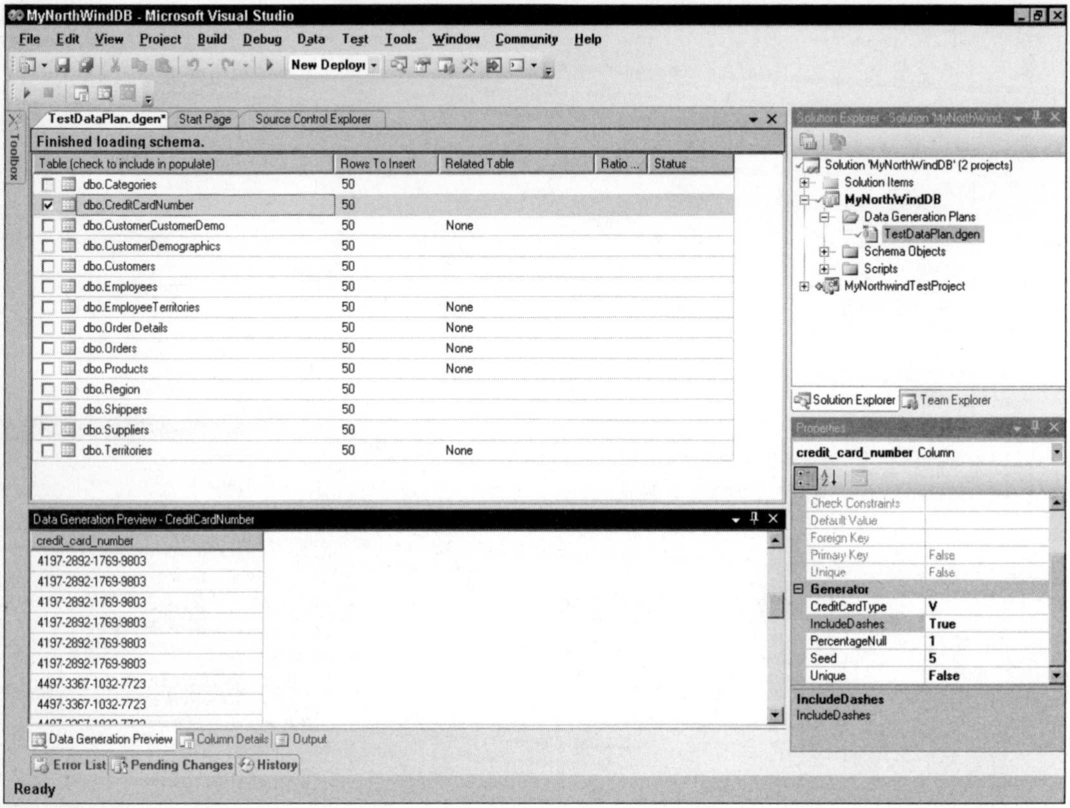

Figure 8-21

Summary

Team Edition for Database Professionals proves itself to be a much needed addition to the Team System family. In conjunction with Team Foundation Server, it provides all the tools you need to manage all the tasks necessary in the data development lifecycle.

You started out this chapter with a basic overview of Team Edition for Database Professionals, and why it is an important product. You then delved into some detailed examples of using the product, including how to import your database schema, make changes to it, deploy those changes, and implement unit testing.

You also discovered some nice new features, including schema compare, for comparing the schema of two different database, and data generation, for generating test data for your application. Finally, you covered how to create your own custom data generator to generate credit card numbers.

Part III
Extensibility and Customization

9

Creating Custom Development Tools

One of the nice things about Team Foundation Server is its extensibility. Team Foundation Server was developed from the ground up with extensibility in mind. While Microsoft tried to provide all the tools and accessories that a development team would need, they also understood that they would not be able to please everyone. As such, they have provided the tools and hooks so anyone can develop add-on tools for Team Foundation Server for a variety of scenarios. By building Team Foundation Server around the principles of objects and Web services, they have made it easy to develop custom tools that work with all the services provided by Team Foundation Server.

This chapter is all about the extensibility of Team Foundation Server, and how you can use that extensibility to build your own custom tools. You start out by looking at the differences between extensibility and customization. Then you move on to get a brief overview of the Team Foundation Core Services. These are Web services used by team foundation server itself to handle all the different functionality for Team Foundation Server.

Then you move into the real meat of the chapter, the Team Foundation Server Object Model. You will use this object model to create your own custom tools, which interact with the Team Foundation Server and the Team Foundation Core Services. Several code samples and sample tools are listed throughout this section, giving you a feel for how you can develop you own custom tools. These code samples provide you with a good starting point for delving into the object model in more detail.

Enough talk; let's start learning how to create some custom tools.

Extensibility versus Customization

Believe it or not, there is a difference between extensibility and customization.

Customization involves modifying your environment, such as Visual Studio 2005 or Team Foundation Server, using the tools that are provided by that environment. There is no coding involved. Rather, by utilizing different user interfaces, you are able to adjust the environment to your needs. Customization can be performed by almost anyone, from end users to developers to project managers.

Extensibility, on the other hand, is concerned with adding new functionality to your environment. Coding is most definitely involved in this. By extending the platform, you are able to create new tools that meet your needs and use built-in aspects of the platform in new and different ways. Such extensions are usually created by internal IT departments or third-party independent software vendors.

Customization Examples

Here are some examples of how you can customize Team Foundation Server:

- Modifying a process template
- Creating a new work item type
- Turning check-in policies on/off
- Modifying the project portal template

These are just a few of the ways you could customize Team Foundation Server. By using provided tools and modifying a few XML files, you can quickly and easily customize the server to work in the manner in which you want.

Extensibility Examples

Some examples of how you can extend Team Foundation Server include the following:

- Raise and subscribe to events
- Add pages to the project creation wizard
- Utilize the object model to create applications that access Team Foundation Server functionality
- Create new check-in policies
- Create new Team Foundation Build tasks

By using the Team Foundation Server Object Model and the Team Foundation Core Services, you can easily extend Team Foundation Server in a variety of ways.

Team Foundation Core Services

The Team Foundation Core Services (TFCS) are a set of services, running on the application tier, which allow you access to different aspects of Team Foundation Server, including administration, security, and events. TFCS consists of five services:

- **Classification service** — Provides access to Team Project information.
- **Eventing service** — Provides access to events thrown by Team Foundation Server
- **Linking service** — Provides ability to link items together, such as work items and files that are version controlled
- **Registration service** — Points Team Foundation Server to the correct tools and services
- **Security service** — Provides ability to manage groups, users, and permissions

These services are implemented as Web services, and are used by Team Explorer and the different areas of Team Foundation Server. When utilizing the Team Foundation Core Services, you should not call the Web services directly. Instead, you should use the Team Foundation Object Model to interact with the Team Foundation Core Services. Microsoft will provide backward compatibility with the object model only, not the Web services, so you should use the object model to ensure your applications work with future versions of Team Foundation Server.

In the following sections, you will learn about each service and what it does. You can learn even more about the Team Foundation Core Services and the Team Foundation Object Model by downloading the Visual Studio 2005 SDK. This SDK contains documentation and examples of both the Team Foundation Core Services and the Team Foundation Object Model, as well as examples on how to extend Team Foundation Server in other ways. You can find it at `http://affiliate.vsipmembers.com`. Membership with the Visual Studio Industry Partner program is required, but membership is free. Just sign up and download the SDK.

Classification Service

The classification service provides access to Team Project information, including the Team Project name and URI, as well as access to the areas and iterations of a Team Project. Remember, the Area and Iterations section of a Team Project is essentially the structure of the project. This service allows you to view project information, and make changes to a project's structure. An example of using this service would be to populate a drop-down list box in your custom tool from which users could select a Team Project. They could then proceed to use your custom tool on the selected Team Project,

Using this service, you can create Team Projects, delete Team Projects, and access all the different properties of your Team Project.

The common pattern for accessing the object model is to first create a connection to the server. Once you have connected to the server, the next step is to ask for a service to use. You will see this in more detail later in this chapter. To access the classification service, you make use of the `ICommonStructureService` service type of the Team Foundation Object Model.

Eventing Service

Team Foundation Server uses events to enable its different services to be loosely coupled. The eventing service is a publish/subscribe system. Third parties can build tools that integrate with Team Foundation Server and register events related to their tools. Team Foundation Server also comes with several preregistered events, such as for work item tracking and version control. For example, Team Foundation Server throws a `WorkItemChanged` event every time a modification is made to a work item.

Users can subscribe to events. When a user subscribes to an event, he can choose to either receive an e-mail concerning that event, or trigger a Web service. When an event is raised, Team Foundation Server looks through its list of subscribed events and triggers the appropriate response.

The Visual Studio 2005 SDK includes a tool called bissubscribe.exe, which you can use to register a user for events. See the section entitled "Example: Subscribe to an Event" later in this chapter for details on using this tool.

To access the eventing service, you make use of the `IEventService` service type of the Team Foundation Object Model.

Linking Service

The linking service allows you to create loosely coupled tools that can offer lightweight data integration. Simply put, by using a standard way to identify the different items in a tool, such as work items used by work item tracking and version control items used by version control, you can link your work items and version control items together, without the different tools knowing the details of the stored data of the other tool.

The linking service does this using the concept of artifacts. Because of this loose coupling, the linking service provides you with a way to discover all the artifacts in Team Foundation Server. In addition, the extensibility of Team Foundation Server allows you to use the linking and registration services to create your own tools and artifacts, and link them with others already in the system. While you can still take the tightly coupled approach if you want, it is recommended you make use of the linking service, to make your tools as extensible. This allows your tools to be used by other tools you might not even know about, such as future parts of Team Foundation Server that have not even been developed yet.

So, what is an artifact? An *artifact* is a piece of information that a tool exposes and that other tools can refer to. For example, a work item is an artifact of the Work Item Tracking tool. An artifact has two required properties, an artifact identifier and an artifact type. To understand the concept of an artifact identifier, you need to understand about Uniform Resource Identifiers (URIs).

The artifact identifier is simply the URI for that artifact. Here is the general syntax for a URI:

```
vstfs:///<tooltype>/<artifacttype>/<tool id>
```

The syntax can be parsed as follows:

- `vstfs` is a custom protocol used by Team Foundation Server. It is converted to a URL and used in that way.
- `<tooltype>` is the interface of the tool that is responsible for answering questions about the artifact. For example, for a work item, the tooltype is `WorkItemTracking`.
- `<artifacttype>` is the specific artifact type for that tool. A tool can handle requests for multiple artifact types. For the Work Item Tracking tool, the artifact type is `WorkItem`.
- `<tool id>` is the unique ID to a particular artifact identifiable by your tool. For example, you might have a work item that has been assigned a number of 50. In this case, the specific tool ID would be 50.

Given the previous example, a URI for work item 52 would be:

```
vstfs:///WorkItemTracking/WorkItem/52
```

For detailed documentation on the linking service, refer to the documentation included with the Visual Studio 2005 SDK.

To access the linking service, you make use of the `ILinking` service type of the Team Foundation Object Model.

Registration Service

The registration service is used to help direct calls to Team Foundation Server to the correct services and tools. Using tools provided with Team Foundation Server, located on the application tier server at `C:\Program Files\Microsoft Visual Studio 2005 Team Foundation Server\Tools`, you can register your tools, artifacts, events, and link types that you have created with Team Foundation Server. You can then use the Team Foundation Object Model to query this registered information for all the tools in Team Foundation Server.

To access the registration service, you make use of the `IRegistration` service type of the Team Foundation Object Model.

Security Service

The security service gives you the ability to manage all the groups, users, and access permissions in Team Foundation Server. There are two primary areas of the security service, Group Security and Authorization.

The Group Security area allows you to manage all the different Team Foundation Server application groups and membership to those groups. The Authorization area allows you to manage the access control lists for the Team Foundation Server.

To access the security service, you make use of the `IGroupSecurityService` and `IAuthorizationService` service types of the Team Foundation Object Model.

Subscribing to an Event

As mentioned earlier when talking about the Eventing Service of the Team Foundation Core Services, there is a tool included with the Visual Studio 2005 SDK which allows you to use the eventing service to subscribe to events. This tool is called bissubscribe`.exe`.

To download the SDK, point your browser to `http://affiliate.vsipmembers.com`. To download the SDK, you must register with the Visual Studio Industry Partner's program. Registration is free and quick.

Once you have downloaded and installed the SDK, look for a folder in the installation directory named `VisualStudioTeamSystemIntegration`. It contains a Utilities directory, and in that folder is a ZIP file called Event Subscription Tool. This zip file contains the bissubscribe utility. Look at the read-me file included in the ZIP file, to determine the correct spot to copy the utility on your machine.

The general syntax for the bissubscribe utility is:

```
Bissubscribe /eventType <MyEvent> /userId <MyDomain\MyId> /address
<MyEmailOrSoapAddress> /deliveryType <EmailHtml|EmailPlainText|Soap> /domain
<MyDomain> /filter <MyFilterString /tag <MyTag>
```

The syntax can be parsed as follows:

- **eventType** — The name (case-sensitive) of the event to which you want to subscribe
- **filter** — A filter expression, if needed
- **userId** — The domain and username for the subscriber
- **address** — The e-mail address or Web service URL for the subscriber
- **tag** — A name that can be used to later identify this subscription
- **domain** — The name of the Team Foundation Server

Let's say you wanted to subscribe to the `ProjectCreatedEvent`. Every time a new Team Project is created, you want to receive an e-mail. Here is the syntax for subscribing a user named User1 located in Domain1:

```
Bissubscribe /eventType ProjectCreatedEvent /userId Domain1\User1 /address
user1@domain1.com /deliveryType EmailPlainText /domain mytfs /tag
User1EmailSubscription1
```

Any time a new team project is created, a `ProjectCreatedEvent` will fire. Team Foundation Server looks through its list of subscribers, finds where User1 subscribed to the `ProjectCreatedEvent`, and sends an e-mail with the creation details to User1.

Team Foundation Server Object Model

Extensibility starts with the Team Foundation Server Object Model (TFSOM). This object model allows you to create applications that can communicate with the application tier of Team Foundation Server. Think of the TFSOM as an API for working with Team Foundation Server. Utilizing the TFSOM, you can work with the following pieces of Team Foundation Server:

- Team Foundation Core Services
- Version Control Object Model
- Work Item Tracking Object Model
- Team Build Object Model
- Team Foundation Data Warehouse Object Model

The Version Control Object Model and the Work Item Tracking Object Model allow you to interact with the version control system and work items, respectively. You will learn more about these in Chapters 11 and 12.

Figure 9-1 shows a visual representation of the extensibility of Team Foundation Server.

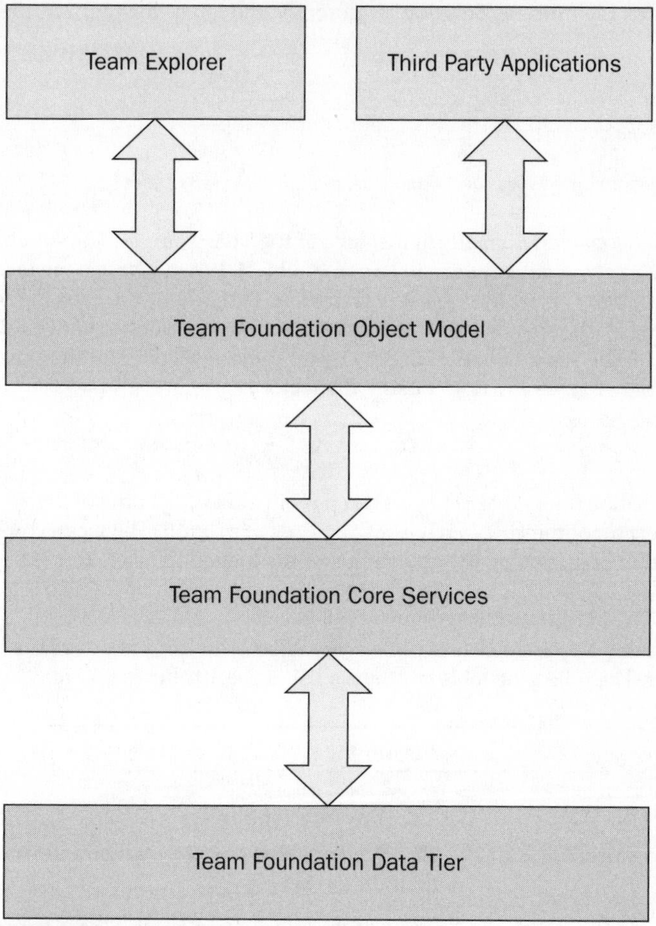

Figure 9-1

The TeamFoundationServer Object

The `TeamFoundationServer` object is where you start with the TFSOM. It contains the basic attributes of the Team Foundation Server. In addition, it provides access to the Team Foundation Core Services, as well as any other services that have been registered with Team Foundation Server, such as version control and work item tracking.

To get started, open Visual Studio 2005 and create a new C# console application. Before you can begin using the `TeamFoundationServer` object, you need to add some references to the Team Foundation Server DLLs to your project. In the Solution Explorer, right-click the References folder and select Add Reference. This opens the Add Reference window. Click the Browse tab, and browse to `C:\Program Files\Microsoft Visual Studio 8\Common7\IDE\PrivateAssemblies`. This directory contains all the Team Foundation Server DLLs. Select the `Microsoft.TeamFoundation.dll` and the `Microsoft.TeamFoundation.Client.dll` files, and click OK.

Open the Program.cs file from the Solution Explorer. At the top of the file, add the following two using statements:

```
using Microsoft.TeamFoundation;
using Microsoft.TeamFoundation.Client;
```

You can now begin working with the `TeamFoundationServer` object.

The first thing you need to do is create an instance of the `TeamFoundationServer` object. You do that using the `TeamFoundationServerFactory` object. When you use the factory to create the `TeamFoundationServer` object, the object is cached, so that any future calls to the object use the same instance. This increases the speed of your application, because it does not have to go through the authentication process with the Team Foundation Server with every call. Here is the sample line of code to create a `TeamFoundationServer` object using the factory:

```
TeamFoundationServer tfs = TeamFoundationServerFactory.GetServer("MSTFS");
```

When making the call to `GetServer()` you can pass in either the name of the Team Foundation Server you want to connect to, or the URL, such as `http://mstfs:8080`. The factory will try to authenticate to the Team Foundation Server using the credentials of the logged on user. You can specify a different user, if you wish.

Once you have created a `TeamFoundationServer` object, you can access various attributes of the Team Foundation Server. The following table contains a list of the attributes you may be interested in:

Attribute Name	Meaning
AuthenticatedUserName	The user that has authenticated to the Team Foundation Server
ClientCacheDirectoryForInstance	The directory that contains cached information for Team Foundation Server
Culture	The culture information for the Team Foundation Server
HasAuthenticated	Tells whether the `TeamFoundationServer` object has authenticated with the Team Foundation Server
InstanceId	Instance ID information for Team Foundation Server
Name	Name of the Team Foundation Server
TimeZone	The time zone for the Team Foundation Server
URI	The Uniform Resource Identifier (URI) for the Team Foundation Server

In your console application, to write out these attributes, you can use the `Console.Writeline()` function. Here is an example of writing out the name and URI of the `TeamFoundationServer` object:

```
Console.Writeline("Name = " + tfs.Name);
Console.Writeline("URI = " + tfs.URI.ToString());
```

The `TeamFoundationServer` object also has several methods, including methods used to authenticate and ensure authentication against the Team Foundation Server, methods used to add and remove services to Team Foundation Server, and a method, called `GetService()`, which is used to access the Team Foundation Core Services, version control system, and work item tracking System.

Here is the code for the Program.cs file of the console application called chp9TFS, to create a `TeamFoundationServer` object and write out its attributes. This sample takes the name of your Team Foundation Server as a command-line argument:

```
using System;
using System.Collections.Generic;
using System.Text;
using Microsoft.TeamFoundation;
using Microsoft.TeamFoundation.Client;

namespace chp9TFS
{
class Program
{
static void Main(string[] args)
{
TeamFoundationServer tfs =
TeamFoundationServerFactory.GetServer(args[0].ToString());

//Write out information about the Team Foundation Server
Console.WriteLine("AuthenticatedUserName = " + tfs.AuthenticatedUserName);
Console.WriteLine("ClientCacheDirectoryForInstance = " +
tfs.ClientCacheDirectoryForInstance);
Console.WriteLine("Culture = " + tfs.Culture.ToString());
Console.WriteLine("HasAuthenticated = " + tfs.HasAuthenticated.ToString());
Console.WriteLine("InstanceId = " + tfs.InstanceId.ToString());
Console.WriteLine("Name = " + tfs.Name);
Console.WriteLine("TimeZone = " + tfs.TimeZone.StandardName);
Console.WriteLine("Uri = " + tfs.Uri.ToString());


}
}
}
```

If you run this code, you should see output similar to Figure 9-2.

Accessing the Service Interfaces

Using the `TeamFoundationServer` object, you can access the Team Foundation Core Services, as well as the version control and work item tracking systems. To gain access to these services, you use the `GetService()` method of the `TeamFoundationServer` object:

```
public object GetService (Type serviceType)
```

For example, to return a `VersionControlServer` object, you would use the following code:

```
VersionControlServer vcs =
(VersionControlServer)tfs.GetService(typeof(VersionControlServer));
```

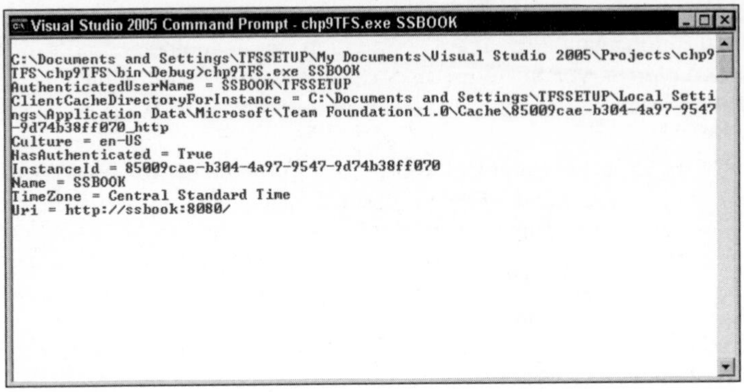

Figure 9-2

Notice how the `GetService()` method returns an object. Therefore, you have to cast the object into the appropriate type. Once you have cast the object into the appropriate type, you can begin accessing that service. In the above example, you could now begin interacting with the Team Foundation Server Version Control system.

The following table lists the different service types that can be used with the `GetService()` method:

Service Type	Used To
IAuthorizationService	Interact with the security service
ICommonStructureService	Interact with the classification service
IEventService	Interact with the eventing service
IGroupSecurityService	Interact with the security service
ILinking	Interact with the linking service
IProcessTemplates	Work with Team Foundation Server process templates
IRegistration	Interact with the registration service
IServerStatusService	Access the Team Foundation Server status
VersionControlServer	Interact with the Team Foundation Server version control system
WorkItemStore	Interact with the Team Foundation Server work item tracking system

The following sections cover each of these services in more detail, including sample code.

IAuthorizationService

`IAuthorizationService` returns an authorization object for interacting with the security service of the Team Foundation Core Services. To access this service type, you need to add the following `using` statement to your code:

```
using Microsoft.TeamFoundation.Server;
```

To create an authorization object, you use the following code:

```
IAuthorizationService a =
(IAuthorizationService)tfs.GetService(typeof(IAuthorizationService));
```

The authorization object allows you to view and make changes to access permissions on objects in Team Foundation Server. While the `IGroupSecurityService` is responsible for creating the application groups, the `IAuthorizationService` is responsible for the access permissions on those groups.

The following code shows the Program.cs file for a console application named chp9IAuthorization, which displays, for all the top level objects in the Team Foundation Server, the access control list options for those objects:

```
using System;
using System.Collections.Generic;
using System.Text;
using Microsoft.TeamFoundation;
using Microsoft.TeamFoundation.Client;
using Microsoft.TeamFoundation.Server;

namespace chp9IAuthorization
{
class Program
{
static void Main(string[] args)
{
TeamFoundationServer tfs =
TeamFoundationServerFactory.GetServer(args[0].ToString());

IAuthorizationService a =
(IAuthorizationService)tfs.GetService(typeof(IAuthorizationService));

foreach (string s in a.ListObjectClasses())
{
Console.WriteLine("Object String = " + s.ToString());
foreach(string s2 in a.ListObjectClassActions(s))
{
Console.WriteLine("Object Actions = " + s2.ToString());
}

Console.WriteLine("\n");
}
Console.ReadLine();
}

}
}
```

Figure 9-3 shows the output from running this sample application.

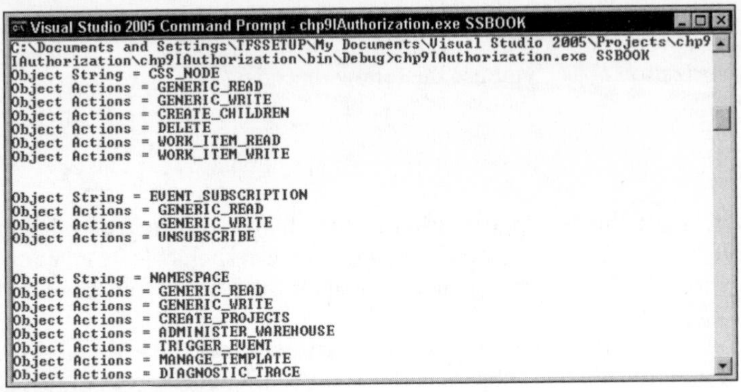

Figure 9-3

ICommonStructureService

The `ICommonStructureService` service type returns a classification object for interacting with the classification service of the Team Foundation Core Services. To access this service type, you need to add the following `using` statement to your code:

```
using Microsoft.TeamFoundation.Server;
```

To create a registration object, you use the following code:

```
ICommonStructureService r =
(ICommonStructureService)tfs.GetService(typeof(ICommonStructureService));
```

The classification object allows you to do a variety of things, including modify the Areas and Iterations section of a project, create projects, delete projects, and review project properties. To access the project information for a particular project, you can use the `GetProjectFromName()` method of the classification object:

```
ProjectInfo ICommonStructureService.GetProjectFromName(string projectName)
```

This returns a project info object. This object contains the project name, status, and URI, as well as any extended project properties.

You can also use the `ListStructures()` method of the classification object to list the different structures located in the areas and iteration section of the Team Project:

```
NodeInfo[] ICommonStructureService.ListStructures(string projectUri)
```

This method returns detailed information on the top level structures, including their name, the URI of their parent node, and their own URI, to name a few.

The following code shows the Program.cs file for a console application named chp9ICSS. This application displays the project name, status, and URI for each project in the Team Foundation Server. It also lists the top-level structures in the Areas and Iterations section for each project.

```
using System;
using System.Collections.Generic;
using System.Text;
using Microsoft.TeamFoundation;
using Microsoft.TeamFoundation.Client;
using Microsoft.TeamFoundation.Server;
using System.Xml;
using System.Collections;

namespace chp9ICSS
{
class Program
{
static void Main(string[] args)
{
TeamFoundationServer tfs =
TeamFoundationServerFactory.GetServer(args[0].ToString());

ICommonStructureService css =
(ICommonStructureService)tfs.GetService(typeof(ICommonStructureService));

string sName;
string sState;
int intTemplateId;
ProjectProperty[] pp;


foreach (ProjectInfo pi in css.ListAllProjects())
{
Console.WriteLine("\n");
Console.WriteLine("ProjectInfo Name = " + pi.Name);
Console.WriteLine("ProjectInfo Status = " + pi.Status);
Console.WriteLine("ProjectInfo Uri= " + pi.Uri);


css.GetProjectProperties(pi.Uri, out sName, out sState, out intTemplateId, out pp);

Console.WriteLine("GetProjectProperties Name = " + sName);
Console.WriteLine("GetProjectProperties State = " + sState);
Console.WriteLine("GetProjectProperties TemplateId = " + intTemplateId.ToString());

foreach (ProjectProperty p in pp)
{
Console.WriteLine("ProjectProperty Name = " + p.Name);
Console.WriteLine("ProjectProperty Value = " + p.Value);
}


foreach (NodeInfo ni in css.ListStructures(pi.Uri))
{
Console.WriteLine("NodeInfo Name = " + ni.Name);
Console.WriteLine("NodeInfo ParentURI = " + ni.ParentUri);
Console.WriteLine("NodeInfo Path = " + ni.Path);
Console.WriteLine("NodeInfo ProjectURI = " + ni.ProjectUri);
Console.WriteLine("NodeInfo StructureType = " + ni.StructureType);
```

```
Console.WriteLine("NodeInfo URI = " + ni.Uri);

foreach (Property p in ni.Properties)
{
Console.WriteLine("NodeInfoProperty Name = " + p.Name);
Console.WriteLine("NodeInfoProperty Value = " + p.Value);
}

}

}

}
}
}
```

Figure 9-4 shows the output from running this sample application.

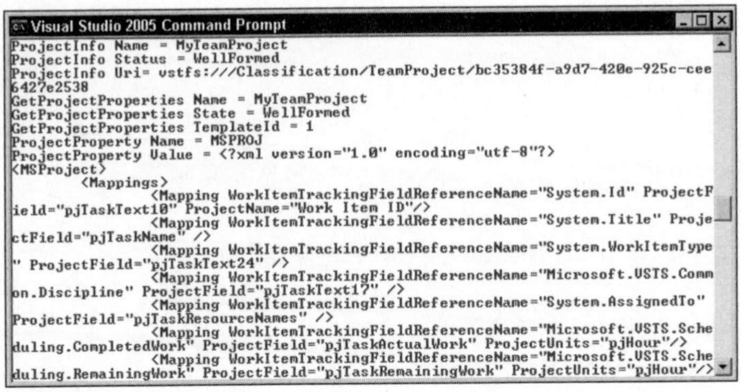

Figure 9-4

The XML values you see in the output are the mappings between Team Foundation Server Work Item Tracking fields and Microsoft Project fields. This mapping is what allows you to synchronize information between the two.

IEventService

The `IEventService` service type returns an event object for interacting with the eventing service of the Team Foundation Core Service. To access this service type, you need to add the following `using` statement to your code:

```
using Microsoft.TeamFoundation.Server;
```

To create a reference to the event service, you use the following code:

```
IEventService es = (IEventService)tfs.GetService(typeof(IEventService));
```

The event object allows you to subscribe to events using `SubscribeEvent()`, unsubscribe from events using `UnsubscribeEvent()`, view the event subscriptions for a given user using `EventSubscriptions()`, and even trigger an event using `FireAsyncEvent()`.

Several different events are configured by default for Team Foundation Server. You can view these by running the `chp9IRegistration` program presented later, or by viewing the `tbl_event_type` in the TfsIntegration database on the data tier. Some of the events are listed as follows:

- AclChangedEvent
- BuildCompletionEvent
- BuildStatusChangedEvent
- BranchMovedEvent
- CheckinEvent
- CommonStructureChangedEvent
- DataChangedEvent
- IdentityChangedEvent
- IdentityCreatedEvent
- IdentityDeletedEvent
- MembershipChangedEvent
- NodeCreatedEvent
- NodePropertiesChangedEvent
- NodeRenamedEvent
- NodeDeletedEvent
- ProjectCreatedEvent
- ProjectDeletedEvent
- WorkItemChangedEvent
- CheckinEvent

The following code shows the Program.cs file for a console application named chp9IEventService, which displays the registered event information for a user. This console application takes two arguments: the name of the Team Foundation Server and the domainname\username for the user in question.

```
using System;
using System.Collections.Generic;
using System.Text;
using Microsoft.TeamFoundation;
using Microsoft.TeamFoundation.Client;
using Microsoft.TeamFoundation.Server;

namespace chp9IEventService
{
```

```
class Program
{
static void Main(string[] args)
{
TeamFoundationServer tfs =
TeamFoundationServerFactory.GetServer(args[0].ToString());

IEventService es = (IEventService)tfs.GetService(typeof(IEventService));

DeliveryPreference dp = new DeliveryPreference();

foreach (Subscription s in es.EventSubscriptions(args[1].ToString()))
{
Console.WriteLine("\n");
Console.WriteLine("Subscriber = " + s.Subscriber);
Console.WriteLine("Condition String = " + s.ConditionString);
Console.WriteLine("Device = " + s.Device);
Console.WriteLine("EventType = " + s.EventType);
Console.WriteLine("ID = " + s.ID.ToString());
Console.WriteLine("Tag = " + s.Tag);

dp = s.DeliveryPreference;

Console.WriteLine("Delivery Preference - Address = " + dp.Address);
Console.WriteLine("Delivery Preference - Schedule = " + dp.Schedule);
Console.WriteLine("Delivery Preference - Type = " + dp.Type);
}
}
}
}
```

This application retrieves the subscription information for a user. For each subscription, it prints the subscription information, including the delivery preferences.

Figure 9-5 shows the output from running this sample application for the SSBOOK Team Foundation Server and the TFSSERVICE user.

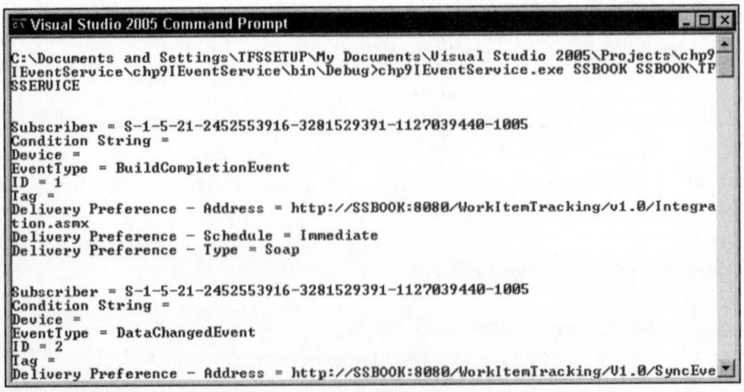

Figure 9-5

IGroupSecurityService

The `IGroupSecurityService` type returns a group-security object for interacting with the security service of the Team Foundation Core Services. To access this service type, you need to add the following `using` statement to your code:

```
using Microsoft.TeamFoundation.Server;
```

To create a group-security object, you use the following code:

```
IGroupSecurityService gss =
(IGroupSecurityService)tfs.GetService(typeof(IGroupSecurityService));
```

The group-security object allows you to create and delete application groups, add and remove members from application groups, and list all the groups for a particular project.

The following code shows the Program.cs file for a console application named chp9IGSS, which displays, for every project in the Team Foundation Server, the application groups and related information:

```
using System;
using System.Collections.Generic;
using System.Text;
using Microsoft.TeamFoundation;
using Microsoft.TeamFoundation.Client;
using Microsoft.TeamFoundation.Server;

namespace chp9IGSS
{
class Program
{
static void Main(string[] args)
{
TeamFoundationServer tfs =
TeamFoundationServerFactory.GetServer(args[0].ToString());

IGroupSecurityService gss =
(IGroupSecurityService)tfs.GetService(typeof(IGroupSecurityService));
ICommonStructureService css =
(ICommonStructureService)tfs.GetService(typeof(ICommonStructureService));

foreach (ProjectInfo pi in css.ListAllProjects())
{
Console.WriteLine("\n");
Console.WriteLine("Project Name = " + pi.Name);
foreach (Identity i in gss.ListApplicationGroups(pi.Uri))
{
Console.WriteLine("\n");
Console.WriteLine("Account Name = " + i.AccountName);
Console.WriteLine("Deleted = " + i.Deleted.ToString());
Console.WriteLine("Description = " + i.Description);
Console.WriteLine("Display Name = " + i.DisplayName);
Console.WriteLine("Distinguished Name = " + i.DistinguishedName);
Console.WriteLine("Domain = " + i.Domain);
```

```
    Console.WriteLine("Mail Address = " + i.MailAddress);
    Console.WriteLine("Security Group = " + i.SecurityGroup.ToString());
    Console.WriteLine("SID = " + i.Sid);

    }
    }
    }
    }
    }
```

Notice how this code uses the `ICommonStructureService` type to retrieve the project URI for each project, and then using this URI, retrieves the application groups using the group-security service object.

Figure 9-6 shows the output from running this sample application.

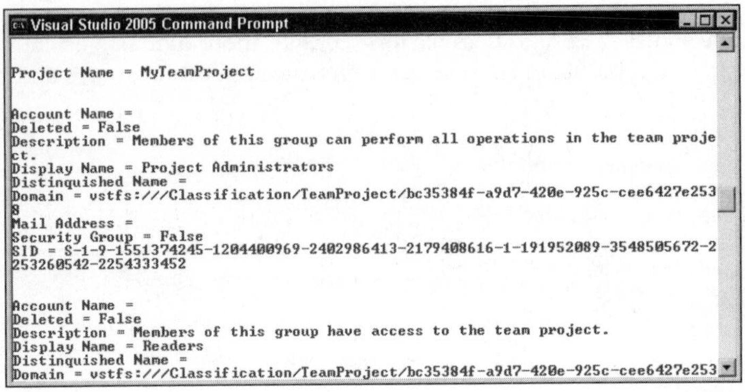

Figure 9-6

ILinking

The `ILinking` service type returns a linking object for interacting with the linking service of the Team Foundation Core Services. To access this service type, you need to add the following `using` statement to your code:

```
using Microsoft.TeamFoundation.Server;
```

You also need to add a reference to the `Microsoft.TeamFoundation.Common.dll`, located at `C:\Program Files\Microsoft Visual Studio 8\Common7\IDE\PrivateAssemblies`.

To create a linking object, you use the following code:

```
ILinking link = (ILinking)tfs.GetService(typeof(ILinking));
```

The linking object allows you to retrieve artifact information, based on artifact URIs, using the `GetArtifacts()` method. Using the `GetArtifactUrl()` method, you can retrieve the URL of an artifact, based on its URI. Finally, using the `GetReferencingArtifacts()` method, you can retrieve a list of referencing artifacts, based on an artifact URI.

Remember that a well-formed URI consists of the following syntax:

```
vstfs:///<tooltype>/<artifacttype>/<tool-specific-id>
```

If you run the chp9IRegistration application listed earlier, you can see, for the WorkItemTracking linking entry type, there is a tool type called WorkItemTracking, with an artifact type called Workitem. Using the Team Explorer, you can run a report to view all work items for a particular project. Each work item is assigned a specific number, such as 32. So a well-formed URI for a Workitem in the WorkItemTracking tool would be:

```
vstfs:///WorkItemTracking/WorkItem/32
```

Using the GetArtifactUrl() method of the linking object, you can obtain a URL, which allows you to view this work item in a Web browser:

```
string url = link.GetArtifactUrl("vstfs:///WorkItemTracking/WorkItem/32");
```

This returns a URL of http://<your-TFS-Server>:8080//WorkItemTracking/WorkItem.aspx?artifactMoniker=32, which, when you put into your Web browser, returns something similar to Figure 9-7.

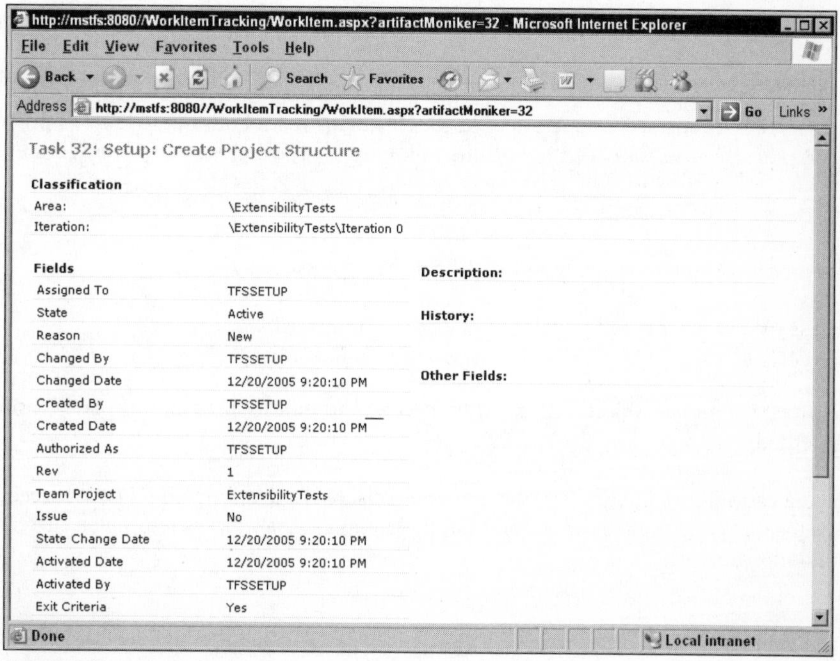

Figure 9-7

The following code shows the Program.cs file for a console application named chp9ILinking, which displays the URL for a given URI:

```
using System;
using System.Collections.Generic;
using System.Text;
using Microsoft.TeamFoundation;
using Microsoft.TeamFoundation.Client;
using Microsoft.TeamFoundation.Server;

namespace chp9ILinking
{
class Program
{
static void Main(string[] args)
{
TeamFoundationServer tfs =
TeamFoundationServerFactory.GetServer(args[0].ToString());

ILinking link = (ILinking)tfs.GetService(typeof(ILinking));

string url = link.GetArtifactUrl("vstfs:///WorkItemTracking/WorkItem/32");

Console.WriteLine("Artifact URL = " + url);
}
}
}
```

IProcessTemplates

The `IProcessTemplates` service type is used to work with Team Foundation Server process templates. To access this service type, you need to add the following `using` statement to your code:

```
using Microsoft.TeamFoundation.Server;
```

To create a process template object, you use the following code:

```
IProcessTemplates pt =
(IProcessTemplates)tfs.GetService(typeof(IProcessTemplates));
```

Using the process template object, you can add, delete, and modify process templates, using a variety of different methods.

The following code shows the Program.cs file for a console application named chp9IProcessTemplates, which calls the `GetTemplateNames()` method, to display all the process templates currently on the Team Foundation Server:

```
using System;
using System.Collections.Generic;
using System.Text;
using Microsoft.TeamFoundation;
using Microsoft.TeamFoundation.Client;
using Microsoft.TeamFoundation.Server;
using System.Xml;

namespace chp9IProcessTemplates
{
```

```
class Program
{
static void Main(string[] args)
{
TeamFoundationServer tfs =
TeamFoundationServerFactory.GetServer(args[0].ToString());

IProcessTemplates pt =
(IProcessTemplates)tfs.GetService(typeof(IProcessTemplates));

XmlNode xn = pt.GetTemplateNames();

Console.WriteLine("\n");
Console.WriteLine("Template Names Inner XML = " + xn.InnerXml.ToString());

Console.WriteLine("\n");

XmlNodeList nl = xn.SelectNodes("/Template");
Console.WriteLine("Nodelist count = " + nl.Count.ToString());

for (int i = 0; i < nl.Count; i++)
{
Console.WriteLine("NodeList Item#\t" + i + " " + nl.Item(i).InnerText);
}
}
}
}
```

Figure 9-8 shows the output from running this sample application.

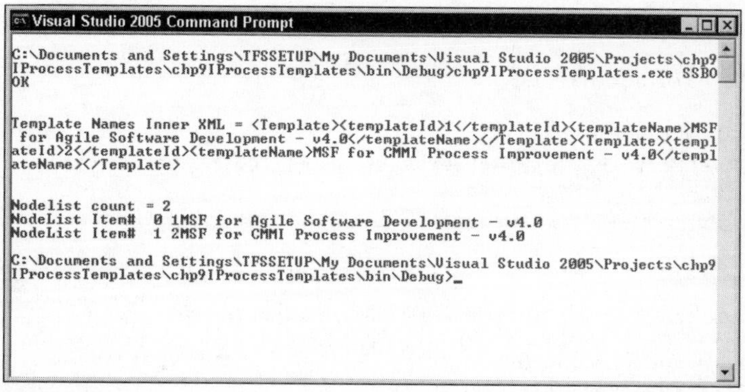

Figure 9-8

IRegistration

The `IRegistration` service type returns a registration object for interacting with the registration service of the Team Foundation Core Services. This allows you to view registration information for tools already registered with Team Foundation Server, as well as register your own tools. To access this service type, you need to add the following `using` statement to your code:

```
using Microsoft.TeamFoundation.Server;
```

To create a registration object, you use the following code:

```
IRegistration r = (IRegistration)tfs.GetService(typeof(IRegistration));
```

The registration object contains multiple registration entries. To access those entries, you use the `GetRegistrationEntries()` method of the registration object:

```
RegistrationEntry[] IRegistration.GetRegistrationEntries(string toolId)
```

The `toolId` is the tool you want to retrieve the registration information for, for example `VersionControl`. If you use an empty string, `""`, in the method call, it will return registration information for all the tools registered with Team Foundation Server.

This method returns a collection of `RegistrationEntry` objects. Each of these objects contains a particular tool that has been registered with Team Foundation Server. From these objects, you can list the tool information, including its associated artifacts, databases, events, extended attributes, and service interfaces.

The following code shows the Program.cs file for a console application named chp9IRegistration, which displays some the registration information for the WorkItemTracking system:

```
using System;
using System.Collections.Generic;
using System.Text;
using Microsoft.TeamFoundation;
using Microsoft.TeamFoundation.Client;
using Microsoft.TeamFoundation.Server;

namespace chp9IRegistration
{
class Program
{
static void Main(string[] args)
{
TeamFoundationServer tfs =
TeamFoundationServerFactory.GetServer(args[0].ToString());

IRegistration r = (IRegistration)tfs.GetService(typeof(IRegistration));

foreach (RegistrationEntry re in r.GetRegistrationEntries("WorkItemTracking"))
{
Console.WriteLine("\n");
Console.WriteLine("Registration Entry Type = " + re.Type);
Console.WriteLine("Registration Entry Change Type = " + re.ChangeType.ToString());

foreach (ArtifactType at in re.ArtifactTypes)
{
Console.WriteLine("ArtifactTypeName = " + at.Name);

foreach (OutboundLinkType olt in at.OutboundLinkTypes)
{
Console.WriteLine("OutboundLinkTypeName = " + olt.Name);
```

```
Console.WriteLine("OutboundLinkTypeTargetArtifactTypeName = " +
olt.TargetArtifactTypeName);
Console.WriteLine("OutboundLinkTypeTargetArtifactTypeTool = " +
olt.TargetArtifactTypeTool);

}

}

foreach (Database db in re.Databases)
{
Console.WriteLine("DbConnectionString = " + db.ConnectionString);
Console.WriteLine("DbDatabaseName = " + db.DatabaseName);
Console.WriteLine("DbExludeBackup = " + db.ExcludeFromBackup);
Console.WriteLine("DbName = " + db.Name);
Console.WriteLine("DbSQLServerName = " + db.SQLServerName);
}

foreach (EventType et in re.EventTypes)
{
Console.WriteLine("Event Type Name = " + et.Name);
//Console.WriteLine("\n" + "Event Type Schema = " + et.Schema + "\n");
}

foreach (RegistrationExtendedAttribute rea in re.RegistrationExtendedAttributes)
{
Console.WriteLine("Reg Extended Att. Name = " + rea.Name);
Console.WriteLine("Reg Extended Att. Value = " + rea.Value);
}
foreach (ServiceInterface si in re.ServiceInterfaces)
{
Console.WriteLine("Service Interface Name = " + si.Name);
Console.WriteLine("Service Interface URL = " + si.Url);
}

}
}
}
}
```

This code retrieves the list of registration objects. For each object, it writes out the artifact, database, event, and extended attribute information.

Figure 9-9 shows the output from running this sample application.

To view the registration information for all registered items, change this line of code:

```
foreach (RegistrationEntry re in r.GetRegistrationEntries("WorkItemTracking"))
```

to

```
foreach (RegistrationEntry re in r.GetRegistrationEntries(""))
```

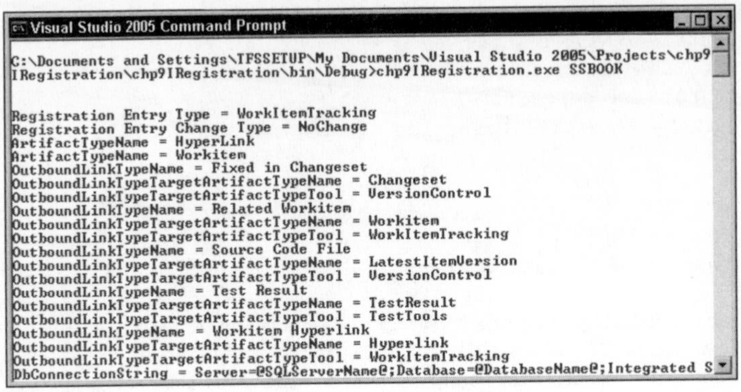

Figure 9-9

IServerStatusService

The `IServerStatusService` service type is used to access the Team Foundation Server status. To access this service type, you need to add the following `using` statement to your code:

```
using Microsoft.TeamFoundation.Server;
```

To create a server status object, you use the following code:

```
IServerStatusType a = (IServerStatusType)tfs.GetService(typeof(IServerStatusType));
```

The primary method of the server status object is the `GetServerStatus()` method. This method returns a collection of `DataChanged` objects, containing two objects. These two objects shows the last time an access control list was changed on the server, and the last time an identity was changed on the server. You might be interested in the access control list change if you were conducting a security audit, and wanted to know the last time someone had modified security on the Team Foundation Server.,

The following code shows the Program.cs file for a console application named chp9IServerStatus, which calls the `GetServerStatus()` method:

```
using System;
using System.Collections.Generic;
using System.Text;
using Microsoft.TeamFoundation;
using Microsoft.TeamFoundation.Client;
using Microsoft.TeamFoundation.Server;


namespace chp9IServerStatus
{
class Program
{
static void Main(string[] args)
{
```

```
TeamFoundationServer tfs =
TeamFoundationServerFactory.GetServer(args[0].ToString());

IServerStatusService s =
(IServerStatusService)tfs.GetService(typeof(IServerStatusService));


foreach (DataChanged dc in s.GetServerStatus())
{
Console.WriteLine("DC DataType = " + dc.DataType);
Console.WriteLine("DC Last Modified = " + dc.LastModified.ToShortDateString());
Console.WriteLine("DC ToString() = " + dc.ToString());
Console.WriteLine("\n");
}
}
}
}
```

This application retrieves the server status information into `DataChanged` objects, and then outputs the contents of those objects to the screen.

Figure 9-10 shows the output from running this sample application.

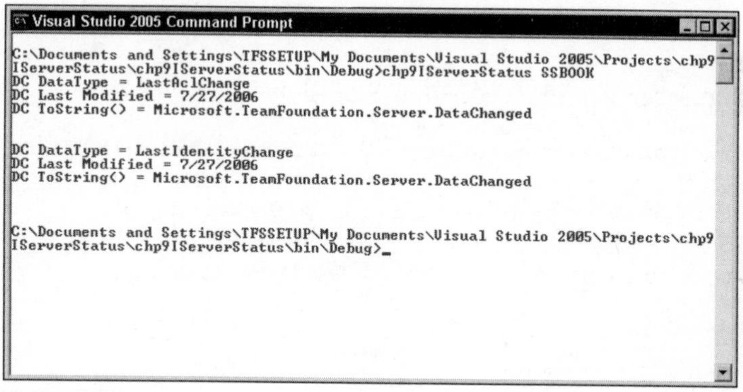

Figure 9-10

VersionControlServer

The `VersionControlServer` service type is used to interact with the Team Foundation Server version control system. To access this service type, you need to add a reference to the `Microsoft.TeamFoundation.VersionControl.Client.dll`. You also need the following `using` statements to your code:

```
using Microsoft.TeamFoundation.Server;
using Microsoft.TeamFoundation.VersionControl;
using Microsoft.TeamFoundation.VersionControl.Client;
```

To create a version-control server object, you use the following code:

```
VersionControlServer vcs =
(VersionControlServer)tfs.GetService(typeof(VersionControlServer));
```

Using the version-control server object, you have full control over the version control system. You can query information, and add, edit, or delete information from the version control system. You learn more about the version control system and using the Team Foundation Object Model with it in Chapter 12.

The following code shows the Program.cs file for a console application named chp9VersionControlServer, which displays some of the information related to the latest changeset in the system.

```
using System;
using System.Collections.Generic;
using System.Text;
using Microsoft.TeamFoundation;
using Microsoft.TeamFoundation.Client;
using Microsoft.TeamFoundation.Server;
using Microsoft.TeamFoundation.VersionControl;
using Microsoft.TeamFoundation.VersionControl.Client;

namespace chp9VersionControlServer
{
class Program
{
static void Main(string[] args)
{
TeamFoundationServer tfs =
TeamFoundationServerFactory.GetServer(args[0].ToString());

VersionControlServer vcs =
(VersionControlServer)tfs.GetService(typeof(VersionControlServer));

Changeset cs = vcs.GetChangeset(vcs.GetLatestChangesetId());

Console.WriteLine("\n");
Console.WriteLine("ChangeSet ID = " + cs.ChangesetId.ToString());
Console.WriteLine("Comment = " + cs.Comment);
Console.WriteLine("Committer = " + cs.Committer);
Console.WriteLine("Creation Date = " + cs.CreationDate.ToShortDateString());
Console.WriteLine("Owner = " + cs.Owner);
}
}
}
```

This application uses the `GetLatestChangeset()` method to retrieve the latest changeset from the version control system, and then outputs the contents of that changeset to the screen.

Figure 9-11 shows the output from running this sample application.

WorkItemStore

The `WorkItemStore` service type is used to interact with the Team Foundation Server work item tracking system. To access this service type, you need to add a reference to the `Microsoft.TeamFoundation.WorkItemTracking.Client.dll`. You also need the following `using` statements to your code:

```
using Microsoft.TeamFoundation.Server;
using Microsoft.TeamFoundation.WorkItemTracking;
using Microsoft.TeamFoundation.WorkItemTracking.Client;
```

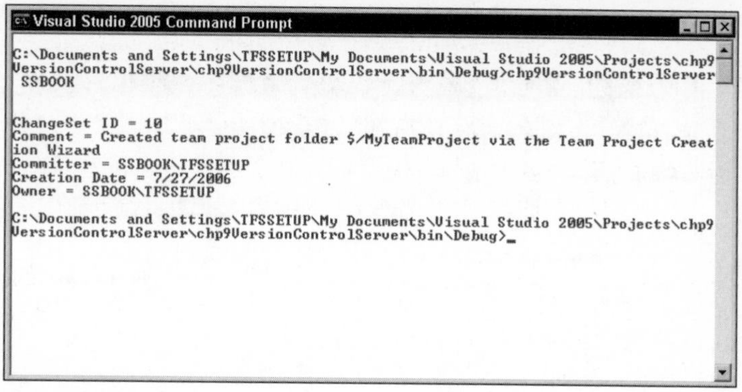

Figure 9-11

To create a work-item store object, you use the following code:

```
WorkItemStore wis = (WorkItemStore)tfs.GetService(typeof(WorkItemStore));
```

Using the work-item store object, you can query and retrieve work items from the work item tracking system. You learn more about work items and using the Team Foundation Object Model with the work item tracking system in Chapter 11.

The following code shows the Program.cs file for a console application named chp9WorkItemStore, which uses the `Diagnostics` attribute of the work item store to display the round-trip time between your application and the work item tracking system in Team Foundation Serve. This time is shown in milliseconds.

```
using System;
using System.Collections.Generic;
using System.Text;
using Microsoft.TeamFoundation;
using Microsoft.TeamFoundation.Client;
using Microsoft.TeamFoundation.Server;
using Microsoft.TeamFoundation.WorkItemTracking;
using Microsoft.TeamFoundation.WorkItemTracking.Client;
namespace chp9WorkItemStore
{
class Program
{
static void Main(string[] args)
{
TeamFoundationServer tfs =
TeamFoundationServerFactory.GetServer(args[0].ToString());
WorkItemStore wis = (WorkItemStore)tfs.GetService(typeof(WorkItemStore));
WorkItemStoreDiagnostics d = wis.Diagnostics;
Console.WriteLine("\n");
Console.WriteLine("Round Trip Time = " + d.RoundTripTime);
}
}
}
```

Figure 9-12 shows the output from running this sample application.

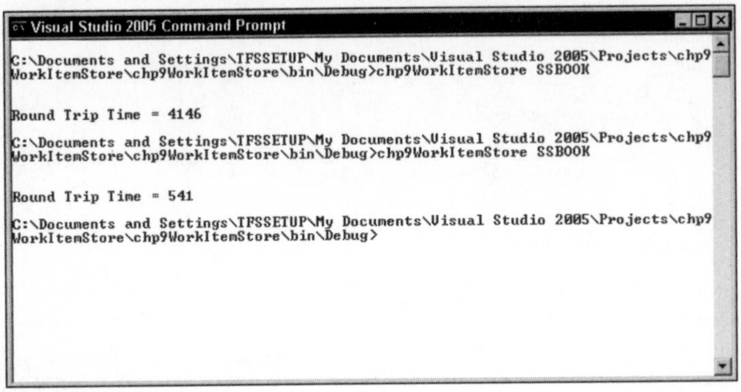

Figure 9-12

Summary

In this chapter, you have learned all about the extensibility of Team Foundation Server. You began the chapter looking at the differences between extensibility and customization, specifically in Team Foundation Server.

You then moved on to learn about Team Foundation Core Services and how they are used by the application tier. After that, you moved into the real meat of the chapter, the Team Foundation Server Object Model. You were presented with several sample applications that you can build off to create custom tools that are even more extensive.

You continue your tour of the extensibility of Team Foundation Server in the next chapter.

10

Extending the Windows SharePoint Team Portal

Each Team Project has a Team Portal. The Team Portal has a pivotal role as it is the centralized area where you can store project documentation, view reports and process guidance, and manage meetings and workflow. In most Team System books that you'll read, you will probably get only surface-level view of what you can do with the portal. Here are some of the core features of Windows SharePoint Services:

- **Team collaboration** — Provides a centralized area for viewing and downloading work products (templates used in your development process), your process guidance, and reports
- **Alerts, instant messaging, and office integration** — Document workflow integration, management of lists and assets on the server
- **Full administrative capabilities** — Including the ability to add and remove lists, discussion boards, tasks, and calendars
- **.NET development** — Has a full object model (OM), Web services, Web Parts development — all available through the Windows SharePoint Services Software Development Kit (SDK)

Figure 10-1 shows the layout and look of the default team portal site.

We aim in this chapter to provide you with the down and dirty details about Windows SharePoint Services and customization of the Team Portal. The unique thing about the chapter is that we will be putting it all in context of Team System and, most important, your development projects.

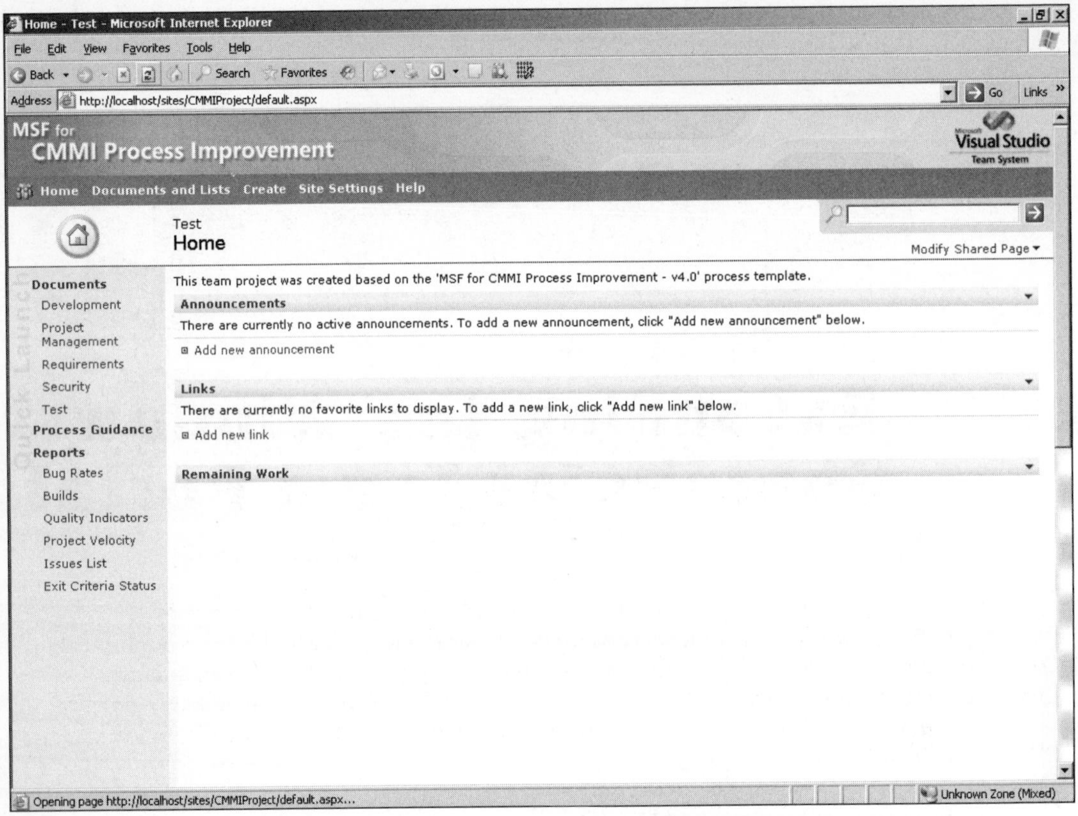

Figure 10-1

Understanding Portal Architecture

To understand how the portal is positioned within Team System, you must clearly understand the underlying implementation. Figure 10-2 shows the architecture of Windows SharePoint Services.

Here is how each component fits into the portal:

- **IIS 6.0** — The Web server is used to store scripts, cascading style sheets, executable files (.exe), dynamic link libraries (.dll), templates, and the Internet Server Applications Program Interface (ISAPI) filter. The ISAPI filter is used to map browser requests to the appropriate sites within each virtual server.
- **Web Parts framework** — The Web Parts framework allows Web Parts to be added and positioned in zones within the screen.
- **ASP.NET** — Multiple sites are grouped together in site collections. These collections contain Web Parts, which are derived from ASP.NET controls.

- **Microsoft SQL Server 2005** — The SQL Server 2005 stores information about what is contained in the templates. The authorization and customization information is also stored in the database.

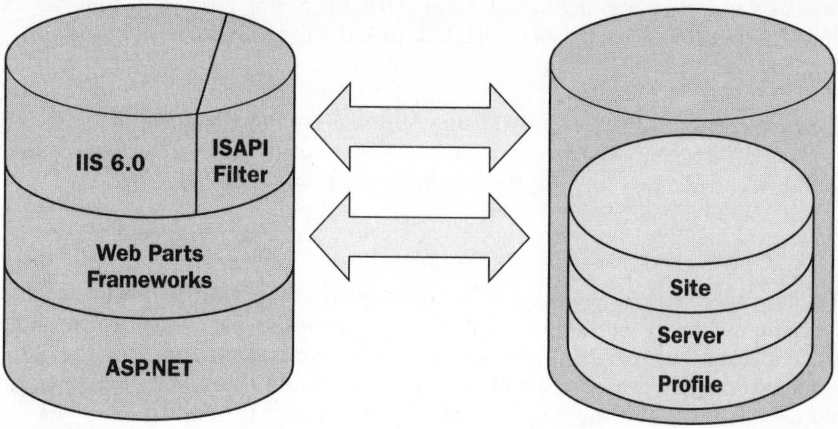

Figure 10-2

> **Windows SharePoint Services is configured as a server farm. This means that multiple team portals can be created with individual settings (as opposed to one set of settings per for the entire site). It allows you to use different security and customizations.**

Integration with Microsoft Office 2003

Using Office 2003, you can integrate with the team portal in interesting ways:

- **Microsoft Office FrontPage 2003** — FrontPage is used primarily to customize the team portal and create analysis reports. You can also add data driven Web Parts to the portal using FrontPage 2003.
- **Microsoft Office Outlook 2003** — You can use Outlook 2003 to manage online calendars and contact lists.
- **Microsoft Office Excel 2003 and Access 2003** — Excel and Access can be used to edit lists on the Windows SharePoint site. For example, you can download the list into Excel and manipulate it in a number of ways. Using Access, you can link a list to a database table.

Extensibility and Customization Overview

Windows SharePoint Services provides many options for customizing and extending your team portal. Customization involves changing settings on an existing control or feature. Extensibility involves creating a brand new feature for the portal.

Creating and Extending Custom Web Parts

Web Parts are preprogrammed page elements on a SharePoint site enabling those who are unfamiliar with Web design and programming to make changes to the portal. Writing custom Web Parts for SharePoint Services can be a challenge for the uninitiated. There are three strategies you can currently take for integrating custom Web Parts:

- You can create a custom Web Part using ASP.NET 1.1 and Visual Studio.NET 2003. The creation of Web Parts with .NET 1.1 is very difficult and involved. You can read about the process in several books and online blogs including this basic tutorial: `sharepointblogs.com/andynoon/archive/2006/06/20/8494.aspx`.

> **We chose not to include a tutorial on creating .NET 1.1 Web Parts in the book because the technology will soon be deprecated and the instructions are really long and prone to error. The real value of a Web Part is to give a nonprogrammer the ability to add and configure controls on a SharePoint site. We provide you with a quick, easy, and effective way of achieving the same results without the pain.**

- Son of SmartParts helps you integrate ASP.NET 2.0 Web Part and User controls within a SharePoint Web Part. ASP.NET 2.0 Web Parts are not available in the current version of Windows SharePoint Services—full ASP.NET 2.0 Web Part support will be available in Windows SharePoint 2007. You can download the Son of SmartParts at `http://workspaces.gotdotnet.com/smartpart`. You can learn in detail how to create an ASP.NET 2.0 Web Part in Peter Vogel's *Professional Web Parts and Custom Controls with ASP.NET 2.0* (from Wrox).
- The last option (and the one we explore in depth) is to integrate ASP.NET 2.0 content into a team portal using the Page Viewer Web Part. One of the biggest customer requests out there is getting work item information displayed on the team portal. The application we build shows the work item list in a `GridView` and allows the user to click links for work item details. A screenshot of the application can be seen in Figure 10-3:

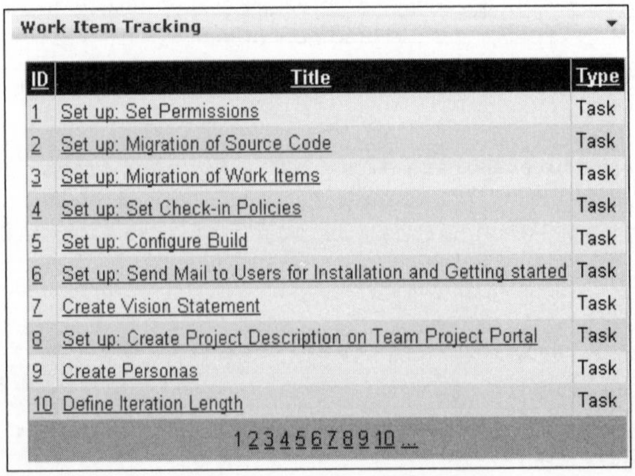

Figure 10-3

Writing custom Web-based work item applications requires special permissions to be set, especially if you are planning to use the work item object model. Some of the tasks you have to complete include setting up the physical architecture, enabling integration authentication, configuring the WIT cache folder, enabling ASP.NET impersonation (and other security settings), and running the Web application under a dedicated application pool. Peter Sheill (`blogs.msdn.com/psheill`) blogged about and posted a document written by Naren Datha with guidelines and requirements for Web-based work item applications. You can download the document at `http://blogs.msdn.com/psheill/attachment/543120.ashx`.

Creating a Custom ASP.NET Work Item Application

First, we need to set up a custom ASP.NET 2.0 application that will interact with our SharePoint portal. The good news is that you don't need a single line of code behind to get the application working—everything will be programmed declaratively. The first thing you need to do is create a C# Web site and set up a standard Web form page called WITDisplay. You'll need to set up a unique virtual site (or Web site) separate from the built-in Team Foundation Server applications.

```
<%@ Page Language="C#"
AutoEventWireup="true"
CodeFile="WITDisplay.aspx.cs"
Inherits="Default" %>
<!DOCTYPE html PUBLIC "-//W3C//DTD XHTML 1.0 Transitional//EN"
"http://www.w3.org/TR/xhtml11/DTD/xhtml11-transitional.dtd">
<html xmlns="http://www.w3.org/1999/xhtml" >
<head runat="server">
<title>WITDisplay</title>
</head>
<body>
<form id="form1" runat="server">
<div>
```

Next, you set up the `GridView`. The first thing you'll notice is that we've allowed paging and sorting with the help of callbacks. The unique key we have provided is `ID`, and the data source is `SqlDataSource1` (which we will define later in code). Included are a few cell, border, and font parameters to establish the look and feel.

```
<asp:GridView AllowPaging="True"
AllowSorting="True"
AutoGenerateColumns="False"
DataKeyNames="ID"
EnableSortingAndPagingCallbacks="True"
ID="GridView1"
DataSourceID="SqlDataSource1"
runat="server"
BackColor="White"
BorderColor="#999999"
BorderStyle="None"
BorderWidth="1px"
CellPadding="3"
```

```
Font-Bold="False"
Font-Names="Arial"
Font-Size="Small"
GridLines="Vertical">
```

Now set up your columns. The first column you'll use is the `ID` column (containing the work item ID). Since you want to make field clickable, use the `asp:HyperLinkField` (instead of an `asp:BoundField`).

```
<Columns>
<asp:HyperLinkField HeaderText="ID"
DataTextField="ID"
DataTextFormatString="{0}"
DataNavigateUrlFields="ID"
```

The `DataNavigateUrlFormatString` establishes the hyperlink. In particular, you will access a native aspx page that displays a work item details page based on the work item's ID (`artifactMoniker`). The results are shown in Figure 10-4.

```
DataNavigateUrlFormatString
="http://TFSRTM:8080/WorkItemTracking/Workitem.aspx?artifactMoniker={0}"
```

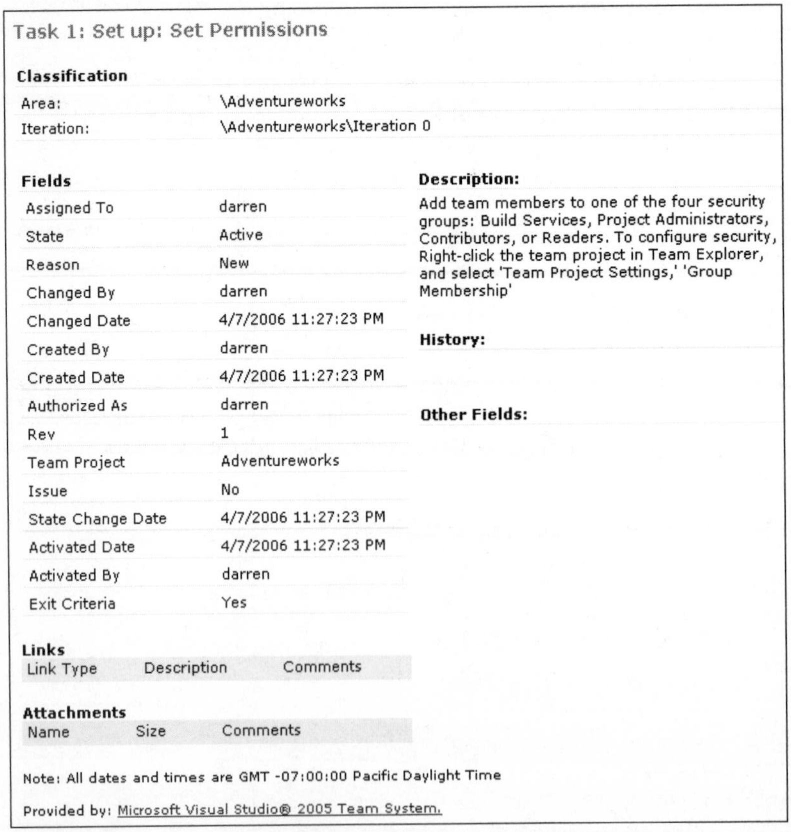
Task 1: Set up: Set Permissions
Classification
Area: \Adventureworks
Iteration: \Adventureworks\Iteration 0
Fields
Assigned To darren
State Active
Reason New
Changed By darren
Changed Date 4/7/2006 11:27:23 PM
Created By darren
Created Date 4/7/2006 11:27:23 PM
Authorized As darren
Rev 1
Team Project Adventureworks
Issue No
State Change Date 4/7/2006 11:27:23 PM
Activated Date 4/7/2006 11:27:23 PM
Activated By darren
Exit Criteria Yes
Description:
Add team members to one of the four security groups: Build Services, Project Administrators, Contributors, or Readers. To configure security, Right-click the team project in Team Explorer, and select 'Team Project Settings,' 'Group Membership'
History:
Other Fields:
Links
Link Type Description Comments
Attachments
Name Size Comments
Note: All dates and times are GMT -07:00:00 Pacific Daylight Time
Provided by: Microsoft Visual Studio® 2005 Team System.

Figure 10-4

You then target a page called `WorkItemDetail` (because no such page has been defined beforehand, clicking a link will spawn a new details page). If a page with the `WorkItemDetail ID` is open in your task bar, the results will keep appearing in the same page.

```
Target="WorkItemDetail"
ItemStyle-Font-Size="10pt"
SortExpression="ID">
<ItemStyle Font-Names="Arial" Font-Size="Small" />
<HeaderStyle Font-Bold="True" Font-Names="Arial" Font-Size="Small" />
</asp:HyperLinkField>
```

You will then define another column for the `Title`. The hyperlink will behave the same as the `ID` field. (It will spawn a new window with the work item details.) The only difference is the `SortExpression` is by title, and the `DataTextField` is obviously `Title`.

```
<asp:HyperLinkField HeaderText="Title"
DataTextField="Title"
DataTextFormatString="{0}"
DataNavigateUrlFields="ID"
DataNavigateUrlFormatString =
"http://TFSRTM:8080/WorkItemTracking/Workitem.aspx?artifactMoniker={0}"
Target="WorkItemDetail"
ItemStyle-Font-Size="10pt"
SortExpression="Title">
<ItemStyle Font-Names="Arial" Font-Size="Small" />
<HeaderStyle Font-Bold="True" Font-Names="Arial" Font-Size="Small" />
</asp:HyperLinkField>
```

This code adds a column for work item tasks. `The SortExpression="WIType"` command allows the user to sort the grid by type. Note that `WIType` is not a native datatype within the work item database; it is an alias for `Work Item Type`.

```
<asp:BoundField DataField="WIType"
HeaderText="Type"
SortExpression="WIType">
<ItemStyle Font-Names="Arial" Font-Size="Small" />
<HeaderStyle Font-Bold="True" Font-Names="Arial" Font-Size="Small" />
</asp:BoundField>
</Columns>
```

The following code defines the Rainy Day color scheme for the entire `GridView`:

```
<FooterStyle BackColor="#CCCCCC"
ForeColor="Black" />
<RowStyle BackColor="#EEEEEE"
Font-Names="Arial"
Font-Size="Small"
ForeColor="Black" />
<SelectedRowStyle BackColor="#008A8C"
Font-Bold="True"
ForeColor="White" />
<PagerStyle BackColor="#999999"
ForeColor="Black"
```

```
HorizontalAlign="Center" />
<HeaderStyle BackColor="#000084"
Font-Bold="True"
Font-Names="Arial"
Font-Size="Small"
ForeColor="White" />
<AlternatingRowStyle BackColor="#DCDCDC" />
</asp:GridView>
```

Finally, you define the connection string and SQL command for the `GridView`. The `SelectCommand` query currently pulls the `ID`, `title`, and `type` for all the work items within the server. However, you can customize the query to pull any kind of information you want. In fact, an interesting customization you can do is integrating a `DropDownList` on the interface to allow your users to select from any query they want.

```
<asp:SqlDataSource ConnectionString="<%$ ConnectionStrings:TfsWarehouse %>"
ID="SqlDataSource1"
runat="server"
SelectCommand="SELECT [ID], [Title], WIType = [Work Item Type] FROM
[TfsWorkItemTracking].[dbo].[WorkItemsLatest]">
</asp:SqlDataSource>
</div>
</form>
</body>
</html>
```

You notice that the connection string refers to `TfsWarehouse`. We've set up the connection string in question within the web.config file. It specifically points to the `Latest Work Item` fact table. It provides up-to-date information about your work items. In the connection string, you use integrated security and target the `TfsWorkItemTracking` database. You can explore the fact tables by opening SQL Server Management Studio, connecting to the database (as opposed to analysis services), and exploring all the tables that start with `Tfs`. Why limit the data to work items? You can customize this application to pull any kind of project data including builds, version control, or test results.

```
<?xml version="1.0"?>
<configuration>
<appSettings/>
<connectionStrings>

<add name="TfsWarehouse" connectionString="Server=TFSRTM;Integrated
Security=True;Database=TfsWorkItemTracking;Persist Security Info=True"
providerName="System.Data.SqlClient" />
</connectionStrings>
 <system.web>
<compilation debug="false">
<assemblies>
<add assembly="Microsoft.SharePoint, Version=11.0.0.0, Culture=neutral,
PublicKeyToken=71E9BCE111E9429C"/></assemblies>
</compilation>
<authentication mode="Windows"/>
</system.web>
</configuration>
```

At this point, you may be wondering why we pulled the data directly from the database instead of resorting to the work item object model. The main reason is performance — the `GridView` has been optimized to pull and page data directly from a database. If we used the object model, we would have to use an intermediate data construct (such as a `DataTable`) to store the results. The results are a lot slower depending on the amount of data you want to pull.

Integrating the Work Item Application into a Web Part

Now it's time to integrate the work item application into the team portal. The first thing you need to do is add a Page Viewer Web Part into one of your SharePoint zones. Start by clicking on Modify Shared Pages in the top-right corner of your portal. Then select Add Web Parts⇨Browse.

The Add Web Parts interface appears on the right (as shown in Figure 10-5). Click the Team Web Site Gallery (as shown), and then click once on the Page Viewer Web Part option to select and highlight it.

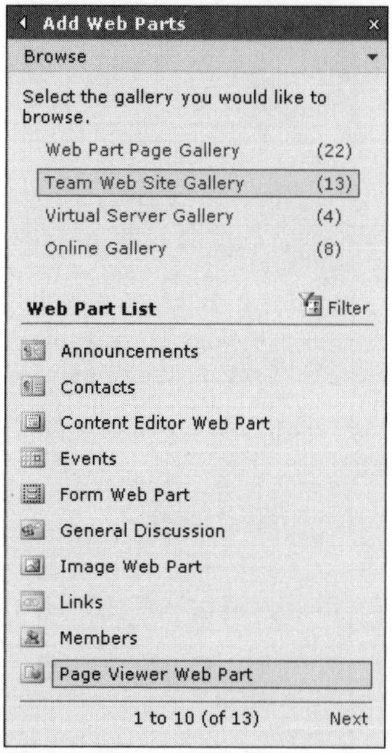

Figure 10-5

Once the option has been highlighted, drag it into one of the SharePoint zones in the middle of the page (as shown in Figure 10-6).

The Page Viewer has now been added to the site. Click the down arrow to the right of the Web Part and select Modify Shared Web Part. The Page Viewer Web Part properties (shown in Figure 10-7) appear on the right of the screen. Change the link to point to your ASP.NET 2.0 application, change the title to say Work Item Tracking, and change the height to 350 pixels. Once you are done, click OK.

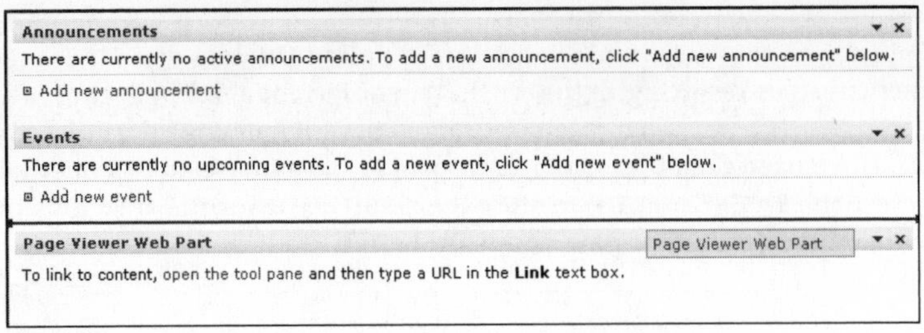

Figure 10-6

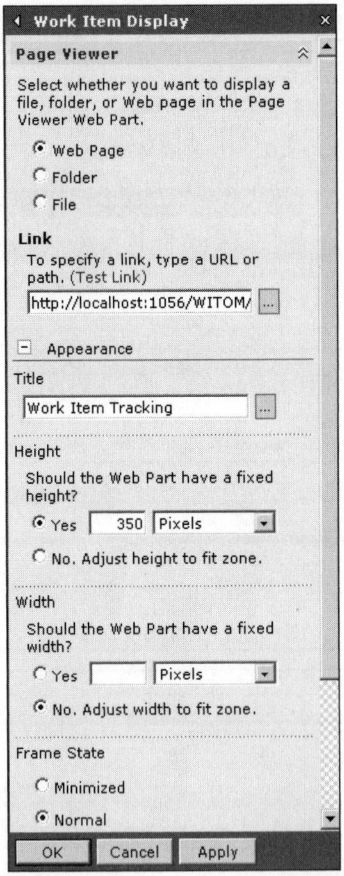

Figure 10-7

Your custom Work Item Tracking Web Part will appear on the team portal (as shown in Figure 10-8).

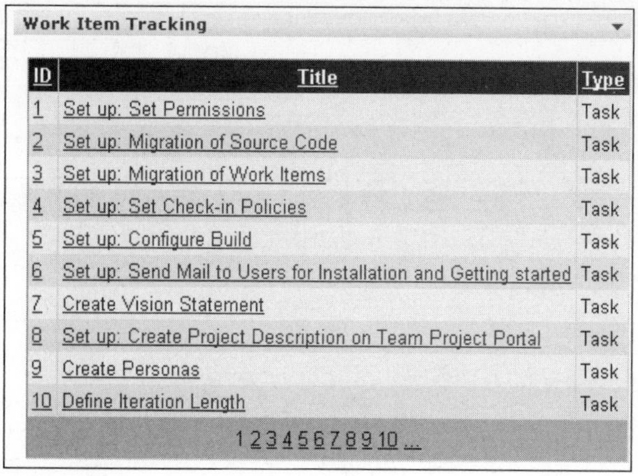

Figure 10-8

Customizing the Team Portal

One of the ways you can establish ownership of the team portal is by customizing it with company colors and logo. The key to customizing the team portal is using Microsoft FrontPage 2003 as your design tool. Because we will be dealing with HTML and Cascading Style Sheets (CSS), it helps if you have some familiarity with Web design.

Let's walk through the process of changing the look and feel of the portal. Later, you will learn how to incorporate those changes into your process template.

1. Launch Microsoft Office FrontPage 2003.
2. Click File⇨Open Site.
3. In the Site name field, type the address of your team portal. For example: `http://TeamFoundationServer/sites/TeamProject` (substituting the names of your own target server and project for *TeamFoundationServer* and *TeamProject*).
4. You may be prompted to for a username and password. Enter them and click OK.

> **You can configure Internet Explorer to avoid having to type in your username and password every time you access the team portal. Simply click Tools⇨Internet Options. Click the Security tab, and then click the Custom Level button. If you scroll down the list of security settings, you'll notice one for User Authentication / Logon. Select Automatic logon with current username and password and click OK. This allows Internet Explorer to authenticate you based on your current security context.**

5. Click Open. The following interface appears (as shown in Figure 10-9).

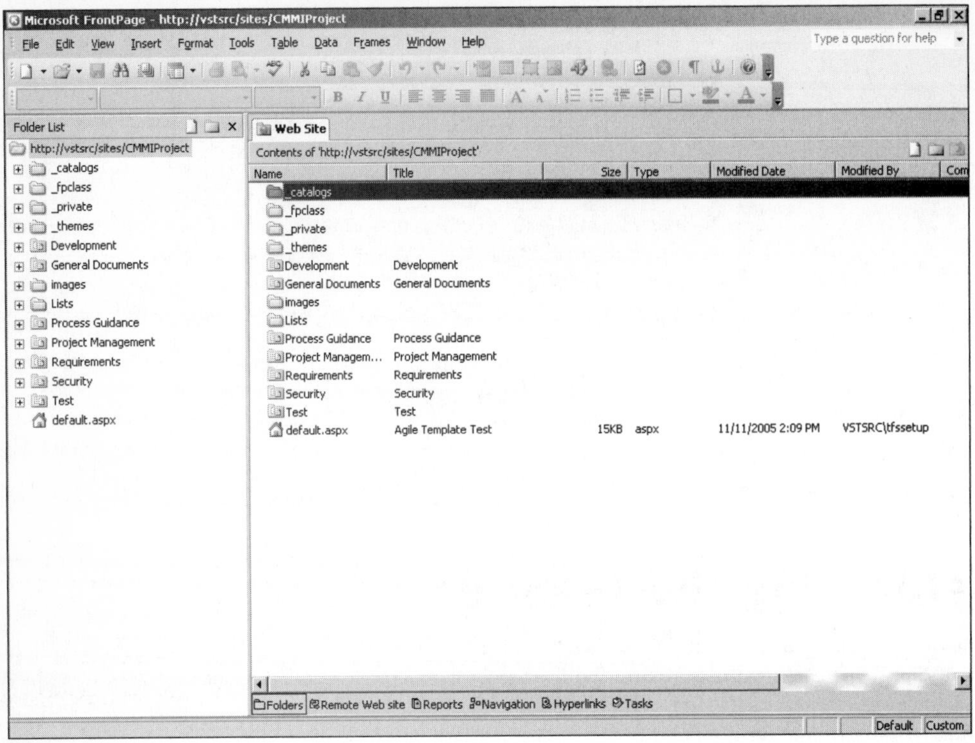

Figure 10-9

Let's look at all the elements in the left menu and find out what they are used for. Note that the following layout was created based on a Team Project using the MSF for Agile Software Development process template. Depending on the template you use to create your project, the folder names may vary:

- **_catalogs** — This folder contains a list of galleries contained on your SharePoint site. By default, you'll find the List Template Gallery, the Web Part Gallery, and the Site Template Gallery.
- **_fpclass** — This is a folder typically found in FrontPage extensions that is used to hold the Hover Button and Banner Ad Manager components. Note that the existence of this folder doesn't mean that the FrontPage Extensions was installed on your server; in fact, you should *never* install FrontPage Extensions on a machine hosting Team Foundation Server. (For details, please refer to the installation documents.)
- **_private** — Whenever you install FrontPage Extensions, this folder is created to hide files that are meant to be hidden on the Web site. The folder itself can't be browsed.
- **_themes** — This folder contains the cascading style sheets (CSS) and .inf configuration files to define the look of your site. If you use the MSF for Agile Software Development and MSF for CMMI Process Improvement, you'll find a SharePoint template in this folder called agile2-default-. It contains the style sheets, MSF logo (header_vsts_logo.gif), and gradient graphic that appear at the top of the page (header-bg.jpg).
- **Development** — This is one of the document libraries.

- **images** — This folder is quite important as it is used to store the images on your Web site. To upload an image to the team portal, all you need to do is drag it from your desktop to the folder. FrontPage will automatically FTP the file over to the site.
- **Lists** — This contains your default lists from SharePoint Services. Lists include Announcements, Contacts, Events, General Discussions, Links, and Tasks. If you created a new list, it will be included here.
- **Process Guidance** — The Process Guidance files are prerendered in HTML and can easily be manipulated using FrontPage 2003. Note that making changes to the process guidance of a particular Team Project will affect that instance only. If you want to make changes to several team projects, the best approach is to incorporate the new guidance within the process template, or manually make changes to the projects one by one.
- **Requirements, Security, and Test** — These folders are generated as part of the process template, and will contain the project templates (or work products) you define within the process template. See the "Customizing the Process Template" section later in this chapter for more details.
- **default.aspx** — This is the main page of the Team Portal. You can make any changes you want to the HTML portion of the file to change its appearance.

Now that you have a handle on the layout of your Team Portal within FrontPage, let's now find out how to make basic customizations to the site.

> **There may be circumstances where you would want to use a pre-existing SharePoint site on a SharePoint server instead of the pre-defined site created with your Team Project. The following TechNote on the MSDN site describes the process of configuring your Team Foundation Server to use a remote SharePoint site for a pre-defined Team Project:** `http://msdn.microsoft.com/vstudio/technotes/tfs/conf_for_remote_ss.aspx`.

Adding a New Logo to the Team Portal

One of the most common customer requests is to find out how to brand a Team Project with a custom company logo. The steps are quite simple:

1. Open up the Team Project you want to modify in Microsoft FrontPage 2003.
2. Double-click default.aspx. This will show the current page layout of the Team Portal in the design screen on the right.
3. Upload your logo to the Web site (either by dragging the graphic file into the images folder within FrontPage or selecting File⇨Import).

> **You can use a similar technique to upload custom Web Parts (.dwp) files. Before clicking the Import option, open up the folder list and select _catalogs⇨wp (Web Part Gallery). That will make it available on the site when you select Modify Shared Page on the portal site.**

4. Select the current MSF logo and hit the Delete key to remove it.

5. Open the images folder from the tree view on the left side of the screen and drag your new custom logo into the placeholder in the design view of the portal.
6. Save your changes.

Customizing the Process Template

From within the process template, you can define elements such as process guidance, document templates, SharePoint templates, and other important files stored on the Team Project Portal. Windows SharePoint Services artifacts are created using the Windows SharePoint plug-in (`Microsoft.ProjectCreationWizard.Portal`).

From within the process guidance folder (Agile or CMMI), the Windows SharePoint Services directory contains all the files you need to manipulate the portal guidance and template. Within this directory, you will find several folders:

- **Process Guidance** — This folder contains HTML and XML versions of your process guidance files. See the section earlier in the chapter entitled "Customizing the Team Portal" for more information on customizing that part of the project.
- **Work Product Folders** — These contain work products (templates and supporting files) for project management, security, project requirements, and tests.

Any directory, file, or template contained in the Windows SharePoint Services directory can be updated and customized to fit your process requirements.

Document Template Schema

The WssTasks.xml file located in the Windows SharePoint Services directory of your process template definition file contains an enumeration of all the SharePoint elements that can be customized once a new Team Project has been created (You can learn more about process template customization in Chapter 6.) The file is divided into three sections. The first section lists the entire document libraries (including titles and descriptions) related to your process. This is a high-level way of categorizing your documents — you can easily add and remove any of these categories based on your specific needs. Please note that these libraries are accessible when you click the Documents and Lists link on the main page of the project portal.

```
<?xml version="1.0" encoding="utf-8" ?>
<tasks>
<task id="SharePointPortal"
name="Create Sharepoint Portal"
plugin="Microsoft.ProjectCreationWizard.Portal"
completionMessage="Project site created.">
<dependencies/>
<taskXml>
<Portal>
<site template="VSTS_MSFAgile" language="1033"/>

<documentLibraries>
<documentLibrary name="Security" description="Documents for the architect team"/>
<documentLibrary name="Test" description="Documents for the test team"/>
...
</documentLibraries>
```

The folders node lists all the folders within specific document libraries. The example defines the folders found in the Process Guidance library:

```
<folders>

<folder documentLibrary="Process Guidance" name="Supporting Files"/>
<folder documentLibrary="Process Guidance" name="Supporting Files/Code" />
<folder documentLibrary="Process Guidance" name="Supporting Files/CSS" />
<folder documentLibrary="Process Guidance" name="Supporting Files/EULA" />
<folder documentLibrary="Process Guidance" name="Supporting Files/HTML" />
<folder documentLibrary="Process Guidance" name="Supporting Files/images" />
<folder documentLibrary="Process Guidance" name="Supporting Files/Other" />
<folder documentLibrary="Process Guidance" name="Supporting Files/Schema" />
<folder documentLibrary="Process Guidance" name="Supporting Files/XML" />
<folder documentLibrary="Process Guidance" name="Supporting Files/XSLs" />
</folders>
```

The Files section of WssTasks.xml lists all the files to be included into a Team Project once your process file has been selected. These include process guidance files and work products:

```
<files>

<file source="Windows SharePoint Services\Process Guidance\ProcessGuidance.html"
target="Process Guidance/ProcessGuidance.html" />
<file source="Windows SharePoint Services\Process Guidance\Supporting
Files\AboutRoles.htm"
target="Process Guidance/Supporting Files/AboutRoles.htm" />
...
</files>
</Portal>
</taskXml>
</task>
</tasks>
```

Adding New Work Products to Your Team Portal

Adding a work product within your process is quite easy using XML. Simply define the path to your source file and the target path of the folder on the server (as defined in the documentLibraries collection):

```
<file source="Windows SharePoint Services\Templates\YourPolicy.doc"
target="Security/YourPolicy.doc" />
```

Customizing the Team Portal Using the Browser

You can perform several activities to customize the team portal without having to do any kind of deep extensibility. The following are among them:

- Add existing Web Parts (calendars, lists, galleries)
- Manage portal contents
- Apply new themes
- Change the display name and description of the portal

Let's look at each one of these customization features of Windows SharePoint Services.

Adding Existing SharePoint Components

Windows SharePoint Services comes with a library of preconfigured Web Parts. You can use these Web Parts to add functionality to a page or change the layout of the controls in a page. To add new Web Parts, click the Modify Shared Pages option at the top-right of the screen. An interface will pop up (as shown in Figure 10-10).

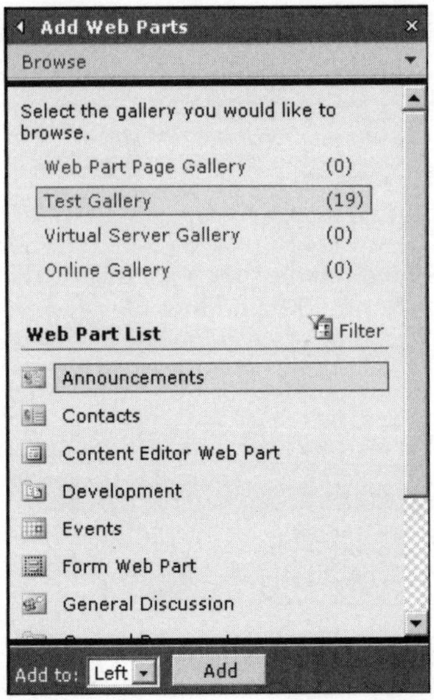

Figure 10-10

You can then drag any of the built-in controls (and your custom controls) to anywhere on your screen.

Modify Site Contents

Windows SharePoint Services allows you to modify any part of the site contents including the Announcements, Contacts, Events, Links, and Tasks. It will also allow you to modify properties for folders specific to team portals (such as Process Guidance). To access these page properties, simply click Site Settings⇨Customizations⇨Modify Site Content (as shown in Figure 10-11).

Applying New Themes

You can change the theme of your team portal by clicking Site Settings⇨Customizations⇨Apply Theme to Site. You find a huge list of predefined themes in Windows SharePoint Services (and you can upload other themes by using the `stsadm.exe` tool). You can view the Apply Theme window (as shown in Figure 10-12).

Once you change the site template, there is no easy way to revert the site to the original one.

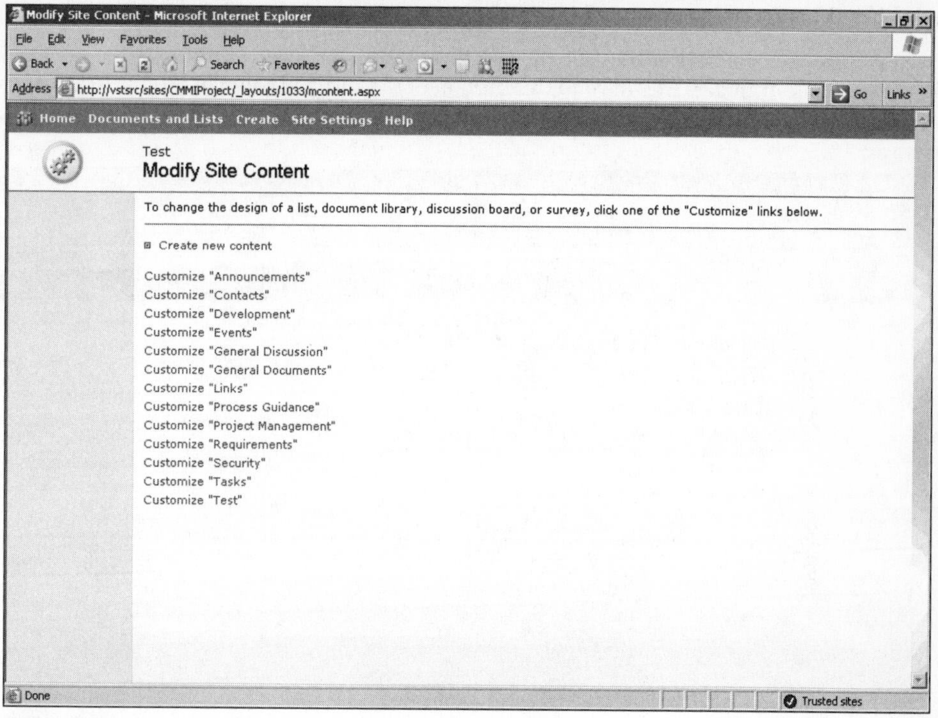

Figure 10-11

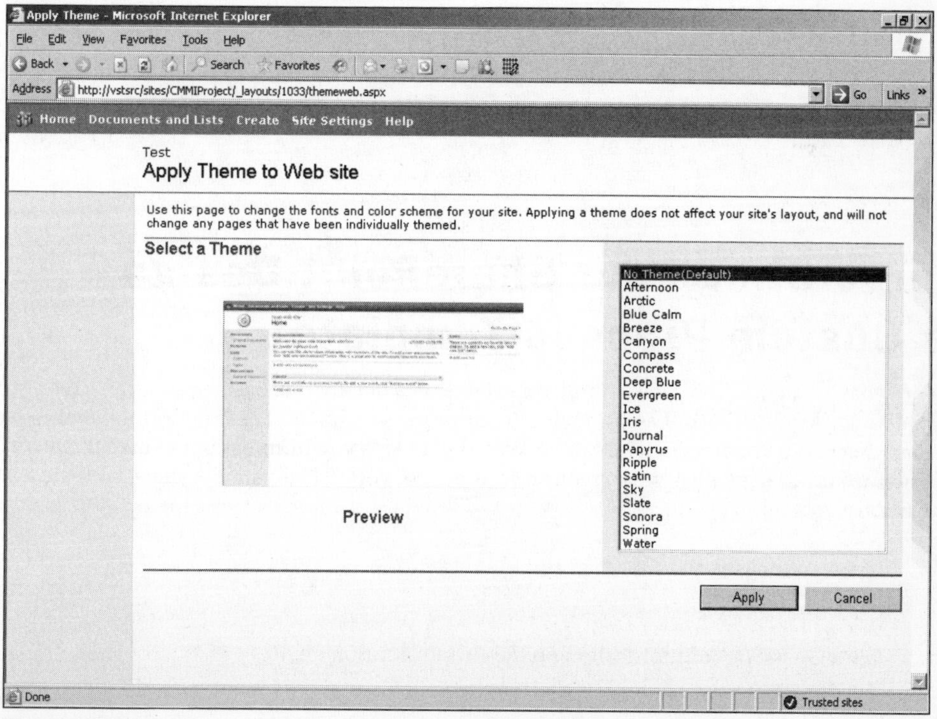

Figure 10-12

Change the Portal Name

You can change the name of the site, simply click Site Settings➪Customizations➪Change Site Title and Description. You can change the title and description of the site (as shown in Figure 10-13) and click OK. You must then return to the root of your team portal to see the changes.

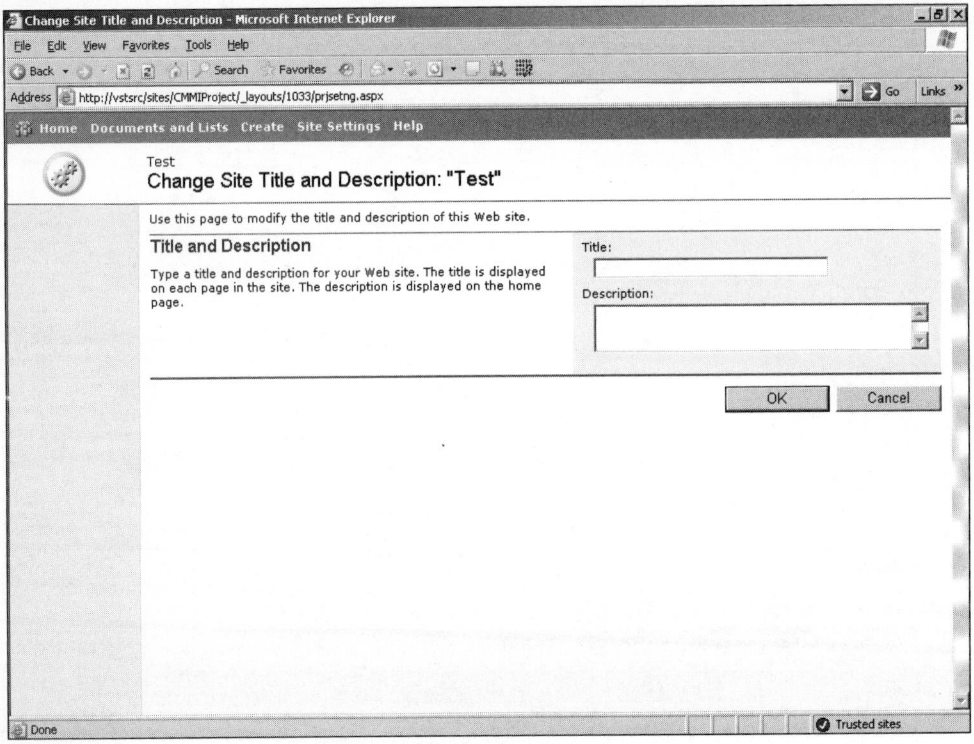

Figure 10-13

Incorporating Your SharePoint Design in a Custom Process Template

You now have a choice: You can customize each site on a one-by-one basis or you can save your work as a SharePoint site template and associate it to your process template. The latter option makes sense if you are planning to reuse a process template repeatedly. It saves you from having to take the manual steps to customize the look and feel after creating each project portal. Here are the steps to create a site template file.

1. Open your customized team portal.
2. Click Site Settings.
3. Click Go to Site Administration on the Administration menu.

4. Under Management and Statistics, click Save Site as Template.
5. You will now have the option of creating a new file name for your custom template (filename.stp). You can also add in a template title and description.

> **We recommend that you omit any spaces from your template file name.**

6. There is a check box on the form that says Include content. This will include all the files that are currently part of your team portal. If you think that you will reuse all the same files on the portal every time you create a Team Project, click the check box. Otherwise, leave it unchecked.
7. Your template has now been saved.

Here are the instructions to obtain a copy of the site template as a .stp file. The .stp file is actually a .cab (Cabinet) file that contains an XML manifest describing the structure of the site and a collection of compressed files with your template's assets. Follow these steps:

1. From the home page of your portal, click Site Settings.
2. Under Administration, click Go to Site Administration.
3. Under Site Collection Galleries, click Manage site Template Gallery.
4. Click your template and download the .stp file to your `C:\` drive.
5. Now, you need to make SharePoint recognize the new template and modify the process template. Assuming that you put your custom .stp file in the root of the `C:\` drive, type the following command using the command prompt and hit Enter:

```
> cd C:\
```

6. Then type the following to add the custom site template to Team Foundation Server:

```
> "C:\Program Files\Common Files\Microsoft Shared\web server
extensions\60\bin\stsadm.exe" -o addtemplate -filename mycustomtemplate.stp -title
customtemplate
```

In the preceding example, the file name for your custom template is `mycustomtemplate.stp`. You also designated `customtemplate` as the identifying title for the template. The title is quite important, as it is used to link the site template to your process template. Once your site template has been added, all you need to do is to make a small customization in your process template.

Integrating a Site Template within a Process Template

At this point, all you need to do is link the process template to the site template. Here are the steps to integrate both together.

1. Download a copy of a process template to your desktop by clicking on Team➪Team Foundation Server Settings➪Process Template Manager. From the Manager, select MSF for Agile Software Development and click the Download button. Once downloaded, open the process template folder.

2. Open the Windows SharePoint Services folder and edit WssTasks.xml in your favorite XML editor.
3. Update this site node, changing the template to your custom template title. For example:

```
<site template="customtemplate" language="1033" />
```

4. Upload your customized process template. (You can do this by using the Upload feature of the Process Template Manager—see Chapter 6 for more details.) Before you do that, you may want to rename the title of the process.

Now every time you create a new Team Project using your custom process, a Team Portal will be generated with your custom logo and colors.

Verifying Your Portal Customizations

The best way to check your custom SharePoint setting is by creating a brand-new project incorporating your custom process template. To test your customized process template, use the following steps:

1. Upload your custom process template to the Team Foundation Server (Team⇨Team Foundation Server Settings⇨Process Template Manager. Then click the Upload button and navigate to your process template).
2. Create a new Team Project using your template.
3. Select the Show Project Portal option by right-clicking on your Team Project within the Team Explorer window.
4. Select the Documents and List option at the top of your project portal.
5. Click Document Libraries to see whether they were properly created.
6. You can then click individual files to determine whether they are located in the right document libraries.

Summary

In this chapter, you learned how to extend, customize, and administer the team portal. First, you learned about the architecture of Windows SharePoint Services. Next, you found out how to create a custom Web Part. We then explored direct customization of the team portal using Microsoft FrontPage 2003 and the built-in customization tools. Finally, you learned how to integrate the site customization into the process template.

Continuing with the theme of customization and extensibility, in the next chapter you will learn how to manipulate work items to make them work within your development environment.

11

Administering and Customizing Work Items

Whether you are building a house or developing a computer application, certain things need to be accomplished. Most people use to-do lists to define what needs to be done on the project and who needs to do it. Every project manager tracks his to-do list differently. Some use applications, such as Microsoft Excel or Microsoft Project. Others develop in-house tools, or buy third-party products to help with the information workload. Still others use Post-it notes on their desk. Sometimes all a project needs is a small Excel spreadsheet to manage it, while other times a detailed Microsoft Project is required. The fact is, there is no need to use a wrecking ball when all you need is a small hammer.

One of the problems with using, say, Microsoft Excel to track the requirements of a development project is providing the information from the spreadsheet to all the members of the team, and keeping the spreadsheet updated with the latest information. Sure, you can share out the spreadsheet on a file share, or possibly make use of Windows SharePoint Services, but you may still run into conflicts with keeping the file updated. With very complicated projects, team members may have great difficulty figuring out what they are supposed to be working on.

There is no good way to tie requirements from that spreadsheet back to the source code that solves that requirement. There is no good automated way to alert testers that a bug they found has been fixed in the latest build of the application, and they need to test it. There is no good way to display the latest status on the project to all the project stakeholders.

Microsoft recognized all these limitations, along with others, in the development process of computer applications, and has tried to address a majority of them with the work item tracking system in Visual Studio Team System. This system tracks all the work that needs to be accomplished to complete your application. It contains mechanisms for assigning the work, tracking its history, and running reports to enable management and project stakeholders to understand the status of a project. All the information for the work item tracking system is stored on the data tier of the Team Foundation Server. Microsoft provided some basic templates for project management, based off their best practices, to enable teams to get up and running with Team System quickly and effectively. Finally, they recognized that each team and project is different. Therefore, they have made the work item tracking system easily customizable and extensible, allowing users to conform the product to how they work, instead of having to change how they work to fit the product.

This chapter covers the work item tracking system of Visual Studio Team System. You will learn the difference between a work item and a work item type. And you will receive a basic introduction to the different work items that are provided for you via the MSF Agile methodology. Next, you create your own custom work item type, import it into your Team Foundation Server, and create a new work item of that type. You will learn how to edit an existing work item type, both by hand and by using a third-party tool. Once you have this basic understanding of work items, you will move into how to administer them. You'll learn about creating a work item, searching for work items, and using Microsoft Excel and Project to access the work item information. Finally, you examine the work item object model, and how you can build a simple ASP.NET Web site to access your custom work item type.

Introducing Work Items Concepts

A work item type (WIT) defines the structure for a particular piece of work that needs to get executed. Work item tracking can differentiate between types of work that need to get done, for example, between fixing bugs, implementing a nonfunctional requirement, or completing a task. Each type of work item has its own definition of the information required to keep track of the work. For example, in a bug work item, the WIT defines the fields associated with that bug, and the layout of the form used by the bug work item. A work item itself is just a specific instance of a work item type. When you create a new work item for a project, you use a work item type to do it. Another way to look at it is that the work item type is the template used to create a specific work item in your project.

Now let's look at some of the different concepts associated with work items and Team Foundation Server.

Work Item Types

You've already learned how, when creating a new team project, you must select a process model. The two process models that ship with Team Foundation Server are MSF Agile and MSF CMMI. These process models define a template for your project. Part of this template definition includes defining all the default work items that are associated with the process model. These are the work items that users will have access to out of the box with Team Foundation Server. When a new team project is created, all the different work item types defined for that project are also created.

For the MSF Agile process model, the following work item types are defined:

- **Bug** — A bug is a work item that provides information about a potential problem in the application. You open a bug to track this problem, and include information on how to re-create the actual issue. The more detailed information you provide on the bug, the easier it will be to fix the problem.
- **Quality of service requirement** — The quality of service requirement is used to track information on how the system is supposed to operate. Certain items such as performance, availability, and maintainability are tracked in this manner, usually in defining how the system should operate in relation to these characteristics. These types of requirements are often referred to as *nonfunctional* requirements.

- **Risk** — All projects have different levels of risk to them. The risk work item tracks all the different possible risks inherent in a project, which could cause the project schedule to slip. If a risk requires some action to prevent it, you can then open the appropriate risk work items. Identifying risks can lead to a more successful project.
- **Task** — A task work item is your basic unit of work in Team Foundation Server. Tasks are very generic, and can be used in pretty much any way you would like. The process guidance for MSF Agile gives some detailed examples of how each role would use the task work item.
- **Scenario** — A scenario is an example of how the end user will interact with the system. It is meant to record a single path that the user takes when trying to accomplish something with the application. A scenario can indicate a successful or unsuccessful outcome.

Detailed information on the entire MSF Agile process model, including the process guidance, can be found at the MSF Agile Web site at `http://msdn.microsoft.com/vstudio/teamsystem/msf/msfagile`.

The CMMI process model has a more extensive collection of work item types. Besides some of the above types it includes the following:

- **Change request** — A change request identifies a change to be made to the application.
- **Issue** — An issue is similar to a risk, in that it identifies something that could cause the project schedule to slip.
- **Requirement** — A requirement lists what an application is supposed to do.
- **Review** — A review identifies the results of an in-depth look into the code or the design of the application.

You learn more concerning the MSF Agile default work item tasks in a later section. And you can always refer to the process guidance that ships with these process models for more detailed information on the work item types and tips on how to use the process models. Finally, as you see later in this chapter, you are not restricted to using these types in the manner prescribed by the process guidance. You can customize these types, or even build your own.

Stored On Data Tier

It's been mentioned before in this book, but it is worth repeating here again: all information related to Team System and Team Foundation Server is stored on the Team Foundation Server data tier. The work item tracking system is no exception. There are two databases devoted directly to the work item tracking system: TfsWorkItemTracking, which contains all the information related to the different work item types, as well as specific instances of work items, and TfsWorkItemTrackingAttachments, which holds any attachments that you might add to a particular work item instance.

Having all this work item information stored in one location on the data tier becomes very useful. It is easy to back up and restore work item information in the event of a catastrophe. In addition, you can use Microsoft Excel to connect to the Team Foundation Server Data Warehouse, allowing you to create useful charts and pivot tables that can give you very detailed information

Work Item Form

Every work item type defines a work item form that is used to fill out a particular instance of the work item type. The form definition and layout is tied directly into the definition of the work item type. When you make changes to an existing work item type, or create a new one, you have to make the appropriate changes to the form definition. For example, if you add a new field to the work item type, you will also need to modify the form definition to allow the user to enter information for that new field.

All the information for the work item type, including what fields are included in the work item type, what fields are available on the work item type form, and the layout of the form, are defined in one XML file. This allows existing work item types to be easily customized, and enables you to extend the platform using new work item types. You learn more about this shortly.

Using the work item form, you can relate work items to changesets in the version control system. You can link to other work items, enabling you to cross-reference information. You can add attachments, such as Word or Excel documents that are related to the work item. Moreover, you can view the work item history to see all the changes that have occurred, when they occurred, and who made them. Talk about a lot of information at your fingertips! You can get all this without ever leaving the Team Explorer tool.

Work item forms can implement rules. For example, you can make fields required, or read-only. You can automatically populate fields with dates or users. You can tie fields back into certain lists. This allows you to make a form that is easier and more intuitive to use, enabling you to capture good clean data in the proper format. These lists can be specific to a work item field, or can be global lists usable by any work item type. We will cover some of these rules later in this chapter. For a more comprehensive look at the rules, we recommend you download the Visual Studio Software Development Kit (VS SDK). This kit contains specific information related to work items, including detailed information on work item forms.

Work Item Work Flow

Tying into the concept of the work item form is the ability to implement a work item workflow. This allows you to automatically change things on a work item form, for example filling out certain fields, based on a series of rules.

For example, when you change a work item from one state to another, say from Open to Closed, the workflow would automatically timestamp the appropriate fields for you. Then let's say, later in the day, someone reopens that work item. You could have a workflow set up so that, when a work item is reopened, it is automatically reassigned to the person who closed it. The person reopening the work item doesn't have to hunt to find out whom to assign the work item to, because the system does this automatically. And all of this workflow information is defined in the work item type definition.

The goal of Team Foundation Server is to support better predictability and quality of projects. And Team Foundation Server, along with the work item tracking system, will allow teams to do a more efficient job with fewer flaws. These little details, such as reassigning the work item to the appropriate person, free up valuable time which, in the long run, ultimately gives team members more time to work on the actual project.

Customizing and Extending

The work item tracking system allows you to export existing work item types, make some modifications to them, and then reimport them back into your existing projects, making the changes easily available.

For example, if you wanted to make a certain field required that was not required before, you could export the work item type, open the XML definition, make the change, then reimport the type back into the particular project. From that point on, that field would be required for all work items of that particular type.

You can also create brand new work item types. Instead of making your process conform to the types presented with the default process models, build types that allow you to work the way you want to. Don't like the built-in bug work item type of MSF Agile? Export it and change it. Better yet, just build your own that works exactly the way you want it to. The point is, Team Foundation Server in general, and the work item tracking system in particular, is designed to give you the power to use the tool the way you want to. Worry about solving your problems, not about how to use the tool.

The work item tracking system also has a built-in object model for doing custom development. We touch on this briefly in Chapter 9, and come back to it later in this chapter. This object model allows you to interact with the work item tracking system, enabling you to build tools that can help you work with the system more effectively. Later in this chapter, we show you how to build a simple ASP.NET page to view a work item.

Work Item Queries

Finally, work items have their own query language, called, not surprisingly, the Work Item Query Language, or WIQL. This language is a SQL-like construct that is used in conjunction with the work item tracking object model to query information from the work item tracking system. You learn more about the WIQL later in this chapter.

The Visual Studio Software Development Kit has detailed information on the WIQL and any of the topics you have heard about so far. This kit is packed with information related to the work item tracking system, including documentation and examples. Some of the examples may be a little out of date, but Microsoft is working on updating the information, so check back regularly.

Work Item Customization and Extensibility

We've covered a bunch of concepts and general information over the past several pages, but now its time to get our hands dirty and delve into this Team Foundation Server work item concept. To do this, we'll help you create a brand new work item type, called the Help Desk Call type. By developing this type, you will get a basic understanding of the XML file that makes up a work item type. While we are intentionally going to make this type very simple, you should be able to build off the information presented here and in the VS SDK, to continue customizing this type to make it as detailed and intricate as you want.

Creating or modifying work item types can become rather tedious, as Microsoft did not ship a visual editor to help with the process. So, you have to make modifications to the XML file by hand, which, for a detailed work item type, can be a little nerve-wracking. You will learn how to make these adjustments by hand, but we will also introduce you to a third-party tool, currently available for free, which makes modifying your work item types, and in fact any part of your process model, much easier.

Before continuing, go ahead and create a test team project called Chp11WIT, using the MSF Agile process model. You'll use this team project throughout the remainder of this chapter.

Work Item Type XML File Overview

Figure 11-1 shows a compact example of the task work item type from the MSF Agile process model.

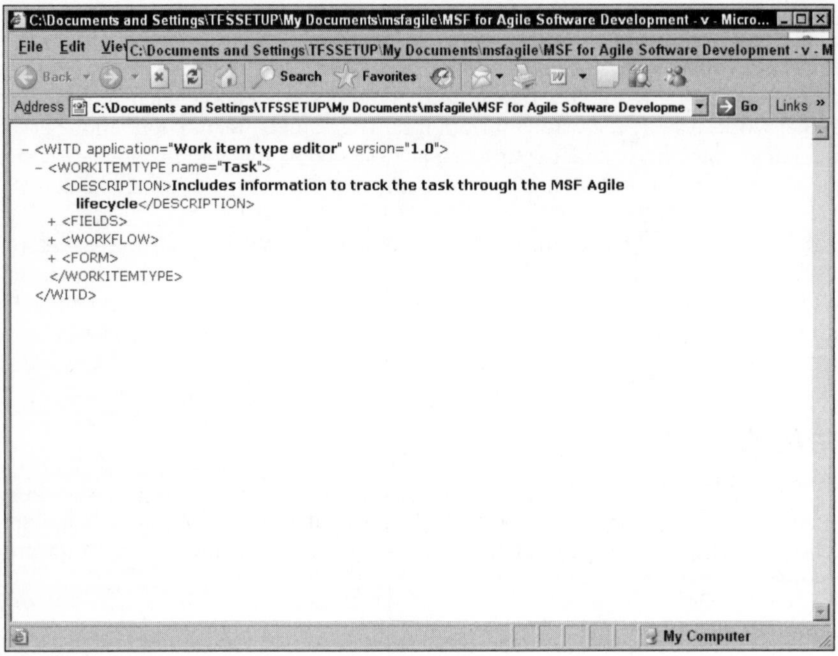

Figure 11-1

As this figure shows, a work item type is made up of several parts:

- A *name* helps identify the work item type. The name must be unique at a team project level, meaning you cannot have two work item types named Task in the same team project.
- A *description* is, as you have probably guessed, a description of the work item type.
- A *collection of fields* defines the information that makes up the work item type. This collection also contains any rules associated with the fields, such as a field being required.
- A *collection of work flow states and transitions* defines the different possible states of the work item type, and what should happen when you move from one state to the next.
- A *form section* defines the layout of the work item type form.

Given these different parts, let's look at the XML code for a very simple help desk form. All this form has is a state (open, closed) and a description of the problem. Obviously, there is much more information we need to make this usable, but this will do for introducing us into the XML syntax for a work item type. A couple of quick housekeeping rules first though. The form must be enclosed in the `<WITD>` tag. The application name can be anything, but the version must be 1.0. You must have at least one field, one state, one state transition, one state transition reason, and something in the form area. Given these basic rules, here is XML declaration for the simple help desk form:

```
<?xml version="1.0" encoding="utf-8"?>
<WITD application="Work item type editor" version="1.0">
<WORKITEMTYPE name="Help Desk Call">
<DESCRIPTION>I am a description of the help desk call</DESCRIPTION>
<FIELDS>

<FIELD name="Id" refname="System.Id" type="Integer" />
<FIELD name="Title" refname="System.Title" type="String">
<HELPTEXT>Short description of the task used to differentiate it in a list or
report</HELPTEXT>
<REQUIRED />
</FIELD>
<FIELD name="State" refname="System.State" type="String">
<HELPTEXT>The workflow state of the task</HELPTEXT>
</FIELD>

</FIELDS>
<WORKFLOW>

<STATES>
<STATE value="Open" />
</STATES>
<TRANSITIONS>
<TRANSITION from="" to="Open">
<REASONS>
<DEFAULTREASON value="New Call Opened" />
</REASONS>
</TRANSITION>
</TRANSITIONS>
</WORKFLOW>
<FORM>

<Layout>
<Control FieldName="System.Title" Type="FieldControl" Label="Title:"
LabelPosition="Left" />
<Control FieldName="System.State" Type="FieldControl" Label="State:"
LabelPosition="Left" />
</Layout>
</FORM>
</WORKITEMTYPE>
</WITD>
```

Let's examine the `FIELDS`, `WORKFLOW`, and `FORM` tags in a little more detail, to explain what you are seeing. Let's look at the `<FIELDS>` tag first.

We declared three fields for this work item type. The first is an ID value for the work item called, obviously, `Id`:

```
<FIELD name="Id" refname="System.Id" type="Integer" />
```

Notice that the field has both a name and a reference name (`refname`). The `name` attribute is the visible identifier for the field. This value is used when constructing queries, and is the basic way of referring to this particular field in the work item. The reference name is a globally unique name for this field. While you can change the `name` attribute on a field, you cannot change the reference name. Reference names are also limited to 70 characters in length. There are two reference name *namespaces* defined with Team Foundation Server: System and Microsoft. System defines the system fields that Team Foundation Server provides for you; Microsoft defines those fields necessary to use the Microsoft process models. You can easily create your own reference name by just changing the value of the `refname` attribute to a unique value. The `type` attribute defines the kind of data that the field is expected to store. The defined types are as follows:

- Double
- DateTime
- HTML
- Integer
- PlainText
- String

You must declare the `name`, `refname`, and `type` attributes when creating a field value.

There is an optional field attribute, called `reportable`, that allows you to specify that the contents of the field be sent to the Team Foundation Server data warehouse. This allows the field to be included in reports. There are three possible values for this attribute:

- **dimension** — This value can be set for Integer, String, and DateTime fields. The data is sent to both the data warehouse and the cube, allowing this field to be used to filter reports.
- **detail** — This value can be set for Integer, Double, String, and DateTime fields. The data is sent to the data warehouse, but not the cube.
- **measure** — This value can be set for Integer and Double fields only and is used for data aggregation purposes.

In the XML listed previously, look at the field value with the name Title. It contains a work item type definition similar to the previous one, but it also contains the following tags:

```
<HELPTEXT>Short description of the task used to differentiate it in a list or
report</HELPTEXT>
<REQUIRED />
```

This is an example of some of the field rules you can apply to a field. Using the `<HELPTEXT>` tag, you can give the field a description to help the user understand its purpose. This information is displayed when the mouse is hovered over the field. The `<REQUIRED />` tag indicates that this field is required, and the work item cannot be saved until something is added to this field. There are various possible field rules, including the following:

- `<ALLOWEXISTINGVALUE />` — This rule allows a field to keep its existing value, even if that value is not allowed.
- `<CANNOTLOSEVALUE />` — This rule does not allow a field to be cleared once a value has been entered.

- `<EMPTY />`—This rule will clear the field when the work item is committed, and the user is not allowed to enter any values in the field.
- `<FROZEN />`—This rule does not allow a field to be modified, after a value has been entered
- `<MATCH pattern="<pattern>" />`—This rule enforces string pattern matching.
- `<NOTSAMEAS field="fieldname" />`—This rule prevents a field from having the same value as another field.
- `<READONLY />`—This rule prevents a field from being modified.
- `<REQUIRED />`—This rule requires a value to be entered for this field.
- `<VALIDUSER />`—This rule requires that the field contain a user who is a valid Team Foundation Server user.

Finally, we declared a `State` field, which, when we open a new help desk form work item, will have a state of `Open`. This field is also required.

Next, let's look at the `<WORKFLOW>` section. Remember, you have to define at least one state, one transition, and a default reason for that transition. In this code, there is one state with a value of Open. There is one transition from nothing (represented by empty quotation marks) to Open, indicating that the work item is being initially created. The default reason for that transition is that a new call has been opened. Obviously, you can add more states, transitions, and reasons as you see fit. If you'll notice, we are not even displaying the reason on the form. We'll fix that in a little bit.

Finally, let's look at the `<FORM>` tag. Inside this tag is the `<Layout>` tag, which will contain all the different fields we want to display. We are currently showing two fields, the `System.Title` and the `System.State`. Notice we are using `refnames` instead of `names`. Because the `names` can always change, but the `refnames` do not, you are required to use the `refnames` when declaring your controls. There are various formatting options you can use to make the form easier to read and use. For right now, you are just going to slap those two controls on the form and go.

Well, you now have you basic help desk call work item type. Go ahead and save this type to the `c:\chp11` directory to a file named HelpDeskCall.xml. Before you can use the type, you must import it into a team project on Team Foundation Server. To do this, you need to use the work item type Import tool, witimport. This tool is located at `c:\Program Files\Microsoft Visual Studio 8\Common7\IDE`. Open a command prompt and navigate to this directory. The format for using the witimport tool is

```
witimport /f filename /t tfs /p teamproject [/v]
```

where `filename` is the work item type XML file, `tfs` is the name of the Team Foundation Server, and `teamproject` is the name of the project you want to import the work item into. The `/v` switch is optional, and allows you to check to make sure the XML file is valid without actually importing it into the Team Foundation Server. To insert your work item type, run the following at the command prompt:

```
witimport /f c:\Chp11\HelpDeskCall.xml /t mstfs /p Chp11WIT
```

If the import runs successfully, you will receive a message saying "Work item type import complete." Otherwise, you will receive an error message, which should help you determine what is wrong with the XML file.

1. Open Visual Studio 2005 and open Team Explorer. Open the Chp11WIT Team Project. Right-click the project name, and select Refresh. This updates the Team Explorer with the latest information from the database.
2. Now, right-click the Work Item folder under the Chp11WIT Team Project, and select Add Work Item. Besides the five work item types installed by default with the MSF Agile process model, you also see the option for your Help Desk Call work item type.
3. Select the Help Desk Call Work Item Type. Figure 11-2 shows you the Work Item Form for that type.

Notice how the State field was populated for us automatically. Remember, we defined a transition in which state is changed to Open when a new help desk call work item is created. Enter a value for the title and click Save. The work item is assigned an ID number, which will appear in the tab of the work item. Make a note of this number, as you will use it in some examples later.

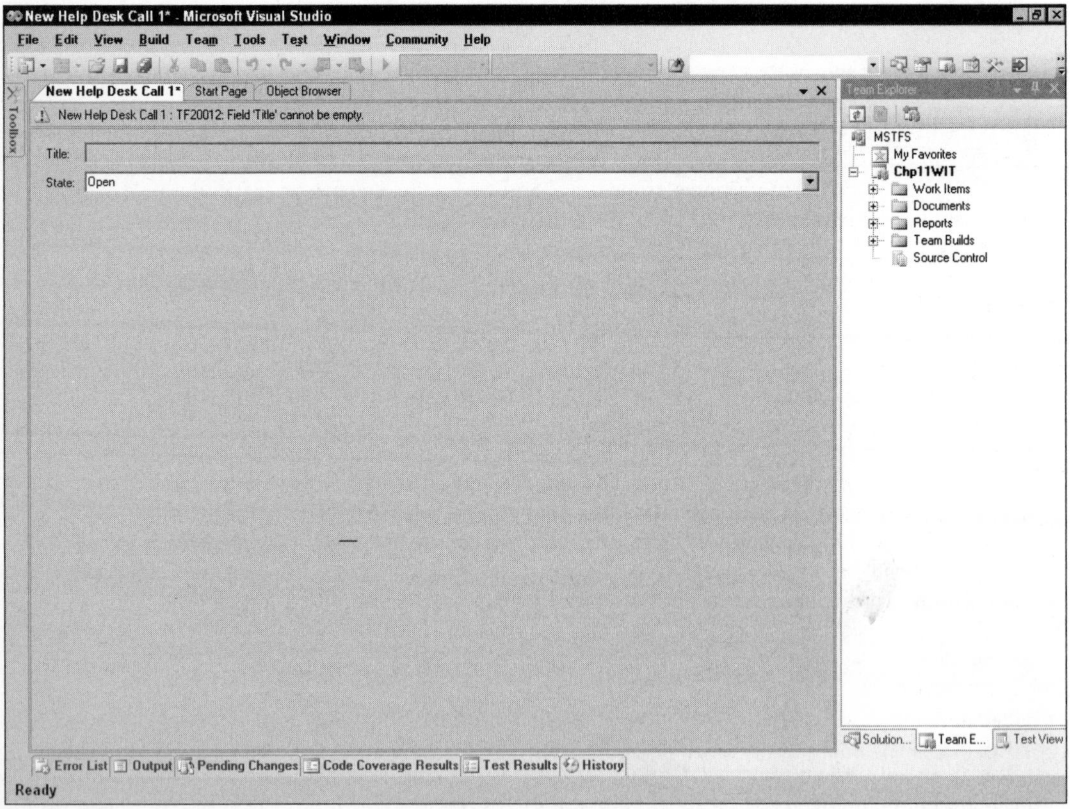

Figure 11-2

And there you go. You have created a custom work item type, imported it into the Team Foundation Server, and created a work item from that type. And with this simple example, you have only touched the surface of what is possible with custom type creation. For a more detailed look, download the SDK. Download the latest process models from the MSF Agile site, open the XML files for the different work items, and see the beauty and complexity of those types. You can make your work item types as simple or as complex as you want, but the fact is, you can make them work the way you want them to. And that is the real power of the work item system in Team Foundation Server.

Customizing an Existing Work Item

You can see in the XML for the Help Desk Call work item type, a reason is declared, but we do not have a field to hold that reason, and are not displaying that reason on the form. Let's fix that problem now. First, we need to export the work item type, so we can make some modifications to it. To do this, you need to use the Work Item Type Export tool, witexport. This tool is located at `c:\Program Files\Microsoft Visual Studio 8\Common7\IDE`. Open a command prompt and navigate to this directory. The format for using the witexport tool is

```
witexport /f filename /t tfs /p teamproject /n witname
```

where `filename` is the destination file you are exporting to, `tfs` is the name of the Team Foundation Server, `teamproject` is the name of the team project containing the work item type, and witname is the name of the work item type to be exported. To export the Help Desk Call work item type to `c:\chp11\hdc.xml`, use the following:

```
witexport /f c:\Chp11\htc.xml /t mstfs /p Chp11WIT /n "Help Desk Call"
```

This exports the work item type to a file named htc.xml. If you open the htc.xml file, you'll see a lot more fields defined than were initially there. The Work Item Tracking System automatically adds any missing system fields to your work item type. These fields are not automatically added to the form, however. As you can see, the Reason field has already been added to the Fields collection. But you still need to add it to the form for it to be displayed.

Once you have exported the work item to a file, you can open it up and make modifications to it. We've shown previously how you can make these modifications by hand. Now we are going to show you a third-party tool, currently free, that allows you to modify your work items in a nicer, graphical environment. This tool is called the Process Template Editor, and was created by Joel Semeniuk, a Microsoft Team System Most Valuable Professional. You can get the latest version of this tool at `gotdotnet.com/Workspaces/Workspace.aspx?id=812a68af-5e74-48c6-9623-1a4469142a84`. Go ahead and download this tool now. It can be used for creating or editing a process model, or for creating and editing work item types. The beauty of this tool is that it can connect to your Team Foundation Server, allowing you to view work item type information that is stored on the server. It even does validation checking to make sure your work item type is configured correctly. Trust me, once you start using a graphical tool for making changes to your work item types, you won't ever go back to Notepad!

Let's open the Process Template Editor, and use it to add the reason field to our work item type and the work item form.

1. Open the Process Template Editor by selecting Start➪All Programs➪Imaginet Resources➪Process Template Editor. This opens the Process Template Editor window. A dialog box appears, asking you to select a Team Foundation Server.

2. Enter the name of your Team Foundation Server, or just click Work Offline. From the main menu, select Work Item Types➪Open From File.

3. Navigate to the `c:\chp11\` and select the htc.xml file that you just exported. Figure 11-3 shows the Process Template Editor with the Help Desk Call work item type open, and the Fields tab selected.

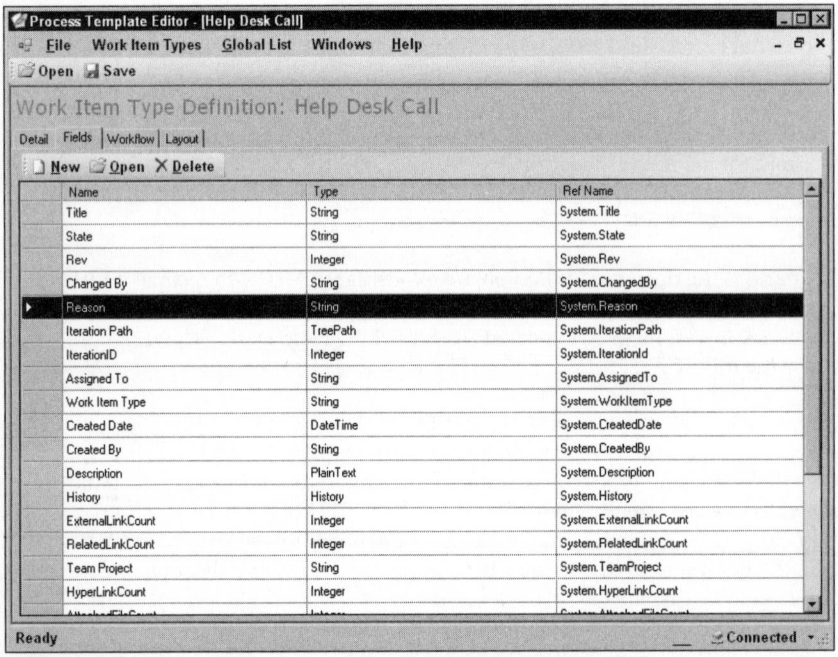

Figure 11-3

The Reason field was added for you automatically when you imported the work item type, but you still need to make this field displayable to the user.

4. Click the Layout tab to begin editing the form.

5. In the tree view on the left side, right-click Layout and select New Control. On the right side of the window, change the Field Name to **System.Reason**, and the Label to be **Reason**. You can even click the Preview Form button to get a general idea of how the form will look.

6. Click the Save button to save the changes to the XML file.

We've only briefly touched on using this graphical tool, but as you can see, it can save a lot of time when editing work item types. You can use this tool to define states, transitions, required fields, and work flow options. This tool is a great example of what you can build using the work item tracking object model.

Now that you have changed the work item type, you need to import it back into the Team Foundation Server. Run the following from the command prompt:

```
witimport /f c:\Chp11\htc.xml /t mstfs /p Chp11WIT
```

Go back to Team Explorer, and add another Help Desk Call work item. As you can see in Figure 11-4, you can now see the Reason field. If you do not see the field, it could be due to Team Foundation Server's caching mechanism. Simply shut down and restart Visual Studio or Team Explorer, and you will be able to see the new field

Notice how the Reason field is filled in for you automatically when you opened the new work item. This is an example of the workflow in the work item tracking system, and how moving from different states can automatically trigger items to change on the form. As with everything else, you can make this as simple or as intricate as you like.

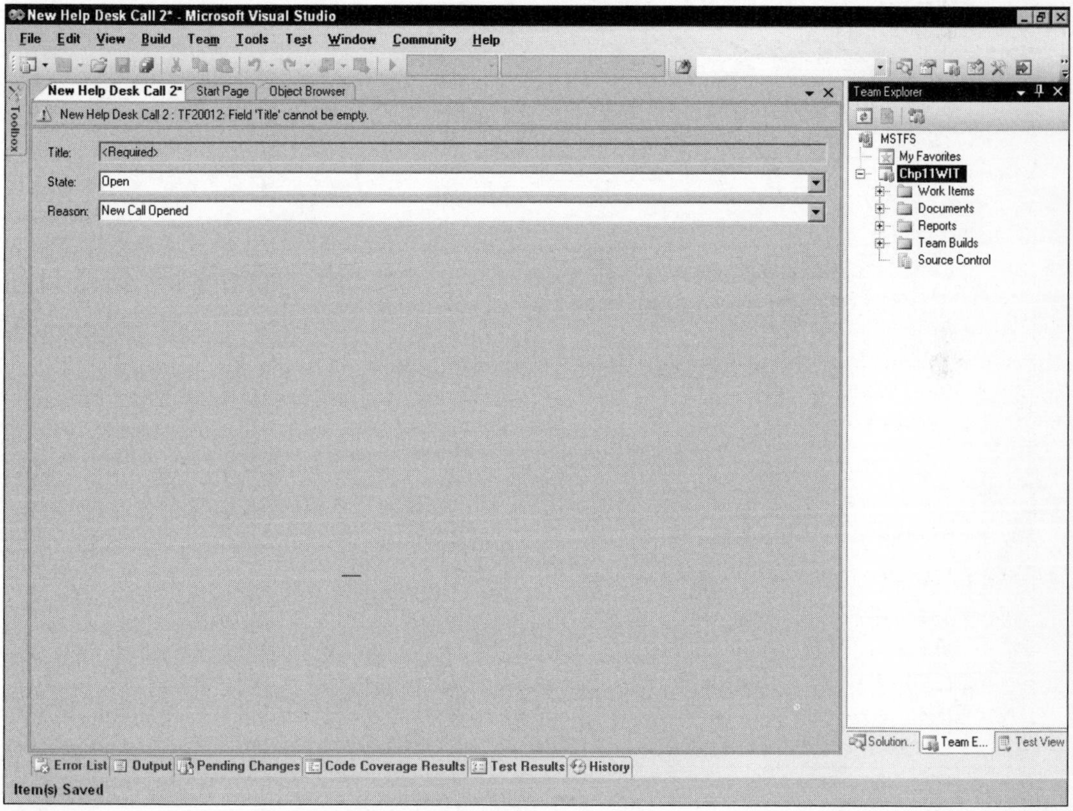

Figure 11-4

Work Item Administration

So far in this chapter, you have examined the guts of a work item, and have a basic understanding of how you can create your own work item, and add it to Team Foundation Server. Now it's time to move on to how you actually interact with the work item tracking system daily. You do this using Team Explorer, and specifically the Work Items folder located in your Team Project. From here you can do anything you need to concerning the work item tracking system: create a new work item, open an existing work item, retrieve lists of work items, and build custom views of work items, just to name a few.

As usual, you can modify all these options, and make them work for you as you need them to.

Creating A Work Item

Creating a new work item is easy. Simply right-click the Work Items folder, Select Add Work Item, and then the work item type you want to create. For example, to create a new task work item, select Task. This opens the task for you to fill out as shown in Figure 11-5.

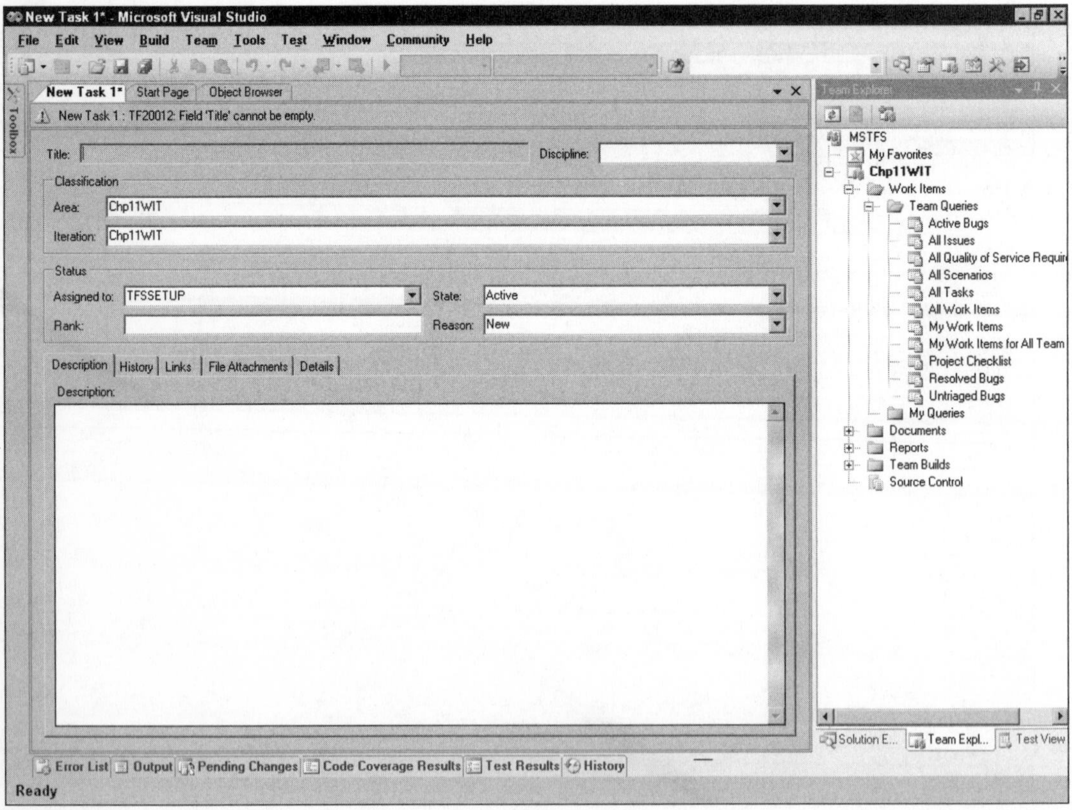

Figure 11-5

Notice how certain fields are filled in for you automatically, like the Assigned To, State, and Reason fields. Enter a title and save the work item. When you save the work item, it will be assigned an ID. Remember this ID, as you will come back to it later.

If you do not fill in all the required fields, you will not be able to save the work item.

Searching the Work Item Store

All work item information is stored in the data tier of the Team Foundation Server. To access this information, you create queries, similar to SQL queries. These queries are stored with the Team Project, and can be set where the entire team can access them, or they can be made private to a particular user.

Figure 11-6 shows the Team Explorer window for the Chp11WIT Team Project. Notice that there are two folders: Team Queries and My Queries. The Team Queries folder contains all the work item queries that are accessible by the entire team. The My Queries are your personal queries for this Team Project.

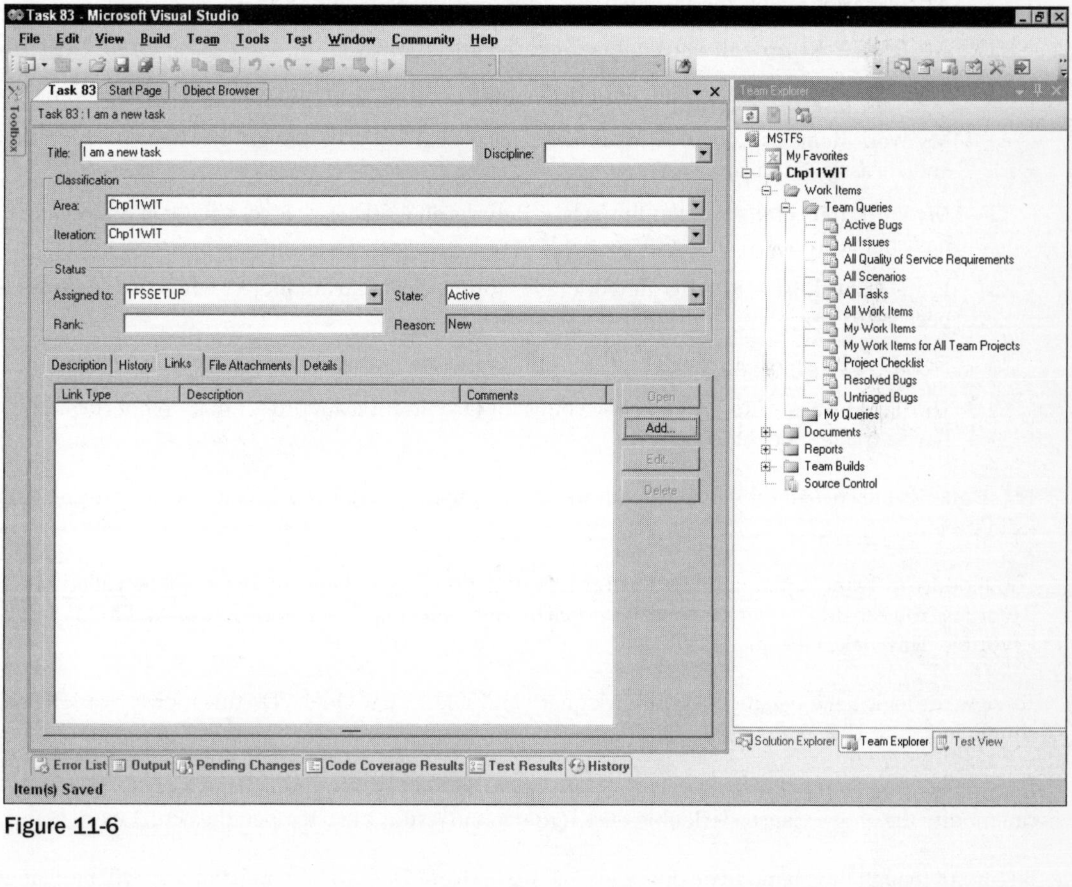

Figure 11-6

You can retrieve a particular work item by using the work item id number. Simply right-click the Work Items folder, and select Go To Work Item. Enter the work item id and it pulls up the details of the work item. This provides a quick way to review a specific work item's information, without having to run a larger query against the database.

Team Queries Folder

As you can see from Figure 11-6, there are several pregenerated queries for you. These include the following:

- Active Bugs — Returns all active bugs for current team project
- All Issues — Returns all work items for the current team project that have been marked as an issue
- **All Quality of Service Requirements** — Returns all active quality of service requirements for current team project
- **All Scenarios** — Returns all active scenarios for current team project
- **All Tasks** — Returns all active tasks for current team project
- **All Work Items** — Returns all work items for the current team project that have not been closed
- **My Work Items** — Returns all work items for the current team project that have not been closed and are assigned to you
- **My Work Items for All Team Projects** — Returns all work items across all team projects that have not been closed and are assigned to you
- **Project Checklist** — Returns all work items for the current team project whose exit criteria has been set to `yes`
- **Resolved Bugs** — Returns all bugs for the current team project that have been resolved
- **Untriaged Bugs** — Returns all active bugs for the current team project that do not currently have a triage state set

These queries are created for you automatically by the process model you selected when you created the team project.

You'll notice in Team Explorer, under the Team Foundation Server name, there is a folder called My Favorites. You can add a query to your favorites by right-clicking on it and selecting Add to My Favorites. This makes the queries you use frequently easily accessible.

To view the logic behind a query, right-click query and select View Query. Do this for My Work Items, as shown in Figure 11-7.

In this view, you can see the `where` clause of the query, as well as the query results in table format. You can modify the `where` clause, or double-click a row in the results view to open the actual work item.

Be careful though. If you modify a query located in the Team Queries folder, that query will be changed for *everyone* who has access to the Team Project. Modifications to Team Queries should be limited to those people who are in charge of the team project. For individual users, it makes more sense to use the My Queries folder.

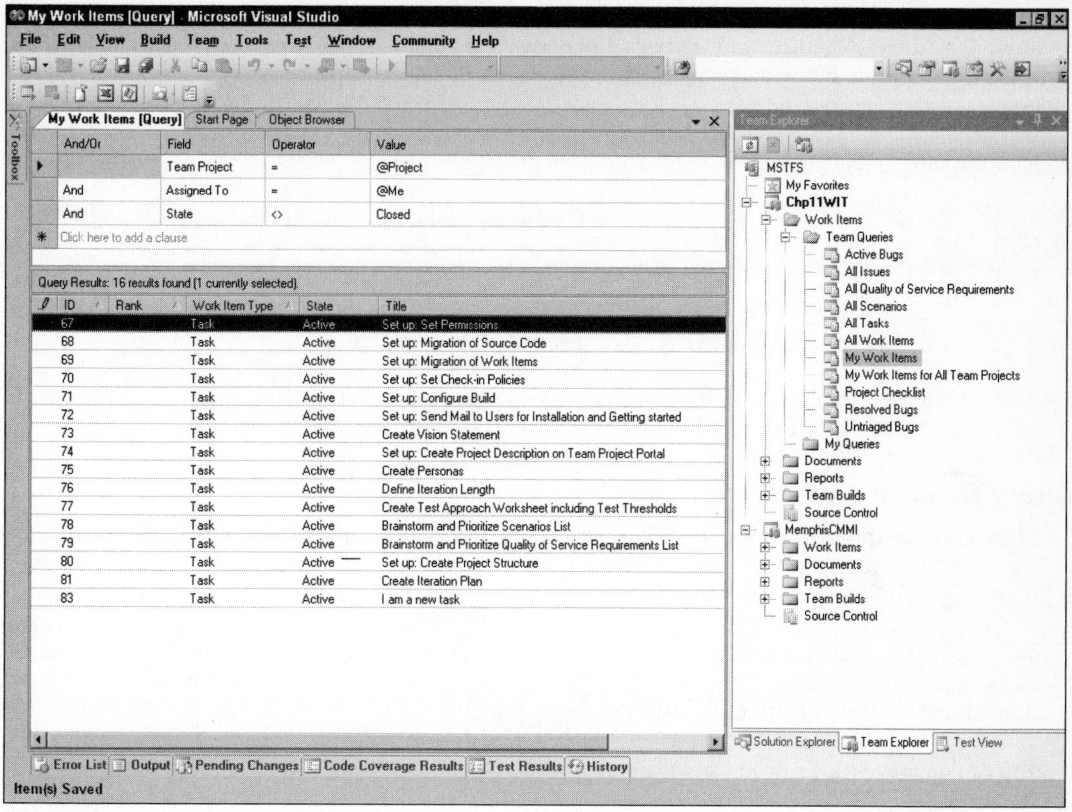

Figure 11-7

My Queries Folder

When a new team project is created, the My Queries folder is empty, which makes sense. This folder is designed to hold any queries you create for this team project, which can only be accessed by you. This allows you to make as detailed a query, or any many queries, as you like, while providing you with a secure, safe place to store and access them.

To create a new query, simply right-click the My Queries folder and select Add Query. This opens a view very similar to Figure 11-7, but with the `where` clause of the query initially empty. Using this query builder, you can easily build a query to retrieve the work item information in which you are interested.

Almost any field from the work item type can be used in the query. When you select the Field column, you will see a list of possible fields from which to choose. Depending on the field you select, you may be provided with a list of possible values. For example, if you select the Assigned To field, you will be presented with a list of all the users in Team Foundation Server. Little touches like this make utilizing the work item tracking system more efficient.

The query builder works like most query builders, so you should grasp it rather quickly. However, you may have already noticed one potential issue. If you are using the Assigned To field to retrieve some work item information and you hard-code a user ID into it, if you want to share that query with other users, they will have to modify it appropriately. While this is not an earth-shattering problem, it can be annoying. Microsoft anticipated that, and has developed a set of macros that allow you to make queries that are more generic. You can actually see these macros in use in the different pregenerated team queries, and in Figure 11-7.

Here are three of the most commonly used macros:

- **@me** — Substitutes the windows account name of the user running the query
- **@Project** — Substitutes the project name of the project containing the query
- **@today** — Substitutes midnight of the current date on the machine running the query. You can also add or subtract days from it, such as @today–4 or @today+7.

And, of course, in keeping with the make-it-work-like-you-want-it-to-work theme, you can create your own custom macros as well, and store them in Team Foundation Server for everyone to use.

Query Results

There are three different views for a work item query. Figure 11-7 already showed you one view of query results, where the query builder is displayed at the top of the window, and table of query results is displayed at the bottom. Now let's look at the other two views.

To actually run a query, just double-click it, or right-click the query and View Results. Running the My Work Items Query, shown in Figure 11-8, shows the table of work items retrieved in the top of the window, and the specific details of the select work item below.

You can double-click a row to view the query full screen, similar to Figure 11-5.

You can also right-click the table, and select which columns are displayed and the sort order for the columns. You can select several work items and print them all at once. Take this screen and modify it so that it works best for you. If you make any changes to how you view the query, these changes will be saved with the query.

View a Work Item's History

The beauty of having all the work item information stored in a database is that every change to the work item can be tracked. This allows you to easily view a history of the work item, from when it was created, to any modifications made to it, to when it is finally closed.

All the pregenerated work item types have a history tab, which displays the history information for the work item. You can also add this history tab to any work item types you create, instantly enabling you to use the same functionality, without having to do any major coding or jump through any hoops.

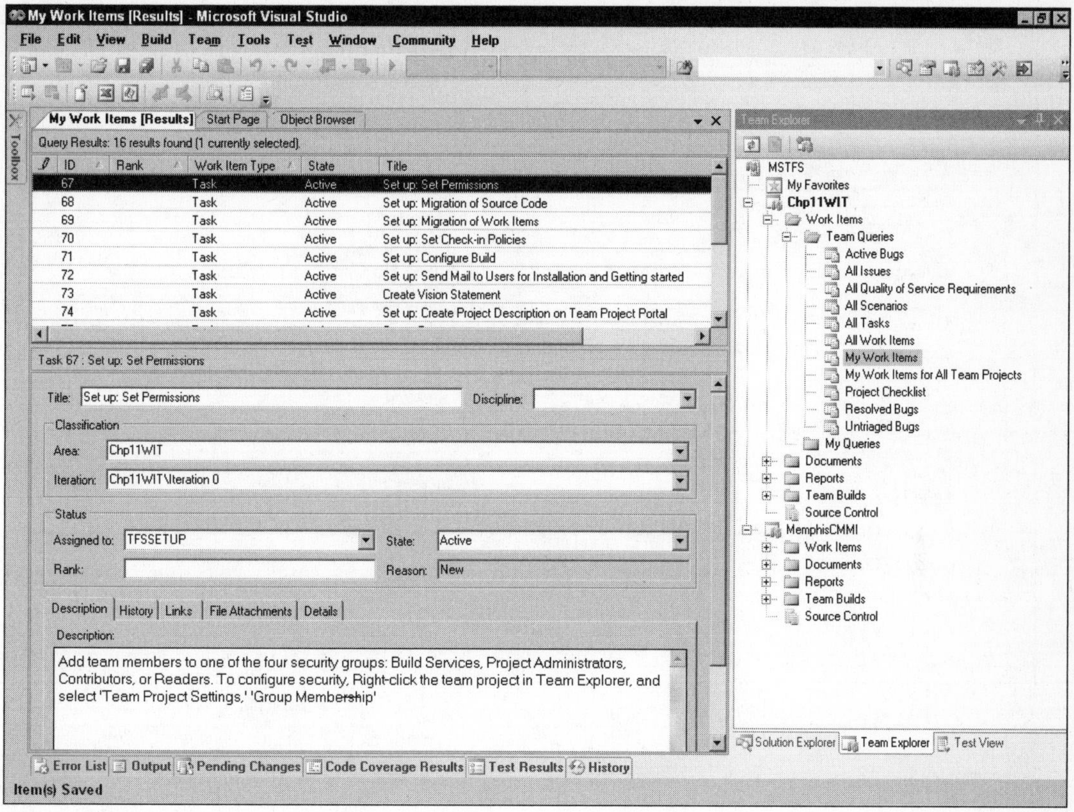

Figure 11-8

Project and Excel Integration

Developers live and breathe in Visual Studio. But managers are sometimes a different breed. Many managers like their Microsoft Excel or Microsoft Project, and don't want to be taken out of their comfort zone. Team Foundation Server takes this into account by allowing managers to open work item information in Microsoft Excel or Microsoft Project.

Doing this is simple. In Team Explorer, right-click the work item query you wish to view. From the context menu, select Open in Microsoft Excel or Open in Microsoft Project. This opens the results of that query in the tool you selected. Figure 11-9 shows the results of opening the All Work Items query in Microsoft Excel.

Now anyone comfortable with Excel can easily view and update this information. The beauty of this is that any changes you make in the spreadsheet can be synched back up with Team Foundation Server. For example, select a row and change the Assigned To field to a different person. Now, under the Team menu option, select Publish Changes. This pushes any changes in the spreadsheet back to the Team Foundation Server. If you now go back into Team Explorer, and pull up the work item you just changed, you will see the Assigned To field has been changed to the new value.

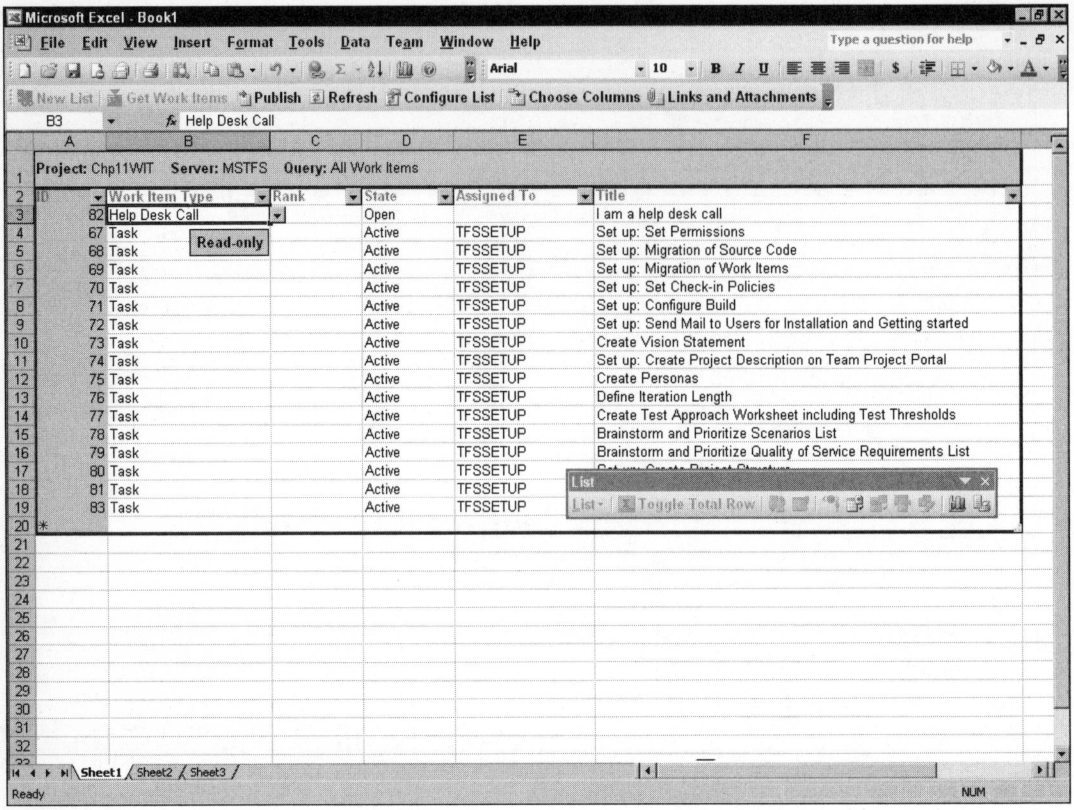

Figure 11-9

All the power of the work item tracking system, with the ability to use it in the tool of your choice, allows you to put the power back into the hands of your users, instead of the users being slaves to a particular tool.

Work Item Tracking Object Model

Chapter 9 introduced the Team Foundation Server Object Model, and briefly touched on the WorkItemStore service type. This WorkItemStore service type allows you access to the Work Item Tracking Object Model, which is the public interface to the work item tracking Web service on the Team Foundation Server. You use this object model to programmatically interact with the work item tracking system.

Each Team Foundation Server defines one and only one work item store. This store contains all the work item information for all the different team projects located on that Team Foundation Server.

Using this work item store, you can access work item information by using the work item ID, or by writing a query in the Work Item Query Language (see the next section). Once you have retrieved a work item, you can examine its contents or make changes and save them back to the Team Foundation Server. The Visual Studio Software Development Kit has some extensive documentation on the work item tracking object model; we would refer you to there for more information.

You have already seen, with the Process Template Editor, one great example of what can be built off the Team Foundation Object Model and the work item tracking object model. Another great example is from a company called Devbiz Business Solutions (`devbiz.com`). They have developed an application called TeamPlain (`teamplain.com`), which gives you a Web-based front-end to the work item tracking system. Everything you can do with Team Explorer and work items, including opening new work items, viewing them, and running queries, you can also do with TeamPlain, without having to install any software on a client machine. Again, another great example of the power and flexibility that these object models give you, to make the system work for you, the way you want it to.

So let's explore how to make a (very) poor man's version of TeamPlain. You are going to see how to create an ASP.NET Web page, which will display a list of team projects. You will select a team project, and a list of work items in that project will be displayed. You can then select a work item, and you will see the details of that work item.

1. Create a new ASP.NET Web site, and name it **Chp11WITWebSite**.
2. Open the Default.aspx page, and add two DropDownList controls. Name the first control **ddlProject** and the second **ddlWorkItem**, and enable AutoPostBack on each control. The first control is going to contain a list of team projects from the Team Foundation Server. When a project is selected, the second control will be populated with a list of work items from that project. Selecting a work item from the second control will display some detailed information for that work item.
3. Add the following code to the `Page_Load` event of the `Default.aspx` page:

```
if (!Page.IsPostBack)
{
TeamFoundationServer tfs = TeamFoundationServerFactory.GetServer("mstfs");
WorkItemStore wis = (WorkItemStore)tfs.GetService(typeof(WorkItemStore));

ProjectCollection pc = wis.Projects;
foreach (Project p in pc)
{
//al.Add(p.Name);

ListItem li = new ListItem();
li.Text = p.Name;
li.Value = p.Name;
ddlProject.Items.Add(li);
li = null;
}
wis = null;
tfs = null;

ddlProject.SelectedIndex = -1;
}
```

This code retrieves all the projects from the work item store. This is a list of all the projects that have work items associated with them. For each project, the code creates a list item and populates the ddlProject drop-down list box.

4. In the `SelectedIndexChanged` event of the `ddlProject` drop-down list box, add the following code:

```
TeamFoundationServer tfs = TeamFoundationServerFactory.GetServer("mstfs");
WorkItemStore wis = (WorkItemStore)tfs.GetService(typeof(WorkItemStore));

WorkItemCollection wic = wis.Query("SELECT System.Id FROM workitems WHERE [Team
Project] = '" + ddlProject.SelectedValue + "'");

ddlWorkItem.Items.Clear();

foreach (WorkItem wi in wic)
{
ListItem li = new ListItem();
li.Text = wi.Id.ToString() + " - " + wi.Title;
li.Value = wi.Id.ToString();
ddlWorkItem.Items.Add(li);
li = null;
}

wic = null;
wis = null;
tfs = null;

ddlWorkItem.SelectedIndex = -1;
```

This code retrieves all the work items for the selected project and populates the ddlWorkItem drop-down list box with those work items.

5. Finally, add the following line of code to the `SelectedIndexChanged` event of the `ddlWorkItem` drop down list box:

```
Response.Redirect("http://mstfs:8080//WorkItemTracking/WorkItem.aspx?artifactMonike
r=" + ddlWorkItem.SelectedValue.ToString());
```

This code uses and ASP.NET page provided by Team Foundation Server to return information on the selected work item. The work item ID is passed into the Web page, and is used to retrieve the work item information.

Figures 11-10 and 11-11 show the Web page and the detailed work item information for a selected work item.

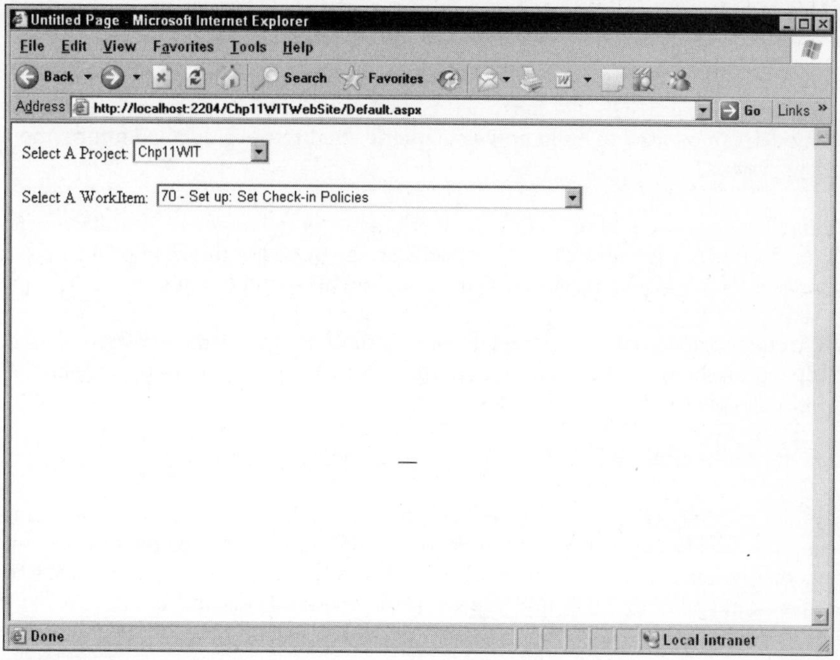

Figure 11-10

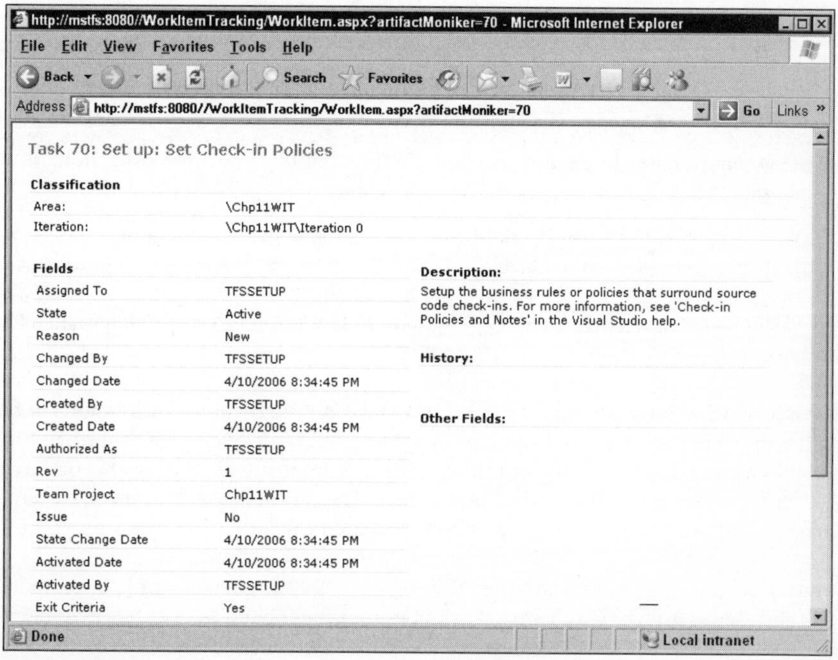

Figure 11-11

Using Work Item Query Language

As mentioned earlier, work items have their own query language, called the Work Item Query Language (WIQL). This language is a SQL-like construct that, when used in conjunction with the work item tracking object model, can be used to build powerful queries that retrieve detailed information from the work item tracking system.

This section will give you a brief primer on the Work Item Query Language. For all the details, you should check out the documentation provided in the Visual Studio SDK. For this brief primer, you will learn about the different aspects of a WIQL query, and then see a short application that uses a WIQL query.

Every WIQL query consists of a `SELECT` statement, containing the fields to retrieve, and a `WHERE` statement to help determine what information to retrieve. So a sample query to retrieve all the work item ids assigned to Developer1 might look like this:

```
System.ID from workitems where System.AssignedTo = 'Developer1'
```

You always must specify the fields you are interested in. When specifying fields, you can use either the friendly name or the reference name. In the above example, we have used the reference name. Best practices dictate that you use reference names at all times, as these will never change, while friendly names may change at some point in the future. You can select any field type in a query, except for plain text fields. And all your standard operators, such as `=`, `>`, and `<`, work in the `WHERE` clause section.

You've already learned about some of the macros you can use, such as `@today`, `@me`, and `@project`. Here is a quick hit list of some behaviors and operators for certain field types:

- String literals, such as Developer1, must be quoted using either single or double quotes.
- The `under` operator is used to check whether an area or iteration path value is within a subtree of a specific node: `WHERE [System.AreaPath] under '\Chp11WIT\Area1\Subarea1'`.
- The `in` operator checks to see if a value is a member of a specified collection: `WHERE System .AssignedTo in ('developer1', developer2', 'developer3')`.
- The `ever` operator tells you if a field has ever been given a certain value. For example, to find all work items ever assigned to Developer1: `WHERE System.AssignedTo ever 'Developer1'`.

You can also use the standard SQL `order by` statement, and `asc` and `desc` statements, to sort the results of your WIQL query.

Finally, the information returned by your query depends on the security permissions of the user running the query. If you try to pull all the work items every assigned to Developer1, but do not have access to all the Team Projects, you will receive information only from those team projects you have the authority to access. There is no warning of any kind that occurs. The moral is to make sure you have access and privileges on all the team projects you are planning to query information from.

Okay, given all the previous information, let's write a quick little console application that will return the `System.ID` and `System.Title` for every work item that the logged in user has ever been assigned to. We'll then display this information to the screen. Create a new console application called `MyWorkItems`, then open the Program.cs file.

As shown in Chapter 9, add references to `Microsoft.TeamFoundation.dll`, `Microsoft.TeamFoundation.WorkItemTracking.dll`, and `Microsoft.TeamFoundation.WorkItemTracking.Client dll`. Then add the following using statements to the `Program.cs` file:

```
using Microsoft.TeamFoundation;
using Microsoft.TeamFoundation.Client;
using Microsoft.TeamFoundation.Server;
using Microsoft.TeamFoundation.WorkItemTracking;
using Microsoft.TeamFoundation.WorkItemTracking.Client;
```

The following code listing goes in the `Main()` function of the Program.cs file:

```
TeamFoundationServer tfs = TeamFoundationServerFactory.GetServer("mstfs");

WorkItemStore wis = (WorkItemStore)tfs.GetService(typeof(WorkItemStore));

WorkItemCollection wic = wis.Query("SELECT System.ID, System.Title FROM workitems
WHERE System.AssignedTo = @Me");

foreach (WorkItem wi in wic)
{
Console.WriteLine("ID = " + wi.Id.ToString());
Console.WriteLine("Title = " + wi.Title.ToString());
}
```

This code creates an instance of the Team Foundation Server Object, and then creates an instance of the work item store associated with the Team Foundation Server Object. Remember, there is only one work item store for each Team Foundation Server.

Next, you run a work item query against the work item store. This query selects the `System.ID` and `System.Title` for all work items that have been assigned to the user running the application. Notice how the `@me` macro was used, to make this query generic. When you run this query against the work item store, it will return all the work items that match the query, and put them in a work item collection.

Finally, you loop through the collection, and for each work item in the collection, you write out the ID and the title. Figure 11-12 shows you a sample output of this application.

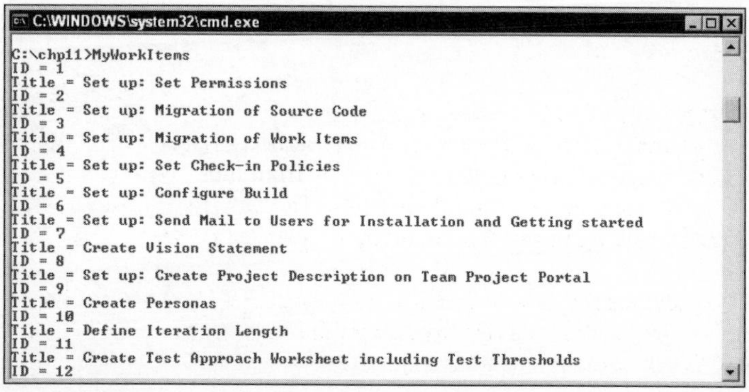

Figure 11-12

Summary

To-do lists. Every project has them, from a simple grocery list to the latest design plans for the next version of an operating system. These lists define the work that needs to be done for a project to be completed successfully. There are many different ways to define these lists. But in development projects, there has not been a good way to tie all these work items together in a way that allows team members to know exactly what they should be working on, and managers and stakeholders to know exactly where the project stands. That is where Team Foundation Server's Work Item Tracking System fits in.

At the beginning of this chapter, you learned about work items, their different components, and some general information about the work items provided for you by the MSF Agile process model.

Next, you got your hands dirty creating a custom work item type. You build the XML code for the work item type, imported the work item type into Team Foundation Server, and created a work item from this work item type. You also exported the work item type, made changes, and reimported it back into Team Foundation Server.

You covered some of the basics of administering work items, including how to create work items, query them, and use Microsoft Excel to view and update work items.

Finally, you explored the work item tracking object model. You created an ASP.NET Web page to view work item information, and you explored the Work Item Query Language by building a console application to display all work items assigned to a particular user.

12

Setting Up Team Foundation Version Control

If you have been developing for any length of time, chances are you have used some sort of version control system. Whether it is an expensive third-party product, a free open-source application, or just a series of directories where you manually copy code after each release or major change, you are implementing some form of change tracking.

Team Foundation Server goes a step beyond most other source control systems with Team Foundation Version Control. This is not just a new version of Visual SourceSafe. This is an enterprise-level version control system, built from the ground up to work with teams both small and large. It makes use of the Team Foundation Server data tier to store all data related to the version control system. It uses Web services on the Team Foundation Server application tier to communicate with the data tier. However, the biggest way in which it differentiates itself from other version control systems is in the way it ties into Team Foundation work item tracking. You can now associate the code you are working on with the problem it is trying to fix. This gives you a completely new level of depth and understanding to your source code, and is just one more way that Team Foundation Server shines.

In this chapter, you are going to learn about Team Foundation Version Control (TFVC). You'll start out by examining some of the current source control systems in use today. From there you will move on to some of the common concepts used in version control systems, and will examine how Team Foundation Version Control implements those concepts. After that you'll get into the essentials of Team Foundation Version Control, including how to configure your team projects to use it, use of the Source Control Explorer, and some of the new features included in TFVC, such as shelving.

Next, you'll take a detailed look at how to convert your old Visual SourceSafe information into Team Foundation Version Control. You'll look at the tools provided by Microsoft, as well as a third-party tool, VS-Converter. You'll learn some best practices for using Team Foundation Version Control to its fullest potential. And to wrap it all up, you'll look at how you can extend Team Foundation Version Control to meet specific needs in your organization.

That's a lot to cover, so let's get started!

Version Control Overview

Ideally, a version control system is supposed to save you time and money. The purpose of a version control system is to enable development teams to track and protect all assets involved in the development of the application. Most important of these assets is the source code, but you also want to track changes to documentation, executables, graphics, and pretty much anything that is involved with the project.

Version control systems allow you to track all the changes made to a file. With this information, it is easy to restore a previous version of a file, if it is needed. Version control systems use security, to ensure that no unauthorized access is permitted to the system. Moreover, a version control system extends beyond just developers. Anyone involved in a project who uses a computer to manage project information can benefit from the use of a version control system.

Different Version Control Systems

There are many systems on the market today. Some are free and some are not. This section discusses three of the most commonly used systems today: Visual SourceSafe, CVS, and Subversion, and then introduces you to Team Foundation Version Control.

Visual SourceSafe

Visual SourceSafe (VSS) is a version control system from Microsoft for use with Microsoft Visual Studio. It is designed to be easy to use right out of the box, and to integrate effectively into Visual Studio. It also provides a command-line tool and separate IDE for accessing the system. VSS also is included with most MSDN subscriptions, making it a natural application to use alongside Visual Studio.

VSS includes the standard features of a version control system, including a repository (file-based), the ability to check files in and out, and the ability to branch and merge files. However, many people have had issues with VSS. VSS relies on file sharing, which can lead to a corrupt database if something happens while a file is being shared. VSS performance can also begin to degrade when a large number of files is involved. While VSS is suitable for small team use, you really need something more robust for larger teams and projects. Moreover, VSS is not easily extensible or easy to access over a slow network connection. This can make using VSS with distributed groups very difficult.

Most versions of VSS support exclusive check-out only, but the latest version VSS 2005, supports shared check-out as well, though it defaults to exclusive.

CVS

CVS started out as a bunch of shell scripts written by Dick Grune. It is a free open-source version control system, designed specifically for use with development projects. It has been around for a very long time, and as such has gotten a lot of use, mostly because it was the only free alternative out there.

CVS uses a file-based repository, similar to VSS. Like VSS, it tracks the history of individual files in the repository, and assigned revision numbers to individual files.

CVS is a command-line only version control system, though there is an offshoot of it called WinCVS that applies a graphical interface to CVS.

Subversion

Subversion is a free open-source version control system that manages a list of files and directories. It was not built specifically for managing development projects. Instead, it is more of a general system that can be used for managing any files, from C# code files to your shopping list for Wal-Mart.

Subversion was actually built by developers who were looking for an alternative to CVS. They felt there were some severe limitations with CVS, and wanted to build something that, while staying true to the ideas of CVS, was more stable and less buggy. The point was to build something similar to CVS, so CVS users could easily switch, but not duplicate any CVS issues.

Subversion also uses a file-based repository. Unlike CVS however, it does not apply revision numbers to individual files. Instead, it applies a revision number to the entire file tree. In effect, each revision number is the state of the entire repository after a committed change.

Team Foundation Version Control

Team Foundation Version Control (TFVC) is a brand new version control system, built from the ground up. Make no mistake; this is not just a newer version of Visual SourceSafe. It is a three-tier application, utilizing Web services and using SQL Server 2005 as the backend repository. It provides both a GUI and command-line tools for accessing the system. It has been designed for enterprise use and provides support for distributed teams. It provides a secure, reliable, and scalable architecture, scaling to well over two thousand users on a single server. Microsoft itself has said that it will move its development onto this platform in the future.

In addition to some of the standard version control features, TFVC has some brand new ideas and concepts. It integrates with the Team Foundation work item system, allowing you to associate checked-in files with work items. It provides atomic check-in capabilities, meaning that either all the files are checked in, or none of the files are checked in. In addition, it implements a new feature called shelving that allows you to store what you are currently doing on the server without checking the changes in.

TFVC is also extensible, providing a rich object model, as well as Web services, that can be used to access TFVC. Using this extensibility, specifically the Web services, partners have been able to leverage the use of TFVC on other platforms, such as Java and Linux.

As you will learn throughout this chapter, TFVC is the way to go for version control, especially with its integration into the rest of Team Foundation Server.

Common Version Control Concepts

All version control systems, regardless of who makes them, have some common concepts. To truly appreciate Team Foundation Version Control, and to make the most of it, you need to have a general understanding of these concepts. In this section, you learn about those concepts. You see quickly how each of the previously mentioned systems implements those concepts, and then learn in more detail how Team Foundation Version Control handles them. In some cases, Team Foundation Version Control appears to handle things in a similar manner to one of the other systems, while in other cases it may seem to be a radical change. Regardless, by the end of this section, you should have a good understanding of version control system concepts. As well, you should have an appreciation for how Team Foundation Version Control handles these concepts. Then, in the next section, building off this information, you get some hands-on experience using Team Foundation Version Control.

Repository

The version control *repository* is the central store of data for the version control system. Any files that are added to the version control system are stored in the repository.

A version control repository can take on different forms. Subversion, for example, uses a file system tree, a collection of folders and files on a file share, as its repository, as does both CVS and Visual SourceSafe. Team Foundation Version Control, on the other hand, uses a backend database, as you will learn about shortly.

The whole point of a version control system is to be able to retrieve, view, and edit previous states, or versions, of files. Different version control systems track changes to files in different ways. However, Subversion, CVS, Visual SourceSafe, and Team Foundation Version Control all use a similar method, called reverse delta technology, for storing changes, which you will also learn about shortly.

The repository for Team Foundation Version Control is the SQL Server 2005 instance used by the Team Foundation Server. Everything related to the version control system is stored in SQL Server. This is an ideal situation for several reasons. By using a database backend, TFS makes use of transactions, to ensure that when you check in, either all the files check in, or none of them do. This is called *atomic check-in;* it allows SQL Server to make sure that the database integrity is maintained. As well, backing up your version control system is now as simple as running a database backup, and restoring is just as easy as running a database restore.

Within the TFVC repository, you have the root directory, represented by `$/`. Beneath that root directory are your different team projects. Inside each team project, you can have multiple folders and files, as shown in Figure 12-1.

This image shows a view of the Source Control Explorer window, which allows you to navigate the repository. As you can see, TFVC allows you to view and interact with the repository as if it were a bunch of files and folders, which conceptually makes it very easy to use. But, as pointed out above, in reality the repository is a database, with all the advantages that databases bring.

Figure 12-2 shows an image from SQL Management Studio of the tables in Team Foundation Server that are associated with the Team Foundation Version Control System.

All these tables are located in the TFSVersionControl database on the data tier of Team Foundation Server.

Team Foundation Version Control gives you a variety of ways to interact with it. With CVS and Subversion, the repository is generally accessed via a command-line tool, though there are some graphical tools available. Team Foundation Version Control can be accessed from directly within Visual Studio, utilizing the Source Control Explorer. There is a command-line tool that can be used for different options. In addition, developers can build applications off the Team Foundation Version Control Object Model.

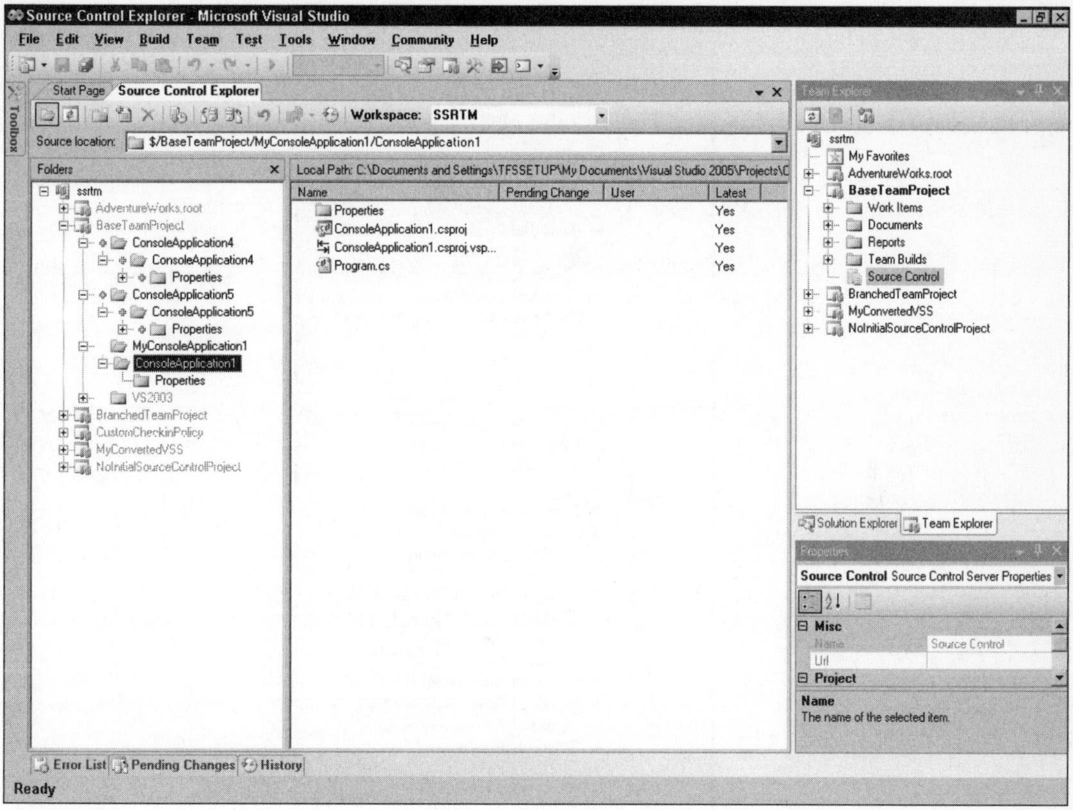

Figure 12-1

Let's talk next in a little more detail about how Team Foundation Version Control stores changes in the repository. It uses a system called *reverse delta technology,* which turns out to be a very efficient system. Basically, only the latest version of a file is the full version. Any earlier versions of a file are stored as deltas of the latest version. When you apply this delta to the latest version, you are able to recreate an earlier version of this file. This is rather counterintuitive to most people. Most people would think that the first version of a file is the full version, and any changes made to the files after that are stored as deltas. But Team Foundation Version Control, as well as other version control systems, have found the reverse delta scheme to be a better methodology to follow. Because most of the time the version that is requested is the latest version of the file, you want the latest version to be the full version.

Finally, although you should always use the object model when writing code to interact with Team Foundation Server and Team Foundation Version Control, there are four Web services that are used by TFS to work with TFVC.

- Administration.asmx
- Integration.asmx
- ProxyStatistics.asmx
- Repository.asmx

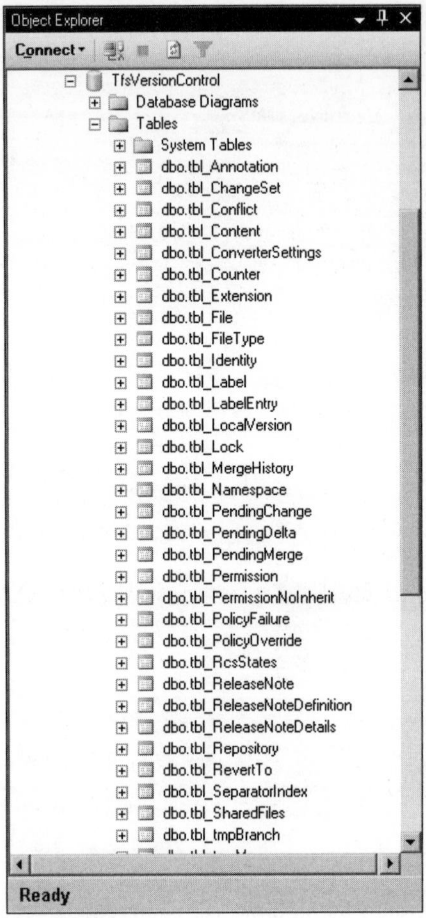

Figure 12-2

The Administration Web service can be used to kill processes on the server, change the server state, optimize the database, and retrieve repository and server information. The Integration Web service is used to delete projects, set up notifications, and retrieve artifacts from TFS. The ProxyStatistics Web service, as you would guess, returns information on the proxy server. The Repository Web service is the main Web service for accessing the Team Foundation Version Control system. It allows you to, among other things, check in items, delete items, and update items.

> **It is not advised that you build applications that use these Web services. These Web services are subject to change in future versions of Team Foundation Server. You should only build applications using the Team Foundation Server Object Model.**

Version Numbers and Changesets

Have you started to figure out yet that every version control system does some things differently? Version numbers are no exception. In Subversion, every time you check in a file, a new version number is applied to all the files and all the folders in the repository. In CVS, each change to a file is a unique version number, same as in Visual SourceSafe.

Team Foundation Version Control introduces a new concept in place of version numbers, called the changeset number. Remember earlier we mention atomic check-ins, and how groups of files are either all checked in together, or none of them is checked in. These groups of files are referred to as changesets. Think of a changeset as an easy-to-manage entity containing all the related pieces of the project on which you have been working.

Changeset numbers are not tied to specific team projects. They are, in fact, a version number used for the entire repository. For example, you check in some files into Team Project 1, and those files are given a changeset number of 6. Someone else then checks in some files into Team Project 2. Those files are then given a changeset number of 7. If you then check more files into Team Project 1, those files will be given a changeset number of 8. So it is not uncommon to view the history of a file in Team Foundation Version Control, and see gaps between the changeset numbers, as shown in Figure 12-3.

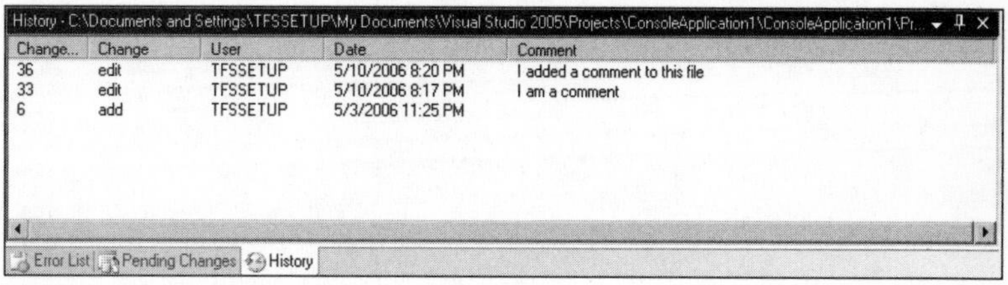

Figure 12-3

This image shows the history for a particular file in the TFVC system. Notice the file has three different changeset numbers. Changeset 6 was when the file was initially added to the version control system. Changesets 33 and 36 represent edits to the file. Notice how the changeset numbers are not sequential. This is due to other files being checked into the version control system before these edits took place.

Workspaces

A *workspace* is where you keep the files and folders that you check out of the repository. It is basically a series of folder mappings on your workstation. Each mapping takes a folder in the repository and associates it with a local folder on your workstation. These mappings allow TFVC to know where to download code onto the local machine when it is checked out. The workspace itself is not just a folder on the local machine though. The workspace is an object, an entity that can contain multiple folder mappings. This allows you to have one workspace that can map all the different projects you are working on, or you could have a separate workspace for each project. Use whatever scenario works best for you.

Team Foundation Server stores your workspace definition on the server. This includes all the file and folder mappings associated with the workspace, version information, and status of the files in your workspace. This allows other developers, with the appropriate security permissions, to duplicate your workspace on their development machines. This can be an effective way to perform a code review or help a remote developer with a coding issue.

There are some rules to follow when creating your workspaces. You cannot map the same repository folder twice in the same workspace. For example, let's say you have a folder in the repository called Folder1. If you have already mapped this repository folder to a local folder, say LocalFolder1, then you cannot add another mapping for Folder1 to go to LocalFolder2, because TFVC would not know which local folder to put the files into. Also, you cannot map two different repository folders to the same local folder in a workspace. For example, you cannot map Folder1 and Folder2 from the repository to LocalFolder1.

Ok, that's enough generalities about workspaces. Let's look at how to actually manipulate these things. As usual, you can manipulate your workspaces using either Source Control Explorer or the command-line tools. If you open the Source Control Explorer, at the top of the window is a workspace drop-down list box. From that list box, select Workspaces to open the Manage Workspaces window, as shown as Figure 12-4.

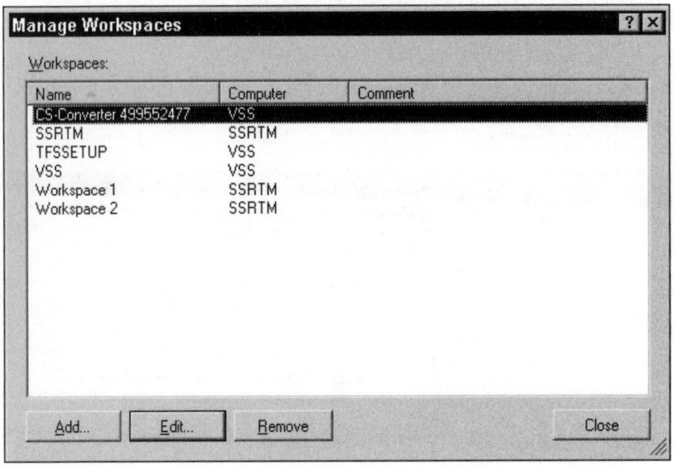

Figure 12-4

This window allows you to add new workspaces, editing existing workspaces, or remove workspaces that are no longer needed. To add a new workspace, simply click Add. This opens the Add Workspace window, as shown in Figure 12-5.

As you can see, you can specify the name of the workspace, the workspace owner, and the computer on which the workspace will reside. As well, you can also specify comments. But of course, the real meat of a workspace are the working folders, the mapping of the local folders to the folders in the repository. In Figure 12-5, you have two projects mapped in this workspace. The BaseTeamProject is mapped to `C:\Workspaces\BaseTeamProject`, and the CustomCheckinPolicy is mapped to `C:\Workspaces\CustomCheckinPolicy`. So the next time you go to retrieve files from the BaseTeamProject project, those files will be stored in the `C:\Workspaces\BaseTeamProject` directory on your local workstation.

You can do the same thing from the command-line tools. Using the Visual Studio 2005 command prompt (Start⇨All Programs⇨Microsoft Visual Studio 2005⇨Visual Studio Tools⇨Visual Studio 2005 Command Prompt), run the following code:

```
tf workspace /new MyCmdWorkspace /noprompt /s:<TFS Server Name>
```

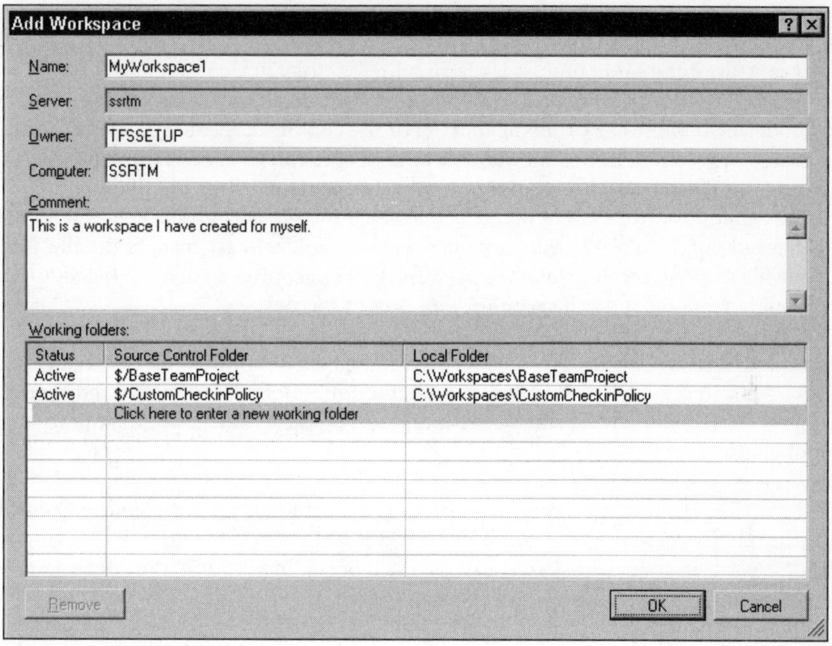

Figure 12-5

This code creates a new workspace called MyCmdWorkspace on the specified Team Foundation Server. If you open the Manage Workspaces window after running this code, you will see the newly created workspace, MyCmdWorkspace. If you do not include the `/noprompt` flag, then the Add Workspace window will open, for you to confirm the creation of the workspace.

You can also use the command-line tools to map local folders to repository folders. After creating the above workspace, run the following code from the command prompt:

```
tf workfold /server:<TFS Server Name> /workspace:MyCmdWorkspace /map
$/BaseTeamProject c:\Workspaces\MyProject
```

This command maps the BaseTeamProject project to `C:\Workspaces\MyProject`. You can verify this by viewing the workspace from the Manage Workspaces window.

Check-In/Check-Out

When you check out a file from a version control system, you are making a copy of that file for you to work on. Once you have made your changes and are done, you add the file back to the repository. This is called the check-in process. All version control systems support check-in/check-out in some form or fashion.

There are two basic models for checking files in and out: exclusive or shared. The *exclusive model,* also known as pessimistic locking or the lock-modify-unlock model, is a method used by several version control systems, including older version of Visual SourceSafe. In this model, one person only can have a file checked out of the repository at a particular time. If User A checks out File A, then User B cannot check out File A until User A checks the file back in. While this ensures that two people can't make modifications to the same file at the same time, it is also a bit restrictive.

The *shared* model, also know as optimistic locking or the copy-modify-merge model, is a method used by VSS 2005 and Subversion. In this model, multiple people can check out the same file at the same time. So User A and User B can both check out File A at the same time. When the file is checked back in to the repository, the version control system will check to see if the file was updated in the repository while you had it checked out. If so, that means you no longer have the latest copy of the file, and you will need to merge your file changes into the latest copy. Most version control systems which support shared check-out provide you with a mechanism for merging these files.

Team Foundation Version Control provides you with the best of both worlds. You can choose to use either the shared or the exclusive check-out model, though it defaults to the shared model, and the shared model is the recommended way to go. It allows you more power and flexibility to achieve your development goals.

As mentioned earlier, the check-in/check-out process in Team Foundation Version Control is atomic. This means that all the changes are applied to the repository, or none of them is. Making use of transactions in SQL Server 2005, you are assured that this will occur. In addition, the check-in process is integrated into the work item tracking system of Team Foundation Server. When you check in your files, you can associate them with one or more work items. This allows you to always have a relationship between the definition of a problem and the code that fixes it. Also, you get e-mail check-in notification right out of the box, so you can be e-mailed any time files are checked into the repository.

Finally, you can define check-in policies. These policies define the rules that determine whether you can check your files into the repository. For example, one rule that ships with Team Foundation Server restricts the check-in process unless you have associated your code with a work item. You cover check-in policies in more detail later in this chapter, and will even learn how to build your own custom policy.

Let's look at some examples of checking files in and out of Team Foundation Version Control. There are several different ways to check out files. One way is to open a development project that is already associated with the version control system. When you then begin to modify files in the project, they will be automatically checked out for you as you begin to make your modifications. Another way is to right-click a file in the Source Control Explorer, and select Check Out for Edit... from the context menu. This opens the Check Out Window, as shown in figure 12-6.

This window shows you the file(s) you want to check out, and allows you to select the lock type you want to use. The default is none, which enables the shared model discussed earlier. You can also select Check Out, which is the exclusive model. Simply click the Check Out button to check out the file. The latest version of the file will be downloaded to your workspace. Simply double-click the file in Source Control Explorer to open and edit it.

Once you have finished editing your file(s), you will want to check them back into the version control system. You can either right-click the file in Source Control Explorer, and select Check In Pending Changes from the context menu, or you can open the Pending Changes window by selecting View⇨Other Windows⇨Pending Changes. Both options open windows with very similar functionality. Figure 12-7 shows the Pending Changes window.

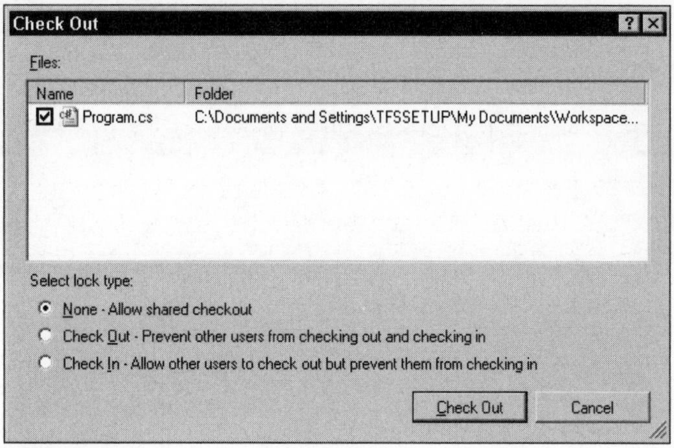

Figure 12-6

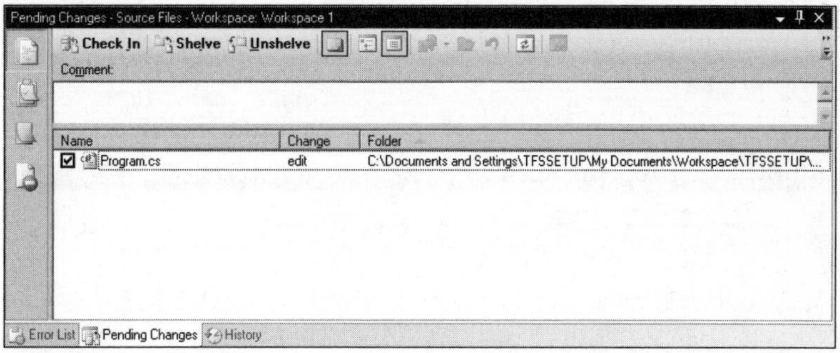

Figure 12-7

This window gives you several options to consider before you check the files back in. You can click the Policy Warnings button to see if you are violating any check-in policies. You can click the Check-in Notes button to enter any check-in notes that are required. You can click the Work Items button to see a list of work items for your team project. You can then select one or more work items and associate them with this check-in. You can enter comments for the check-in, and even decide to shelve your changes until a later date.

One last thing to look at is the ability to resolve conflicts when checking files back into the system. Specifically, let's look at the scenario where you have checked a file out, and someone else checks out the same file. The second person makes a change to the file, and checks it back in. You then make a change to your copy, and go to check it back in. However, at this point, you no longer have the latest version of the file from the repository, so you are going to have some conflicts. When you click the Check In button, the Resolve Conflicts window appears, as shown in Figure 12-8.

This window is telling you that a newer version of the file you are trying to check in already exists on the server. As such, you are going to have to resolve this conflict. If you click the Auto Merge All button, it will attempt to resolve the conflicts for you automatically. If you click the Resolve button, it opens a new window, where you can decide how you would like to resolve this situation. You have the option of merging changes using the merge tool, undoing your local changes, or discarding the server changes. Figure 12-9 shows an example of the merge tool in action.

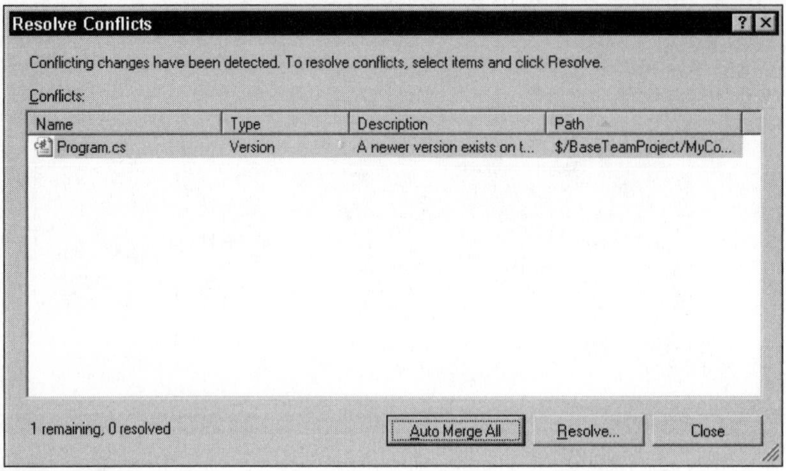

Figure 12-8

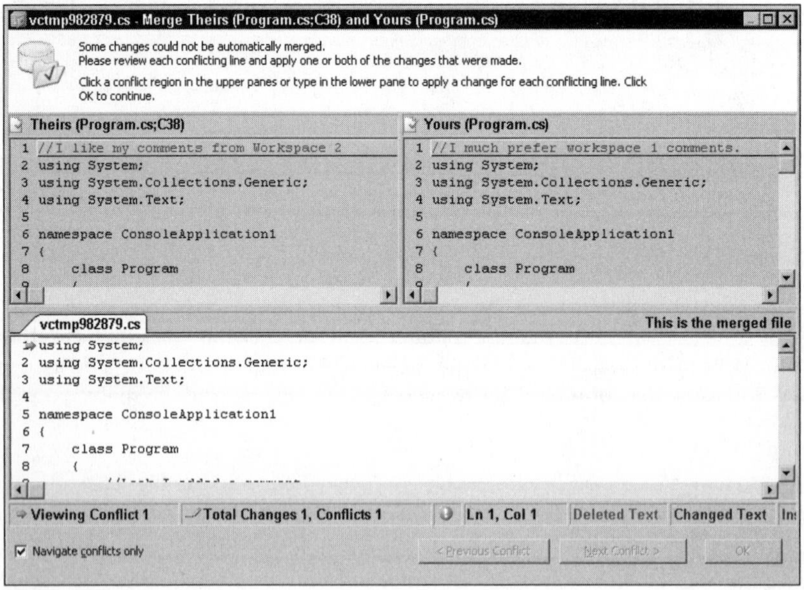

Figure 12-9

If you use Visual SourceSafe, this tool will seem very familiar to you. It allows you to go through each conflicting file, and choose what code goes into the final file, resolving your conflicts. Once all the conflicts are resolved, the new file is then saved into your workspace. You can then try to check the files in again, and they should check into the repository with no problems.

Branching and Merging

Branching is a way for you to isolate code into a separate area for development. It allows a collection of files to diverge on two or more different paths. There are several reasons you might want to branch your code. You might need to create a bug fix for a problem that was found in your production code. You might want to segment your application development into the different functional areas of your application. In this case, you would have a main folder, and then branch off that main folder for each functional area. In the best practices section later in this chapter, you learn some of the best ways to use branching in your environment.

> **Microsoft has recently published a primer on how to properly branch and merge code on MSDN. You can refer to the article here:** `http://msdn.microsoft.com/vstudio/default.aspx?pull=/library/en-us/dnvs05/html/BranchMerge.asp`

Obviously, there are times where you will want to take your changes from your branch, and put them back into the folder from which you branched. Alternatively, you might want to take new changes from the original folder, and move them into your branch. This process is called *merging*. As you have seen in the previous section on check-in/check-out, Team Foundation Version Control has a nice merge process in place to help you walk through this merge process. In addition, the section later in this chapter on best practices discusses several concepts related to when you should merge different branches.

Team Foundation Version Control uses a method called the *path space branching model*. Basically, it creates new copies of items based on their path. This allows easy logical access to the branch, because you can think of everything in terms of files and folders. This is different from other version control systems, which use a version number branching model, where each branch has a different version number. The path space branching model is easier and more intuitive to use.

Let's look at some basic examples of how to branch and merge items in Team Foundation Version Control. Please note this is a rather simplistic example, which shows some basic branch and merge functionality. When you get to the best practices section later in this chapter, you see some more-detailed examples.

Follow these steps to create a new team project and console application to use for the following example:

1. Start off by creating a new team project called BranchExample. To do this, open Team Explorer, right-click your Team Foundation Server, and select New Team Project. This will start the New Team Project Creation Wizard. Simply follow the directions to create your team project,
2. Now create a console application called BranchTest. Select File⇨New⇨Project to open the New Project window. Select Visual C# as the project type, and Console Application as the template. Enter **BranchTest** as the name of the application, check the Add to Source Control check box, and click OK to create the project. When prompted to select a team project location, select the BranchExample Team Project.
3. Finally, check the console application into version control. Open the Pending changes window by selecting View⇨Other Windows⇨Pending Changes, and click the Check In button, to check in the application.
4. Open the Program.cs file, and add the following comment to the `Main` method:

```
//Comment added from main folder of version control system.
```

5. Open the pending check in window and check this new change into the version control system. Open Team Explorer, open the BranchExample Team Project, and double-click the Source Control icon to open the Source Control Explorer. If you open the BranchExample folder in Source Control Explorer, you'll see the folder for the BranchTest project you were just making changes to.

Next, let's create a branch off this BranchTest folder.

1. Right-click the BranchTest folder, and select Branch from the context menu. This opens the Branch window, shown in Figure 12-10.

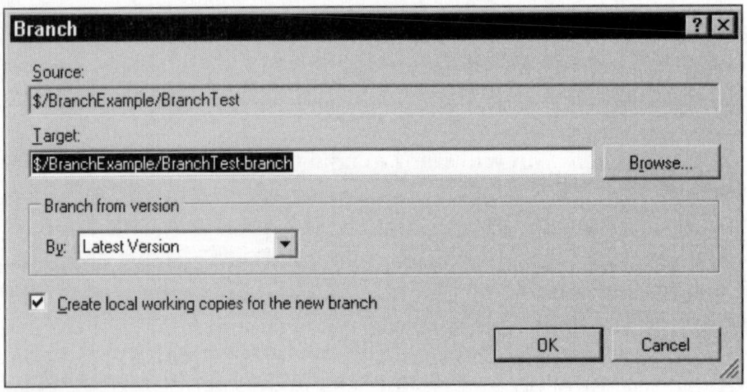

Figure 12-10

This window shows you the source folder or file you are branching from. In this case, it is $/BranchExample/BranchTest. It then allows you to select the Target, which is the new branch that you want to form. You can either type in the new branch, or select the Browse button to use a graphical interface. For now, simply accept the default name and location for the branch.

2. You have five different options for creating your branch. You can select a specific changeset, date, or label to branch from. You can branch based off a workspace version. Or you can take the default, which is to branch off the latest version of the code in the repository. You can also have the branch files automatically downloaded into your workspace. For this example, leave everything as the defaults, and click OK.

   Figure 12-11 shows the new branch in the Source Control Explorer window.

3. Once you have created your new branch, you have a bunch of files in your Pending Changes window that need to be checked in to complete the branching process. Open your Pending Changes window and check those changes back in.

4. So now you have two folders in your Team Project, BranchTest and BranchTest-branch. Next, you want to modify a file in the branch so you can merge it back. Using the Source Control Explorer, navigate to the BranchTest-branch folder in the BranchExample Team Project, and double-click the BranchTest.sln to open the console application. Then double-click the Program.cs file to open it and add the following comment:

```
//I am a comment from the branch
```

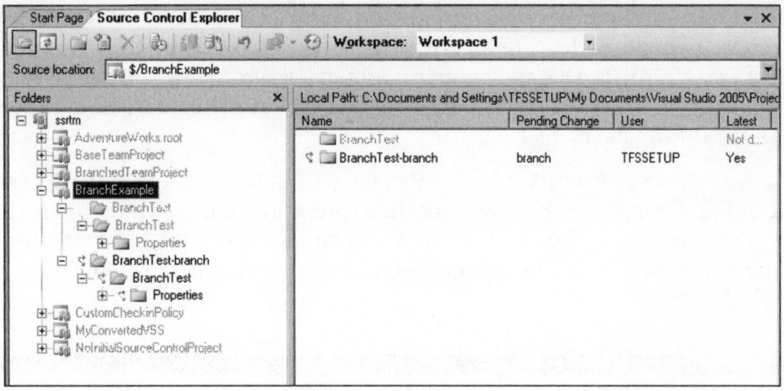

Figure 12-11

5. Save your changes, then open the Pending Changes window and check your changes back into the branch. At this point, you are now ready to merge the branch back with the original folder.

6. In the Source Control Explorer, right-click the BranchTest-branch folder and select Merge. This starts the Source Control Merge Wizard, as shown in Figure 12-12.

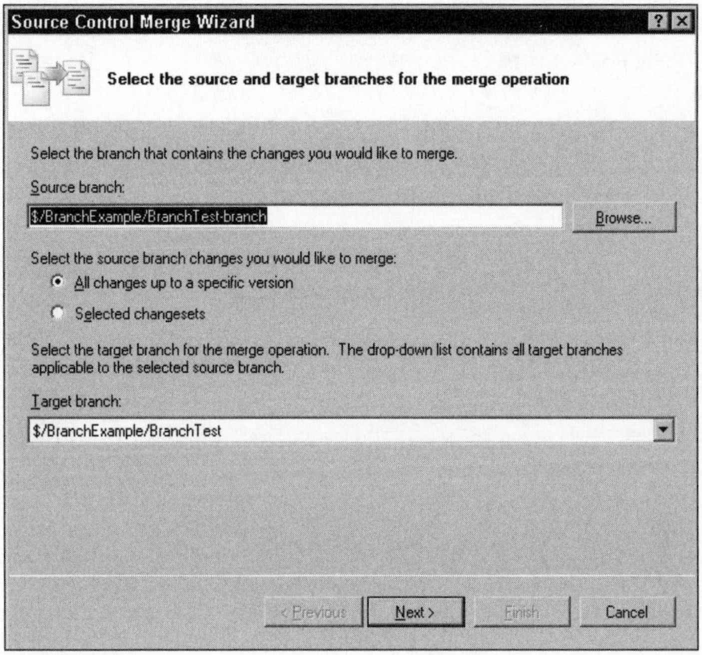

Figure 12-12

7. From this window, you can specify the source branch and the target branch. Notice that the target branch defaults to the parent folder that you branched from. Click Next to go to the next step of the wizard. On this page is a drop-down list box where you can select which version of the branch you want to merge. Keep the default of Latest Version and click Next; then click Finish to perform the merge.

8. Again, as when you branched earlier, you have to check the merged files back into TVFC. Open the Pending Changes window and click the Check In button to check in the changes. If you now navigate to the Program.cs file in the BranchTest, right-click the file, and select View, you will see the comment from the branch has been merged back into the main folder, as shown in Figure 12-13.

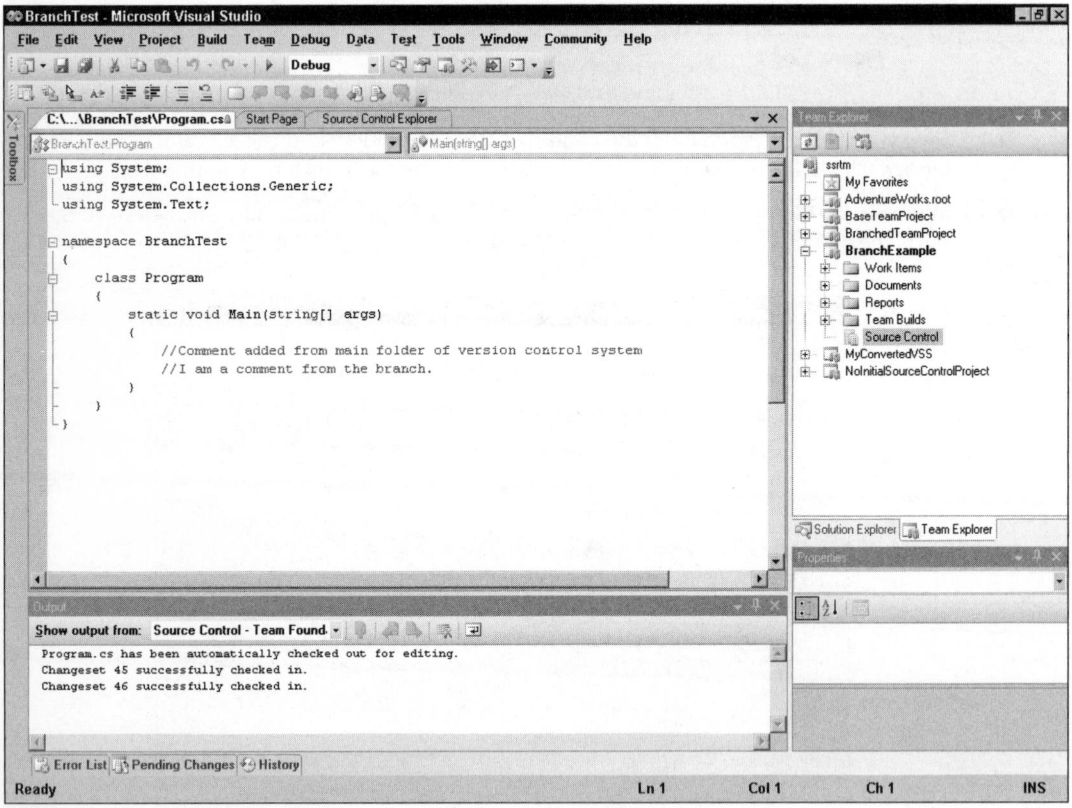

Figure 12-13

Team Foundation Version Control Essentials

In this section, you learn some of the basics of interacting with Team Foundation Version Control. You've already seen the basics of checking items in and out and branching and merging, so that will not be repeated here.

Here you learn how to add version control to a team project, how to add files to version control, and security considerations. You look at the Source Control Explorer, shelving, and check-in policies.

Configuring Team Foundation Version Control

To get started using Team Foundation Version Control, you need to set up your team projects to have access to the version control system. Once they have access to the system, then you can begin to add items into version control, enabling you to track changes made to objects in the system. Configuring your access to Team Foundation Version Control is relatively simple, and can be done from the GUI or the command-line interface.

Adding Version Control to a Team Project

There are two ways to add version control to a team project. You can associate the team project with the version control system when you initially create the project, or you can do it at a later point and time.

Figure 12-14 shows the Specify Source Control Settings windows, which is one of the steps in the Team Project Creation Window.

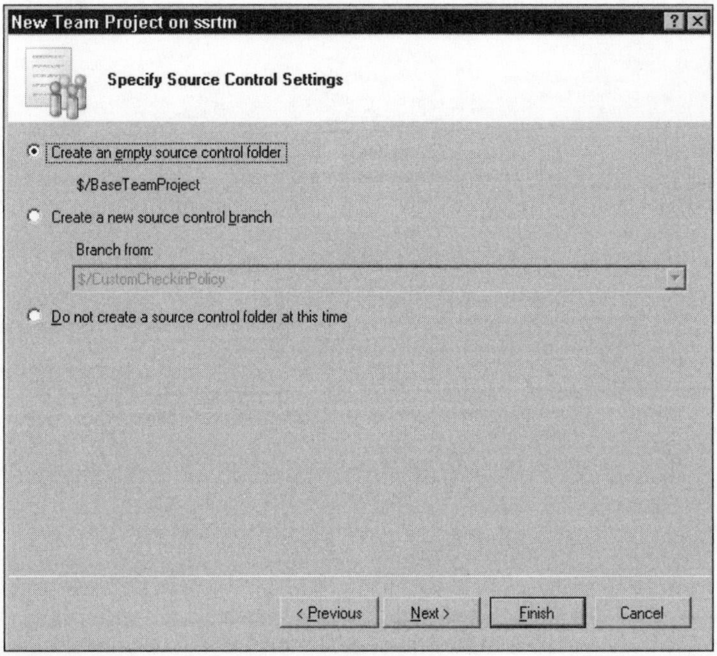

Figure 12-14

You have three options for specifying your source control during the creation of your team project. You can choose to create an empty source control folder. This folder will default to the name of your team project, and will be located right off the root of the repository, represented by a $. The second option is to choose to create a branch from an existing area of the repository. Using the drop-down list box, you can select which area you want to branch from. This will create a new folder in the repository off the root of the repository, with the same name as the team project you are creating. However, the difference between this and the first option is that this project is a branch off an existing folder, so it includes the latest version of all the files in the folder. The third option is to not create a source control folder at this time. This creates your team project, but does not associate it with the version control repository. As you will see shortly, you can then manually associate the team project with the version control system.

If you choose not to associate your team project with the version control system at creation time, you can do it at any point in the future. Simply open Team Explorer, navigate to your project, and double-click Source Control. You will be asked if you want to create a folder for this team project at $/<Team Project Name>.

Adding Source Files to Version Control

To add source files, follow these steps:

1. Open Visual Studio 2005 and create a new console application (File ➪New ➪Project➪Visual C# Console Application) and name it **ConsoleApplication1**. Figure 12-15 shows you the New Project creation window.

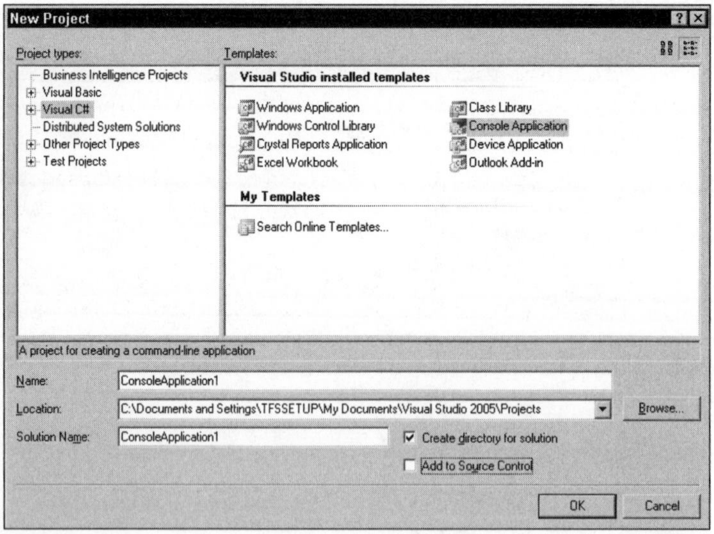

Figure 12-15

2. When you create a new project, not a team project but a regular development project, you can choose to add it to source control at the time the project is created. Simply click the Add to Source Control check box. This opens another window, where you select the team project and the folder you want to add your development project to, as shown in Figure 12-16.

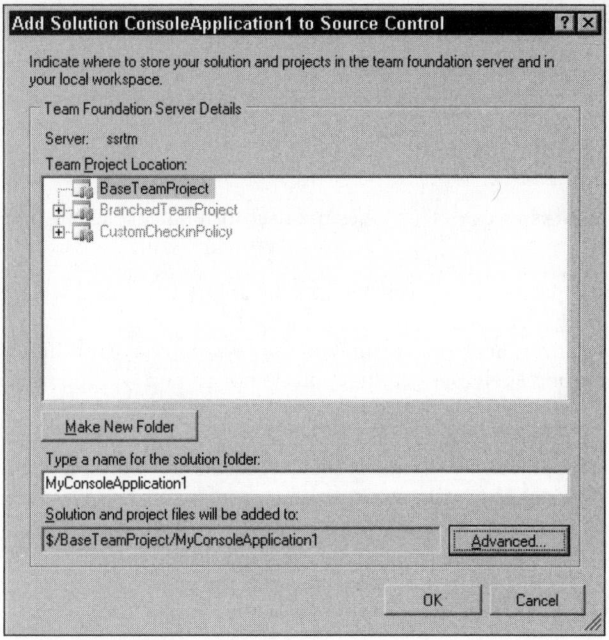

Figure 12-16

As you can see from the figure, you are adding the ConsoleApplication1 project to the BaseTeamProject Team Project. By default, a folder is created under the team project called ConsoleApplication1. You can add folders under the listed team projects by clicking the Make New Folder button. You can also type in a different name for the solution folder if you would like.

3. Go ahead and change the name for the solution folder to be **MyConsoleApplication1**. The solution and project files are added to the `$/BaseTeamProject/MyConsoleApplication1`. Click OK to finish creating the project.

4. You have now added the ConsoleApplication1 development project to the Team Project named BaseTeamProject. Notice in the Solution Explorer, as shown in Figure 12-11, that all the files in the project have a plus sign beside them, as was discussed earlier. To check these files in, open the Pending Changes window and click the Check In button.

If you choose to add an application to source control later, you simply right-click the solution node in Solution Explorer and select Add Project To Source Control. This opens the window shown in Figure 12-16, where you can follow the same steps.

> **You can associate multiple development projects with a single team project. It is not just a one-to-one correspondence. In fact, it is expected there will be multiple solutions under each team project.**

Security Considerations

From a security perspective, you can set important permissions on a global and a project scale. The global permissions a user can have for the version control system are:

- **Administer shelved changes** — This gives the user the ability to delete shelvesets that have been created by other users.
- **Administer workspaces** — This gives the user the ability to create and delete workspaces for other users.
- **Create a workspace** — This gives the user the ability to create a workspace for themselves.

Depending on the organization of your team, you may want to have multiple people with the ability to work with workspaces and shelvesets, so that you do not end up waiting for one person to administer your workspaces and shelvesets.

Besides these global permissions, you can set security levels at a team project level, a folder level, or even an individual file level. You will explore this more in the next section concerning the Source Control Explorer.

Source Control Explorer

The Source Control Explorer is the main access point into Team Foundation Version Control. The Source Control Explorer is integrated into the IDE, making it very easy to find and use. To open the Source Control Explorer, you can either double-click the Source Control icon in a team project, or select View⇨Other Windows⇨Source Control Explorer. Figure 12-17 shows the Source Control Explorer.

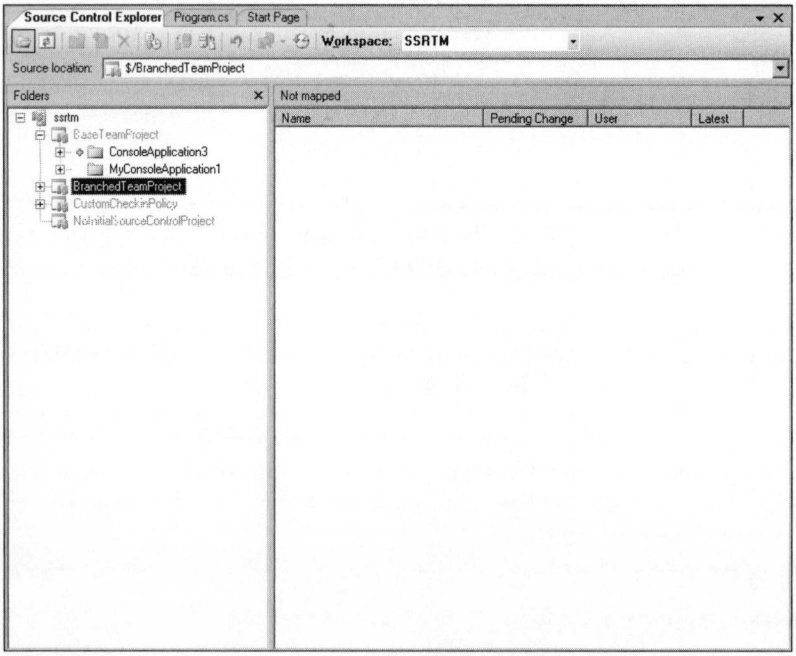

Figure 12-17

Once you are in the Source Control Explorer, you have several different options available to you. You can manage your workspaces as was discussed earlier in the chapter. You can click the Add Files button to add files to a particular project. You can delete files and folders. You can get the latest versions of a file and store them in your workspace. You can check items in and out.

> **Make sure your workspace is mapped to the repository and to a local folder. If the option to add files and folders to your project is not available (grayed out) in the Source Control Explorer, then you do not have the appropriate mappings in your workspace.**

If you right-click a file, the context menu offers several options. You can choose to get a specific version of a file instead of the latest version. Your options with this include retrieving a file by changeset, date, label, latest version, or workspace version. If you try to retrieve a version that is already located in your workspace, it will not overwrite the version in your workspace, unless you check the Force get check box in the Get window.

You can right-click a file or folder and lock it. You can set it so other uses cannot check a file in or out, or allow them to check a file out, but not check it back in. You can also right-click a file and select Compare. This allows you to compare a file in your workspace with a version of the file from the repository, allowing you to see how the files differ textually. You have already seen earlier how you can branch and merge.

The Source Control Explorer is the main window into the Team Foundation Version Control system. You will probably spend a lot of time here, so take some time to become comfortable with the environment.

Setting Security Using Source Control Explorer

The beauty of using a path-based source control system is that you can set permissions on folders and even individual files. This allows you very granular control over your version control system. To modify the security permissions for a particular file or folder, simply right-click the file or folder in the Source Control Explorer, and select Properties. When the properties window opens, click the Security tab.

On this tab, you can add and remove Team Foundation Server groups, and Windows Users or Groups. You can also specify the permissions for the groups, to either Allow or Deny certain security permissions. By default, if a permission is not set to Allow, it is automatically assumed to be Deny.

> **Team Foundation Server grants certain access rights to certain groups by default. Be very careful about modifying the rights of these groups.**

The following are some of the permissions you can set on a file or folder:

- **Read** — Read the file
- **Check out** — Check Out the file
- **Check in** — Check In the file
- **Label** — Add a label to a file

- ❑ **Lock** — Lock a file
- ❑ **Revise other users' changes** — Revise committed changes made by other users
- ❑ **Unlock other users' changes** — Ability to remove a lock on a file by another user
- ❑ **Undo other users' changes** — Ability to rollback changes from a user
- ❑ **Administer labels** — Create, delete, and modify labels
- ❑ **Manipulate security settings** — Ability to modify security settings
- ❑ **Check in other users' changes** — Ability to check in changes on behalf of another user

The ability to provide this granular level of control from a security perspective is just one more aspect of Team Foundation Version Control and Team Foundation Server that make it so appealing.

Shelving

Shelving is a new feature to version control and is specific to Team Foundation Version Control. The best way to understand shelving is with an example. Say you are working on a project and are in the middle of adding some new features to the application when your boss walks in and tells you he needs you to fix a bug that has been found. You can't fix the bug in the code currently in your workspace, because when you check the bug fix in, you will also be adding your new features, which may not be ready yet. Normally in this case, you would back up the files you had been working on, delete them from your working directory, download the old code, fix it, check the bug fix back in, then restore the files you had been working on — a rather cumbersome process.

Shelving automates this process for you. Using shelving, you can automatically store what you have been working on onto Team Foundation Server. It does not check the files back in, but it moves them to the Team Foundation Server. This allows you to then download the old code into your workspace and make the changes. Then, when you are done, you can unshelve your new code back into your workspace.

Besides the bug fix scenario described, here are some reasons you might want to shelve your code:

- ❑ You may not be finished with some coding changes before you go home, but you want to make sure your code gets backed up, so you shelve it to TFS to have it backed up in the nightly backup.
- ❑ You want someone else to review your new code. You shelve your changes, and another developer unshelves them and does a code review. Then that developer can check the changes in if they pass.

Shelving your pending changes is easy. In the Pending Changes window, just click the Shelve button. You enter a name for your shelveset, an optional comment, and select the items you want to shelve. You can also associate the shelved items with work items at this stage. You also have the option of keeping your pending changes in your workspace, or undoing them as part of the shelving process. Once you are ready, click the Shelve button to shelve your changes. You can create as many different shelvesets as you would like.

To unshelve a shelveset, simply open the Pending Changes window, and click the Unshelve button. This opens the Unshelve window, as shown in Figure 12-18.

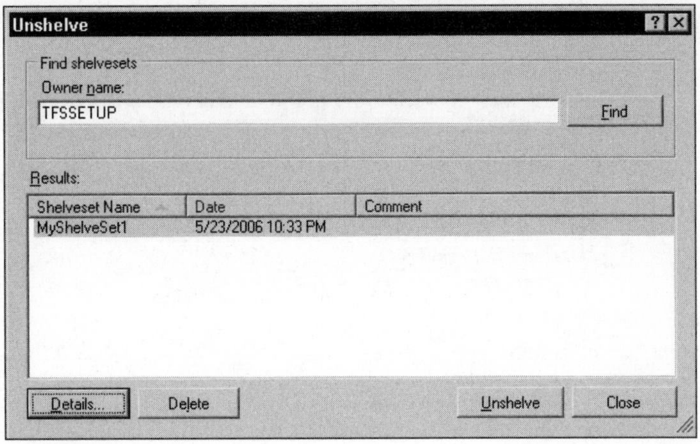

Figure 12-18

In this window, you can search for the shelvesets that have been created by a particular user. Once you have found a shelveset, you can click the Details button to view the files contained in the shelveset. You can also delete the shelveset, or unshelve it to your workspace.

Setting Source Control Options

You can specify Source Control Settings on a per team project basis. Right-click your team project in Team Explorer, and select Team Project Settings⇨Source Control. This opens the Source Control Settings window for your team project.

There are three tabs on this window. The first tab is the Check-out Settings tab. This tab allows multiple check-outs, or shared check-outs. By default, this is allowed. You can deselect the check box to turn off shared check-outs.

The second is the Check-in Policy tab. This is where you select which check-in policies you want to apply to your team project. A check-in policy is a way to stipulate requirements for how code is checked into the system. Team Foundation Server ships with the following three check-in policies:

- **Code analysis** — You must run code analysis before check-in.
- **Testing policy** — Tests must be successfully executed before check-in.
- **Work items** — Work items must be associated with check-in.

Besides the shipped policies, you can create your own, as you learn to do later in this chapter.

The final tab is the Check-in Notes tab. This tab allows you to add or remove items from the Check-in Notes page. By default, there are three titles on this page: Code Reviewer, Security Reviewer, and Performance Reviewer. You can also make these fields required, meaning that someone has to add their names to these fields before the check-in can occur.

You can also elect to be notified via e-mail anytime an item is checked in. To do this, right-click your Team Project and select Project Alerts. This opens the Project Alerts window, as shown in Figure 12-19.

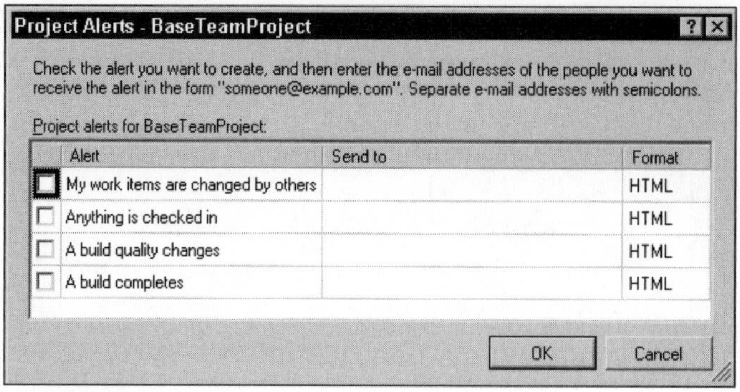

Figure 12-19

As you can see, you can sign yourself up for several different notification events. To be alerted anytime something is checked in, simply check the Anything is checked in check box, and enter your e-mail in the Send to box.

Converting from Other Version Control Systems

One of the critical areas that you need to consider is how you are going to move your data from your current version control system to Team Foundation Server. Obviously, you want to retain as much history and information as you can from your old system, while converting the necessary pieces into the new Team Foundation Version Control terminology, such as changesets. Using the Team Foundation Server Object Model, you could create your own conversion utility. That is one option. If you are using a custom-built version control system right now, that is probably your only option.

However, if you are using one of the major third-party tools now on the market, such as CVS, Subversion, or Visual SourceSafe, then you have another option. Microsoft provides free with Team Foundation Server a conversion tool called VSSConverter, which allows you to convert Visual SourceSafe information into Team Foundation Version Control. And third-party companies, such as ComponentSoftware (`.componentsoftware.com`) are providing utilities to convert Subversion, CVS, and several other version control systems, including Visual SourceSafe.

In this section, you learn how to convert your Visual SourceSafe project, using the free VSSConverter tool provided with Team Foundation Server. You learn about some of the pros and cons of converting using this tool. Next, you look at converting the same Visual SourceSafe database using the CS-Converter tool provided by ComponentSoftware. This tool converts information in a slightly different way than the VSSConverter tool provided by Microsoft, so it is worth looking at.

While you won't see a specific example of converting Subversion or CVS to Team Foundation Server, the CS-Converter tool by ComponentSoftware will convert these version control systems in a manner similar to the one shown for Visual SourceSafe.

Using VSSConverter to Convert Visual SourceSafe

The VSSConverter tool is provided free with Visual Studio Team System by Microsoft, for use in converting your Visual SourceSafe projects into Team Foundation Version Control. This tool is located at `c:\Program Files\Microsoft Visual Studio 8\Common7\IDE\VSSConverter.exe`. It is a command-line only tool, which uses XML configuration files to convert a single VSS project or an entire VSS database, depending on how you configure the application to run.

> **The MSDN documentation (`http://msdn2.microsoft.com`) contains a wealth of information concerning the VSSConverter tool. While some of the most pertinent information concerning the tool is presented here, check the online documentation for the latest and most complete information.**

All the code mentioned here is available for download at `wrox.com`.

VSSConverter Information

Before you get started with VSSConverter, you need to briefly understand what it will and won't do for you. VSSConverter does its best to convert as much of the historical information in the VSS database over into Team Foundation Server Version Control. However, some features of VSS, such as sharing, are not supported in TFS. As such, any historical information related to the use of these features will be lost.

The history for all the following items will be preserved with VSSConverter:

- Adding a file or a folder
- Deleting or undeleting a file or a folder
- Renaming a file or a folder
- Moving a folder
- Editing a file
- Modifying a label

The following actions are not supported in Team Foundation Server, and all historical information related to these actions will be lost:

- Sharing
- Branching
- Pinning

Sharing is not supported in Team Foundation Server. When a shared file is migrated, the version of the file that was originally shared is copied to its destination folder. After that, any changes that had been made to the shared file are copied to its original destination folder, and to any other copies of the shared file in other folders.

While branching is supported in Team Foundation Server, it is not supported in the manner that VSS used it. In VSS, sharing a file was a prerequisite to branching the file. When migrating a branched file, the original file is copied to its destination folder. At the point of the branch event, any changes made to a branch are copied to their appropriate area in Team Foundation Version Control.

Team Foundation Server Version Control provides no support for pinning. When a pinned file is migrated, two labels are created for the file: PINNED_LATEST and PINNED. The PINNED label applies only to the pinned versions of the pinned files, while the PINNED_LATEST label is applied to all the PINNED labeled files, as well as the latest version of any unpinned files.

There are two other things to be aware of when using VSSConverter. The conversion tool does not modify the source control bindings on the files. The files will still think they are bound to Visual SourceSafe when you try to open them. You can either change the bindings before you open the files, or Visual Studio 2005 prompts you to change them when you try to open them.

Finally, the timestamp associated with a specific action in VSS will not be preserved when converting over to Team Foundation Server Version Control. Instead, the timestamp associated with the action will be set to the date and time of the conversion. The original timestamp will be stored in the comments field though, so the information is not lost.

Before You Begin

Before you can begin converting your project using VSSConverter, there are some things you need to do, and some security issues you need to be aware of.

Prerequisites

First thing you need to do is find a machine to run the conversion on. This machine will need the following software installed on it:

- Visual SourceSafe 2005
- SQL Server Express
- Team Explorer

Next, you need to make sure your VSS database is ready for the conversion. Have all the users check in their files; then, make a backup copy of the database. Finally, run the VSS Analyze tool to find and fix any errors contained in your VSS database. Once you are convinced your database is ready, copy it over to the conversion machine.

> **The VSS database must be version 6.0 or later. If you are using an earlier version, you must first convert to VSS 2005.**

You need to log into the conversion machine with administrative privileges. Also, you will need to know the administrator password for your VSS database.

Finally, you need to go ahead and create a new team project, or a folder in an existing team project, to convert the VSS information into.

Let's get things set up for you to covert the example in this chapter. Go ahead and install all the prerequisites. Using the downloaded code for this chapter, unzip the MyVSS.zip file to `c:\MyVSS` on your conversion machine. If you like, you can open Visual SourceSafe 2005 and connect to this database, to view the files, as shown in Figure 12-20. This database contains two projects, VSSTest.root and VSSTest ver2. For this example, are just going to convert the VSSTest.root project.

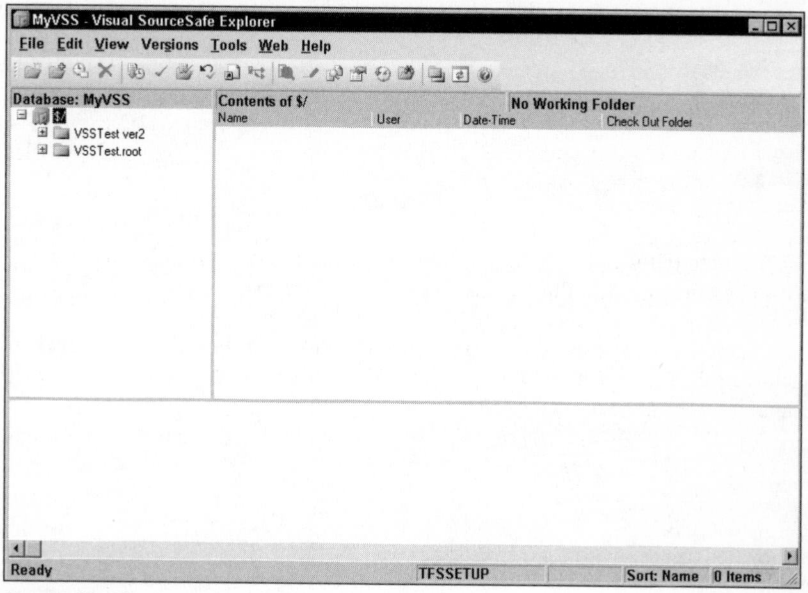

Figure 12-20

Open Team Explorer, and create a new Team Project called MyConvertedVSS. Go ahead and associate with the version control system when the project is created, using $/MyConvertedVSS.

Security Concerns

You should be aware of several security elements when performing this conversion. You need to be logged into the conversion machine with administrative privileges. You also need to have administrative privileges on the Visual SourceSafe database, and know the administrative password for the VSS database.

You need to be a member of the Team Foundation Administrators security group in Team Foundation Server.

Finally, you need to be a member of the sysadmin role for SQL Express. If you were logged in when you installed SQL Express, then you are added to this group by default.

Analyze the Projects

Once you have the conversion machine configured, you are ready to analyze the projects you want to convert. This analysis will look at the VSS projects, and notify you of any potential errors or loss of data that may occur with the conversion. To run this analysis, you need to create a XML configuration file that contains the settings for the VSSConverter tool. The configuration file contains the following information:

```
<?xml version="1.0" encoding="utf-8"?>
<SourceControlConverter>
<ConverterSpecificSetting>
<Source name="VSS">
<VSSDatabase name=""></VSSDatabase>
</Source>
<ProjectMap>
<Project Source=""></Project>
</ProjectMap>
</ConverterSpecificSetting>
<Settings>
</Settings>
</SourceControlConverter>
```

The `VSSDatabase` tag defines the location of the Visual SourceSafe database to convert. The `Project` tag defines the specific project in the database you want to convert.

1. To continue with this example, create a new directory off the `C:` drive of the conversion machine, called **Convert**. Add a new file to that director called settings.xml. Add the following code to the settings.xml file:

```
<?xml version="1.0" encoding="utf-8"?>
<SourceControlConverter>
<ConverterSpecificSetting>
<Source name="VSS">
<VSSDatabase name="c:\MyVSS"></VSSDatabase>
</Source>
<ProjectMap>
<Project Source="$/VSSTest.root"></Project>
</ProjectMap>
</ConverterSpecificSetting>
<Settings>
</Settings>
</SourceControlConverter>
```

Notice in the `VSSDatabase` tag now contains the name of the VSS database, `C:\MyVss`. You are going to convert the `VSSTest.root` project, so that has been added in the `Project` tag.

> **To migrate the entire VSS database, use the tag `<Project Source="$/"></Project>`. It is recommended that you try several smaller conversions before attempting to do the entire database at once.**

2. Once you have created the settings.xml file, it is time to run the analysis. Go to Start➪All Programs➪Microsoft Visual Studio 2005➪Visual Studio Tools➪Visual Studio 2005 Command Prompt, and run the command prompt. Once the prompt opens, type `CD c:\Convert`, to switch to the directory where the settings.xml file is located. Now run the following command:

```
vssconverter analyze settings.xml
```

3. You will be asked for the VSS administrator password. For this example, it is blank, so simply press the Enter key. The converter application analyzes the `VSSTest.root` project in the MyVSS database, makes some modifications to the settings.xml file, and outputs the results of the analysis.

Reviewing Analysis Results

After the VSSConverter has run its analysis, it outputs an analysis report. This report is located in the same directory as you ran the conversion analysis from, and is called VSSAnalysisReport.xml. Figure 12-21 shows the report for our example:

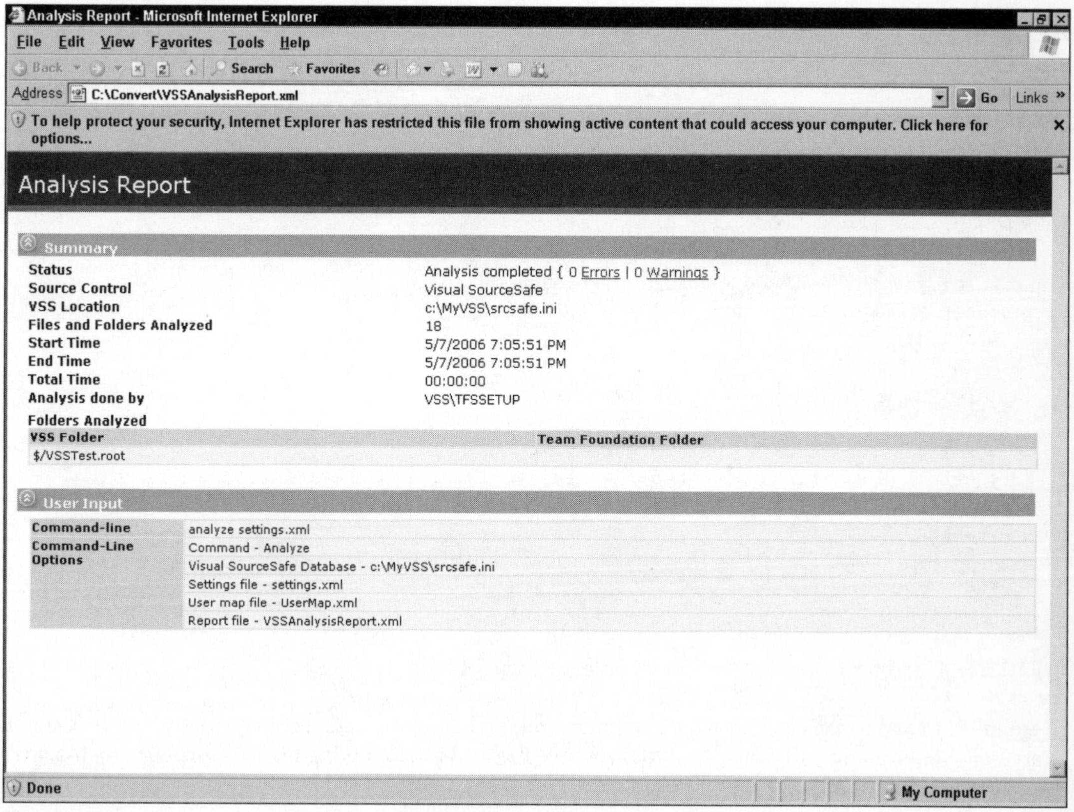

Figure 12-21

This report shows you the number of files and folders that were analyzed, and will list any potential warnings or errors that may occur during the actual conversion. It will give you a good indication of how your conversion process will go, and what things you should watch out for, or check for after the conversion is complete.

Now that you have reviewed the analysis results, you are ready to proceed with the conversion. Before you begin though, you need to make some more changes to the settings.xml file. As well, the analysis run has added another configuration file to your directory, the UserMap.xml file, which also needs your attention.

Customizing Files for Conversion

When the analysis of the database is run, a UserMap.xml file is created. This file can be used to map VSS users to Team Foundation Server users. For example, you may have a user John in VSS, but on Team Foundation Server his name is JohnSmith. This file allows you to map the name John in VSS to JohnSmith in TFS. So, when the VSS data is converted, any files associated with the name John would then be associated with the name JohnSmith in TFS.

> **You do not have to do this. If you choose not to associate certain names, then the VSS names will be inserted into the TFS database.**

The following is an example of what the `UserMap.xml` file would look like:

```
<?xml version="1.0" encoding="utf-8"?>
<UserMappings xmlns:xsi="http://www.w3.org/2001/XMLSchema-instance"
xmlns:xsd="http://www.w3.org/2001/XMLSchema">
<UserMap From="John" To="JohnSmith" />
</UserMappings>
```

For our example, the `UserMap.xml` file looks like this:

```
<?xml version="1.0" encoding="utf-8"?>
<UserMappings xmlns:xsi="http://www.w3.org/2001/XMLSchema-instance"
xmlns:xsd="http://www.w3.org/2001/XMLSchema">
<UserMap From="DEV1" To="" />
<UserMap From="DEV2" To="" />
<UserMap From="ADMIN" To="" />
</UserMappings>
```

Feel free to add users to the `TO` attribute, or leave them blank if you wish.

You need to make some changes to the settings.xml file before the actual conversion can be run. If you are going to be using a UserMap.xml file, you need to add the following tag in the `<Source>` tag, just under the `<VSSDatabase>` tag:

```
<UserMap name="[PathToUserMap.xmlFile]"></UserMap>
```

This tag tells the VSSConverter application that you want to use a user-mapping file and where the UserMap file is located.

For each of the `<Project>` tags, you need to add a `Destination` attribute. This attribute tells the VSSConverter application where in the Team Foundation Version Control system to covert the VSS project:

```
<Project Source="$/VssProject1" Destination="$/TeamProject1"></Project>
```

Finally, you need to add a new set of tags after the `<ConverterSpecificSetting>` tag. This tag is called `<Settings>` and is used to define which Team Foundation Server you want to convert to:

```
<Settings>
<TeamFoundationServer name="[ServerName]" port="[PortNumber]"
protocol="[Protocol]"></TeamFoundationServer>
</Settings>
```

You specify the name of your Team Foundation Server, the port number (most likely 8080), and the protocol (either http or https).

So, for the example, after making the appropriate changes, the settings.xml file should look like this:

```
<?xml version="1.0" encoding="utf-8"?>
<SourceControlConverter>
<ConverterSpecificSetting>
<Source name="VSS">
<VSSDatabase name="c:\MyVSS"></VSSDatabase>
<UserMap name="C:\Convert\UserMap.xml"></UserMap>
</Source>
<ProjectMap>
<Project Source="$/VSSTest.root" Destination="$/MyConvertedVSS></Project>
</ProjectMap>
</ConverterSpecificSetting>
<Settings>
<TeamFoundationServer name="SSRTM" port="8080"
protocol="http"></TeamFoundationServer>
</Settings>
</SourceControlConverter>
```

You are using the UserMap.xml file located in the `C:\Covert` directory. You are converting to the MyConvertedVSS Team Project, so you added that to the `Destination` attribute. And you have added the appropriate Team Foundation Server settings for your server.

You are now ready to run the conversion.

Converting and Viewing Results

To start the conversion, go back to the command prompt you opened earlier, and while still in the `C:\Convert` directory:

1. Run the following:

```
vssconverter migrate settings.xml
```

2. You are asked if you want to start the migration. Press Y to start it. You are then asked for the VSS administrator password (again, for this example, the password is blank, so simply press Enter). The conversion continues. Once the conversion is complete, you will be notified of the success or failure of the process.

3. VSSConverter uses SQL Express during the migration process. If the conversion process uses more than 4GB, it will fail. You fix this by using SQL Server instead of SQL Express, and adding the following tag to the `<Source>` tag:

```
<SQL Server="SQLServerName"></SQL>
```

When the conversion is finished, it writes out a report to the file VSSMigrationReport.xml, as shown in Figure 12-22.

This report gives you the details of the conversion, including any possible warnings or errors that may have occurred, so you know what to look for in Team Foundation Server.

Of course, the true test of the conversion will be to see it in Team Foundation Server. Once you have converted the example, open Team Explorer, and navigate to the MyConvertedVSS Team Project. Double-click the Source Control icon in the project to open Source Control Explorer. You can then drill down into the MyConvertedVSS folder, and verify the files have been converted, and the history has been maintained, as shown in Figure 12-23.

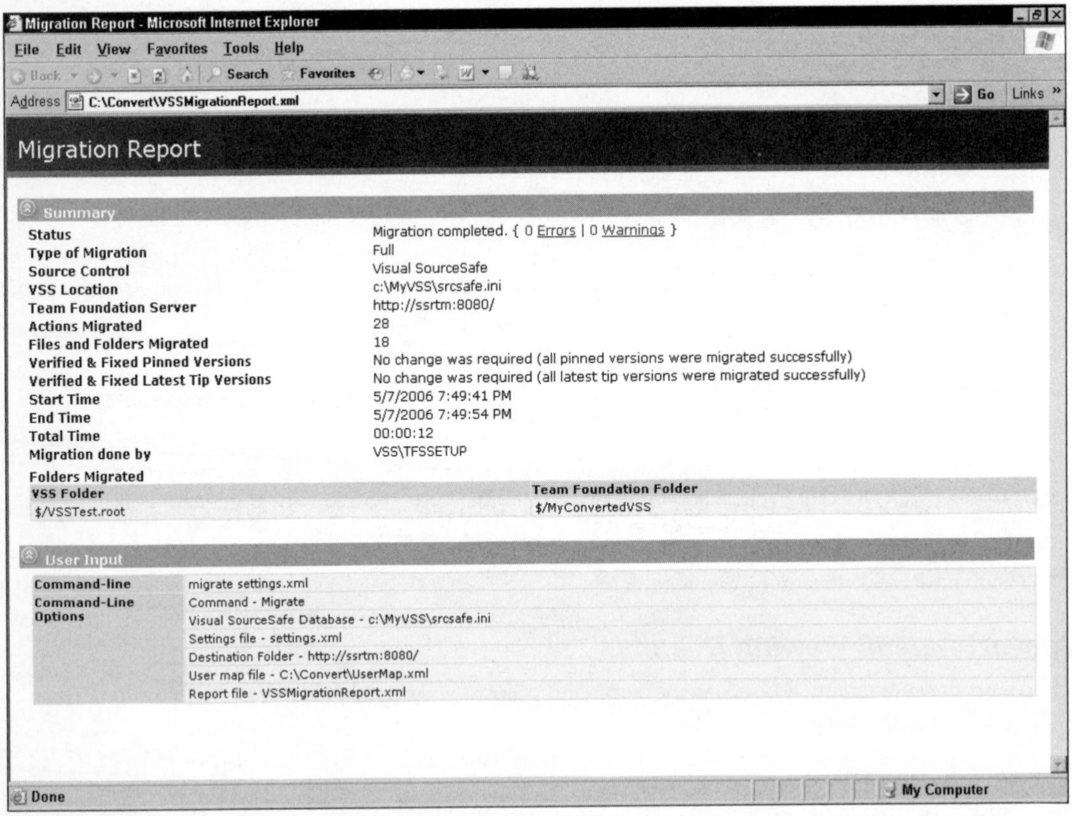

Figure 12-22

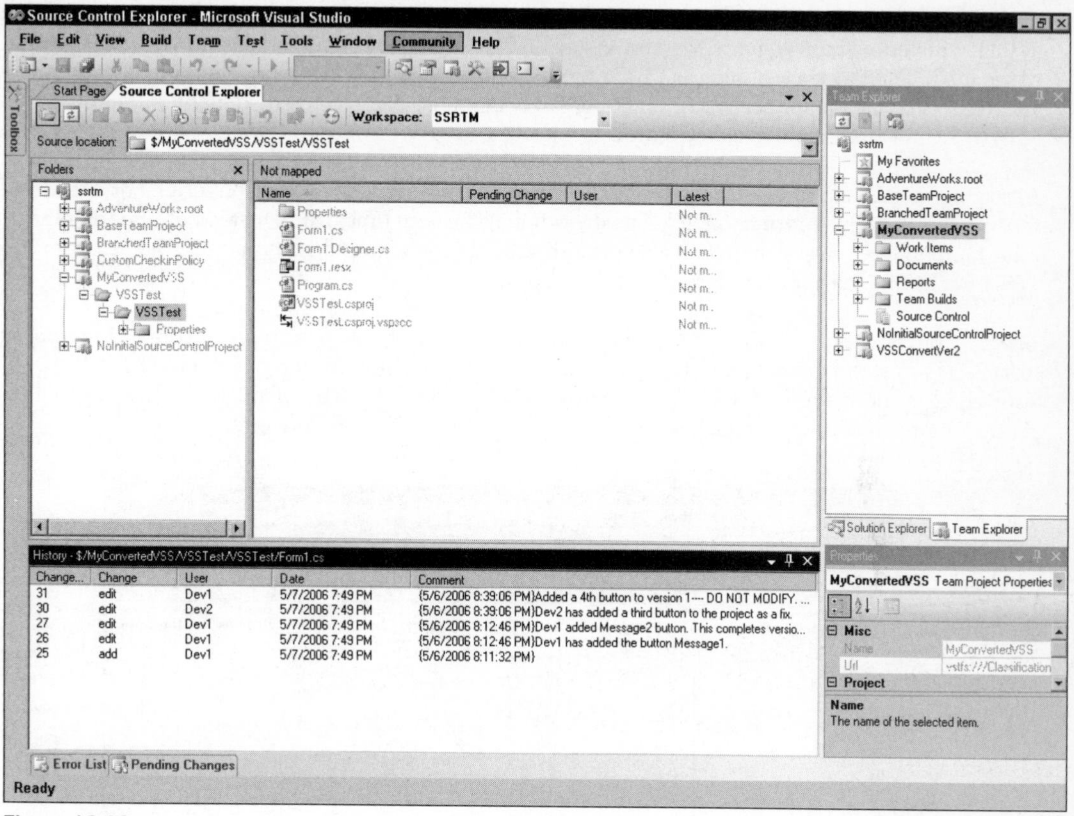

Figure 12-23

There you go, you have successfully migrated a Visual SourceSafe project into Team Foundation Version Control!

Using CS-Converter to Convert Visual SourceSafe

As you have seen, Microsoft provides a free tool, VSSConverter, for converting your Visual SourceSafe information over into Team Foundation Version control. One drawback of the tool is that it is completely command-line driven, requiring you to run the conversion from the command prompt, as well as edit XML configuration files by hand. Another potential issue is that the VSSConverter application can only be used to convert Visual SourceSafe projects, so users of other version control systems, such as Subversion or CVS, must find other means to convert their information into TFS.

One solution is to make use of the Team Foundation Server Object Model, and create a customized tool for running the conversion. However, if you do not want to go that route, there are some third-party tools on the market that will do the conversion for you. One of these tools is CS-Converter, by ComponentSoftware (`componentsoftware.com`).

CS-Converter is a graphical conversion tool, which can be used to migrate a variety of version control systems, including Subversion, CVS, and Visual SourceSafe, onto Team Foundation Version Control. One of the main benefits of a tool such as CS-Converter is that it is a graphical conversion tool, making it easier to use by a majority of people. Another benefit is that it is able to convert so many different other systems to Team Foundation Version Control.

According to the help file for CS-Converter, it has several advantages of VSSConverter. For example, when converting the information, it keeps the original check-in timestamp, instead of updating the timestamp to the conversion date. It also provides the ability to graphically map user names from VSS to TFS, by selecting the appropriate user from a drop-down list box.

The CS-Converter help file does a great job of providing a step-by-step example of converting from VSS to TFS, so you won't go into that here. If you are interested in a graphical tool for converting Visual SourceSafe, or need a tool to convert from Subversion or CVS, it is recommended you investigate this product more on your own. Figure 12-24 shows a screenshot from CS-Converter.

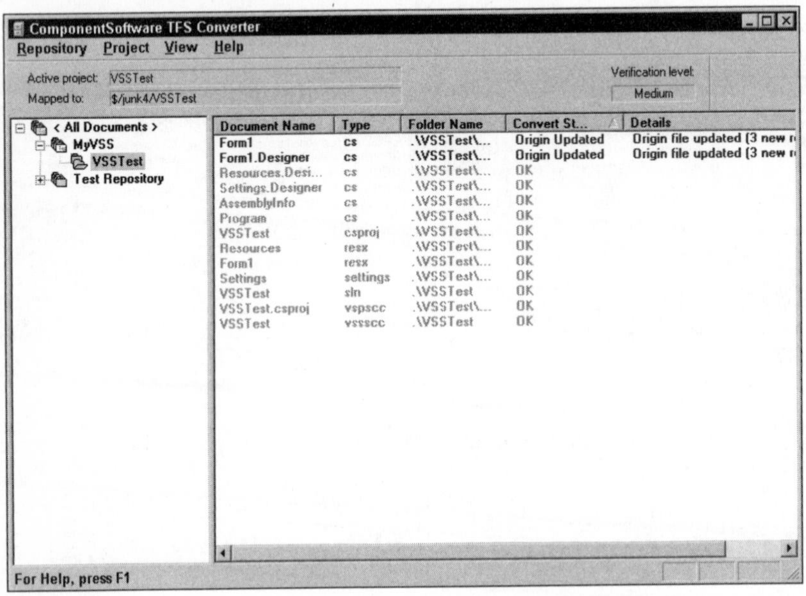

Figure 12-24

Team Foundation Version Control Best Practices

Team Foundation Server and Team Foundation Version Control are brand new products, having just been released in the first quarter of 2006. As such, there is not a lot of best practice information built up around them. This section of the chapter attempts to outline what the authors believe to be some good ways to use Team Foundation Version Control. Some of the points presented here hold true regardless of the version control system you are using. You should take the following information and build off it to develop the best practices that work best for you and your organization.

The Trunk

Regardless of what you are developing, you want to have a copy of your code that will always compile, allowing you to create a product release of your code. This copy is referred to by Vincent Maraia in *The Build Masters* as the mainline, or trunk. The purpose of the trunk is to make it easy to create a release of your product. As such, no code is merged or added to the trunk until you are sure it compiles and passes any appropriate tests. This ensures the trunk is always in pristine condition.

Always start a top-level folder underneath a new team project to serve as a mainline or trunk. Create a folder called main, and put all the source code for the main branch in this folder. When a new branch needs to be created, you can branch from the main folder directly.

Check-In and Check-Out

Always use the shared check-out model. This model allows you to make the most efficient use of the source files and your team. You will not have developers waiting to check out files to make changes, allowing more work to be completed in a shorter length of time.

If you have source files checked out for a long period, do not just try to check them back into the repository when you are done. Depending on how long you have had the files checked out into your workspace, there may be many changes that have taken place in the repository. As such, it may be difficult to check your code back in, due to all the conflicts. Instead, while you are working on your code, periodically get the latest code from the repository and merge it into your workspace. This allows you to make sure the changes you are making will play nice with the other changes that have taken place in the repository. That way, when you do finally check your changes back into the repository, you have already resolved most of the conflicts, making the check-in process relatively painless.

This leads to the next point, which is *never* check code into the repository unless it compiles and is ready for consumption by other members of the team. Remember, you want to have a trunk of code in the repository that you can ensure will always compile.

When you check in your code to the repository, you should always associate it with a work item, so you can track why the change was made and what the changes addresses. However, you should only associate one work item per check-in. Do not associate multiple work items with a check-in, as this makes it difficult to determine what code changes go with what work item.

Finally, even though you can, don't override a check-in policy unless you *really* have to! Check-in policies exist not to make your life difficult, but to ensure that code changes meet certain requirements, to ensure the reliability of the repository. When you override a check-in policy, you potentially introduce instability into the system, such as causing a build to break. If you need to stop working on a project for a while, or want to make sure your files are backed up on the server nightly, use shelving instead.

Branching and Merging

The following bullet points are some branching and merging best practices:

- You should merge frequently. Whether you are merging the latest changes from the repository into your workspace, or vice versa, you should do this often to ensure compatibility between changes. As well, you should do full merges instead of cherry-pick merges. This will simplify the merge process as a whole.

- When you perform a merge, make sure you always check that merge in completely before you perform another merge. Otherwise, things can become confusing.
- Always build and run tests after performing a merge, but before you check the merge into the repository. This ensures that you have tested the merges, to make sure nothing is broken. Remember, you never want to perform a check-in of code that will not build or pass its tests. Also, when renames are part of a merge, pay particular attention to the path the tool recommends for the renames, and make changes as appropriate.

Branching and merging tie into a concept called promotion modeling. Promotion modeling is a strategy where you maintain your source code at various levels of readiness. For example, your developers will always be working on the latest version of the source files, which might be relatively unstable, while the testers are looking at the latest version of the stable code. Using promotion modeling, once the developers have stabilized their code and are ready for the testers to look at it, they move it, or promote it, into an area where the testers can take advantage of the new code.

With Team Foundation Version Control, if you are going to use promotion modeling, you need to establish a branch for every promotion level. For example, you might have a development branch, a test branch, and a production branch in your team project. When code is checked into the development branch, and is ready to be promoted to the test branch, you simply merge the development branch changes into the test branch. This promotes the files, allowing the testers to have access to the new code. Then, when the testers are satisfied, they can promote the code to the production branch. The moral of this story is to use branching and merging to establish your promotion model scenario.

Remember, you are always going to have your main trunk, which is your pristine copy of your code. The trunk is always supposed to compile. All changes will ultimately be merged into the trunk.

Shelving

You should always shelve your code before you quit working. That ensures your latest changes are backed up when the Team Foundation Server is backed up. Moreover, never check in code that does not compile or pass your tests. If you need to put it back on the server for some reason, shelve it.

You should also use shelving to conduct peer code reviews. This provides an easy way for other developers to look at your code from their own workstations.

Team Foundation Version Control Extensibility

Extensibility has been a constant theme throughout this book concerning Team Foundation Server, and Team Foundation Version Control is no exception. TFVC gives you the ability to build your own custom check-in policies, allowing you to implement your specific organization rules concerning how items are checked into the repository. As well, TFVC makes use of the Team Foundation Server Object Model. While you won't learn much about that in this chapter, you make use of it in future chapters where continuous integration and Team Build are discussed. Finally, Microsoft has provided a MSSCCI Provider for Team Foundation Version Control, allowing you to access TFVC from older development environments, such as Visual Studio 2003. This allows you to take advantage of the version control system in Team Foundation Server, without having to immediately port all your development over to Visual Studio 2005.

Custom Check-In Policies

One of the nice things about check-in policies is that you can create your own for almost any situation for which you want to write some code. Basically, a custom check-in policy is just a managed .NET assembly containing one or more classes. These classes are added to the Windows Registry, allowing Team Foundation Server Version Control to find and manage the check-in policies. The Visual Studio SDK has some detailed documentation concerning creating a custom check-in policy.

Included with the code for this chapter is a Policies.zip file. This file contains a custom check-in policy project called PendingCheckinComments. The purpose of this policy is to force the user to enter comments in the Pending Checkins window, before allowing the modified code to be checked in. Unzip this code to the `C:\Policies` directory; then open the `PendingCheckinComments` solution file in VS 2005 to view the code. This project is just a C# Class Library project.

There is only one class in this project, called Comment.cs. This class implements your custom check-in policy. You should be able to take this class file, and use it as a template for creating your own custom policies. While we won't go into detail about every aspect of this file, we need to point out a couple of things to you concerning this custom policy.

You need to add the following using statements to any custom policy you make:

```
using System.Windows.Forms;
using Microsoft.TeamFoundation.VersionControl.Client;
using System.Collections;
using System.IO;
```

You will have to add a reference to `System.Windows.Form`. As well, you will need to add a reference to `C:\Program Files\Microsoft Visual Studio 8\Common7\IDE\PrivateAssemblies\Microsoft.TeamFoundationVersionControl.Client.dll`.

A custom policy is persisted as a serialized .NET object. As such, it needs to be marked with the `[Serializable]` attribute. The class also needs to inherit from `PolicyBase`, which defines the basic policy interface.

```
[Serializable]
public class Comments : PolicyBase
{
...
}
```

> **Some of methods for `PolicyBase` are abstract and therefore you have to define them. One easy way to create these is to right-click PolicyBase and select Implement Abstract Class.**

Notice the list of strings at the top of the class:

```
static string pType = "Pending Checkin Comments Policy";
static string pDescription = "This policy ensures that the pending comments field
has comments.";
static string pInstallationInstructions = "None available at this time.";
static string pTypeDescription = pType + " Description";
static string pDisposedMessage = pType + " Object has been disposed.";
static string pHelp = "No help available at this time";
static string pMessage = "Pending Checkin comments are empty.";
```

These strings contain the different messages and text strings that a custom policy might need. Listing them all in one place makes it easy to find and modify them.

All the methods listed in Comments.cs need to be implemented as listed. Most of the methods listed in Comments.cs will be the same regardless of your custom policy. The main method, which does your work for you, is the `PolicyFailure` method:

```
public override PolicyFailure[] Evaluate()
{
//If this object has been disposed of, throw an exception
if (this.Disposed)
{
throw new ObjectDisposedException(pType, pDisposedMessage);
}

//Create an array list of policy failures
ArrayList policyFailures = new ArrayList();

//If the Pending Changes Comment field is empty
if (this.PendingCheckin.PendingChanges.Comment.Length == 0)
{
//Create a new policy failure object and add it to the collection
PolicyFailure failure = new PolicyFailure(pMessage, this);
policyFailures.Add(failure);
}

//Return the policy failures collection
return (PolicyFailure[])policyFailures.ToArray(typeof(PolicyFailure));

}
```

This is the method you will be modifying to implement your custom logic for your check-in policy. For the example code, the first thing you do is check to see if the custom check-in object has been disposed of. If it has, then you throw an exception:

```
//If this object has been disposed of, throw an exception
if (this.Disposed)
{
throw new ObjectDisposedException(pType, pDisposedMessage);
}
```

Next, you create an array list to hold any policy failures that may occur:

```
//Create an array list of policy failures
ArrayList policyFailures = new ArrayList();
```

Then you check to see if the Pending Changes comment field is empty. If it is, you create a new policy failure object, and add it to the array list:

```
//If the Pending Changes Comment field is empty
if (this.PendingCheckin.PendingChanges.Comment.Length == 0)
{
//Create a new policy failure object and add it to the collection
PolicyFailure failure = new PolicyFailure(pMessage, this);
policyFailures.Add(failure);
}
```

Finally, you return the array list of policy failures. If the array list has at least one member, the policy will be violated, and you will be warned:

```
//Return the policy failures collection
return (PolicyFailure[])policyFailures.ToArray(typeof(PolicyFailure));
```

All the other methods in this class can pretty much be cut and pasted from policy to policy, as they should rarely change, if ever.

Be aware that the Edit method must return a true value:

```
public override bool Edit(IPolicyEditArgs policyEditArgs)
{
//This function must return true, due to a bug in V1
return true;
}
```

Due to a bug in version 1 of Team Foundation Server, if you do not have this method return a true value, then you will not be able to add your custom check-in policy to your source control settings in Team Explorer.

Once you have created your policy (or in this case, unzipped it) and compiled it, you have to add a registry key for your policy, so Visual Studio Team System will see it and use it. To do this, open a command prompt and type **regedit** to run the registry editor. Drill down to the following registry key:

```
HKEY_LOCAL_MACHINE\SOFTWARE\Microsoft\VisualStudio\8.0\TeamFoundation\SourceControl\
Checkin Policies
```

Add a new string value with the same name as your DLL, but without the .dll extension. For this example, add a new string value with a name of **PendingCheckinComments**. Double-click this string value, and enter the full path to the DLL file. If you have unzipped the included code to the specified directory, this path should be:

```
C:\Policies\PendingCheckinComments\PendingCheckinComments\bin\Debug\
PendingCheckinComments.dll
```

Once you have added this path, you can close the registry editor.

All right, you have now created a check-in policy, and have associated it with Visual Studio. Let's see the policy in action.

1. Open Visual Studio and go to one of your Team Projects. Right-click the project, and select Team Project Settings⇨Source Control. This opens the Source Control Settings window for that team project.
2. Click the Check-in Policy tab; then click the Add button to add a Check-in Policy to this Team Project. You see a window similar to Figure 12-25. As you can see, the policy you have created, Pending Checkin Comment Policy, is listed in the window.

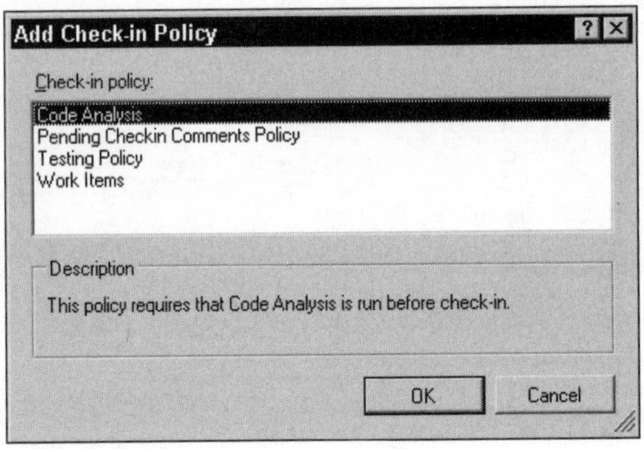

Figure 12-25

3. Select your custom policy and click OK. You will now see the policy listed in the Check-in Policy tab of the Source Control Settings window.
4. Create a new console application, and associate it with the team project you just enabled your custom policy on. Open the Pending Changes window, and click the Policy Warnings button. Figure 12-26 shows you that you are violating a check-in policy, because you do not have any comments in the comments field.

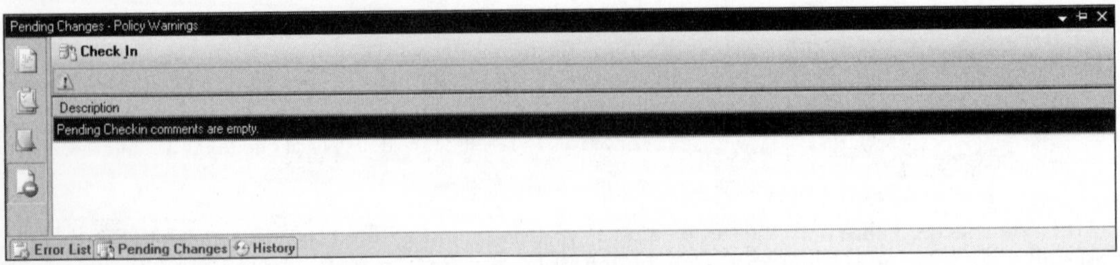

Figure 12-26

If you try to check in your changes, you will be warned that you are violating a check-in policy. You always have the option to override a check-in policy, but this is not recommended.

Object Model

Team Foundation Version Control contains its own rich object model, built off the Team Foundation Server Object Model. You learned the basics of using this object model in Chapter 9. Utilizing the object model, you can interact with all aspects of the version control system. Everything you can do with the Source Control Explorer you can also do with the object model. You will learn more about using the object model in the next chapter, when you look at how to implement continuous integration with Team Build.

MSSCCI Provider

The Microsoft Source Code Control Interface, or MSSCCI, was brought into being with Visual SourceSafe, and is now supported by many different IDEs. Microsoft recognized that many developers would like to use the more powerful version control located in Team Foundation Server but would not be able to immediately begin development using Visual Studio Team System. As such, they created a MSSCCI client for Team Foundation Version Control, allowing users of older IDEs the ability to interface with Team Foundation Version Control.

The provider can be downloaded from the Microsoft Download site at `microsoft.com/downloads/details.aspx?FamilyId=87E1FFBD-A484-4C3A-8776-D560AB1E6198&displaylang=en`. While this MSSCCI client was developed by Microsoft, it is not officially supported. However, Microsoft is very interested in seeing the client succeed, and has provided a special e-mail address, `tfsmsscci@microsoft.com`, for you to provide feedback on the client. As well, the Team Foundation Server Version Control forum (`http://forums.microsoft.com/MSDN/ShowForum.aspx?ForumID=478&SiteID=1`) located at the MSDN Forums (`http://forums.microsoft.com/MSDN`) is a great place to get questions answered and provide feedback for this MSSCCI client.

The MSSCCI client works with the following products:

- Visual Studio 2003
- Visual C++ 6 SP6
- Visual Basic 6 SP6
- Visual Foxpro 9 SP1
- Microsoft Access 2003 SP2
- SQL Server Management Studio
- Sparx Systems Enterprise Architect
- Sybase Powerbuilder 10.5

> **You must have Team Explorer installed on your machine, before you install the MSSCCI client.**

As you start to use the MSSCCI provider in your IDE of choice, you'll notice that many of the screens and windows are remarkably similar to their Visual Studio 2005 counterparts. Microsoft has done a nice job of integrating the dialogs and windows from VS 2005, making it very intuitive to use.

There are a couple of gotchas that you need to watch out for. First, the code analysis and the testing check-in policies are not going to work. These policies rely on pieces of Visual Studio Team System to run, so it makes sense they would not work in a non-VSTS environment. Requiring a check-in to be associated with a work item will still work though, as will most custom check-in policies.

A second issue to watch for is if you have multiple MSSCCI providers installed on one machine, for example the VSS MSSCCI client and the TFS MSSCCI client. There will be times when you need to switch between one provider or the other. Ed Hintz, on his blog at `http://blogs.msdn.com/edhintz/archive/2006/04/10/572826.aspx`, gives the details on how to handle this issue. Basically, you need to set the value of `the ProviderRegKey` in the registry at `HKEY_LOCAL_MACHINE\Software\SourceCodeControlProvider` to a value listed under `the Installed SCCProviders` key.

Let's look at a quick example of using the MSSCCI provider. Take a machine that you have Visual Studio 2003 installed on. Install Team Explorer on the machine, then download and install the Team Foundation Server MSSCCI client. Following the instructions from Ed Hintz's blog, make sure the registry is configured to use Team Foundation Server.

1. Open Visual Studio 2003 and create a new console application. Now that you have a new project created, you need to add it to Team Foundation Version Control.
2. Select File⇨Source Control⇨Add Solution To Source Control. You are prompted to connect to a Team Foundation Server, with a dialog box very similar to that used in Visual Studio 2005. You can select a server from the drop-down list box, or click the Servers button and add a new server.
3. Next, you need to choose a team project and folder to put the application in. You can also select a local workspace to map to this folder. Once you are done, click OK.
4. The Check-in window opens. In this window, as normal, you can view the files that are being checked in. You can enter comments. You can associate the changeset with a work item. You can enter check-in notes, and even view policy warnings. Figure 12-27 shows an example of this window.

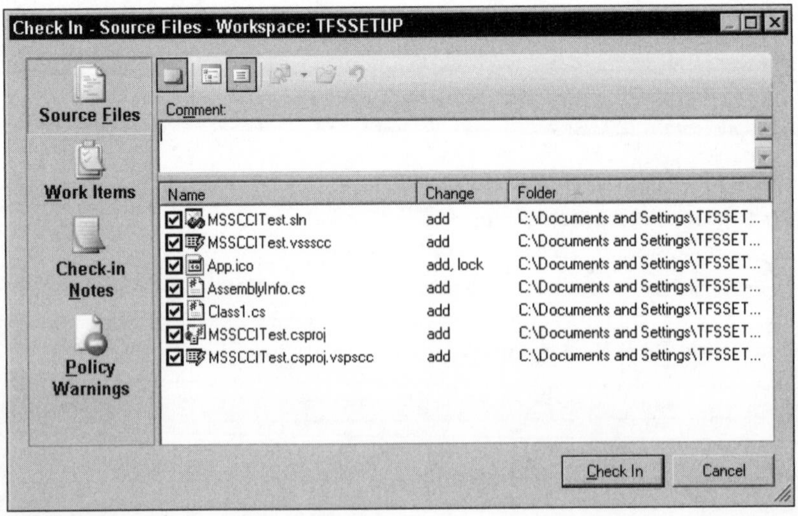

Figure 12-27

As you can see, it looks exactly like the window from Visual Studio 2005. Click the check-in button to check the files in.

5. Now open Visual Studio 2005. Using Team Explorer, open the Source Control Explorer for the team project you added the project to. You can see the folders that were added, and can see the files, the associated work items, everything. You can have most of the power and functionality of Team Foundation Version Control, yet continue to develop in the environment you are most comfortable in. It is the best of both worlds.

Summary

You started out this chapter by examining some of the version control systems in use today and then covered some basic concepts related to version control systems, with an emphasis on how those concepts are implemented in Team Foundation Version Control.

After that, you jumped into some of the essentials of TFVC, including the Source Control Explorer, and some of the new features, such as shelving. Following that discussion was a detailed look at how to convert your Visual SourceSafe information over into Team Foundation Version Control, and some suggested best practice information.

Finally, you learned how you can extend TFVC through the creation of custom check-in policies, and how you can use other development environments, such as Visual Studio 2003, with TFVC using a MSSCCI control.

There is a lot to Team Foundation Version Control; in some ways, you have just scratched the surface in this chapter. However, you should have learned enough to navigate your way around the system and begin to understand how you can apply it to you and your organization's needs.

Chapter 9 goes into detail on automating Team System. In that chapter, you'll go into more depth on the Team Foundation Version Control Object Model, and how it can be used to automate your build processes.

Part IV
Management

13

Managing Your Team Projects

You have installed Team System and set up your first Team Project. How do you properly configure it? The Microsoft Solutions Framework (MSF) has some good guidance, but most people seem to be stuck when trying to figure out where to go next. What is the optimal way of setting up your areas and iterations? What exactly is an iteration? In this chapter, we provide a context around these questions and many more.

> **You should read this chapter before implementing a Team Project. We provide important information here on how to structure it.**

Effectively leveraging the artifacts in Team System involves an understanding of the underlying goals of the product. One of the reoccurring themes you will see is the implementation of software engineering principles in your development process. However, it's much more than that — many processes out there provide the rigor, but no agility. Team System is a remarkable suite of tools as it supports the best of both worlds. Sam Guckenheimer in his book *Software Engineering with Microsoft Visual Studio Team System* (ISBN: 0321278720) refers to this amalgamation of agility and mathematical precision as the "Value Up" approach. It makes a great deal of sense because both the Agile and Software Engineering movements seek to scope out how software is developed and drive predictability.

Software project management is a complex set of tasks that involves the balancing act of managing project dependencies and resources. You can easily write an entire book on the subject. (In fact, hundreds have been written on the topic.) One authoritative compilation software project management wisdom is the Project Management Body of Knowledge (PMBOK) developed by the Project Management Institute (PMI). The PMBOK covers most aspects of the project management discipline, and provides guidance on areas that can be managed using Team System. It also covers additional areas such as project management for human resources, procurement, and cost management (to name a few). You can learn more about the PMBOK at `www.pmi.org`.

In this chapter, we look at some the guidance provided by the PMBOK, and then compare and contrast it with the capabilities of Team System. We also provide a pragmatic guide to setting up a Team Project, and running it through to its conclusion. You will come to understand how all the pieces of the project puzzle fit together. Finally, you get a solid overview of how to manage your test infrastructure within the scope of a Team Project.

Working with Team Members

Central to MSF is the concept of the Team Model. The Team Model is a 180-degree move away from a hierarchical process structure (the waterfall approach) to embrace the concept that all team members are equal stakeholders in the software development process. This may sound simple in theory, but is actually very difficult to implement and requires cooperation and support from the very highest level of management to work.

The PMBOK discusses key stakeholders such as project managers, customers, sponsors, but—in what we regard as a huge omission from that list—neglects to discuss the rest of the team! Process methodologies were first designed with the premise that project members needed to be brought in line and controlled with an iron fist. This is really a reaction to product slips, delays, bugs, and so forth. Most process management books that you can find at a bookstore are large bricks. The emphasis is to bring a team under control and measure time very closely. However, the developer isn't always to blame for project slippages! Often, the chief cause of delays is a lack of visibility and understanding of the velocity of your team (which leads to bad estimation). Figure 13-1 shows the process flow of most waterfall projects.

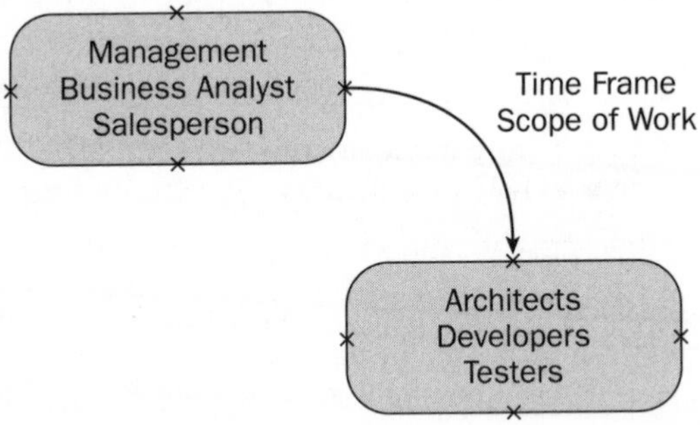

Figure 13-1

As you can see, there is no feedback loop. The management and sales personnel have no idea how long a feature takes to develop. Yet, they frame the work in an artificial timeframe and expect the developers to deliver. Figure 13-2 shows the Team Model.

The Team Model is characterized by and builds trust, whereas trust is not a feature of the waterfall process. Another characteristic of the Team Model is that there is feedback between all team members at all stages of development.

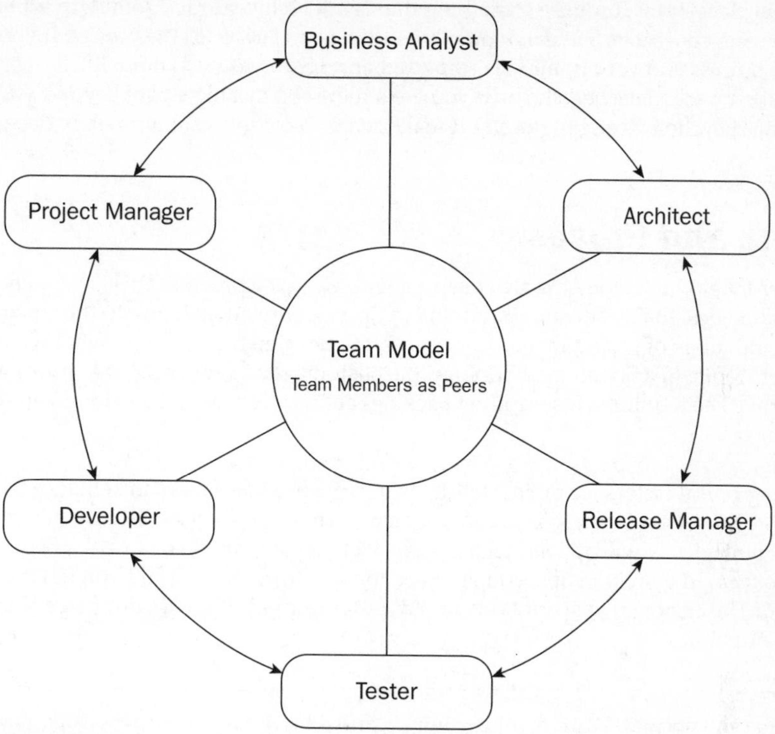

Figure 13-2

Advocacy and Ownership

A big theme in the Team Model is the concept of advocacy. If you care about and have a stake in the product, you will want to work as hard as possible to deliver it. In a waterfall approach, the developer is focused on time-to-task and meeting the deadline at any cost (even allowing bugs or sloppy code).

In the Team Model, each role within the team is an advocate for the part of the process for which they are responsible. For example, the business analyst is responsible and advocates for the needs of the customer. The developer advocates for the needs of the application. In a true Team Model configuration, a developer has equal say in what decisions are made for the application, even over management because in a trusting respectful environment, the developer really wants what's best for the product. Just because you are a project manager doesn't mean you stop making mistakes. If you are used to a waterfall like approach, the everyone-is-equal approach may seem unpalatable and radical. However, the model was not conceived in a vacuum. There is repeated precedent showing companies that are extremely successful using this management structure.

The Team Model stands for advocacy and equal representation but also communication. It's difficult for a single person (or a small group of people) to capture the big picture, every single risk, technical challenge, and so forth. One of the reasons it works so well is that it eliminates situations such as when the businessperson, who may not understand the architectural needs of the application, may, without consulting the developers, promise something that is not architecturally sound. In a Team Model environment, we gain consensus and every member of the team *buys in* to the project. If you feel that you are a part of the process and your opinion is respected and heard, you will more likely work harder on a project than if you feel detached and as if you are a mere cog in a big wheel beyond your control. The basis for this is psychological, but doesn't it make sense? Isn't software ultimately designed by human beings?

Customers and Process

In the Team Model, the customer is also deeply involved in the process. This is very characteristic of agile methodologies. In Extreme Programming (XP), a close relationship with the customer is key. Why focus on the minutiae of project management artifacts and timeframes when what really counts is what the customer wants. In a Scrum methodology, the customer has a say in what features get developed within a sprint. The requirements (product backlog) are carefully managed along with the expectations of the customer.

One of the big causal factors for project failure is unrealistic expectation on behalf of the customer. The customer or sales person in a waterfall arrangement wants a product as fast as you can produce it, and expects that it magically will appear. There is a lack of visibility in the process — therefore, you can't really blame them. If a project slips, you get questions such as "Why didn't you tell me that it would take longer?" The customer is mainly concerned with the application of your piece of software from a business standpoint.

If you can't accurately predict how long a project will take, then you can guarantee that the customer also has no idea how long it will take. It is your responsibility to get a handle on your process and manage the expectations of the customer.

The term customer is used loosely here. A customer may be the CEO of your company, a business analyst, or even your development lead.

Setting Up Team Meetings

It is always a good practice to get the team together to discuss the initial steps of the project. It is in this phase where you can work out the requirements; decompose them into manageable tasks (usually one to three days long). Another key reason for a team meeting is to get everyone's feedback on the programmable elements. As key advocates in the process, each can contribute to the project and provide a sanity check on the structural, business, and implementation details.

Microsoft has released a Requirements Authoring Starter Kit that you can integrate with Team System. You can download the kit from `microsoft.com/downloads/details.aspx?FamilyId=E96CCC54-8759-452F-BF68-3A261C663B66&displaylang=en`.

Structuring Your Project

You have three tools at your disposal to organize your project: Microsoft Project, Microsoft Excel, and Team Explorer. No matter what processes you choose to use for your project (agile approach, MSF, or other), a consistent theme should be always apparent. To this end, you need to come up with a vision statement of some sort along with a set of requirements that define the features of the application. In Extreme Programming, the story card is used for that purpose. In MSF, you use scenarios and personas to define the parameters of your project.

> **There are many ways you can define scenarios. On his blog, Randy Miller (the creator of MSF for Agile Software Development) provides his take on how to formulate a scenario. Please refer to** `http://blogs.msdn.com/randymiller/archive/2006/08/02/686701.aspx`**.**

There is an mismatch with the ways Team System and Microsoft Project handle workflow. Microsoft Project is designed to handle complicated relationships, hierarchies, dependencies, managing tasks cross iteration, and time tracking. Team System, on the other hand, is designed to handle lists (for example, a backlog) only. This makes Team System perfect for managing agile projects but a little more challenging for more structured and complicated projects. You mainly have to rethink the techniques you are used to implement in enterprise project management (EPM).

Team System's project management infrastructure is quite simply a tool created by *developers* for *developers*. It is a good area for third-party partners and independent software vendors (ISVs) to fill in the gaps. This chapter provides several insider techniques to make the most out of the available project management tools.

Let's start setting up our workflow.

1. To load in your work items into Microsoft Project or Microsoft Excel, simply click the Choose Team Project button. The interface shown in Figure 13-3 should appear.

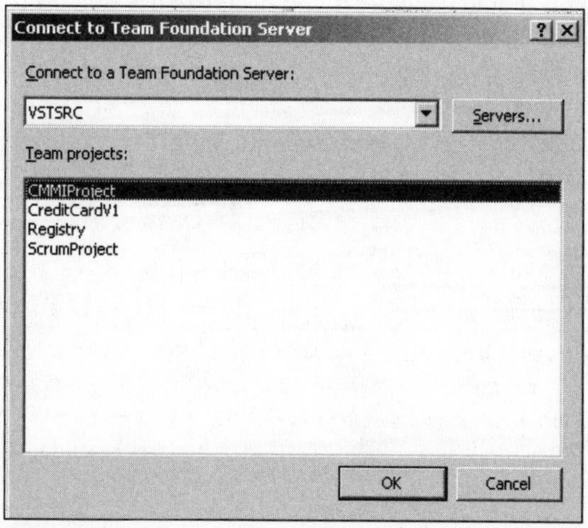

Figure 13-3

> **If you can't find the Choose Team Project button in Microsoft Project or Microsoft Excel, chances are that Team Explorer didn't install correctly, or you installed Microsoft Office *after* installing Team Explorer. The fix is to go into Start⇨Control Panel, Add/Remove Programs and reinstall or repair Team Explorer. The Team Explorer client application is available on the Team Foundation Server media (CD or DVD) or you can download a copy using the following link:** `http://download.microsoft.com/download/2/a/d/2ad44873-8ccb-4a1b-9c0d-23224b3ba34c/VSTFClient.img`**.**

2. Once you have selected your Team Project, you can get a list of work items, publish the changes you made to the project plan or refresh the current view using the toolbar in Microsoft Project (as shown in Figure 13-4).

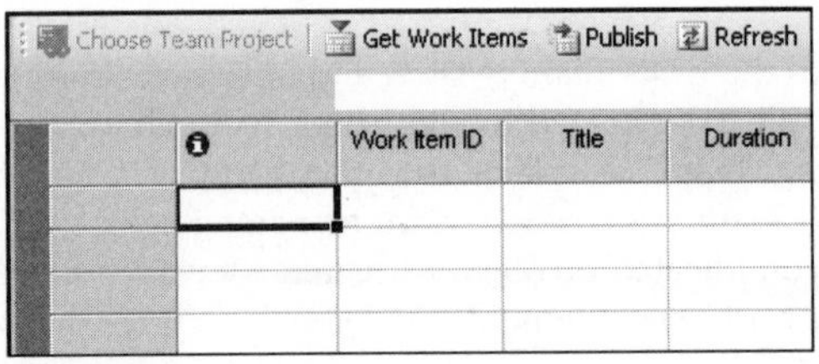

Figure 13-4

There are many additional options available in Microsoft Project including a link to your process guidance from the Help menu. From the Team menu, you can access the mappings between work items on Team Foundation Server and Project; add links and attachments to your work items; and edit your areas and iterations. Microsoft Excel has similar options.

Work Item Synchronization

There are a few points you should consider if you decide to use Microsoft Project to develop your work breakdown structure. Team System is currently designed to manage task list hierarchies really well. Figure 13-5 shows a summary task Requirement, associated to a list of dependent Tasks.

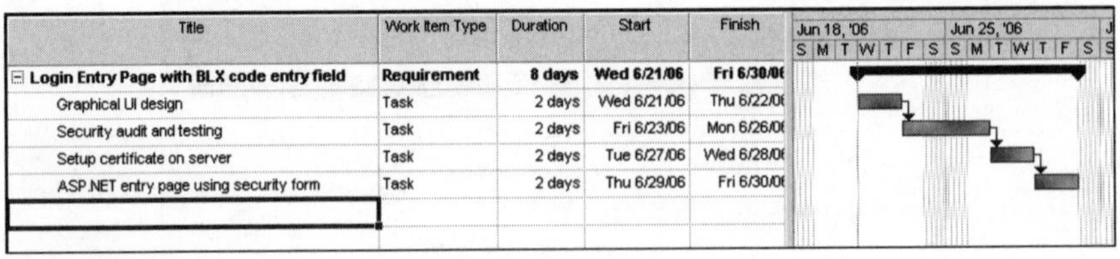
Title
Work Item Type
Duration
Start
Finish
Jun 18, '06
Jun 25, '06
Login Entry Page with BLX code entry field
Requirement
8 days
Wed 6/21/06
Graphical UI design
Task
2 days
Wed 6/21/06
Security audit and testing
Task
2 days
Fri 6/23/06
Setup certificate on server
Task
2 days
Tue 6/27/06
ASP.NET entry page using security form
Task
2 days
Thu 6/29/06

Figure 13-5

What happens when you try to synchronize this task list with Team Foundation Server? The information you entered in Project and Excel is for the most part preserved. For example, if you open up the Setup certificate on server Task in Team Explorer and click the Details tab, you'll notice a field called Task Hierarchy that has the following value: Login Entry Page with BLX code entry field⇨Setup certificate on server.

A problem occurs when you try to sync back the work items to a blank Microsoft Project worksheet. As shown in Figure 13-6, the summary tasks, time and date tracking, dependencies, and the rollup have all disappeared. Your nicely formatted Gantt chart also won't show up.

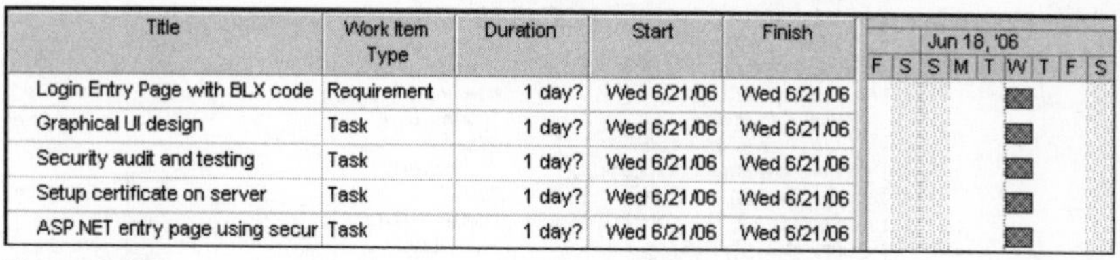

Title	Work Item Type	Duration	Start	Finish
Login Entry Page with BLX code	Requirement	1 day?	Wed 6/21/06	Wed 6/21/06
Graphical UI design	Task	1 day?	Wed 6/21/06	Wed 6/21/06
Security audit and testing	Task	1 day?	Wed 6/21/06	Wed 6/21/06
Setup certificate on server	Task	1 day?	Wed 6/21/06	Wed 6/21/06
ASP.NET entry page using secur	Task	1 day?	Wed 6/21/06	Wed 6/21/06

Figure 13-6

> **In light of these limitations as well as a best practice, it is recommended that you save and back up your Microsoft Project or Excel file once you have worked out the work breakdown structure (WBS) for your Team System software development projects.**

In this chapter, we examine how to work around synchronization issues with the following Project file elements:

- Summary tasks
- Rollups
- Start and Finish dates
- Predecessors

Team System is configured to map out the value of specific Project fields with Team Foundation Server, based on an XML file found in your Classification process template folder, called FileMappings.xml. This file is quite important, especially when you want to create your own customized work items. To view the current mappings in your project, simply click Team⇨View Column Mappings (as shown in Figure 13-7).

> **Field mapping customization is covered in some depth on the MSDN Web site. You can view the documentation by visiting the following link:** `http://msdn2.microsoft.com/en-us/library/ms404684.aspx`

When you update a Task work item in the MSF for CMMI Process Improvement process, the following fields are updated in the work item (as shown in Figure 13-8).

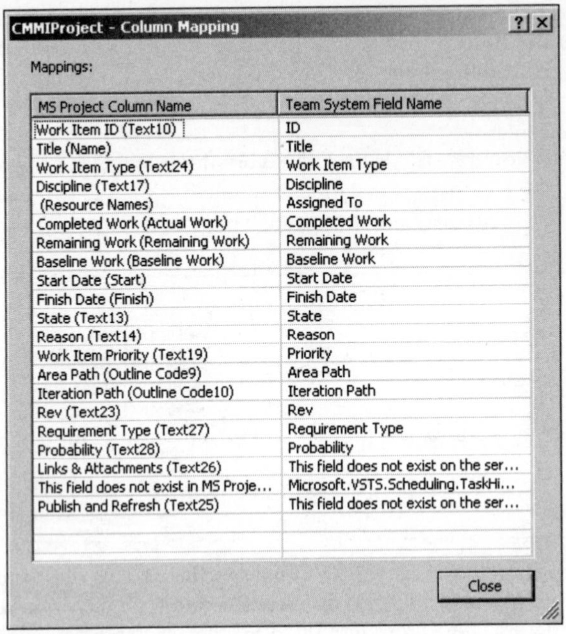

Figure 13-7

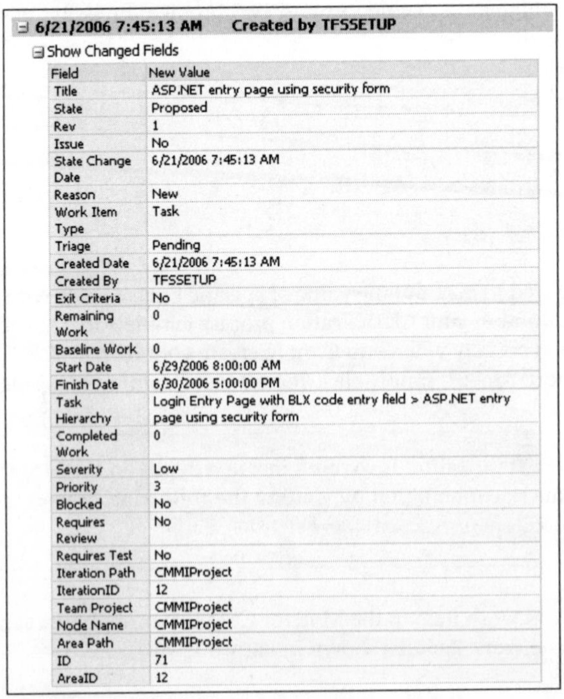
6/21/2006 7:45:13 AM Created by TFSSETUP
Show Changed Fields
Field
New Value
Title
ASP.NET entry page using security form
State
Proposed
Rev
1
Issue
No
State Change Date
6/21/2006 7:45:13 AM
Reason
New
Work Item Type
Task
Triage
Pending
Created Date
6/21/2006 7:45:13 AM
Created By
TFSSETUP
Exit Criteria
No
Remaining Work
0
Baseline Work
0
Start Date
6/29/2006 8:00:00 AM
Finish Date
6/30/2006 5:00:00 PM
Task Hierarchy
Login Entry Page with BLX code entry field > ASP.NET entry page using security form
Completed Work
0
Severity
Low
Priority
3
Blocked
No
Requires Review
No
Requires Test
No
Iteration Path
CMMIProject
IterationID
12
Team Project
CMMIProject
Node Name
CMMIProject
Area Path
CMMIProject
ID
71
AreaID
12

Figure 13-8

Let's take a look at some strategies for mitigating these issues, including unique names and work item management, managing summary tasks, time tracking and rolling up results, and using pivot tables to view result summaries.

Naming and Managing Work Items

One of the issues you may encounter when you are working with work items is similarly named tasks, requirements, or scenarios. They may appear because you need to accomplish the same task in two iterations. For example, in Figure 13-9, a requirement called "Ability to scan and link documents" appears twice.

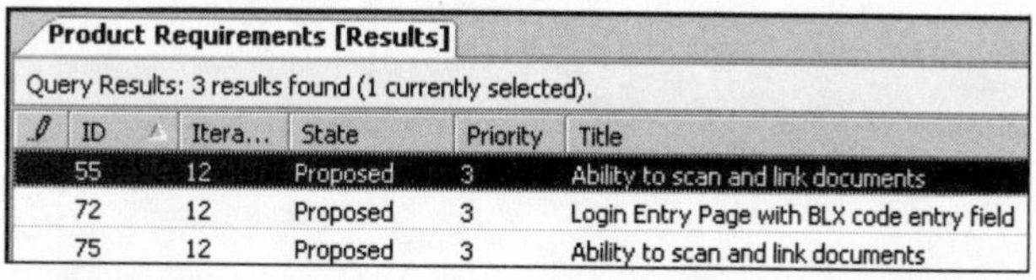

Product Requirements [Results]

Query Results: 3 results found (1 currently selected).

ID	Itera...	State	Priority	Title
55	12	Proposed	3	Ability to scan and link documents
72	12	Proposed	3	Login Entry Page with BLX code entry field
75	12	Proposed	3	Ability to scan and link documents

Figure 13-9

There are two approaches you can take to get around this problem. The first involves changing the title of the work item and indicating the iteration. For example, "Iteration 0: Ability to scan and link documents" (as seen in Figure 13-10). By doing this, you will instantly be able to know where the work item belongs. With your team, you should establish good practices with the naming of your work items. For example, a work item called bug will not provide any context as to what bug it is and to what part of your application it applies.

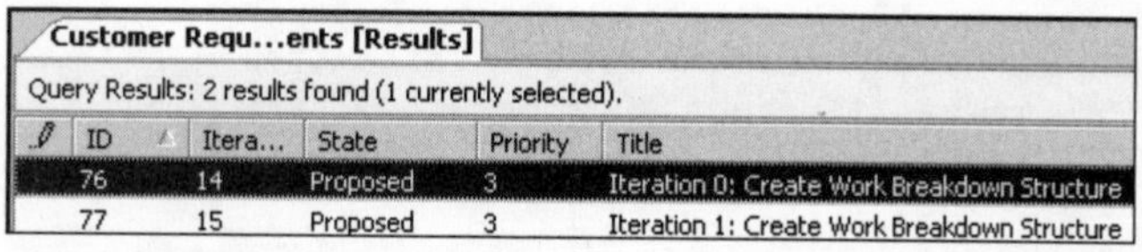

Customer Requ...ents [Results]

Query Results: 2 results found (1 currently selected).

ID	Itera...	State	Priority	Title
76	14	Proposed	3	Iteration 0: Create Work Breakdown Structure
77	15	Proposed	3	Iteration 1: Create Work Breakdown Structure

Figure 13-10

The second approach to filter your work item results by iteration is by creating custom queries. The example in Figure 13-11 shows the query editor, which you can access by right-clicking the Work Items folder in your team project, and selecting Add Query. The query defines the team project, the work item type (which is a scenario in the example, but can be changed to any type you want), and setting the iteration path to the right value.

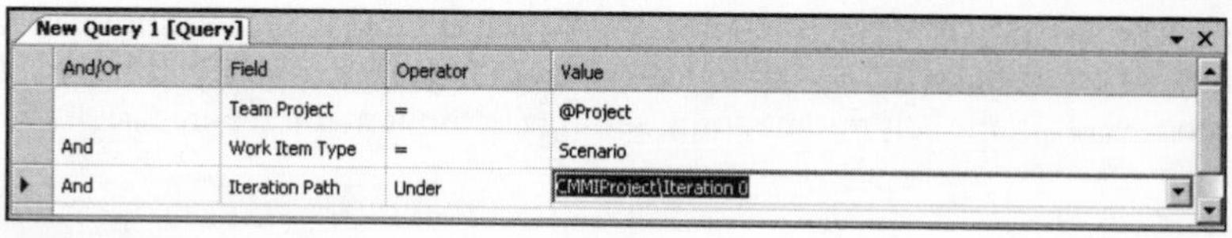

New Query 1 [Query]

And/Or	Field	Operator	Value
	Team Project	=	@Project
And	Work Item Type	=	Scenario
And	Iteration Path	Under	CMMIProject\Iteration 0

Figure 13-11

Once you have completed the query and you are ready to save it, you can provide a descriptive name for your query (in Figure 13-12, the query is called "Customer Scenarios for Iteration 0"). You can define if the query will be local or accessible to the entire team by picking the appropriate save location.

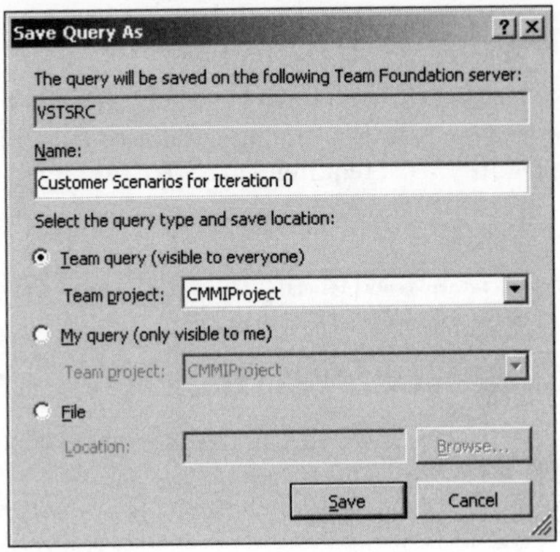

Figure 13-12

Customers commonly ask how to assign a work item to more than one individual. You can assign a work item to a group (such as all your developers) by making the following `ALLOWEDVALUES` modification to the `AssignedTo` field in your work item:

```
<FIELD refname="System.AssignedTo">
<ALLOWEDVALUES expanditems="true" filteritems="excludegroups">
<LISTITEM value="[Project]\Business Analysts" />
<LISTITEM value="[Project]\Developers" />
<LISTITEM value="[Project]\Testers" />
</ALLOWEDVALUES>

</FIELD>
```

To learn more about work item customization, refer to Chapter 11.

Managing Summary Tasks

The standard work breakdown structure in the Microsoft Solutions Framework (MSF) is arranged by a set of scenarios broken down in component tasks. As you learned earlier, Team Foundation Server records but does not maintain the hierarchy tasks. As such, you can specify not to publish the information over to the server in the column mapping settings without many repercussions.

> **When you create a summary task in Microsoft Project, the relationship is written into a field called Task Context. Team System supports writing to this field (when you synchronize your work items to Team Foundation); however the Office plug-in will not read from the field to reconstitute the relationship when you try to pull work items into Microsoft Project. Microsoft is looking into the possibility of building in this functionality in the next version of the product (codename Orcas).**

One of the ways you can filter hierarchies and partition your tasks is by using areas and iterations. The main purpose for areas and iterations is to filter work items and provide structure for your process. Areas stand for feature area (or functional area). You can store categories for functional portions of your application (for example the data layer, user interface) in the areas. Some choose to add the names of their customers in the Area portion of the Team Project, so that they can divide their work items by customer.

> **If you do use regular summary tasks within Microsoft Project, one of the techniques to avoid strange results is to completely disable summary task synchronization with Team Foundation Server. Simply right-click your summary tasks, and select Task Information. Click the Custom Fields tab, and select the Publish and Refresh (Text 25) field. Change Yes to No, and click OK.**

Iterations denote a scope of time for completing a set of tasks. Within each feature area, you may have a set of iterations. Therefore, you can organize your areas as shown below:

```
User Interface
Business Logic
Data Access Layer
```

Then you can organize your iterations to represent the iterative cycle within each area:

```
User Interface
  Iteration 0
  Iteration 1
  Iteration 2
Business Logic
  Iteration 0
  Iteration 1
  Iteration 2
Data Access Layer
  Iteration 0
  Iteration 1
  Iteration 2
```

You can even further break down your iterations to represent each scenario, use case, or requirement. For example:

```
User Interface
  Iteration 0
    Create Work Breakdown Structure
Business Logic
  Iteration 0
    Create Work Breakdown Structure
```

Setting Up Your Work Items Hierarchically

Let's look at how we can set up these logical groupings within Team Foundation Server.

1. To begin, access the Areas and Iterations options within your Team Project by right-clicking on your Team Project and selecting Team Project Settings⇨Areas and Iterations. In Microsoft Project, you can access this window by clicking Team⇨Edit Areas and Iterations. If you click the Iteration tab, you'll see the following display (as shown in Figure 13-13).

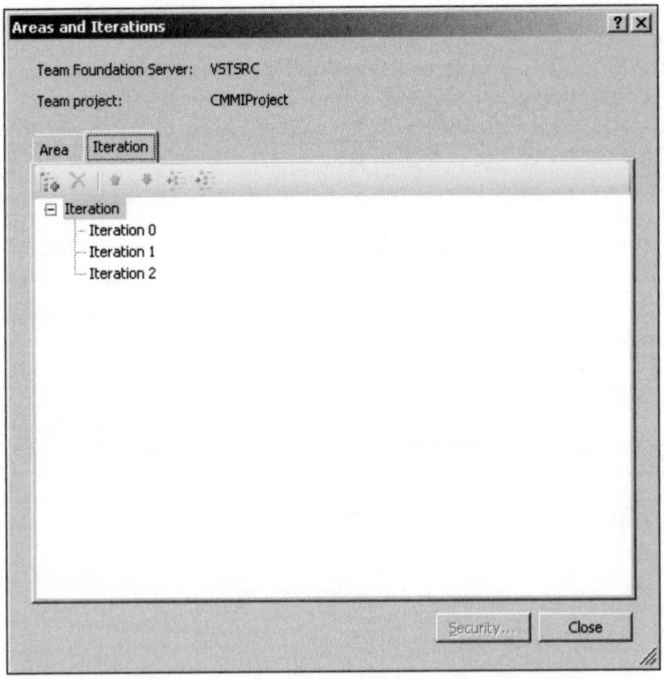

Figure 13-13

2. Click Iteration 0 to highlight the node, and then click the little blue plus sign icon to add a subnode. In the subnode, type **Create Work Breakdown Structure**. Repeat as shown in Figure 13-14.

   Adding and maintaining your requirements/scenarios may seem like extra work, but it provides an interesting benefit of enabling you to recreate the hierarchy in Microsoft Project with sync back from Team Foundation Server.

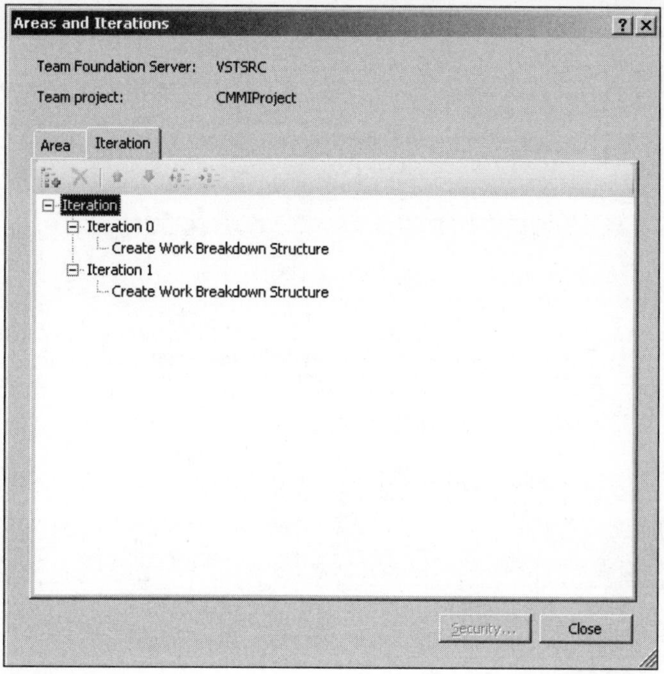

Figure 13-14

3. The next step involves changing the area and path of each scenario/requirement and task and assigning it appropriately (as shown in Figure 13-15).

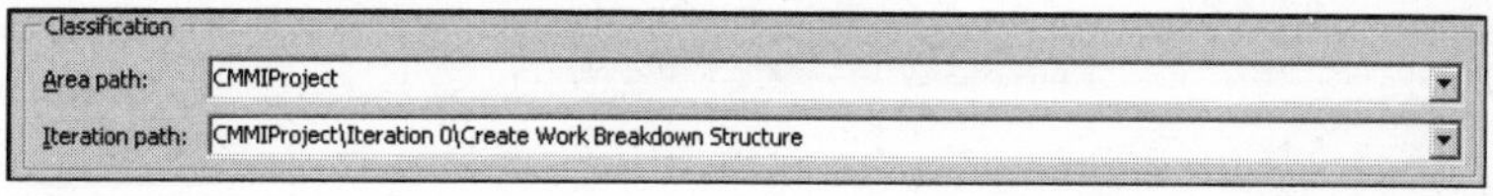

Figure 13-15

Re-creating the Hierarchy in Microsoft Project

To re-create the hierarchy:

1. Open Microsoft Project. Click Choose Team Project (and select the Team Project appropriate to you). Then click Get Work Items and the Get Work Items dialog box appears (Figure 13-16).
2. Select the query to pull in the appropriate tasks, scenarios, and requirements. Once the work items appear in Microsoft Project, click Project⇨Group By: No Group⇨Customize Group By. The Customize Group By dialog box appears (Figure 13-17).

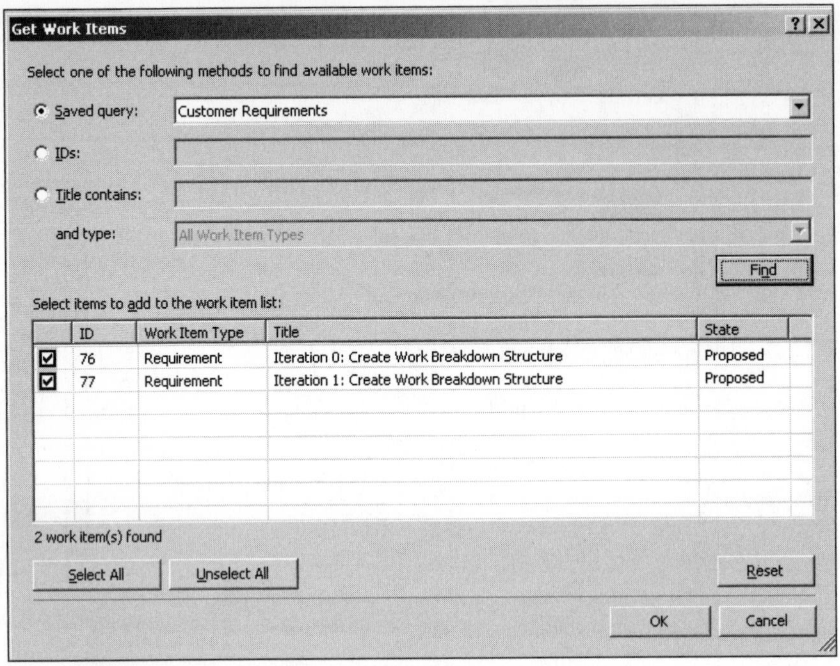

Figure 13-16

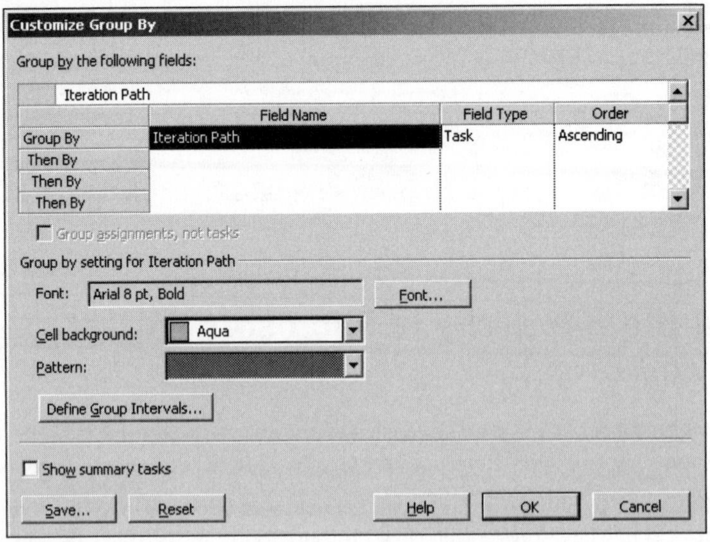

Figure 13-17

3. Finally, when you click OK you will see your scenarios and tasks organized hierarchically (Figure 13-18). From this point on, you can resynchronize your work items from Team Foundation to a new worksheet; follow the preceding steps in the recreation process and you'll get consistent results every time.

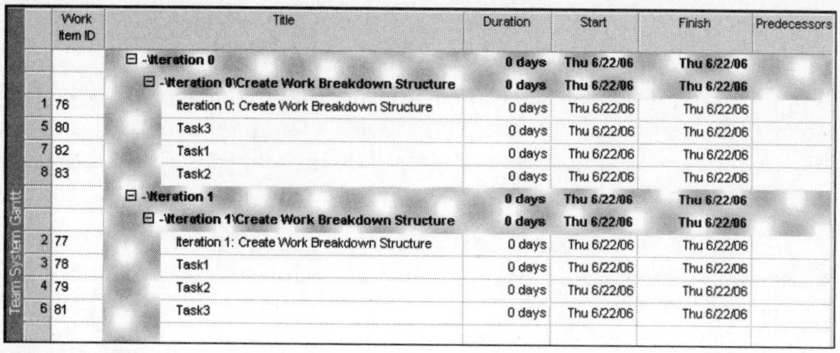

	Work Item ID	Title	Duration	Start	Finish	Predecessors
		⊟ -\Iteration 0	0 days	Thu 6/22/06	Thu 6/22/06	
		⊟ -\Iteration 0\Create Work Breakdown Structure	0 days	Thu 6/22/06	Thu 6/22/06	
1	76	Iteration 0: Create Work Breakdown Structure	0 days	Thu 6/22/06	Thu 6/22/06	
5	80	Task3	0 days	Thu 6/22/06	Thu 6/22/06	
7	82	Task1	0 days	Thu 6/22/06	Thu 6/22/06	
8	83	Task2	0 days	Thu 6/22/06	Thu 6/22/06	
		⊟ -\Iteration 1	0 days	Thu 6/22/06	Thu 6/22/06	
		⊟ -\Iteration 1\Create Work Breakdown Structure	0 days	Thu 6/22/06	Thu 6/22/06	
2	77	Iteration 1: Create Work Breakdown Structure	0 days	Thu 6/22/06	Thu 6/22/06	
3	78	Task1	0 days	Thu 6/22/06	Thu 6/22/06	
4	79	Task2	0 days	Thu 6/22/06	Thu 6/22/06	
6	81	Task3	0 days	Thu 6/22/06	Thu 6/22/06	

Figure 13-18

From a functional perspective, if you need to view the Gantt charts, the best approach is to use a preconfigured Project file with your work breakdown structure, back it up, and work primarily through one-way synchronization with Team Foundation Server. In Microsoft Project, you have two views you can use: the Team System Gantt and the Team System Task Sheet. You can access both views by clicking the View menu. (Note that these views are context-sensitive and you must connect to a Team Project on Team Foundation Server for the options to appear.)

> **On a related note, if you choose to delete work items in your Microsoft Project or Excel file, be aware that the work item will *not* be deleted within the Team System data warehouse. For auditing purposes, work item data is persisted permanently. There are techniques for "expiring" work items — see Chapter 19 for more details.**

Time Tracking and Results Roll-Ups

Time tracking and time-to-task approaches aren't terribly effective techniques in software project management. Time boxing is ineffective unless you (a) have solid historical metrics on the velocity of your team, (b) you can completely assess the complexity of a task, and (c) you are a practitioner of process improvement. If your estimation is missing any of these elements, there is a good chance that your estimation and time boxing may be closer to guesswork than reality.

However, that said, in many circumstances time tracking may be a requirement in a process. The default MSF for CMMI Process Improvement Task work item has the following time tracking interface (shown in Figure 13-19).

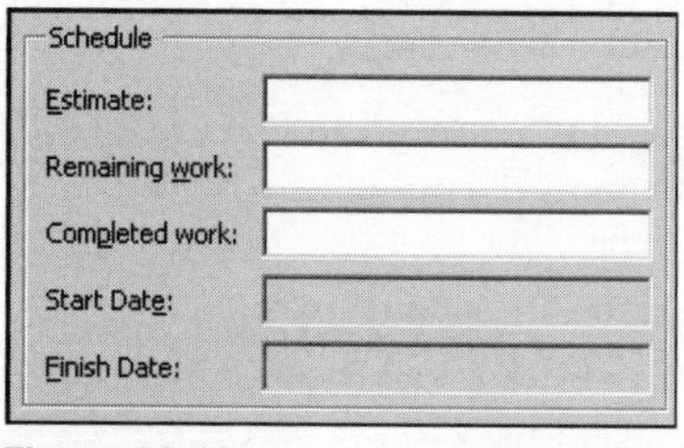

Figure 13-19

Manipulating Mapping Files

By default, the Start and Finish dates are read-only for anyone using work item tracking. There may be circumstances where you would want members of your team to change the dates. Here is how you can manipulate the mapping file (FileMapping.xml) to make the Start and Finish fields fully configurable:

1. Open up the Visual Studio 2005 Command Prompt (Start⇨All Programs⇨Microsoft Visual Studio 2005⇨Visual Studio Tools⇨Visual Studio 2005 Command Prompt).
2. Type in the following command in the command prompt and press Enter (substitute TFS:8080 with your own Team Foundation Server, and TeamProject for the name of your actual Team Project on the server):

```
tfsfieldmapping download http://TFS:8080 TeamProject C:\
FileMappings.xml
```

3. Edit `FileMappings.xml` from your C:\ drive.
4. Change the "`PublishOnly`" attribute from "`True`" to "`False`" for both of the following date fields:

```
Microsoft.VSTS.Scheduling.StartDate
Microsoft.VSTS.Scheduling.FinishDate
```

5. Save your changes.
6. Upload your file using the following command:

```
tfsfieldmapping upload http://TFS:8080 TeamProject C:\
FileMappings.xml
```

Here is a breakdown of each field within the task work item:

- **Estimate** — This field is used to provide an estimation of work. It should never be used by your development team. Read the note below for more details.
- **Remaining work** — Within the timeframe set by the project manager, the team member can indicate how much work has been done. You should indicate the value as a percentage, for example: 40.
- **Completed work** — The team member (developer, tester, architect, database professional, or other) can indicate how much work is completed as a percentage. For example, if the remaining work value is 40 percent, an appropriate value to put in the Completed Work field is 60 to round out the total work to 100 percent.
- **Start date** — This field has a `READONLY` value. As a project manager, you can set and change the start date, but your team members can only view it.
- **Finish date** — This field also has a `READONLY` value.

Make it a best practice for your entire team to leave the Estimate field blank when working with task work items. The reason for this is that Project will inappropriately roll up the values of all the estimates and provide inaccurate information. This happens because Team System work item fields have no concept of a local value or a global value.

The default MSF for Agile Software Development task work item has this interface (which can be accessed by clicking on the Details tab)—minus Estimate. The CMMI has Estimate Remaining Work and Completed work. The scenario work item has the interface shown in Figure 13-20.

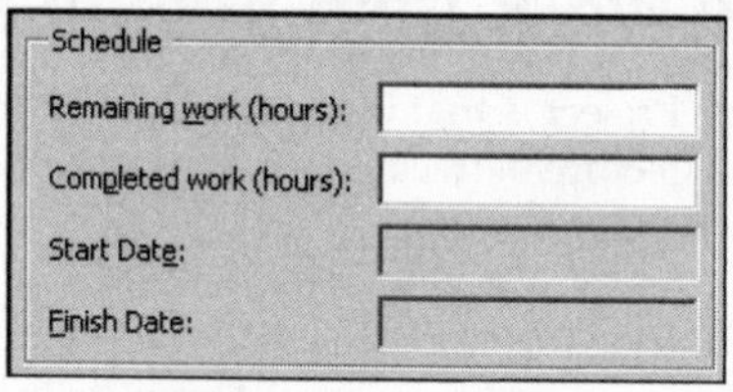

Figure 13-20

Notice that in the scenario work item in MSF for Agile Software Development, the Start Date and Finish Date fields are not available (and read-only). The Rough Order of Magnitude field (which is equivalent to the agile concept of Nebulous Units of Time) is used to assess the complexity of the feature on a scale of one to three. One denotes a scenario of light complexity; a three represents a scenario of heavy complexity. If you have too many threes in your project, you should decompose your scenarios down to smaller units of complexity (as shown in Figure 13-21):

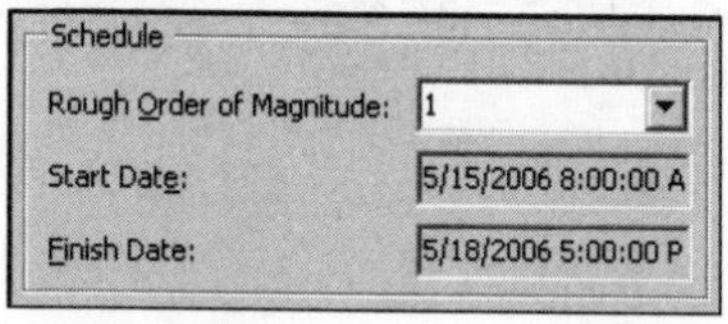

Figure 13-21

Remaining Work

The Remaining Work and Completed Work fields integrate nicely with Team Foundation Server. You should advise your entire team to use the feature and fill out the field when appropriate. In Figure 13-22, the developer has completed 60 percent of his (or her) tasks and has 40 percent remaining. As a project manager, you can judge the progress of work using the reports and the Gantt chart.

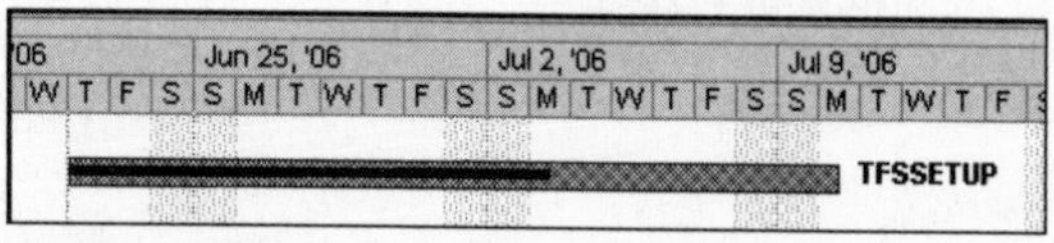

Figure 13-22

> **Note that Team Foundation Server has no support for predecessors. You can manage the dependencies between tasks manually. Another approach is to create an extensibility point where work items are automatically updated and assigned. The Work Item Tracking API and the Team Foundation Eventing service are the backbone for such an approach. Look at the Visual Studio 2005 SDK (`http://msdn.microsoft.com/vstudio/extend/`) and the following MSDN article on automating state transitions for further details: `http://msdn2.microsoft.com/en-us/library/ms194990.aspx`.**

Using Pivots to View Work Item Summaries

One of the issues with Microsoft Project is that it won't effectively roll up results from Team Foundation Server. Due to the technical architecture between both products, the roll-ups from work items will provide you with incorrect values for the most part.

It is here where Excel comes to the rescue. You can use Excel pivot tables to tally up several fields from work items and more effectively manage the process of your team.

1. The first step you have to undertake is to start up a new Excel worksheet and click the New List button. The New List dialog box appears as shown in Figure 13-23.

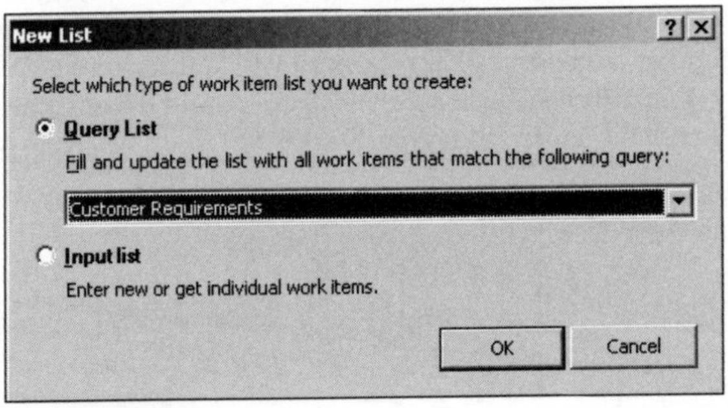

Figure 13-23

2. Select the appropriate query and click OK. Your worksheet will fill up (as shown in Figure 13-24).
3. Now the environment is ready. The first thing you need to do is add all the work item fields into the worksheet. You can pick columns by clicking on Team⇨Choose Columns option. The dialog box shown in Figure 13-25 shows up as a result. Highlight all the work item fields on the left (in the Available columns list) and click the top arrow button to bring all the fields to the right-most Selected columns list.
4. Next, you need to set up your pivot table. You can pivot by a number of fields including iterations, type, state, and tasks, for example. Highlight the first three rows of your work items in your work list (Work Item Type, Rank, and State) as shown in Figure 13- 26.

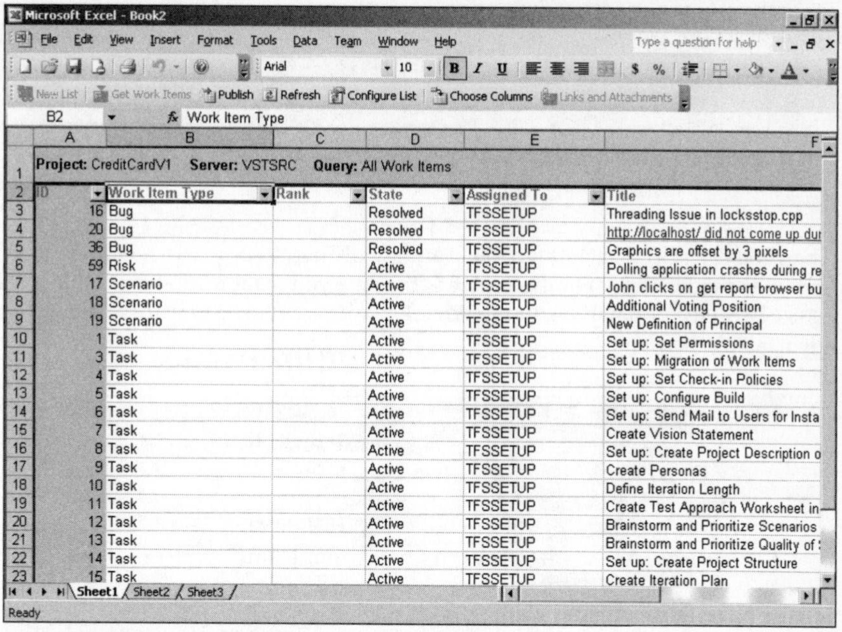

Figure 13-24

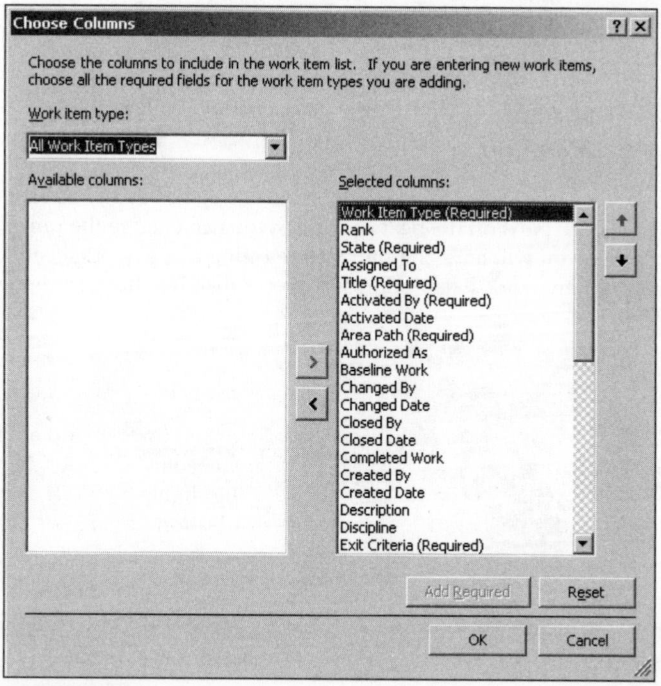

Figure 13-25

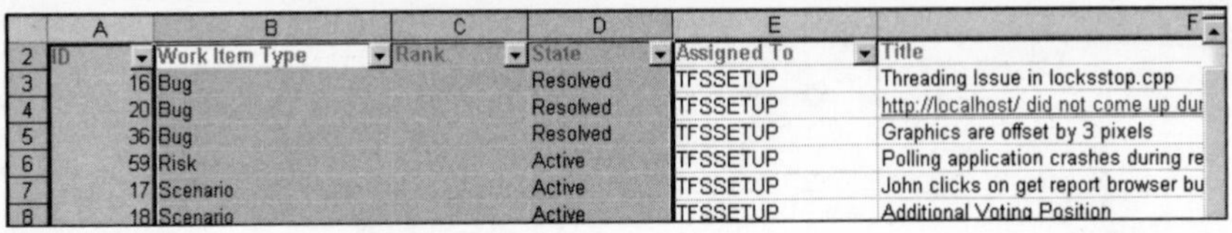

Figure 13-26

5. Then you can select Data⇨PivotTable and PivotChart Reports. This launches the pivot table shown in Figure 13-27. For the Where is the data you want to analyze? option, select Microsoft Office Excel list or database. In the What kind of report do you want to create? option, select PivotTable. Click Next.

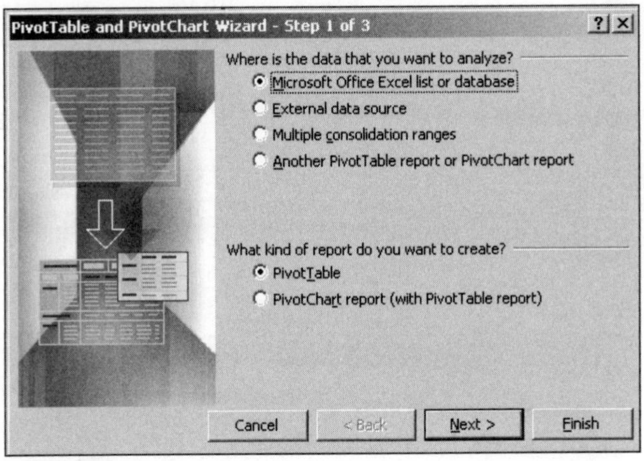

Figure 13-27

6. You can then click Next on the next screen (or you can change the range of values you want to pivot on). Then you will have the choice of selecting a new worksheet or use an existing worksheet. Pick the new worksheet option and click Finish (as shown in Figure 13-28).

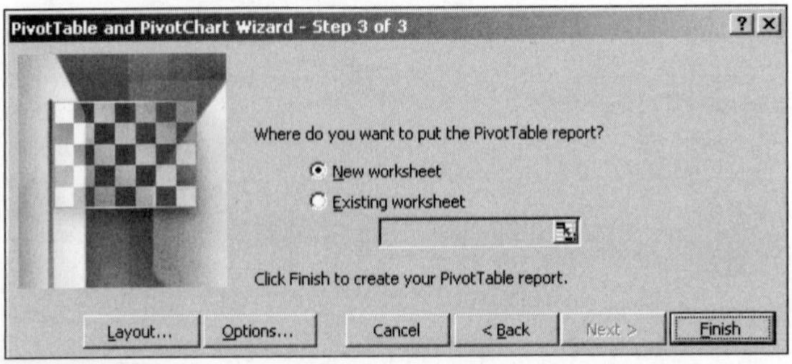

Figure 13-28

The pivot table appears on the worksheet (shown in Figure 13-29). Notice the pivot table field list on the right of the screen.

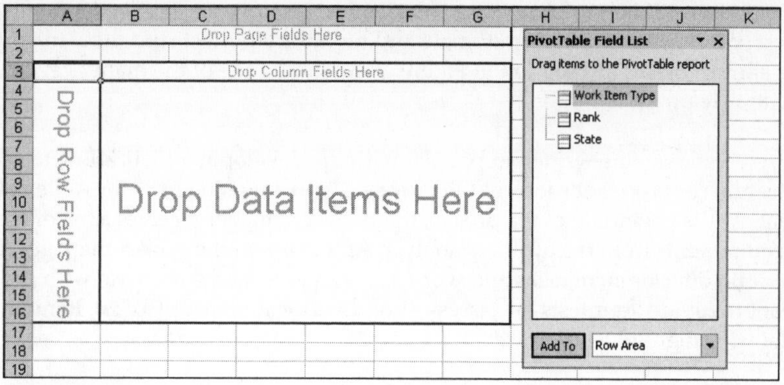

Figure 13-29

7. The last step you need to make is to drag the work item fields into the appropriate spots on the pivot. Drag the Work Item Type field to the portion of the pivot that says "Drop Row Fields Here." You can then drag the State field into the part of the pivot that says "Drop Data Items Here." The result will look a lot like Figure 13-30 (assuming you have enough work items in your Team Project).

3	Count of State	
4	Work Item Type	Total
5	Bug	4
6	Risk	1
7	Scenario	3
8	Task	16
9	(blank)	
10	Grand Total	24

Figure 13-30

Managing Test Cases

One of the management tasks that run concurrently with your development includes test case management. Good code is derived from good tests. Moreover, as with any aspect of a software development project, careful planning will determine the effectiveness of your test approach. Truth be told, it's easy to get lost in all of Team System's testing capabilities. This section runs through a practical scenario and shows you how tests are managed end-to-end.

> **In this section, we are assuming you are familiar with Team System tests, have successfully run them, and so forth. If you are new to the Team System Test Framework, we greatly encourage that you read and try the demos and walkthroughs for Team Edition for Software Testers on the MSDN Web site (http://msdn2.microsoft.com/en-us/library/ms182409.aspx) or look at *Professional Visual Studio 2005 Team System* (ISBN:0764584367) for a deeper exploration of the topic.**

Test case management involves more than the organization of tests. You need to manage how to properly write test specifications, how to automate and monitor your test runs, how to write effective bug work items, and so forth. The diagram in Figure 13-31 shows one of the many ways tests cases can be managed within Team System.

As you can see, test cases are written in parallel with the development workflow to verify the functionality of each feature (or task). Let's look at the process if you are using MSF for Agile Software Development. At the beginning of the project, the project manager receives a list of scenarios and quality of service requirements from the business analyst. At this point, the project manager must break down the scenarios into development tasks and work out tests to test each scenario with the designated tester. You may want to divide your tests in classes—build verification tests (BVTs), iteration (or milestone) tests, and daily (or nightly) tests.

Let's say we are developing a Web front-end log-in page for an ASP.NET application. Most applications go through a mock-up before development. The target application has to have the same look and feel and functionality as the graphic (shown in Figure 13-32).

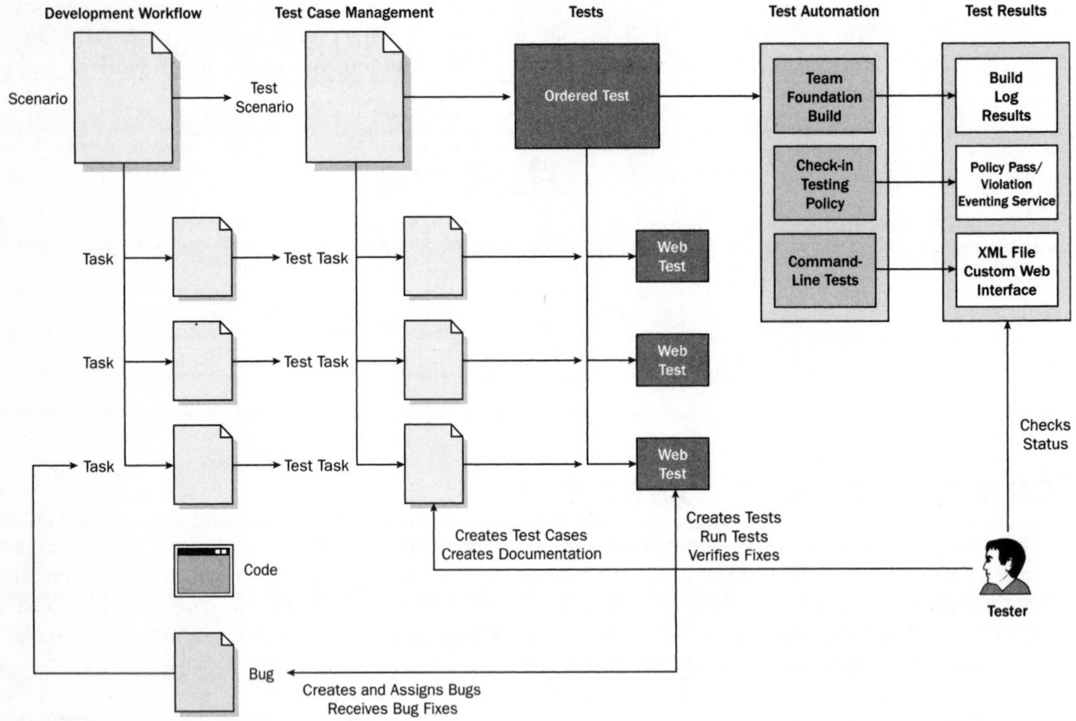

Figure 13-31

Figure 13-32

As a project manager, you are given the feature to build as a requirement (or scenario). In MSF, scenarios are written out very specifically. For example, "Harry, the manager, wants to access the administrative site. He clicks on the log-in button on the main page of the portal and is led to a page with a user name and password field. He visits the site quite often therefore he clicks on the Remember Me check box to remember his credentials. He then clicks on the log-in button to quickly enter the desired site." Some business analysts and project managers prefer to write more-functional generic specifications, such as "Build log-in screen to access administrative site." The project manager then has to decompose this scenario or requirement into a set of development tasks. Figure 13-33 shows our scenario as a summary task, and the subtasks in Microsoft Project.

	Title	Work Item Type	Duration	Start	Finish
1	**⊟ Build Login Screen to Access Administrative Site**	**Scenario**	**17 days**	**Wed 7/26/06**	**Thu 8/17/06**
2	Plan and Design Graphical User Interface (GUI)	Task	2 days	Wed 8/2/06	Thu 8/3/06
3	Remember User Checkbox Functionality	Task	2 days	Fri 8/4/06	Mon 8/7/06
4	Successful Login	Task	3 days	Tue 8/8/06	Thu 8/10/06
5	New User Login Functionality	Task	3 days	Tue 8/15/06	Thu 8/17/06
6	Unsuccessful Login	Task	3 days	Wed 7/26/06	Fri 7/28/06

Figure 13-33

As the project manager starts figuring out the development tasks, it's also a good time to work out the test process for each task (or feature). In Microsoft Excel, test scenarios and test tasks are created that correspond to our development scenarios and tasks (as shown in Figure 13-34). Note that you can create a new work item type called "test case" to manage all your tests. A question you might be asking is, why create a new work item for each scenario and task? Isn't it duplication? There are several answers to these questions: First, you are establishing workflow for your tester separate from your development workflow. (Team System does not support assigning a work item to two individuals — although you can assign a work item to an entire group in special cases.) Second, these test work items are used to fully document your test approach.

	A	B	C
1	**Project:** I	**Server:** TFSRTM **Query:** [None]	
2	ID	Title	Work Item Type
3		Test: Verify Login Screen to Access Administrative Screen	Scenario
4		Test: Verify Successful Login	Task
5		Test: Verify Unsuccessful Login	Task

Figure 13-34

> **Sara Ford has a great blog post called "Developing a Test Specification" in which she describes the elements of a great test plan and specification. You can learn more by reading her post at** `http://blogs.msdn.com/saraford/archive/2004/10/28/249135.aspx`**.**

As soon as features are implemented, tests are set up side-by-side to make sure that the application is functionally correct. In our scenario, we are building a Web application; therefore, the most logical way to test it is using Team System Web tests. In Figure 13-35, we've built Web tests for two test tasks:

- Verify successful login
- Verify unsuccessful login

In the real world, you will likely want to set up different log-in verification Web tests according to personas, using different credentials for each persona. We can roll up all these Web tests into a single Ordered test, which represents one of our main scenarios (also shown in Figure 13-35).

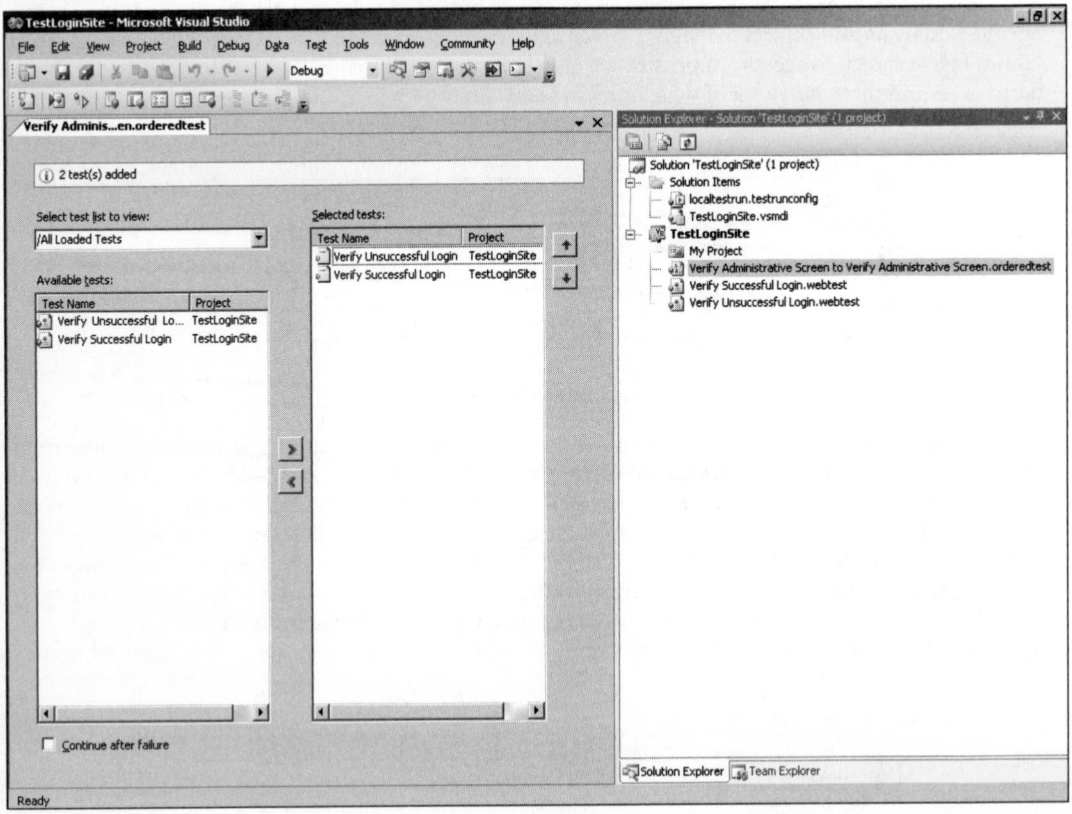

Figure 13-35

Note that you can use the Test Manager to manage, query, order, and filter your tests. You can access the Test Manager by selecting Test➪Windows➪Test Manager, or click the Test Manager button on the Test Tools toolbar. To run a test, you can right-click and select Run Checked Tests. You can disable a test by right-clicking and selecting Disable. Test Lists also allow you to filter, sort, and group tests. You can create a new test list by selecting Test➪Create New Test List.

Manual Test Cases

Manual testing is the process of testing software by hand and writing down the steps to reproduce bugs and errors. Before you start manually testing an application, you should formulate a solid set of test cases. Automated tests are predefined in scope, and can only confirm or deny the existence of specific bugs. However, an experienced tester has the advantage of being able to explore facets of the application and find bugs in the most unlikely places. Because software isn't completely written by machines (yet), human error can creep into the design and structure of an application. It takes the eye of a good tester to find these flaws and correct them. You can create and structure manual tests in the same way as your automated tests (as shown in Figure 13-36).

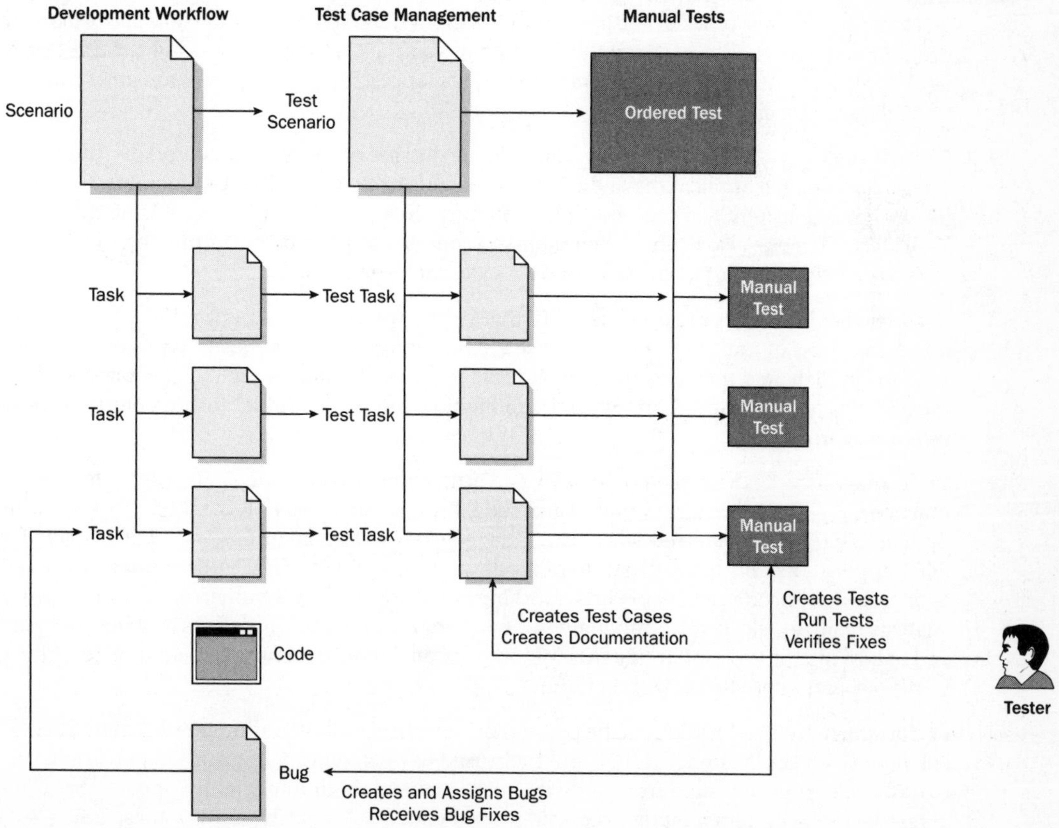

Figure 13-36

You can also use manual tests to document how to reproduce (repro) a bug. The Microsoft Word file can then be attached to (or associated to) a bug work item and then assigned to the developer.

Other Test Types

What kind of tests can be automated? Team System provides several test types that support automation. These test types include:

- **Web tests** — Web tests enable verification that a Web application's behavior is correct. They issue an ordered series of HTTP requests against a target Web application and analyze each response for expected behaviors. You can use the integrated Web test recorder to create a test by observing your interaction with a target Web site through a browser window. Once the test is recorded, you can then use that Web test to ensure that you get the same results every time. The great thing about a Web test is that you can perform regression testing on a Web site when a new feature is added without having to manually go through the steps. (The tester can intervene only when a bug or error is found.)
- **Unit tests** — Unit testing involves writing code to verify a system at a lower and more granular level than with other types of testing. Unit tests are written to ensure that code performs as the programmer expects — you assert the functionality, inputs, and error handling capabilities of your application. If new code "breaks" the way the application is supposed to work, your unit test will generate errors.
- **Generic tests** — Generic tests enable you to reach outside of the test framework by running external executable applications, which return results back to Team Test. Generic tests are useful for supporting current test processes that you may already have in place by wiring them to Team Test. They are also useful when there are complex steps to be performed by third-party tools, or when you want to create your own external testing tools.
- **Load tests** — Load tests are used to verify that your application will perform as expected while under the stress of multiple concurrent users. You configure the levels and types of load you wish to simulate and then execute the load test. A series of requests will be generated against the target application and Team System will monitor the system under test to determine how well it performs.
- **Code analysis** — Code analysis consists of a verification of your code against set rules and best practices. When dealing with unmanaged code, the code analysis tool is called PREfast. In Team System, the feature is referred to as "Unmanaged Code Analysis for C/C++." For managed .NET applications, the engine that drives code analysis is FxCop. You can consider code analysis as an automated code review of sorts. Nothing can really replace a human code review, but code analysis really excels at verifying that your code adheres to your guidelines and best practices, and at looking for issues with regards to nonfunctional requirements (for example, security, performance, and internationalization issues).
- **Performance tests** — Profiling is the process of observing and recording metrics about the behavior of an application. Profilers are tools used to help identify application performance issues. Issues typically stem from code that performs slowly or inefficiently or code that causes excessive use of system memory. A profiler helps you to more easily identify these issues so they can be corrected. Profiling sessions can be automated alongside other types of tests.

Test Automation

Now that we've identified the kinds of tests we can automate, let's look at the different ways we can trigger test automation within Team System:

- **Code check-in integration** — You can create a test check-in policy by right-clicking on your Team Project in Team Explorer, and selecting Team Project Settings⇨Source Control. If you click the Add button under the Check-in Policy tab and select Testing Policy, you are prompted for a metadata (.vsmdi) file. Once the policy is in place, every time the developer checks in code, your tests will run to verify said code. If the tests fail, Team System automatically generates a policy violation and the developer will have to fix the errors (or override the policy) to proceed. The disadvantage of this approach is that the violation is only immediately visible to the developer (although it is possible to capture policy violation overrides using the extensibility capabilities of Team Foundation Server and alert the project manager or tester).
- **Build integration** — Tests can be automated as part of a build type, or triggered as a custom `EXEC` build task. The tester will then have to refer to the hourly, daily (or nightly) build logs to find any build breaks and track down testing errors.
- **Eventing service and extensibility** — The Team Foundation Server Eventing service can be used to trigger test runs. Events can be triggered from work items, version control — almost any feature of Team System. Once an event is detected, a handler can launch your custom application or tool. You can also programmatically launch test runs.
- **Command-line integration** — `MSTEST.EXE`, the command-line tool for Team Edition for Software Testers can be used to launch a test. You can use the Windows Scheduled Tasks (schtasks.exe) tool to execute Ordered tests using the command-line tool at predetermined times (such as a nightly test).

> **To get the benefit of check-in and build integration, you must place your test cases in an ordered list.**

Let's take a closer look at the command-line testing tool (MSTEST.EXE). The command-line testing tool can trigger individual tests or .vsmdi files. The .vsmdi file contains your custom test lists, and refers to the tests within your lists. Here are the options available with `MSTEST`:

MSTEST Option	Description
`/noisolation:`	This option will run the tests in-process.
`/publish:`	This option will publish the test results to a Team Foundation Server. You need to also specify the build you want to associate the results (`publishbuild`), the `flavor` (release or debug), the `platform` (x86 for example), and the Team Project (`teamproject`).
`/resultsfile:`	The `resultsfile` option will generate a file with the test results (in XML format). Simply specify what directory and filename you want (for example: `C:\results.xml`).

Table continued on following page

MSTEST Option	Description
`/runconfig:`	This denotes the path to the run configuration file you want to execute.
`/testcontainer:`	This specifies the test you want to load and run.
`/testlist:`	You can specify what tests you want to launch from a test list using the `/testlist` option. Write out the full path to the file in question.
`/testmetadata:`	You can use `/testmetadata` to specify what tests to load from the metadata file.

To publish anything to Team Foundation Server, you need at least one successful build in one of your Team Projects. To create a successful build, check-in some code, create a build type, and build it once. To learn why builds are required to publish tests, refer to Chapter 16.

Let's say we wanted to trigger the Ordered test corresponding to our test case "Build login screen to access administrative site." First, you need to open the Visual Studio 2005 Command Prompt (Start⇨All Programs⇨Microsoft Visual Studio 2005⇨Visual Studio Tools⇨Visual Studio 2005 Command Prompt). Then you specify the test you want to run (`Verify Administrative Screen to Verify Administrative Screen.orderedtest`) and then the file and directory you want to output the results (`C:\ results.xml`):

```
C:\Program Files\Microsoft Visual Studio 8\VC>mstest /testcontainer:"C:\
TestLoginSite\TestLoginSite\Verify Administrative Screen to Verify Administrative
Screen.orderedtest" /resultsfile:"C:\results.xml"
```

Once you run the test, you'll notice that the results.xml file is quite long. If you scroll down the file a bit, you will find the `result` node with the results of your test. Notice that the Ordered test contains three tests, three tests were executed, and three passed:

```
<result type="Microsoft.VisualStudio.TestTools.Common.RunResultAndStatistics">
<runInfoList type="System.Collections.Generic.List`1[[
 Microsoft.VisualStudio.TestTools.Common.RunInfo,
 Microsoft.VisualStudio.QualityTools.Common,
 Version=8.0.0.0, Culture=neutral,
 PublicKeyToken=b03f5f7f11d50a3a]]">
<_size type="System.Int32">0</_size>
<_version type="System.Int32">0</_version>
</runInfoList>

<totalTestCount type="System.Int32">3</totalTestCount>
<executedTestCount type="System.Int32">3</executedTestCount>
<passedTestCount type="System.Int32">3</passedTestCount>
<stdout type="System.String" />
<stderr type="System.String" />
<debugTrace type="System.String" />
<outcome type="Microsoft.VisualStudio.TestTools.Common.TestOutcome">
<value__ type="System.Int32">11</value__>
```

```
</outcome>
<counters type="System.Int32">0,0,0,0,0,0,0,0,0,0,3,0,6,0</counters>
<isPartialRun type="System.Boolean">False</isPartialRun>
</result>
```

Using the command line tools, you can copy over the XML results file in a virtual directory, read it with an ASP.NET page, and create a custom dashboard for your testers. CruiseControl.NET comes with an .xsl file called MsTestSummary.xsl. The file may save you some time in trying to format the output.

Once the tester has analyzed the results of the test, they can assign bugs, rerun tests and create tests (according to the requirements). Test Results (.trx) files can be attached or linked to a bug work item. There are many integration possibilities out there.

> **What about automated UI testing for WinForms? This is probably one of the biggest feature requests that keep coming up with Team System. Microsoft has included a UI Automation framework within the .NET Framework 3.0. Specifically, UI Automation is an accessibility feature of the Windows Presentation Foundation. To learn more about the UI Automation framework, visit the Windows SDK (`http://windowssdk.msdn.microsoft.com/en-us/library/ms747327.aspx`) and the UI Automation forums on the Microsoft MSDN Web site at `http://forums.microsoft.com/MSDN/ShowForum.aspx?ForumID=352&SiteID=1&PageID=0`.**

Project Server Integration

One of the most highly requested project management features of Team Foundation Server is deep integration with Microsoft Project Server. This would allow project managers to apply enterprise project management (EPM) capabilities within Team System.

Unfortunately, Team Foundation Server (version 1.0) does not have any Project Server integration points built in. However, you can use the project plan (.mpp) as the intermediary between both servers to create a loose integration between both products.

There are other solutions available from third-party providers:

- Avanade (`avanade.com`) is working on a Software Lifecycle Process (SLP) that will provide support for industrialized project management capabilities within Team System. The SLP solution will include a solution for integrating Team Foundation Server with Microsoft Project Server. You can learn more on the following Web site: `http://msdn.microsoft.com/vstudio/why/avanade/default.aspx`.
- There is a GotDotNet (`gotdotnet.com`) project called the Project Server-Visual Studio Team System Connector. It provides some tools for more tightly integrating both products together using the Project Creation Wizard and a COM add-in for Microsoft Project. At the time of writing, the connector is available for Team Foundation Server Beta 3 only. However, there are plans for updating the product for the RTM version of Team Foundation Server. To obtain the connector, visit the following link: `gotdotnet.com/Workspaces/Workspace.aspx?id=b9f69ea5-ace1-4a21-846f-6222a507cc9c`.

Summary

In Chapters 6 and 7, you learned how to integrate your process into a process template and effectively kick start a new Team Project. Chapter 11 provided you with an overview of work item extensibility. Following the next logical step in the software development lifecycle, this chapter provided you with pragmatic information on how to manage your team using Team System and Team Foundation Server. Specifically, you learned how to set up a Team Project, how to cope with summary tasks, hierarchies, and roll ups, and organize your workflow using areas and iterations. You then found out how to manage test cases within Team System in a practical scenario. In the next chapter, you'll find out how to improve the communication channels within your development team.

14

Effective Team Communication

Communication is the lifeblood of any project, but it is especially important in the software development world. Gathering the requirements that a particular application is supposed to handle, managing and communicating those requirements to everyone on the team, and ensuring that the application comes in on time and on budget are large issues to most project teams. Every person and every team is different, which means that the most effective way you communicated on one team may not work on another team. What are you supposed to do?

Well, Team Foundation Server may not solve every communication problem you encounter with your project team, but it goes a long way toward handling a majority of them. Moreover, with its ease of extensibility, you can modify Team Foundation Server and your process to make things work for you, to enable greater communication among project members, and ultimately to lead to project success.

In this chapter, you learn how Team Foundation Server can help you and your team to communicate better and more effectively. First, we discuss some of the communication challenges that face teams today, and look at some of the current methods that are used to address those challenges. After that, you look at how Team Foundation Server provides a sure, strong foundation for meeting your team communication needs. Finally, you learn about some existing third-party tools that integrate with Team Foundation Server and the e-mail program most everyone uses, Microsoft Outlook. We look at some existing tools and discuss some ideas for tools that might not be out yet, but that you could build yourself using the Team Foundation Core Services. One such tool has Team Foundation Server send out instant message alerts.

Current Communication Challenges

Application development has always been carried out by teams, with team members playing various roles in the project. In most cases, no single solution has tied all the team members together. Instead, each role used a product or service that worked well for that role, regardless of whether that solution communicated easily and seamlessly with products used by other roles. This is one example of the communication challenges between team members. Such problems with communication ultimately lead to problems with your project.

With agile processes and projects, communication plays a major role. Most agile projects stress a close relationship with customers, including effective communication using tools and methods they know and understand. The MSF for Agile Software Development Process attempts to address some of the communication challenges with two of its guiding principles. One is to foster open communication. MSF for Agile Software Development advocates that for team members to be their most effective, all information must be readily available and transparently shared among all team members. In addition, this sharing of information and increase in communication, leads to working toward a shared vision, another MSF principle.

Also, developers and other project members who have to communicate over disparate platforms, including Linux, Macintosh, and Windows, face severe challenges. Enabling communication among different tools on different platforms can be a monumental process. Luckily, as you will see shortly, Team Foundation Server's extensibility is able to overcome this issue.

The Cons of Current Methods

Let's look at an example of communicating the old way, using the different roles from MSF for Agile Software Development. Obviously not all teams will do things exactly as described, but the roles as described are valid enough to prove the point.

Let's imagine project development the old way: The business analyst defines the project vision and requirements using Microsoft Word; then he passes this document off to the project manager. The project manager begins to create a Microsoft Project plan, breaking the requirements into tasks for the developers to execute. While doing this, the business analyst discovers two more requirements. Instead of updating his Word document, he just e-mails the new requirements to the project manager included in his project plan. Of course, the e-mail server is offline at that time, so the project manager never receives it.

Meanwhile, the project manager has printed out the project plan for each developer, and given each a copy, showing them the work they are to do. The next day, however, one of the developers leaves the company. The project manager goes back to his project plan, and begins to readjust everyone's schedule. With the schedule readjusted, he e-mails the new project plan to everyone, with their new duties.

However, one of the developers, whose duties have changed in the new project plan, doesn't check his e-mail. Instead, he continues to work from the original plan that was printed out, and begins to duplicate work being done by another developer. As well, the business analyst discovers another requirement, and e-mails it to the project manager. Because it seems to be a simple thing, the Project Manager simply forwards the e-mail to a developer, and does not add it to the project plan.

At this point, you have out-of-date requirements and project plans, developers duplicating code, and nothing that ties any code development back to specific requirements. The project seems to be spiraling out of control — all because of the lack of good communication between different members of the team.

The following are all good technologies to use, and they have their place. However, they each have some weaknesses, which take some effort to overcome, especially if you don't have a central way of tracking your projects, such as Team Foundation Server.

E-mail

Pretty much everyone lives in their e-mail application. For many, that application is Microsoft Outlook. And, e-mail itself can generally be a very useful tool. You can easily pop off e-mails to different team members, asking for updates or answering questions. However, e-mail can also lead to problems. Response times with e-mails are a major factor. You may e-mail someone about a critical feature, and they don't respond for several days. What are they doing? Are they working on the feature? Is there something else even more pressing that is taking their attention?

As well, normally your e-mail client does not tie into your development environment. You can e-mail a new requirement or bug to the project manager, but the project manager still has to enter that information into whatever they are using to track project issues. Wouldn't it be nice if you could just open a new trouble ticket from your e-mail client, since you are in it all day anyway?

Many users use Microsoft Outlook to organize their task lists of what they need to work on that day. Again, they have to take the tasks they are working on, and manually add them to Outlook to track them there. Wouldn't it be nice if you could quickly and easily view all your tasks for a development project, without having to cut and paste them from your tracking system?

Telephone

The telephone is great for getting the answer to a quick or an in-depth question. The ability to easily talk to another team member, regardless of location, is a great asset. The telephone allows you to overcome the impersonality and incompleteness of e-mail and instant messaging, enabling you to quickly get an answer to a question or resolve an issue.

There are some drawbacks to relying on the telephone though. For multinational teams, language might be a barrier. However, the biggest drawback is its convenience. It's easy to call someone up to get the answer to a question. Then, when you get off the phone, you go "yep, I'll remember what they said." So, you don't write it down in a central location where others can also find the answer to that question. And so, the same or similar question get asked again and again. Not very efficient, is it?

File Shares

Every developer has done this at some point and time. They have copied their code onto a public file share, accessible by others, so other developers can look at their code. Every project manager at some point has copied his Excel spreadsheet or Microsoft Project file onto a file share, where it can be accessed by other team members. This is a quick and easy way to share project files with other team members, but it can ultimately lead to a lot of heartache.

If the file share is not secure, you are opening all your sensitive project data up to malicious users. And if you don't have the permissions set correctly on the share, other team members could overwrite your vital project data with old information, or even delete it accidentally. There is no tracking of previous versions of files either. It's just a bomb waiting to go off.

So far, you have looked at the negatives of how teams currently communicate — or don't communicate, as the case may be. In most cases, individual role members of a team are isolated from each other by the tools they use. Business analysts use Microsoft Word or Excel, developers use Visual Studio, project managers use Microsoft Project, just to name a few. Moreover, there are all the other tools out there for use by developers and testers in their every day environment. Again, many of these tools do not play nice with each other.

Using Team Foundation Server to Communicate Better

This is where Team Foundation Server enters the picture. It provides one tool that easily and effectively allows all the different roles on the team to work together. By facilitating effective communication between team members, it improves project productivity and success.

Let's look at some of the ways Team Foundation Server will help your team members communicate better. While we covered some of these topics in detail earlier in the book, it's worth another look here.

- **Centralized information** — This is by far the most important point, and one of the most important things you can take away from this book. The ability to store all the information about your project in one place is seriously powerful. Having all your source code, design documents, meeting notes, wish lists, and bugs, just to name a few, makes it easy to gauge the overall health and status of your project.

  Moreover, having a central store of all your data makes it easy to cross-reference that data, allowing you to tie your bugs to the source code that fixes them and to associate your requirements with specific areas of code. Instead of lots of different systems, Team Foundation Server gives you one place to go to find out everything about the project. This centralized store of information is also easy to back up and maintain.

- **Document management** — Many people overlook the fact that Team Foundation Server can do much more than just track work items or versions of source code. You can also use it to track changes made to any documents related to your project. In effect, you are version controlling your documents, which is a very effective way of doing document management.

  You can track every change made to your documents, regardless of the document type — Word, Excel, PowerPoint, it doesn't matter. You will always know who made what changes, and when they made them. In addition, you can use the security model built into Team Foundation Server to allow or restrict access to any document in the project, enabling you to keep documents restricted to those who have the appropriate access. Finally, and this point ties back into the previous section, you have all your documents in one place; anyone interested in project information knows where to go to find the latest version, plus any previous versions, of any documentation.

- **Work item tracking** — This is best way that Team Foundation Server enables teams to communicate more effectively. No more will you be bedeviled by e-mails that get lost or misinterpreted. No more will you be faced by Excel spreadsheets containing requirements, where you have to wonder whether a particular requirement has been completed, or even if this is the latest spreadsheet with the requirements.

The work item tracking system gives you a quick, effective, in-depth way of tracking all the different tasks associated with your projects. Combined with the reports in Team Foundation Server, it gives you an excellent snapshot at any time of your project's health. Instead of having to spend hours compiling project information from myriad files, you can quickly run a couple of reports that will probably provide richer, more in-depth information than your old way of doing things.

- **Seamless tool integration** — The ability to allow users to use the tools they are comfortable with to work with project data makes them very productive. The ability to review work items, create new work items, and update work item statuses, all without having to leave his comfort zone of Microsoft Project, makes for a happy project manager. In addition, with the Microsoft Office Integration being mostly seamless, users will be able to quickly and easily access and make the most of the data in Team Foundation Server.

  Let's not overlook the benefit to the developers. Having all the work item tracking and source control integrated into Visual Studio just makes their life that much easier. No more having to switch to a different application to review and track bugs. No more having to switch to a different application to access the source control system. Instead, everything can be done from the comfort of the IDE. And because all the other project members are hooked into Team Foundation Server via Team Explorer or some other environment, all project data are quickly and easily communicated to all the team members.

Communication across Multiple Platforms

Using the Team Foundation Object Model, you can solve the problem of team members working in multiple platforms. In fact, a Microsoft partner company called Teamprise (`www.teamprise.com`) has already solved this problem for you. Many enterprises do Java development in addition to .NET development. Teamprise has developed a Team Foundation Server client that is written entirely in Java. The advantage of this approach is that it will run from any location that has a suitable Java Runtime Environment (JRE) such as Linux, Unix, Solaris, Windows, and even Mac OS X.

Figure 14-1 shows how the Teamprise plug-in looks within the Eclipse IDE on Windows.

By bringing together both of the main development platforms used today, Java and .NET, you can use Team Foundation Server to manage all your IT development. By using the Team Foundation Server's version control and work item tracking elements together for all your development, you can easily generate reports that span your entire development team.

Besides the Eclipse plug-in, Teamprise also provides a cross-platform standalone client for Team Foundation Server, similar to Team Explorer. This client provides most of the same abilities as Team Explorer, but, as with the Eclipse plug-in, it runs on multiple platforms. Teamprise also provides a command-line client similar to the one that comes with Team Foundation Server. This client could be highly useful in a Unix or Linux environment, particularly when used in automating builds.

In previous chapters, you learned about TeamPlain from devbiz Business Solutions (`www.teamplain.com`). It provides a nice way to access the work item tracking system of Team Foundation Server through a Web browser. This product, built off the Team Foundation Object Model, allows users on multiple platforms to leverage their Team Foundation Server for maximum use. Figure 14-2 shows a screenshot of this Web application.

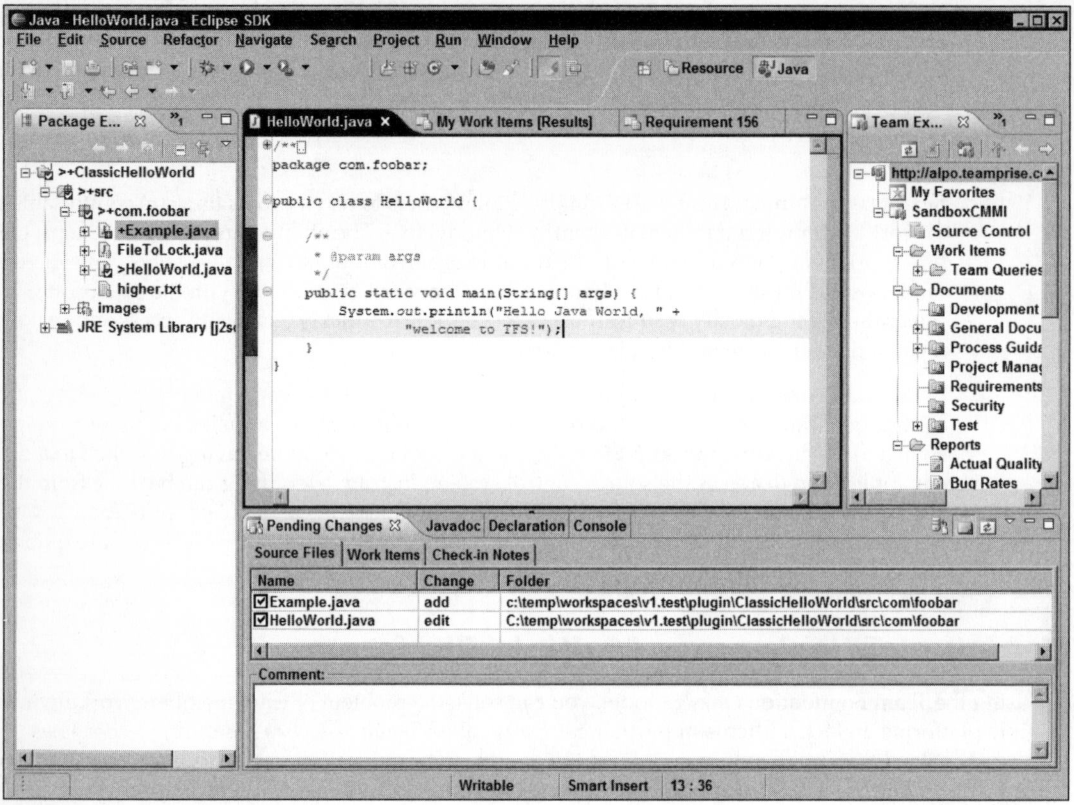

Figure 14-1

Also, recall that in Chapter 11 you built a very simple Web application for accessing the work item tracking system. This is another example of extending Team Foundation Server across multiple platforms. Please refer to that chapter for the details of that application.

Communicating the New Way

Let's now go back to our communication example from the previous section, and see how you could use Team Foundation Server to enable a better flow of communication between the different roles. Again, this is not necessarily how to do things, but it is an example of how Team Foundation Server can help.

The business analyst begins defining requirements in Team Foundation Server, using scenario work items. To create these work items, he opens Team Explorer, navigates to the appropriate team project, right-clicks on the Work Items folder, and selects Add Work Item⇨Scenario. This opens a new scenario work item. As he creates these work items, he assigns them to the project manager, by selecting the manager's name in the Assigned To field of the Status section of the form.

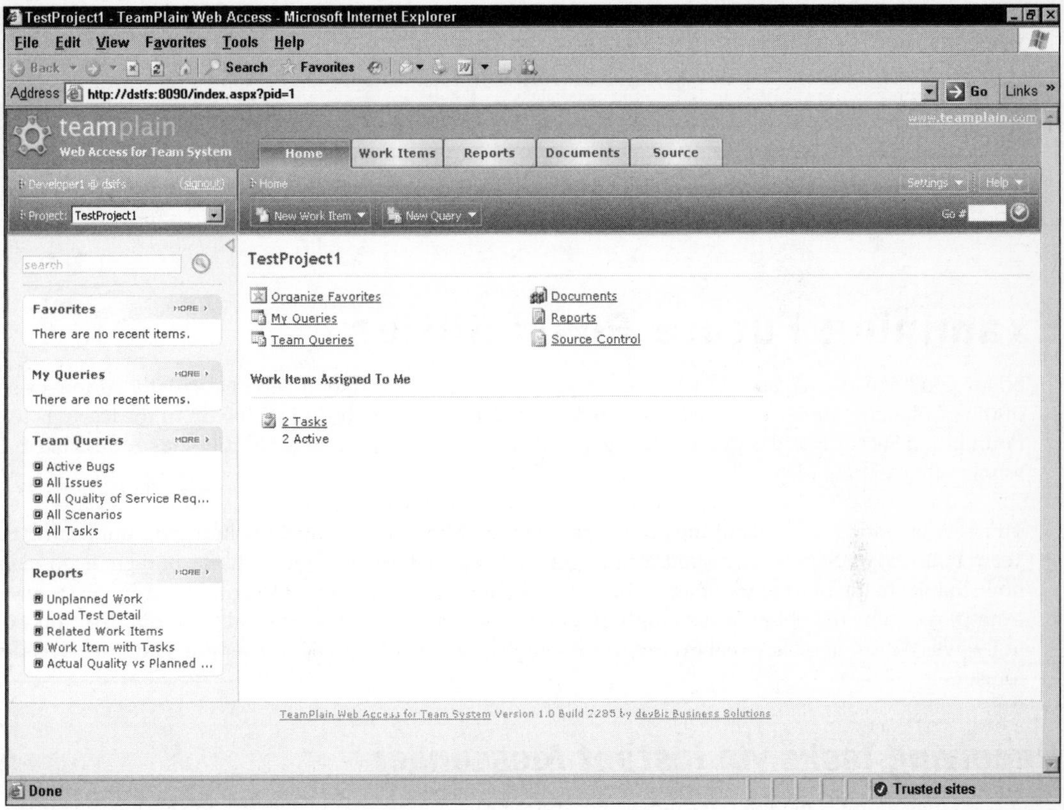

Figure 14-2

The project manager checks his assigned work items in Team Explorer by running the "My Work Items" query in Team Explorer. To run this, he navigates to the team project, opens the Work Items folder, then the Team Queries folder, and double-clicks the "My Work Items" query. This shows him there are new scenarios that have been assigned to him. He begins to break the scenarios into tasks for his developers, using Microsoft Project. He can get a head start on this by opening the Development Project Plan project file that exists in the team project. In the Documents folder for the team project, under the Project Management folder, is a Microsoft Project file called Development Project Plan.mpp. Double-clicking this file opens it in Microsoft Project, where the manager can then connect to Team Foundation Server and begin making tasks. When he is done, he synchronizes Microsoft Project with Team Foundation Server, creating new work items in Team Foundation Server for the developers. While he is doing this, the business analyst has discovered more requirements. Instead of sending an e-mail, he adds the scenario work items to Team Foundation Server. The Project Manager, later that day, reruns his "My Work Items" query, sees the new scenarios, modifies his project plan, and syncs his plan again with Team Foundation Server.

Each developer runs the "My Work Items" query to see what work items he has been assigned in Team Foundation Server. Seeing the new work items that were created by the project manager, they begin their work. The next day, one of the developers leaves the company. The project manager opens his project plan, begins to reassign work items to developers, and syncs again with Team Foundation Server. Now, when developers pull their list of work items to work on the next day, their schedules will be automatically adjusted to take into account the missing developer.

As you can see, having a central repository for all the information related to the project really does play a crucial role in providing effective communication among team members. The integration with tools that team members are used to using, such as Microsoft Project, the work item tracking system, and the version control system, all play a vital part in increasing the power of communication within the team.

Examining Future Possibilities

So far you have learned about the different ways that Team Foundation Server currently addresses some of the challenges related to teams and communication. However, this is just the tip of the iceberg. Team Foundation Server was designed with extensibility in mind, and this extensibility makes possible a whole range of new ideas.

This section addresses some of the possible scenarios for the future, which include communicating with Team Foundation Server via instant messenger and Microsoft Outlook. In fact, one of them is possible now, thanks to the hard work of a third-party company called Personify Design. These are just a few examples of how the object model might be used to leverage Team Foundation Server in new and exciting ways. We also look at a real example of having Team Foundation Server send instant message alerts to users.

Receiving Tasks via Instant Messenger

Instant messaging is here to stay, and corporations are working on determining the best way to integrate it into their daily processes. You know that you can already set up Team Foundation Server to e-mail you if there is a problem with your build, or whenever code is checked into the Team Foundation source control system. However, you don't always check your e-mail right away, so you may not be alerted in as timely a manner as you would like.

What if you had Team Foundation Server send you an instant message about the build instead? Or what if you had Team Foundation Server send you an instant message any time you had a new task assigned to you in the Team Foundation work item tracking system? Utilizing the Team Foundation Server Object Model and the Team Foundation eventing service, this scenario, and others like it, are just some coding away from reality. So enough talk, let's try to actually write some code that enables Team Foundation Server to send you an instant message.

Here is the scenario: You have a manager, named Developer2, who wants to be alerted via instant messenger anytime a work item has been changed. And yes, while this could lead to a *lot* of alerts, he wants it, so you are going to give it to him. No matter what is changed on the work item, he wants to be made aware of it through an instant message.

First, there are some prerequisites. You need to be running Microsoft Live Communication Server 2005, and have an Active Directory. Users need to be using Microsoft Office Communicator, and Office Communicator needs to be installed on the Team Foundation Server. Finally, you need to set up a user in your Active Directory that will be used for sending instant messages, and give that user access to the Live Communication Server. These are things your network administrator should be able to help you with.

The first thing you need is a way to actually send an instant message programmatically. For this particular example, you need a way to send an instant message from the command line. To do this, you need to install the Windows Real-Time Communication Client API SDK 1.3 on the Team Foundation Server. This SDK is available for download at `microsoft.com/downloads/details.aspx?familyid=C3A7BD15-FD1C-4BF7-A505-3F8FAF1E120A&displaylang=en`. This SDK installs the latest version of the real-time communication DLL, which is needed for the code samples.

Once this SDK is installed, you need to download the cmdSendIMApp.zip from the Wrox Web site (`wrox.com`). Unzip the contents of this archive to the `C:\cmdSendIM` directory. Before you can use this application, you need to configure it by telling it what user to log onto the Live Communication Server as. Team Foundation Server will send instant messages as this user. To do this, open the app.config file located in the `C:\cmdSendIM` directory. Find the `<appSettings>` section of the configuration file. There are four key settings you need to change:

- `domainuser` — This is the domain user you want to send the IM message from. The format is `<domain>\<username>`.
- **password** — This is the password for the domain user.
- **sip** — This is the `sip` value for the domain user for Live Communication Server. More than likely it will be `sip: <username>@<domain>`.
- **server** — This is the Live Communication Server name.

To view the actual code for this utility, download the cmdSendIMCode.zip file from Wrox. This code is based on code by Glen Scales from his blog post on sending an instant message programmatically via Live Communication Server (`outlookexchange.com/articles/glenscales/lcssprg1.asp`).

To send an instant message using this command-line application, open a command-prompt window, and navigate to `c:\cmdSendIM`. The syntax for sending a message is:

```
cmdSendIM <user> <message>
```

So, to send a message to Developer2, run the following in the command prompt window:

```
cmdsendIM developer2@vsts.com Here is a test message
```

If Developer2 is online in Office Communicator, he will receive an instant message, similar to that shown in Figure 14-3.

You want Team Foundation Server to alert Developer2 anytime a work item changes. To do this, you need to build a Web service that will listen for the `WorkItemChangedEvent` from Team Foundation Server. When this event is fired, this Web service uses the above command-line application to send the work item details in an instant message.

> **You need to grant the TFSSERVICE user read and execute privileges to the `cmdSendIM` directory. This allows TFSSERVICE to run this application from the Web service.**

Figure 14-3

To download the Web service files, download the SendIMWS.zip file. To download the project and code for this Web service, download the WorkItemChangedWSSendIM.zip file.

Let's examine the code for this Web service, `WorkItemChangedWSSendIM.asmx`, to get a basic understanding of how it works. Every Web service that is going to tie into the Team Foundation Server eventing service must implement the following method:

```
[SoapDocumentMethod(Action = "http://schemas.microsoft.com/TeamFoundation/2005/06/
Services/Notification/03/Notify", RequestNamespace = "http://schemas.microsoft.com/
TeamFoundation/2005/06/Services/Notification/03")]
[WebMethod]
public void Notify(string eventXml, string tfsIdentityXml)
{
...
}
```

You need to add `using` System.XML and `using System.Diagnostics` to the top of the Web service to utilize the XML services and process services in this example.

Team Foundation Server will call this Notify method. eventXml will hold the event information written in an XML format. tfsIdentityXml holds the name of the Team Foundation Server that called the Web service.

The following code is contained in the `Notify` method.

```
XmlDocument myXmlDoc = new XmlDocument();
myXmlDoc.LoadXml(eventXml);
XmlElement myData = myXmlDoc.DocumentElement;

//Retrieve Information From the Document
string title = myData.SelectSingleNode("Title").InnerText;

//Create IM message
string Msg = "Work Item Has Changed. Title = " + title.ToString();

Process p = new Process();

p.EnableRaisingEvents = false;

string strCmdLine = "/C C:\\cmdSendIM\\cmdSendIM.exe developer2@vsts.com " +
Msg.ToString();

p = Process.Start("C:\\cmdSendIM\\CMD.exe", strCmdLine);

p.Close();
```

The first three lines of code take the XML data sent by Team Foundation Server, and loads it into an XML document, so you can search over and manipulate it. For this instant message example, you are grabbing the `<Title>` element from the message, which contains the team project name, the work item name, and the work item number, and sending that title information in an instant message. Using the `myData` variable, you can select the title out of the XML document.

Once you have this title, you create a string that contains the message you want to send. Remember, you are going to call our command-line application to actually send the instant message. To call an external application from a Web service, you use `System.Diagnostic.Process` by opening a command-prompt window, and then calling the cmdSendIM.exe application.

First, create the string that you want to run from the command line:

```
string strCmdLine = "/C C:\\cmdSendIM\\cmdSendIM.exe developer2@vsts.com " +
Msg.ToString();
```

`/C` tells the command prompt to carry out the command in this string, and then terminate the command prompt. As you can see from the string, you are executing the `cmdSendIM` application, sending a message to `developer2@vsts.com`, with the contents of the message being the string you built previously.

Next, you need to actually trigger the process to run:

```
p = Process.Start("C:\\cmdSendIM\\CMD.exe", strCmdLine);
```

This line of code opens a command prompt, and then runs the previously mentioned string. Finally, once the process has finished running, you close the process.

Now that you have a basic understanding of how the Web service will work, let's get it installed. Unzip the contents of the SendIMWS.zip file to `C:\SendIM` on the Team Foundation Server. This directory contains a Web service called `WorkItemChangedWSSendIM.asmx`. To use this Web service, you need to set up a virtual directory in ISS under the Team Foundation Server Web site, which points to this directory:

1. To do this, right-click the My Computer icon, and select Manage. This opens the Computer Management window.
2. Navigate to Services and Applications⇨IIS Manager⇨Web Sites⇨Team Foundation Server.
3. Right-click Team Foundation Server and select New⇨Virtual Directory. Following the steps of the wizard, name the virtual directory **WorkItemChangedWSSendIM**, and point it to the `C:\SendIM directory.`

Currently, the user to send an instant message to is hard-coded in the Web service. To make this example work, you will need to edit the Web service to change the user to a user on your network.

Once the virtual directory is set up with the Web service, the next step is to link the Web service into the Team Foundation Server event model. To do this, you need a tool called BisSubscribe, located in the Visual Studio 2005 SDK. This SDK is available for free download at `http://msdn.microsoft.com/vstudio/extend`. The bissubscribe.exe utility is a command-line utility you can use to register your Web service with Team Foundation Server. It allows you to link your Web service to events that are fired with Team Foundation Server, so that when specific events are called, you can have Team Foundation Server trigger your Web service as well. It also allows you to subscribe to events via e-mail.

The general syntax for using bissubscribe is

```
Bissubscribe /eventType <MyEvent> /userId <MyDomain\\MyID> /address <webservice>
```

There are some other optional parameters. For a full list of parameters for bissubscribe, run `bissubscribe.exe /?` from the command prompt.

Developer2 is interested in receiving notifications any time there is a change in the work item. Therefore, he is interested in the `WorkItemChangedEvent` event type. To register your Web service for Developer2, you would use the following command:

```
Bissubscribe.exe /eventType WorkItemChangedEvent /userID vsts\Developer2 /address
http://dstfs:8080/WorkItemchangedWSSendIM/WorkItemChangedWSSendIM.asmx
```

This command registers Developer2 for the event type `WorkItemChangedEvent`. Any time that event is fired, the `WorkItemChangedWSSendIM.asmx` Web service will be called.

Everything has been set up, so now it is time to put this Web service to use.

1. Log on to Office Communicator as Developer2.
2. Open Team Explorer, navigate to a Team Project, right-click the Work Items folder, and select Add Work Item⇨Scenario.

3. Enter a title for the scenario, and click Save. The work item is saved, and shortly thereafter, an instant message will be sent to Developer2, alerting him that a work item has been changed, as shown in Figure 14-4.

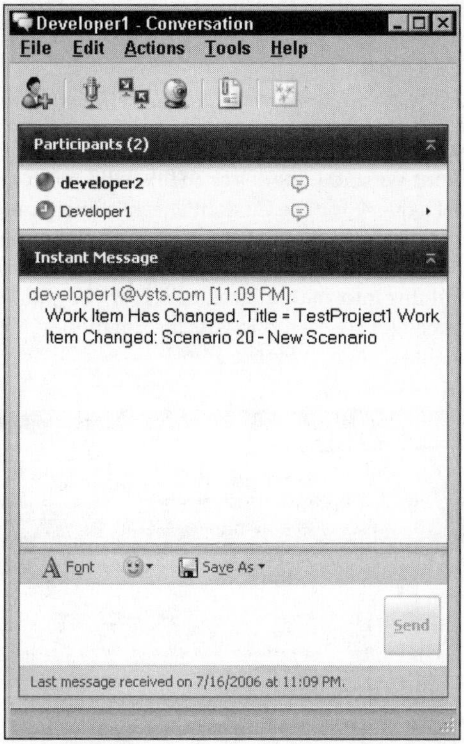

Figure 14-4

Some final caveats with the code provided in this example. The user you are sending an instant message to is hard-coded into the Web service at this time, which makes this option a bit limited. One possible enhancement would be to take the work item information, extract the user it is assigned to, query the active directory to find his instant messaging address, and then send him that instant message. This would allow people to be notified whenever a work item assigned specifically to them is modified. This code gives you a foundation for instant messaging to build off, to create the solution you need. And it is yet another example of how the extensibility of Team Foundation Server can be used in new and creative ways.

Tracking Project Status via Outlook

Most people who deal with Microsoft technologies live in Microsoft Outlook. They would be much more comfortable interacting with Team Foundation Server, and much more likely to do it on a consistent basis, if they could do it from Outlook. One option you have is to write your own extension to Outlook, utilizing the Team Foundation Server Object Model, to allow users to access different parts of your Team Foundation Server. Or you could turn to an already existing solution from a company called Personify Design (`www.personifydesign.com`).

More and more people are becoming involved in the software development lifecycle. Personify Design has developed an extension called TeamLook for Microsoft Outlook 2003 that allows all project users to communicate more effectively and accurately on the project status using one of the most commonly used and understood communication tools. This extension connects to Team Foundation Server and allows you to view work items, reports, and other information stored on the data tier. You can connect to multiple Team Foundation Servers, and multiple projects on those servers.

Figure 14-5 shows an example of what TeamLook looks like in Outlook.

As you can see, all the different team projects you are interested in are listed on the left side. For each team project, you can view your personal queries or the reports and team queries defined for the project. This image shows the All Tasks query for the CustomCheckInPolicy project. Notice the tool bar along the top. By highlighting a task, you can create a new e-mail or meeting invitation, with the work item embedded in the message. You can reassign the work item to another team member or change the state of a work item, and update all this information back into Team Foundation Server without leaving Outlook. You can double-click a work item to view its information in a window almost identical to what is displayed in Team Explorer, as shown in Figure 14-6.

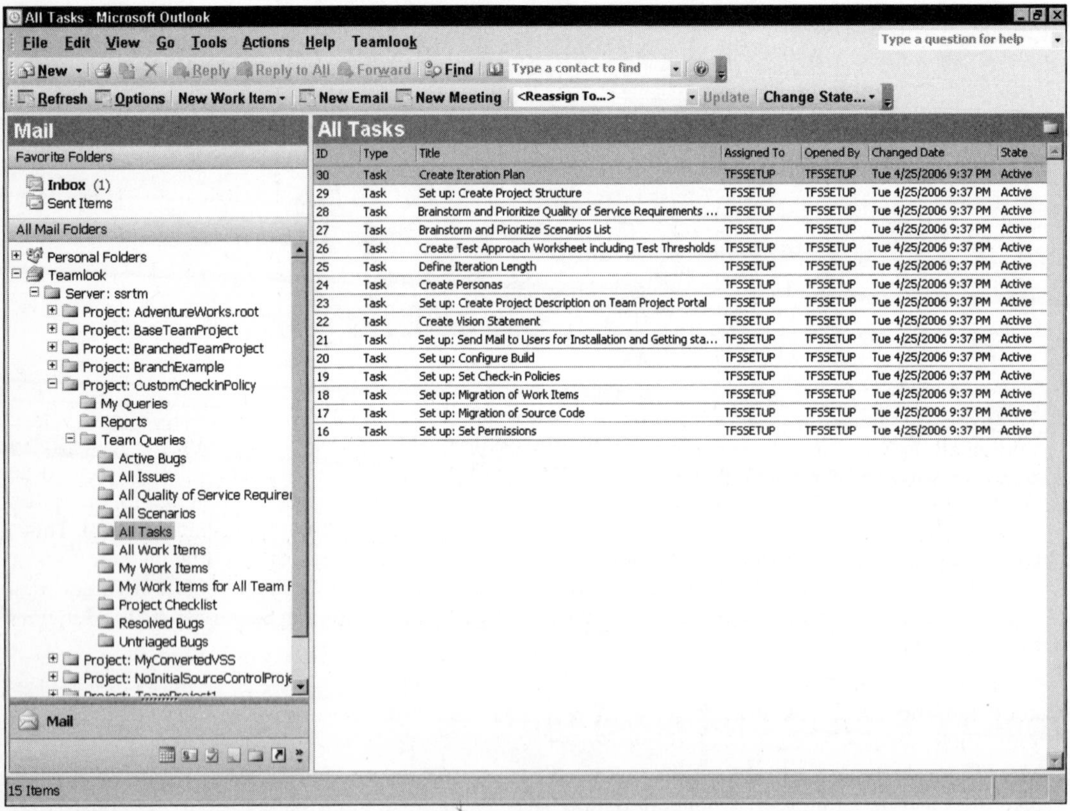

Figure 14-5

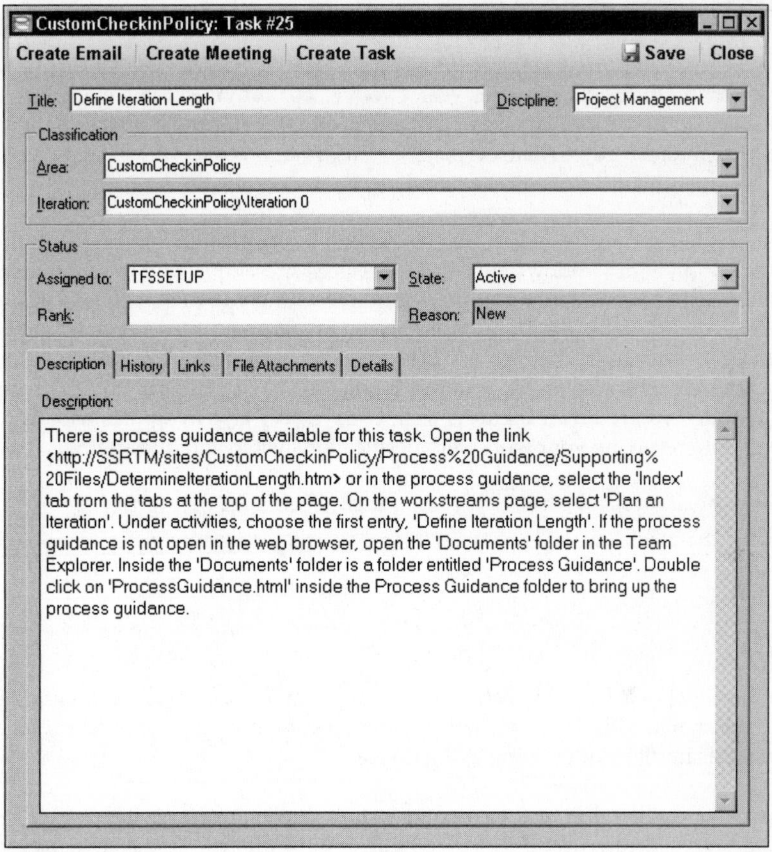

Figure 14-6

Here you are seeing Task #25. This window looks very similar to the one you see in Team Explorer, containing all the work item information. However, notice the three buttons running along the top of the window. You can click any of those buttons to create a new e-mail, meeting invitation, or personal task. And when you do, it will automatically copy of the contents of the work item into whatever you have created. Using this tool, you have a nice way to continue using Outlook, without having to cut and paste, or jump through a lot of hoops to get information from Team Foundation Server.

Another great feature is the ability to run reports against Team Foundation Server from directly inside Outlook, and then create an e-mail with the report as an attachment. Moreover, if you create a meeting invitation based off a work item, TeamLook actually figures out who should be invited, based on the context of the work item. TeamLook allows you to use both Team Foundation Server and Microsoft Outlook in synergy, creating an effective project management communication tool. It even allows you to view the team project portal from within Outlook.

For your users who can't live without Outlook, and don't want to open a separate tool for accessing Team Foundation Server, TeamLook or a custom-built in-house plug-in, are definitely the way to go.

Microsoft Groove 2007

Microsoft will be releasing a new version of their collaborative environment software, Groove 2007, alone with Microsoft Office 2007 later this year. Groove 2007 provides users the ability to create a collaborative workspace on their machine and to invite people to participate in that workspace. This makes it easy to keep team members up to date on the latest information concerning the project. This workspace provides all the tools and information that team members need in one place.

So how does this tie back into Team Foundation Server? There are a couple of possibilities. Groove 2007 can share information with Windows SharePoint Services sites. You could tie your Groove workspace into a particular Team Foundation Server project site, enabling you to quickly and effectively access information from the project site without leaving your workspace. In addition, it may be possible to create custom Groove controls, enabling accesses to different pieces of Team Foundation Server, such as work item tracking information. None of this exists now, but by building off the Team Foundation Server Object Model, you could create it. As well, Groove 2007 also integrates with Communicator 2005, which ties back into receiving your work item notifications via instant messaging.

> For more information on Groove 2007, visit www.microsoft.com/office/preview/programs/groove.

Summary

Communication is going to be only as effective as you want to make it. But as mentioned at the beginning of this chapter, it is critically important to the success of any project, whether you are writing software for the space shuttle — or building a dog house.

In this chapter, you examined some the communication challenges facing teams today, and some of the ways team communicate today, such as with e-mail, and telephones. You even looked at an example of using all these communications, and how it can lead to project failure.

After that, you dove into how Team Foundation Server helps you overcome all these communication challenges. With its central store of information, document management, work item tracking, and the ability to communicate across multiple platforms, Team Foundation Server is ideally placed to solve a majority of your communication needs.

Finally, you wrapped up the chapter learning about some possible uses of Team Foundation Server in the future. In the case of TeamLook, a communication tool from Personify Design, that future is now. You also learned how to write your own code to have Team Foundation Server send instant messages. The future looks very bright for Team Foundation Server, as more and more people take advantage of its extensibility to mold it to their needs.

This chapter on effective team communication should have you thinking about the best way for your team members to work with each other to achieve your goals. The next chapter should help you build on this way of thinking to make the most of your distributed teams.

15

Working with Geographically Distributed Teams

Outsourcing is one of the most prevalent trends in software development today. We are working in a global economy with greater competition and choice. There are many reasons you may be working with a distributed team. Here are a few examples:

- Your company has grown and expanded and has several field offices.
- Your company contracts out portions of development to third parties.
- A merger has occurred and two companies need to work interactively over great distances.

As more companies adopt Agile methodologies, it becomes apparent that they don't scale all too well between great distances. To work around this, agilists have devised the Team-of-Teams approach. In decomposing the features of a product, each component is broken down to a set of features that are assigned to a small development team that makes up the greater team. In Figure 15-1, the large circle represents an entire company spanning several continents. The smaller circles represent feature areas that are handled by each smaller team.

There is an inherent problem if you take this approach using Agile methodologies. To break down a project and teams in such a way, you have to have some sort of implied architectural plan before you start. One of the core principles in Agile is to avoid big planning up front. Therefore, the challenge is bringing in the architectural role and keeping it lightweight and responsive during the development of your project.

Microsoft has worked in a Team-of-Teams approach on many projects including Team System. For example, on Team Foundation Server, Team Foundation Build was designed by Microsoft India in Bangalore. Team Foundation Version Control was designed by the Visual Studio team in Raleigh, North Carolina, and work items and the Visual Studio 2005 Team Editions were worked on primarily in Redmond, Washington.

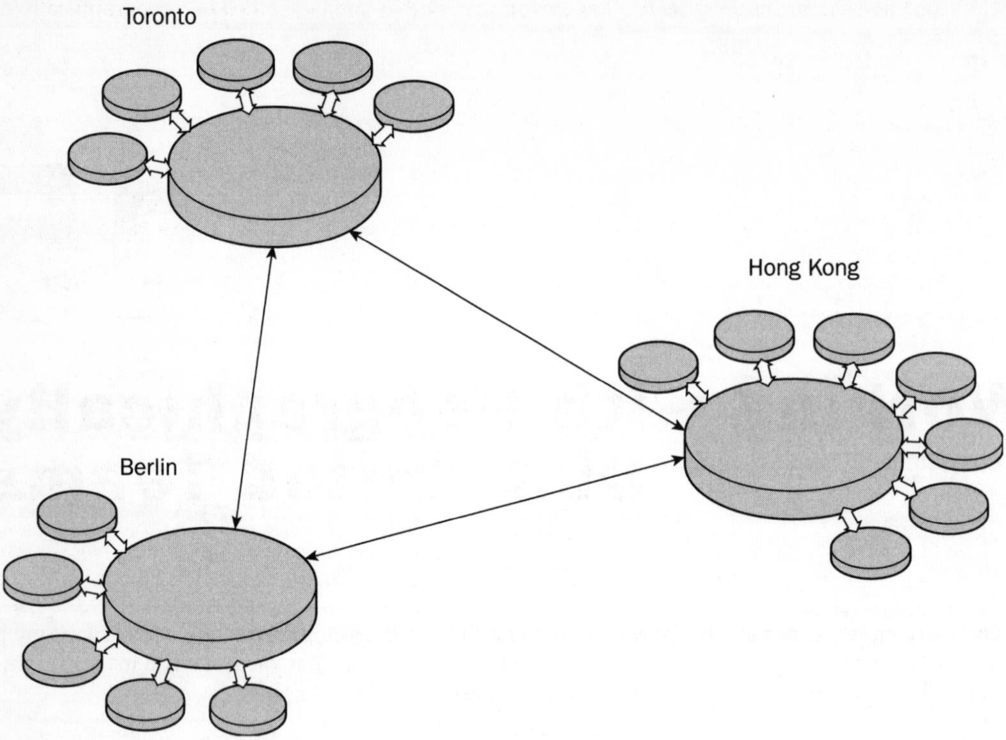

Figure 15-1

Identifying the Challenges

The process of working in a distributed team is called geographically distributed development (GDD). Interesting challenges come up when you look at the cultures and approaches of each team. You may have a project that spans several geographies. Additionally, separate projects may be worked on in separate field offices. Other interesting issues that come up are development culture, language differences, process differences, and tools. To address these challenges, you have to look at each project and assess if they are good candidates for Team System. The features, elements, and components that can be distributed include:

- Team Foundation Server
- Branch office infrastructure
- Team portal
- Team Foundation Version Control
- Distributed load testing
- Team Foundation Build

Let's look at each one of these features and explore how they can be applied to a geographically distributed development environment.

Team Foundation Server over The WAN

For secure communication with Team Foundation Server, it is recommended that you access it using a virtual private network (VPN). Most of the applications that connect to Team Foundation Server use a series of Web services. In its release of the server, Microsoft directly supports Integrated Windows Authentication. The problem with Integrated Authentication is that it may not be able to connect through a proxy server (and many ISPs have implemented proxies). Firewalls may also pose a problem for the very same reason. The limitations are well documented in the following knowledge base article: `http://support.microsoft.com/kb/916845`.

Team Foundation Server Service Pack 1 brings in support for basic and digest authentication. You can see an example of this on Codeplex (`codeplex.com`), a Microsoft community site hosting open-source applications. This has been implemented using an ISAPI filter that allows Basic Authentication on your extranet.

You can make Team Foundation Server visible on the Web using secure connections such as Secure Socket Layer (SSL). Without Service Pack 1, there are risks involved in exposing the server; so, you should do a thorough analysis. There have been reports of successes using Microsoft Internet Security and Acceleration Server.

Setting Up Your Branch Office Infrastructure

Most companies will have established network and directory infrastructures in each branch office. But how do you integrate them? Setting up a branch office infrastructure involves mass consolidation of services and applications. The goal here is to make administration a lot easier and to simplify authentication and management of users and applications across geographies.

An Enterprise-level branch office reorganization is typically a complex, involved, and expensive process. Microsoft has created a guide called the Branch Office Infrastructure Solution (BOIS) to help simplify the process using Windows Server 2003 R2. You can learn more about BOIS at the following link: `www.microsoft.com/technet/itsolutions/branch/`.

How does a branch office infrastructure impact Team System? The impact is most felt on two fronts: during deployment and day-to-day management. With regards to deployment, you have to look at scalability and design of your team projects. Will a single Team Foundation Server support your team? Will you need to create different team projects to support different languages, approaches, and methodologies?

From a management perspective, you may need to administer users from different countries using Active Directory. The challenge here is to set up the security structure appropriately to remove dependencies on having to access the server to administer your privileges. Chapter 4 has a great overview on how to consolidate all security administration within Active Directory (AD).

The elements that will make a distributed development environment work are standardization and consolidation. There is nothing more difficult to manage than a potpourri of development practices across a company. By setting standards in process, best practices, and protocols, development will be much easier to manage.

Deploying Your Team Portal on The Web

There are technical considerations to keep in mind if you want to deploy Windows SharePoint Services as an extranet application. Windows SharePoint Services dynamically generates hyperlinks; thanks to Service Pack 2, it now supports reverse proxies, and many Secure Socket Layer (SSL) configurations (such as SSL terminations). A reverse proxy is a single proxy server that acts as a gateway to a farm of Web servers (as shown in Figure 15-2).

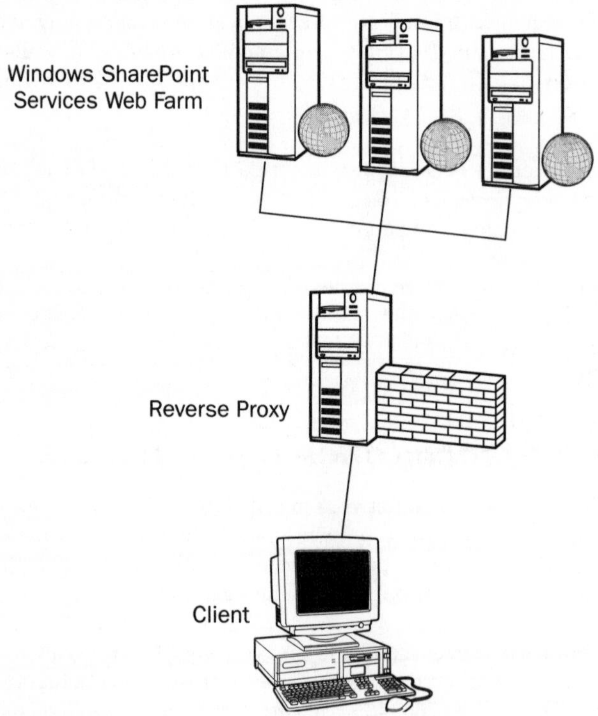

Figure 15-2

> **One of the most asked questions asked about the portal is if the portal can be suppressed or if another established SharePoint site can be used in its place. There is one main strategy you can apply here. To begin, you can create the Team Portal during the Team Project creation process and then change the code in `default.aspx` in the root of your portal to contain a simple `Response.Redirect` to your existing or new SharePoint site. (You can use `Server.Transfer` for performance reasons if your SharePoint site is contained on the same server.) The main disadvantage of this approach is that you will have to recreate the assets (links to reports, work products, and the like) on the other site.**

Another scenario is that a reverse proxy may change the header of a SharePoint site in the following way. The client requests a page on the SharePoint site (for example, `http://teamportal/default.aspx`). The reverse proxy may change the URL to reflect the internal address of the site (`http://internal.teamportal`). Since the external user doesn't have access to the network past the proxy, the link will be invalid. Windows SharePoint Services Service Pack 2 provides the ability to define both the external and internal URLs to avoid this problem. Check out this blog post on the WSS URL Zone Administration Utility for more information: `graphicalwonder.com/?p=122`.

Setting Up the Tools

Team System has several tools that were designed out of the box to work in a distributed environment. These include Team Foundation Version Control, the load agent and controller, and Team Foundation Build. This next section looks at each one of these tools and how to deploy them in your development environments.

Shared Repositories

A large part of the implementation of distributed teams is standardization. By standardizing development, testing, and project management practices, your team will get benefits such as predictability and productivity. Another advantage is that your project assets will be easier to manage, therefore cutting down on costs and effort. When deploying Team System, an important part of the process is reexamining the way software is developed from an end-to-end perspective.

Shared repositories can help in the standardization process. To share resources, you need software that allows you to connect across corporate firewalls and networks, and you need to establish standards and practices. The Internet-connected software has to provide great performance across wide topologies.

Another advantage with a shared repository will provide your entire team with up to date information about your project. Several different types of repositories are used in a distributed environment:

- **Workflow** — Every team member can benefit from connecting from a common Team Foundation Server. As requirements change and specifications need to be updated for business reasons, everyone remains in the loop. Team Foundation Server online capabilities enable workflow, change management, and requirements management.
- **Version control** — Team Foundation Server Proxy allows teams outside of the immediate network to retrieve the latest source code files without performance problems.
- **Test case management** — Assuming that Team Foundation Server has a copy of Team Suite or Team Edition for Software Testers installed, it can run a variety of tests during the build and check-in process. The load controller and agents allows your team to perform distributed load testing on a server farm to stress test your Web applications under real-world conditions. Test case management in a distributed scenario also allows you to track test plans and results for your entire development team.

Team Foundation Server Proxy

The Team Foundation Server File Cache Proxy is an important tool to help enable branch offices and geographically distributed teams to connect to a common source repository. The proxy was designed because of internal testing within Microsoft. In "dog fooding" their product, they realized that better performance was required to use Team System between the Raleigh office and the Redmond office.

Figure 15-3 shows how Team Foundation Server Proxy fits in with the rest of the Team System architecture.

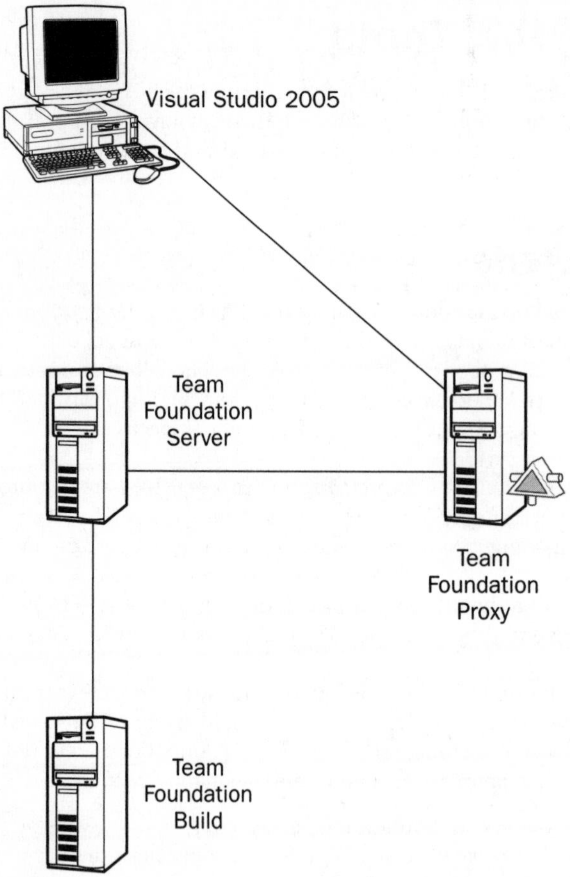

Figure 15-3

Installing the Proxy

It's important that you follow the instructions found in the Team Foundation Server Installation Guide (also found in the Team Foundation Server media). In particular, make sure you have a sufficiently large hard drive for your files. The main reason is that you would likely want to cache as many files as possible, which will in turn increase the cache hits (and increase performance). Make sure you install Team

Foundation Server first, test it out, and then install the proxy. Otherwise, it will be more difficult to troubleshoot whether installation problems will be attributed to the proxy or the server. The proxy server typically runs on port 8081.

You may also want to create a script to pull the latest files into the proxy and use the Task Scheduler to run the script at a predefined interval (for example, every 5 to 10 minutes). This will assure that your users will have access to the latest files and it will improve the performance of your server (from an end-user perspective).

> **Each of the files stored in the cache contain a unique id to allow multiple versions of the same file. The file versions that will be cached will depend on whether the user did a "get latest" or get a specific version of a changeset.**

Since the cached version control artifacts are stored locally, it's super important that you secure the assets. Access to the file system should be locked down as a result.

> **The Team Foundation Proxy is available on the Team Foundation Server media. Simply look for a directory called "`proxy`" on the CD or DVD. Double-click setup.exe to start the installation process.**

How GET Works in Team Foundation Proxy

To effectively use the Team Foundation Proxy, it's important to understand how it works internally. The following describes a get latest scenario of a cache miss in both the server and proxy behind the scenes:

1. When you do a get operation, Visual Studio communicates with Team Foundation Server. Team Foundation Server in turn performs a `prc_Get` to the data tier to retrieve and validate your authentication information. The client never authenticates directly with the proxy.
2. Team Foundation Server then runs a security filter. If you are an authenticated user, the server creates the download tickets.
3. The client receives the download ticket and then uses them to start the download of the items. The client (Visual Studio 2005) now does an HTTP Get operation, but rather than communicate with Team Foundation Server, it communicates directly with the proxy. Note that the ticket system is enabled using the exchange of private and public keys (PKI).
4. The HTTP Get operation is made from the proxy to Team Foundation Server (if the file is not in the proxy cache).
5. If Team Foundation Server does not have the requested items in cache, Team Foundation Server performs a `prc_GetItemContent` to the data tier. This retrieves the desired code (or other assets) from version control.
6. The file contents are then sent to the proxy and saved into the proxy cache (using `WriteToFileCache`).
7. The file contents are then sent to the client machine.

8. An `UpdateLocalVersion` is run from the client to Team Foundation, and then to the data tier to update the server with the information on what are the latest files that were downloaded in your workspace

Here is a representation of the SOAP request and response from the client. You can obtain this by enabling tracing on the client in the tf.exe.config file. In Visual Studio, you can configure it in devenv.exe.config as shown below:

```
<appSettings>
<add key="VersionControl.EnableSoapTracing" value="True" />

<add key="VersionControl.TraceDownloadContent" value="True" />
</appSettings>
```

The following request sets the recursion level, and tells the server what file is requested. This SOAP message is automatically generated by Team Explorer (or the command-line tool) during a GET operation:

```
<GetRequest>
<ItemSpec recurse="OneLevel" item="C:\Application.cs" />
<VersionSpec xsi:type="LatestVersionSpec" />
</GetRequest>
```

Once the request has been authenticated, the following response will be generated:

```
<GetResponse
xmlns=http://schemas.microsoft.com/TeamFoundation/2005/06/VersionControl/ClientServ
ices/02>
<GetResults>
<ArrayOfGetOperations>
<GetOperation type="File"
itemid="7"
slocal="C\Application.cs"
tlocal=" C\Application.cs"

titem="$/NewProject/Files/Application.cs"
sver="4"
lver="4"

durl="sfid=1025,0,0,0,0,0,0,0,0,0&amp;
ts=5635763534534534534 5&amp;
s=A4e3hUiIOlGuy7t;
fid=1025" >
<HashValue>+gdGH7fI9C3bVD59s12i0aaN</HashValue>
</GetOperation>
</ArrayOfGetOperation>
</GetResults>
</GetResponse>
```

`titem` contains the path to the requested file in Team Foundation Version Proxy. The `sfid` is the signed file download ticket that the application tier generated for the request. The `ts` variable contains an expiry time stamp. The `s` variable contains a Base64 encrypted hash string and `fid` stands for File ID.

> **A commonly asked question is if the Team Foundation Server goes offline, can a user continue working with just the proxy. The answer is no — Team Foundation Proxy uses a Team Foundation Server ticket to authenticate the user.**

Client and Server Configuration

To configure your Visual Studio 2005 client to connect to the proxy, you must first change the proxy settings — your Visual Studio clients will not automatically detect a proxy. To start, click Tools⇨Options. Then expand the Source Control node and select Visual Studio Team Foundation. As shown in Figure 15-4, you need to select "Use proxy server" and specify the server name for your proxy and the port. Finally, you have to define whether your proxy connection will be done over HTTP or HTTPS.

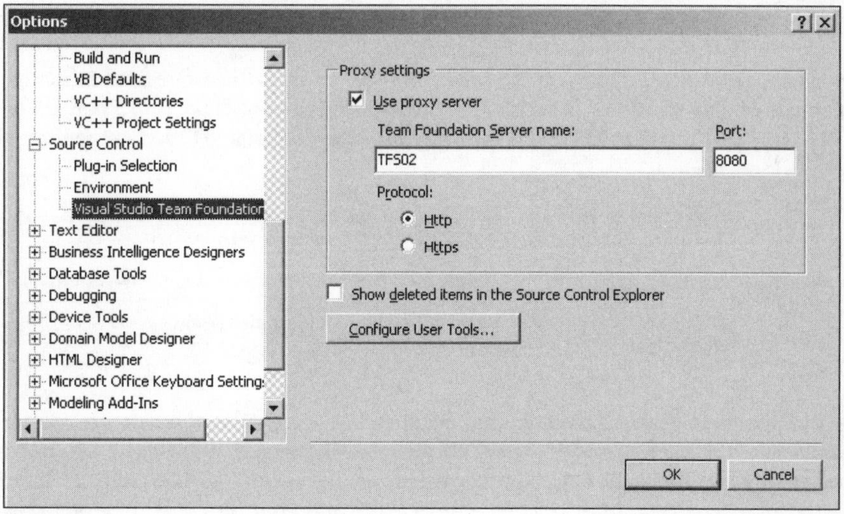

Figure 15-4

> **The Plug-In Selection settings allow you to easily switch over from different version control systems including Visual SourceSafe or Team Foundation Version Control.**

On the server, you will have to modify the proxy.config configuration file located in the Web services directory. Specifically, the file can be found (assuming that you installed the proxy on the C: drive) at the following location: `C:\Program Files\Microsoft Visual Studio 2005 Team Foundation Server\Web Services\VersionControlProxy`.

When you open up this file, the first thing you notice is a node called `Servers`. Here you can specify what Team Foundation Server Version Control systems you want to cache. Between the `Server` nodes, you can add as many `Uri` references to as many servers as you need. In case you are wondering, `@H_TFSSERVER@` refers to the current server:

```
<?xml version="1.0"?>
<ProxyConfiguration
xmlns:xsd="http://www.w3.org/2001/XMLSchema"
xmlns:xsi="http://www.w3.org/2001/XMLSchema-instance">
<Servers>
<Server>

<Uri>@H_TFSSERVER@/VersionControl</Uri>
</Server>
</Servers>
```

Next, you need to specify the proxy file cache root folder. This is the folder specified during the installation process that contains the cache data:

```
<CacheRoot>C:\Program Files\Microsoft Visual Studio 2005 Team Foundation Server\Web
Services\VersionControlProxy\Data\</CacheRoot>
```

It is now time to set the cache limit on the proxy. You can express the cache limit in many ways including as a percentage of disk space (for example, the proxy cache can only take up 75 percent of your hard drive space. As a best practice, Microsoft typically uses the percentage based cache limit policy:

```
<CacheLimitPolicy>
<PercentageBasedPolicy>75</PercentageBasedPolicy>
```

You can also express your cache limit as a fixed number of megabytes (as shown below):

```
<FixedSizeBasedPolicy>1000</FixedSizeBasedPolicy>
</CacheLimitPolicy>
```

Once the limit has been reached, you need to decide what percentage of the cache size needs to be freed. The `CacheDeletionPercent` node below indicates that 10 percent of the cache will be freed up. It's important to note that the cache is freed according to an algorithm (`CacheLimit = (AvailableSpace + CurrentCacheSize * CacheLimitPercent)/100`) and your files will be removed according to the `LastWriteTime`. Note that the last writes will be removed first.

```
<CacheDeletionPercent>10</CacheDeletionPercent>
```

The `StatisticsPersistTime` shows how many hours the proxy statistics logs should be persisted to a file. This setting is especially important to set depending on the number of users accessing the proxy and whether you are using the proxy server to do some performance monitoring:

```
<StatisticsPersistTime>1</StatisticsPersistTime>
```

Finally, we have the `ReaderChunkSize` and `WriterChunkSize`, which indicate in what size chunk the data should be propagated in and out of the proxy. `ReaderChunkSize` specifies what packet size is read from the application tier to the proxy, and `WriterChunkSize` denotes the packet size written to the client.

```
<ReaderChunkSize>1048576</ReaderChunkSize>
<WriterChunkSize>1048576</WriterChunkSize>
</ProxyConfiguration>
```

Managing the Proxy

At this point, Team Foundation Proxy has been appropriately configured. Once you install Team Foundation Proxy, it initiates several performance counters behind the scenes including the following:

- Current cache size
- Total cache hits (count and percentage)
- Total download requests
- Total files in cache
- Total cache miss (count and percentage)

There are two ways you can monitor the proxy, either by using the Web service, or by using the Performance Monitor (perfmon.msc). You can access the Web service by following these instructions.

1. Type this address in your preferred Web browser: `http://localhost:8081/VersionControlProxy/v1.0/proxystatistics.asmx`.
2. You will get access to a Web service.
3. Click the `QueryProxyStatistics` method.
4. Click Invoke to bring up the proxy statistics in XML format.

```
<ProxyStatisticsInfo CurrentCacheSize="102403" NoOfRequests="112"
OverallCacheHits="22" NoOfFilesInCache="22" OverallCacheMisses="22"
CacheHitsPercentage="50" CacheMissPercentage="50" ServerId="123c55a2-2d45-75a2-
a353-1aa3b3ff2ddf" ServerUrl="http://VSTSRTM:8080/VersionControl" />
```

You can learn a lot from proxy statistics; in fact, it's like a scorecard. For example, the `OverallCacheHits` in the example is 22 percent. That isn't a good sign at all. It means that your proxy is constantly retrieving the files from the application tier — a best practice is to try to get this number up to 80 percent or greater. Also, notice that the proxy contains a very small number of files (22), and thereby is reduced in effectiveness. The `CurrentCacheSize` provides a view into what is currently cached on the server — if you compare it to your total cache size, it will provide an indication of how much cache you have left.

The Performance Monitor is accessible by clicking Start⇨Administrative Tools⇨Performance. A window appears as shown in Figure 15-5.

To configure the counters, simply right-click the System Monitor pane (the graph) and select Add Counters. A configuration window appears as shown in Figure 15-6.

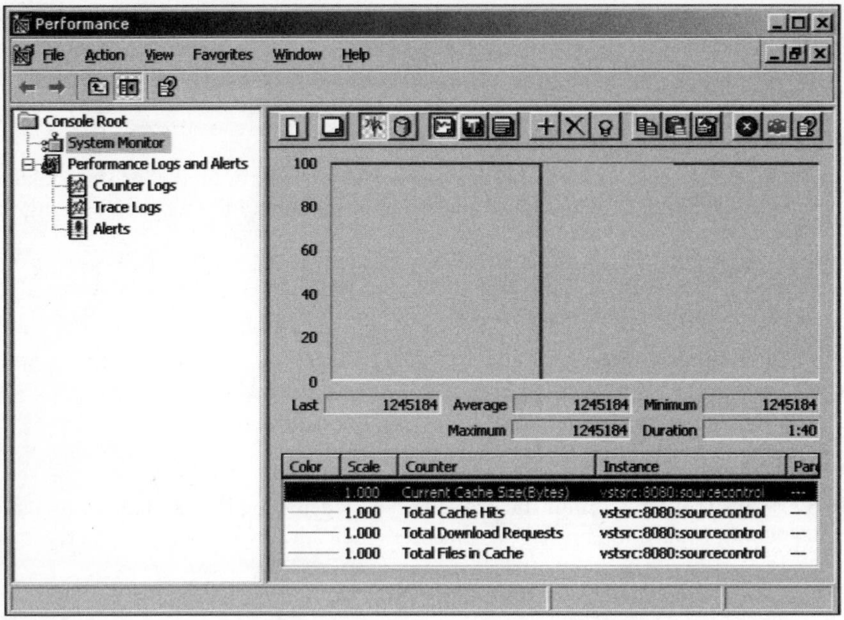

Figure 15-5

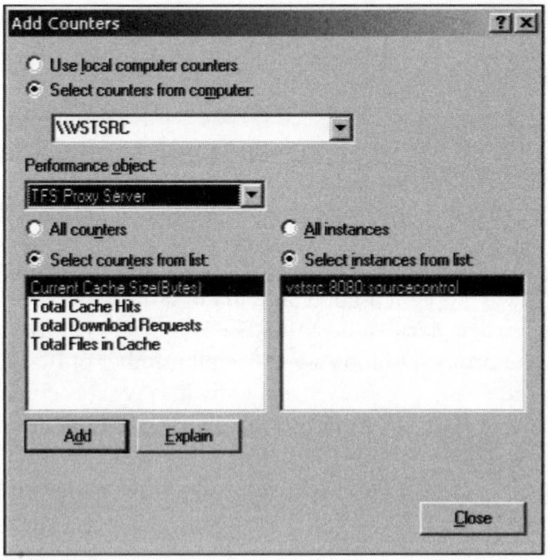

Figure 15-6

From the Performance object drop-down menu, select TFS Proxy Server. You can then select the counters from the list and add them to the display by clicking on the Add button. You will now be able to see your counters on the System Monitor pane and print them off for analysis. You can also obtain log information about the proxy server and correlate them with application logs to troubleshoot any problems that may come up. From a day-to-day perspective, a typical proxy administrator retrieves proxy statistics (weekly or every two weeks), sets up proxy security (including account credentials), and configures the cache settings. Here are pragmatic best practices targeted to Team Foundation Proxy administrators, some of which will improve your performance dramatically:

- Use Team Foundation Proxy in high-performance, high-bandwidth environments. Using Team Foundation Proxy within a LAN reduces CPU and memory stress on your Team Foundation Server and SQL Server 2005.
- If you want to access files from a Team Foundation Server for a short amount of time, connect directly to the server rather than add the proxy to the proxy.config file. The common sense reason for this is that the proxy will turn around and cache files that will be unused for the most part.
- If the proxy needs to go offline for maintenance or any other reasons, tell your team members to turn off the proxy settings within Visual Studio. Visual Studio is designed to reconnect to a proxy server every five minutes. This will cause unnecessary network traffic.
- If you are proxying large files, you should reset the `executionTimeout` to a higher value to compensate.

Working Offline

There may be scenarios where your users may need to work offline. Team Foundation Server does not support this scenario out of the box, however you can use the Team Foundation Power Toy online utility (found in the Visual Studio 2005 SDK in the Utilities folder) to integrate your offline work. To invoke the online tool, simply navigate to your workspace using the command prompt and type in a command such as this one:

```
C:\Visual Studio 2005 SDK\tfpt.exe online
```

The utility scans your workspace for writeable files and then creates a changeset. The workspace scan is shown in Figure 15-7.

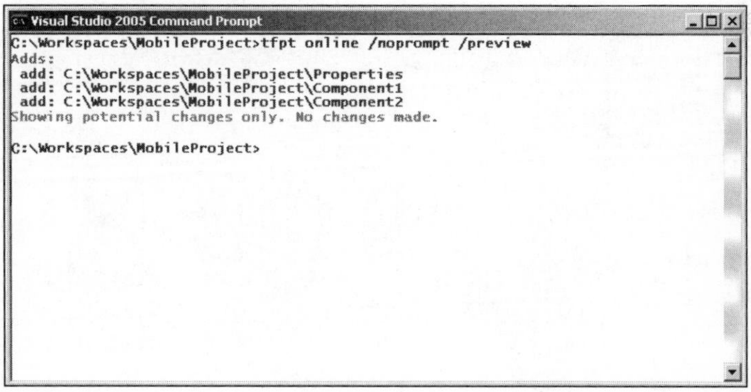

Figure 15-7

Don't try to undo changes made by the online tool; make sure the changeset contains exactly what you want checked in. (You can do this by using the `/preview` flag to give you a sneak peek.) If you are planning to use the tool, there are very specific instructions you must follow:

- When in offline mode, remove the read-only flag on the files you want to edit. You can do this by right-clicking the folder or file, select Properties, and uncheck Read Only.
- Don't rename files while offline. Team Foundation Server will not know the difference between a renamed file and a new file.
- When you regain connectivity, before doing anything else run the online tool and check in the pending changeset that is generated. That way, there will be no confusion between the new online work you will be doing and your offline work. If you don't do this and you do a "get latest," there is a chance you may overwrite your work.
- You can add and delete files offline. Make sure the files you are deleting are marked writeable before you proceed.

For more information about the tool, please refer to the most current version of the Visual Studio 2005 SDK, which can be downloaded for free at `http://msdn.microsoft.com/vstudio/extend/`.

Distributed Load Testing

Team System supports a scenario where you can test an application under load using multiple servers. This type of testing isn't specific to geographically distributed teams. In fact, in most cases you will want to run test rigs within a self-contained Web farm (rather than set up agents in distant geographies). You might be asking at this point, why include this topic in a book called *Professional Team Foundation Server,* and specifically in this chapter? In this book, we try to take a scenario and theme approach (as opposed to a feature-centric approach).

We are covering the topic here to specifically show how you can set up distributed tests, and specifically provide a scenario where you need to test the performance of an Enterprise-grade Web application under load of thousands of virtual users. For example, a tester in Hyderabad can connect to Team Foundation Server in Toronto, run his tests on a Canadian test rig then receive results back in India (as shown in Figure 15-8).

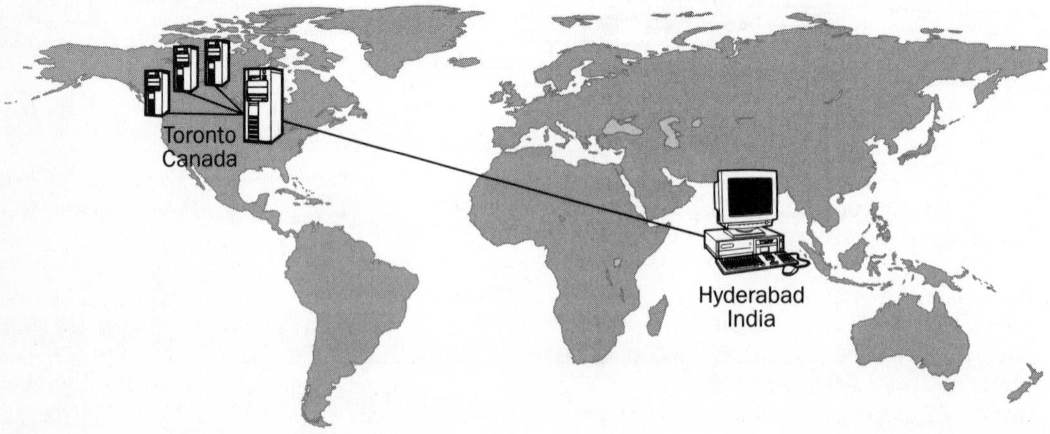

Figure 15-8

Note that the load controller and agents are sold separately from Team System. You can learn more about the product by visiting the following link: `http://go.microsoft.com/fwlink/?linkid=64719`**. It is highly recommended that you read the Team Foundation Server installation and administration guides for in-depth configuration information.**

There are two key points to consider when installing the test controller and agents. First is not to install the controller on a domain controller. This configuration isn't supported and will most likely fail. The second important point is that you shouldn't install any of the agents until the controller has been installed. If you do so, your installation has a great likelihood of failing.

Once installed, you can administer your test controller by clicking Test➪Administer Test Controller. You will see an interface as shown in Figure 15-9.

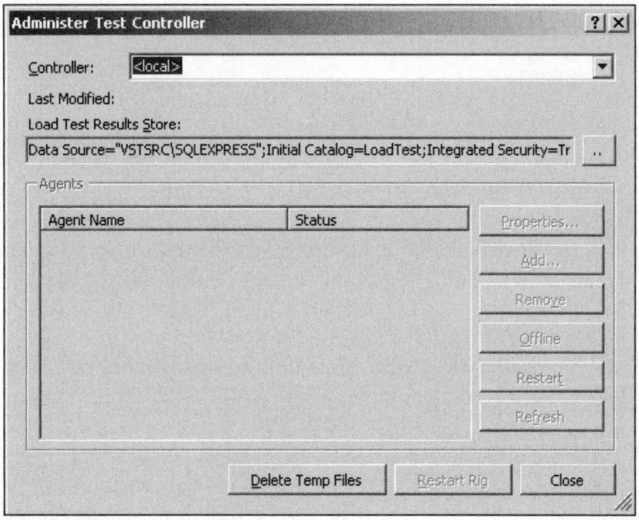

Figure 15-9

This interface allows you to delete temporary files, restart rigs, and add, remove, and manipulate controllers and agents. You can learn more about the process by looking at the official MSDN documentation at `http://msdn2.microsoft.com/en-us/library/ms182637.aspx`.

We will now look at how to set up a load test and associate it to a rig. We provide you with the step-by-step instructions on how to do this. However, if you want a great deal of depth on the topic, we would highly recommend you pick up *Professional Visual Studio 2005 Team System* published by Wrox Press. To start a load test, you must first create a test project. You can create one by clicking File➪New➪Project. A window appears with multiple project types. Expand Test Projects and select Test Documents (as shown in Figure 15-10).

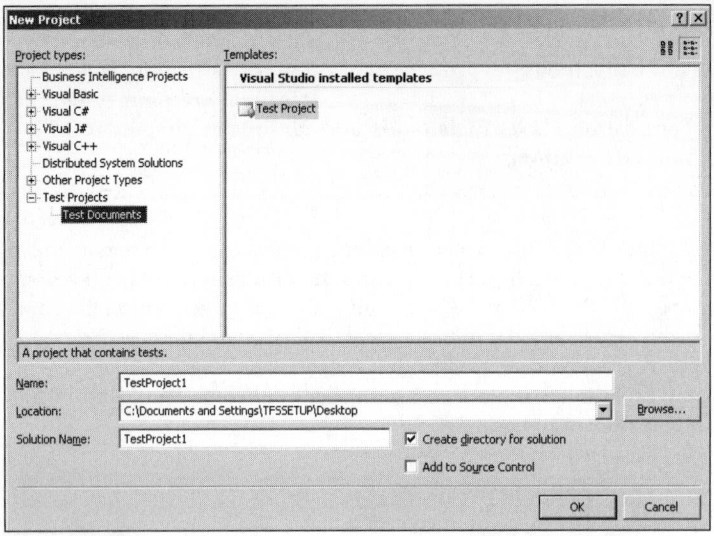

Figure 15-10

You should now create Web tests to use as the basis for your load test. In many development shops, usability tests are done against functional requirements to see if the Web site fulfills the business needs of the application. In many cases, this process is slow and manual. Web tests allow you to automate these manual tests, making regression testing really easy. On top of that, you get full integration of the tests with the rest of Team System, allowing you to create work items if a bug is found, or integrate the tests within a build (or check-in).

To create a Web test, all you need to do is right-click your test project and select Add⇨Web Test. Once the test is created, Internet Explorer launches along with the Web Test Recorder (as shown in Figure 15-11).

> **You'll notice the above example is a Web test of the team portal. In most real-world scenarios, you will want to Web test your own production and development applications.**

1. Once all of your Web tests have been created, right-click your project name in Solution Explorer, and select Add⇨Load Test. The New Load Test Wizard (Figure 15-12) provides you with the opportunity to configure your load tests, including your agent and controller settings.
2. Click Next to move on to the Test Scenario. You can define the recorded think times. You can also set up the think time between iterations (shown in Figure 15-13).
3. You can then add your mix of tests to a load test, and then set the load distribution of each test (as shown in Figure 15-14).

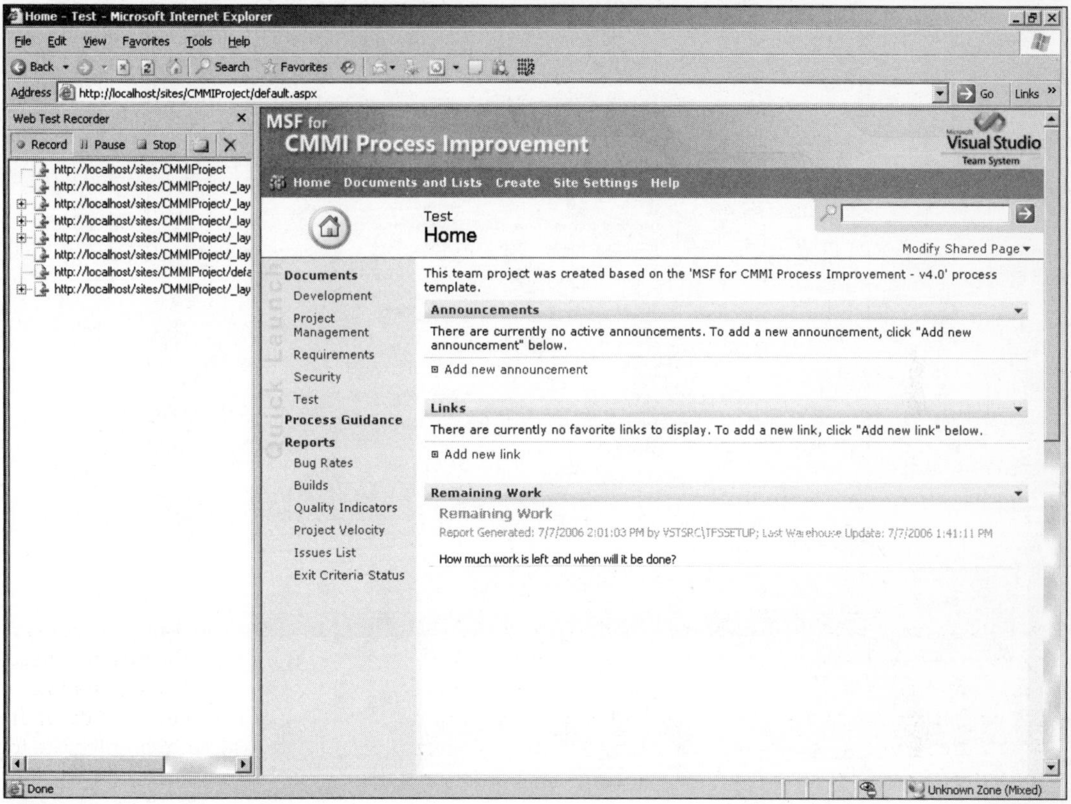

Figure 15-11

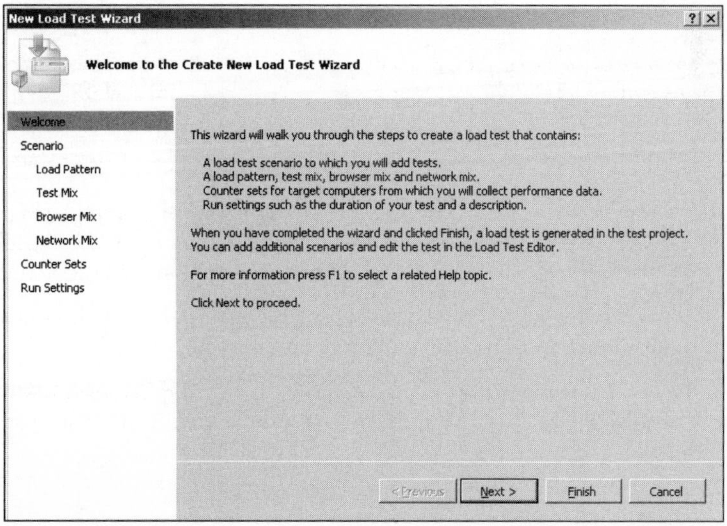

Figure 15-12

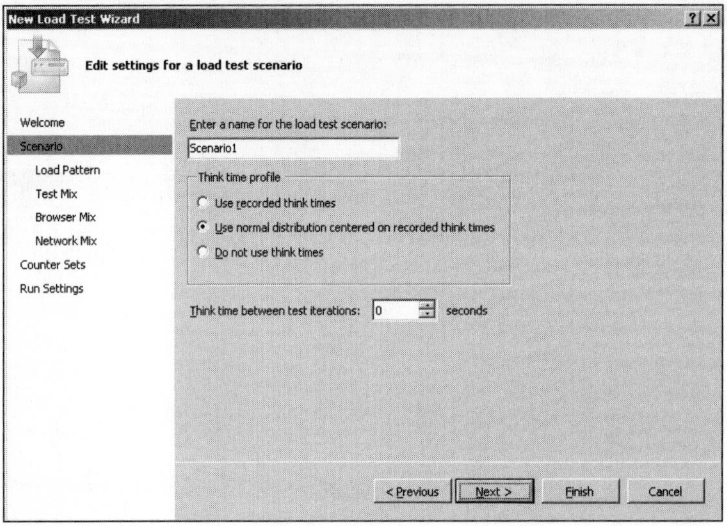

Figure 15-13

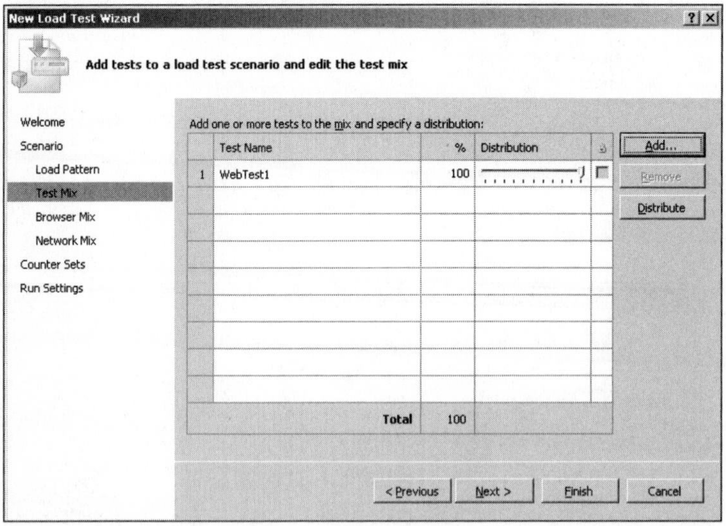

Figure 15-14

4. Next, you can add the mix and distribution of browsers (Figure 15-15).
5. You can then add the network type mix, including LAN, 56k dial-up, and distribute it according your user profile. You can figure out the normal profile for your Web site based on statistics (Figure 15-16).

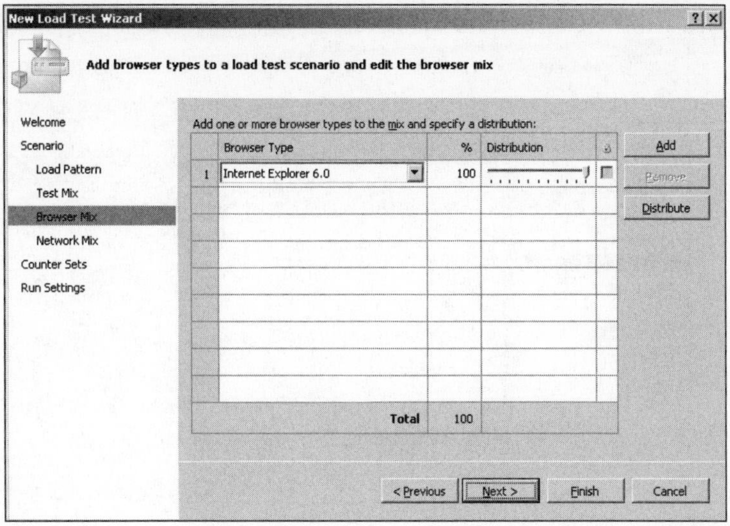

Figure 15-15

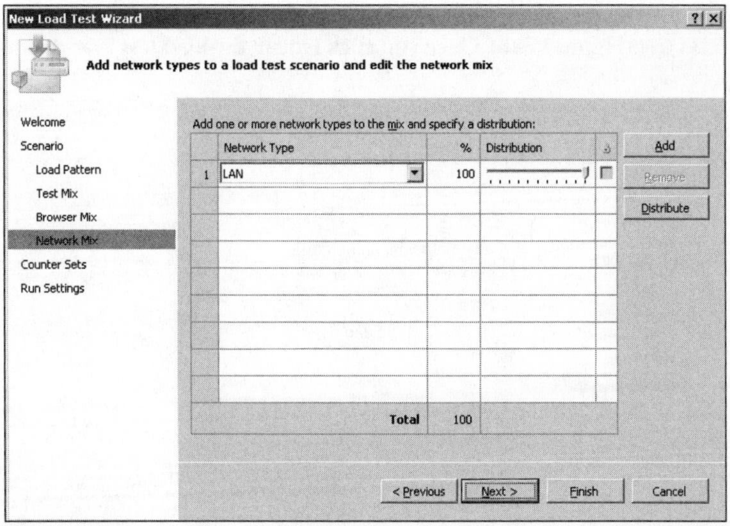

Figure 15-16

6. At this point, you can specify the controllers and agents to monitor, and include the results within the load test (seen in Figure 15-17):

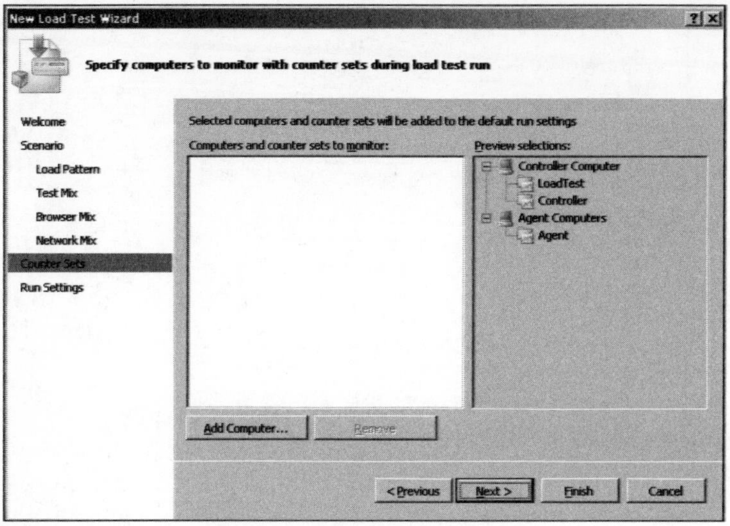

Figure 15-17

7. At the end of the process, you can set the timings, a description, and set the validation level for your load test (Figure 15-18). Once you click Finish, the load test is added to your project.

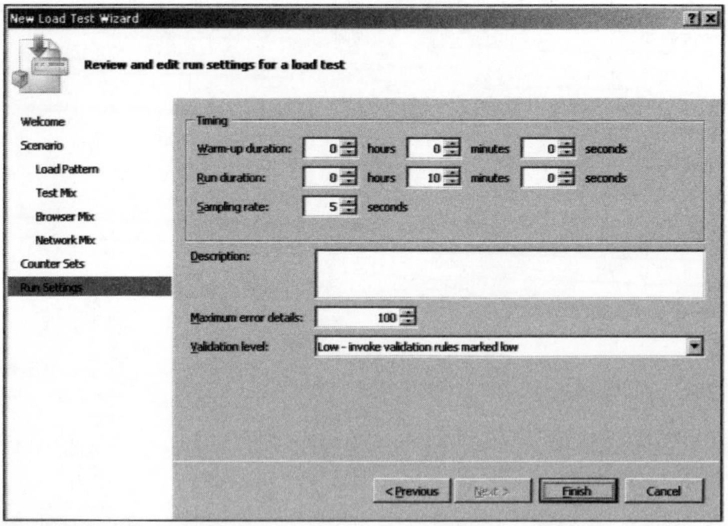

Figure 15-18

Figure 15-19 shows the various counters that are measured on the controller. It includes memory, network interfaces, process, processor, and system.

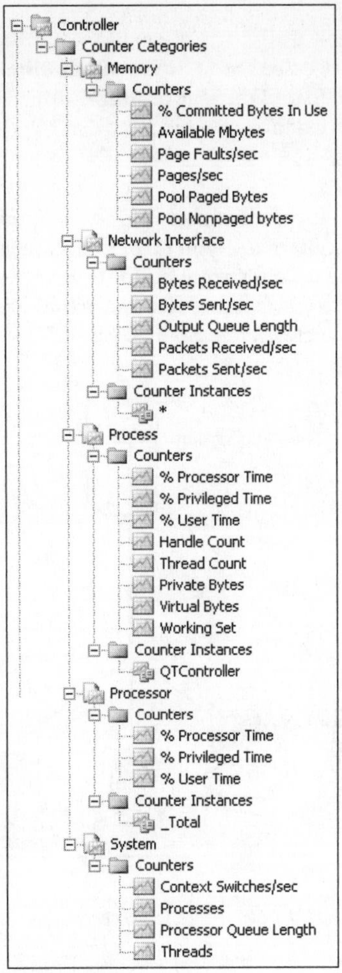

Figure 15-19

Team Foundation Build

Depending on the configuration of your remote teams, projects, and what hardware you have at your disposal, you may decide to deploy one (or several) build servers in your infrastructure. The most common scenario with most companies is one build server in the center of the development environment. If your builds take a long time to complete or you have several distributed projects with unique build requirements, you may want to set up a farm of build servers. If your builds are also performance intensive, the extra horsepower will definitely come in handy.

One of the advantages of doing this is that the licensing is quite flexible in the deployment of multiple build servers. The rule of thumb is that you can deploy as many build servers as you want as long as the users accessing or triggering builds have a client access license (CAL).

To install Team Foundation Build, simply explore the Team Foundation Server media and find a directory called `build`. Simply double-click setup.exe to start the process—you can install Team Foundation Build directly on your Team Foundation Server or on a standalone machine.

In Figure 15-20, you can see a deployment of multiple Team Foundation Build servers partitioned by project. This is but one of many scenarios—you have to decide what is applicable in your environment. Another logical scenario is setting up a separate build server for every phase of development—a daily development/integration server, a test/quality assurance build server for intensive testing, and a release build server dedicated for creating clean, release-ready builds.

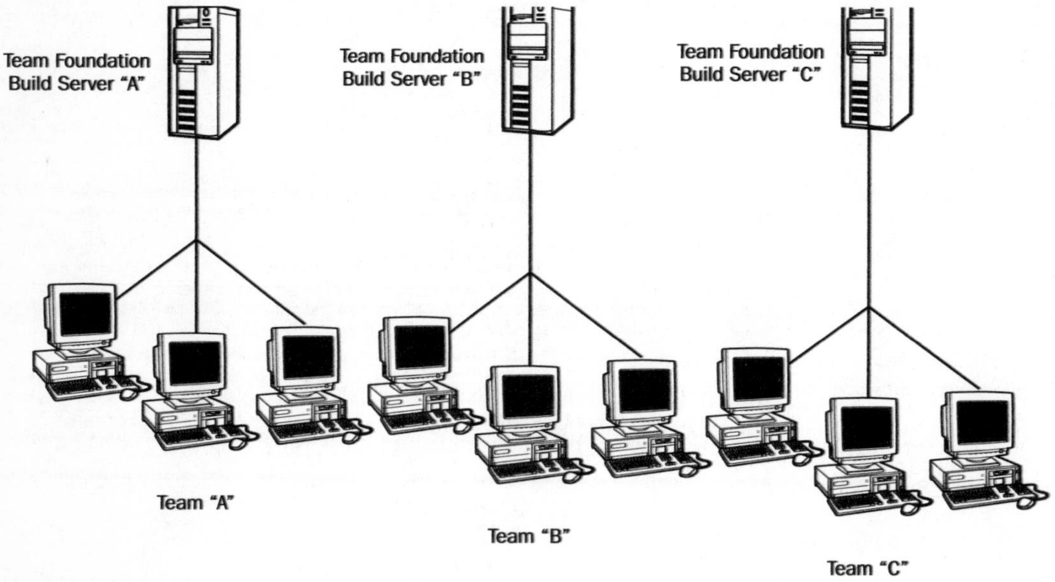

Figure 15-20

You can target any of your build servers within a build script when you create a build type. Right-click the Team Builds folder of your team project (within Team Explorer) and select New Team Build Type. The following table is a decision chart to help guide you through the process of planning a multiple Team Foundation Build deployment:

Single Build Server	Multiple Build Servers
Daily or nightly build: A single server can run at off-peak hours to build the code.	**Continuous Integration:** Code is built continuously at every check-in.
Small development team: A single build server is adequate for a small development team.	**Large development team:** The volume of build requests may increase with a larger number of team members. A build farm would help alleviate the load of requests.

Single Build Server	Multiple Build Servers
Localized team: If the entire development team is in one location, you won't have the same concerns as a distributed team — for example, communication and operational delays due to differences in time zone.	**Distributed team:** A build server per location may alleviate lag time in generating and retrieving builds. This scenario has to be assessed on a case-by-case basis based on the responsibilities of each of the teams.
Short build cycles: Builds take 5 to 15 minutes without disruption.	**Long build cycles:** If your builds take several hours to run, you may want to set up multiple build servers to load balance your builds.

Internationalization

When dealing with distributed teams, one of the important considerations is language and culture across continental boundaries. Team Foundation Server is not designed to work with multiple languages; you can install only one per server. If you try to get language-specific versions of Team Suite accessing a Team Foundation Server that has been set to a different culture and language, you may get unexpected results such as error messages and other user interfaces (UI) in other languages. As a best practice, we greatly encourage that you match up the language of your clients with the server.

Here is an important consideration. You can install the English version of Team Foundation Server on Windows Server 2003 localized to most languages (such as Korean). However, you cannot install a localized version of Team Foundation Server without its localized Windows Server equivalent. For example, if you are installing the Korean version of Team Foundation Server, you must install Team Foundation Server on a Windows Server 2003 also localized to Korean.

The following matrix explains what language combination of servers are supported:

Team Foundation Server	Windows Server 2003	Windows SharePoint Services Service Pack 2
English version	English version	English version
English version	Localized version	Must be English version
Localized version	English version	Must be localized to same language as Team Foundation Server
Localized version	Localized (must be localized to the same language as Team Foundation Server)	Localized (must be localized to the same language as Team Foundation Server)

> **Visual Studio 2005 is currently available in nine different languages including Simplified and Traditional Chinese, English, French, German, Italian, Japanese, Korean, and Spanish.**

The configuration of the collation settings in SQL Server 2005 (shown in Figure 15-21) facilitates support for multiple languages. Collations determine the ordering of your data. Note that the incorrect collation settings will prevent your Team Foundation Server from functioning properly. Depending on what language you are working with, you need to make sure that you consider a collation that handles accents, kana, and width sensitivity. (Some languages use glyphs that rely on double-byte character sets.) In general, you should use case-insensitive collations.

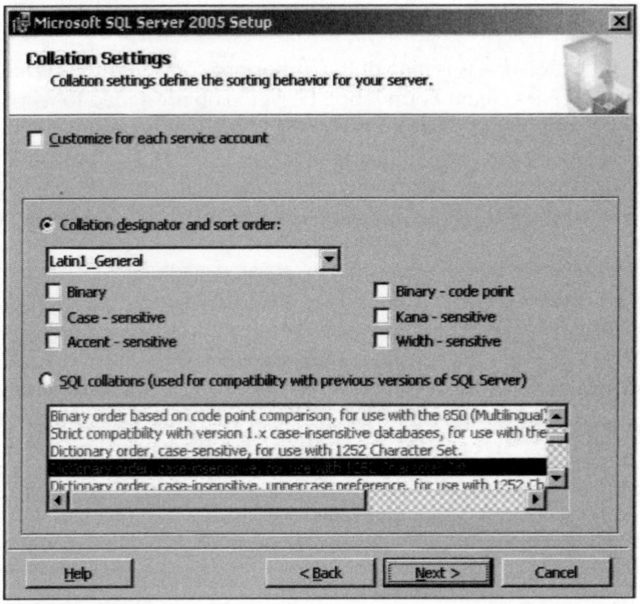

Figure 15-21

Here is a matrix chart to help you choose the right collation settings for Team Foundation Server based on internationalization requirements:

Language	Condition	Collation Setting
US-English	Default installation	SQL Server collation (for backward compatibility)
US-English	Extra U.S. English characters	Latin1_General
English	Default installation	Windows collation
Other Languages	Default installation	Windows collation

Language	Condition	Collation Setting
Other Language	Extra Unicode support (for example, Unicode CJK Extension A characters, Unicode Surrogates, etc.)	"_90" collation. For example, "Japanese_90"
Japanese	Hiragana/Katakana support	Enable Kana and Width sensitivity

> **Note that Team Foundation Server does not support binary, binary2, case sensitive, and accent insensitive collations.**

You can customize other aspects of the team project, such as the reports and the team portal. In your custom report, simply set the Language property to blank to allow Internet Explorer to dynamically change the culture of the report (in terms of dates and time).

To change the language of the team portal, you can use the Microsoft Windows SharePoint Services 2.0 Language Template Pack, which you can download at `www.microsoft.com/downloads/details.aspx?FamilyID=e7eec77d-4365-4b66-8e8d-9d079c509679&DisplayLang=en`.

Deploying it is quite straightforward; simply install it on the same machine as your Team Foundation Server. You can then create a custom process template to bring up the foreign language features. In WssTasks.xml, simply change the site template to:

```
<site template="STS#0" language="1031" />
```

This example creates a Team Portal with a German language template. Upload your custom process template, create a Team Project, and *dort ist es* (there it is) — your German team portal appears. Simply change the language attribute to the appropriate value to change languages. Here is a matrix with the languages supported by Visual Studio 2005, and the values that need to be added in to effect a change:

Language	Locale ID
Chinese (People's Republic of China)	2052
English (United States)	1033
French (France)	1036
German (Germany)	1031
Italian (Italy)	1040
Japanese	1041
Korean	1042
Spanish (Spain — Traditional Sort)	1034

For a complete list of Locale IDs, please refer to the Web page at `www.microsoft.com/globaldev/reference/lcid-all.mspx`.

> **To learn more on how you can internationalize Team Foundation Server (and specific steps on how to change the language of the Windows SharePoint Services portal), refer to the informative blog post at** `http://blogs.msdn.com/team_foundation/archive/2005/05/09/415838.aspx`**.**

Summary

In this chapter, you learned how to plan and manage a geographically distributed development (GDD) environment. You found out the challenges and then explored the assets and tools found in Team System. We delved deeper into the Team Foundation Proxy and the distributed load testing tools, and we examined different scenarios where you could apply a deployment of multiple Team Foundation Build servers. Finally, we explored internationalization issues.

In the next chapter, we will look at reporting and how it can be used to measure both distributed teams and centralized development teams.

16

Monitoring Your Team Project Metrics Using SQL Server Reporting Services

Metrics are undoubtedly one of the most important features of Team System. Team System's reporting infrastructure provides visibility and transparency within your Team Project. It is the key area to help you effectively manage software development projects using software engineering techniques. For example, you can track the velocity of your team and react to potential bottlenecks (instances of special cause variation) using the Remaining Work report.

The Team System reporting infrastructure has value to all the members of your team: the project manager can use summary reports to understand the big picture; developers and testers can look at meaningful data (such as code coverage) to get a view of their particular slice of the project.

You can look at a project metrics two main ways. The traditional (also referred to as waterfall view), shows a view of common project management elements such as time, resources, functionality, and quality. In this project management approach, you track the progress of tasks against set requirements. Within a time scope, your developers will try to develop an application against a range of specifications. In his book *Software Engineering using Visual Studio Team System,* Sam Guckenheimer refers to this approach as "Work Down."

Team System provides you with the tools to approach software development using a completely opposite "Value Up" approach — a combination of Agile techniques mixed in with established software engineering practices. In "Value Up," rather than prescribe the flow of work, Team System provides a descriptive view of your work. In this paradigm, you can measure the true velocity of your team and other metrics such as bug rates and code churn.

You don't necessarily need a deep technical knowledge of SQL Server Reporting Services to create reports (for example, Excel pivot table reports). However, what you do need is a solid understanding of how to store your data in the data warehouse and how to extract it. If you look at it in statistical terms, only a small number of people (approximately 5 percent) in your organization will know how to create a useful report without additional training or books. You can create ad hoc reports that can provide historical (and current) data. Team System also ships with a number of preconfigured reports that are integrated within the MSF for Agile Software Development and MSF for CMMI Process Improvement process templates.

At the heart of Team System's reports is SQL Server Reporting Services and SQL Server 2005 Analysis Services. Data warehousing, business intelligence (BI), and advanced report customizations are complex topics that can easily take up several books. The goal in this chapter is to provide you with enough working knowledge of SQL Server Reporting Services and OLAP to work with reports within the context of Team System.

> **If you want to go really deep on the subject, we suggest you read books such as *Professional SQL Server Analysis Services 2005 with MDX* (ISBN: 0764579185) and *Professional SQL Server 2005 Reporting Services* (ISBN: 0764568787) published by Wrox Press. The product documentation (`http://msdn.microsoft.com`) and the process guidance in MSF for Agile Software Development and MSF for CMMI Process Improvement will provide you with the fundamental data points around reporting.**

To be able to leverage the Team System reports, it helps to have a good understanding of OLAP, metrics gathering within a mature process and process improvement. You should read and absorb other chapters of this book to get a solid understanding of how process is handled within Team System. For example, if you are not sure how work items are managed through the lifecycle, how can you identify trends and troubleshoot problems?

Reporting Services Architecture

SQL Server Reporting Services (SSRS) relies on the SQL Server 2005 database, SQL Server 2005 Analysis Services, and online analytical processing (OLAP) to mine project data. Figure 16-1 illustrates the overall architecture of Team System's data warehouse.

In Team System, metrics from every tool (testing tools, build, version control, and work items) are automatically pushed into several relational databases (operational stores), and then processed into an analysis cube (called `TFSWarehouse`). The default reports that ship with Team System tap into the warehouse to quickly generate graphs that provide a near-real-time view of the progress of your project.

> **SQL Server Analysis Services is an OLAP database system.**

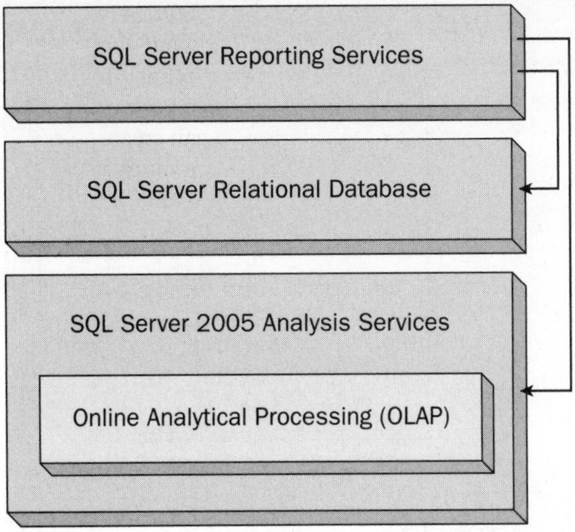

Figure 16-1

Online Analytical Processing (OLAP)

Online analytical processing (OLAP) is a term that was coined by Dr. Edgar F. Codd, considered by many as the inventor of the relational database model. Dr. Codd came up with 12 rules that allow anyone to correctly identify any OLAP system. For example, the OLAP approach is designed to provide summarized data very quickly, is typically used in business or sales applications, and is an important component of business intelligence (BI).

You aren't restricted to use Microsoft tools to access an OLAP cube. Several third-party products can help you interact with them (for example, ProClarity). Team System provides two primary ways of creating cube-based reports: via Microsoft Excel and the Business Intelligence Projects within Team Suite.

All the default Team System reports use the TfsWarehouse OLAP cube as the primary data source.

Team System relies on multidimensional OLAP (or MOLAP) to manage the data warehouse. By multidimensional, we mean that you can correlate many of the metrics of Team System; for example, you can view the work items by build-by date. Another example is a view by changeset, test results and work items. OLAP uses multidimensional expressions (MDX) query language to manipulate multidimensional databases.

A cube is a database structure that is specifically designed for OLAP, and provides a way for team members to collect and view aggregated data. For example, totals for work items, builds, test results, and much more.

Think of your typical database table; it is flat and represented in two dimensions. One axis represents the fields in your table. The other axis contains the rows of data in your table. An OLAP cube can represent data in three or more dimensions. Figure 16-2 shows an OLAP cube with three dimensions (including builds, changesets, and work items).

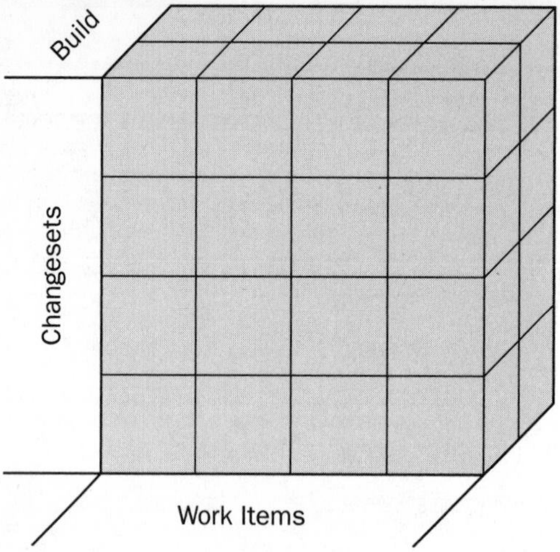

Figure 16-2

Team System Data Warehouse Structure

The Team System data warehouse is composed of four core components:

- **Operational stores** — The operational stores gather live information about each component of Team System such as build, version control and work items. For example, the data source for work items is called `TfsWorkItemTracking`.
- **Adapters** — The adapters handle a variety of tasks, including managing cube processing cycles, and adapting and customizing the data warehouse as your process templates begin to change (through customization). These adapters tap into the data warehouse API and Web services to perform the tasks in question.
- **Relational database (fact tables)** — The relational database correlates and normalizes the data from each operational store. Because the information is integrated, it is a lot easier to manage and report against. Each of these tables contains measures, dimensions, and details.
- **OLAP Cube** — Aggregates and optimizes the Team Project data to be processed in reports.

Figure 16-3 outlines how Team Project data flows through the warehouse. Your project data are captured within each operational store. Adapters normalize the data into an established format, which makes it easier to interrelate. The data are then pulled on a periodic basis into the OLAP cube.

> **If you ever try to publish your test results to Team Foundation Server, you'll sometimes notice that the IDE complains that a build is not present within your current (or new) Team Project. The reason is that the test data are typically contained in the Team Foundation Build operational store.**

Figure 16-3 shows the structure of Team System's data warehouse.

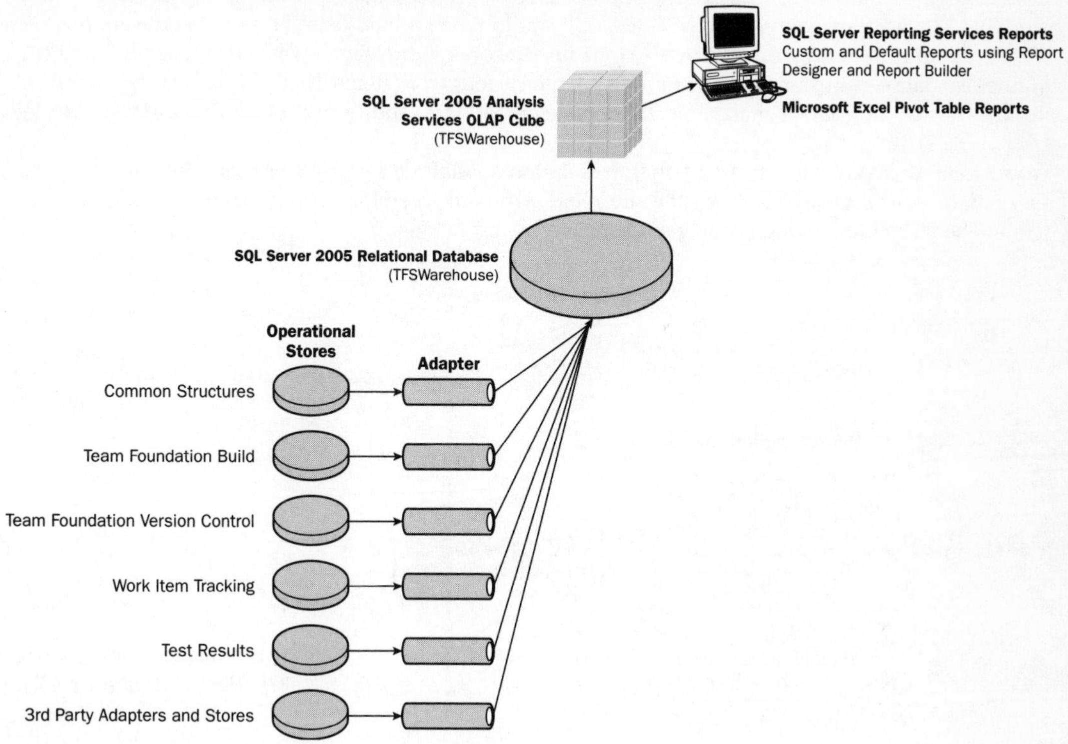

Figure 16-3

Operational Stores and Adapters

The operational stores contain raw data about test results, builds, code churn, work items, and so forth. Each store has a unique schema tailored to each Team System feature and your operational stores are optimized to contain live data. The adapters perform a variety of tasks including data synchronization and correlation (for example, correlating builds and work items) and the normalization of data into the relational database. Adapters are also used in the processing of the cube.

When you create custom work items (or other types of customizations), the adapters also perform the task of synchronizing these new custom fields on the fly within the OLAP and relational schemas. All the adapters implement the `IWarehouseAdapter` interface, and are DLLs stored in the following directory: `C:\Program Files\Microsoft Visual Studio 2005 Team Foundation Server\Web Services\Warehouse\bin\Plugins`. For example, the build adapter is called `Microsoft.TeamFoundation.Build.Adapter.dll`.

Relational Database (Fact Tables)

Fact tables are simply used to aggregate and relate Team Project data. For example, the fact table will tell you that 12 work items are associated to a specific build for a specific Team Project. If you want precise details about each build, then you have to look into the operational tables. Fact tables usually contain numerical data — for example, summaries of all the current work items. Fact tables also help provide a historical view of your data. For example, fact tables contain dates and record counts that can be correlated.

You'll hear Microsoft say repeatedly that the relational database system uses a star schema. What exactly does that mean? Figure 16-4 shows the star relationship between the operational stores and the fact table. The fact tables contain measures, dimensions, and details.

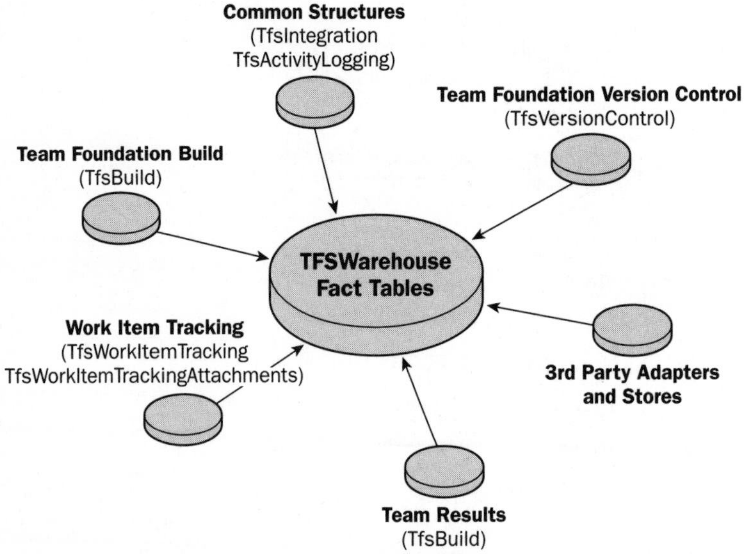

Figure 16-4

The Team System relational database contains a variety of metrics pertaining to work items, changesets, builds, test results, and much more. Fact tables establish relationships between different project metric types — for example, work items and changesets, or builds and work items. Fact tables don't actually contain any details, only raw numerical data.

The default Team System reports access the relational warehouse to get a timestamp. But you can easily report against the relational database (especially if all you want is an up-to-the-minute view of the data, or you just want to query a list — such as a list of work items).

For example, the Build Changeset fact table only contains a list of unique identifiers for builds and their associated changesets. The table shown in Figure 16-5 was obtained by connecting to the SQL Server 2005 database using the SQL Server Management Studio, expanding the `TfsWarehouse` table, and generating a database diagram:

You'll notice that it contains a field for work items, a field for changesets, and a field for Team Projects. Work item and changesets are the dimensions of that particular fact table. Running a `SELECT *` query on the table reveals the following information shown in Figure 16-6.

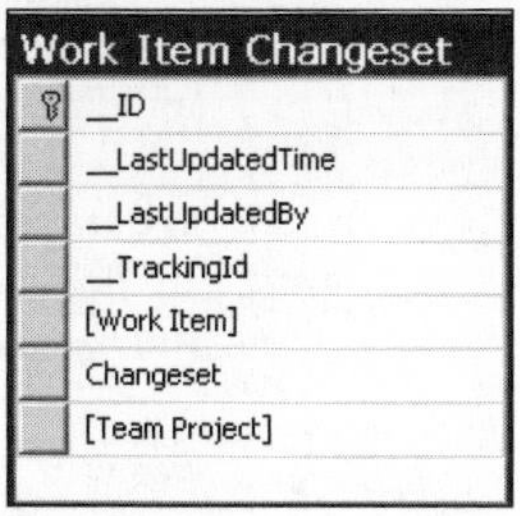

Figure 16-5

Results | Messages

	__ID	__LastUpdatedTime	__LastUpdatedBy	__TrackingId	Work Item	Changeset	Team Project
1	1	2006-05-11 19:11:55.720		16-2|9	17	6	1
2	2	2006-05-12 14:05:18.277		16-3|9	34	6	1
3	3	2006-05-13 17:10:53.707		16-4|9	35	6	1
4	4	2006-05-15 18:29:09.263		16-5|9	54	6	1
5	5	2006-05-16 17:54:10.133		2-4|32	92	32	1
6	6	2006-05-16 17:54:10.193		2-5|32	93	32	1
7	7	2006-05-16 20:07:37.610		20-2|42	98	43	1
8	8	2006-05-16 20:07:37.860		16-6|9	99	6	1
9	9	2006-05-16 20:07:37.870		16-6|42	99	43	1
10	10	2006-05-16 20:07:38.000		36-2|42	100	43	1
11	11	2006-05-17 15:54:00.250		57-2|44	105	44	1
12	12	2006-05-17 15:54:00.420		57-3|44	106	44	1

Figure 16-6

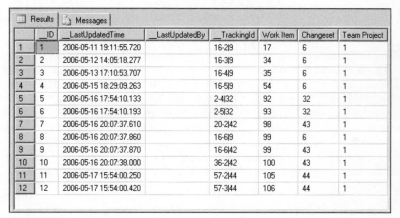

As you can see, the unique identifiers (foreign keys) for both of the work items and changesets establish a relationship between the project data types.

Terminology

There is a lot of terminology associated with OLAP, warehouses, and reporting. Let's get some clearer meaning of the terminology to get a better idea of how the parts all work together.

Measures

Measures allow you to tally up, count, and aggregate your data in a Team System report. For example, in the Build perspective, you have measures such as a build count and a build project count. These counts are stored in the relational warehouse within the fact table. Team System's OLAP cube contains seventeen measure groups (as shown in Figure 16-7).

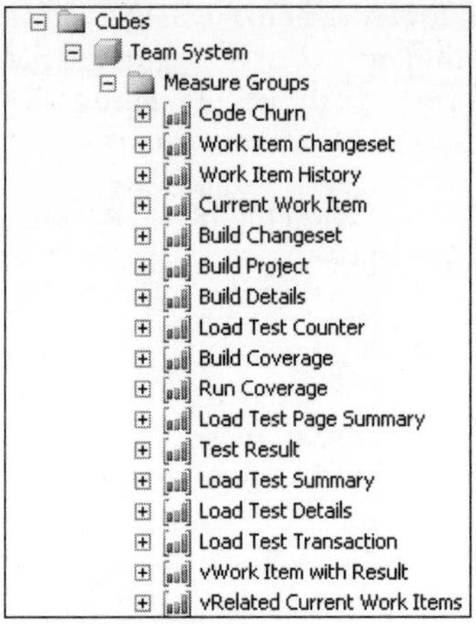

Figure 16-7

Dimensions

A *dimension* is used within an OLAP cube to provide a summary of measures and contain dimension attributes. The entire column name in dimensions are Reference Names and some of the data rows are designed to be an internal resource within the OLAP cube. If you are planning to use dimensions within relational warehouse reports, you should use SQL views (set up in a separate database) to make the tables easier to work with. You can also set up indexes to boost up your performance. The separate database is important because it separates out the customizations you have made to the actual product, and prevents issues if the database schema is changed for whatever reason (for example, a service pack). Otherwise, all of your reports will break. Figure 16-8 shows all the dimensions available in the OLAP data cube.

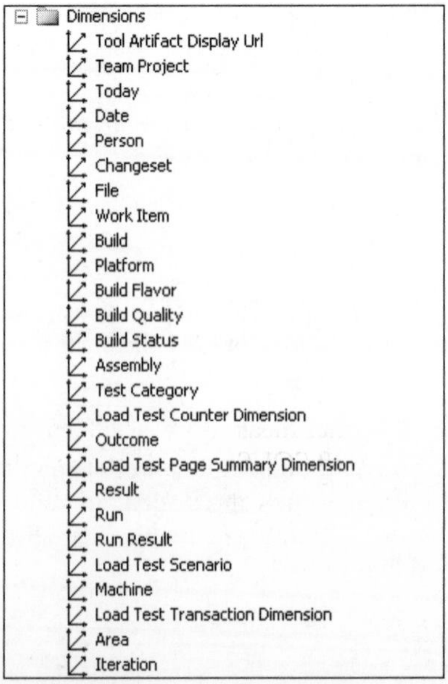

Figure 16-8

As you can see, some examples of dimensions include Rank, Person, Date, and so forth. Dimensions are useful for slicing up report data. For example, you may have a list of work items. If you filter them using the Date dimension, you will get a view of all the work items by date values. Dimensions are implemented in the relational database as a set of tables that tie into the fact table.

Dimension members are a named instance of a dimension. For example, you can have dimension members for changesets called Changeset1, Changeset2, and so forth. This also applies to dates and other dimensions. If you try to do a query within a pivot table, you may find that too much information is returned. A *filter* is a collection of dimension members that limit (or filter) the amount of data provided in a query.

You can also view a dimensions hierarchy. For example, the Date dimension has a hierarchy as shown in Figure 16-9:

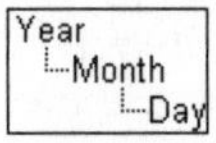

Figure 16-9

Details

Details provide titles that are used in list reports in the relational database. They are composed of strings of text that can be used within reports, for example as a descriptive list. In a nutshell, details are used to provide more "detail" in an OLAP report.

Perspectives

The amount of data contained in the Team Foundation OLAP cubes is massive. Trying to create custom reports can be tricky because it can be difficult to filter out only the information that you need. You can use *perspectives* to filter your data and reduce the complexity and manageability of your reports. Perspectives will make any element of your data cube visible or invisible, based on your needs. Across all cubes, you have a shared set of dimensions across all cube perspectives. They include the following:

- **Team Project**
- **Area**
- **Iteration**
- **Person**
- **Date**

You can use them to tie them against other measure groups. Note that you can only use perspectives if you install Team System with Microsoft SQL Server 2005 Enterprise Edition (x86 or x64) as your data tier.

This section of the chapter is meant to provide a solid overview of the concepts around Team System's data warehouse. There is so much information that it would be quite easy to write an entire book on the topic. If you are craving deeper details, the best source of information bar none is the MSDN documentation. Refer to "Team Foundation Server Data Warehouse" at `http://msdn2.microsoft.com/en-us/library/ms244712.aspx`**.**

Using MSF Documentation as a Guide

The Microsoft Solutions Framework provides a good starting point in trying to understand what the Team System reports are for. To navigate to the list of reports, you can click Index⇨Reports in MSF for Agile Software Development and Index⇨Reports in MSF for CMMI Process Improvement. The documentation provides diagnosis information such as healthy and unhealthy examples of report data. You can then do a project course correction to fix the issues.

Planning Custom VSTS Reports

Now that you have a basic understanding of the components of the data warehouse, let's look at how you can take that data and manipulate it to get useful customized reports. Reports are great for making all elements of your project more visible. You can also easily identify trends. For example, look at Figure 16-10.

```
Year
 └Month
   └Day
```

Figure 16-10

As you can see, there is a dotted line that is traveling from the lower part of the graph (the closed scenarios). Currently, the closed scenarios are 56 percent completed. If we were to estimate, you can see that the project will extend well past October 28. In fact, if you add more dates to the right of the graphic and used a rule, you could predict when the project would be completed at the current rate.

The whole point of creating a report is to not only identify trends but also look at the past. For example, historical data can provide details that help in the process of estimation. Finally, reports provide a way of making better decisions. Your knowledge and the effectiveness of your project management approach are only as good as the data you are receiving.

When designing a custom report, you must consider what tools you will use to build the report and what the report will actually contain. If you need ad hoc reporting, then perhaps an Excel pivot table might be appropriate. You may want to compare the data you would like to get out of Team System with the project data you are used to getting. If Team System isn't collecting what you need, you may want to customize work items and create separate tables for storing the data, then integrate both into a report. The approach you will take will depend on your needs, your environment, and your circumstances.

Creating Custom Team System Reports

The default project types in Team System provide a nice, consistent view into the development lifecycle. More often than not, you'll need other types of reports to supplement your project. For example, you may want visibility.

> **SQL Server 2005 Enterprise provides better field names for your reports than other versions of SQL Server. For example, a field in SQL Server 2005 Standard may be represented as "WorkItem.WorkItem." In SQL Server 2005 Enterprise, it is represented as simply "WorkItem."**

Mining Project Data Using an Excel Pivot Table Report

You can view your project data using an Excel pivot table. One of the key advantages of using a pivot table is simplicity; Microsoft Excel mines the data warehouse directly and has the built-in capability to display rich graphs and charts. Here is how you can set up Excel to view your project data:

1. Open Microsoft Excel.
2. Select Data⇨PivotTable and PivotChart Report.
3. Select External Data Source and Pivot Table and then click Next.
4. Click the Get Data button.
5. Select the OLAP Cube tab, select New Data Source, and then click OK.
6. Write a custom name for your data source. (If you are unsure, write in something like TFSDATA.) To use pivot tables, you need to first download the OLEDB 9.0 drivers. If you want to install the drivers without having to install all the SQL client tools, refer to the package at `www.microsoft.com/downloads/details.aspx?FamilyID=D09C1D60-A13C-4479-9B91-9E8B9D835CDC&displaylang=en`.

> **If the OLEDB drivers have been installed and you encounter an "Initialization of the data source failed" error, simply go to Start⇨Run, and type** `Regsvr32 "C:\Program Files\Common Files\System\Ole DB\msolap90.dll"`.

7. Select the Microsoft OLE DB Provider for Analysis Services 9.0 and click Connect.
8. A new window entitled Multidimensional Connection 9.0 pops up.
9. Select Analysis Server; under Server, enter (local).
10. Enter your administrative credentials in the User ID and Password fields. (The wizard warns you if your credentials are invalid.) Theoretically, you should not need credentials, but you need to be a member of the `TFSDataWarehouseReader` role on the cube. You can set this up using the SQL Server Management Studio.

If you enter incorrect credentials or credentials that don't have sufficient permissions to access the cube, you may receive an "error occurred in the transport layer" message. You can avoid the error message by entering valid user names and passwords.

11. Select the TFSWarehouse database and click Finish.
12. Select Team System, check Save My User ID and Password, and click Yes. You may get a warning that your user name and password will not be encrypted. The wizard will not allow you to move forward until you accept the warning. It's an important consideration if you are not in a secure environment for example, if you are working from a coffee house hotspot.

If you need to create reports in that kind of environment, you should consider replicating your database locally. (Team Edition for Database Professionals will enable you to create a local instance of your Team Foundation Server data warehouse.) For more information, please refer to Chapter 8.

13. Click OK in the Create New Data Source dialog box; click OK once more.
14. Click Finish in the PivotTable dialog box.

At this point, you can select any fields you want to view in the pivot table. Select the items that interest you and drag them into the pivot table. For example, you may be interested in seeing ChangeSet information. The information will automagically appear in the Excel spreadsheet within the pivot table (as shown in Figure 16-11). You can then save the sheet or choose to manipulate it at will.

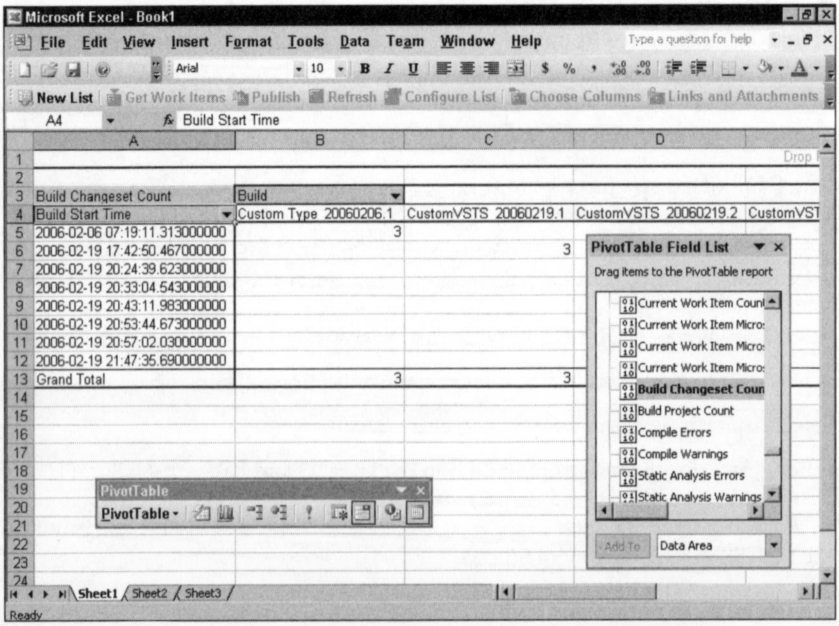

Figure 16-11

It is important to understand the role of the row and column axes. The row axis defines a collection of dimension members that represent row labels. The column axis represents column labels. Here is the layout of a typical pivot report: the project dimension is used as a filter, the date dimension is used on the row axis, and the measures from many measure groups are sliced up using the same dimension.

Creating Custom Reports with the Report Designer

To create an effective report, it is important to be able to distinguish between the different data sources and show the appropriate use of each. `TfsReportDS` is used in conjunction with the Team Foundation Server relational database. The relational database is perfect for getting lists and summary data, plus it contains the most recent data. An example of an appropriate use of the relational database is pulling the most recent work items from the data warehouse. Note that you may need to index the relational database in a separate table to get good performance for reports.

> **You should download and install the latest SQL Server 2005 Service Pack on your data tier before attempting to create a custom report. Otherwise, you may experience some difficulties, such as crashes — Service Pack 1 includes a great number of bug fixes. Here is a direct link to SQL Server 2005 Service Pack 1 (SP1):** `microsoft.com/downloads/details.aspx?familyid=cb6c71ea-d649-47ff-9176-e7cac58fd4bc&displaylang=en`.

`TfsOlapReportDS` is the data source for the Team Foundation Server OLAP cube. OLAP is perfect for obtaining multidimensional data and correlated data without incurring a performance hit (as opposed to having to create a complex spaghetti mess of joins to obtain the same results).

SQL Server Reporting Services reports are based on the .rdl file format (which stands for Report Definition Language). The reports can be built within Visual Studio 2005 and managed in Team Foundation Version Control (alongside all the other code assets). Your custom reports can also be deployed within a process template, to make them available every time you create a new Team Project.

> **The effective use of Report Designer is not for the faint of heart. If your custom reports are primarily based on OLAP, you should learn how to use multidimensional expressions (MDX). Some of your queries will require Visual Basic expressions, and the manipulation of parameters. Before attempting your first Team System report, take the time to learn the basics and try changing existing reports. The best way to learn is through trial and error, and don't expect to be creating amazing reports overnight (unless you are SQL Server Reporting Services expert and you code MDX in your sleep).**

Here are the steps to create a report in Report Designer that pulls from the Work Item History fact table, specifically bug assignments by priority.

1. First, create a new project by clicking File⇨New⇨Project.
2. Select Business Intelligence Projects.
3. Under templates, select Report Project. Add a custom name for your project and select OK.

4. In the Reports Project, right-click the Reports folder, and select Add New Report.
5. This triggers the Report Wizard. Click Next.
6. Next, you have to select a data source. Select Microsoft SQL Server Analysis Services (to leverage the OLAP cube). Click Next.
7. Select the New data source option. Under name, enter `VSTSRC`. Under type, make sure Microsoft SQL Server Analysis Services is selected. Under data source, enter the following: `Data source=VSTSRC;initial catalog=TFSWarehouse`. Click Next.
8. Click Query Builder. The Query Builder for Analysis Services appears.
9. In the top-left corner, you see a label that says AssemblyFact. Click the button next to it.
10. You see a list of fact tables to select. Select WorkItem_Fact table and click Next.
11. Now you can drag metadata from the Work Item History cube into the filter area or the measures level.
12. Expand the Measures node in the left menu. Drag RecordCount into the Measures area on the right.
13. Expand the Assigned To node. Drag Alias to the Measures area on the right of the screen.
14. Scroll down and expand Work Item Type. Further expand WorkItemType⇨WorkItemType⇨Bug, and then drag Bug into the Dimension window at the top-right of the screen.
15. Expand the State node. From there, further expand State⇨State⇨Active. Drag Active to the top right window on the screen
16. Drag the Priority node into the Measures area on the right of the screen
17. Click OK
18. Select the Matrix type of report. Click Next.
19. Select RecordCount to be in the Details area.
20. Select Alias for the Column level.
21. Select Priority for the Row level. Click Next.
22. Select a style for your report. If you are unsure what style, select Bold.
23. Enter a name for your report (Bug Assignments by Priority), and click Finish.

Using the Report Builder

We would be remiss if we didn't include the Report Builder in this chapter. Report Builder is a ClickOnce application that is integrated in SQL Server Reporting Services. It's designed for business users and developers who wish to create custom reports quickly and easily. You can launch it by clicking the Report Builder option on the Report Manager menu bar. (You can bring up the Report Manager by right-clicking on a project Reports folder in Team Explorer and selecting Show Report Site.)

Before you can access Team System data, you'll have to create a Semantic Model Definition Language (`.SMDL`) model. The SDML model can be created against both the relational warehouse and the OLAP cube. To get a usable model with the relational warehouse, you'll need to customize it considerably to get any useful data out of it. On the other hand, you can use the OLAP data source (`TfsOlapReportDS`), but keep in mind that creating reports against the model will have some impact from a performance and usability perspective. The rule of thumb is, if you want to create a custom report, use the Report Designer. In case you are curious, here is the process for creating an SDML model and setting up a Report Builder report:

1. Go to the Home page of SQL Reporting Services (the URL is `http://<your application tier>/Reports/`).
2. Click the TfsOlapReportDS data source link.
3. Click the Generate Model button. (It's at the bottom of the page.)
4. You are then be prompted for a name, description, and location. Name the model `TfsOlapReportDS`.
5. Once you are finished, you are ready to start building a report. Launch the Report Builder by clicking on the link from the front page of the Report Manager site. (You can access the Report Manager by right-clicking on your Team Project reports folder in Team Explorer)
6. Once the application launches, you can choose whether your report is a matrix, chart, or columnar table. Select the TfsOlapReportDS model and select your report type, then click OK.
7. A report template appears with an area where you can drag data fields onto it. To create a build report, click the Build entity and select the fields you want to appear on the report. You can also drag entities. (Entities are a logical collection of fields and other data types.) You can then save your report by clicking File➪Save. Once you click Save, you'll have the option of placing your report in any Team Project you want.

You can mix and match the entities and fields to get unique views of your project data. For example, you can mix your build data with changeset data.

Advanced Customization and Extensibility

Team System comes with many customization and extensibility features to allow you to create unique reports. For example, you can include custom fields within your work items and designate them as reportable. The adapters will automatically re-create the field in the data warehouse and start collecting data alongside all the other Team Project data.

Most custom fields that are created are used as *dimensions*. For example, if the field has a `VALIDVALUE` list, it is most likely a dimension, and can be used to summarize measures. If it has arbitrary values, the field may be a *detail*.

Here is a sample reportable field that represents a custom status, which is reportable (thanks to the `reportable="dimension"` attribute). It includes a list of statuses (based on traffic lights):

```
<FIELD name="Issue" type="String" refname="Stormpixel.TeamProject1.CustomStatus"
 reportable="dimension">
<HELPTEXT>Provides a custom status on a work item.</HELPTEXT>
<REQUIRED/>
<ALLOWEDVALUES>
<LISTITEM value="GreenStatus"/>
<LISTITEM value="YellowStatus"/>
<LISTITEM value="RedStatus"/>
```

```
</ALLOWEDVALUES>
<DEFAULT from="value" value="YellowStatus"/>
</FIELD>
```

Note that once you create a reportable field, it can't be changed. You have to carefully select the appropriate type that makes sense and keep in mind the impact of your field on the rest of your projects. Note that all custom fields are stored in the same cube; therefore, naming becomes very important. If you use similar fields in different work items, you may want to delineate them in some way.

You can customize a report in a variety of ways including in a drilldown view (where you can expose additional details by clicking on a chart), navigation view (where you can show alternate views of information based on selected parameters), and calculations (using averages).

You may also want to create customizations to render reports in unsupported formats (such as XML binary). Or, you might compose a report that emits a special format — such as XHTML.

You can download examples of advanced customized Team System reports from Tom Patton's blog. Tom is a program manager with the Visual Studio Team Foundation Server team. He works specifically on the reporting features: `http://blogs.msdn.com/tompatton/archive/2006/05/07/591713.aspx`.

Deploying Reports in Team System

A report can be deployed in Team System using the process template. To download a copy of the template, simply right-click your server in Team Explorer and select Team Project Settings⇨Process Template Manager. (Alternatively, you can click Team⇨Team Foundation Server Settings⇨Process Template Manager.) A window appears as shown in Figure 16-12.

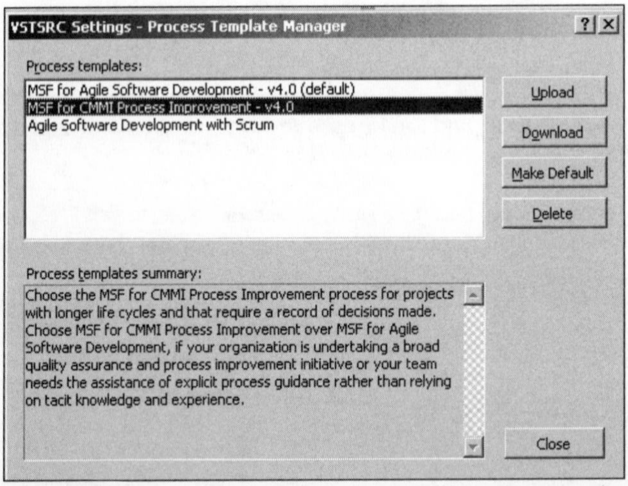

Figure 16-12

Click MSF for CMMI Process Improvement - v4.0, select Download, and select your desktop. A copy of the process template downloads after that. Click the process template folder, then Reports and you'll see the files shown in Figure 16-13.

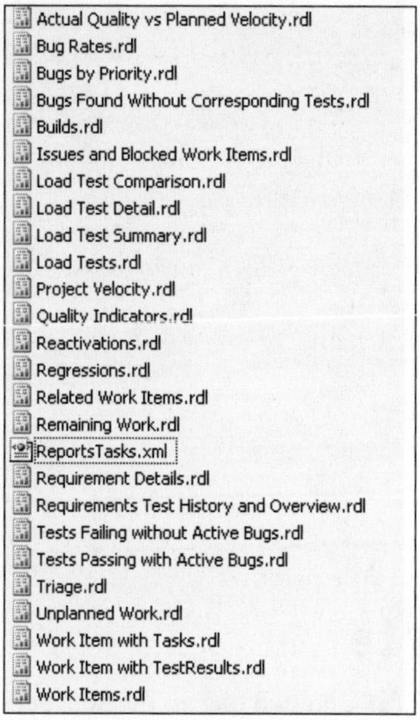

Figure 16-13

Each of the .rdl files represents a report that ships with MSF for CMMI Process Improvement. ReportTask.xml contains an enumeration of the reports that are included in the process template, along with a link to the physical file in the process template folder, the cache expiration properties, and the data source to be used for the report. (In all cases, the data source is TfsOlapReportDS.) The following code shows a sample of the XML found in ReportTask.xml (which you can customize at will).

```
<?xml version="1.0" encoding="utf-8" ?>
<tasks>
<task
id="Site"
plugin="Microsoft.ProjectCreationWizard.Reporting"
completionMessage="Project Reporting site created.">
<dependencies/>
<taskXml>
<ReportingServices>
<site />
</ReportingServices>
</taskXml>
</task>
<task id="Populate Reports"
plugin="Microsoft.ProjectCreationWizard.Reporting"
completionMessage="Project site created.">
<dependencies>
<dependency taskId="Site"/>
```

```
</dependencies>
<taskXml>
<ReportingServices>
<reports>

<report name="Custom Report"
filename="Reports\CustomReport.rdl"
folder=""
cacheExpiration="30">
<properties>
<property name="Hidden" value="true"/>
</properties>
<datasources>
<reference name="/TfsOlapReportDS" dsname="TfsOlapReportDS"/>
</datasources>
</report>
</reports>
</ReportingServices>
</taskXml>
</task>
</tasks>
```

Managing Reports

The reports in Team System are located in two places: the SQL Server reporting portal and within Team Explorer. You can access the reports in the SQL Server reporting portal by expanding your Team Project within Team Explorer, right-clicking on the Reports node, and selecting Show Report Site. You can alternatively access your Team System project reports by typing in the following in your Web browser: `http://localhost/Reports/`.

There are several ways you can share a report using Windows SharePoint Services. You can use the SQL Reporting Services Web Parts or the page viewer, which allows redirection based on a URL. To make any modifications to the team portal, you need Microsoft FrontPage. You can also use the Web Part Manager to drag the appropriate parts and specify the report URL. Here are the steps to add a report to the team portal using the Page Viewer Web Part:

1. Click Modify Shared Page⇨Design This Page.
2. Click Modify Shared Page⇨Add Web Part. You are then presented with the following options: Browse, Search and Import.
3. Select Browse and then select the Page Viewer Web Part.
4. You can then drag the part to the left portion of the screen.
5. Click the down-arrow at the corner of the Web part and select Modify Shared Web Part.
6. In the Link section on the right, enter **http://<servername>/Reports/**.
7. Click OK.

You can run the reports by double-clicking on them in Team Explorer. Reports can also be executed by clicking on the links on the SQL Server Reporting Services Web site. As easily, you can delete a report on Team Explorer by selecting Delete. On the reporting site, your reports can be deleted by clicking on the Show Detail option, checking off the report you want to delete and clicking on the Delete option.

> **Note that deleting a report in this way will remove it from your Team Project permanently, but will not affect the process template you used to instantiate the project.**

Unfortunately, you cannot really export reports from Team Explorer. All you can do is print from the interface by clicking on the printer icon. On the reporting site, you can export in a variety of formats including the following:

- XML file with report data
- Comma delimited (CSV)
- TIFF file
- Acrobat (PDF) file
- Web archive
- Excel

The Excel and PDF formats are very handy for creating redistributable versions of the reports.

Troubleshooting the Data Warehouse

One of the common issues that come up when you first generate a Team Project is that you try to generate a report and nothing comes up, or you'll get an error message such as "`An error has occurred during report processing.(rsProcessingAborted)`" or "`rsErrorExecutingCommand`." First, consider that your project initially doesn't have any data in it; therefore, you won't see much in the reports. Second, if you do have data in your project (for example, you have added work items), the warehouse refresh occurs only once an hour.

Another common problem when you first set up a Team Project is that you may see a little red *x* next to the Reports node. This means that you didn't set the appropriate permissions on the reporting site. Please follow the instructions in Chapter 4 for details on how to set up privileges using the Report Manager.

> **MSDN has great information on troubleshooting the data warehouse (`http://msdn2.microsoft.com/en-us/library/ms244674.aspx`) and troubleshooting SQL Server Reporting Services (`http://msdn2.microsoft.com/en-us/library/ms244677.aspx`).**

Administering and Refreshing the Warehouse

Typically, the data warehouse refreshes data every hour. What happens is that the data are aggregated from the operational stores to the fact tables. Once that operation has occurred, then the cube is refreshed. There may be circumstances where the stakeholders in the project may need the report information to be refreshed more frequently.

> **If you use SQL Server 2005 Enterprise Edition, optimizations have been made to the product for parallel processing in increments. Whenever you are modifying the refresh frequency, be mindful of the overhead and the impact on your operations especially if you are planning to refresh more frequently.**

The default refresh rate is once per hour. To change the refresh rate, you must have administrative privileges on the data tier. You can change the setting by using the `WarehouseController` Team Foundation Server Web service. Here are the specific steps:

1. Launch Internet Explorer (or your browser of choice) and type in the following link:

```
http://localhost:8080/Warehouse/v1.0/warehousecontroller.asmx
```

2. Go to the ControllerService page and click the ChangeSetting link.
3. Type in **RunIntervalSeconds** in the `settingsID` input field.
4. Type in the number of seconds between refreshes in the `newValue` input field. For example, an hour is 3600 seconds (60 minutes × 60 seconds). To set the interval to half an hour, write in 1800 (30 minutes × 60 seconds).
5. Click the Invoke button.

The Web service in question appears as shown in Figure 16-14.

Once you have set up the new refresh rate, you can verify it using the `GetWarehouseStatus` method. There are three default statuses that can come up: Idle, RunningAdapters, or ProcessingOlap. Once the data warehouse has been processed, the status will return to Idle.

SetupWarehouse

There may be instances where you will need to completely rebuild the data warehouse. The Team Foundation Server Warehouse Setup Tool (`SetupWarehouse`) allows you to fix up either the relational database or the OLAP cube. You can access the tool at `C:\Program Files\Microsoft Visual Studio 2005 Team Foundation Server\Tools`.

You can rebuild the relational database using this command:

```
SetupWarehouse -rebuild -mturl MidTierURL -s ServerName -d TFSWarehouse-c
wareHouseSchema.xml -a TFSServiceAccount -ra TFSReportAccount -edt
TeamBuildDataBase
```

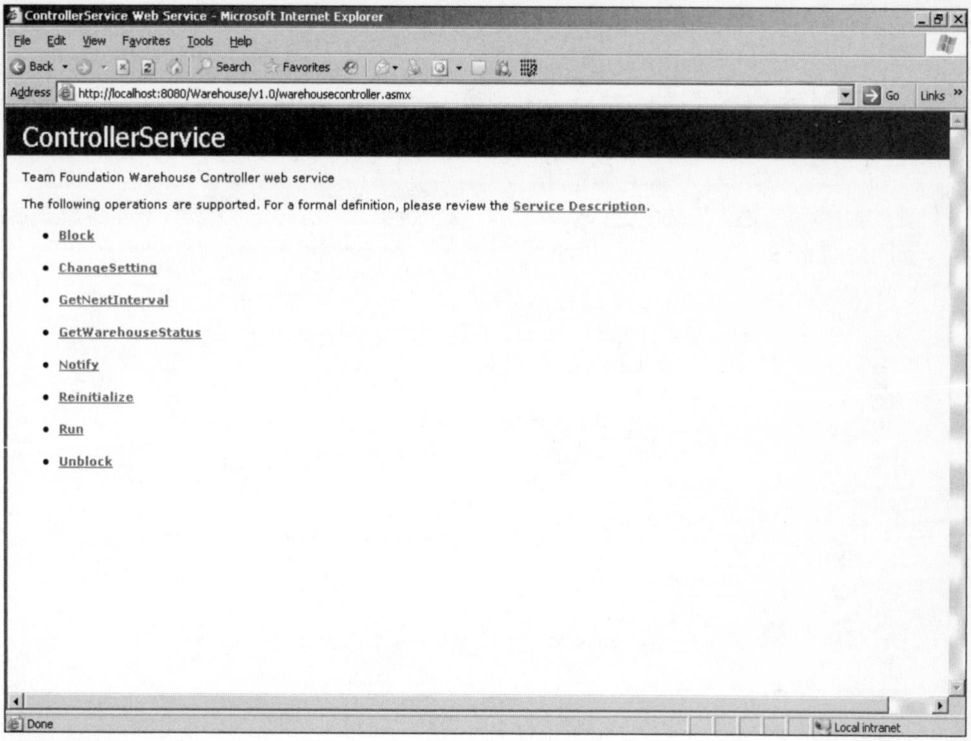

Figure 16-14

You can also rebuild the OLAP cube using the following command:

```
SetupWarehouse -o -s YourDataTierServer -d TFSWarehouse -c warehouseSchema.xml -a
TFSServiceAccount -ra TFSReportAccount
```

A list of all the available options is available online at `http://msdn2.microsoft.com/en-us/library/ms400783.aspx`. You can also get a list of commands by typing the following in the command prompt:

```
SetupWarehouse /?
```

Setting Security Permission on Reports

The SharePoint project portal and the team reporting sites have to be configured separately from the rest of Team Foundation Server. As with Team Foundation Server, you can simply add server groups to the report site to provide easy administration. Or, you can opt to add individual users to provide a higher level of granularity in your security approach per report.

You can access the security setting for your site by first opening up the reports site. Right-click Reports in Team Explorer, and select View Report Site. Once the Report Manager site appears, click the Site Settings link on the upper-right corner of the page. At the bottom of the new page, you will have the option of configuring site-wide security, configuring item-level role definitions, and configuring system-level role definitions (as shown in Figure 16-15).

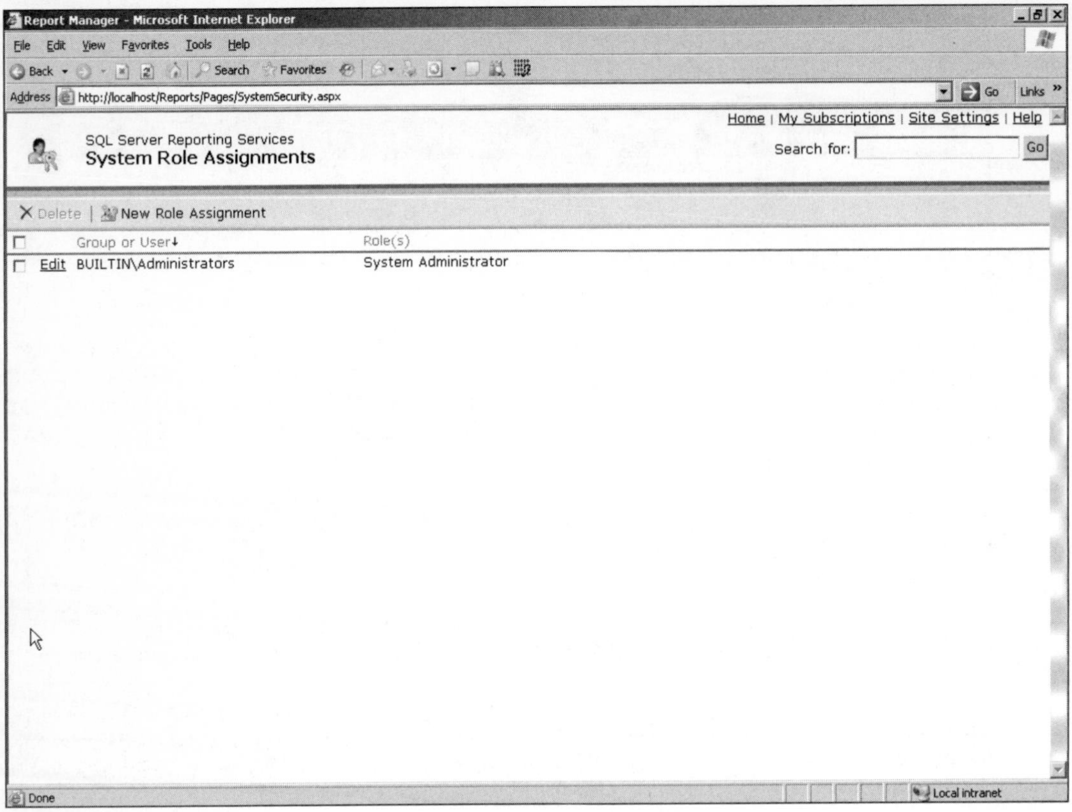

Figure 16-15

The Team Foundation Server data warehouse has an interesting security model. First, all Team Projects on the server share one data warehouse (as explained earlier in the chapter). If you want to tighten security, you can do periodical password resets on the data sources. In order for the reporting to work correctly, the service account (`TFSSERVICE`) needs at the very minimum access to the OLAP database. You can also willfully constrain what other accounts access the OLAP cube and other parts of the warehouse. To access Reporting Services, a user needs at least Contributor rights. One of the first steps you need to take when deploying Team System is making sure that the credentials have been set up on both the team portal and SQL Server Reporting Services. Otherwise, your users will only see a red *x* on the Reports node of the Team Project and will be unable to view reports. There are some scenarios where this is desirable, perhaps if you have built custom reports to assess the performance of each employee, for example. However, we would recommend that you should allow your team to view progress reports and bug reports to promote transparency and allow your team to perform self-corrections when needed.

As recommended in the security chapter (Chapter 4), you should consolidate your security within security groups, either on Active Directory or in Windows Server 2003 groups in Workgroup mode. Name the security groups as follows:

- ReportingServices
- AnalysisServices
- SQLServer2005

You can also set up a group for managing access to Windows SharePoint Services. The server administrators should typically be placed in the Content Manager group at the root level. Project administrators should also be placed in this group at the project level. Project contributors, on the other hand, should be placed in the Browser group at the project level. These permission levels allow you to control access to the Report Server.

At the project level, don't inherit security from the root. You should provide access directly to the cube for the cube browsers. If you are a project manager and are planning to use Microsoft Excel to create a pivot-table report, you should use the report authors permission level. Administrators have full access to warehouse data (such as when the last time the cube has been processed). They also have access to all the projects (and project data) on the data tier.

You can access the tables containing the role and permissions in the Team Foundation Server Warehouse by following these steps:

1. Open SQL Server Management Studio.
2. Connect to Analysis Services. Select your Team Foundation Server as the server name.
3. Expand the Database node.
4. Expand the TFSWarehouse database. This is the OLAP database that is used by the default reports in Team System, as well as any custom reports that require correlation of data and Excel pivot tables.
5. Expand the Roles node.
6. Double-click the TfsWarehouseDataReader role.
7. Click the Membership tab. You'll notice that the `TFSREPORTS` account has been designated as the main service account for SQL Server Reporting Services.

Summary

In this chapter, you learned the architecture of SQL Server Reporting Services as it relates to Team Foundation Server. Included in the overview was a glossary of terminology and concepts commonly used in OLAP reporting. Next, you learned how to generate custom reports using Microsoft Excel, Report Designer, and Report Builder. Not only did you get an overview of the steps to build a report but also hints and best practices to get the best performance and capabilities out of Team System reporting. You found out how to incorporate your custom reports within the team portal, manage the reports, and define and set security on a project and report level. Once your project is completed, historical data derived from reports will provide the data you need to implement process improvement. You'll learn more about that in the next chapter.

17

Completing Software Projects

We have now arrived at the end of the road. Throughout this book, you learned how to create and manage a software project. At the final stage, you need to consider release management issues such as making sure your project has undergone final quality assurance (QA) and releasing and deploying your application to clients. From an operational perspective, we can look at the retirement of applications. This chapter outlines a series of strategies for wrapping up a project, analyzing your assets, and conducting a postmortem for process improvements. There are two processes you need to consider:

- A series of conventional release management steps for wrapping up a software development project
- A series of tasks you need to run through to complete a project in Team System

The build and release of a project should be considered one of the most important elements of the software development lifecycle. Think of it, the justification for the existence of a software development team is to successfully release software. If your builds are failing or you have an inadequate release process, you won't be as successful and your results will be uneven. As with other parts of the development process, you can tie release management to software engineering principles in general, and specifically to the Microsoft Solution Framework and the Microsoft Operations Framework. Let's look at how it all ties in together.

Release Management within the Microsoft Solutions Framework (MSF)

The Microsoft Solutions Framework has very specific process guidance on release management. In the MSF for Agile Software Development process, you can break down release management tasks using the following steps:

- **Execute a release plan**—A release plan includes all the steps needed to successfully release the product, including scheduling quality assurance tests, creating a series of steps for your rollout (which you can document using work items), and so forth. By setting up your plan as a series of work items, you can then track the progress using a cumulative flow diagram (just like the project manager wanting to manage a software development effort). Some agilists would scoff at the idea of all this documentation and tracking. To those individuals, we can say that the work item database at the very least provides the benefit for a centralized area to manage your work items (much like story cards). The release plan could include the coordination of sales and marketing efforts, but should focus primarily on the delivery of the application to the target environment and the logistics around deployment.
- **Validate a release**—This phase involves final quality assurance (QA) on a release. You should test the release using customer or user acceptance tests and requirements validation tests. From a functional perspective, you can create a specific branch for testing the release and run regression tests on your unit tests. Basically, unit tests verify the fidelity of data coming in and out of your classes and methods. On a conceptual level, you can use unit tests to enforce business requirements. For example, if you are creating a credit card processing application, you can verify that the input contains only numerical data, has only a certain number of digits, has specific prefixes, and so forth. By incorporating business requirements as unit tests, you can run both regression and validation tests on the application. If bugs are found, bug work items can be created to forward to the rest of your development team.
- **Create release notes**—This is the documentation step that involves writing down the environment requirements, installation steps, new features, and bug fixes from the previous versions, known bugs, and limitations. If you are creating a commercial product (for example, a shareware application) the documentation is typically leveraged to create part of the marketing package for the software release.
- **Deploy the product**—This final step of the process involves creating a deployment package. If you are commercial software development company, you may need to create a master CD or DVD for your product to ship to a mass manufacturer.

The MSF for CMMI Process Improvement release management process has more complexity and auditing requirements to take into account. Figure 17-1 shows the release manager documentation in the CMMI process template.

The CMMI process template begins with entry criteria such as user acceptance tests, build, system test results, critical quality factors, and requirements. You need, for example, a stable build to establish as a release candidate (if it fulfills the customer requirements). The release management activities for MSF for CMMI Process Improvement include the following:

- **Establish a user acceptance test environment**—You need to set up a location and equipment to run your tests. This involves planning up-front to book the rooms and coordination with the operations team to get the needed resources.
- **Establish validation guidelines**—This step involves the establishment of a test plan framework (including test cases) to check the stability of the software and make sure it conforms to the customer's specifications.
- **Select a release candidate**—This involves selecting a stable build that will be subject to user acceptance testing (in other words, the build that most satisfies the customer requirements). You need to designate a set of functional exit criteria and validate the release against those criteria.

Figure 17-1

- **Create a rollout and deployment plan**—The rollout and deployment plan has a strong training component; it should include the end users, trainers, sales staff, helpdesk, and operations. A project management component involves a list of requirements for deployment, assessing risks and issues, and working closely with operations to capture the operational and management challenges before deployment.
- **User acceptance testing**—These tests allow you to evaluate the end product against the vision statement outlined at the beginning of the project. They also help you determine if the release fulfills a need in the market (in the case of commercial software), and meets the quality standards that are expected by the customer or end user.
- **Analyze user acceptance test results**—In this step, you are measuring your test steps against the tests. This includes critical-to-quality (CTQ) factors as determined by the customer. The CTQ are represented in a project as a series of scenarios capturing the customer requirements.
- **Accept product for release**—In this phase, you set up a meeting with all stakeholders to agree to a specific release and demo of the product. The easiest way to gain consensus is to get everyone to physically sign off on the release.

- **Package product**—You decide on the right packaging and sales approach for the product. It will differ based on the type of development project. If you are working on commercial software, it may be boxed or distributed online. In-house software development projects don't require packaging per se, and may only need a brochure explaining the core features to upper management. The exact makeup of the package depends greatly on the software being produced.
- **Execute rollout plan**—If you instantiate a rollout plan in work item form, all you need is to assign the tasks appropriately and work through them with your team. You can also track variation (much like a software development plan) to mitigate risks and issues in future rollouts.
- **Create release notes**—As in MSF for Agile Software Development, the release notes contain any upgrade details or bug fixes for the new release. They also provide installation information and a list of new features.

The exit criteria for the CMMI release management process are that change requests are generated for usability and testing, notice is created that a release is available in package form, the product is available, and the release candidate has been certified by the team in a milestone review.

Implementing Release Management Tasks in Team System

Are there any components of Team Foundation Server and Team System that can assist in the process of releasing software? Indeed, there is. You can slice up the release management process as a lifecycle within the larger software development lifecycle. In a nutshell, release management involves four phases:

- **Planning**—The process of creating a release plan
- **Implementation**—Executing the release plan
- **Testing**—The final QA and user acceptance testing process
- **Deployment**—Shipping the product

The release plan can be created using the same tools that a project manager would use, Microsoft Excel or Project. You can create an area within the Team Project called Release (by right-clicking on Team Project, selecting Team Project Settings⇨Areas and Iterations, and adding a Release node to the project, as shown in Figure 17-2).

Then you can associate all your release management oriented tasks to this area.

You could alternatively create a custom work item called Release Task for this purpose. How do you effectively choose whether to create an area or a custom work item? If your tasks are structurally the same as other tasks in Team System (in other words, there are no custom transitions and so forth), you should pick the area approach. If customization is required, then the new work item approach will work well for you.

You should execute a release management project just as you would a software development project. You can identify risk at the beginning, track the progress of your project, and make note of blocking issues that may arise.

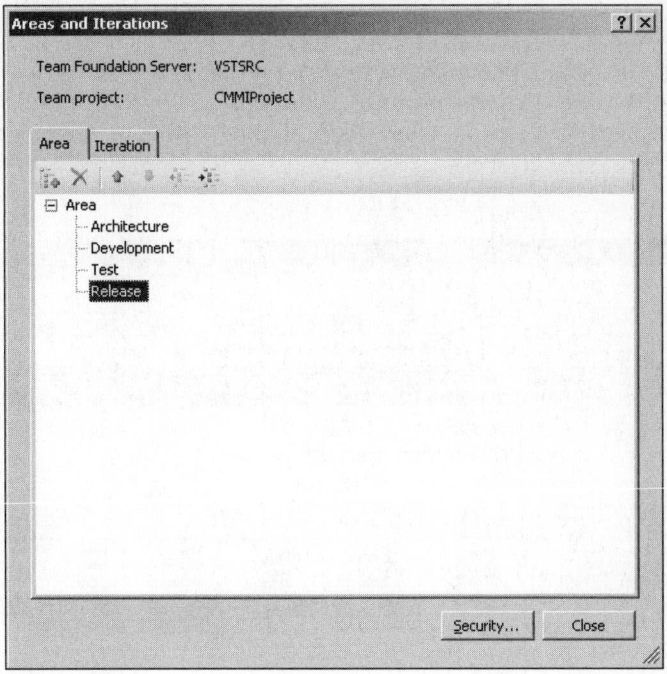

Figure 17-2

The next phase involves testing the application. You can store your test cases (for user acceptance testing) in manual tests, which would then allow you to create a last-minute change request if the desired functionality has not been obtained (or if hidden bugs are uncovered). You can automate your user acceptance testing to some degree by using unit tests that enforce your business requirements. Finally, you can use tools such as the Framework for Integrated Testing (FIT) to allow customers to test all of your business logic. FIT works by providing the user with a table in Word format. Into this table, the user inserts a range of values and the expected outputs. Then the user's data are compared to the output generated from your classes. You can learn more about FIT on its Web site at `http://fit.c2.com/`.

The deployment piece of the release management cycle involves shipping a master CD to a manufacturer. Team Foundation Server fits in during the creation of a custom build that cleans up your project for deployment. Postdeployment, you can also look over the effectiveness of your release and do a postmortem on the process.

Finalizing Projects in Team System

Once the software development project has been wrapped up, you can back up your Team System assets and analyze the project for bugs, defects, risks, and issues that came up along the way.

Exporting and Saving Your Project Artifacts

The first important step of the process is exporting and saving your project artifacts. This can include your work products, which are templates and documents in use during the project. In your team portal, you can download the files by clicking on one of the document libraries in the left menu bar (in this case, Project Management), click Explorer View, select all your work items and drag them onto your desktop (or backup media) as shown in Figure 17-3.

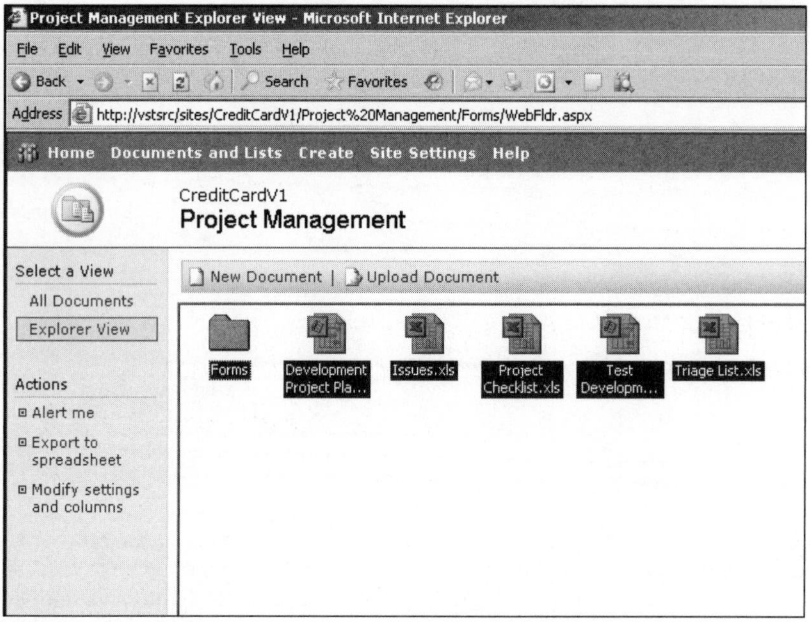

Figure 17-3

You can also export your environment settings by clicking Tools⇨Import and Export Settings in any of the Team Edition IDEs within Team System (as shown in Figure 17-4).

Postmortems

The real value of undertaking a software engineering approach is process improvement. You can accomplish this through the postmortem, which is the dissection of a project after completion.

In MSF for CMMI Process Improvement, a postmortem is referred to as a Project Retrospective, and found within the project manager's Governance track.

A postmortem is a perfect opportunity to discover the risks and issues in your project and to mitigate them in the future. Another value in a postmortem is to identify the things that went right—best practices and approaches that delivered value during the course of the project. Finally, the postmortem provides a chance for everyone to sign off on the project in a postmortem report.

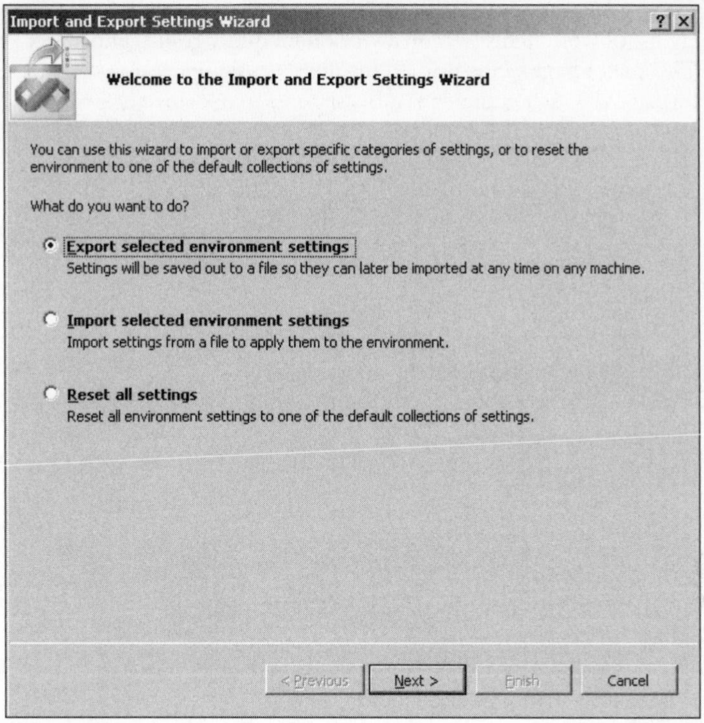

Figure 17-4

To do an effective postmortem, make sure you get your entire team for a day or two and try to schedule the meeting very soon after the project has been completed (rather than wait a few weeks or months). That way, all the details will be fresh in people's minds. Think about bringing the customer into the meetings, as they are a stakeholder in the process. If your project was subject to scope creep (in other words, constantly changing scenarios or requirements), then involve customers in the process of finding mitigation paths and approaches. As with any development project, the most important thing is that the business requirements are met; however, providing a framework for your developers will make them more productive in the future. A postmortem plan and report can be divided up into three logical parts:

1. **Effective processes** — Identify the processes that worked within the project. You may be able to incorporate them into other team projects as check-in policies or at the very least include it into your process guidance document.
2. **Issues and risk** — This is a key area we will explore in-depth in this chapter. Team System provides work items to help track these elements in an integrated way. You can use specific reports and queries to pull that information from the data warehouse. Also don't underestimate the human factor. Members of your team may be able to provide feedback that was not recorded during the course of the project. The key here is free and open communication.
3. **Action items** — This step is where you take the feedback you have gathered and create actionable tasks on an ongoing basis for future projects. The action item phase may require you to modify your process templates and process guidance. It may involve restructuring your processes.

To get a complete view of your work items, you may want to print them out. To print work items, simply right-click any list of work items (within a work item query result) and select Print Selected Work Items. Figure 17-5 shows a page of the printed results.

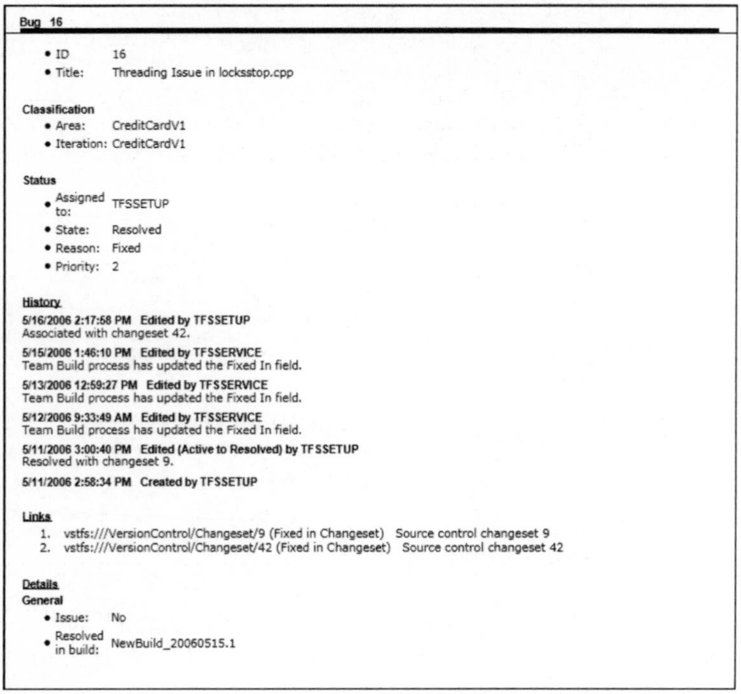

Bug 16

- ID 16
- Title: Threading Issue in locksstop.cpp

Classification

- Area: CreditCardV1
- Iteration: CreditCardV1

Status

- Assigned to: TFSSETUP
- State: Resolved
- Reason: Fixed
- Priority: 2

History

5/16/2006 2:17:58 PM Edited by TFSSETUP
Associated with changeset 42.

5/15/2006 1:46:10 PM Edited by TFSSERVICE
Team Build process has updated the Fixed In field.

5/13/2006 12:59:27 PM Edited by TFSSERVICE
Team Build process has updated the Fixed In field.

5/12/2006 9:33:49 AM Edited by TFSSERVICE
Team Build process has updated the Fixed In field.

5/11/2006 3:00:40 PM Edited (Active to Resolved) by TFSSETUP
Resolved with changeset 9.

5/11/2006 2:58:34 PM Created by TFSSETUP

Links

1. vstfs:///VersionControl/Changeset/9 (Fixed in Changeset) Source control changeset 9
2. vstfs:///VersionControl/Changeset/42 (Fixed in Changeset) Source control changeset 42

Details

General

- Issue: No
- Resolved in build: NewBuild_20060515.1

Figure 17-5

Improving Your Process through Lessons Learned

Once you have done a full postmortem on your project, you should document all the improvements and best practices gathered by your team. At the very least, you should write them down. A more effective way of retaining the value of the lessons learned is to modify your process templates, immediately transforming the recommendations into templates, policies, work items, and workflow. For example, you may want to include steps in your work item instance (the default work items that appear when you create a team project). You may want to enforce code policies (for example, making sure that all your classes and methods include documentation) and add best practices documentation to the project portal.

You can improve your process by studying the special cause variation on a project. A lot of the mechanics behind formal processes are designed for the purpose of accountability and conformance to specification — in other words, documenting, evaluating and auditing each step of the process to make sure the quality of the end product remains high. In agile methodologies, trust is inherent in the process; you have to trust that your developers will build quality features and build trust with your customers. MSF for Agile Software Development and MSF for CMMI Process Improvement foster agility by allowing your team members to focus on their core activities, automating documentation and policies, and, most importantly, building quality within the process.

One of the vehicles for incorporating your best practices in your process is the Guidance Automation Toolkit. It allows you to compile your guidance and enact guidance through mechanisms such as code automation.

You can learn from your process by looking at the risks and issues that came up during the course of your project. You should query them, aggregate the data, and create an action plan for future projects.

Removing a Project from the Server

There will be circumstances where you will want to remove a project from the server, be it for cleaning up or to improve the speed of your data warehouse (by limiting the scope of data being queried).

Deleting a Team Project

Deleting a team project is a drastic move; therefore it is not available through the user interface (UI). Rather you must use the `TfsDeleteProject` command-line tool.

> **When you delete a team project, Team System removes references to the project in Team Explorer, SharePoint portal site, and Reporting Services. What it won't delete is your project data within the data warehouse.**

One of the most common questions around the delete tool is why version control branches related to the team project can't truly be deleted. You can delete and hide them (using the source control options). One of the answers is that in CMMI, the code and project artifacts need to remain for auditing purposes. Another good reason is that it allows you to restore a version control asset that you may accidentally delete. For example, if you right-click any deleted tree or branch, you can select Undelete to recover the item.

> **Since the server retains data from a deleted project, you will be unable to create a new team project with the same name as a previously deleted project.**

To hide the deleted branch in version control, you can click Tools⇨Options, then Source Control⇨Visual Studio Team Foundation Server. You'll find an option that says "Show deleted items in the Source Control Explorer." Make sure it is unchecked and click Apply.

> **Do not attempt to hack the data warehouse and try to delete data directly from the tables within SQL Server 2005. The data schemas and relationships are more complex than they appear and the likelihood of corrupting your database and environment is very high.**

Another project artifact you can't delete is a work item. The proof of this is that when you look into the Work Item Tracking API, you won't find a delete method. If you want to delete a work item, the best approach is to customize each work item and provide an extra Deleted state. Here is the code to include in your work items to incorporate the Deleted state:

```
<FIELD name="Tracking" refname="Stormpixel.Tracking" type="String">
<HELPTEXT>This field is used to track the workflow</HELPTEXT>
</FIELD>
```

Within the workflow of the work item in question, you need to designate the different states. In the example below, we've added a `Deleted` state within a Task work item:

```
<WORKFLOW>
<STATES>
<STATE value="Active">
<FIELDS>
<FIELD refname="Microsoft.VSTS.Common.ClosedDate"><EMPTY/></FIELD>
<FIELD refname="Microsoft.VSTS.Common.ClosedBy"><EMPTY/></FIELD>
</FIELDS>
</STATE>
<STATE value="Closed"></STATE>

<STATE value="Deleted"></STATE>
</STATES>
```

Once you have designated your new state, you have to set up your state transitions. In the example below, we have set up:

```
<TRANSITION from="Not Done" to="Deleted">
<REASONS>
<DEFAULTREASON value="Item has been marked for deletion"/>
</REASONS>
<FIELDS>
<FIELD refname="Stormpixel.Tracking">
<DEFAULT from="value" value="0" />
</FIELD>
</FIELDS>
</TRANSITION>

<TRANSITION from="Deleted" to="Not Done">
<REASONS>
<DEFAULTREASON value="Item has been marked for restoration"/>
</REASONS>
<FIELDS>
<FIELD refname="Stormpixel.Tracking">
<DEFAULT from="value" value="0" />
</FIELD>
</FIELDS>
</TRANSITION>
```

You can then create a query called Deleted Items to show all work items set to the deleted state. Here is the .wiq (work item query) to display all your deleted items (`DeletedWorkItems.wiq`):

```
<?xml version="1.0" encoding="utf-8"?>
<WorkItemQuery Version="1">
<Wiql>SELECT [System.Id], [System.WorkItemType], [System.AssignedTo],
 [System.CreatedBy], [Microsoft.VSTS.Common.Priority], [System.Title]
FROM WorkItems

WHERE [System.TeamProject] = @project AND [System.State] = 'Deleted'
ORDER BY [Microsoft.VSTS.Common.Priority], [System.Id]
</Wiql>
</WorkItemQuery>
```

Then you can modify all other queries to exclude all items that have been set to `Deleted`. Here is an example of a query that pulls up all work items that aren't set to a `Deleted` state: (`NonDeletedWorkItems.wiq`):

```
<?xml version="1.0" encoding="utf-8"?>
<WorkItemQuery Version="1">
<Wiql>SELECT [System.Id], [System.WorkItemType], [System.AssignedTo],
 [System.CreatedBy], [Microsoft.VSTS.Common.Priority], [System.Title]
FROM WorkItems
WHERE [System.TeamProject] = @project

AND [System.State] NOT CONTAINS 'Deleted'
ORDER BY [Microsoft.VSTS.Common.Priority], [System.Id]
</Wiql>
</WorkItemQuery>
```

Please refer to Chapter 6 for more information on how to manipulate and customize a process template and work item types.

Using the TfsDeleteProject Commands

Assuming you installed Visual Studio on your `C:\` drive, you can find the `TfsDeleteProject` tool at the following link: `C:\Program Files\Microsoft Visual Studio 8\Common7\IDE\PrivateAssemblies\`.

Before you use the TfsDeleteProject command, be sure you clean up your assets. For example, if you have any pending changesets, you should check them in (or delete them). In fact, it would be a good idea to delete your code and commit the changes; it will be a lot cleaner in the end. Here is the command to delete a project:

```
TfsDeleteProject.exe
```

Here is a table with all the common commands for this tool:

Option	Description
/q	This option allows you to delete files quietly; no prompt will appear to confirm the deletion.
/force	When you are deleting a project, there are sometimes circumstances that will prevent a portion of it from being deleted (for example, if a file lock exists on a particular file). The /force option will make the uninstaller continue the process even if some parts cannot be deleted.
/server:servername	The name of the Team Foundation Server where the team project is located. This is required in multiserver environments.

You can't undo the deletion of a team project! All the project files relating to your SharePoint site, SQL Server Reporting Services, and Team Foundation Server will be deleted.

If there are any spaces in the project name or the server name, you should use quotation marks. You need administrative privileges to connect to Team Foundation Server and perform the `TFSDeleteProject` operation.

Uninstalling Team System

There are very concise instructions in the installation guide (`TFSInstall.chm`) to delete the components of Team System. The key for getting a clean uninstall is to follow those instructions in the correct order. Of course, you must have administrative privileges to perform the uninstall.

The simplest way of managing Team System (including the uninstall process) is to set it up in Microsoft Virtual Server 2005 R2, which is available as a free download from the Microsoft site (`microsoft.com/windowsserversystem/virtualserver`). The most important point is that the uninstall will be unnecessary. All you will need to do is to back up and remove the .vhd files from the server.

When you uninstall SQL Server 2005, the data files are retained in the `Program Files/Microsoft SQL Server` directory. If you are uninstalling to install a more recent version of SQL Server (for example, you may be running a Beta version and want to upgrade to a full retail version), keep in mind that the data will magically reappear in your new installation of Team Foundation Server and you may get installation errors if you install SQL Server in the same directory as the old one without "cleaning it up first.

In case you are wondering, you can find the data contained in folders with names such as MSSQL.1. If you are planning to re-install SQL Server 2005, your best bet is to delete the existing Microsoft SQL Server directory before reattempting a new installation.

If you are working with a Beta version and you need to remove or uninstall, Microsoft has created a tool to facilitate the job. You can download the uninstall tool at `http://msdn.microsoft.com/vstudio/support/uninstall/default.aspx`.

If your plan is to install a new version of Team System and you are getting configuration errors, use the `devenv /ResetUserData` and `devenv /ResetSettings` commands. In some cases, these commands will do the trick. If you are unsure that all the components have been uninstalled, you can use an MSI Inventory tool called msiinv.exe to detect what is installed on your system. You can download the tool at `huydao.net/setup/msiinv.zip`.

> **Aaron Stebner has good coverage on how to use the MSI Inventory tool on his Web log. Visit** `http://blogs.msdn.com/astebner/archive/2005/07/01/434814.aspx`**.**

The tool is especially useful if you can't remove an application using the Add/Remove Programs control panel applet (because it's not appearing for a reason or another), yet you know that the application hasn't been uninstalled. First, run the `msiinv` tool using the following command:

```
msiinv >C:\msilog.txt
```

An application like Team Suite will generate an entry that looks something like this:

```
Microsoft Visual Studio 2005 Team Suite - ENU

Product code: {1862162E-3BBC-448F-AA63-49F33152D54A}
Product state: (5) Installed.
Package code: {A2BF1D84-54D1-4630-9613-058629EFACF4}
Version: 8.0.50727.42
AssignmentType: 1
Publisher: Microsoft Corporation
Language: 1033
Suggested installation location: C:\Program Files\Microsoft Visual Studio 8\
Installed from: d:\vs\
Package: vs_setup.msi
Local package: C:\WINDOWS\Installer\60381.msi
Install date: 2005\12\15
Registered to: Jean-Luc David,
Serial Code: xxxxx-xxx-xxxxxx-xxxxx
58 features.
0 features are not used.
0 features are advertised.
0 features are absent.
58 features installed to run local.
0 features installed to run from source.
0 features installed for default.
0 features in some other state.
6797 components.
0 qualified.
17 permanent.
1529 shared.
0 patch packages.
```

Notice the highlighted product code. To remove Team Suite, you can use the `msiexec` command using the code as shown below.

```
msiexec /x {1862162E-3BBC-448F-AA63-49F33152D54A}
```

> **One of the common culprits of this scenario is the Microsoft Visual J# Redistributable Package. It won't show up in Add/Remove, but, lo and behold, the inventory tool will display it in the list.**

If after uninstalling Team Suite, you try to reinstall it and you start getting "Package Load Failure" issues, it means that the .NET Framework 2.0 installation has likely failed. You can get around the problem by following the advice outlined on Aaron Stebner's blog at `http://blogs.msdn.com/astebner/archive/2005/04/16/408856.aspx`.

Another fantastic resource for install/uninstall issues is the Microsoft Forums (`http://forums.microsoft.com`). It's a great resource because frankly, it is frequently accessed by members of the product group.

Creating a New Version of an Existing Application

The completion of the entire development lifecycle will often spawn into a new project. How do you deal with setting up a version 2.0 and what are some of the best practices for Team System? Here is a little bit of guidance:

Create a New Team Project

The logical place to start is creating a new team project. This will allow you to designate new work items for your project (thus isolating them from the previous project). You can also assign new team members and a new workflow based on process improvement strategies outlined in this book.

There may be some circumstances where you will want to start development of your new version of an existing project within an existing team project. The main determination of whether a new team project is warranted should be based on factors such as the following:

- **Team members**—If the personnel will remain relatively the same on both projects, then you can have the choice of either starting a new team project or sticking to the existing one. If you are starting with a considerably different team, then we would recommend starting a new team project.
- **Process**—If your new project is substantially different from original one (for example, you are creating a Web-based version of a WinForms application), then creating a new team project makes sense. If you want to build the new application using a process that differs from the original project (for example, you used Extreme Programming on the first project and now you want to implement Scrum on the derivative project), then a new team project is of course warranted.
- **Version control and workflow isolation**—One of the advantages of starting a new team project is to isolate a new project. For example, a new project will contain new iterations and features; when combined with an existing project it may add up to a lot of assets to manage.

- **Complexity**—If you have a huge number of work items, or your version control tree for the existing project has grown, adding yet another project on top of it may make it hard to manage. Creating a new team project will allow you to simplify the process. In the case of source code, a single branch will be created using your stable release from the previous project. From a work item perspective, all the new work items will be scoped within the new project, allowing you to isolate them effectively.

There are other considerations, but this list should get you in the right mindset. The main argument for wanting to start over with a new team project is process improvement. You can apply the outcomes and action items from the postmortem investigation to the new project, and benefit from lessons learned.

In approaching a new team project, you should keep in mind the Team System's application. limits. For example, Team Foundation Version Control can maintain 10GB of source code, with a theoretical limit of 250GB. For a complete list of features and theoretical limits, please refer to the MSDN Web site (`http://msdn2.microsoft.com`) and this blog post by Brian Harry: `http://blogs.msdn.com/bharry/archive/2005/11/28/497666.aspx`.

You may want to continue a project within an existing team project if you are working with the same development team using the same process, and complexity is not an issue.

Implement Version Control Migration

When you run the New Team Project Wizard, it provides the option of copying an existing branch as the basis for your new project. This is the perfect launch pad for a V2 because your production code is ostensibly very mature. Figure 17-6 shows the dialog in question, where a project called CreditCardV2 is created based on a branch called CreditCardV1.

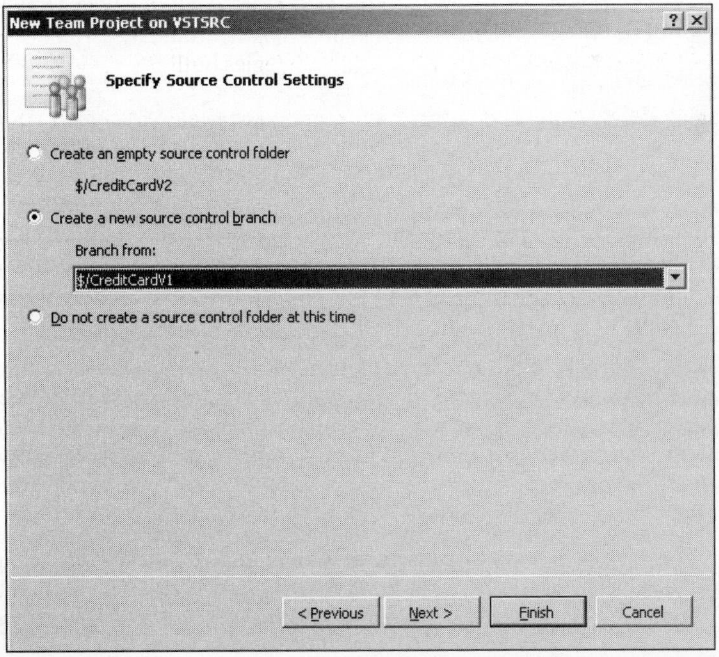

Figure 17-6

You may refer to Chapter 12 for more information about how to set up and manage Team Foundation Version Control.

Migrate Workflow

Team System enables you to transfer work items one-by-one by right-clicking each one and then using the Create Copy of Work Item option. (You can obtain it by right-clicking on a work item from a query result.) Of course, if you have more than 50 work items (which is likely in any active project) the one-work-item-at-a-time approach will not scale. The main strategy for migrating your work items en masse is creating a custom application using the extensibility API. Eric Lee has created a project on GotDotNet.com called the Team Foundation Server Work Item Utility. You can download the source code and the functional application at the following link: `gotdotnet.com/codegallery/codegallery.aspx?id=b29d4456-c4ba-474e-a422-0479471776e1`.

Bulk Migration of Work Items

When we say migrating work items, we mean to copy them over from one project to another. Team System does not allow you to delete work items from a team project per se (for auditing purposes). Another strategy for moving your work items from one project is to use an Excel spreadsheet. Here is an overview of the process:

1. Create two spreadsheets: one for your existing team project (Project A) and one for your new team project (Project B
2. For the Project A spreadsheet, connect to Team Foundation Server (using the New List option (Team⇨New List), then select the All Work Items query to get all the work items from Project A.
3. For the Project B spreadsheet, connect to Team Foundation Server and select the Input List option, which creates a blank spreadsheet ready for new work items.
4. Select and copy the work items in Project A you want to copy over to Project B.
5. Paste the work items from Project A into Project B.
6. Click Publish in the Project B spreadsheet.

You may receive validation errors, especially if the status of some work items is set to Resolved. The reason being is that new work items can only start with the Active status. Also, keep in mind that you can transfer only those work item types that are supported in both projects. For example, you can't transfer an MSF for CMMI Process Improvement Review work item to an MSF for Agile Software Development project (which doesn't contain that work item type).

You can use Microsoft Project to do a work item migration. We recommend you look at the post by Yogita Manghnani on the Microsoft Forums at `http://forums.microsoft.com/msdn/showpost.aspx?postid=273633` to associate an .mpp file from one Team Project to another:

If you are working on an especially complex migration (for example, a half-million to millions of work items), we would highly recommend you contact a Team System consultant or specialist to assist.

Migrating Other Assets

You might also opt to migrate assets, such as check-in policies, project alerts, and other extensibility changes you made to the original project.

Of course, you must, do all the normal setup tasks within your project such as setting up your permissions, setting up your new feature areas, and so forth.

Team Foundation Server Future Directions

There are many new developments in store for the next version of Team Foundation Server. Microsoft has altered its shipping schedules for developer tools, shortening the release cycles. That means that Team System and Team Foundation Server will likely have fewer new features, but instead will contain many enhancements, fixes, and improvements.

One of the big developments in Team System is the internal adoption of the tool. The Developer Division (DevDiv) product group was the first team to test-drive Team Foundation Server (ironically to develop Team System!). Next on the list is the Office group and looking in the near future, the Windows group. The term using your own software is called *dogfooding*. One of the important additions to Team Foundation Server is the Team Foundation Server Proxy, which was added because of cross development between the Visual Studio North Carolina (responsible for Team Foundation Version Control) and the Redmond campus. Through testing, it was found that accessing and checking out code from Team Foundation Server over HTTP (and long distances) needed a boost for scalability and performance.

What does this mean in terms of Team Foundation Server vNext? Primarily, it will be more scalable. (The current limit for Team Foundation Server in v1 is three thousand users.) As they adapt the tools for their development environment, many of the enhancements will be pushed out in the next product. Many of the painful areas of the product (for example, having to edit XML to create or modify process templates) can be solved with external tools such as the Process Template Customization tool.

Expect many out-of-band releases from Microsoft, Partners, and the community at large. For example, there is Codeplex — a GotDotNet-like (`gotdotnet.com`) open source project directory driven by Team Foundation Server. You can learn more about Codeplex by visiting it online at `codeplex.com`.

> **Brian Harry announced that a Team Foundation Server service pack will be available Q2/2006 period. You can learn about the challenges of implementing Team System within the Developer Division and about the Service Pack on his blog at** `http://blogs.msdn.com/bharry/archive/2006/05/17/599817.aspx`**.**

Summary

In this chapter, you learned how to manage the final stage of the software development lifecycle. You learned how to wrap up your projects and to work on an effective postmortem (to gain visibility on the issues and how to overcome them). You learned how to remove assets, a project, and even Team System from a server (and the challenges that removal may entail). We provided a roadmap for your completed projects if they are to end up as launching pads for a new development effort. Finally, we looked into the crystal ball to see what Team Foundation Server (and Team System) has in store for the future.

Overall, this book provided you from a pragmatic, cradle-to-grave view of how to set up and manage team projects. This book is meant to supplement the documentation provided by Microsoft and give you shortcuts on how to use the tools effectively. We would love to hear your feedback and experiences with the product. Feel free to contact us at `support@stormpixel.com` and `mickey_gousset@hotmail.com`.

Index

Index

Symbols and Numerics

A

B

D

E

H

I

J

K

L

M

N

O

P

U

V

X